ACCA

Advanced Financial Management

Practice & Revision Kit

For exams in September 2021, December 2021, March 2022 and June 2022

First edition 2007
Fifteenth edition February 2021

ISBN 9781 5097 3753 6
(previous ISBN 9781 5097 8396 0)

e-ISBN 9781 5097 3903 5

British Library Cataloguing-in-Publication Data
A catalogue record for this book
is available from the British Library

Published by

BPP Learning Media Ltd
BPP House, Aldine Place
142–144 Uxbridge Road
London W12 8AA

www.bpp.com/learningmedia

Printed in the United Kingdom

Your learning materials, published by BPP Learning Media Ltd, are printed on paper obtained from traceable, sustainable sources.

The contents of this book are intended as a guide and not professional advice. Although every effort has been made to ensure that the contents of this book are correct at the time of going to press, BPP Learning Media makes no warranty that the information in this book is accurate or complete and accepts no liability for any loss or damage suffered by any person acting or refraining from acting as a result of the material in this book.

We are grateful to the Association of Chartered Certified Accountants for permission to reproduce past examination questions. The suggested solutions in the Practice & Revision Kit have been prepared by BPP Learning Media Ltd, except where otherwise stated.

Contents

Finding questions

Question index

The headings in this checklist/index indicate the main topics of questions, but questions often cover several different topics. Since September 2015 there have been four exam sittings per year, but ACCA only publish a sample of the questions from the March and June papers, and from the September and December papers; these questions are denoted as 'Mar/Jun' and 'Sept/Dec' in the index below.

Topic index

Listed below are the key AFM syllabus topics and the numbers of the questions in this Kit covering those topics. We have also included a reference to the relevant Chapter of the BPP AFM Workbook, the companion to the BPP AFM Practice and Revision Kit, in case you wish to revise the information on the topic you have covered.

If you need to concentrate your practice and revision on certain topics or if you want to attempt all available questions that refer to a particular subject, you will find this index useful.

Syllabus topic	Question numbers	Workbook chapter
A1: Role of senior financial advisor	1, 8, 21, 59, ME2 Q1	1
A2: Financial strategy formulation	1, 3, 4, 5, 6, 7, 8, 10, 29, 30, 48, 49, 50, 51, 57, 59, ME4 Q1	2
A3: Ethical and governance issues	1, 3, 24, 30, 52, 54, ME1 Q1, ME1 Q3, ME2 Q1, ME3 Q1, ME4 Q1	1
A4: Management of international trade and finance	4, 36, 51	16
A5: Strategic business and financial planning	2, 5	16
A6: Dividend policy and transfer pricing	3, 4, 7, 9, 26, 38, 56, ME4 Q2	16
B1: Discounted cash flow techniques	13, 14, 15, 16, 35, 51, 52, 59, ME3 Q1	3
B2: Option pricing theory	11, 12, 17, 18, 19, 52, ME3 Q1, ME4 Q3	4
B3: Impact of financing and APV	20, 22, 23, 33, 44, 46, 48, 54, 59, ME1 Q1, ME2 Q2, ME4 Q1	6 and 7
B4: Valuation and free cash flows	9, 21, 27, 35, 54, 56, ME1 Q1	8
B5: International investment and financing	49, 50, 53, ME4 Q2	5
C1: Acquisitions and other growth strategies	24, 25, 27, 29, 49, 50, 53, 54, 55, 58, ME2 Q3	9
C2: Valuation for acquisition and mergers	24, 25, 26, 27, 28, 29, 51, 54, 55, 56, 58, ME1 Q1, ME2 Q3	8
C3: Regulatory issues	54, 55, ME4 Q1	9
C4: Financing acquisitions and mergers	24, 25, 27, 28	10
D1: Financial reconstruction	31, 32, 34, 48, 57	14
D2: Business reorganisation	30, 33, 34, 35, 49, 55, 57, 58, ME1 Q3, ME3 Q3	15
E1: Treasury function	12, 35, 38, 41, 42, 44	11 and 12
E2: Foreign exchange hedging	36, 37, 38, 39, 40, 53, 56, ME1 Q2, ME2 Q1	12 and 13
E3: Interest rate hedging	35, 37, 41, 42, 44, 45, 46, 47, ME3 Q2, ME4 Q3	13

ME1 is Mock Exam 1, ME2 is Mock Exam 2 etc.

The exam

Computer-based exams

With effect from the March 2020 sitting, ACCA have commenced the launch of computer-based exams (CBEs) for this exam with the aim of rolling out into all markets internationally over a short period. BPP materials have been designed to support you, whichever exam format you are studying towards. For more information on these changes and when they will be implemented, please visit the ACCA website.

Approach to examining the syllabus

The Advanced Financial Management syllabus is assessed by a 3 hour 15 minute exam. The pass mark is **50%**. All questions in the exam are **compulsory**.

Examining team's general comments

If you are preparing to sit AFM you should pay particular attention to the following in order to maximise your chances of success.

1   *Know your stuff*

- Develop a sound knowledge of the entire AFM syllabus. Augment studying the manuals with wider reading of the financial press, finance textbooks, articles in Student Accountant and financial journals.

- You should expect and be prepared for questions from a range of syllabus areas and more than one area may be tested in a single question. Be prepared for questions that require you to consider a number of areas of the syllabus within one question.

2   *Question practice*

- Work through the past exam questions under exam conditions and to time. Doing past questions will help you build efficiency in answering questions and help you build knowledge of how to make your answer relevant to the scenario in the question.

3   *Address the requirement and scenario*

- Your answer must relate to the scenario in question. Context is very important for higher-level exams. General answers will gain fewer or even no marks.

- In your exams, good time management techniques and habits are essential in ensuring success. Make sure that you are able to answer all parts of each question and manage your time effectively so that you make a reasonable attempt at each part of each question. Good time management skills are essential.

- Often parts of a requirement may ask for more than one aspect. Make sure that you can answer, and do answer, everything each part of each requirement is asking for.

- Make sure you answer the requirements correctly. For example, if the question asks you to explain, it is not enough just to list. If the question asks you to assess, it is not enough just to explain.

4   *Communicate concisely*

- For the written parts of any question, remember it is generally a mark for each relevant point. Repeating a point does not get you any extra marks and it wastes time. Avoid repetition.

- Don't use incomplete sentences when making a point. Marks are awarded for complete points made in full sentences. However, you can use bullet points and numbered paragraphs, and headings when appropriate, to structure an answer to a question. But points made should be in complete sentences.

5   *Think before you start and manage your time*

- Pay attention to the number of marks available – this provides you with a clear indication of the amount of time you should spend on each question part.

- Use your exam time effectively. The questions may contain a substantial amount of information that you will need to sort out and apply properly and you should plan your answer before beginning to write it.

Marks available in respect of professional skills

The presentation of your answers is critical. It is very important to pay regard to neatness, organisation and structure of your answers. Professional exams are extremely time-pressured but giving your answers a structure will help you organise your thoughts and work more effectively. Make sure that your answers are legible because markers cannot award marks for something that they cannot read.

Format of the exam

100 marks, two sections, each section 50 marks	Marks
Section A One compulsory question. Longer questions will cover topics from across the syllabus but will tend to be based on one major area – for example a cross-border merger question (major topic) might bring in ethical issues (smaller topic). **Four professional marks are available.** The examining team has emphasised that in order to gain all the marks available, students must write in the specified format (such as a report or memo). Reports must have terms of reference, conclusion, appendices and appropriate headings.	50
Section B Two compulsory 25-mark questions (from September 2018). From the September 2018 exam, all topics and syllabus sections will be examinable in either Section A or Section B of the exam, but every exam will have questions which have a focus on syllabus Sections B (advanced investment appraisal) and E (advanced risk management). There will no longer be any wholly narrative questions (although some still appear in this Revision Kit as preparation questions).	50

Analysis of past exams

The table below provides details of when each element of the syllabus has been examined in the ten most recent sittings and the question number and section in which each element was examined. We have also included a reference to the relevant Chapter of the BPP AFM Workbook, the companion to the BPP AFM Practice and Revision Kit, in case you wish to revise the information on the topic covered.

Note that in exams before June 2018 there were three questions in Section B (of which two had to be answered) so that five questions in total are referenced.

Workbook chapter		Sep/ Dec 2020	Mar 2020	Sep/ Dec 2019	Mar/ Jun 2019	Dec 2018	Sep 2018	Mar/ Jun 2018	Sep/ Dec 2017	Mar /Jun 2017	Sep/ Dec 2016
	ROLE OF SENIOR FINANCIAL ADVISER										
1	Financial strategy formulation	A		B	A			B	A		A, B
2	Financial strategy evaluation	A		B			B		B		
16	Planning and trading issues for multinationals	B									
	ADVANCED INVESTMENT APPRAISAL										
3	Discounted cash flow techniques		B	A	A				B		B
4	Application of option pricing theory to investment decisions	B			A						
5	International investment	B		A			A			B	
6	Cost of capital and changing risk				B	B		B			A
7	Financial and credit risk	A							A	B	

Workbook chapter		Sep/Dec 2020	Mar 2020	Sep/Dec 2019	Mar/Jun 2019	Dec 2018	Sep 2018	Mar/Jun 2018	Sep/Dec 2017	Mar/Jun 2017	Sep/Dec 2016
	ACQUISITIONS AND MERGERS										
8	Valuation techniques		A	B		A	B	A	B		B
9	Strategic and regulatory issues	A	A	B			B	A		A	
10	Financing acquisitions		A	B		A	B			A	
	CORPORATE RECONSTRUCTION AND REORGANISATION										
14	Financial reconstruction								A		
15	Business reorganisation				B	A			B	A	
	TREASURY AND ADVANCED RISK MANAGEMENT TECHNIQUES										
11	Role of the treasury function		B		B			A	B		A
12	Managing foreign currency risk		B	A		B	A			B	
13	Managing interest rate risk	B			B				B		B

IMPORTANT! The table above gives a broad idea of how frequently major topics in the syllabus are examined. It should **not** be used to question spot and predict, for example, that Topic X will not be examined because it came up two sittings ago. The examining team's reports indicate that they are well aware that some students try to question spot. They avoid predictable patterns and may, for example, examine the same topic two sittings in a row, particularly if there has been a recent change in legislation.

Syllabus and Study Guide

The complete AFM syllabus and study guide can be found by visiting the exam resource finder on the ACCA website.

Helping you with your revision

BPP Learning Media – ACCA Approved Content Provider

As an **ACCA Approved Content Provider**, BPP Learning Media gives you the opportunity to use revision materials reviewed by the ACCA examining team. By incorporating the ACCA examining team's comments and suggestions regarding the depth and breadth of syllabus coverage, the BPP Learning Media Practice & Revision Kit provides excellent, **ACCA-approved** support for your revision.

These materials are reviewed by the ACCA examining team. The objective of the review is to ensure that the material properly covers the syllabus and study guide outcomes, used by the examining team in setting the exams, in the appropriate breadth and depth. The review does not ensure that every eventuality, combination or application of examinable topics is addressed by the ACCA Approved Content. Nor does the review comprise a detailed technical check of the content as the Approved Content Provider has its own quality assurance processes in place in this respect.

BPP Learning Media do everything possible to ensure the material is accurate and up-to-date when sending to print. In the event that any errors are found after the print date, they are uploaded to the following website: www.bpp.com/learningmedia/Errata.

The structure of this Practice & Revision Kit

This Practice & Revision Kit is divided into two sections. The questions in Section A are 25 mark questions which are mainly focused on specific syllabus areas. Section B contains a number of 50 mark questions which generally cover at least two different syllabus areas. There are also four mock exams which provide sufficient opportunity to refine your knowledge and skills as part of your final exam preparations.

Question practice

Question practice under timed conditions is absolutely vital. We strongly advise you to create a revision study plan which focuses on question practice. This is so that you can get used to the pressures of answering exam questions in limited time, develop proficiency in the Specific AFM skills and the Exam success skills. Ideally, you should aim to cover all questions in this Kit, and very importantly, all four mock exams.

Selecting questions

To help you plan your revision, we have provided a full topic index which maps the questions to topics in the syllabus (see page vii).

Making the most of question practice

At BPP Learning Media we realise that you need more than just questions and model answers to get the most from your question practice.

- Our **Top tips** included for certain questions provide essential advice on tackling questions, presenting answers and the key points that answers need to include.

- We show you how you can pick up **Easy marks** on some questions, as we know that picking up all readily available marks often can make the difference between passing and failing.

- We include **marking guides** to show you what the examining team rewards.

Attempting mock exams

This Kit has four mock exams, including the ACCA Specimen Exam, which provide practice at coping with the pressures of the exam day. We strongly recommend that you attempt them under exam conditions. All the mock exams reflect the question styles and syllabus coverage of the exam.

Topics to revise

Any part of the syllabus could be tested in the compulsory Section A question, therefore it is essential that you learn the entire syllabus to maximise your chances of passing. There are no short cuts – trying to spot topics is dangerous and will significantly reduce the likelihood of success.

As this is an advanced level exam, it assumes knowledge of the topics covered in *Financial Management (FM)*, including business valuation techniques, investment appraisal techniques, cost of capital and risk management. You should revise these topics if necessary as they impact on your understanding of the more advanced techniques.

From September 2018 every exam will contain a question which has a clear focus on syllabus Section B (advanced investment appraisal) and on Section E (treasury and advanced risk management) so these syllabus sections are especially important.

It's also useful to keep reading the business pages during your revision period and not just narrowly focus on the syllabus. Remember that the examining team has stressed that this exam is about how organisations respond to real-world issues, so the more you read, the more practical examples you will have of how organisations have tackled real-life situations.

Essential skills areas to be successful in Advanced Financial Management

We think there are two areas you should develop in order to achieve exam success in Advanced Financial Management:

(1) Specific AFM skills

(2) Exam success skills

These are shown in the diagram below.

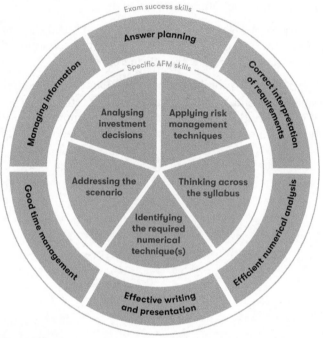

Specific AFM skills

These are the skills specific to AFM that we think you need to develop in order to pass the exam.

In the Workbook, there are five Skills Checkpoints which define each skill and show how it is applied in answering a question. A brief summary of each skill is given below.

Skill 1: Addressing the scenario

All of the questions in your Advanced Financial Management (AFM) exam will be scenario-based.

It is vital to spend time reading and assimilating the scenario as part of your answer planning. Both with your numerical and (especially) discursive points it will be important for you **to address them to** the requirements of the question and the problem as presented in **the scenario**.

A common complaint from the ACCA examining team is that 'Less satisfactory answers tended to give more general responses rather than answers specific to the scenario'. This skill is relevant to all syllabus areas and is likely to be important in every question in your AFM exam.

BPP recommends a step-by-step technique to develop this skill:

Step 1	Allow about 20% of your allotted time for planning.
Step 2	Prepare an answer plan using key words from the question's requirements.
Step 3	Read the scenario; identify specific points from the scenario that are relevant to the question being asked.
Step 4	Write your answer using short paragraphs, relating each point to the scenario as far as is possible.

Skills Checkpoint 1 in the BPP Workbook for AFM covers this technique in detail through application to an exam-standard question. Consider revisiting Skills Checkpoint 1 to improve this skill.

Skill 2: Analysing investment decisions

Analysing investments to select those which are most likely to benefit shareholders is probably the most important activity for a senior financial adviser.

Section B of the AFM syllabus is 'advanced investment appraisal' and directly focusses on the skill of 'analysing investment decisions'. The AFM exam will always contain a question that have a focus on this syllabus area, so this skill is extremely important.

BPP recommends a step-by-step technique to develop this skill:

Step 1	Spend time analysing the scenario and considering why numerical information has been provided and how long you will have to analyse it.
Step 2	Plan your answer carefully; check your analysis matches the question's requirements.
Step 3	Complete your calculations in a time-efficient manner – if necessary, make simplifying assumptions in order to complete the question in the time allowed.
Step 4	Write your answer using short paragraphs; don't forget to explain the meaning of your numbers.
Step 5	Write up your answer; do not try to correct errors identified at this late stage.

Skills Checkpoint 2 in the BPP Workbook for AFM covers this technique in detail through application to an exam-standard question. Consider revisiting Skills Checkpoint 2 to improve this skill.

Skill 3: Identifying the required numerical analysis

Some exam questions will not directly state which numerical techniques should be used and you may have to use clues in the scenario of the question to select an appropriate technique.

This issue commonly arises in syllabus Section C, acquisitions and mergers. Often you will need to assess from the scenario what type of valuation is required and what techniques can be used given the details that are provided in the scenario.

In syllabus Section B, investment appraisal questions will also sometimes be formulated so that you will have to infer that specific techniques (such as real options or adjusted present value) are required ie the question may not always specifically tell you to use these techniques.

A step-by-step technique for developing this skill is outlined below.

Step 1	Don't panic if you do not immediately see which technique needs to be used – spend time considering the range of techniques that could potentially be applied in the scenario presented.
Step 2	Next, carefully analyse the scenario and consider why numerical information has been provided and which of the techniques that you have identified in Step 1 can be used given this information.
Step 3	Complete your numerical analysis.

Skills Checkpoint 3 in the BPP Workbook for AFM covers this technique in detail through application to an exam-standard question. Consider revisiting Skills Checkpoint 3 to improve this skill.

Skill 4: Applying risk management techniques

Section E of the AFM syllabus covers treasury and advanced risk management techniques and directly focuses on the skill of 'applying risk management techniques'.

The AFM exam will always contain a question that will have a clear focus on this syllabus area, so this skill is extremely important.
Successful application of this skill will require a strong technical knowledge of this syllabus area, especially of setting up arrangements to manage risk using futures and options.

Additionally, you will need to be able to forecast the outcome of a technique quickly and efficiently under exam conditions.

Finally, as well as being able to apply the techniques numerically you need to be able to discuss the advantages and disadvantages of using them, the meaning of the numbers and their suitability given the scenario (as discussed in Skills Checkpoint 1).

A step-by-step technique for developing this skill is outlined below.

Step 1	Spend time analysing the scenario and requirements to ensure that you understand the nature of the risk being faced. Work out how many minutes you have to answer each part of the question.
Step 2	Plan your answer. Double check that you are applying the correct type of risk management analysis given the nature of the risk that is faced and the techniques mentioned in the scenario. Identify a time-efficient approach.
Step 3	Complete your numerical analysis. Don't overcomplicate it – aim for a set of clear relevant numbers. Be careful not to overrun on time with your calculations.
Step 4	Explain the meaning of your numbers – relating your points to the scenario wherever possible.

Skills Checkpoint 4 in the BPP Workbook for AFM covers this technique in detail through application to an exam-standard question. Consider revisiting Skills Checkpoint 4 to improve this skill.

Skill 5: Thinking across the syllabus

A common cause for failure in the AFM exam is that students focus on mastering the key numerical parts of the syllabus (typically investment appraisal, valuation techniques and risk management) but leave gaps in their knowledge, in two senses:

(1)   Failing to carefully revise discussion areas within a given syllabus section

(2)   Neglecting some syllabus sections entirely; for example, syllabus Sections A and D are often neglected because they do not contain complex numerical techniques

The structure of the AFM exam exposes students that have knowledge gaps because:

- Exams are designed so that question-spotting does not work

- The 50-mark question is structured to test multiple syllabus areas

- The 25-mark questions, although often focusing on a specific syllabus section, normally contain three requirements which often means that a wide variety of topics within this syllabus area are tested

- And, of course, there are no optional questions

It is therefore crucial that you prepare yourself for the exam by revising across the whole syllabus, even if your knowledge is deeper in some areas than others there must not be any 'gaps', and that you practice questions that force you to address a problem from a variety of perspectives. This skill will often involve thinking outside the confines of one specific chapter of the workbook and thinking across the syllabus.

A step-by-step technique for developing this skill is outlined below.

Step 1	Analyse the scenario and requirements. Consider the wording of the requirements carefully to understand the nature of the problem being faced.
Step 2	Next, plan your answer. Double-check that you are applying the correct knowledge and that you are not neglecting other syllabus areas that would help to support your analysis.
Step 3	Produce your answer, explaining the meaning of your points – and relating them to the scenario wherever possible.

Skills Checkpoint 5 in the BPP Workbook for AFM covers this technique in detail through application to an exam-standard question. Consider revisiting Skills Checkpoint 5 to improve this skill.

Exam success skills

Passing the AFM exam requires more than applying syllabus knowledge and demonstrating the specific AFM skills; it also requires the development of excellent exam technique through question practice.

We consider the following six skills to be vital for exam success. The Skills Checkpoints show how each of these skills can be applied in the exam.

Exam success skill 1

Managing information

Questions in the exam will present you with a lot of information. The skill is how you handle this information to make the best use of your time. The key is determining how you will approach the exam and then actively reading the questions.

Advice on developing this skill

To avoid being overwhelmed by the quantity of information provided, you must take an **active approach** to reading each question.

Active reading means focussing on the question's requirements first, highlighting key verbs such as 'evaluate', 'analyse', 'explain', 'discuss', to ensure you answer the question properly. Then, now that you have an understanding of what the question will require you to do, read the rest of the question, highlighting important and relevant information, and making notes of any relevant technical information you think you will need.

Computer-based exam

In a computer-based exam (CBE) the **highlighter tool** provided in the toolbar at the top of the screen offers a range of colours:

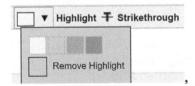

This allows you to choose **different colours to answer different aspects to a question**. For example, if a question asked you to discuss the pros and cons of an issue then you could choose a different colour for highlighting pros and cons within the relevant section of a question.

The **strikethrough function** allows you to delete areas of a question that you have dealt with – this can be useful in managing information if you are dealing with numerical questions because it can allow you to ensure that all numerical areas have been accounted for in your answer.

The CBE also allows you to **resize windows** by clicking on the bottom right-hand corner of the window as highlighted in the following section:

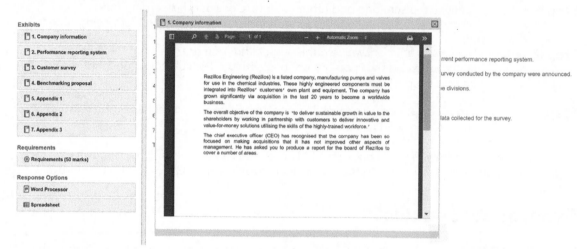

This functionality allows you to **display a number of windows at the same time**, so this could allow you review:

- The question requirements and the exhibit relating to that requirement at the same time; or

- The window containing your answer (whether a word processing or spreadsheet document) and the exhibit relating to that requirement, at the same time.

Exam success skill 2

Correct interpretation of the requirements

The active verb used often dictates the approach that written answers should take (eg 'explain', 'discuss', 'evaluate'). It is important you identify and use the verb to define your approach. The correct interpretation of the requirements skill means correctly producing only what is being asked for by a requirement. Anything not required will not earn marks.

Advice on developing this skill

This skill can be developed by analysing question requirements and applying this process:

Step 1	Read the requirement
	Firstly, read the requirement a couple of times slowly and carefully and **highlight the active verbs.** Use the active verbs to define what you plan to do. Make sure you identify any sub-requirements within a requirement; this **often signalled by the use of the word 'and'** within a requirement.
	Important active verbs for AFM include the following.

Verb	Meaning
Advise	This requires you to provide someone with useful information, or to **tell them what you think they should do** based on a consideration of the issues presented in a scenario.
Analyse	This requires you **break an issue into separate parts** and discuss, examine, or interpret each part.
	This may require you to **give reasons for** the current situation or what has happened.
Apply	This requires you to put a concept into action by applying it **to the scenario** in a relevant way.
Assess	This requires you to **judge the importance** or estimate the nature, quality or significance of an issue.

	Discuss	This will require you to consider and debate/argue about the **pros and cons** of an issue.	
	Estimate	Calculate an **approximate value** based on reasonable assumptions, and explain those assumptions, where appropriate.	
	Evaluate	This will require you to present a **'balanced' discussion** of an issue looking at both the positive and negative issues. Where numbers feature in a question, an evaluation will require you to use the numbers provided to create a value from which **a judgement** can be made.	
	Explain	This involves making an idea clear and could require you to, for example, show logically how a concept is developed, or to **give the reason for** an event.	
	Recommend	If you are asked to **'recommend'** then you are expected to **use details presented in the scenario** to create a logical and **justified** course of action.	
Step 2	Read the rest of the question		
	By reading the requirement first, you will have an idea of what you are looking out for as you read through the case overview and exhibits. This is a great time saver and means you don't end up having to read the whole question in full twice. You should do this in an active way – see Exam success skill 1: Managing Information.		
Step 3	Read the requirement again		
	Read the requirement again to remind yourself of the exact wording before starting your written answer. This will capture any misinterpretation of the requirements or any missed requirements entirely. This should become a habit in your approach and, with repeated practice, you will find the focus, relevance and depth of your answer plan will improve.		

Exam success skill 3

Answer planning: Priorities, structure and logic

This skill requires the planning of the key aspects of an answer which accurately and completely responds to the requirement.

Advice on developing this skill

Everyone will have a preferred style for an answer plan. For example, it may be a mind map, bullet-pointed lists or simply annotating the question paper. Choose the approach that you feel most comfortable with, or, if you are not sure, try out different approaches for different questions until you have found your preferred style.

For a discussion question, annotating the question paper is likely to be insufficient. It would be better to draw up a separate answer plan in the format of your choosing (eg a mind map or bullet-pointed lists).

In a **computer-based exam** you can use the copy and paste functions to **copy the question requirements to the beginning of your answer.** This will allow you to ensure that your answer plan addresses all parts of the question requirements.

You can also **copy the question requirements to the main body your answer.** This will allow you to create sub-headings for your answer, again ensuring that your answer addresses all parts of the question requirements.

Copying and pasting simply involves highlighting the relevant information and either right clicking to access the copy and paste functions, or alternatively using Ctrl C to copy and Ctrl V to paste.

Exam success skill 4

Efficient numerical analysis

This skill aims to maximise the marks awarded by making clear to the marker the process of arriving at your answer. This is achieved by laying out an answer such that, even if you make a few errors, you can still score subsequent marks for follow-on calculations. It is vital that you do not lose marks purely because the marker cannot follow what you have done.

Advice on developing this skill

This skill can be developed by applying the following process:

Step 1	**Use a standard proforma working where relevant**
	If answers can be laid out in a standard proforma then always plan to do so. This will help the marker to understand your working and allocate the marks easily. It will also help you to work through the figures in a methodical and time-efficient way.
Step 2	**Show your workings**
	Keep your workings as clear and simple as possible and ensure they are cross-referenced to the main part of your answer. Where it helps, provide brief narrative explanations to help the marker understand the steps in the calculation. This means that if a mistake is made you do not lose any subsequent marks for follow-on calculations.
Step 3	**Keep moving!**
	It is important to remember that, in an exam situation, it is difficult to get every number 100% correct. The key is therefore ensuring you do not spend too long on any single calculation. If you are struggling with a solution then make a sensible assumption, state it and move on.

In a **computer-based exam** (CBE) it is important to show the marker where numbers have come from, ie it is not sensible to perform the calculations on a calculator and then manually transfer them to the spreadsheet.

The marker needs to be able to see where the numbers have come from, for example in the following spreadsheet the marker can see that the highlighted calculation in cell F12 is calculated as 8% on a loan of $10,250m because this is what is recorded in the spreadsheet cell (as shown in the first row).

F12		▼	:	×	✓	*fx*	=-0.08*10250					
	A	B	C	D	E	F	G	H	I	J	K
2		part a	Workings								
3											
4			increase in revenue								
5			20X6	op profit 2678		133900		2% margin			
6			20X5	3% growth vs 20X5		130000					
7				change		3900					
8											
9			Answer			$m					
10											
11				operating profit		2678					
12				interest		-820					
13						1858					
14				tax 30%		-557.4					
15											
16				spending on new capacity		-975		25% of increase in revenue			
17											
18				dividend capacity		325.6					

If the workings are visible in the cell as shown here, then there is **less need to show detailed workings.** It will still sometimes be helpful to produce workings because they can reduce the likelihood of errors being made if calculations are complex.

For example, in cell F16 in the previous spreadsheet extract, workings are helpful, although there is no real need for the narrative in cell H16, as the marker will be able to follow the logic by looking at the basis for the calculation in F16, which will be something like =F7*0.25).

In a **computer-based exam** (CBE) you can also use useful spreadsheet short-cuts to improve the efficiency of numerical analysis. For AFM, useful short-cuts include the ability to calculate totals and averages, to insert different currency symbols and also to calculate NPV, IRR and MIRR.

Further details are given in the following table.

Function	Guidance & examples
Sum	=SUM(A1:A10) adds all the numbers in spreadsheet cells A1 to A10.
Average	=AVERAGE(A1:A10) averages the numbers in spreadsheet cells A1 to A10.
NPV	Net present value is based on future cash flows, assuming that the first cash flow is in one year's time.
	For example, if the future cash flows from a project arise over five years and need to be discounted at 10% then the formula could be as follows:
	=NPV(0.1, B10:F10)
	This would give the present value of cash flows from time period 1-5, the cash outflow in time 0 would then need to be deducted to calculate the net present value.
IRR	Internal rate of return is based on future cash flows (looking at cash outflows and inflows) in each year of a project, from time 0 onwards.
	For example, to identify the internal rate of return of a project arising over five years (involving time periods 0-5), the formula could be as follows:
	=IRR(A10:F10)
MIRR	Modified internal rate of return is based on future cash flows (looking at cash outflows and inflows) in each year of a project, from time 0 onwards.
	The formula is =MIRR (values, finance rate, reinvestment rate). The finance rate and reinvestment rate will normally be the same.
	For example, to identify the MIRR of the future cash flows from a project arising over five years (involving time periods 0-5) where the cost of capital to be applied to cash outflows (the finance rate) and cash inflows (reinvestment rate) is 10%, then the formula could be as follows:
	=MIRR(A10:F10, 0.1, 0.1)
Ln	This natural log function is useful in calculation of d1 in the Black-Scholes model. To use this, insert = LN and then highlight the cells containing the values for Pa and Pe. For example:
	=LN(A5/A6)
EXP	This raises 'e' to the power of a given number and is useful in the calculation of the value of a call or put option using the Black-Scholes model. To use this, insert = EXP and then highlight the cells containing the values for -rt. For example:
	=EXP(A5*A6)

Where numerical calculations require commentary then this can be provided in a word processing document with a **reference to calculations provided within the spreadsheet.**

Exam success skill 5

Effective writing and presentation

Written answers should be presented so that the marker can clearly see the points you are making, presented in the format specified in the question. The skill is to provide efficient written answers with sufficient breadth of points that answer the question, in the right depth, in the time available.

Advice on developing this skill

Step 1	Use headings
	Using the headings and sub-headings from your answer plan will give your answer structure, order and logic. This will ensure your answer links back to the requirement and is clearly signposted, making it easier for the marker to understand the different points you are making. Underlining your headings will also help the marker.
Step 2	Write your answer in short, but full, sentences
	Use short, clear sentences with the aim that every sentence should say something different and generate marks. Write in full sentences, ensuring your style is professional.

For AFM there are four professional marks in question 1 of the exam:

These can be obtained by:

(1) Providing a suitable, simple heading to the answer (eg a simple report format)
(2) Providing a short introduction paragraph outlining the structure of the report
(3) Providing a clear answer (eg referencing spreadsheet calculations where appropriate)
(4) Providing a conclusion to complete the report

None of these steps should be time consuming, and each will earn 1 mark.

Exam success skill 6

Good time management

This skill means planning your time across all the requirements so that all tasks have been attempted at the end of the 3 hours 15 minutes available and actively checking on time during your exam. This is so that you can flex your approach and prioritise requirements which, in your judgement, will generate the maximum marks in the available time remaining.

Advice on developing good time management

The exam is 3 hours 15 minutes long, which translates to 1.95 minutes per mark. Therefore a 10-mark requirement should be allocated a maximum of 20 minutes to complete your answer before you move on to the next task. At the beginning of a question, work out the amount of time you should be spending on each requirement and write the finishing time next to each requirement on your exam paper.

In **AFM** it is **crucial to spend time planning before starting to write your answer**. This allows time for a candidate to immerse themselves in the question scenarios.

Planning time can be built into time management by amending the 1.95 minutes per mark approach to allow for planning time. The total time for planning your answer should be about 20% of the total time you would allocate to a question. This means that for a section A question planning time would be 50 marks × 1.95 × 0.2 = (approximately) 20 minutes and for a section B question planning time would be 25 marks × 1.95 × 0.2 = 10 minutes.

Allowing 20% of time for planning means allocating 80% of the time for writing so the 1.95 minutes per mark approach becomes, ie 0.8 × 1.95 = 1.56 minutes per mark for writing your answer.

Keep an eye on the clock

Aim to attempt all requirements, but be ready to be ruthless and move on if your answer is not going as planned. The challenge for many is sticking to planned timings. Be aware this is difficult to achieve in the early stages of your studies and be ready to let this skill develop over time.

If you find yourself running short on time and know that a full answer is not possible in the time you have, consider recreating your plan in overview form and then add key terms and details as time allows. Remember, some marks may be available, for example, simply stating a conclusion which you don't have time to justify in full.

Question practice

Question practice is a core part of learning new topic areas. When you practise questions, you should focus on improving the Exam success skills – personal to your needs – by obtaining feedback or through a process of self-assessment.

If sitting this exam as a computer-based exam, practising as many exam-style questions as possible in the ACCA CBE practice platform will be the key to passing this exam. You should attempt questions under **timed conditions** and ensure you produce full answers to the discussion parts as well as doing the calculations. Also ensure that you attempt all mock exams under exam conditions.

ACCA have launched a free on-demand resource designed to mirror the live exam experience helping you to become more familiar with the exam format. You can access the platform via the Study Support Resources section of the ACCA website navigating to the CBE question practice section and logging in with your myACCA credentials.

Questions

1 Preparation question: Mezza (6/11, amended)   49 mins

[Note that from September 2018 questions that are wholly narrative will not be set]

Mezza Co is a large food manufacturing and wholesale company. It imports fruit and vegetables from countries in South America, Africa and Asia, and packages them in steel cans and plastic tubs and as frozen foods, for sale to supermarkets around Europe. Its suppliers range from individual farmers to government-run co-operatives, and farms run by its own subsidiary companies. In the past, Mezza Co has been very successful in its activities, and has an excellent corporate image with its customers, suppliers and employees. Indeed, Mezza Co prides itself on how it has supported local farming communities around the world and has consistently highlighted these activities in its annual reports.

However, in spite of buoyant stock markets over the last couple of years, Mezza Co's share price has remained static. Previously announcements to the stock market about growth potential led to an increase in the share price. It is thought that the current state is because there is little scope for future growth in its products. As a result the company's directors are considering diversifying into new areas. One possibility is to commercialise a product developed by a recently acquired subsidiary company. The subsidiary company is engaged in researching solutions to carbon emissions and global warming, and has developed a high carbon absorbing variety of plant that can be grown in warm, shallow sea water. The plant would then be harvested into carbon-neutral bio-fuel. This fuel, if widely used, is expected to lower carbon production levels.

Currently there is a lot of interest among the world's governments in finding solutions to climate change. Mezza Co's directors feel that this venture could enhance its reputation and result in a rise in its share price. They believe that the company's expertise would be ideally suited to commercialising the product. On a personal level, they feel that the venture's success would enhance their generous remuneration package which includes share options. It is hoped that the resulting increase in the share price would enable the options to be exercised in the future.

Mezza Co has identified the coast of Maienar, a small country in Asia, as an ideal location, as it has a large area of warm, shallow waters. Mezza Co has been operating in Maienar for many years and as a result, has a well-developed infrastructure to enable it to plant, monitor and harvest the crop, although a new facility would be needed to process the crop after harvesting. The new plant would employ local people. Mezza Co's directors have strong ties with senior government officials in Maienar and the country's politicians are keen to develop new industries, especially ones with a long-term future.

The area identified by Mezza Co is a rich fishing ground for local fishermen, who have been fishing there for many generations. However, the fishermen are poor and have little political influence. The general perception is that the fishermen contribute little to Maienar's economic development. The coastal area, although naturally beautiful, has not been well developed for tourism. It is thought that the high carbon absorbing plant, if grown on a commercial scale, may have a negative impact on fish stocks and other wildlife in the area. The resulting decline in fish stocks may make it impossible for the fishermen to continue with their traditional way of life.

Required

(a) Discuss the key issues that the directors of Mezza Co should consider when making the decision about whether or not to commercialise the new product, and suggest how these issues may be mitigated or resolved. **(17 marks)**

(b) Advise the board on what Mezza Co's integrated report should disclose about the impact of undertaking the project on Mezza Co's capitals. **(8 marks)**

(Total = 25 marks)

2 Preparation question: Bournelorth (Mar/Jun 17)   49 mins

[Note that from September 2018 questions that are wholly narrative will not be set]

Bournelorth Co is an IT company which was established by three friends ten years ago. It was listed on a local stock exchange for smaller companies nine months ago.

Bournelorth Co originally provided support to businesses in the financial services sector. It has been able to expand into other sectors over time due to the excellent services it has provided and the high quality staff whom its founders recruited. The founders have been happy with the level of profits which the IT services have generated. Over time they have increasingly left the supervision of the IT services in the hands of experienced managers and focused on developing diagnostic applications (apps). The founders have worked fairly independently of each other on development work. Each has a small team of staff and all three want their teams to work in an informal environment which they believe enhances creativity.

Two apps which Bournelorth Co developed were very successful and generated significant profits. The founders wanted the company to invest much more in developing diagnostic apps. Previously they had preferred to use internal funding, because they were worried that external finance providers would want a lot of information about how Bournelorth Co is performing. However, the amount of finance required meant that funding had to be obtained from external sources and they decided to seek a listing, as two of Bournelorth Co's principal competitors had recently been successfully listed.

25% of Bournelorth Co's equity shares were made available on the stock exchange for external investors, which was the minimum allowed by the rules of the exchange. The founders have continued to own the remaining 75% of Bournelorth Co's equity share capital. Although the listing was fully subscribed, the price which new investors paid was lower than the directors had originally hoped.

The board now consists of the three founders, who are the executive directors, and two independent non-executive directors, who were appointed when the company was listed. The non-executive directors have expressed concerns about the lack of frequency of formal board meetings and the limited time spent by the executive directors overseeing the company's activities, compared with the time they spend leading development work. The non-executive directors would also like Bournelorth Co's external auditors to carry out a thorough review of its risk management and control systems.

The funds obtained from the listing have helped Bournelorth Co expand its development activities. Bournelorth Co's competitors have recently launched some very successful diagnostic apps and its executive directors are now afraid that Bournelorth Co will fall behind its competitors unless there is further investment in development. However, they disagree about how this investment should be funded. One executive director believes that Bournelorth Co should consider selling off its IT support and consultancy services business. The second executive director favours a rights issue and the third executive director would prefer to seek debt finance. At present Bournelorth Co has low gearing and the director who is in favour of debt finance believes that there is too much uncertainty associated with obtaining further equity finance, as investors do not always act rationally.

Required

(a) Discuss the factors which will determine whether the sources of finance suggested by the executive directors are used to finance further investment in diagnostic applications (apps).

(8 marks)

(b) (i) Identify the risks associated with investing in the development of apps and describe the controls which Bournelorth Co should have over its investment in development.

(6 marks)

(ii) Discuss the issues which determine the information Bournelorth Co communicates to external finance providers.

(3 marks)

(c) (i) Explain the insights which behavioural finance provides about investor behaviour.

(3 marks)

(ii) Assess how behavioural factors may affect the share price of Bournelorth Co.

(5 marks)

(Total = 25 marks)

3 Cadnam (Sep/Dec 19)   49 mins

Cadnam Co is a large company in the support services sector.

Cadnam Co's most recent annual report, for the year ended 31 December 20X5, acknowledged challenges for the company, including financing the major investment programme required to meet its clients' increasing expectations. Cadnam Co also faced upward pressure on employment costs, fuelled by a 'fair wage' campaign which adversely compared wage rises in the support services sector with increases in dividends and directors' remuneration, and a consequent government enquiry into low pay in the sector.

Cadnam Co's board, however, was confident that the company would be able to renew a number of large contracts that were coming up for review. The report stressed the strength of Cadnam Co's senior management team as a vital success factor. Directors' remuneration packages thus reflected the need to, in a competitive labour market, retain its directors at senior level.

In the stakeholder engagement section of its annual report, Cadnam Co highlighted that it had fulfilled its aim of guaranteeing investors a consistent rise in dividends, and its board was confident that Cadnam Co would be able to maintain the recent rate of dividend increase. The report also stated that Cadnam Co was looking to publish a full integrated report over the next couple of years.

Dividend policy

At Cadnam Co's last annual general meeting, there were no questions about the level of profits, dividends or directors' remuneration. However, a recent investment analysts' report on the support services sector highlighted Cadnam Co as a company which might have problems in the next few years. The report suggested that Cadnam Co's investment and dividend policies could not both be maintained. It highlighted one of Cadnam Co's principal competitors, Holmsley Co, as a company whose policies it believed would sustain long-term growth. It highlighted directors' remuneration as an area where Holmsley Co's policies were more likely to encourage long-term value creation and share price increases than Cadnam Co's policies.

Cadnam Co's board is currently considering the comments made by the investment analysts, and also assessing what the dividend for 20X6 should be.

Cadnam Co

	20X2 $m	20X3 $m	20X4 $m	20X5 $m
Profit after tax	1,380	1,490	1,550	1,580
Dividends	765	840	925	1,020
Investment in additional assets	282	312	584	864
Share price ($)	$4.88	$5.35	$5.61	$5.75
Gearing (debt/(debt + equity)) (market value) × 100%	33.0%	33.2%	35.0%	38.8%

Holmsley Co

	20X2 $m	20X3 $m	20X4 $m	20X5 $m
Profit after tax	1,485	1,590	1,700	1,830
Dividends	560	590	621	654
Investment in additional assets	595	625	660	690
Share price	$5.04	$5.23	$5.55	$5.93
Gearing (debt/(debt + equity)) (market value) × 100%	35.1%	35.2%	34.9%	34.7%

Average gearing in the support services sector since 20X1 has been stable at around 34%. There have been no changes in the issued share capital of Cadnam Co and Holmsley Co since 20X1.

Directors' remuneration

	Cadnam Co	Holmsley Co
Average salary executive director	$550,000	$550,000
Performance bonus	Maximum 25% of salary	Maximum 30% of salary
Loyalty bonus	Maximum 10% of salary	None
Share options	None	Options to be exercised on 31 December 20X8 at an exercise price of $7.00

Cadnam Co 20X6 forecast

Forecasts prepared by Cadnam Co's finance director for 20X6 predict that:

- Cadnam Co's pre-tax operating profit for 20X6 will be $2,678 million, an increase of 3% compared with 20X5. The operating profit margin will be 2%, the same as for 20X5.

- The tax rate will be 30%.

- Average debt in 20X6 will be $10,250 million and predicted year-end gearing will be 41.3%. The average pre-tax interest rate on the debt will be 8%.

- The investment required to keep the non-current asset base at its present productive capacity in 20X6 will be $2,430 million, which has been included in the calculation of operating profit as depreciation.

- Investment required in additional assets in 20X6 will be $0.25 for every $1 increase in revenue.

Required

(a) Calculate the forecast dividend capacity of Cadnam Co for 20X6. **(5 marks)**

(b) Discuss the viability and financial impacts of Cadnam Co seeking to maintain its current dividend policy, supporting your answers with relevant calculations.

Note. 6 marks are available for calculations in part (b). **(12 marks)**

(c) Discuss the governance and ethical issues associated with Cadnam Co's dividend and directors' remuneration policies. **(8 marks)**

(Total = 25 marks)

4 Chawan (6/15)

The treasury department of Chawan Co, a listed company, aims to maintain a portfolio of around $360 million consisting of equity shares, corporate bonds and government bonds, which it can turn into cash quickly for investment projects. Chawan Co is considering disposing of 27 million shares, valued at $2.15 each, which it has invested in Oden Co. The head of Chawan Co's treasury department is of the opinion that, should the decision be made to dispose of its equity stake in Oden Co, this should be sold through a dark pool network and not sold on the stock exchange where Oden Co's shares are listed. In the last few weeks, there have also been rumours that Oden Co may become subject to a takeover bid.

Oden Co operates in the travel and leisure (T&L) sector, and the poor weather conditions in recent years, coupled with a continuing recession, have meant that the T&L sector is underperforming. Over the past three years, sales revenue fell by an average of 8% per year in the T&L sector. However, there are signs that the economy is starting to recover, but this is by no means certain.

Given below are extracts from the recent financial statements and other financial information for Oden Co and the T&L sector.

ODEN CO
YEAR ENDING 31 MAY

	20X3 $m	20X4 $m	20X5 $m
Total non-current assets	972	990	980
Total current assets	128	142	126
Total assets	1,100	1,132	1,106
Equity			
Ordinary shares ($0.50)	300	300	300
Reserves	305	329	311
Total equity	605	629	611
Non-current liabilities			
Bank loans	115	118	100
Bonds	250	250	260
Total non-current liabilities	365	368	360
Current liabilities			
Trade and other payables	42	45	37
Bank overdraft	88	90	98
Total current liabilities	130	135	135
Total equity and liabilities	1,100	1,132	1,106

ODEN CO
YEAR ENDING 31 MAY

	20X3 $m	20X4 $m	20X5 $m
Sales revenue	1,342	1,335	1,185
Operating profit	218	203	123
Finance costs	(23)	(27)	(35)
Profit before tax	195	176	88
Taxation	(35)	(32)	(16)
Profit for the year	160	144	72

OTHER FINANCIAL INFORMATION (BASED ON ANNUAL FIGURES TILL 31 MAY OF EACH YEAR)

	20X2	20X3	20X4	20X5
Oden Co average share price ($)	2.10	2.50	2.40	2.20
Oden Co dividend per share ($)	0.15	0.18	0.20	0.15
T&L sector average share price ($)	3.80	4.40	4.30	4.82
T&L sector average earnings per share ($)	0.32	0.36	0.33	0.35
T&L sector average dividend per share ($)	0.25	0.29	0.29	0.31
Oden Co's equity beta	1.5	1.5	1.6	2.0
T&L sector average equity beta	1.5	1.4	1.5	1.6

The risk-free rate and the market return have remained fairly constant over the last ten years at 4% and 10% respectively.

Required

(a) Explain what a dark pool network is and why Chawan Co may want to dispose of its equity stake in Oden Co through one, instead of through the stock exchange where Oden Co's shares are listed. **(5 marks)**

(b) Discuss whether or not Chawan Co should dispose of its equity stake in Oden Co. Provide relevant calculations to support the discussion.

Note. Up to 10 marks are available for the calculations. **(20 marks)**

(Total = 25 marks)

5 High K (Sep/Dec 17) 49 mins

High K Co is one of the three largest supermarket chains in the country of Townia. Its two principal competitors, Dely Co and Leminster Co, are of similar size to High K Co. In common with its competitors (but see below), High K Co operates three main types of store:

- Town centre stores – these sell food and drink and a range of small household items. High K Co's initial growth was based on its town centre stores, but it has been shutting them over the last decade, although the rate of closure has slowed in the last couple of years.

- Convenience stores – these are smaller and sell food and drink and very few other items. Between 20X3 and 20Y3, High K Co greatly expanded the number of convenience stores it operated. Their performance has varied, however, and since 20Y3, High K Co has not opened any new stores and closed a number of the worst-performing stores.

- Out-of-town stores – these sell food and drink and a full range of household items, including large electrical goods and furniture. The number of out-of-town stores which High K Co operated increased significantly until 20Y0, but has only increased slightly since.

The majority of town centre and out-of-town stores premises are owned by High K Co, but 85% of convenience stores premises are currently leased.

High K Co also sells most of its range of products online, either offering customers home delivery or 'click and collect' (where the customer orders the goods online and picks them up from a collection point in one of the stores).

High K Co's year end is 31 December. When its 20Y6 results were published in April 20Y7, High K Co's chief executive emphasised that the group was focusing on:

- Increasing total shareholder return by improvements in operating efficiency and enhancement of responsiveness to customer needs

- Ensuring competitive position by maintaining flexibility to respond to new strategic challenges

- Maintaining financial strength by using diverse sources of funding, including making use in future of revolving credit facilities

Since April 20Y7, Dely Co and Leminster Co have both announced that they will be making significant investments to boost online sales. Dely Co intends to fund its investments by closing all its town centre and convenience stores, although it also intends to open more out-of-town stores in popular locations.

The government of Townia was re-elected in May 20Y7. In the 18 months prior to the election, it eased fiscal policy and consumer spending significantly increased. However, it has tightened fiscal policy since the election to avoid the economy overheating. It has also announced an investigation into whether the country's large retail chains treat their suppliers unfairly.

Extracts from High K Co's 20Y6 financial statements and other information about it are given below:

HIGH K CO
STATEMENT OF PROFIT OR LOSS EXTRACTS
YEAR ENDING 31 DECEMBER (ALL AMOUNTS IN $m)

	20Y4	20Y5	20Y6
Sales revenue	23,508	23,905	24,463
Gross profit	1,018	1,211	1,514
Operating profit	204	407	712
Finance costs	(125)	(115)	(100)
Profit after tax	52	220	468
Dividends	150	170	274

HIGH K CO STATEMENT OF FINANCIAL POSITION EXTRACTS
YEAR ENDING 31 DECEMBER (ALL AMOUNTS IN $m)

	20Y4	20Y5	20Y6
Non-current assets	10,056	9,577	8,869
Cash and cash equivalents	24	709	1,215
Other current assets	497	618	747
Total non-current and current assets	10,577	10,904	10,831
Equity			
Ordinary shares ($1)	800	800	800
Reserves	7,448	7,519	7,627
Total equity	8,248	8,319	8,427
Non-current liabilities	1,706	1,556	1,246
Current liabilities	623	1,029	1,158
Other information			
Market price per share (in $, $3.89 at end of 20Y3, $3.17 currently)	3.54	3.34	3.23
Staff working in shops ('000)	78	75	72
Segment information			
Revenue ($m)			
Town centre stores	5,265	5,189	5,192
Convenience stores	3,786	3,792	3,833
Out-of-town stores	10,220	10,340	10,547
Store revenue	19,271	19,321	19,572
Online sales	4,237	4,584	4,891
Number of stores			
Town centre stores	165	157	153
Convenience stores	700	670	640
Out-of-town stores	220	224	227

Required

(a) Evaluate High K Co's financial performance. You should indicate in your discussion areas where further information about High K Co would be helpful. Provide relevant calculations for ratios and trends to support your evaluation.

Note. Up to 10 marks are available for calculations. **(21 marks)**

(b) Discuss how High K Co may seek to finance an investment programme. **(4 marks)**

(Total = 25 marks)

BPP
LEARNING
MEDIA

6 Tillinton (Sep 18)   49 mins

Tillinton Co is a listed company which has traditionally manufactured children's clothing and toys with long lives. Five years ago, it began manufacturing electronic toys and has since made significant investment in development and production facilities. The first electronic toys which Tillinton Co introduced into the market were received very well, partly as it was seen to be ahead of its competitors in making the most of the technology available.

The country where Tillinton Co is listed has seen a significant general increase in share prices over the last three years, with companies in the electronic goods sector showing particularly rapid increases.

Statement by Tillinton Co's chief executive

Assume it is now September 20X3. Tillinton Co's annual report for the year ended 31 March 20X3 has just been published. Its chief executive commented when announcing the company's results:

> I am very pleased to report that revenue and gross profits have shown bigger increases than in 20X2, resulting in higher post-tax earnings and our company being able to maintain increases in dividends. The sustained increase in our share price clearly demonstrates how happy investors are with us. Our cutting-edge electronic toys continue to perform well and justify our sustained investment in them. Our results have also benefited from improvements in operational efficiencies for our older ranges and better working capital management. We are considering the development of further ranges of electronic toys for children, or developing other electronic products for adults. If necessary, we may consider scaling down or selling off our operations for some of our older products.

Steph Slindon represents an institutional investor who holds shares in Tillinton Co. Steph is doubtful whether its share price will continue to increase, because she thinks that Tillinton Co's situation may not be as good as its chief executive suggests and because she believes that current share price levels generally may not be sustainable.

Financial information

Extracts from Tillinton Co's financial statements for the last three years and other information about it are given below.

TILLINTON CO STATEMENT OF PROFIT OR LOSS IN YEARS ENDING 31 MARCH
(ALL AMOUNTS IN $m)

	20X1	20X2	20X3
Sales revenue	1,385	1,636	1,914
Gross profit	381	451	528
Operating profit	205	252	300
Finance costs	(46)	(50)	(66)
Profit before tax	159	202	234
Taxation	(40)	(51)	(65)
Profit after tax	119	151	169
Dividends	(60)	(72)	(84)

TILLINTON CO STATEMENT OF FINANCIAL POSITION IN YEARS ENDING 31 MARCH
(ALL AMOUNTS IN $m)

	20X1	20X2	20X3
Non-current assets	2,070	2,235	2,449
Cash and cash equivalents	10	15	15
Other current assets	150	130	125
Total non-current and current assets	2,230	2,380	2,589
Equity			
Ordinary shares ($0.50)	400	400	400
Reserves	805	884	969
Total equity	1,205	1,284	1,369
Non-current liabilities	920	970	1,000
Current liabilities	105	126	220
Total equity and liabilities	2,230	2,380	2,589

Other information

	20X1	20X2	20X3
Market price per $0.50 share ($2.50 at 31 March 20X0, $5.06 in Sept 20X3)	$2.76	$3.49	$4.44
Earnings per share ($)	0.15	0.19	0.21
Dividend per share ($)	0.075	0.09	0.105
Analysis of revenue			
Electronic toys	249	319	390
Non-electronic toys	302	350	404
Clothing	834	967	1,120
	1,385	1,636	1,914
Analysis of gross profit			
Electronic toys	100	112	113
Non-electronic toys	72	88	105
Clothing	209	251	310
	381	451	528

Note. None of Tillinton Co's loan finance in 20X3 is repayable within one year.

Required

(a) Evaluate Tillinton Co's performance and business prospects in the light of the chief executive's comments and Steph Slindon's concerns. Provide relevant calculations for ratios and trends to support your evaluation.

Note. 10 marks are available for the calculations. **(20 marks)**

(b) Discuss how behavioural factors may have resulted in Tillinton Co's share price being higher than is warranted by a rational analysis of its position. **(5 marks)**

(Total = 25 marks)

7 Limni Co (6/13) 49 mins

Limni Co is a large company manufacturing hand-held electronic devices such as mobile phones and tablet computers. The company has been growing rapidly over the last few years, but it also has high research and development expenditure. It is involved in a number of projects worldwide, developing new and innovative products and systems in a rapidly changing industry. Due to the nature of the industry, this significant growth in earnings has never been stable, but has depended largely on the success of the new innovations and competitor actions. However, in the last two years it seems that the rapid period of growth is slowing, with fewer products coming to market compared to previous years.

Limni Co has never paid dividends and has financed projects through internally generated funds and with occasional rights issues of new share capital. It currently has insignificant levels of debt. The

BPP
LEARNING
MEDIA

retained cash reserves have recently grown because of a drop in the level of investment in new projects.

The company has an active treasury division which invests spare funds in traded equities, bonds and other financial instruments; and releases the funds when required for new projects. The division also manages cash flow risk using money and derivative markets. The treasury division is currently considering investing in three companies with the following profit after tax (PAT) and dividend history:

	Company Theta		Company Omega		Company Kappa	
Year	PAT	Dividends	PAT	Dividends	PAT	Dividends
	$'000	$'000	$'000	$'000	$'000	$'000
20X7	57,100	22,840	93,300	60,560	162,400	44,100
20X6	54,400	21,760	90,600	57,680	141,500	34,200
20X5	52,800	21,120	88,000	54,840	108,900	26,300
20X4	48,200	19,280	85,400	52,230	105,700	20,250
20X3	45,500	18,200	82,900	49,740	78,300	15,700

All three companies' share capital has remained largely unchanged since 20X3.

Recently, Limni Co's board of directors (BoD) came under pressure from the company's larger shareholders to start returning some of the funds, currently retained by the company, back to the shareholders. The BoD thinks that the shareholders have a strong case to ask for repayments. However, it is unsure whether to pay a special, one-off large dividend from its dividend capacity and retained funds, followed by small annual dividend payments, or to undertake a periodic share buyback scheme over the next few years.

Limni Co is due to prepare its statement of profit or loss shortly and estimates that the annual sales revenue will be $600 million, on which its profit before tax is expected to be 23% of sales revenue. It charges depreciation of 25% on a straight-line basis on its non-current assets of $220 million. It estimates that $67 million investment in current and non-current assets was spent during the year. It is due to receive $15 million in dividends from its subsidiary companies, on which annual tax of 20% on average has been paid. Limni Co itself pays annual tax at 26%, and the tax authorities where Limni Co is based charge tax on dividend remittances made by overseas subsidiary companies, but give full credit on tax already paid on those remittances. In order to fund the new policy of returning funds to shareholders, Limni Co's BoD wants to increase the current estimated dividend capacity by 10%, by asking the overseas subsidiary companies for higher repatriations.

Required

(a) Discuss Limni Co's current dividend, financing and risk management policies, and suggest how the decision to return retained funds back to the shareholders will affect these policies.
(8 marks)

(b) Evaluate the dividend policies of each of the three companies that Limni Co is considering investing in, and discuss which company Limni Co might select. **(8 marks)**

(c) Calculate, and briefly comment on, how much the dividends from overseas companies need to increase by, to increase Limni Co's dividend capacity by 10%. **(6 marks)**

(d) Discuss the benefits to Limni Co's shareholders of receiving repayments through a share buyback scheme as opposed to the dividend scheme described above. **(3 marks)**

(Total = 25 marks)

8 Arthuro (Mar/Jun 18)   49 mins

Arthuro Co is based in Hittyland and is listed on Hittyland's stock exchange. Arthuro Co has one wholly-owned subsidiary, Bowerscots Co, based in the neighbouring country of Owlia. Hittyland and Owlia are in a currency union and the currency of both countries is the $.

Arthuro Co purchased 100% of Bowerscots Co's share capital three years ago. Arthuro Co has the power under the acquisition to determine the level of dividend paid by Bowerscots Co. However, Arthuro Co's board decided to let Bowerscots Co's management team have some discretion when making investment decisions. Arthuro Co's board decided that it should receive dividends of 60% of Bowerscots Co's post-tax profits and has allowed Bowerscots Co to use its remaining retained earnings to fund investments chosen by its management. A bonus linked to Bowerscots Co's after-tax profits is a significant element of Bowerscots Co's managers' remuneration.

Bowerscots Co operates in a very competitive environment. Recently, a senior member of its management team has left to join a competitor.

Arthuro Co's dividend policy

Until three months ago, Arthuro Co had 90 million $2 equity shares in issue and $135 million 8% bonds. Three months ago it made a 1 for 3 rights issue. A number of shareholders did not take up their rights, but sold them on, so there have been changes in its shareholder base. Some shareholders expressed concern about dilution of their dividend income as a result of the rights issue. Therefore, Arthuro Co's board felt it had to promise, for the foreseeable future, at least to maintain the dividend of $0.74 per equity share, which it paid for the two years before the rights issue.

Arthuro Co's board is nevertheless concerned about whether it will have sufficient funds available to fulfil its promise about the dividend. It has asked the finance director to forecast its dividend capacity based on assumptions about what will happen in a 'normal' year. The finance director has made the following assumptions in the forecast:

(1) Sales revenue can be assumed to be 4% greater than the most recent year's of $520 million.

(2) The operating profit margin can be assumed to be 20%.

(3) Operating profit can be assumed to be reported after charging depreciation of $30 million and profit on disposal of non-current assets of $5.9 million. The cost of the non-current assets sold can be assumed to be $35 million and its accumulated depreciation to be $24.6 million. Depreciation is allowable for tax and the profit on disposal is fully chargeable to tax.

(4) The net book value of non-current assets at the year end in the most recent accounts was $110 million. To maintain productive capacity, sufficient investment to increase this net book value figure 12 months later by 4% should be assumed, in line with the increase in sales. The calculation of investment required for the year should take into account the depreciation charged of $30 million, and net book value of the non-current assets disposed of during the year.

(5) A $0.15 investment in working capital can be assumed for every $1 increase in sales revenue.

(6) Bowerscots Co's pre-tax profits can be assumed to be $45 million.

Arthuro Co's directors have decided that if there is a shortfall of dividend capacity, compared with the dividends required to maintain the current dividend level, the percentage of post-tax profits of Bowerscots Co paid as dividend should increase, if necessary up to 100%.

Taxation

Arthuro Co pays corporation tax at 30% and Bowerscots Co pays corporation tax at 20%. A withholding tax of 5% is deducted from any dividends remitted by Bowerscots Co. There is a bilateral tax treaty between Hittyland and Owlia. Corporation tax is payable by Arthuro Co on profits declared by Bowerscots Co, but Hittyland gives full credit for corporation tax already paid in Owlia. Hittyland gives no credit for withholding tax paid on dividends in Owlia.

Required

(a) (i) Estimate Arthuro Co's forecast dividend capacity for a 'normal' year.   **(11 marks)**

(ii) Estimate the level of dividend required from Bowerscots Co to give Arthuro Co sufficient dividend capacity to maintain its dividend level of $0.74 per equity share.
(3 marks)

(b)   Arthuro Co has decided to increase its level of dividend from Bowerscots Co if its dividend capacity is insufficient.

Required

(i)   From Arthuro Co's viewpoint, discuss the financial benefits of, and problems with, this decision.   **(5 marks)**

(ii)   Discuss the agency problems, and how they might be resolved, with this decision.

(6 marks)

(Total = 25 marks)

9 Lamri (12/10, amended)   49 mins

Lamri Co (Lamri), a listed company, is expecting sales revenue to grow to $80 million next year, which is an increase of 20% from the current year. The operating profit margin for next year is forecast to be the same as this year at 30% of sales revenue. In addition to these profits, Lamri receives 75% of the after-tax profits from one of its wholly owned foreign subsidiaries, Magnolia Co (Magnolia), as dividends. However, its second wholly owned foreign subsidiary, Strymon Co (Strymon), does not pay dividends.

Lamri is due to pay dividends of $7.5 million shortly and has maintained a steady 8% annual growth rate in dividends over the past few years. The company has grown rapidly in the last few years as a result of investment in key projects and this is likely to continue.

For the coming year it is expected that Lamri will require the following capital investment.

• An investment equivalent to the amount of depreciation to keep its non-current asset base at the present productive capacity. Lamri charges depreciation of 25% on a straight-line basis on its non-current assets of $15 million. This charge has been included when calculating the operating profit amount.

• A 25% investment in additional non-current assets for every $1 increase in sales revenue.

• $4.5 million additional investment in non-current assets for a new project.

Lamri also requires a 15% investment in working capital for every $1 increase in sales revenue.

Strymon produces specialist components solely for Magnolia to assemble into finished goods. Strymon will produce 300,000 specialist components at $12 variable cost per unit and will incur fixed costs of $2.1 million for the coming year. It will then transfer the components to Magnolia at full cost price, where they will be assembled at a cost of $8 per unit and sold for $50 per unit. Magnolia will incur additional fixed costs of $1.5 million in the assembly process.

Tax-Ethic (TE) is a charitable organisation devoted to reducing tax avoidance schemes by companies operating in poor countries around the world. TE has petitioned Lamri's board of directors to reconsider Strymon's policy of transferring goods at full cost. TE suggests that the policy could be changed to cost plus 40% mark-up. If Lamri changes Strymon's policy, it is expected that Strymon would be asked to remit 75% of its after-tax profits as dividends to Lamri.

Other information

1   Lamri's outstanding non-current liabilities of $35 million, on which it pays interest of 8% per year, and its 30 million $1 issued equity capital will not change for the coming year.

2   Lamri's, Magnolia's and Strymon's profits are taxed at 28%, 22% and 42% respectively. A withholding tax of 10% is deducted from any dividends remitted from Strymon.

3   The tax authorities where Lamri is based charge tax on profits made by subsidiary companies but give full credit for tax already paid by overseas subsidiaries.

4   All costs and revenues are in $ equivalent amounts and exchange rate fluctuations can be ignored.

Required

(a) Calculate Lamri's dividend capacity for the coming year prior to implementing TE's proposal and after implementing the proposal. **(14 marks)**

(b) Comment on the impact of implementing TE's proposal and suggest possible actions Lamri may take as a result. **(6 marks)**

(c) Outline the mechanisms that the tax authorities could use to prevent transfer price manipulation by Lamri. **(5 marks)**

(Total = 25 marks)

10 Moonstar (Sep/Dec 15)   49 mins

Moonstar Co is a property development company which is planning to undertake a $200 million commercial property development. Moonstar Co has had some difficulties over the last few years, with some developments not generating the expected returns and the company has at times struggled to pay its finance costs. As a result Moonstar Co's credit rating has been lowered, affecting the terms it can obtain for bank finance. Although Moonstar Co is listed on its local stock exchange, 75% of the share capital is held by members of the family who founded the company. The family members who are shareholders do not wish to subscribe for a rights issue and are unwilling to dilute their control over the company by authorising a new issue of equity shares. Moonstar Co's board is therefore considering other methods of financing the development, which the directors believe will generate higher returns than other recent investments, as the country where Moonstar Co is based appears to be emerging from recession.

Securitisation proposals

One of the non-executive directors of Moonstar Co has proposed that it should raise funds by means of a securitisation process, transferring the rights to the rental income from the commercial property development to a special purpose vehicle. Her proposals assume that the leases will generate an income of 11% per year to Moonstar Co over a ten-year period. She proposes that Moonstar Co should use 90% of the value of the investment for a collateralised loan obligation which should be structured as follows:

- 60% of the collateral value to support a tranche of A-rated floating rate loan notes offering investors LIBOR plus 150 basis points

- 15% of the collateral value to support a tranche of B-rated fixed rate loan notes offering investors 12%

- 15% of the collateral value to support a tranche of C-rated fixed rate loan notes offering investors 13%

- 10% of the collateral value to support a tranche as subordinated certificates, with the return being the excess of receipts over payments from the securitisation process

The non-executive director believes that there will be sufficient demand for all tranches of the loan notes from investors. Investors will expect the income stream from the development to be low risk, as they will expect the property market to improve with the recession coming to an end and enough potential lessees to be attracted by the new development.

The non-executive director predicts that there would be annual costs of $200,000 in administering the loan. She acknowledges that there would be interest rate risks associated with the proposal, and proposes a fixed for variable interest rate swap on the A-rated floating rate notes, exchanging LIBOR for 9.5%.

However, the finance director believes that the prediction of the income from the development that the non-executive director has made is over-optimistic. He believes that it is most likely that the total value of the rental income will be 5% lower than the non-executive director has forecast. He believes that there is some risk that the returns could be so low as to jeopardise the income for the C-rated fixed rate loan note holders.

Islamic finance

Moonstar Co's chief executive has wondered whether Sukuk finance would be a better way of funding the development than the securitisation.

Moonstar Co's chairman has pointed out that a major bank in the country where Moonstar Co is located has begun to offer a range of Islamic financial products. The chairman has suggested that a Mudaraba contract would be the most appropriate method of providing the funds required for the investment.

Required

(a) Calculate the amounts in $ which each of the tranches can expect to receive from the securitisation arrangement proposed by the non-executive director and discuss how the variability in rental income affects the returns from the securitisation. **(11 marks)**

(b) Discuss the benefits and risks for Moonstar Co associated with the securitisation arrangement that the non-executive director has proposed. **(6 marks)**

(c) (i) Discuss the suitability of Sukuk finance to fund the investment, including an assessment of its appeal to potential investors. **(4 marks)**

   (ii) Discuss whether a Mudaraba contract would be an appropriate method of financing the investment and discuss why the bank may have concerns about providing finance by this method. **(4 marks)**

(Total = 25 marks)

ADVANCED INVESTMENT APPRAISAL

Questions 11 to 23 cover advanced investment appraisal, the subject of Chapters 3-7 of the BPP Workbook for AFM.

11 Preparation question: Cathlynn   29 mins

(a)   The current share price of Cathlynn plc is £3.50. Using the Black-Scholes model, estimate the value of a European call option on the shares of the company that has an exercise price of £3.30 and three months to run before it expires. The risk-free rate of interest is 8% and the variance of the rate of return on the share has been 12%.

Note. The Black-Scholes formula shows call price for a European option P_c where

$P_c = P_s N(d_1) - Xe^{-rT} N(d_2)$

Where N(d) = cumulative distribution function

$$d_1 = \frac{\ln(P_s / X) + rT}{\sigma\sqrt{T}} + 0.5\sigma\sqrt{T}$$

$d_2 = d_1 - \sigma\sqrt{T}$

P_s = share price

e = the exponential constant 2.7183

X = exercise price of option

r = annual (continuously compounded) risk-free rate of return

T = time of expiry of option in years

σ = share price volatility, the standard deviation of the rate of return on shares

$N(d_x)$ = delta, the probability that a deviation of less than d_x will occur in a normal distribution with a mean of zero and a standard deviation of one

ln = natural log

Normal distribution tables are in the appendix to this Kit.   (10 marks)

(b)   Discuss the main limitations of the Black-Scholes model.   (5 marks)

(Total = 15 marks)

12 Preparation question: Faoilean (6/14)   49 mins

[Note that from September 2018 questions that are wholly narrative will not be set]

The Chief Executive Officer (CEO) of Faoilean Co has just returned from a discussion at a leading university on the 'application of options to investment decisions and corporate value'. She wants to understand how some of the ideas which were discussed can be applied to decisions made at Faoilean Co. She is still a little unclear about some of the discussion on options and their application, and wants further clarification on the following:

1   Faoilean Co is involved in the exploration and extraction of oil and gas. Recently there have been indications that there could be significant deposits of oil and gas just off the shores of the Republic of Ireland. The government of the Republic of Ireland has invited companies to submit bids for the rights to commence the initial exploration of the area to assess the likelihood and amount of oil and gas deposits, with further extraction rights to follow. Faoilean Co is considering putting in a bid for the rights. The speaker leading the discussion suggested that using options as an investment assessment tool would be particularly useful to Faoilean Co in this respect.

2   The speaker further suggested that options were useful in determining the value of equity and default risk, and suggested that this was why companies facing severe financial distress could still have a positive equity value.

3   Towards the end of the discussion, the speaker suggested that changes in the values of options can be measured in terms of a number of risk factors known as the 'greeks', such as the 'vega'. The CEO is unclear why option values are affected by so many different risk factors.

Required

(a) With regard to (1) above, discuss how Faoilean Co may use the idea of options to help with the investment decision in bidding for the exploration rights, and explain the assumptions made when using the idea of options in making investment decisions.   **(11 marks)**

(b) With regard to (2) above, discuss how options could be useful in determining the value of equity and default risk, and why companies facing severe financial distress still have positive equity values.   **(9 marks)**

(c) With regard to (3) above, explain why changes in option values are determined by numerous different risk factors and what 'vega' determines.   **(5 marks)**

(Total = 25 marks)

13 Fernhurst (Sep/Dec 16)   49 mins

Fernhurst Co is a manufacturer of mobile communications technology. It is about to launch a new communications device, the Milland, which its directors believe is both more technologically advanced and easier to use than devices currently offered by its rivals.

Investment in the Milland

The Milland will require a major investment in facilities. Fernhurst Co's directors believe that this can take place very quickly and production be started almost immediately.

Fernhurst Co expects to sell 132,500 units of the Milland in its first year. Sales volume is expected to increase by 20% in Year 2 and 30% in Year 3, and then be the same in Year 4 as Year 3, as the product reaches the end of its useful life. The initial selling price in Year 1 is expected to be $100 per unit, before increasing with the rate of inflation annually.

The variable cost of each unit is expected to be $43.68 in Year 1, rising by the rate of inflation in subsequent years annually. Fixed costs are expected to be $900,000 in Year 1, rising by the rate of inflation in subsequent years annually.

The initial investment in non-current assets is expected to be $16,000,000. Fernhurst Co will also need to make an immediate investment of $1,025,000 in working capital. The working capital will be increased annually at the start of each of Years 2 to 4 by the inflation rate and is fully recoverable at the end of the project's life. Fernhurst Co will also incur one-off marketing expenditure of $1,500,000 post-inflation after the launch of the Milland. The marketing expenditure can be assumed to be made at the end of Year 1 and be a tax-allowable expense.

Fernhurst Co pays company tax on profits at an annual rate of 25%. Tax is payable in the year that the tax liability arises. Tax-allowable depreciation is available at 20% on the investment in non-current assets on a reducing balance basis. A balancing adjustment will be available in Year 4. The realisable value of the investment at the end of Year 4 is expected to be zero.

The expected annual rate of inflation in the country in which Fernhurst Co is located is 4% in Year 1 and 5% in Years 2 to 4.

The applicable cost of capital for this investment appraisal is 11%.

Other calculations

Fernhurst Co's finance director has indicated that besides needing a net present value calculation based on this data for the next board meeting, he also needs to know the figure for the project's duration, to indicate to the board how returns from the project will be spread over time.

Failure of launch of the Milland

The finance director would also like some simple analysis based on the possibility that the marketing expenditure is not effective and the launch fails, as he feels that the product's price may be too high. He has suggested that there is a 15% chance that the Milland will have negative net cash flows for Year 1 of $1,000,000 or more. He would like to know by what percentage the selling price could be reduced or increased to result in the investment having a zero net present value, assuming demand remained the same.

Assessment of new products

Fernhurst Co's last board meeting discussed another possible new product, the Racton, and the finance director presented a range of financial data relating to this product, including the results of net present value and payback evaluations. One of the non-executive directors, who is not a qualified accountant, stated that they found it difficult to see the significance of the different items of financial data. Their understanding was that Fernhurst Co merely had to ensure that the investment had a positive net present value and shareholders were bound to be satisfied with it, as it would maximise their wealth in the long term. The finance director commented that, in reality, some shareholders looked at the performance of the investments which Fernhurst Co made over the short term, whereas some were more concerned with the longer term. The financial data he presented to board meetings included both short- and long-term measures.

Required

(a)   Evaluate the financial acceptability of the investment in the Milland and calculate and comment on the investment's duration.   **(15 marks)**

(b)   Calculate the percentage change in the selling price required for the investment to have a zero net present value, and discuss the significance of your results.   **(5 marks)**

(c)   Discuss the non-executive director's understanding of net present value and explain the importance of other measures in providing data about an investment's short- and long-term performance.   **(5 marks)**

(Total = 25 marks)

14 Tisa Co (6/12, amended)   49 mins

Tisa Co is considering an opportunity to produce an innovative component which, when fitted into motor vehicle engines, will enable them to utilise fuel more efficiently. The component can be manufactured using either process Omega or process Zeta. Although this is an entirely new line of business for Tisa Co, it is of the opinion that developing either process over a period of four years and then selling the production rights at the end of four years to another company may prove lucrative.

The annual after-tax cash flows for each process are as follows:

Process Omega

Year	0	1	2	3	4
After-tax cash flows ($'000)	(3,800)	1,220	1,153	1,386	3,829

Process Zeta

Year	0	1	2	3	4
After-tax cash flows ($'000)	(3,800)	643	546	1,055	5,990

Tisa Co has 10 million 50c shares trading at 180c each. Its loans have a current value of $3.6 million and an average after-tax cost of debt of 4.50%. Tisa Co's capital structure is unlikely to change significantly following the investment in either process.

Elfu Co manufactures electronic parts for cars including the production of a component similar to the one being considered by Tisa Co. Elfu Co's equity beta is 1.40, and it is estimated that the equivalent equity beta for its other activities, excluding the component production, is 1.25. Elfu Co has 400 million 25c shares in issue trading at 120c each. Its debt finance consists of variable rate

BPP
LEARNING
MEDIA

loans redeemable in seven years. The loans paying interest at base rate plus 120 basis points have a current value of $96 million. It can be assumed that 80% of Elfu Co's debt finance and 75% of Elfu Co's equity finance can be attributed to other activities excluding the component production. Both companies pay annual corporation tax at a rate of 25%. The current base rate is 3.5% and the market risk premium is estimated at 5.8%.

Required

(a) Provide a reasoned estimate of the cost of capital that Tisa Co should use to calculate the net present value of the two processes. Include all relevant calculations. **(8 marks)**

(b) Calculate the internal rate of return (IRR) and the modified internal rate of return (MIRR) for Process Omega. Given that the IRR and MIRR of Process Zeta are 26.6% and 23.3% respectively, recommend which process, if any, Tisa Co should proceed with and explain your recommendation. **(8 marks)**

(c) Elfu Co has estimated an annual standard deviation of $800,000 on one of its other projects, based on a normal distribution of returns. The average annual return on this project is $2,200,000.

   (i) Estimate the project's value at risk (VaR) at a 99% confidence level for 1 year and over the project's life of 5 years. Explain what is meant by the answers obtained. **(4 marks)**

   (ii) Apart from the use of VaR, briefly explain methods that Elfu Co can use to deal with risk and uncertainty in investment appraisal and their drawbacks. **(5 marks)**

(Total = 25 marks)

15 Riviere (12/14)   49 mins

Riviere Co is a small company based in the European Union (EU). It produces high quality frozen food which it exports to a small number of supermarket chains located within the EU as well. The EU is a free trade area for trade between its member countries.

Riviere Co finds it difficult to obtain bank finance and relies on a long-term strategy of using internally generated funds for new investment projects. This constraint means that it cannot accept every profitable project and often has to choose between them.

Riviere Co is currently considering investment in one of two mutually exclusive food production projects: Privi and Drugi. Privi will produce and sell a new range of frozen desserts exclusively within the EU. Drugi will produce and sell a new range of frozen desserts and savoury foods to supermarket chains based in countries outside the EU. Each project will last for five years and the following financial information refers to both projects.

PROJECT DRUGI ANNUAL AFTER-TAX CASH FLOWS EXPECTED AT THE END OF EACH YEAR

Year	Current	1	2	3	4	5
Cash flows (€'000)	(11,840)	1,230	1,680	4,350	10,240	2,200

	Privi	Drugi
Net present value	€2,054,000	€2,293,000
Internal rate of return	17.6%	Not provided
Modified internal rate of return	13.4%	Not provided
Value at risk (over the project's life)		
95% confidence level	€1,103,500	Not provided
90% confidence level	€860,000	Not provided

Both projects' net present value has been calculated based on Riviere Co's nominal cost of capital of 10%. It can be assumed that both projects' cash flow returns are normally distributed and the annual standard deviation of project Drugi's present value of after-tax cash flows is estimated to be €400,000. It can also be assumed that all sales are made in € (Euro) and therefore the company is not exposed to any foreign exchange exposure.

Notwithstanding how profitable project Drugi may appear to be, Riviere Co's board of directors is concerned about the possible legal risks if it invests in the project because they have never dealt with companies outside the EU before.

Required

(a) Discuss the aims of a free trade area, such as the EU, and the possible benefits to Riviere Co of operating within the EU. **(5 marks)**

(b) Calculate the figures which have not been provided for project Drugi and recommend which project should be accepted. Provide a justification for the recommendation and explain what the value at risk measures. **(13 marks)**

(c) Discuss the possible legal risks of investing in project Drugi which Riviere Co may be concerned about and how these may be mitigated. **(7 marks)**

(Total = 25 marks)

16 Arbore (12/12, amended)   49 mins

Arbore Co is a large listed company with many autonomous departments operating as investment centres. It sets investment limits for each department based on a three-year cycle. Projects selected by departments would have to fall within the investment limits set for each of the three years. All departments would be required to maintain a capital investment monitoring system, and report on their findings annually to Arbore Co's board of directors.

The Durvo department is considering the following five investment projects with three years of initial investment expenditure, followed by several years of positive cash inflows. The department's initial investment expenditure limits are $9,000,000, $6,000,000 and $5,000,000 for Years one, two and three respectively. None of the projects can be deferred and all projects can be scaled down but not scaled up.

	Investment required at start of year			
	Year one			Project net
Project	(Immediately)	Year two	Year three	present value
PDur01	$4,000,000	$1,100,000	$2,400,000	$464,000
PDur02	$800,000	$2,800,000	$3,200,000	$244,000
PDur03	$3,200,000	$3,562,000	$0	$352,000
PDur04	$3,900,000	$0	$200,000	$320,000
PDur05	$2,500,000	$1,200,000	$1,400,000	Not provided

PDur05 project's annual operating cash flows commence at the end of Year four and last for a period of 15 years. The project generates annual sales of 300,000 units at a selling price of $14 per unit and incurs total annual relevant costs of $3,230,000. Although the costs and units sold of the project can be predicted with a fair degree of certainty, there is considerable uncertainty about the unit selling price. The department uses a required rate of return of 11% for its projects, and inflation can be ignored.

The Durvo department's managing director is of the opinion that all projects which return a positive net present value (NPV) should be accepted and does not understand the reason(s) why Arbore Co imposes capital rationing on its departments. Furthermore, she is not sure why maintaining a capital investment monitoring system would be beneficial to the company.

Required

(a) (i) Calculate the NPV of project PDur05. Calculate and comment on what percentage fall in the selling price would need to occur before the NPV falls to zero. **(6 marks)**

   (ii) Explain the strengths and weaknesses of NPV as a basis for making investment decisions in a capital rationing situation. **(5 marks)**

(b) Formulate an appropriate capital rationing model, based on the above investment limits, that maximises the NPV for department Durvo. Finding a solution for the model is not required. **(3 marks)**

(c) Assume the following output is produced when the capital rationing model in part (b) above is solved:

Category 1: Total final value

$1,184,409

Category 2: Adjustable final values

Project PDur01: 0.958

Project PDur02: 0.407

Project PDur03: 0.732

Project PDur04: 0.000

Project PDur05: 1.000

Category 3:

Constraints utilised	Slack
Year one: $9,000,000	Year one: $0
Year two: $6,000,000	Year two: $0
Year three: $5,000,000	Year three: $0

Required

Explain the figures produced in each of the three output categories. **(5 marks)**

(d) Provide a brief response to the managing director's opinions by:

(i) Explaining why Arbore Co may want to impose capital rationing on its departments. **(2 marks)**

(ii) Explaining the features of a capital investment monitoring system and discussing the benefits of maintaining such a system. **(4 marks)**

(Total = 25 marks)

17 MMC (6/11, amended) 49 mins

MesmerMagic Co (MMC) is considering whether to undertake the development of a new computer game based on an adventure film due to be released in 22 months. It is expected that the game will be available to buy two months after the film's release, by which time it will be possible to judge the popularity of the film with a high degree of certainty. However, at present, there is considerable uncertainty about whether the film, and therefore the game, is likely to be successful. Although MMC would pay for the exclusive rights to develop and sell the game now, the directors are of the opinion that they should delay the decision to produce and market the game until the film has been released and the game is available for sale.

MMC has forecast the following end of year cash flows for the four-year sales period of the game.

Year	1	2	3	4
Cash flows ($ million)	25	18	10	5

MMC will spend $7 million at the start of each of the next two years to develop the game and the gaming platform, and to pay for the exclusive rights to develop and sell the game. Following this, the company will require $35 million for production, distribution and marketing costs at the start of the four-year sales period of the game.

It can be assumed that all the costs and revenues include inflation. The relevant cost of capital for this project is 11% and the risk-free rate is 3.5%. MMC has estimated the likely volatility of the cash flows at a standard deviation of 30%.

Required

(a) Estimate the financial impact of the directors' decision to delay the production and marketing of the game. The Black-Scholes option pricing model may be used, where appropriate. All relevant calculations should be shown. **(12 marks)**

(b) Briefly discuss the implications of the answer obtained in part (a) above. **(7 marks)**

(c) Discuss how a decrease in the value of each of the determinants of the option price in the Black-Scholes option pricing model for European options is likely to change the price of a call option. **(6 marks)**

(Total = 25 marks)

18 Marengo (12/10, amended)

49 mins

The treasury division of Marengo Co, a large quoted company, holds equity investments in various companies around the world. One of the investments is in Arion Co, in which Marengo holds 200,000 shares, which is around 2% of the total number of Arion Co's shares traded on the stock market. Over the past year, due to the general strength in the equity markets following optimistic predictions of the performance of world economies, Marengo's investments have performed well. However, there is some concern that the share price of Arion Co may fall in the coming two months due to uncertainty in its markets. It is expected that any fall in share prices will be reversed following this period of uncertainty.

The treasury division managers in Marengo, Wenyu, Lola and Sam, have met with the Chief Executive Officer (CEO), Edward, to discuss what to do with the investment in Arion Co and they each made a different suggestion as follows:

1   Wenyu was of the opinion that Marengo's shareholders would benefit most if no action were taken. He argued that the courses of action proposed by Lola and Sam, below, would result in extra costs and possibly increase the risk to Marengo Co.

2   Lola proposed that Arion Co's shares should be sold in order to eliminate the risk of a fall in the share price.

3   Sam suggested that the investment should be hedged using an appropriate derivative product.

4   Edward does not understand why Marengo Co holds equity investments at all. He believes all shares should be sold.

Although no exchange-traded derivative products exist on Arion Co's shares, a bank has offered over-the-counter (OTC) option contracts at an exercise price of 350 cents per share in a contract size of 1,000 shares each, for the appropriate time period. Arion Co's current share price is 340 cents per share, although the volatility of the share prices could be as high as 40%.

It can be assumed that Arion Co will not pay any dividends in the coming few months and that the appropriate inter-bank lending rate will be 4% over that period.

Required

(a)   Estimate the number of OTC put option contracts that Marengo Co will need to hedge against any adverse movement in Arion Co's share price. Provide a brief explanation of your answer.

Note. You may assume that the delta of a put option is equivalent to $N(-d_1)$.   **(7 marks)**

(b)   Discuss possible reasons for the suggestions made by each of the three managers and the CEO.   **(18 marks)**

(Total = 25 marks)

19 Furlion Co (Mar/Jun 16)

49 mins

Furlion Co manufactures heavy agricultural equipment and machinery which can be used in difficult farming conditions. Furlion Co's chief executive has been investigating a significant opportunity in the country of Naswa, where Furlion Co has not previously sold any products. The government of Naswa has been undertaking a major land reclamation programme and Furlion Co's equipment is particularly suitable for use on the reclaimed land. Because of the costs and other problems involved in transporting its products, Furlion Co's chief executive proposes that Furlion Co should establish a plant for manufacturing machinery in Naswa. He knows that the Naswan government is keen to encourage the development of sustainable businesses within the country.

Initial calculations suggest that the proposed investment in Naswa would have a negative net present value of $1.01 million. However, Furlion Co's chief executive believes that there may be opportunities for greater cash flows in future if the Naswan government expands its land reclamation programme. The government at present is struggling to fund expansion of the programme out of its own resources and is looking for other funding. If the Naswan government obtains this funding, the chief executive has forecast that the increased demand for Furlion Co's products would justify $15 million additional expenditure at the site of the factory in three years' time. The expected net present value for this expansion is currently estimated to be $0.

It can be assumed that all costs and revenues include inflation. The relevant cost of capital is 12% and the risk-free rate is 4%. The chief executive has estimated the likely volatility of cash flows at a standard deviation of 30%.

One of Furlion Co's non-executive directors has read about possible changes in interest rates and wonders how these might affect the investment appraisal.

Required

(a) Assess, showing all relevant calculations, whether Furlion Co should proceed with the significant opportunity. Discuss the assumptions made and other factors which will affect the decision of whether to establish a plant in Naswa. The Black-Scholes pricing model may be used, where appropriate. **(16 marks)**

(b) Explain what is meant by an option's rho and discuss the impact of changes in interest rates on the appraisal of the investment. **(5 marks)**

(c) Discuss the possibility of the Naswan Government obtaining funding for further land reclamation from the World Bank, referring specifically to the International Development Association. **(4 marks)**

(Total = 25 marks)

20 Toltuck (Mar/Jun 17) 49 mins

Toltuck Co is a listed company in the building industry which specialises in the construction of large commercial and residential developments. Toltuck Co had been profitable for many years, but has just incurred major losses on the last two developments which it has completed in its home country of Arumland. These developments were an out-of-town retail centre and a major residential development. Toltuck Co's directors have blamed the poor results primarily on the recent recession in Arumland, although demand for the residential development also appears to have been adversely affected by it being located in an area which has suffered serious flooding over the last two years.

As a result of returns from these two major developments being much lower than expected, Toltuck Co has had to finance current work-in-progress by a significantly greater amount of debt finance, giving it higher gearing than most other construction companies operating in Arumland. Toltuck Co's directors have recently been alarmed by a major credit agency's decision to downgrade Toltuck Co's credit rating from AA to BBB. The directors are very concerned about the impact this will have on the valuation of Toltuck Co's bonds and the future cost of debt.

The following information can be used to assess the consequences of the change in Toltuck Co's credit rating.

Toltuck Co has issued an 8% bond, which has a face or nominal value of $100 and a premium of 2% on redemption in three years' time. The coupon on the bond is payable on an annual basis.

The government of Arumland has three bonds in issue. They all have a face or nominal value of $100 and are all redeemable at par. Taxation can be ignored on government bonds. They are of the same risk class and the coupon on each is payable on an annual basis. Details of the bonds are as follows:

Bond	Redeemable	Coupon	Current market value $
1	1 year	9%	104
2	2 years	7%	102
3	3 years	6%	98

Credit spreads, published by the credit agency, are as follows (shown in basis points):

Rating	1 year	2 years	3 years
AA	18	31	45
BBB	54	69	86

Toltuck Co's shareholder base can be divided broadly into two groups. The majority of shareholders are comfortable with investing in a company where dividends in some years will be high, but there will be low or no dividends in other years because of the cash demands facing the business. However, a minority of shareholders would like Toltuck Co to achieve at least a minimum dividend each year and are concerned about the company undertaking investments which they regard as very speculative. Shareholders from both groups have expressed some concerns to the board about the impact of the fall in credit rating on their investment.

Required

(a) Calculate the valuation and yield to maturity of Toltuck Co's $100 bond under its old and new credit ratings. **(10 marks)**

(b) Discuss the factors which may have affected the credit rating of Toltuck Co published by the credit agency. **(8 marks)**

(c) Discuss the impact of the fall in Toltuck Co's credit rating on its ability to raise financial capital and on its shareholders' return. **(7 marks)**

(Total = 25 marks)

21 Coeden (12/12, amended)   49 mins

Coeden Co is a listed company operating in the hospitality and leisure industry. Coeden Co's board of directors met recently to discuss a new strategy for the business. The proposal put forward was to sell all the hotel properties that Coeden Co owns and rent them back on a long-term rental agreement. Coeden Co would then focus solely on the provision of hotel services at these properties under its popular brand name. The proposal stated that the funds raised from the sale of the hotel properties would be used to pay off 70% of the outstanding non-current liabilities and the remaining funds would be retained for future investments.

The board of directors is of the opinion that reducing the level of debt in Coeden Co will reduce the company's risk and therefore its cost of capital. If the proposal is undertaken and Coeden Co focuses exclusively on the provision of hotel services, it can be assumed that the current market value of equity will remain unchanged after implementing the proposal.

Coeden Co financial information

EXTRACT FROM THE MOST RECENT STATEMENT OF FINANCIAL POSITION

	$'000
Non-current assets (revalued recently)	42,560
Current assets	26,840
Total assets	69,400
Share capital (25c per share par value)	3,250
Reserves	21,780
Non-current liabilities (5.2% redeemable bonds)	42,000
Current liabilities	2,370
Total capital and liabilities	69,400

Coeden Co's latest free cash flow to equity of $2,600,000 was estimated after taking into account taxation, interest and reinvestment in assets to continue with the current level of business. It can be assumed that the annual reinvestment in assets required to continue with the current level of business is equivalent to the annual amount of depreciation. Over the past few years, Coeden Co has consistently used 40% of its free cash flow to equity on new investments while distributing the remaining 60%. The market value of equity calculated on the basis of the free cash flow to equity model provides a reasonable estimate of the current market value of Coeden Co.

The bonds are redeemable at par in three years and pay the coupon on an annual basis. Although the bonds are not traded, it is estimated that Coeden Co's current debt credit rating is BBB but would improve to A+ if the non-current liabilities are reduced by 70%.

Other information

Coeden Co's current equity beta is 1.1 and it can be assumed that debt beta is 0. The risk-free rate is estimated to be 4% and the market risk premium is estimated to be 6%.

There is no beta available for companies offering just hotel services, since most companies own their own buildings. The average asset beta for property companies has been estimated at 0.4. It has been estimated that the hotel services business accounts for approximately 60% of the current value of Coeden Co and the property company business accounts for the remaining 40%.

Coeden Co's corporation tax rate is 20%. The three-year borrowing credit spread on A+ rated bonds is 60 basis points and 90 basis points on BBB rated bonds, over the risk-free rate of interest.

Required

(a)   Calculate, and comment on, Coeden Co's cost of equity and weighted average cost of capital before and after implementing the proposal. Briefly explain any assumptions made.

(20 marks)

(b)   Discuss the validity of the assumption that the market value of equity will remain unchanged after the implementation of the proposal.

(5 marks)

(Total = 25 marks)

22 Tippletine (Mar/Jun 18)   49 mins

Tippletine Co is based in Valliland. It is listed on Valliland's stock exchange but only has a small number of shareholders. Its directors collectively own 45% of the equity share capital.

Tippletine Co's growth has been based on the manufacture of household electrical goods. However, the directors have taken a strategic decision to diversify operations and to make a major investment in facilities for the manufacture of office equipment.

Details of investment

The new investment is being appraised over a four-year time horizon. Revenues from the new investment are uncertain and Tippletine Co's finance director has prepared what she regards as cautious forecasts. She predicts that it will generate $2 million operating cash flows before marketing costs in Year 1 and $14.5 million operating cash flows before marketing costs in Year 2, with operating cash flows rising by the expected levels of inflation in Years 3 and 4.

Marketing costs are predicted to be $9 million in Year 1 and $2 million in each of Years 2 to 4.

The new investment will require immediate expenditure on facilities of $30.6 million. Tax allowable depreciation will be available on the new investment at an annual rate of 25% reducing balance basis. It can be assumed that there will either be a balancing allowance or charge in the final year of the appraisal. The finance director believes the facilities will remain viable after four years, and therefore a realisable value of $13.5 million can be assumed at the end of the appraisal period.

The new facilities will also require an immediate initial investment in working capital of $3 million. Working capital requirements will increase by the rate of inflation for the next three years and any working capital at the start of Year 4 will be assumed to be released at the end of the appraisal period.

Tippletine Co pays tax at an annual rate of 30%. Tax is payable with a year's time delay. Any tax losses on the investment can be assumed to be carried forward and written off against future profits from the investment.

Predicted inflation rates are as follows:

Year	1	2	3	4
	8%	6%	5%	4%

Financing the investment

Tippletine Co has been considering two choices for financing all of the $30.6 million needed for the initial investment in the facilities:

- A subsidised loan from a government loan scheme, with the loan repayable at the end of the four years. Issue costs of 4% of the gross finance would be payable. Interest would be payable at a rate of 30 basis points below the risk-free rate of 2.5%. In order to obtain the benefits of the loan scheme, Tippletine Co would have to fulfil various conditions, including locating the facilities in a remote part of Valliland where unemployment is high.

- Convertible loan notes, with the subscribers for the notes including some of Tippletine Co's directors. The loan notes would have issue costs of 4% of the gross finance. If not converted, the loan notes would be redeemed in six years' time. Interest would be payable at 5%, which is Tippletine Co's normal cost of borrowing. Conversion would take place at an effective price of $2.75 per share. However, the loan note holders could enforce redemption at any time from the start of Year 3 if Tippletine Co's share price fell below $1.50 per share. Tippletine Co's current share price is $2.20 per share.

Issue costs for the subsidised loan and convertible loan notes would be paid out of available cash reserves. Issue costs are not allowable as a tax-deductible expense.

In initial discussions, the majority of the board favoured using the subsidised loan. The appraisal of the investment should be prepared on the basis that this method of finance will be used. However, the chairman argued strongly in favour of the convertible loan notes, as, in his view, operating costs will be lower if Tippletine Co does not have to fulfil the conditions laid down by the government of Valliland. Tippletine Co's finance director is sceptical, however, about whether the other shareholders would approve the issue of convertible loan notes on the terms suggested. The directors will decide which method of finance to use at the next board meeting.

Other information

Humabuz Co is a large manufacturer of office equipment in Valliland. Humabuz Co's geared cost of equity is estimated to be 10.5% and its pre-tax cost of debt to be 5.4%. These estimates are based on a capital structure comprising $225 million 6% irredeemable bonds, trading at $107 per $100, and 125 million $1 equity shares, trading at $3.20 per share. Humabuz Co also pays tax at an annual rate of 30% on its taxable profits.

Required

(a) Calculate the adjusted present value for the investment on the basis that it is financed by the subsidised loan and conclude whether the project should be accepted or not. Show all relevant calculations. **(17 marks)**

(b) Discuss the issues which Tippletine Co's shareholders who are not directors would consider if its directors decided that the new investment should be financed by the issue of convertible loan notes on the terms suggested.

Note. You are not required to carry out any calculations when answering part (b).

(8 marks)

(Total = 25 marks)

23 Amberle (Dec 18)   49 mins

Amberle Co is a listed company with divisions that manufacture cars, motorbikes and bicycles. Over the last few years, Amberle Co has used a mixture of equity and debt finance for its investments. However, it is about to make a new investment of $150 million in facilities to produce electric cars, which it proposes to finance solely by debt finance.

Project information

Amberle Co's finance director has prepared estimates of the post-tax cash flows for the project, using a four-year time horizon, together with the realisable value at the end of four years:

Year	1	2	3	4
	$m	$m	$m	$m
Post-tax operating cash flows	28.50	36.70	44.40	50.90
Realisable value				45.00

Working capital of $6 million, not included in the estimates above and funded from retained earnings, will also be required immediately for the project, rising by the predicted rate of inflation for each year. Any remaining working capital will be released in full at the end of the project.

Predicted rates of inflation are as follows:

Year	1	2	3	4
	8%	6%	5%	4%

The finance director has proposed the following finance package for the new investment:

	$m
Bank loan, repayable in equal annual instalments over the project's life, interest payable at 8% per year	70
Subsidised loan from a government loan scheme over the project's life on which interest is payable at 3.1% per year	80
	150

Issue costs of 3% of gross proceeds will be payable on the subsidised loan. No issue costs will be payable on the bank loan. Issue costs are not allowable for tax.

Financial information

Amberle Co pays tax at an annual rate of 30% on profits in the same year in which profits arise.

Amberle Co's asset beta is currently estimated at 1.14. The current return on the market is estimated at 11%. The current risk-free rate is 4% per year.

Amberle Co's chairman has noted that all of the company's debt, including the new debt, will be repayable within three to five years. He is wondering whether Amberle Co needs to develop a longer-term financing policy in broad terms and how flexible this policy should be.

Required

(a) Calculate the adjusted present value (APV) for the project and conclude whether the project should be accepted or not. **(15 marks)**

(b) Discuss the factors which may determine the long-term finance policy which Amberle Co's board may adopt, and the factors which may cause the policy to change. **(10 marks)**

(Total = 25 marks)

ACQUISITIONS AND MERGERS

Questions 24 to 29 cover acquisitions and mergers, the subject of Chapters 8-10 of the BPP Workbook for AFM.

24 Kerrin (Sep/Dec 19)   49 mins

A new client has approached you for advice on a potential acquisition. Kerrin Co is a consumer electronics manufacturer and retailer. The company obtained a listing eight years ago with the founders retaining a 20% stake in the business. Whilst Kerrin Co had previously experienced rapid growth in earnings before tax, problems arose soon after the listing as competition intensified. Although the company remains profitable, annual growth has declined significantly and is currently 3%.

The board is concerned by the lack of future growth opportunities. The current share price reflects these concerns, trading well below the offer price of eight years ago. In response, the directors have decided to invest in a market development strategy for future growth, utilising significant cash reserves to acquire companies in other areas of the country where competition is less intense. The board has identified a potential target, Danton Co.

Danton Co

Danton Co is a privately-owned consumer electronics company, established ten years ago. Significant unrelieved losses were incurred in the early years of development, although the company is now profitable and achieving growth in earnings before tax of 6% per year. However, cash reserves are low. Access to capital has acted as a severe constraint on Danton Co's reinvestment potential throughout this period. The founders and their families own 60% of the shares with the balance held by a venture capitalist organisation, which acquired its equity stake around six years ago.

Acquisition information

Kerrin Co's board is keen to ensure that Danton Co's founders remain as directors after the acquisition and the company has sufficient cash reserves to purchase Danton Co outright.

Early discussions between the directors of both companies suggest Danton Co's shareholders would approve a cash offer of $13.10 per share. As an alternative, the board is considering a share-for-share exchange to fund the acquisition in order to preserve cash for future acquisitions and dividend payments. Recent mergers have attracted an acquisition premium of around 25%–30% and Danton Co's directors indicated their shareholders would be expecting a premium towards the higher end of this scale for a share-for-share offer. Kerrin Co has therefore asked you to design a share-for-share offer scheme which will allow for a 30% acquisition premium. You have been provided with extracts from the latest financial statements for both companies.

Extracts from the most recent financial statements

	Kerrin Co	Danton Co
	$m	$m
Operating profit	448.6	201.8
Earnings before tax	381.9	116.3

Additional financial information

The book value of Kerrin Co's $0.50 ordinary shares is $375 million. These shares are currently trading at $5.28 and the finance director expects the price earnings (PE) ratio to increase by 10% if the acquisition proceeds.

Danton Co upgraded its main manufacturing facility during the previous year and expects to make annual pre-tax cost savings of $2.5 million from the start of the current financial year. The book value of Danton Co's $0.25 ordinary shares is $35 million. Based on an analysis of companies of a comparable size and cost structure, it is estimated that Danton Co's PE ratio is 20% higher than Kerrin Co's current PE ratio.

Kerrin Co's chief executive officer estimates annual pre-tax revenue and cost synergies of $15.2 million to arise as a result of the acquisition. In addition, the finance director anticipates annual pre-tax financial synergies of $5.3 million, although she insists this is a cautious estimate after reading an article on recent merger and acquisition activity where post-acquisition synergies have either been overestimated or failed to materialise.

The rate of corporation tax relevant to both companies is 20%.

Required

(a)   Discuss possible sources of financial synergy arising from Kerrin Co's acquisition of Danton Co and comment on the finance director's concern that synergy is often overestimated, including any steps which could be taken by Kerrin Co's board to address this problem.

(8 marks)

(b)   Advise the directors on a suitable share-for-share exchange offer which meets the criteria specified by Danton Co's shareholders and calculate the effect of the cash and share-for-share offers on the post-acquisition wealth of both Kerrin Co's and Danton Co's shareholders.

(13 marks)

(c)   Discuss the likely reaction of Kerrin Co's and Danton Co's shareholders to the cash and share-for-share offers.

(4 marks)

(Total = 25 marks)

25 Selorne (Sep 18)

49 mins

Selorne Co

Selorne Co is one of the biggest removal companies in Pauland, offering home and business removals. It has a number of long-term contracts with large businesses, although it has not won any new major contracts in the last two years. Selorne Co is listed on Pauland's stock market for smaller companies. Selorne Co is financed by a mixture of equity and short and long-term debt, but its gearing level is below the average for its sector.

Selorne Co has four executive directors, who each own 20% of the company's share capital, with the other 20% owned by external shareholders. Selorne Co has paid a constant dividend since it has been listed and its share price has risen slightly over the last three years.

Selorne Co is based in a number of the large cities and towns in Pauland and owns the majority of the sites where it is located. Many of its employees have worked for the company for a long time. Drivers of the lorries used by Selorne Co are required to have a special, heavy vehicles licence. Salary levels at Selorne Co are relatively high compared with other companies in the sector.

Chawon Co

Selorne Co is currently considering making a bid for Chawon Co, an unlisted company specialising in distribution and delivery services. Chawon Co is owned 100% by its founder, Chris Chawon. Chawon Co has built up a portfolio of small contracts over time. It has made unsuccessful bids for two larger contracts over the last 12 months, the bids being rejected primarily because Chawon Co was not felt to be big enough to be able to guarantee the level of service required.

Chawon Co is based in many of the same cities and towns where Selorne Co is located, although Chawon's premises are all rented. The drivers of Chawon's vehicles do not require a heavy vehicles licence. Chawon Co has a few long-serving employees who are mostly centre managers. Most of its drivers and staff, however, stay at Chawon Co for only a short time. Salary levels are low, although Chawon Co pays high levels of overtime and high bonuses if target profit levels are achieved. Chawon Co is highly geared, leading to recent media speculation about its financial viability.

Terms of bid for Chawon Co

In initial discussions about the acquisition, Chris Chawon indicated that he would prefer the consideration to be a share-for-share exchange, the terms being one Chawon Co share for five Selorne Co shares.

Chawon Co has 2 million $1 shares in issue, and Selorne Co has 50 million $0.50 shares in issue. Each Selorne Co share is currently trading at $6.50, which is a multiple of 8 of its free cash flow to equity. The multiple of 8 can be assumed to remain unchanged if the acquisition takes place. Chawon Co's free cash flow to equity is currently estimated at $7 million, with an expected annual growth rate of 3%, and it is expected to generate a return on equity of 15%. Chris Chawon expects that the total free cash flows to equity of the combined company will increase by $5 million due to synergy benefits. He believes that Selorne Co will be able to win more contracts because it is larger and because it will be diversifying the services which it offers. He also believes that significant operational synergies can be achieved, pointing out the time Selorne Co drivers spend idle during the winter months when removal activity is traditionally lower. Chris Chawon believes that he can achieve the synergies if he is given management responsibility for the operational reorganisation, including dealing with the staff employment and retention issues. Chris Chawon thinks that synergies could also be achieved in central administration and in premises costs.

The chief executive and the finance director of Selorne Co are in favour of bidding for Chawon Co. However, one of the other executive directors is opposed to the bid. He is sceptical about the level of synergies which can be achieved and does not want Chris Chawon to be brought into the management of Selorne Co. He suggests that if the bid is to go ahead, it should be a cash offer rather than a share exchange. Selorne Co's chief executive has responded that Chris Chawon is likely to ask for a higher equivalent price if the purchase is for cash.

Financing the bid for Chawon Co

Selorne Co's finance director has pointed out that Selorne Co will need additional funding if Chawon Co is purchased for cash. He has suggested that there may be a number of possible sources of finance:

- A rights issue
- A fixed rate, long-term, bank loan
- A three-year, unsecured, mezzanine loan facility
- Convertible debt, with conversion rights being exercisable in five years' time

Required

(a) (i)   Estimate the equity value of the combined company and the expected additional value arising from the combination of Selorne Co and Chawon Co. **(6 marks)**

(ii) Estimate the share of the gain from the combination created for Chris Chawon and the share of the gain created for Selorne Co's shareholders and comment on your results. **(6 marks)**

(b) Evaluate how reliable the estimates of the synergies for the combined company are likely to be and discuss the factors which may prevent the forecast synergies from being achieved. **(7 marks)**

(c) Discuss the factors which Selorne Co's board will consider when determining which source or sources of finance are chosen to finance a possible cash bid for the share capital of Chawon Co. **(6 marks)**

(Total = 25 marks)

26 Chithurst (Sep/Dec 16)

49 mins

Chithurst Co gained a stock exchange listing five years ago. At the time of the listing, members of the family who founded the company owned 75% of the shares, but now they only hold just over 50%. The number of shares in issue has remained unchanged since Chithurst Co was listed. Chithurst Co's directors have continued the policy of paying a constant dividend per share each year which the company had before it was listed. However, investors who are not family members have become increasingly critical of this policy, saying that there is no clear rationale for it. They would prefer to see steady dividend growth, reflecting the increase in profitability of Chithurst Co since its listing.

The finance director of Chithurst Co has provided its board with details of Chithurst Co's dividends and investment expenditure, compared with two other similar-sized companies in the same sector, Eartham Co and Iping Co. Each company has a 31 December year end.

	Chithurst Co			Eartham Co			Iping Co		
	Profit for year after interest and tax $m	Dividend paid $m	New investment expenditure $m	Profit for year after interest and tax $m	Dividend paid $m	New investment expenditure $m	Profit for year after interest and tax $m	Dividend paid $m	New investment expenditure $m
20X2	77	33	18	95	38	30	75	35	37
20X3	80	33	29	(10)	15	15	88	17	64
20X4	94	33	23	110	44	42	118	39	75
20X5	97	33	21	120	48	29	132	42	84

Other financial information relating to the three companies is as follows:

	Chithurst Co	Eartham Co	Iping Co
Cost of equity	11%	14%	12%
Market capitalisation $m	608	1,042	1,164
Increase in share price in last 12 months	1%	5%	10%

Chithurst Co's finance director has estimated the costs of equity for all three companies.

None of the three companies has taken out significant new debt finance since 20X1.

Required

(a) Discuss the benefits and drawbacks of the dividend policies which the three companies appear to have adopted. Provide relevant calculations to support your discussion.

Note. Up to 5 marks are available for the calculations. **(15 marks)**

(b) Discuss how the market capitalisation of the three companies compares with your valuations calculated using the dividend valuation model. Use the data provided to calculate valuations based on growth rates for the most recent year and for the last three years.

Note. Up to 5 marks are available for the calculations. **(10 marks)**

(Total = 25 marks)

27 Louieed (Mar/Jun 16)

49 mins

Louieed Co, a listed company, is a major supplier of educational material, selling its products in many countries. It supplies schools and colleges and also produces learning material for business and professional exams. Louieed Co has exclusive contracts to produce material for some examining bodies. Louieed Co has a well-defined management structure with formal processes for making major decisions.

Although Louieed Co produces online learning material, most of its profits are still derived from sales of traditional textbooks. Louieed Co's growth in profits over the last few years has been slow and its directors are currently reviewing its long-term strategy. One area in which they feel that Louieed Co must become much more involved is the production of online testing materials for exams and to validate course and textbook learning.

Bid for Tidded Co

Louieed Co has recently made a bid for Tidded Co, a smaller listed company. Tidded Co also supplies a range of educational material, but has been one of the leaders in the development of online testing and has shown strong profit growth over recent years. All of Tidded Co's initial five founders remain on its board and still hold 45% of its issued share capital between them. From the start, Tidded Co's directors have been used to making quick decisions in their areas of responsibility. Although listing has imposed some formalities, Tidded Co has remained focused on acting quickly to gain competitive advantage, with the five founders continuing to give strong leadership.

Louieed Co's initial bid of five shares in Louieed Co for three shares in Tidded Co was rejected by Tidded Co's board. There has been further discussion between the two boards since the initial offer was rejected and Louieed Co's board is now considering a proposal to offer Tidded Co's shareholders two shares in Louieed Co for one share in Tidded Co or a cash alternative of $22.75 per Tidded Co share. It is expected that Tidded Co's shareholders will choose one of the following options:

1   To accept the two shares for one share offer for all the Tidded Co shares;

2   To accept the cash offer for all the Tidded Co shares; or

3   60% of the shareholders will take up the two shares for one share offer and the remaining 40% will take the cash offer.

In the case of the third option being accepted, it is thought that three of the company's founders, holding 20% of the share capital in total, will take the cash offer and not join the combined company. The remaining two founders will probably continue to be involved in the business and be members of the combined company's board.

Louieed Co's Finance Director has estimated that the merger will produce annual post-tax synergies of $20 million. He expects Louieed Co's current price/earnings (P/E) ratio to remain unchanged after the acquisition.

Extracts from the two companies' most recent accounts are shown below:

	Louieed $m	Tidded $m
Profit before finance cost and tax	446	182
Finance costs	(74)	(24)
Profit before tax	372	158
Tax	(76)	(30)
Profit after tax	296	128
Issued $1 nominal shares (m)	340	90
P/E ratios, based on most recent accounts	14	15.9
Long-term liabilities (market value) ($m)	540	193
Cash and cash equivalents ($m)	220	64

The tax rate applicable to both companies is 20%.

Assume that Louieed Co can obtain further debt funding at a pre-tax cost of 7.5% and that the return on cash surpluses is 5% pre-tax.

Assume also that any debt funding needed to complete the acquisition will be reduced instantly by the balances of cash and cash equivalents held by Louieed Co and Tidded Co.

Required

(a)   Discuss the advantages and disadvantages of the acquisition of Tidded Co from the viewpoint of Louieed Co.   **(6 marks)**

(b)   Calculate the P/E ratios of Tidded Co implied by the terms of Louieed Co's initial and proposed offers, for all three of the above options.   **(5 marks)**

(c)   Calculate, and comment on, the funding required for the acquisition of Tidded Co and the impact on Louieed Co's earnings per share and gearing, for each of the three options given above.

   Note. Up to 10 marks are available for the calculations.   **(14 marks)**

(Total = 25 marks)

BPP
LEARNING
MEDIA

28 Makonis (12/13)

49 mins

Makonis Co, a listed company producing motor cars, wants to acquire Nuvola Co, an engineering company involved in producing innovative devices for cars. Makonis Co is keen to incorporate some of Nuvola Co's innovative devices into its cars and thereby boost sales revenue.

The following financial information is provided for the two companies:

	Makonis Co	Nuvola Co
Current share price	$5.80	$2.40
Number of issued shares (m)	210	200
Equity beta	1.2	1.2
Asset beta	0.9	1.2

It is thought that combining the two companies will result in several benefits. Free cash flows to firm of the combined company will be $216 million in current value terms, but these will increase by an annual growth rate of 5% for the next four years, before reverting to an annual growth rate of 2.25% in perpetuity. In addition to this, combining the companies will result in cash synergy benefits of $20 million per year, for the next four years. These synergy benefits are not subject to any inflationary increase and no synergy benefits will occur after the fourth year. The debt to equity ratio of the combined company will be 40:60 in market value terms and it is expected that the combined company's cost of debt will be 4.55%.

The corporation tax rate is 20%, the current risk-free rate of return is 2% and the market risk premium is 7%. It can be assumed that the combined company's asset beta is the weighted average of Makonis Co's and Nuvola Co's asset betas, weighted by their current market values.

Makonis Co has offered to acquire Nuvola Co through a mixed offer of one of its shares for two Nuvola Co shares plus a cash payment, such that a 30% premium is paid for the acquisition. Nuvola Co's equity holders feel that a 50% premium would be more acceptable. Makonis Co has sufficient cash reserves if the premium is 30%, but not if it is 50%.

Required

(a) Estimate the additional equity value created by combining Nuvola Co and Makonis Co, based on the free cash flows to firm method. Comment on the results obtained and briefly discuss the assumptions made. **(13 marks)**

(b) Estimate the impact on Makonis Co's equity holders if the premium paid is increased to 50% from 30%. **(5 marks)**

(c) Estimate the additional funds required if a premium of 50% is paid instead of 30% and discuss how this premium could be financed. **(7 marks)**

(Total = 25 marks)

29 Vogel (6/14)

49 mins

Vogel Co, a listed engineering company, manufactures large-scale plant and machinery for industrial companies. Until ten years ago, Vogel Co pursued a strategy of organic growth. Since then, it has followed an aggressive policy of acquiring smaller engineering companies, which it feels have developed new technologies and methods, which could be used in its manufacturing processes. However, it is estimated that only between 30% and 40% of the acquisitions made in the last ten years have successfully increased the company's shareholder value.

Vogel Co is currently considering acquiring Tori Co, an unlisted company, which has three departments. Department A manufactures machinery for industrial companies, Department B produces electrical goods for the retail market, and the smaller Department C operates in the construction industry. Upon acquisition, Department A will become part of Vogel Co, as it contains the new technologies which Vogel Co is seeking, but Departments B and C will be unbundled, with the assets attached to Department C sold and Department B being spun off into a new company called Ndege Co.

Given below are extracts of financial information for the two companies for the year ended 30 April 20X4.

	Vogel Co $m	Tori Co $m
Sales revenue	790.2	124.6
Profit before depreciation, interest and tax (PBDIT)	244.4	37.4
Interest	13.8	4.3
Depreciation	72.4	10.1
Pre-tax profit	158.2	23.0
Non-current assets	723.9	98.2
Current assets	142.6	46.5
7% unsecured bond	–	40.0
Other non-current and current liabilities	212.4	20.2
Share capital (50c/share)	190.0	20.0
Reserves	464.1	64.5

Share of current and non-current assets and profit of Tori Co's three departments:

	Department A	Department B	Department C
Share of current and non-current assets	40%	40%	20%
Share of PBDIT and pre-tax profit	50%	40%	10%

Other information

1　It is estimated that for Department C, the realisable value of its non-current assets is 100% of their book value, but its current assets' realisable value is only 90% of their book value. The costs related to closing Department C are estimated to be $3 million.

2　The funds raised from the disposal of Department C will be used to pay off Tori Co's other non-current and current liabilities.

3　The 7% unsecured bond will be taken over by Ndege Co. It can be assumed that the current market value of the bond is equal to its book value.

4　At present, around 10% of Department B's PBDIT come from sales made to Department C.

5　Ndege Co's cost of capital is estimated to be 10%. It is estimated that in the first year of operation Ndege Co's free cash flows to firm will grow by 20%, and then by 5.2% annually thereafter.

6　The tax rate applicable to all the companies is 20%, and Ndege Co can claim 10% tax-allowable depreciation on its non-current assets. It can be assumed that the amount of tax-allowable depreciation is the same as the investment needed to maintain Ndege Co's operations.

7　Vogel Co's current share price is $3 per share and it is estimated that Tori Co's price/earnings (P/E) ratio is 25% higher than Vogel Co's P/E ratio. After the acquisition, when Department A becomes part of Vogel Co, it is estimated that Vogel Co's P/E ratio will increase by 15%.

8　It is estimated that the combined company's annual after-tax earnings will increase by $7 million due to the synergy benefits resulting from combining Vogel Co and Department A.

Required

(a)　Discuss the possible reasons why Vogel Co may have switched its strategy of organic growth to one of growing by acquiring companies. **(4 marks)**

(b)　Discuss the possible actions Vogel Co could take to reduce the risk that the acquisition of Tori Co fails to increase shareholder value. **(7 marks)**

(c)　Estimate, showing all relevant calculations, the maximum premium Vogel Co could pay to acquire Tori Co, explaining the approach taken and any assumptions made. **(14 marks)**

(Total = 25 marks)

BPP
LEARNING
MEDIA

CORPORATE RECONSTRUCTION AND REORGANISATION

Questions 30 to 35 cover corporate reconstruction and reorganisation, the subject of Chapters 14-15 of the BPP Workbook for AFM.

30 Newimber (Mar/Jun 19)   49 mins

Newimber Co is a listed company which has always manufactured formal clothing for adults and children. It obtained a listing ten years ago after years of steady growth. 70% of shares in the company are owned by its directors or their relatives, with the remaining 30% owned by external investors, including institutional investors.

Sportswear division

Eight years ago it set up a division to manufacture sportswear. This investment has been very successful and the sportswear division now accounts for 40% of total group revenue, having grown much quicker than the original formal clothing division.

Newimber Co's board has given divisional management at the sportswear division more authority over time, although the board has continued to make major policy and investment decisions relating to the division. Initially, relations between Newimber Co's board and management of the sportswear division were good, but there have been problems over the last couple of years. The sportswear division's management has been frustrated by the board's refusal to approve their recent investment plans on the grounds that they were too risky. In order to achieve operational efficiencies, the sportswear division's management would also like to pursue stricter policies for managing operational staff and suppliers than Newimber Co's board has so far allowed.

In addition, Newimber Co started to prepare an integrated report three years ago, but Newimber Co's board has had difficulties in obtaining all the information it requires for the report from the sportswear division.

Restructuring

A few months ago, the management of the sportswear division approached Newimber Co's board with a proposal for a management buyout of the sportswear division. However, the price the sportswear division's management was able to offer was insufficient to persuade Newimber Co's board to sell the sportswear division to them.

Newimber Co's board has subsequently decided that the sportswear division should be demerged into a new company, Poynins Co. The shareholders and proportion of shares held would be the same for Poynins Co as it currently is for Newimber Co. The sportswear division's senior management team would become the board of Poynins Co and Poynins Co would seek an immediate listing on the same stock exchange as Newimber Co.

Financial information

The market capitalisation of Newimber Co's share capital is currently $585 million. Newimber Co also currently has $200 million 5.9% loan notes. The loan notes are redeemable in five years' time at a premium of 5%. Newimber Co's equity beta is currently estimated at 1.4. Newimber Co's current cost of equity is 11.8% and its current before-tax cost of debt is 4.5%.

The asset beta of the formal clothing division is estimated to be 1.21. The weighting in estimating Newimber Co's overall asset beta is 60% for the formal clothing division to 40% for the sportswear division. The debt beta can be assumed to be zero.

In return for 40% of the issued share capital of Newimber Co, its current shareholders will receive 100% of the issued share capital of Poynins Co, corresponding to the assets and liabilities being transferred. The shares in Newimber Co which shareholders have given up will be cancelled. After the demerger, Newimber Co's new market capitalisation can be assumed to be $351 million. Poynins Co will have no long-term debt, the liability for the $200 million loan notes remaining with Newimber Co.

The current risk-free rate of return is estimated to be 3.4%. The market risk premium is estimated to be 6%. A tax rate of 28% is applicable to all companies.

The sportswear division currently has $36 million operating cash flows. Its managers believe that operating cash flows can increase by the following rates once Poynins Co has been listed:

Year	%
1	25
2	20
3	15
4 onwards	2

The sportswear division's managers believe that Poynins Co will require a $20 million investment of additional assets in Year 1, rising to $22 million in each of Years 2 and 3, and to $25 million annually from Year 4 onwards.

Required

(a) Discuss the advantages and disadvantages of demerging the sportswear division into a new company. **(5 marks)**

(b) Calculate:

    (i) The change in the weighted average cost of capital of Newimber Co if the demerger of the sportswear division takes place; and

    (ii) The valuation of Poynins Co using free cash flows, based on the information and assumptions given and briefly discuss your results. **(15 marks)**

(c) Discuss the factors which may determine the policies Poynins Co should adopt for communication of information to its shareholders and other significant stakeholders.

(5 marks)

(Total = 25 marks)

31 Flufftort (Sep/Dec 15)   **49 mins**

Five years ago the Patel family invested in a new business, Flufftort Co, which manufactures furniture. Some family members became directors of Flufftort Co, others have not been actively involved in management. A venture capital firm, Gupte VC, also made a 20% investment in Flufftort Co. A representative of Gupte VC was appointed to Flufftort Co's board. Flufftort Co also took out a long-term 8.5% bank loan.

Sales have generally been disappointing. As a result, members of the Patel family have been reluctant to invest further in Flufftort Co. Over the last year Gupte VC has taken a tougher attitude towards Flufftort Co. Gupte VC pressurised Flufftort Co to pay a dividend of $2 million for the year ended 30 June 20X5. Gupte VC has also said that if Flufftort Co's financial results do not improve, Gupte VC may exercise its right to compel Flufftort Co to buy back its shares at par on 30 June 20X6.

However, Flufftort Co's most recent product, the Easicushion chair, has been a much bigger success than expected. In order to produce enough Easicushion chairs to affect its results substantially, Flufftort Co will need to make significant expenditure on manufacturing facilities and additional working capital.

EXTRACTS FROM STATEMENT OF PROFIT OR LOSS FOR YEAR ENDED 30 JUNE 20X5 AND FORECAST STATEMENT OF PROFIT OR LOSS FOR YEAR ENDED 30 JUNE 20X6

	20X5 $m	20X6 forecast $m
Operating profit	8.0	6.0
Finance cost	(3.0)	(3.0)
Profit before tax	5.0	3.0
Tax on profits (20%)	(1.0)	(0.6)

	20X5	20X6 forecast
	$m	$m
Profit for the period	4.0	2.4
Dividends	(2.0)	–
Retained earnings	2.0	2.4

Note. The forecast statement of profit or loss for the year ended 30 June 20X6 is not affected by the proposed investment. This can be assumed only to affect results after 30 June 20X6. The figure shown for retained earnings in the 20X6 forecast can be assumed to be the net increase in cash for the year ended 30 June 20X6.

SUMMARISED STATEMENT OF FINANCIAL POSITION AS AT 30 JUNE 20X5

	$m
Assets	
Non-current assets	69.0
Current assets excluding cash	18.0
Cash	7.6
Total assets	94.6
Equity and liabilities	
Share capital ($1 shares)	50.0
Retained earnings	2.6
Total equity	52.6
Long-term liabilities	
8.5% bank loan	30.0
9% loan note	5.0
Total long-term liabilities	35.0
Current liabilities	7.0
Total liabilities	42.0
Total equity and liabilities	94.6

Notes

1   55% of shares are owned by the members of the Patel family who are directors, 25% by other members of the Patel family and 20% by Gupte VC.

2   The bank loan is secured on the non-current assets of Flufftort and is due for repayment on 31 December 20X9. The loan is subject to a covenant that the ratio of equity to non-current liabilities should be greater than 1.3 on a book value basis. Flufftort has also been granted an overdraft facility of up to $5 million by its bank.

3   The loan note is held by Rajiv Patel, a member of the Patel family who is not a director. The loan note is unsecured, is subordinated to the bank loan and has no fixed date for repayment.

4   If no finance is available for investment in manufacturing facilities, non-current assets, current assets excluding cash, the bank loan, loan note and current liabilities can be assumed to be the same at 30 June 20X6 as at 30 June 20X5.

However, the chief executive and finance director of Flufftort Co intend to propose that the company should be refinanced to fund the expanded production of the Easicushion chair. They have not yet consulted anyone else about their proposals.

Details of the proposed refinancing are as follows:

1   The members of the Patel family who are directors would subscribe to an additional 15 million $1 shares at par.

2   Gupte VC would subscribe to an additional 20 million $1 shares at par.

3   The 8.5% bank loan would be renegotiated with the bank and the borrowing increased to $65 million, to be repaid on 30 June 20Y2. The expected finance cost of the loan would be 10% per year.

4   Rajiv Patel's loan note would be replaced by 5 million $1 shares.

5   The refinancing would mean non-current assets would increase to $125 million, current assets other than cash would increase to $42 million and current liabilities would increase to $12 million.

6   Operating profits would be expected to increase to $20 million in the first full year after the facilities are constructed (year ended 30 June 20X7) and $25 million in the second year (year ended 30 June 20X8). No dividends would be paid for these two years, as cash surpluses would be used for further investment as required. Tax on company profits can be assumed to remain at 20%.

Required

(a)   (i)   Prepare a projected statement of financial position as at 30 June 20X6, on the assumption that Gupte VC exercises its rights and Gupte VC's shares are repurchased and cancelled by Flufftort Co.   **(4 marks)**

        (ii)   Prepare a projected statement of financial position as at 30 June 20X6 on the assumption that the proposed refinancing and investment take place.   **(4 marks)**

        (iii)   Prepare projected statements of profit or loss for the years ended 30 June 20X7 and 30 June 20X8 on the basis that the profit forecasts are correct.   **(4 marks)**

(b)   Evaluate whether the suggested refinancing scheme is likely to be agreed by all finance providers. State clearly any assumptions which you make.   **(13 marks)**

                                                                        (Total = 25 marks)

32 Ennea (6/12)   **49 mins**

Three proposals were put forward for further consideration after a meeting of the executive directors of Ennea Co to discuss the future investment and financing strategy of the business. Ennea Co is a listed company operating in the haulage and shipping industry.

Proposal 1

To increase the company's level of debt by borrowing a further $20 million and use the funds raised to buy back share capital.

Proposal 2

To increase the company's level of debt by borrowing a further $20 million and use these funds to invest in additional non-current assets in the haulage strategic business unit.

Proposal 3

To sell excess non-current haulage assets with a net book value of $25 million for $27 million and focus on offering more services to the shipping strategic business unit. This business unit will require no additional investment in non-current assets. All the funds raised from the sale of the non-current assets will be used to reduce the company's debt.

Ennea Co financial information

EXTRACTS FROM THE FORECAST FINANCIAL POSITION FOR THE COMING YEAR

	$m
Non-current assets	282
Current assets	66
Total assets	348
Equity and liabilities	
Share capital (40c per share)	48
Retained earnings	123
Total equity	171
Non-current liabilities	140
Current liabilities	37
Total liabilities	177
Total liabilities and equity	348

Ennea Co's forecast after-tax profit for the coming year is expected to be $26 million and its current share price is $3.20 per share. The non-current liabilities consist solely of a 6% medium-term loan redeemable within seven years. The terms of the loan contract stipulate that an increase in borrowing will result in an increase in the coupon payable of 25 basis points on the total amount borrowed, while a reduction in borrowing will lower the coupon payable by 15 basis points on the total amount borrowed.

Ennea Co's effective tax rate is 20%. The company's estimated after-tax rate of return on investment is expected to be 15% on any new investment. It is expected that any reduction in investment would suffer the same rate of return.

Required

(a) Estimate and discuss the impact of each of the three proposals on the forecast statement of financial position, the earnings and earnings per share, and gearing of Ennea Co.

(20 marks)

(b) An alternative suggestion to Proposal 3 was made where the non-current assets could be leased to other companies instead of being sold. The lease receipts would then be converted into an asset through securitisation. The proceeds from the sale of the securitised lease receipts asset would be used to reduce the outstanding loan borrowings.

Required

Explain what the securitisation process would involve and what would be the key barriers to Ennea Co undertaking the process. **(5 marks)**

(Total = 25 marks)

33 Nubo (12/13)   49 mins

Nubo Co has divisions operating in two diverse sectors: production of aircraft parts and supermarkets. Whereas the aircraft parts production division has been growing rapidly, the supermarkets division's growth has been slower. The company is considering selling the supermarkets division and focusing solely on the aircraft parts production division.

Extracts from Nubo Co's most recent financial statements are as follows:

Year ended 30 November	20X3
	$m
Profit after tax	166
Non-current assets	550
Current assets	122
Non-current liabilities	387
Current liabilities	95

About 70% of Nubo Co's non-current assets and current assets are attributable to the supermarkets division and the remainder to the aircraft parts production division. Each of the two divisions generates roughly half of the total profit after tax. The market value of the two divisions is thought to be equivalent to the price/earnings (P/E) ratios of the two divisions' industries. The supermarket industry's P/E ratio is 7 and the aircraft parts production industry's P/E ratio is 12.

Nubo Co can either sell the supermarkets division as a going concern or sell the assets of the supermarkets division separately. If the assets are sold separately, Nubo Co believes that it can sell the non-current assets for 115% of the book value and the current assets for 80% of the book value. The funds raised from the sale of the supermarkets division will be used to pay for all the company's current and non-current liabilities.

Following the sale of the supermarkets division and paying off the liabilities, Nubo Co will raise additional finance for new projects in the form of debt. It will be able to borrow up to a maximum of 100% of the total asset value of the new downsized company.

One of the new projects which Nubo Co is considering is a joint venture with Pilvi Co to produce an innovative type of machinery which will be used in the production of light aircraft and private jets. Both companies will provide the expertise and funding required for the project equally.

Representatives from both companies will make up the senior management team and decisions will be made jointly. Legal contracts will be drawn up once profit-sharing and other areas have been discussed by the companies and agreed on.

Pilvi Co has approached Ulap Bank for the finance it requires for the venture, based on Islamic finance principles. Ulap Bank has agreed to consider the request from Pilvi Co but, because the financing requirement will be for a long period of time and because of uncertainties surrounding the project, Ulap Bank wants to provide the finance based on the principles of a Musharaka contract, with Ulap Bank requiring representation on the venture's senior management team. Normally Ulap Bank provides funds based on the principles of a Mudaraba contract, which the bank provides for short-term, low-risk projects, where the responsibility for running a project rests solely with the borrower.

Required

(a)   Advise Nubo Co whether it should sell the supermarkets division as a going concern or sell the assets separately and estimate the additional cash and debt funds which could be available to the new, downsized company. Show all relevant calculations.   **(7 marks)**

(b)   An alternative to selling the supermarkets division would be to demerge both the divisions. In this case, all of Nubo Co's liabilities would be taken over by the demerged supermarkets division. Also, either of the demerged companies can borrow up to 100% of their respective total asset values.

Required

Discuss whether a demerger of the supermarkets division may be more appropriate than a sale.   **(6 marks)**

(c)   Discuss why Ulap Bank may want to consider providing the finance based on a Musharaka contract instead of a Mudaraba contract, and the key concerns Nubo Co may have from the arrangement between Pilvi Co and Ulap Bank.   **(12 marks)**

(Total = 25 marks)

34 Bento (6/15)   49 min

In order to raise funds for future projects, the management of Bento Co, a large manufacturing company, is considering disposing of one of its subsidiary companies, Okazu Co, which is involved in manufacturing rubber tubing. It is considering undertaking the disposal through a management buyout (MBO) or a management buy-in (MBI). Bento Co wants $60 million from the sale of Okazu Co.

Given below are extracts from the most recent financial statements for Okazu Co:

YEAR ENDING 30 APRIL

	20X5 $'000
Total non-current assets	40,800
Total current assets	12,300
Total assets	53,100
Equity	24,600
Non-current liabilities	16,600
Current liabilities	
Trade and other payables	7,900
Bank overdraft	4,000
Total current liabilities	11,900
Total equity and liabilities	53,100

YEAR ENDING 30 APRIL

	20X5
	$'000
Sales revenue	54,900
Operating profit	12,200
Finance costs	1,600
Profit before tax	10,600
Taxation	2,120
Profit for the year	8,480

Notes relating to the financial statements above:

1   Current assets, non-current assets and the trade and other payables will be transferred to the new company when Okazu Co is sold. The bank overdraft will be repaid by Bento Co prior to the sale of Okazu Co.

2   With the exception of the bank overdraft, Bento Co has provided all the financing to Okazu Co. No liabilities, except the trade and other payables specified above, will be transferred to the new company when Okazu Co is sold.

3   It is estimated that the market value of the non-current assets is 30% higher than the book value and the market value of the current assets is equivalent to the book value.

4   The group finance costs and taxation are allocated by Bento Co to all its subsidiaries in pre-agreed proportions.

Okazu Co's senior management team has approached Dofu Co, a venture capital company, about the proposed MBO. Dofu Co has agreed to provide leveraged finance for a 50% equity stake in the new company on the following basis:

- $30 million loan in the form of an 8% bond on which interest is payable annually, based on the loan amount outstanding at the start of each year. The bond will be repaid on the basis of fixed equal annual payments (constituting of interest and principal) over the next four years.

- $20 million loan in the form of a 6% convertible bond on which interest is payable annually. Conversion may be undertaken on the basis of 50 equity shares for every $100 from the beginning of Year 5 onwards.

- 5,000,000 $1 equity shares for $5,000,000.

Okazu Co's senior management will contribute $5,000,000 for 5,000,000 $1 equity shares and own the remaining 50% of the equity stake.

As a condition for providing the finance, Dofu Co will impose a restrictive covenant that the new company's gearing ratio will be no higher than 75% at the end of its first year of operations, and then fall to no higher than 60%, 50% and 40% at the end of Year 2 to Year 4 respectively. The gearing ratio is determined by the book value of debt divided by the combined book values of debt and equity.

After the MBO, it is expected that earnings before interest and tax will increase by 11% per year and annual dividends of 25% on the available earnings will be paid for the next four years. It is expected that the annual growth rate of dividends will reduce by 60% from Year 5 onwards following the MBO. The new company will pay tax at a rate of 20% per year. The new company's cost of equity has been estimated at 12%.

Required

(a)   Distinguish between an MBO and an MBI. Discuss the relative benefits and drawbacks to Okazu Co if it is disposed through an MBO instead of an MBI.   **(5 marks)**

(b)   Estimate, showing all relevant calculations, whether the restrictive covenant imposed by Dofu Co is likely to be met.   **(12 marks)**

(c)   Discuss, with supporting calculations, whether or not an MBO would be beneficial for Dofu Co and Okazu Co's senior management team.   **(8 marks)**

(Total = 25 marks)

35 Eview Cinemas (Sep/Dec 17)

49 mins

Eview Cinemas Co is a long-established chain of cinemas in the country of Taria. 20 years ago Eview Cinemas Co's board decided to convert some of its cinemas into sports gyms, known as the EV clubs. The number of EV clubs has expanded since then. Eview Cinemas Co's board brought in outside managers to run the EV clubs, but over the years there have been disagreements between the clubs' managers and the board. The managers have felt that the board has wrongly prioritised investment in, and refurbishment of, the cinemas at the expense of the EV clubs.

Five years ago, Eview Cinemas Co undertook a major refurbishment of its cinemas, financing this work with various types of debt, including loan notes at a high coupon rate of 10%. Shortly after the work was undertaken, Taria entered into a recession which adversely affected profitability. The finance cost burden was high and Eview Cinemas Co was not able to pay a dividend for two years.

The recession is now over and Eview Cinemas Co has emerged in a good financial position, as two of its competitors went into insolvency during the recession. Eview Cinemas Co's board wishes to expand its chain of cinemas and open new, multiscreen cinemas in locations which are available because businesses were closed down during the recession.

In two years' time Taria is due to host a major sports festival. This has encouraged interest in sport and exercise in the country. As a result, some gym chains are looking to expand and have contacted Eview Cinemas Co's board to ask if it would be interested in selling the EV clubs. Most of the directors regard the cinemas as the main business and so are receptive to selling the EV clubs.

The finance director has recommended that the sales price of the EV clubs be based on predicted free cash flows as follows:

(1)   The predicted free cash flow figures in $m for EV clubs are as follows:

Year	1	2	3	4
	390	419	455	490

(2)   After Year 4, free cash flows should be assumed to increase at 5.2% per year.

(3)   The discount rate to be used should be the current weighted average cost of capital, which is 12%.

(4)   The finance director believes that the result of the free cash flow valuation will represent a fair value of the EV clubs' business, but Eview Cinemas Co is looking to obtain a 25% premium on the fair value as the expected sales price.

Other information supplied by the finance director is as follows:

(1)   The predicted after-tax profits of the EV clubs are $454 million in Year 1. This can be assumed to be 40% of total after-tax profits of EV Cinemas Co.

(2)   The expected proceeds which Eview Cinemas Co receives from selling the EV clubs will be used firstly to pay off the 10% loan notes. Part of the remaining amount from the sales proceeds will then be used to enhance liquidity by being held as part of current assets, so that the current ratio increases to 1.5. The rest of the remaining amount will be invested in property, plant and equipment. The current net book value of the non-current assets of the EV clubs to be sold can be assumed to be $3,790 million. The profit on the sale of the EV clubs should be taken directly to reserves.

(3)   Eview Cinemas Co's asset beta for the cinemas can be assumed to be 0.952.

(4)   Eview Cinemas Co currently has 1,000 million $1 shares in issue. These are currently trading at $15.75 per share. The finance director expects the share price to rise by 10% once the sale has been completed, as he thinks that the stock market will perceive it to be a good deal.

(5)   Tradeable debt is currently quoted at $96 per $100 for the 10% loan notes and $93 per $100 for the other loan notes. The value of the other loan notes is not expected to change once the sale has been completed. The overall pre-tax cost of debt is currently 9% and can be assumed to fall to 8% when the 10% loan notes are redeemed.

(6)   The current tax rate on profits is 20%.

(7)   Additional investment in current assets is expected to earn a 7% pre-tax return and additional investment in property, plant and equipment is expected to earn a 12% pre-tax return.

(8)   The current risk-free rate is 4% and the return on the market portfolio is 10%.

Eview Cinemas Co's current summarised statement of financial position is shown below. The CEO wants to know the impact the sale of the EV clubs would have immediately on the statement of financial position, the impact on the Year 1 forecast earnings per share and on the weighted average cost of capital.

	$m
Assets	
Non-current assets	15,621
Current assets	2,347
Total assets	17,968
Equity and liabilities	
Called-up share capital	1,000
Retained earnings	7,917
Total equity	8,917
Non-current liabilities	
10% loan notes	3,200
Other loan notes	2,700
Bank loans	985
Total non-current liabilities	6,885
Current liabilities	2,166
Total equity and liabilities	17,968

Required

(a)   Calculate the expected sales price of the EV clubs and demonstrate its impact (ie the impact of the sale) on Eview Cinemas Co's statement of financial position, forecast earnings per share and weighted average cost of capital.   **(17 marks)**

(b)   Evaluate the decision to sell the EV clubs.   **(8 marks)**

(Total = 25 marks)

36 Kenduri Co (6/13)   **49 mins**

Kenduri Co is a large multinational company based in the UK with a number of subsidiary companies around the world. Currently, foreign exchange exposure as a result of transactions between Kenduri Co and its subsidiary companies is managed by each company individually. Kenduri Co is considering whether or not to manage the foreign exchange exposure using multilateral netting from the UK, with the sterling pound (£) as the base currency. If multilateral netting is undertaken, spot mid-rates would be used.

The following cash flows are due in three months between Kenduri Co and three of its subsidiary companies. The subsidiary companies are Lakama Co, based in the US (currency US$), Jaia Co, based in Canada (currency CAD), and Gochiso Co, based in Japan (currency JPY).

Owed by	Owed to	Amount
Kenduri Co	Lakama Co	US$4.5m
Kenduri Co	Jaia Co	CAD 1.1m
Gochiso Co	Jaia Co	CAD 3.2m
Gochiso Co	Lakama Co	US$1.4m
Jaia Co	Lakama Co	US$1.5m
Jaia Co	Kenduri Co	CAD 3.4m
Lakama Co	Gochiso Co	JPY 320m
Lakama Co	Kenduri Co	US$2.1m

Exchange rates available to Kenduri Co

	US$/£1	CAD/£1	JPY/£1
Spot	1.5938–1.5962	1.5690–1.5710	131.91–133.59
Three-month forward	1.5996–1.6037	1.5652–1.5678	129.15–131.05

Currency options available to Kenduri Co

Contract size £62,500, Exercise price quotation: US$/£1, Premium: cents per £1

	Call options		Put options	
	3-month expiry	6-month expiry	3-month expiry	6-month expiry
Exercise price				
1.60	1.55	2.25	2.08	2.23
1.62	0.98	1.58	3.42	3.73

It can be assumed that option contracts expire at the end of the relevant month.

Annual interest rates available to Kenduri Co and subsidiaries

	Borrowing rate	Investing rate
UK	4.0%	2.8%
US	4.8%	3.1%
Canada	3.4%	2.1%
Japan	2.2%	0.5%

Required

(a) Advise Kenduri Co on, and recommend, an appropriate hedging strategy for the US$ cash flows it is due to receive or pay in three months, from Lakama Co. Show all relevant calculations to support the advice given.   **(12 marks)**

(b) Calculate, using a tabular format (transactions matrix), the impact of undertaking multilateral netting by Kenduri Co and its three subsidiary companies for the cash flows due in three months. Briefly discuss why some governments allow companies to undertake multilateral netting, while others do not.   **(10 marks)**

BPP
LEARNING
MEDIA

(c)   When examining different currency options and their risk factors, it was noticed that a long call option had a high gamma value. Explain the possible characteristics of a long call option with a high gamma value.

(3 marks)

(Total = 25 marks)

37 Massie (Sep/Dec 15)   49 mins

The Armstrong Group is a multinational group of companies. Today is 1 September. The treasury manager at Massie Co, one of Armstrong Group's subsidiaries based in Europe, has just received notification from the group's head office that it intends to introduce a system of netting to settle balances owed within the group every six months. Previously inter-group indebtedness was settled between the two companies concerned.

The predicted balances owing to, and owed by, the group companies at the end of February are as follows:

Owed by	Owed to	Local currency (m)
Armstrong (US)	Horan (South Africa)	US$12.17
Horan (South Africa)	Massie (Europe)	SA R42.65
Giffen (Denmark)	Armstrong (US)	D Kr21.29
Massie (Europe)	Armstrong (US)	US$19.78
Armstrong (US)	Massie (Europe)	€1.57
Horan (South Africa)	Giffen (Denmark)	D Kr16.35
Giffen (Denmark)	Massie (Europe)	€1.55

The predicted exchange rates, used in the calculations of the balances to be settled, are as follows:

	D Kr	US$	SA R	€
1 D Kr =	1.0000	0.1823	1.9554	0.1341
1 US$ =	5.4855	1.0000	10.7296	0.7358
1 SA R =	0.5114	0.0932	1.0000	0.0686
1 € =	7.4571	1.3591	14.5773	1.0000

Settlement will be made in dollars, the currency of Armstrong Group, the parent company. Settlement will be made in the order that the company owing the largest net amount in dollars will first settle with the company owed the smallest net amount in dollars.

Note. D Kr is Danish Krone, SA R is South African Rand, US$ is United States dollar and € is euro.

Required

(a)   (i)   Calculate the inter-group transfers which are forecast to occur for the next period.

(8 marks)

(ii)   Discuss the problems which may arise with the new arrangement.   (3 marks)

(b)   The most significant transaction which Massie Co is due to undertake with a company outside the Armstrong Group in the next six months is that it is due to receive €25 million from Bardsley Co on 30 November. Massie Co's treasury manager intends to invest this money for the six months until 31 May, when it will be used to fund some major capital expenditure. However, the treasury manager is concerned about changes in interest rates. Predictions in the media range from a 0.5% rise in interest rates to a 0.5% fall.

Because of the uncertainty, the treasury manager has decided to protect Massie Co by using derivatives. The treasury manager wishes to take advantage of favourable interest rate movements. Therefore she is considering options on interest rate futures or interest rate collars as possible methods of hedging, but not interest rate futures. Massie Co can invest at LIBOR minus 40 basis points and LIBOR is currently 3.6%.

The treasury manager has obtained the following information on euro futures and options. She is ignoring margin requirements.

Three-month euro futures, €1,000,000 contract, tick size 0.01% and tick value €25.

September	95.94
December	95.76
March	95.44

Options on three-month euro futures, €1,000,000 contract, tick size 0.01% and tick value €25. Option premiums are in annual %.

Calls			Strike	Puts		
September	December	March		September	December	March
0.113	0.182	0.245	96.50	0.002	0.123	0.198
0.017	0.032	0.141	97.00	0.139	0.347	0.481

It can be assumed that settlement for the contracts is at the end of the month. It can also be assumed that basis diminishes to zero at contract maturity at a constant rate and that time intervals can be counted in months.

Required

Based on the choice of options on futures or collars which Massie Co is considering and assuming the company does not face any basis risk, recommend a hedging strategy for the €25 million receipt. Support your recommendations with appropriate comments and relevant calculations.

(14 marks)

(Total = 25 marks)

38 Adverane (Mar/Jun 18)

49 mins

The Adverane Group is a multinational group of companies, with its headquarters in Switzerland. The Adverane Group consists of a number of fully-owned subsidiaries and Elted Co, an associate company based in the USA, in which Adverane Group owns 30% of the ordinary equity share capital. Balances owing between the parent, Adverane Co, and its subsidiaries, and between subsidiaries, are settled by multilateral netting. Transactions between the parent and Elted Co are settled separately.

Transactions with Elted Co

Adverane Co wishes to hedge transactions with Elted Co which are due to be settled in four months' time in US$. Adverane Co will owe Elted Co US$3.7 million for a major purchase of supplies and Elted Co will owe Adverane Co US$10.15 million for non-current assets. Adverane Group's treasury department is considering whether to use money markets or exchange-traded currency futures for hedging.

Annual interest rates available to Adverane Co:

	Investing rate	Borrowing rate
Switzerland	2.7%	3.9%
USA	2.5%	3.7%

Exchange traded currency futures

Contract size CHF125,000, price quotation US$ per CHF1

Three-month expiry: 1.1213

Six-month expiry: 1.1204

Netting

The balances owed to and owed by members of Adverane Group when netting is to take place are as follows:

Owed by	Owed to	Local currency (m)
Adverane (Switzerland)	Bosha (Eurozone)	CHF15.90
Adverane (Switzerland)	Diling (Brazil)	CHF4.46
Bosha (Eurozone)	Cogate (USA)	€24.89
Bosha (Eurozone)	Diling (Brazil)	€18.57
Cogate (USA)	Adverane (Switzerland)	US$27.08
Cogate (USA)	Diling (Brazil)	US$5.68
Diling (Brazil)	Adverane (Switzerland)	BRL38.80
Diling (Brazil)	Bosha (Eurozone)	BRL51.20

Spot rates are currently as follows:

	CHF	€	US$	BRL
1 CHF =	1.0000	0.9347–0.9369	1.1196–1.1222	3.1378–3.1760

The group members will make settlement in Swiss francs. Spot mid-rates will be used in calculations. Settlement will be made in the order that the company owing the largest net amount in Swiss francs will first settle with the company owed the smallest net amount in Swiss francs.

Transfer price arrangements

The Adverane Group board has been reviewing the valuation of inter-group transactions, as it is concerned that the current system is not working well. Currently inter-group transfer prices are mostly based on fixed cost plus a mark-up negotiated by the buying and selling divisions. If they cannot agree a price, either the sale does not take place or the central treasury department determines the margin. The board has the following concerns:

- Both selling and buying divisions have claimed that prices are unfair and distort the measurement of their performance.

- Significant treasury department time is being taken up dealing with disputes and then dealing with complaints that the price it has imposed is unfair on one or the other division.

- Some parts of the group are choosing to buy from external suppliers rather than from suppliers within the group.

As a result of the review, the Adverane Group board has decided that transfer prices should in future be based on market prices, where an external market exists.

Note. CHF is Swiss Franc, € is Euro, US$ is United States dollar and BRL is Brazilian Real.

Required

(a) Advise Adverane Co on, and recommend, an appropriate hedging strategy for the US$ cash flows it is due to receive from, or pay to, Elted Co. **(9 marks)**

(b) (i) Calculate the inter-group transfers which are forecast to take place. **(7 marks)**

   (ii) Discuss the advantages of multilateral netting by a central treasury function within the Adverane Group. **(3 marks)**

(c) Evaluate the extent to which changing to a market-price system of transfer pricing will resolve the concerns of the Adverane Group board. **(6 marks)**

(Total = 25 marks)

39 Nutourne (Dec 18)

49 mins

Nutourne Co is a company based in the USA, supplying medical equipment to the USA and Europe.

It is 30 November 20X8. Nutourne Co's treasury department is currently dealing with a sale to a Swiss customer of CHF12.3 million which has just been agreed, where the customer will pay for the equipment on 31 May 20X9. The treasury department intends to hedge the foreign exchange risk on this transaction using traded futures or options as far as possible. Any amount not hedged by a futures or option contract will be hedged on the forward market.

Exchange rates (quoted as US$/CHF 1)

Spot	1.0292–1.0309
Three months forward	1.0327–1.0347
Six months forward	1.0358–1.0380

Currency futures (contract size CHF125,000, futures price quoted as US$ per CHF1)

	Futures price
December	1.0318
March	1.0345
June	1.0369

Currency options (contract size CHF125,000, exercise price quotation US$ per CHF1, premium: US cents per CHF1)

	Calls			Puts		
Exercise price	December	March	June	December	March	June
1.0375	0.47	0.50	0.53	0.74	0.79	0.86

Futures and options contracts mature at the month end.

Non-executive director's comments

A new non-executive director has recently been briefed about the work of the treasury department and has a number of questions about hedging activities. He wants to understand the significance of basis risk in relation to futures. He also wants to know the significant features of over-the-counter forward contracts and options, and why Nutourne Co prefers to use exchange-traded derivatives for hedging.

The non-executive director has also heard about the mark-to-market process and wants to understand the terminology involved, and how the process works, using the transaction with the Swiss customer as an example. The treasury department has supplied relevant information to answer his query. The contract specification for the CHF futures contract states that an initial margin of US$1,450 per contract will be required and a maintenance margin of US$1,360 per contract will also be required. The tick size on the contract is US$0.0001 and the tick value is US$12.50. You can assume that on the first day when Nutourne Co holds the futures contracts, the loss per contract is US$0.0011.

Required

(a) Evaluate which of the exchange-traded derivatives would give Nutourne Co the higher receipt, considering scenarios when the options are and are not exercised. **(12 marks)**

(b) Discuss the benefits and drawbacks for Nutourne Co in using forward contracts compared with using over-the-counter currency options, and explain why Nutourne Co may prefer to use exchange-traded derivatives rather than over-the-counter derivatives to hedge foreign currency risk. **(7 marks)**

(c) Explain to the non-executive director how the mark-to-market process would work for the CHF futures, including the significance of the data supplied by the treasury department. Illustrate your explanation with calculations showing what would happen on the first day, using the data supplied by the treasury department. **(6 marks)**

(Total = 25 marks)

40 Buryecs (Mar/Jun 17)

49 mins

Buryecs Co is an international transport operator based in the Eurozone which has been invited to take over a rail operating franchise in Wirtonia, where the local currency is the dollar ($). Previously this franchise was run by a local operator in Wirtonia but its performance was unsatisfactory and the government in Wirtonia withdrew the franchise.

Buryecs Co will pay $5,000 million for the rail franchise immediately. The government has stated that Buryecs Co should make an annual income from the franchise of $600 million in each of the next three years. At the end of the three years the government in Wirtonia has offered to buy the franchise back for $7,500 million if no other operator can be found to take over the franchise.

Today's spot exchange rate between the Euro and Wirtonia $ is €0.1430 = $1. The predicted inflation rates are as follows:

Year	1	2	3
Eurozone	6%	4%	3%
Wirtonia	3%	8%	11%

Buryecs Co's finance director has contacted its bankers with a view to arranging a currency swap, since he believes that this will be the best way to manage financial risks associated with the franchise. The swap would be for the initial fee paid for the franchise, with a swap of principal immediately and in three years' time, both these swaps being at today's spot rate. Buryecs Co's bank would charge an annual fee of 0.5% in € for arranging the swap. Buryecs Co would take 60% of any benefit of the swap before deducting bank fees, but would then have to pay 60% of the bank fees.

Relevant borrowing rates are:

	Buryecs Co	Counterparty
Eurozone	4.0%	5.8%
Wirtonia	Wirtonia bank rate + 0.6%	Wirtonia bank rate + 0.4%

In order to provide Buryecs Co's board with an alternative hedging method to consider, the finance director has obtained the following information about over-the-counter options in Wirtonia $ from the company's bank.

The exercise price quotation is in Wirtonia $ per €1, premium is % of amount hedged, translated at today's spot rate.

Exercise price	Call options	Put options
7.75	2.8%	1.6%
7.25	1.8%	2.7%

Assume a discount rate of 14%.

Required

(a) Discuss the advantages and drawbacks of using the currency swap to manage financial risks associated with the franchise in Wirtonia. **(6 marks)**

(b) (i) Calculate the annual percentage interest saving which Buryecs Co could make from using a currency swap, compared with borrowing directly in Wirtonia, demonstrating how the currency swap will work. **(4 marks)**

    (ii) Evaluate, using net present value, the financial acceptability of Buryecs Co operating the rail franchise under the terms suggested by the government of Wirtonia and calculate the gain or loss in € from using the swap arrangement. **(8 marks)**

(c) Calculate the results of hedging the receipt of $7,500 million using the currency options and discuss whether currency options would be a better method of hedging this receipt than a currency swap. **(7 marks)**

(Total = 25 marks)

41 Lurgshall (Mar/Jun 19)

Lurgshall Co is a listed electronics company. Lurgshall Co has recently appointed a new chief executive, who has a number of plans to expand the company. The chief executive also plans to look carefully at the costs of all departments in Lurgshall Co's head office, including the centralised treasury department.

The first major investment which the chief executive will oversee is an investment in facilities to produce application-specific components. To finance the planned investment, it is likely that Lurgshall Co will have to borrow money. It is now 1 May. At present, it seems that Lurgshall Co will need to borrow $84 million on 1 September for a period of six months, though both the amount and the period of borrowing are subject to some uncertainty. The treasurer plans to borrow the funds at a variable rate of LIBOR plus 50 basis points. LIBOR is currently 4.5% but is expected to rise by up to 0.6% between now and 1 September.

So far, the possibility of hedging a rise in LIBOR of 0.6% using a forward rate agreement or September $ futures has been investigated. The results of the calculations for these instruments were as follows:

4–10 Forward rate agreement from Birdam Bank: 5.38%

Three-month traded September $ futures: 5.36%

Lurgshall Co's treasurer also wants to consider using options on futures to hedge loans.

Although Lurgshall Co has not previously used swaps for hedging purposes, the treasurer has asked Birdam Bank to find a counterparty for a potential swap arrangement.

Relevant information about options and swaps is as follows:

Options

The current price for three-month $ September futures, $2 million contract size is 95.05. The price is quoted in basis points at 100 − annual % yield.

Options on three-month September $ futures, $2 million contract size, option premiums are in annual %

September calls	Strike price	September puts
0.132	95.25	0.411

It can be assumed that futures and options contracts are settled at the end of each month. Basis can be assumed to diminish to zero at contract maturity at a constant rate, based on monthly time intervals. It can also be assumed that there is no basis risk and there are no margin requirements.

Swap

Birdam Bank has found a possible counterparty to enter into a swap with Lurgshall Co. The counterparty can borrow at an annual floating rate of LIBOR + 1.5% or a fixed rate of 6.1%. Birdam Bank has quoted Lurgshall Co a notional fixed rate of 5.6% for it to borrow. Birdam Bank would charge a fee of 10 basis points to each party individually to act as the intermediary of the swap. Both parties would share equally the potential gains from the swap contract.

Treasury staffing

Lurgshall Co's new chief executive has made the following comments:

> I understand that the treasury department has a number of day-to-day responsibilities, including investing surplus funds for the short-term liquidity management and hedging against currency and interest rates. However, these tasks could all be carried out by the junior, less experienced, members of the department. I do not see why the department needs to employ experienced, expensive staff, as it does not contribute to the strategic success of the company.

BPP LEARNING MEDIA

Required

(a)   Compare the results of hedging the $84 million, using the options and the swap, with the results already obtained using the forward rate agreement and futures, and comment on the results. Show all relevant calculations, including how the interest rate swap would work.   **(15 marks)**

(b)   Discuss the advantages and disadvantages of using swaps as a means of hedging interest rate risk for Lurgshall Co.   **(5 marks)**

(c)   Criticise the views of the chief executive about the work carried out by the treasury department and the staff required to do this work.   **(5 marks)**

(Total = 25 marks)

42 Awan (12/13)   49 mins

Awan Co is expecting to receive $48,000,000 on 1 February 20X4, which will be invested until it is required for a large project on 1 June 20X4. Due to uncertainty in the markets, the company is of the opinion that it is likely that interest rates will fluctuate significantly over the coming months, although it is difficult to predict whether they will increase or decrease.

Awan Co's treasury team want to hedge the company against adverse movements in interest rates using one of the following derivative products:

*   Forward rate agreements (FRAs)
*   Interest rate futures
*   Options on interest rate futures

Awan Co can invest funds at the relevant inter-bank rate less 20 basis points. The current inter-bank rate is 4.09%. However, Awan Co is of the opinion that interest rates could increase or decrease by as much as 0.9% over the coming months.

The following information and quotes are provided from an appropriate exchange on $ futures and options. Margin requirements can be ignored.

Three-month $ futures, $2,000,000 contract size

Prices are quoted in basis points at 100 – annual % yield

December 20X3:   94.80
March 20X4:   94.76
June 20X4:   94.69

Options on three-month $ futures, $2,000,000 contract size, option premiums are in annual %

	Calls		Strike	Puts		
December	March	June		December	March	June
0.342	0.432	0.523	94.50	0.090	0.119	0.271
0.097	0.121	0.289	95.00	0.312	0.417	0.520

Voblaka Bank has offered the following FRA rates to Awan Co:

1–7:   4.37%
3–4:   4.78%
3–7:   4.82%
4–7:   4.87%

It can be assumed that settlement for the futures and options contracts is at the end of the month and that basis diminishes to zero at contract maturity at a constant rate, based on monthly time intervals. Assume that it is 1 November 20X3 now and that there is no basis risk.

Required

(a)   Based on the three hedging choices Awan Co is considering, recommend a hedging strategy for the $48,000,000 investment, if interest rates increase or decrease by 0.9%. Support your answer with appropriate calculations and discussion.   **(19 marks)**

(b)   A member of Awan Co's treasury team has suggested that if option contracts are purchased to hedge against the interest rate movements, then the number of contracts purchased should be determined by a hedge ratio based on the delta value of the option.

Required

Discuss how the delta value of an option could be used in determining the number of contracts purchased.

(6 marks)

(Total = 25 marks)

43 Wardegul (Sep/Dec 17)   49 mins

Wardegul Co, a company based in the Eurozone, has expanded very rapidly over recent years by a combination of acquiring subsidiaries in foreign countries and setting up its own operations abroad. Wardegul Co's board has found it increasingly difficult to monitor its activities and Wardegul Co's support functions, including its treasury function, have struggled to cope with a greatly increased workload. Wardegul Co's board has decided to restructure the company on a regional basis, with regional boards and appropriate support functions. Managers in some of the larger countries in which Wardegul Co operates are unhappy with reorganisation on a regional basis, and believe that operations in their countries should be given a large amount of autonomy and be supported by internal functions organised on a national basis.

Assume it is now 1 October 20W7. The central treasury function has just received information about a future transaction by a newly-acquired subsidiary in Euria, where the local currency is the dinar (D). The subsidiary expects to receive D27,000,000 on 31 January 20X8. It wants this money to be invested locally in Euria, most probably for five months until 30 June 20X8.

Wardegul Co's treasury team is aware that economic conditions in Euria are currently uncertain. The central bank base rate in Euria is currently 4.2% and the treasury team believes that it can invest funds in Euria at the central bank base rate less 30 basis points. However, treasury staff have seen predictions that the central bank base rate could increase by up to 1.1% or fall by up to 0.6% between now and 31 January 20X8.

Wardegul Co's treasury staff normally hedge interest rate exposure by using whichever of the following products is most appropriate:

- Forward rate agreements (FRAs)
- Interest rate futures
- Options on interest rate futures

Treasury function guidelines emphasise the importance of mitigating the impact of adverse movements in interest rates. However, they also allow staff to take into consideration upside risks associated with interest rate exposure when deciding which instrument to use.

A local bank in Euria, with which Wardegul Co has not dealt before, has offered the following FRA rates:

4–9:   5.02%
5–10:   5.10%

The treasury team has also obtained the following information about exchange traded Dinar futures and options:

Three-month D futures, D500,000 contract size

Prices are quoted in basis points at 100 − annual % yield:

December 20W7:   94.84
March 20X8:   94.78
June 20X8:   94.66

Options on three-month D futures, D500,000 contract size, option premiums are in annual %

	Calls		Strike price		Put	
December	March	June		December	March	June
0.417	0.545	0.678	94.25	0.071	0.094	0.155
0.078	0.098	0.160	95.25	0.393	0.529	0.664

It can be assumed that futures and options contracts are settled at the end of each month. Basis can be assumed to diminish to zero at contract maturity at a constant rate, based on monthly time intervals. It can also be assumed that there is no basis risk and there are no margin requirements.

Required

(a) Recommend a hedging strategy for the D27,000,000 investment, based on the hedging choices which treasury staff are considering, if interest rates increase by 1.1% or decrease by 0.6%. Support your answer with appropriate calculations and discussion. **(18 marks)**

(b) Discuss the advantages of operating treasury activities through regional treasury functions compared with:

    (i) Each country having a separate treasury function.
    (ii) Operating activities through a single global treasury function. **(7 marks)**

(Total = 25 marks)

44 Keshi (12/14)   49 mins

Keshi Co is a large multinational company with a number of international subsidiary companies. A centralised treasury department manages Keshi Co and its subsidiaries' borrowing requirements, cash surplus investment and financial risk management. Financial risk is normally managed using conventional derivative products such as forwards, futures, options and swaps.

Assume it is 1 December 20X4 today and Keshi Co is expecting to borrow $18,000,000 on 1 February 20X5 for a period of seven months. It can either borrow the funds at a variable rate of LIBOR plus 40 basis points or a fixed rate of 5.5%. LIBOR is currently 3.8% but Keshi Co feels that this could increase or decrease by 0.5% over the coming months due to increasing uncertainty in the markets.

The treasury department is considering whether or not to hedge the $18,000,000, using either exchange-traded March options or over-the-counter swaps offered by Rozu Bank.

The following information and quotes for $ March options are provided from an appropriate exchange. The options are based on three-month $ futures and $1,000,000 contract size and option premiums are in annual %.

March calls	Strike price	March puts
0.882	95.50	0.662
0.648	96.00	0.902

Option prices are quoted in basis points at 100 minus the annual percentage yield and settlement of the options contracts is at the end of March 20X5. The current basis on the March futures price is 44 points and it is expected to be 33 points on 1 January 20X5, 22 points on 1 February 20X5 and 11 points on 1 March 20X5.

Rozu Bank has offered Keshi Co a swap on a counterparty variable rate of LIBOR plus 30 basis points or a fixed rate of 4.6%, where Keshi Co receives 70% of any benefits accruing from undertaking the swap, prior to any bank charges. Rozu Bank will charge Keshi Co 10 basis points for the swap.

Keshi Co's chief executive officer believes that a centralised treasury department is necessary in order to increase shareholder value, but Keshi Co's new chief financial officer (CFO) thinks that having decentralised treasury departments operating across the subsidiary companies could be more beneficial. The chief financial officer thinks that this is particularly relevant to the situation which Suisen Co, a company owned by Keshi Co, is facing.

Suisen Co operates in a country where most companies conduct business activities based on Islamic finance principles. It produces confectionery products including chocolates. It wants to use Salam contracts instead of commodity futures contracts to hedge its exposure to price fluctuations of cocoa. Salam contracts involve a commodity which is sold based on currently agreed prices, quantity and quality. Full payment is received by the seller immediately, for an agreed delivery to be made in the future.

Required

(a) Based on the two hedging choices Keshi Co is considering, recommend a hedging strategy for the $18,000,000 borrowing. Support your answer with appropriate calculations and discussion. **(15 marks)**

(b) Discuss how a centralised treasury department may increase value for Keshi Co and the possible reasons for decentralising the treasury department. **(6 marks)**

(c) Discuss the key differences between a Salam contract, under Islamic finance principles, and futures contracts. **(4 marks)**

(Total = 25 marks)

45 Daikon (6/15)   49 mins

For a number of years Daikon Co has been using forward rate agreements to manage its exposure to interest rate fluctuations. Recently its chief executive officer (CEO) attended a talk on using exchange-traded derivative products to manage risks. She wants to find out by how much the extra cost of the borrowing detailed below can be reduced, when using interest rate futures, options on interest rate futures, and a collar on the options, to manage the interest rate risk. She asks that detailed calculations for each of the three derivative products be provided and a reasoned recommendation be made.

Daikon Co is expecting to borrow $34,000,000 in five months' time. It expects to make a full repayment of the borrowed amount in 11 months' time. Assume it is 1 June 20X5 today. Daikon Co can borrow funds at LIBOR plus 70 basis points. LIBOR is currently 3.6%, but Daikon Co expects that interest rates may increase by as much as 80 basis points in five months' time.

The following information and quotes from an appropriate exchange are provided on LIBOR-based $ futures and options.

Three-month $ December futures are currently quoted at 95.84. The contract size is $1,000,000, the tick size is 0.01% and the tick value is $25.

Options on three-month $ futures, $1,000,000 contract, tick size 0.01% and tick value $25. Option premiums are in annual %

December calls	Strike price	December puts
0.541	95.50	0.304
0.223	96.00	0.508

Initial assumptions

It can be assumed that settlement for both the futures and options contracts is at the end of the month; that basis diminishes to zero at a constant rate until the contract matures and time intervals can be counted in months; that margin requirements may be ignored; and that if the options are in-the-money, they will be exercised at the end of the hedge instead of being sold.

Further issues

In the talk, the CEO was informed of the following issues:

(1) Futures contracts will be marked to market daily. The CEO wondered what the impact of this would be if 50 futures contracts were bought at 95.84 on 1 June and 30 futures contracts were sold at 95.61 on 3 June, based on the $ December futures contract given above. The closing settlement prices are given below for four days:

Date	Settlement price
1 June	95.84
2 June	95.76
3 June	95.66
4 June	95.74

(2)   Daikon Co will need to deposit funds into a margin account with a broker for each contract they have opened, and this margin will need to be adjusted when the contracts are marked to market daily.

(3)   It is unlikely that option contracts will be exercised at the end of the hedge period unless they have reached expiry. Instead, they are more likely to be sold and the positions closed.

Required

(a)   Based on the three hedging choices available to Daikon Co and the initial assumptions given above, draft a response to the CEO's request made in the first paragraph of the question.   **(15 marks)**

(b)   Discuss the impact on Daikon Co of each of the three further issues given above. As part of the discussion, include the calculations of the daily impact of the mark-to-market closing prices on the transactions specified by the CEO.   **(10 marks)**

(Total = 25 marks)

46 Sembilan (6/12, amended)   49 mins

Sembilan Co, a listed company, recently issued debt finance to acquire assets in order to increase its activity levels. This debt finance is in the form of a floating rate bond, with a face value of $320 million, redeemable in four years. The bond interest, payable annually, is based on the spot yield curve plus 60 basis points. The next annual payment is due at the end of Year 1.

Sembilan Co is concerned that the expected rise in interest rates over the coming few years would make it increasingly difficult to pay the interest due. It is therefore proposing to either swap the floating rate interest payment to a fixed rate payment, or to raise new equity capital and use that to pay off the floating rate bond. The new equity capital would either be issued as rights to the existing shareholders or as shares to new shareholders.

Ratus Bank has offered Sembilan Co an interest rate swap, whereby Sembilan Co would pay Ratus Bank interest based on an equivalent fixed annual rate of 3.76¼% in exchange for receiving a variable amount based on the current yield curve rate. Payments and receipts will be made at the end of each year, for the next four years. Ratus Bank will charge an annual fee of 20 basis points if the swap is agreed and will also guarantee the swap. The current annual spot yield curve rates are as follows:

Year	1	2	3	4
Rate	2.5%	3.1%	3.5%	3.8%

The current annual forward rates for Years 2, 3 and 4 are as follows:

Year	2	3	4
Rate	3.7%	4.3%	4.7%

Required

(a)   Based on the above information, calculate the amounts Sembilan Co expects to pay or receive every year on the swap (excluding the fee of 20 basis points). Explain why the fixed annual rate of interest of 3.76¼% is less than the four-year yield curve rate of 3.8%.
                                                                                      (6 marks)

(b)   (i)   Demonstrate that Sembilan Co's interest payment liability does not change, after it has undertaken the swap, whether the interest rates increase or decrease. **(5 marks)**

       (ii)   Discuss the advantages and disadvantages of the swap for Sembilan Co. **(5 marks)**

(c)   Discuss the factors that Sembilan Co should consider when deciding whether it should raise equity capital to pay off the floating rate debt.   **(9 marks)**

(Total = 25 marks)

47 Pault (Sep/Dec 16)

Pault Co is currently undertaking a major programme of product development. Pault Co has made a significant investment in plant and machinery for this programme. Over the next couple of years, Pault Co has also budgeted for significant development and launch costs for a number of new products, although its finance director believes there is some uncertainty with these budgeted figures, as they will depend upon competitor activity amongst other matters.

Pault Co issued floating rate loan notes, with a face value of $400 million, to fund the investment in plant and machinery. The loan notes are redeemable in ten years' time. The interest on the loan notes is payable annually and is based on the spot yield curve, plus 50 basis points.

Pault Co's finance director has recently completed a review of the company's overall financing strategy. His review has highlighted expectations that interest rates will increase over the next few years, although the predictions of financial experts in the media differ significantly.

The finance director is concerned about the exposure Pault Co has to increases in interest rates through the loan notes. He has therefore discussed with Millbridge Bank the possibility of taking out a four-year interest rate swap. The proposed terms are that Pault Co would pay Millbridge Bank interest based on an equivalent fixed annual rate of 4.847%. In return, Pault Co would receive from Millbridge Bank a variable amount based on the forward rates calculated from the annual spot yield curve rate at the time of payment minus 20 basis points. Payments and receipts would be made annually, with the first one in a year's time. Millbridge Bank would charge an annual fee of 25 basis points if Pault Co enters the swap.

The current annual spot yield curve rates are as follows:

Year	1	2	3	4
Rate	3.70%	4.25%	4.70%	5.10%

A number of concerns were raised at the recent board meeting when the swap arrangement was discussed.

- Pault Co's chairman wondered what the value of the swap arrangement to Pault Co was, and whether the value would change over time.

- One of Pault Co's non-executive directors objected to the arrangement, saying that in his opinion the interest rate which Pault Co would pay and the bank charges were too high. Pault Co ought to stick with its floating rate commitment. Investors would be critical if, at the end of four years, Pault Co had paid higher costs under the swap than it would have done had it left the loan unhedged.

Required

(a) (i) Using the current annual spot yield curve rates as the basis for estimating forward rates, calculate the amounts Pault Co expects to pay or receive each year under the swap (excluding the fee of 25 basis points). **(6 marks)**

   (ii) Calculate Pault Co's interest payment liability for Year 1 if the yield curve rate is 4.5% or 2.9%, and comment on your results. **(6 marks)**

(b) Advise the chairman on the current value of the swap to Pault Co and the factors which would change the value of the swap. **(4 marks)**

(c) Discuss the disadvantages and advantages to Pault Co of not undertaking a swap and being liable to pay interest at floating rates. **(9 marks)**

(Total = 25 marks)

50 MARK QUESTIONS

Questions 48 to 59 are a bank of mixed 50 mark questions which cover a range of syllabus areas.

48 Conejo (Sep/Dec 17)   98 mins

Conejo Co is a listed company based in Ardilla and uses the $ as its currency. The company was formed around 20 years ago and was initially involved in cybernetics, robotics and artificial intelligence within the information technology industry. At that time due to the risky ventures Conejo Co undertook, its cash flows and profits were very varied and unstable. Around ten years ago, it started an information systems consultancy business and a business developing cyber security systems. Both these businesses have been successful and have been growing consistently. This in turn has resulted in a stable growth in revenues, profits and cash flows. The company continues its research and product development in artificial intelligence and robotics, but this business unit has shrunk proportionally to the other two units.

Just under eight years ago, Conejo Co was successfully listed on Ardilla's national stock exchange, offering 60% of its share capital to external equity holders, whilst the original founding members retained the remaining 40% of the equity capital. The company remains financed largely by equity capital and reserves, with only a small amount of debt capital. Due to this, and its steadily growing sales revenue, profits and cash flows, it has attracted a credit rating of A from the credit rating agencies.

At a recent board of directors (BoD) meeting, the company's chief financial officer (CFO) argued that it was time for Conejo Co to change its capital structure by undertaking a financial reconstruction, and be financed by higher levels of debt. As part of her explanation, the CFO said that Conejo Co: is now better able to bear the increased risk resulting from higher levels of debt finance; would be better protected from predatory acquisition bids if it was financed by higher levels of debt; and could take advantage of the tax benefits offered by increased debt finance. She also suggested that the expected credit migration from a credit rating of A to a credit rating of BBB, if the financial reconstruction detailed below took place, would not weaken Conejo Co financially.

Financial reconstruction

The BoD decided to consider the financial reconstruction plan further before making a final decision. The financial reconstruction plan would involve raising $1,320 million ($1.32 billion) new debt finance consisting of bonds issued at their face value of $100. The bonds would be redeemed in five years' time at their face value of $100 each. The funds raised from the issue of the new bonds would be used to implement one of the following two proposals:

- Either buy back equity shares at their current share price, which would be cancelled after they have been repurchased; or

- Invest in additional assets in new business ventures.

Conejo Co, financial information

EXTRACT FROM THE FORECAST FINANCIAL POSITION FOR NEXT YEAR

	$m
Non-current assets	1,735
Current assets	530
Total assets	2,265
Equity and liabilities	
Share capital ($1 per share par value)	400
Reserves	1,700
Total equity	2,100
Non-current liabilities	120
Current liabilities	45
Total liabilities	165
Total liabilities and capital	2,265

Conejo Co's forecast after-tax profit for next year is $350 million and its current share price is $11 per share.

The non-current liabilities consist solely of 5.2% coupon bonds with a face value of $100 each, which are redeemable at their face value in three years' time. These bonds are currently trading at $107.80 per $100. The bond's covenant stipulates that should Conejo Co's borrowing increase, the coupon payable on these bonds will increase by 37 basis points.

Conejo Co pays tax at a rate of 15% per year and its after-tax return on the new investment is estimated at 12%.

Other financial information

Current government bond yield curve

Year	1	2	3	4	5
	1.5%	1.7%	1.9%	2.2%	2.5%

Yield spreads (in basis points)

	1 year	2 years	3 years	4 years	5 years
A	40	49	59	68	75
BBB	70	81	94	105	112
BB	148	167	185	202	218

The finance director wants to determine the percentage change in the value of Conejo Co's current bonds, if the credit rating changes from A to BBB. Furthermore, she wants to determine the coupon rate at which the new bonds would need to be issued, based on the current yield curve and appropriate yield spreads given above.

Conejo Co's chief executive officer (CEO) suggested that if Conejo Co paid back the capital and interest of the new bond in fixed annual repayments of capital and interest through the five-year life of the bond, then the risk associated with the extra debt finance would be largely mitigated. In this case, it was possible that credit migration, by credit rating companies, from A rating to BBB rating may not happen. He suggested that comparing the duration of the new bond based on the interest payable annually and the face value in five years' time with the duration of the new bond where the borrowing is paid in fixed annual repayments of interest and capital could be used to demonstrate this risk mitigation.

Required

(a) Discuss the possible reasons for the finance director's suggestions that Conejo Co could benefit from higher levels of debt with respect to risk, from protection against acquisition bids, and from tax benefits. **(7 marks)**

(b) Prepare a report for the board of directors of Conejo Co which:

   (i) Estimates, and briefly comments on, the change in value of the current bond and the coupon rate required for the new bond, as requested by the CFO; **(6 marks)**

   (ii) Estimates the Macaulay duration of the new bond based on the interest payable annually and face value repayment, and the Macaulay duration based on the fixed annual repayment of the interest and capital, as suggested by the CEO; and **(6 marks)**

   (iii) Estimates the impact of the two proposals on how the funds may be used on next year's forecast earnings, forecast financial position, forecast earnings per share and on forecast gearing. **(11 marks)**

   (iv) Using the estimates from (b)(i), (b)(ii) and (b)(iii), discusses the impact of the proposed financial reconstruction and the proposals on the use of funds on:

   - Conejo Co;
   - Possible reaction(s) of credit rating companies and on the expected credit migration, including the suggestion made by the CEO;
   - Conejo Co's equity holders; and
   - Conejo Co's current and new debt holders. **(16 marks)**

Professional marks will be awarded in part (b) for the format, structure and presentation of the report. **(4 marks)**

(Total = 50 marks)

49 Chrysos (Mar/Jun 17)

98 mins

The eight-member board of executive directors (BoD) of Chrysos Co, a large private, unlisted company, is considering the company's long-term business and financial future. The BoD is considering whether or not to undertake a restructuring programme. This will be followed a few years later by undertaking a reverse takeover to obtain a listing on the stock exchange in order to raise new finance. However, a few members of the BoD have raised doubts about the restructuring programme and the reverse takeover, not least the impact upon the company's stakeholders. Some directors are of the opinion that an initial public offering (IPO) would be a better option when obtaining a listing compared to a reverse takeover.

Chrysos Co was formed about 15 years ago by a team of five senior equity holders who are part of the BoD and own 40% of the equity share capital in total; 30 other equity holders own a further 40% of the equity share capital but are not part of the BoD; and a consortium of venture capital organisations (VCOs) own the remaining 20% of the equity share capital and have three representatives on the BoD. The VCOs have also lent Chrysos Co substantial debt finance in the form of unsecured bonds due to be redeemed in ten years' time. In addition to the BoD, Chrysos Co also has a non-executive supervisory board consisting of members of Chrysos Co's key stakeholder groups. Details of the supervisory board are given below.

Chrysos Co has two business units: a mining and shipping business unit, and a machinery parts manufacturing business unit. The mining and shipping business unit accounts for around 80% of Chrysos Co's business in terms of sales revenue, non-current and current assets, and payables. However, it is estimated that this business unit accounts for around 75% of the company's operating costs. The smaller machinery parts manufacturing business unit accounts for the remaining 20% of sales revenue, non-current and current assets, and payables; and around 25% of the company's operating costs.

The following figures have been extracted from Chrysos Co's most recent financial statements:

Profit before depreciation, interest and tax for the year to 28 February 20X7

	$m
Sales revenue	16,800
Operating costs	(10,080)
Profit before depreciation, interest and tax	6,720

Financial position as at 28 February 20X7

	$m
Non-current assets	
Land and buildings	7,500
Equipment	5,400
Current assets	
Inventory	1,800
Receivables	900
Total assets	15,600
Equity	
Share capital ($1 par value per share)	1,800
Reserves	5,400
Non-current liabilities	
4.50% unsecured bonds 20Y6 (from the VCOs)	4,800
Other debt	1,050
Current liabilities	
Payables	750
Bank overdraft	1,800
Total equity and liabilities	15,600

Corporate restructuring programme

The purpose of the restructuring programme is to simplify the company's gearing structure and to obtain extra funding to expand the mining and shipping business in the future. At present, Chrysos Co is having difficulty obtaining additional funding without having to pay high interest rates.

Machinery parts manufacturing business unit

The smaller machinery parts manufacturing business unit will be unbundled either by having its assets sold to a local supplier for $3,102 million after its share of payables have been paid or the smaller machinery parts manufacturing business unit will be unbundled through a management buy-out by four managers. In this case, it is estimated that its after-tax net cash flows will increase by 8% in the first year only and then stay fixed at this level for the foreseeable future. The cost of capital related to the smaller business unit is estimated to be 10%. The management buy-out team will pay Chrysos Co 70% of the estimated market value of the smaller machinery parts manufacturing business unit.

Mining and shipping business unit

Following the unbundling of the smaller machinery parts manufacturing business unit, Chrysos Co will focus solely on the mining and shipping business unit, prior to undertaking the reverse takeover some years into the future.

As part of the restructuring programme, the existing unsecured bonds lent by the VCOs will be cancelled and replaced by an additional 600 million $1 shares for the VCOs. The VCOs will pay $400 million for these shares. The bank overdraft will be converted into a 15-year loan on which Chrysos Co will pay a fixed annual interest of 4.50%. The other debt under non-current liabilities will be repaid. In addition to this, Chrysos Co will invest $1,200 million into equipment for its mining and shipping business unit and this will result in its profits and cash flows growing by 4% per year in perpetuity.

Additional financial information

Chrysos Co aims to maintain a long-term capital structure of 20% debt and 80% equity in market value terms. Chrysos Co's finance director has assessed that the 4.50% annual interest it will pay on its bank loan is a reasonable estimate of its long-term cost of debt, based on the long-term capital structure above.

Although Chrysos Co does not know what its cost of capital is for the mining and shipping business unit, its finance director has determined that the current ungeared cost of equity of Sidero Co, a large quoted mining and shipping company, is 12.46%. Chrysos Co's finance director wants touse Sidero Co's ungeared cost of equity to calculate itscost of capital for the mining and shipping business unit.

The annual corporation tax rate on profits applicable to all companies is 18% and it can be assumed that tax is payable in the year incurred. All the non-current assets are eligible for tax allowable depreciation of 12% annually on the book values. The annual reinvestment needed to keep operations at their current levels is equivalent to the tax allowable depreciation.

Details of the supervisory board

The non-executive supervisory board provides an extra layer of governance over the BoD. It consists of representatives from the company's internal stakeholder groups including the finance providers, employees and the company's management. It ensures that the actions taken by the BoD are for the benefit of all the stakeholder groups and to the company as a whole. Any issues raised in board meetings are resolved through negotiation until an agreed position is reached.

Required

(a) Explain what a reverse takeover involves and discuss the relative advantages and disadvantages to a company, such as Chrysos Co, of obtaining a listing through a reverse takeover as opposed to an initial public offering (IPO). **(9 marks)**

(b) Prepare a report for the board of directors of Chrysos Co which includes:

   (i)   An extract of the financial position and an estimate of Chrysos Co's value to the equity holders, after undertaking the restructuring programme. **(18 marks)**

   (ii) An explanation of the approach taken and assumptions made in estimating Chrysos Co's value to the equity holders, after undertaking the restructuring programme. **(5 marks)**

   (iii) A discussion of the impact of the restructuring programme on Chrysos Co and on the venture capital organisations. **(10 marks)**

   Professional marks will be awarded in part (b) for the format, structure and presentation of the report. **(4 marks)**

(c) Discuss why the attention Chrysos Co pays to its stakeholders represented on the supervisory board may change once it has obtained a listing. **(4 marks)**

(Total = 50 marks)

50 Yilandwe (6/15)   98 mins

Yilandwe, whose currency is the Yilandwe Rand (YR), has faced extremely difficult economic challenges in the past 25 years because of some questionable economic policies and political decisions made by its previous governments. Although Yilandwe's population is generally poor, its people are nevertheless well educated and ambitious. Just over three years ago, a new government took office and since then it has imposed a number of strict monetary and fiscal controls, including an annual corporation tax rate of 40%, in an attempt to bring Yilandwe out of its difficulties. As a result, the annual rate of inflation has fallen rapidly from a high of 65% to its current level of 33%. These strict monetary and fiscal controls have made Yilandwe's government popular in the larger cities and towns, but less popular in the rural areas which seem to have suffered disproportionately from the strict monetary and fiscal controls.

It is expected that Yilandwe's annual inflation rate will continue to fall in the coming few years as follows:

Year	Inflation rate
1	22.0%
2	14.7%
3 onwards	9.8%

Yilandwe's government has decided to continue the progress made so far, by encouraging foreign direct investment into the country. Recently, government representatives held trade shows internationally and offered businesses a number of concessions, including:

1 Zero corporation tax payable in the first two years of operation; and

2 An opportunity to carry forward tax losses and write them off against future profits made after the first two years.

The government representatives also promised international companies investing in Yilandwe prime locations in towns and cities with good transport links.

Imoni Co

Imoni Co, a large listed company based in the US with the US dollar ($) as its currency, manufactures high tech diagnostic components for machinery, which it exports worldwide. After attending one of the trade shows, Imoni Co is considering setting up an assembly plant in Yilandwe where parts would be sent and assembled into a specific type of component, which is currently being assembled in the US. Once assembled, the component will be exported directly to companies based in the European Union (EU). These exports will be invoiced in euro (€).

Assembly plant in Yilandwe: financial and other data projections

It is initially assumed that the project will last for four years. The four-year project will require investments of YR21,000 million for land and buildings, YR18,000 million for machinery and YR9,600 million for working capital to be made immediately. The working capital will need to be increased annually at the start of each of the next three years by Yilandwe's inflation rate and it is assumed that this will be released at the end of the project's life.

It can be assumed that the assembly plant can be built very quickly and production started almost immediately. This is because the basic facilities and infrastructure are already in place as the plant will be built on the premises and grounds of a school. The school is ideally located, near the main highway and railway lines. As a result, the school will close and the children currently studying there will be relocated to other schools in the city. The government has kindly agreed to provide free buses to take the children to these schools for a period of six months to give parents time to arrange appropriate transport in the future for their children.

The current selling price of each component is €700 and this price is likely to increase by the average EU rate of inflation from Year 1 onwards.

The number of components expected to be sold every year are as follows:

Year	1	2	3	4
Sales component units ('000)	150	480	730	360

The parts needed to assemble into the components in Yilandwe will be sent from the US by Imoni Co at a cost of $200 per component unit, from which Imoni Co would currently earn a pre-tax contribution of $40 for each component unit. However, Imoni Co feels that it can negotiate with Yilandwe's government and increase the transfer price to $280 per component unit. The variable costs related to assembling the components in Yilandwe are currently YR15,960 per component unit. The current annual fixed costs of the assembly plant are YR4,600 million. All these costs, wherever incurred, are expected to increase by that country's annual inflation every year from Year 1 onwards.

Imoni Co pays corporation tax on profits at an annual rate of 20% in the US. The tax in both the US and Yilandwe is payable in the year that the tax liability arises. A bilateral tax treaty exists between Yilandwe and the US. Tax-allowable depreciation is available at 25% per year on the machinery on a straight-line basis.

Imoni Co will expect annual royalties from the assembly plant to be made every year. The normal annual royalty fee is currently $20 million, but Imoni Co feels that it can negotiate this with Yilandwe's government and increase the royalty fee by 80%. Once agreed, this fee will not be subject to any inflationary increase in the project's four-year period.

If Imoni Co does decide to invest in an assembly plant in Yilandwe, its exports from the US to the EU will fall and it will incur redundancy costs. As a result, Imoni Co's after-tax cash flows will reduce by the following amounts:

Year	1	2	3	4
Redundancy and lost contribution	20,000	55,697	57,368	59,089

Imoni Co normally uses its cost of capital of 9% to assess new projects. However, the finance director suggests that Imoni Co should use a project-specific discount rate of 12% instead.

Other financial information

Current spot rates

Euro per dollar	€0.714/$1
YR per euro	YR142/€1
YR per dollar	YR101.4/$1

Forecast future rates based on expected inflation rate differentials

Year	1	2	3	4
YR/$1	120.1	133.7	142.5	151.9

Year	1	2	3	4
YR/€1	165.0	180.2	190.2	200.8

Expected inflation rates

EU expected inflation rate: Next two years	5%
EU expected inflation rate: Year 3 onwards	4%
US expected inflation rate: Year 1 onwards	3%

Required

(a) Discuss the possible benefits and drawbacks to Imoni Co of setting up its own assembly plant in Yilandwe, compared to licensing a company based in Yilandwe to undertake the assembly on its behalf. **(5 marks)**

(b) Prepare a report which:

   (i) Evaluates the financial acceptability of the investment in the assembly plant in Yilandwe; **(21 marks)**

   (ii) Discusses the assumptions made in producing the estimates, and the other risks and issues which Imoni Co should consider before making the final decision; and **(17 marks)**

   (iii) Provides a reasoned recommendation on whether or not Imoni Co should invest in the assembly plant in Yilandwe. **(3 marks)**

   Professional marks will be awarded in part (b) for the format, structure and presentation of the report. **(4 marks)**

   (Total = 50 marks)

51 Avem (12/14)   98 mins

Nahara Co and Fugae Co

Nahara Co is a private holding company owned by the government of a wealthy oil-rich country to invest its sovereign funds. Nahara Co has followed a strategy of risk diversification for a number of years by acquiring companies from around the world in many different sectors.

One of Nahara Co's acquisition strategies is to identify and purchase undervalued companies in the airline industry in Europe. A recent acquisition was Fugae Co, a company based in a country which is part of the European Union (EU). Fugae Co repairs and maintains aircraft engines.

A few weeks ago, Nahara Co stated its intention to pursue the acquisition of an airline company based in the same country as Fugae Co. The EU, concerned about this, asked Nahara Co to sell Fugae Co before pursuing any further acquisitions in the airline industry.

Avem Co's acquisition interest in Fugae Co

Avem Co, a UK-based company specialising in producing and servicing business jets, has approached Nahara Co with a proposal to acquire Fugae Co for $1,200 million. Nahara Co expects to receive a premium of at least 30% on the estimated equity value of Fugae Co, if it is sold.

Given below are extracts from the most recent statements of financial position of both Avem Co and Fugae Co.

	Avem Co $m	Fugae Co $m
Share capital (50c/share)	800	100
Reserves	3,550	160
Non-current liabilities	2,200	380
Current liabilities	130	30
Total capital and liabilities	6,680	670

Each Avem Co share is currently trading at $7.50, which is a multiple of 7.2 of its free cash flow to equity. Avem Co expects that the total free cash flows to equity of the combined company will increase by $40 million due to synergy benefits. After adding the synergy benefits of $40 million, Avem Co then expects the multiple of the total free cash flow of the combined company to increase to 7.5.

Fugae Co's free cash flow to equity is currently estimated at $76.5 million and it is expected to generate a return on equity of 11%. Over the past few years, Fugae Co has returned 77.3% of its annual free cash flow to equity back to Nahara Co, while retaining the balance for new investments.

Fugae Co's non-current liabilities consist entirely of $100 nominal value bonds which are redeemable in four years at the nominal value, on which the company pays a coupon of 5.4%. The debt is rated at B+ and the credit spread on B+ rated debt is 80 basis points above the risk-free rate of return.

Proposed luxury transport investment project by Fugae Co

In recent years, the country in which Fugae Co is based has been expanding its tourism industry and hopes that this industry will grow significantly in the near future. At present tourists normally travel using public transport and taxis, but there is a growing market for luxury travel. If the tourist industry does expand, then the demand for luxury travel is expected to grow rapidly. Fugae Co is considering entering this market through a four-year project. The project will cease after four years because of increasing competition.

The initial cost of the project is expected to be $42,000,000 and it is expected to generate the following after-tax cash flows over its 4-year life:

Year	1	2	3	4
Cash flows ($'000)	3,277.6	16,134.3	36,504.7	35,683.6

The above figures are based on the tourism industry expanding as expected. However, it is estimated that there is a 25% probability that the tourism industry will not grow as expected in the first year. If this happens, then the present value of the project's cash flows will be 50% of the original estimates over its four-year life.

It is also estimated that if the tourism industry grows as expected in the first year, there is still a 20% probability that the expected growth will slow down in the second and subsequent years, and the present value of the project's cash flows would then be 40% of the original estimates in each of these years.

Lumi Co, a leisure travel company, has offered $50 million to buy the project from Fugae Co at the start of the second year. Fugae Co is considering whether having this choice would add to the value of the project.

If Fugae Co is bought by Avem Co after the project has begun, it is thought that the project will not result in any additional synergy benefits and will not generate any additional value for the combined company, above any value the project has already generated for Fugae Co.

Although there is no beta for companies offering luxury forms of travel in the tourist industry, Reka Co, a listed company, offers passenger transportation services on coaches, trains and luxury vehicles. About 15% of its business is in the luxury transport market and Reka Co's equity beta is 1.6. It is estimated that the asset beta of the non-luxury transport industry is 0.80. Reka Co's shares are currently trading at $4.50 per share and its debt is currently trading at $105 per

$100. It has 80 million shares in issue and the book value of its debt is $340 million. The debt beta is estimated to be zero.

General information

The corporation tax rate applicable to all companies is 20%. The risk-free rate is estimated to be 4% and the market risk premium is estimated to be 6%.

Required

(a) Discuss whether or not Nahara Co's acquisition strategies, of pursuing risk diversification and of purchasing undervalued companies, can be valid. **(7 marks)**

(b) Discuss why the European Union (EU) may be concerned about Nahara Co's stated intention and how selling Fugae Co could reduce this concern. **(4 marks)**

(c) Prepare a report for the board of directors of Avem Co, which:

    (i) Estimates the additional value created for Avem Co, if it acquires Fugae Co without considering the luxury transport project; **(10 marks)**

    (ii) Estimates the additional value of the luxury transport project to Fugae Co, both with and without the offer from Lumi Co; and **(18 marks)**

    (iii) Evaluates the benefit attributable to Avem Co and Fugae Co from combining the two companies with and without the project, and concludes whether or not the acquisition is beneficial. The evaluation should include any assumptions made. **(7 marks)**

Professional marks will be awarded in part (c) for the format, structure and presentation of the report. **(4 marks)**

(Total = 50 marks)

52 Talam (Mar/Jun 19)   98 mins

Talam Co, a listed company, aims to manufacture innovative engineering products which are environmentally friendly and sustainable. These products have been highly marketable because of their affordability. Talam Co's mission statement also states its desire to operate to the highest ethical standards. These commitments have meant that Talam Co has a very high reputation and a high share price compared to its competitors.

Talam Co is considering a new project, the Uwa Project, to manufacture drones for use in the agricultural industry, which are at least 50% biodegradable, at competitive prices. The drones will enable farmers to increase crop yields and reduce crop damage. Manufacture of drones is a new business area for Talam Co. The project is expected to last for four years.

Talam Co will also work on the Jigu Project (a follow-on project to the Uwa Project) to make 95%+ biodegradable drones. It is expected that the Jigu Project will last for a further five years after the Uwa Project has finished. If the Uwa Project is discontinued or sold sooner than four years, the Jigu Project could still be undertaken after four years.

Uwa Project

The following number of drones are expected to be produced and sold:

Year	1	2	3	4
Number of drones produced and sold	4,300	19,200	35,600	25,400

In the first year, for each drone, it is expected that the selling price will be $1,200 and the variable costs will be $480. The total annual direct fixed costs will be $2,700,000. After the first year, the selling price is expected to increase by 8% annually, the variable costs by 4% annually and the fixed costs by 10% annually, for the next three years. Training costs are expected to be 200% of the variable costs in Year 1, 60% in Year 2, and 10% in each of Years 3 and 4. There is substantial uncertainty about the drones produced and sold, and Talam Co estimates the project to have a standard deviation of 30%.

At the start of every year, the Uwa Project will need working capital. In the first year, this will be 20% of sales revenue. In subsequent years, the project will require additional or a reduction in working capital of 10% for every $1 increase or decrease in sales revenue respectively. The working capital is expected to be fully recovered when the Uwa Project ceases.

The Uwa Project will need $35,000,000 of machinery to produce the drones at the start of the project. Tax allowable depreciation is available on the machinery at 15% per year on a straight-line basis. The machinery is expected to be sold for $7,000,000 (post-inflation) at the end of the project. Talam Co makes sufficient profits from its other activities to take advantage of any tax loss relief. Tax is paid in the year it falls due.

Jigu Project as a real option

Talam Co estimates that Jigu Project's cash flows are highly uncertain, and its standard deviation is 50%. It is estimated that $60,000,000 will be required at the start of the project in four years' time. Using conventional net present value, Talam Co's best estimate is that net present value will be $10,000,000 at the start of the project.

The following figures were estimated for the Jigu Project using the real options method. Asset value (P_a) = $46,100,000 (to nearest 100,000)

Exercise price (P_e) = $60,000,000
Exercise date (t)   = 4 years
Risk-free rate (r)   = 2.30%
Volatility (s) = 50%

d_1 = 0.329 d_2 = –0.671 $N(d_1)$ = 0.6288 $N(d_2)$ = 0.2510

Call option value: $15,258,399

It can be assumed that the call option value is accurate.

Talam Co's finance director wants to know how the asset value of $46,100,000 has been estimated.

Honua Co's offer

Honua Co, whose main business is drone production, has approached Talam Co with an offer to buy the Uwa Project in its entirety from Talam Co for $30,000,000 at the start of the third year of the project's life.

Talam Co has calculated some figures to assess the value of Honua Co's offer using the real options method, as follows:

d_1 = 0.779 d_2 = 0.355 $N(d_1)$ = 0.7821 $N(d_2)$ = 0.6387

Talam Co's finance director has requested that the value of Honua Co's offer is estimated using the real options method. She has also requested to know the amounts of the initial variables which would have been used to calculate the d_1, d_2, $N(d_1)$ and $N(d_2)$ figures.

It can be assumed that the d_1, d_2, $N(d_1)$ and $N(d_2)$ figures are accurate.

Additional information

Both Honua Co and Talam Co pay corporation tax at an annual rate of 20%. Talam Co has estimated Uwa Project's and Jigu Project's risk-adjusted cost of capital at 11%, based on Honua Co's asset beta. Talam Co believes that LIBOR, which is currently 2.30%, provides a good estimate of the risk-free rate of interest.

Required

(a)   Discuss how incorporating real options into net present value decisions may help Talam Co with its investment appraisal decisions.   **(5 marks)**

(b)   Prepare a report for the board of directors (BoD) of Talam Co which:

(i)   Estimates, showing all relevant calculations, the net present value of the Uwa Project before considering the offer from Honua Co and the Jigu Project;   **(12 marks)**

(ii) Addresses the requests made by the finance director about the initial variables and estimated value of the offer from Honua Co using the real options method; and

(9 marks)

(iii) Assesses whether the Uwa Project should be undertaken, using the results from, and discussing the assumptions made in, the calculations in (b)(i) and (b)(ii) above.

(10 marks)

Professional marks will be awarded in part (b) for the format, structure and presentation of the report.

(4 marks)

(c) At a recent trade show, the biodegradable drones attracted considerable interest from organisations worldwide. Nevertheless, some expressed concern about the drone price, which they felt was too high.

Talam Co estimates that even a modest reduction in each drone's price would make the projects unprofitable. Therefore, the operations director suggested that costs could be reduced if drone components were produced in Dunia, a country where Talam Co already gets some of its other products made.

However, the public relations director brought up an issue concerning Dunia. He said that several companies in Dunia, which Talam Co trades with, employ young teenage children. These companies pay the education fees for the teenagers, and the companies argued that stopping this practice would harm the teenagers' families financially.

Required

Discuss the impact on Talam Co and its aims arising from the possible sustainability and ethical issues above, and advise on how these issues may be addressed. **(10 marks)**

(Total = 50 marks)

53 Washi (Sep 18)   98 mins

Washi Co is a large, unlisted company based in Japan and its local currency is the Japanese Yen (JPY). It manufactures industrial equipment and parts. Initially Washi Co's customers consisted of other Japanese companies, but over the last 12 years it has expanded into overseas markets and also sources its materials from around the world. The company's board of directors (BoD) believes that the strategy of overseas investments, through subsidiary companies, branches and joint ventures, has directly led to the company's substantial increase in value in the past few years.

Washi Co's BoD is considering investing in a project based in Airone, whose currency is the Airone Rand (ARD). It believes that the project will be an important addition to the company's portfolio of investments, because Washi Co does not currently have a significant presence in the part of the world where Airone is located. It is intended that the project will commence in one year's time. Details of the project are given below.

Washi Co intends to finance the project through proceeds from an agreed sale of a small European subsidiary, with any remaining funding requirement being met by additional debt finance issued in Japanese Yen. The company is due to receive the proceeds from the sale of a European subsidiary company in six months' time and it will then invest these funds in short-dated Japanese treasury bills for a further six months before they are needed for the project. Washi Co has a centralised treasury department, which hedges expected future cash flows against currency fluctuations.

Funding and financial information

The agreed proceeds from the sale of the European subsidiary company receivable in six months' time are Euro (EUR) 80 million. The BoD is concerned about a negative fluctuation in EUR/JPY rate between now and in six months when the EUR 80 million will be received. Therefore, it has asked Washi Co's treasury department to hedge the expected receipt using one of currency forwards, currency futures or exchange traded currency options. Washi Co's treasury department has obtained the following information:

	JPY per EUR 1	ARD per EUR 1
Spot	129.2–132.4	92.7–95.6
Six-month forward rate	125.3–128.6	

Currency futures (contract size EUR 125,000, quotation JPY per EUR 1)

Four-month expiry	126.9
Seven-month expiry	125.2

Currency options (contract size EUR 125,000, exercise price quotation: JPY per EUR 1, premium quotation: JPY per EUR 1)

At an exercise price of JPY 126.0 per EUR 1

	Four-month expiry	Seven-month expiry
Calls	2.3	2.6
Puts	3.4	3.8

Annualised yield on short-dated Japanese treasury bills = 1.20%

Airone's annual inflation rate is 9% currently, but has fluctuated markedly in the last five years. The Japanese annual inflation rate is 1.5% and has been stable for many years.

Pato Bank has offered Washi Co the possibility of using over-the-counter options to hedge the EUR receipt instead of exchange traded currency options.

Airone project information

A member of Washi Co's finance team has produced the following estimates of the Airone project which is expected to last for four years. The estimates are based on the notes given below but not on the further information. The estimates have been checked and verified independently for their numerical accuracy.

All figures are in ARD millions.

Project year	0	1	2	3	4
Sales revenue		13,000	30,800	32,300	4,500
Costs		(10,200)	(24,200)	(24,500)	(3,200)
Tax allowable depreciation		(1,000)	(1,000)	(1,000)	(1,000)
Pre-tax profits		1,800	5,600	6,800	300
Tax at 15%		(270)	(840)	(1,020)	(45)
Tax allowable depreciation		1,000	1,000	1,000	1,000
Working capital	(400)				400
Investment in buildings	(5,750)				
Investment in machinery	(4,000)				
Cash flows in ARD	(10,150)	2,530	5,760	6,780	1,655

Notes (incorporated into the estimates above):

1   The estimates are based on using the end of the first year, when the project commences, as the start of the project (Year 0). The numbers are given in ARD million.

2   The total investment required for the project is ARD 10,150 million and separated into buildings, machinery and working capital in the table above. The machinery is eligible for tax allowable depreciation on a straight-line basis and the working capital is redeemable at the end of the project.

3   The impact of inflation has been incorporated into the sales revenue and cost figures, at Airone's current annual inflation figures.

4   Corporation tax has been included based on Airone's annual rate of 15%. The tax is payable in the year that the tax liability arises.

Further information (not incorporated into the estimates above):

1   Undertaking the Airone project will result in lost sales for Washi Co. These sales would have generated a pre-tax contribution of JPY 110 million in the first year of the project, rising by the Japanese rate of inflation in the following Years 2 to 4 of the project.

2   The Airone project costs include components which are made in Japan by Washi Co and would be imported to the Airone project. The pre-inflation revenues generated from the sale of the components are estimated to be as follows:

In JPY millions

Project year	1	2	3	4
Components revenue	1,200	2,400	2,500	300

These revenues are expected to increase by the Japanese inflation rate in Years 2 to 4 of the project. The contribution which Washi Co expects to earn on these components is 25% of revenue.

3   The Japanese annual corporation tax rate is 30% and tax is payable in the year that the tax liability arises. A bilateral tax treaty exists between Japan and Airone, which permits offset of overseas tax against any Japanese tax liability on overseas earnings.

4   Washi Co's finance department has estimated a cost of capital of 12% to be used as a discount rate for the project.

Required

(a)   Discuss how investing in overseas projects may enable Washi Co to gain competitive advantage over its competitors, who only invest in domestic projects.   **(5 marks)**

(b)   Discuss the advantages and drawbacks of exchange traded option contracts compared with over-the-counter options.   **(5 marks)**

(c)   Prepare a report for the board of directors of Washi Co which:

    (i)   Estimates the expected amount of JPY receivable under each hedge choice and the additional debt finance needed to fund the Airone project for the preferred hedge choice;   **(12 marks)**

    (ii)   Estimates the net present value of the Airone project in Japanese yen, based on the end of year one being the start of the project (Year 0);   **(9 marks)**

    (iii)   Evaluates the preferred hedge choice made, the debt finance needed and whether the Airone project should be undertaken, considering both financial and non-financial factors.   **(8 marks)**

Professional marks will be awarded in part (c) for the format, structure and presentation of the report.   **(4 marks)**

(d)   Washi Co's chief operations officer (COO) has suggested that it would be more beneficial for the company to let its major subsidiary companies have their own individual treasury departments, instead of having one centralised treasury department for the whole company.

    Required

    Discuss the validity of the COO's suggestion.   **(7 marks)**

(Total = 50 marks)

54 Chikepe (Mar/Jun 18)   **98 mins**

Chikepe Co is a large listed company operating in the pharmaceutical industry, with a current market value of equity of $12,600 million and a debt to equity ratio of 30:70, in market value terms. Institutional investors hold most of its equity shares. The company develops and manufactures antibiotics and anti-viral medicines. Both the company and its products have an established positive reputation among the medical profession, and its products are used widely. However, its rate of innovation has slowed considerably in the last few years and it has fewer new medical products coming into the market.

At a recent meeting of the board of directors (BoD), it was decided that the company needed to change its current strategy of growing organically to one of acquiring companies, in order to maintain the growth in its share price in the future. The members of the BoD had different opinions on the type of acquisition strategy to pursue.

Director A was of the opinion that Chikepe Co should follow a strategy of acquiring companies in different business sectors. She suggested that focusing on just the pharmaceutical sector was too risky and acquiring companies in different business sectors will reduce this risk.

Director B was of the opinion that Director A's suggestion would not result in a reduction in risk for shareholders. In fact, he suggested that this would result in agency related issues with Chikepe Co's shareholders reacting negatively and as a result, the company's share price would fall. Instead, Director B suggested that Chikepe Co should focus on its current business and acquire other established pharmaceutical companies. In this way, the company will gain synergy benefits and thereby increase value for its shareholders.

Director C agreed with Director B but suggested that Chikepe Co should consider relatively new pharmaceutical companies, as well as established businesses. In her opinion, newer companies might be involved in research and development of innovative products, which could have high potential in the future. She suggested that using real options methodology with traditional investment appraisal methods such as net present value could help establish a more accurate estimate of the potential value of such companies.

The company has asked its finance team to prepare a report on the value of a potential target company, Foshoro Co, before making a final decision.

Foshoro Co

Foshoro Co is a non-listed pharmaceutical company established about ten years ago. Initially Foshoro Co grew rapidly, but this rate of growth slowed considerably three years ago, after a venture capital equity backer exited the company by selling its stake back to the founding directors. The directors had to raise substantial debt capital to buy back the equity stake. The company's current debt to equity ratio is 60:40. This high level of gearing means that the company will find it difficult to obtain funds to develop its innovative products in the future.

The following financial information relates to Foshoro Co:

Extract from the most recent statement of profit or loss

	$m
Sales revenue	878.1
Profit before interest and tax	192.3
Interest	78.6
Tax	22.7
Profit after tax	91.0

In arriving at the profit before interest and tax, Foshoro Co deducted tax allowable depreciation and other non-cash expenses totalling $112.0 million. It requires a cash investment of $98.2 million in non-current assets and working capital to continue its operations at the current level.

Three years ago, Foshoro Co's profit after tax was $83.3 million, and this has been growing steadily to their current level. Foshoro Co's profit before interest and tax and its cash flows grew at the same growth rate as well. It is likely that this growth rate will continue for the foreseeable future if Foshoro Co is not acquired by Chikepe Co. Foshoro Co's cost of capital has been estimated at 10%.

Combined company: Chikepe Co and Foshoro Co

Once Chikepe Co acquires Foshoro Co, it is predicted that the combined company's sales revenue will be $4,200 million in the first year, and its operating profit margin on sales revenue will be 20% for the foreseeable future.

After the first year, the sales revenue is expected to grow at 7% per year for the following three years. It is anticipated that after the first four years, the growth rate of the combined company's free cash flows will be 5.6% per year.

The combined company's tax allowable depreciation is expected to be equivalent to the amount of investment needed to maintain the current level of operations. However, as the company's sales revenue increases over the four-year period, the combined company will require an additional investment in assets of $200 million in the first year and then $0.64 per $1 increase in sales revenue for the next three years.

It can be assumed that the asset beta of the combined company is the weighted average of the individual companies' asset betas, weighted in proportion of the individual companies' value of equity. It can also be assumed that the capital structure of the combined company remains at Chikepe Co's current capital structure level, a debt to equity ratio of 30:70. Chikepe Co pays interest on borrowings at a rate of 5.3% per year.

Chikepe Co estimates that it will be able to acquire Foshoro Co by paying a premium of 30% above its estimated equity value to Foshoro Co's shareholders.

Other financial information

	Equity beta	Asset beta
Chikepe Co	1.074	0.800
Foshoro Co	2.090	0.950

The current annual government borrowing base rate is 2% and the annual market risk premium is estimated at 7%.

Both companies pay tax at an annual rate of 20%.

Chikepe Co estimates equity values in acquisitions using the free cash flow to firm method.

Future acquisitions

The BoD agreed that in the future it is likely that Chikepe Co will target both listed and non-listed companies for acquisition. It is aware that when pursuing acquisitions of listed companies, the company would need to ensure that it complied with regulations such as the mandatory bid rule and the principle of equal treatment to protect shareholders. The BoD is also aware that some listed companies may attempt to defend acquisitions by employing anti-takeover measures such as poison pills and disposal of crown jewels.

Required

(a)   Compare and contrast the reasons for the opinions held by Director A and by Director B, and discuss the types of synergy benefits which may arise from the acquisition strategy suggested by Director B.
(9 marks)

(b)   Discuss how using real options methodology in conjunction with net present value could help establish a more accurate estimate of the potential value of companies, as suggested by Director C.
(5 marks)

(c)   Prepare a report for the board of directors of Chikepe Co which:

(i)   Estimates the current equity value of Foshoro Co;
(6 marks)

(ii)   Estimates the equity value arising from combining Foshoro Co with Chikepe Co;
(11 marks)

(iii)   Evaluates whether the acquisition of Foshoro Co would be beneficial to Chikepe Co's shareholders and discusses the limitations of the valuation method used in (c)(i) and (c)(ii) above.
(7 marks)

Professional marks will be awarded in part (c) for the format, structure and presentation of the report.
(4 marks)

(d)   Discuss how the mandatory bid rule and the principle of equal treatment protects shareholders in the event of their company facing a takeover bid, and discuss the effectiveness of poison pills and disposal of crown jewels as defensive tactics against hostile takeover bids.
(8 marks)

(Total = 50 marks)

55 Cigno (Sep/Dec 15)

Cigno Co is a large pharmaceutical company, involved in the research and development (R&D) of medicines and other healthcare products. Over the past few years, Cigno Co has been finding it increasingly difficult to develop new medical products. In response to this, it has followed a strategy of acquiring smaller pharmaceutical companies which already have successful products in the market and/or have products in development which look very promising for the future. It has mainly done this without having to resort to major cost cutting and has therefore avoided large-scale redundancies. This has meant that not only has Cigno Co performed reasonably well in the stock market, but it has also maintained a high level of corporate reputation.

Anatra Co is involved in two business areas: the first area involves the R&D of medical products, and the second area involves the manufacture of medical and dental equipment. Until recently, Anatra Co's financial performance was falling, but about three years ago a new chief executive officer (CEO) was appointed and she started to turn the company around. Recently, the company has developed and marketed a range of new medical products, and is in the process of developing a range of cancer-fighting medicines. This has resulted in a good performance in the stock market, but many analysts believe that its shares are still trading below their true value. Anatra Co's CEO is of the opinion that the turnaround in the company's fortunes makes it particularly vulnerable to a takeover threat, and she is thinking of defence strategies that the company could undertake to prevent such a threat. In particular, she was thinking of disposing of some of the company's assets and focusing on its core business.

Cigno Co is of the opinion that Anatra Co is being held back from achieving its true potential by its equipment manufacturing business and that by separating the two business areas, corporate value can be increased. As a result, it is considering the possibility of acquiring Anatra Co, unbundling the manufacturing business, and then absorbing Anatra Co's R&D of medical products business. Cigno Co estimates that it would need to pay a premium of 35% to Anatra Co's shareholders to buy the company.

Financial information: Anatra Co

Given below are extracts from Anatra Co's latest statement of profit or loss and statement of financial position for the year ended 30 November 20X5.

	20X5 $m
Sales revenue	21,400
Profit before interest and tax (PBIT)	3,210
Interest	720
Pre-tax profit	2,490
Non-current liabilities	9,000
Share capital (50c/share)	3,500
Reserves	4,520

Anatra Co's share of revenue and profits between the two business areas are as follows:

	Medical products R&D	Equipment manufacturing
Share of revenue and profit	70%	30%

Post-acquisition benefits from acquiring Anatra Co

Cigno Co estimates that following the acquisition and unbundling of the manufacturing business, Anatra Co's future sales revenue and profitability of the medical R&D business will be boosted. The annual sales growth rate is expected to be 5% and the profit margin before interest and tax is expected to be 17.25% of sales revenue, for the next four years. It can be assumed that the current tax-allowable depreciation will remain equivalent to the amount of investment needed to maintain the current level of operations, but that the company will require an additional investment in assets of 40c for every $1 increase in sales revenue.

After the four years, the annual growth rate of the company's free cash flows is expected to be 3% for the foreseeable future.

Anatra Co's unbundled equipment manufacturing business is expected to be divested through a sell-off, although other options such as a management buy-in were also considered. The value of the sell-off will be based on the medical and dental equipment manufacturing industry. Cigno Co has estimated that Anatra Co's manufacturing business should be valued at a factor of 1.2 times higher than the industry's average price/earnings ratio. Currently the industry's average earnings per share is 30c and the average share price is $2.40.

Possible additional post-acquisition benefits

Cigno Co estimates that it could achieve further cash flow benefits following the acquisition of Anatra Co, if it undertakes a limited business reorganisation. There is some duplication of the R&D work conducted by Cigno Co and Anatra Co, and the costs related to this duplication could be saved if Cigno Co closes some of its own operations. However, it would mean that many redundancies would have to be made, including employees who have worked in Cigno Co for many years. Anatra Co's employees are considered to be better qualified and more able in these areas of duplication, and would therefore not be made redundant.

Cigno Co could also move its headquarters to the country where Anatra Co is based and thereby potentially save a significant amount of tax, other than corporation tax. However, this would mean a loss of revenue for the government where Cigno Co is based.

The company is concerned about how the government and the people of the country where it is based might react to these issues. It has had a long and beneficial relationship with the country and its people.

Cigno Co has estimated that it would save $1,600 million after-tax free cash flows to the firm at the end of the first year as a result of these post-acquisition benefits. These cash flows would increase by 4% every year for the next three years.

Estimating the combined company's weighted average cost of capital

Cigno Co is of the opinion that as a result of acquiring Anatra Co, the cost of capital will be based on the equity beta and the cost of debt of the combined company. The asset beta of the combined company is the individual companies' asset betas weighted in proportion of the individual companies' market value of equity. Cigno Co has a market debt to equity ratio of 40:60 and an equity beta of 1.10.

It can be assumed that the proportion of market value of debt to market value of equity will be maintained after the two companies combine.

Currently, Cigno Co's total firm value (market values of debt and equity combined) is $60,000 million and Anatra Co's asset beta is 0.68.

Additional information

- The estimate of the risk-free rate of return is 4.3% and of the market risk premium is 7%.

- The corporation tax rate applicable to all companies is 22%.

- Anatra Co's current share price is $3 per share, and it can be assumed that the book value and the market value of its debt are equivalent.

- The pre-tax cost of debt of the combined company is expected to be 6.0%.

Important note

Cigno Co's board of directors (BoD) does not require any discussion or computations of currency movements or exposure in this report. All calculations are to be presented in $ million. Currency movements and their management will be considered in a separate report. The BoD also does not expect any discussion or computations relating to the financing of acquisition in this report, other than the information provided above on the estimation of the cost of capital.

Required

(a) Distinguish between a divestment through a sell-off and a management buy-in as forms of unbundling.

(4 marks)

(b)   Prepare a report for the BoD of Cigno Co which:

  (i)   Estimates the value attributable to Cigno Co's shareholders from the acquisition of Anatra Co before taking into account the cash benefits of potential tax savings and redundancies, and then after taking these into account **(18 marks)**

  (ii) Assesses the value created from (b)(i) above, including a discussion of the estimations made and methods used **(8 marks)**

  (iii) Advises the BoD on the key factors it should consider in relation to the redundancies and potential tax savings **(4 marks)**

  Professional marks will be awarded in part (b) for the format, structure and presentation of the report. **(4 marks)**

(c)   Discuss whether the defence strategy suggested by Anatra Co's CEO of disposing assets is feasible. **(6 marks)**

(d)   Takeover regulation, where Anatra Co is based, offers the following conditions aimed at protecting shareholders: the mandatory-bid condition through sell-out rights, the principle of equal treatment, and squeeze-out rights.

  Required

  Explain the main purpose of each of the three conditions. **(6 marks)**

  (Total = 50 marks)

56 Lirio (Mar/Jun 16)   **98 mins**

Lirio Co is an engineering company which is involved in projects around the world. It has been growing steadily for several years and has maintained a stable dividend growth policy for a number of years now. The board of directors (BoD) is considering bidding for a large project which requires a substantial investment of $40 million. It can be assumed that the date today is 1 March 20X6.

The BoD is proposing that Lirio Co should not raise the finance for the project through additional debt or equity. Instead, it proposes that the required finance is obtained from a combination of funds received from the sale of its equity investment in a European company and from cash flows generated from its normal business activity in the coming two years. As a result, Lirio Co's current capital structure of 80 million $1 equity shares and $70 million 5% bonds is not expected to change in the foreseeable future.

The BoD has asked the company's treasury department to prepare a discussion paper on the implications of this proposal. The following information on Lirio Co has been provided to assist in the preparation of the discussion paper.

Expected income and cash flow commitments prior to undertaking the large project for the year to the end of February 20X7

Lirio Co's sales revenue is forecast to grow by 8% next year from its current level of $300 million, and the operating profit margin on this is expected to be 15%. It is expected that Lirio Co will have the following capital investment requirements for the coming year, before the impact of the large project is considered:

1   A $0.10 investment in working capital for every $1 increase in sales revenue;

2   An investment equivalent to the amount of depreciation to keep its non-current asset base at the present productive capacity. The current depreciation charge already included in the operating profit margin is 25% of the non-current assets of $50 million;

3   A $0.20 investment in additional non-current assets for every $1 increase in sales revenue; and

4    $8 million additional investment in other small projects.

In addition to the above sales revenue and profits, Lirio Co has one overseas subsidiary – Pontac Co, from which it receives dividends of 80% on profits. Pontac Co produces a specialist tool which it sells locally for $60 each. It is expected that it will produce and sell 400,000 units of this specialist tool next year. Each tool will incur variable costs of $36 per unit and total annual fixed costs of $4 million to produce and sell.

Lirio Co pays corporation tax at 25% and Pontac Co pays corporation tax at 20%. In addition to this, a withholding tax of 8% is deducted from any dividends remitted from Pontac Co. A bi-lateral tax treaty exists between the countries where Lirio Co is based and where Pontac Co is based. Therefore, corporation tax is payable on profits made by subsidiary companies, but full credit is given for corporation tax already paid.

It can be assumed that receipts from Pontac Co are in $ equivalent amounts and exchange rate fluctuations on these can be ignored.

Sale of equity investment in the European country

It is expected that Lirio Co will receive euro (€) 20 million in three months' time from the sale of its investment. The € has continued to remain weak, while the $ has continued to remain strong through 20X5 and the start of 20X6. The financial press has also reported that there may be a permanent shift in the €/$ exchange rate, with firms facing economic exposure. Lirio Co has decided to hedge the € receipt using one of currency forward contracts, currency futures contracts or currency options contracts.

The following exchange contracts and rates are available to Lirio Co.

	Per €1
Spot rates	$1.1585–$1.1618
Three-month forward rates	$1.1559–$1.1601

Currency futures (contract size $125,000, quotation: € per $1)

March futures	€0.8638
June futures	€0.8656

Currency options (contract size $125,000, exercise price quotation € per $1, premium € per $1)

	Calls		Puts	
Exercise price	March	June	March	June
0.8600	0.0255	0.0290	0.0267	0.0319

It can be assumed that futures and options contracts expire at the end of their respective months.

Dividend history, expected dividends and cost of capital, Lirio Co

Year to end of February	20X3	20X4	20X5	20X6
Number of $1 equity shares in issue ('000)	60,000	60,000	80,000	80,000
Total dividends paid ($'000)	12,832	13,602	19,224	20,377

It is expected that dividends will grow at the historic rate, if the large project is not undertaken.

Expected dividends and dividend growth rates if the large project is undertaken:

Year to end of February 20X7	Remaining cash flows after the investment in the $40 million project will be paid as dividends.
Year to end of February 20X8	The dividends paid will be the same amount as the previous year.
Year to end of February 20X9	Dividends paid will be $0.31 per share.
In future years from February 20X9	Dividends will grow at an annual rate of 7%.

Lirio Co's cost of equity capital is estimated to be 12%.

Required

(a) With reference to purchasing power parity, explain how exchange rate fluctuations may lead to economic exposure.

(6 marks)

(b) Prepare a discussion paper, including all relevant calculations, for the BoD of Lirio Co which:

(i) Estimates Lirio Co's dividend capacity as at 28 February 20X7, prior to investing in the large project **(9 marks)**

(ii) Advises Lirio Co on, and recommends, an appropriate hedging strategy for the euro (€) receipt it is due to receive in three months' time from the sale of the equity investment **(14 marks)**

(iii) Using the information on dividends provided in the question, and from (b)(i) and (b)(ii) above, assesses whether or not the project would add value to Lirio Co **(8 marks)**

(iv) Discusses the issues of proposed methods of financing the project which need to be considered further **(9 marks)**

Professional marks will be awarded in part (b) for the format, structure and presentation of the discussion paper. **(4 marks)**

(Total = 50 marks)

57 Morada (Sep/Dec 16)   98 mins

Morada Co is involved in offering bespoke travel services and maintenance services. In addition to owning a few hotels, it has built strong relationships with companies in the hospitality industry all over the world. It has a good reputation of offering unique, high quality holiday packages at reasonable costs for its clients. The strong relationships have also enabled it to offer repair and maintenance services to a number of hotel chains and cruise ship companies.

Following a long discussion at a meeting of the board of directors (BoD) about the future strategic direction which Morada Co should follow, three directors continued to discuss one particular issue over dinner. In the meeting, the BoD had expressed concern that Morada Co was exposed to excessive risk and therefore its cost of capital was too high. The BoD feared that several good projects had been rejected over the previous two years, because they did not meet Morada Co's high cost of capital threshold. Each director put forward a proposal, which they then discussed in turn. At the conclusion of the dinner, the directors decided to ask for a written report on the proposals put forward by the first director and the second director, before taking all three proposals to the BoD for further discussion.

First director's proposal

The first director is of the opinion that Morada Co should reduce its debt in order to mitigate its risk and therefore reduce its cost of capital. He proposes that the company should sell its repair and maintenance services business unit and focus just on offering bespoke travel services and hotel accommodation. In the sale, the book value of non-current assets will reduce by 30% and the book value of current liabilities will reduce by 10%. It is thought that the non-current assets can be sold for an after-tax profit of 15%.

The first director suggests that the funds arising from the sale of the repair and maintenance services business unit and cash resources should be used to pay off 80% of the long-term debt. It is estimated that as a result of this, Morada Co's credit rating will improve from Baa2 to A2.

Second director's proposal

The second director is of the opinion that risk diversification is the best way to reduce Morada Co's risk and therefore reduce its cost of capital. He proposes that the company raise additional funds using debt finance and then create a new strategic business unit. This business unit will focus on construction of new commercial properties.

The second director suggests that $70 million should be borrowed and used to invest in purchasing non-current assets for the construction business unit. The new debt will be issued in the form of four-year redeemable bonds paying an annual coupon of 6.2%. It is estimated that if this amount of debt is raised, then Morada Co's credit rating will worsen to Ca3 from Baa2. Current liabilities are estimated to increase to $28 million.

Third director's proposal

The third director is of the opinion that Morada Co does not need to undertake the proposals suggested by the first director and the second director just to reduce the company's risk profile. She feels that the above proposals require a fundamental change in corporate strategy and should be considered in terms of more than just tools to manage risk. Instead, she proposes that a risk management system should be set up to appraise Morada Co's current risk profile, considering each type of business risk and financial risk within the company, and taking appropriate action to manage the risk where it is deemed necessary.

MORADA CO EXTRACTS FROM THE FORECAST FINANCIAL POSITION FOR THE COMING YEAR

	$'000
Non-current assets	280,000
Current assets	48,000
Total assets	328,000

Equity and liabilities

Share capital (40c/share)	50,000
Retained earnings	137,000
Total equity	187,000
Non-current liabilities (6.2% redeemable bonds)	120,000
Current liabilities	21,000
Total liabilities	141,000
Total liabilities and equity capital	328,000

Other financial information

Morada Co's forecast after-tax earnings for the coming year are expected to be $28 million. It is estimated that the company will make a 9% return after tax on any new investment in non-current assets, and will suffer a 9% decrease in after-tax earnings on any reduction in investment in non-current assets.

Morada Co's current share price is $2.88 per share. According to the company's finance division, it is very difficult to predict how the share price will react to either the proposal made by the first director or the proposal made by the second director. Therefore, it has been assumed that the share price will not change following either proposal.

The finance division has further assumed that the proportion of the book value of non-current assets invested in each business unit gives a fair representation of the size of each business unit within Morada Co.

Morada Co's equity beta is estimated at 1.2, while the asset beta of the repairs and maintenance services business unit is estimated to be 0.65. The relevant equity beta for the new, larger company including the construction unit relevant to the second director's proposals has been estimated as 1.21.

The bonds are redeemable in four years' time at face value. For the purposes of estimating the cost of capital, it can be assumed that debt beta is zero. However, the four-year credit spread over the risk-free rate of return is 60 basis points for A2 rated bonds, 90 basis points for Baa2 rated bonds and 240 basis points for Ca3 rated bonds.

A tax rate of 20% is applicable to all companies. The current risk-free rate of return is estimated to be 3.8% and the market risk premium is estimated to be 7%.

Required

(a)   Explain how business risk and financial risk are related; and how risk mitigation and risk diversification can form part of a company's risk management strategy.   **(6 marks)**

(b)   Prepare a report for the board of directors of Morada Co which:

   (i)   Estimates Morada Co's cost of equity and cost of capital, based on market value of equity and debt, before any changes and then after implementing the proposals put forward by the first and by the second directors;   **(17 marks)**

   (ii)   Estimates the impact of the first and second directors' proposals on Morada Co's forecast after-tax earnings and forecast financial position for the coming year; and   **(7 marks)**

   (iii)   Discusses the impact on Morada Co of the changes proposed by the first and second directors and recommends whether or not either proposal should be accepted. The discussion should include an explanation of any assumptions made in the estimates in (b)(i) and (b)(ii) above.   **(9 marks)**

   Professional marks will be awarded in part (b) for the format, structure and presentation of the report.   **(4 marks)**

(c)   Discuss the possible reasons for the third director's proposal that a risk management system should consider each risk, before taking appropriate action.   **(7 marks)**

                                                                            (Total = 50 marks)

58 Opao (Dec 18)   **98 mins**

Around seven years ago, Opao Co, a private conglomerate company involved in many different businesses, decided to obtain a listing on a recognised stock exchange by offering a small proportion of its equity shares to the public. Before the listing, the company was owned by around 100 shareholders, who were all closely linked to Opao Co and had their entire shareholding wealth invested in the company. However, soon after the listing these individuals started selling their shares in Opao Co, and over a two-year period after the listing, its ownership structure changed to one of many diverse individual and institutional shareholders.

As a consequence of this change in ownership structure, Opao Co's board of directors (BoD) commenced an aggressive period of business reorganisation through portfolio and organisational restructuring. This resulted in Opao Co changing from a conglomerate company to a company focusing on just two business sectors: financial services and food manufacturing. The financial press reported that Opao Co had been forced to take this action because of the change in the type of its shareholders. The equity markets seem to support this action, and Opao Co's share price has grown strongly during this period of restructuring, after growing very slowly initially.

Opao Co recently sold a subsidiary company, Burgut Co, through a management buy-in (MBI), although it also had the option to dispose of Burgut Co through a management buy-out (MBO). In a statement, Opao Co's BoD justified this by stating that Burgut Co would be better off being controlled by the MBI team.

Opao Co is now considering acquiring Tai Co and details of the proposed acquisition are as follows:

Proposed acquisition of Tai Co

Tai Co is an unlisted company involved in food manufacturing. Opao Co's BoD is of the opinion that the range of products produced by Tai Co will fit very well with its own product portfolio, leading to cross-selling opportunities, new innovations, and a larger market share. The BoD also thinks that there is a possibility for economies of scale and scope, such as shared logistic and storage facilities, giving cost saving opportunities. This, the BoD believes, will lead to significant synergy benefits and therefore it is of the opinion that Opao Co should make a bid to acquire Tai Co.

Financial information related to Opao Co, Tai Co and the combined company

Opao Co

Opao Co has 2,000 million shares in issue and are currently trading at $2.50 each.

BPP
LEARNING
MEDIA

Tai Co

Tai Co has 263 million shares in issue and the current market value of its debt is $400 million. Its most recent profit before interest and tax was $132.0 million, after deducting tax allowable depreciation and non-cash expenses of $27.4 million. Tai Co makes an annual cash investment of $24.3 million in non-current assets and working capital. It is estimated that its cash flows will grow by 3% annually for the foreseeable future. Tai Co's current cost of capital is estimated to be 11%.

Combined company

If Opao Co acquires Tai Co, it is expected that the combined company's sales revenue will be $7,351 million in the first year and its annual pre-tax profit margin on sales will be 15.4% for the foreseeable future. After the first year, sales revenue will grow by 5.02% every year for the next three years. It can be assumed that the combined company's annual depreciation will be equivalent to the investment required to maintain the company at current operational levels. However, in order to increase the sales revenue levels each year, the combined company will require an additional investment of $109 million in the first year and $0.31 for every $1 increase in sales revenue for each of the next three years.

After the first four years, it is expected that the combined company's free cash flows will grow by 2.4% annually for the foreseeable future. The combined company's cost of capital is estimated to be 10%. It expected that the combined company's debt to equity level will be maintained at 40:60, in market value terms, after the acquisition has taken place.

Both Opao Co and Tai Co pay corporation tax on profits at an annual rate of 20% and it is expected that this rate will not change if Opao Co acquires Tai Co. It can be assumed that corporation tax is payable in the same year as the profits it is charged on.

Possible acquisition price offers

Opao Co's BoD is proposing that Tai Co's acquisition be made through one of the following payment methods:

- A cash payment offer of $4.40 for each Tai Co share; or

- Through a share-for-share exchange, where a number of Tai Co shares are exchanged for a number of Opao Co shares, such that 55.5% of the additional value created from the acquisition is allocated to Tai Co's shareholders and the remaining 44.5% of the additional value is allocated to Opao Co's shareholders; or

- Through a mixed offer of a cash payment of $2.09 per share and one Opao Co share for each Tai Co share. It is estimated that Opao Co's share price will become $2.60 per share when such a mixed offer is made.

Similar acquisitions in the food manufacturing industry have normally attracted a share price premium of between 15% and 40% previously.

Required

(a) Distinguish between a management buy-out (MBO) and a management buy-in (MBI), and discuss why Opao Co's board of directors (BoD) might have sold Burgut Co through an MBI. **(4 marks)**

(b) Explain what portfolio restructuring and organisational restructuring involve, and discuss possible reason(s) why the change in the type of shareholders may have made Opao Co change from being a conglomerate to one focusing on just two business sectors. **(5 marks)**

(c) Prepare a report for the board of directors of Opao Co which:

    (i) Estimates the value of equity of Opao Co and of Tai Co before the acquisition, and of the combined company after the acquisition; **(10 marks)**

    (ii) Estimates the percentage gain in value for each Opao Co share and Tai Co share, under each of the cash, the share-for-share, and the mixed offers; and

    (12 marks)

(iii) Evaluates the likely reaction of Opao Co's and Tai Co's shareholders to the acquisition offers. **(7 marks)**

Professional marks will be awarded in part (c) for the format, structure and presentation of the report. **(4 marks)**

(d) Following the MBI, the BoD of Burgut Co announced that its intention was to list the company on a recognised stock exchange within seven years. The BoD is discussing whether to obtain the listing through an initial public offering (IPO) or through a reverse takeover, but it does not currently have a strong preference for either option.

Required

Distinguish between an IPO and a reverse takeover, and discuss whether an IPO or a reverse takeover would be an appropriate method for Burgut Co to obtain a listing.

(8 marks)

(Total = 50 marks)

59 Okan (Sep/Dec 19)   98 mins

Okan Co, a large listed company located in Yasailand (which uses the currency Y$), manufactures engines and engine parts. It is considering whether or not to invest in one of two new four-year projects: Project Alpha or Project Beta. Details of both projects are given separately. Previously, Okan Co has used relevant risk-adjusted discount rates to calculate the net present value (NPV) of projects. However, the finance director believes that calculating adjusted present values (APV) of projects would be more appropriate. Okan Co wants to base its decision on which project to invest in; the returns generated by the projects; the projects' risk as measured by their project durations; and important non-financial aspects. Both projects are due to commence in six months' time.

Funding for projects Alpha and Beta

Project Alpha or Project Beta will each require the same amount of initial funding of Y$50,000,000.

Proceeds from the sale of a factory based in Europe in six months' time, for Euro (€)10,000,000, will provide part of the funding and the balance will be financed by debt borrowing.

Okan Co expects to hedge the €10,000,000 using either forward markets or money markets. The following information is available on these markets:

Foreign exchange rates

	Y$/€1
Spot	2.5210–2.5862
Six months forward	2.5462–2.6121

Bank interest rates

	Investing	Borrowing
Yasailand	2.40%	5.00%
Eurozone	1.05%	2.20%

The balance of funding raised by domestic debt borrowing will be through a four-year subsidised loan on which interest is payable at 2.1%, although Okan Co's normal borrowing rate is 5%. Issue costs related to raising this finance will be 3% of the gross proceeds.

Project Alpha details

Project Alpha's base case NPV and APV in six months' time when the project will commence should be estimated using the following information.

The sales revenues and production costs related to Project Alpha in six months' time, before any annual price or cost increases, are estimated as follows:

Year	1	2	3	4
Sales revenue (Y$ 000s)	15,750	28,350	47,250	23,100
Production cost (Y$ 000s)	6,120	10,710	21,420	8,160

It is expected that the sales price will increase at an annual inflation rate of 10%. Domestic production costs are likely to increase at Yasailand's annual inflation rate.

In addition to the above, components will be imported from the UK (currency £), at the following current cost:

Year	1	2	3	4
Component costs (£ 000s)	1,200	1,800	3,700	1,400

The costs of components from the UK are fixed and not subject to inflation.

The funds of Y$50,000,000 for Project Alpha will be used to purchase plant and equipment needed for manufacturing purposes. Tax allowable depreciation is available on the value of the plant and equipment at 25% per year on a reducing balance basis, with a balancing allowance or charge applicable at the end of the project. The plant and equipment is expected to be sold for Y$10,000,000 (post-inflation) at the end of the project.

At the start of every year, Project Alpha will require working capital. In the first year this will be 10% of the estimated Year 1 sales revenue. In subsequent years, the project will require an increase or a reduction in working capital of 15% for every $1 increase or decrease in sales revenue respectively. The working capital is expected to be fully released when Project Alpha ceases.

The expected spot exchange rate between the Y$ and the £, in six months' time, is expected to be Y$3.03 per £1. The annual inflation rates are currently 2% in the UK and 4% in Yasailand. It can be assumed that these inflation rates will not change for the foreseeable future.

The cost of capital for appraising the base case net present value of Project Alpha is 10%. Okan Co pays tax at an annual rate of 20%. Tax is payable in the same year as the profits it is based on. Okan Co makes sufficient profits from its other activities to take advantage of any tax loss relief.

Project Beta details

Given below are Project Beta's base case present values, based on the project start date in six months' time, discounted at the project's relevant risk-adjusted all-equity financed discount rate:

Year	1	2	3	4
Present values (Y$ 000s)	8,450	19,360	22,340	4,950

It can be assumed that any working capital requirements for Project Beta are included in the annual cash flows.

Project Beta's duration has been calculated as 2.43 years, based on its base case present values.

Economic risk and risk categories

One of Okan Co's subsidiary companies in Yasailand, which produces and sells all its products domestically, has still found that it is exposed to economic risk (economic exposure). The directors of the subsidiary believe that this is because Yasailand's government has maintained comparatively higher interest rates, even though the inflation in Yasailand is now under control.

Okan Co categorises the risks inherent in its projects according to the severity of their impact and the frequency of their occurrence, as follows: (i) severe and frequent; (ii) not severe but frequent; (iii) severe but not frequent; and (iv) neither severe nor frequent.

Required

(a) Discuss why a company may prefer to use the adjusted present value (APV) method rather than the net present value (NPV) method.
(4 marks)

(b) Prepare a report for the board of directors (BoD) of Okan Co which:

(i) Estimates the minimum amount of debt borrowing Okan Co would require;
(4 marks)

(ii)   Estimates:

    (1)   Project Alpha's and Project Beta's base case NPV, in six months' time, before considering the financing side effects;   **(12 marks)**

    (2)   Project Alpha's and Project Beta's APV, in six months' time; and   **(6 marks)**

    (3)   Project Alpha's duration based on its base case present values of cash flows;   **(2 marks)**

(iii) Evaluates and justifies which project Okan Co should choose, basing the decision on the factors Okan Co considers to be important. The evaluation should include a discussion of the assumptions made.   **(8 marks)**

Professional marks will be awarded in part (b) for the format, structure and presentation of the report.   **(4 marks)**

(c)   Discuss why Okan Co's subsidiary company may be exposed to economic risk (economic exposure) and how it may be managed.   **(4 marks)**

(d)   Discuss how each category of risk, in terms of severity and frequency, may be managed.   **(6 marks)**

(Total = 50 marks)

Answers

Advanced Financial Management

1 Preparation question: Mezza

Marking scheme

		Marks
(a)	Overarching corporate aim	1–2
	Discussion of the project adding value and issues relating to return and risk	3–4
	Possible suggestions for mitigating the negative issues to above discussion	3–4
	Discussion of the ethical and environmental issues	3–4
	Possible suggestions for mitigating the ethical and environmental issues	3–4
	Other relevant key issues and suggestions for mitigation	2–3
		Max 17
(b)	1–2 marks per capital discussed	Max 8
		25

(a) **Overarching corporate aim**

The main aim of the directors is to maximise shareholder value and any decisions should be taken with this objective in mind. However, the company has other stakeholders and directors should be sensitive to potential negative implications from implementing the project.

Key issue (1) – will the project add value?

The first issue to consider is whether the project will add value to the company.

Positive factors

At first glance it would appear that the project would be adding value, as it is meeting an identifiable market need (tackling climate change). There are likely to be positive effects on the company's reputation and ultimately its share price as Mezza Co is demonstrating a desire and ability to tackle climate change. If Mezza Co champions the work being done by its subsidiary, there are likely to be future opportunities for the subsidiary to work on similar projects.

Other factors to consider

Before progressing with the project, further investigation into its likely value is required. Whilst there is no doubt that such a project should be well received, there are risks that must be considered, not just from the project itself but also from the behaviour of the directors. Share options form part of the directors' remuneration package and they may be tempted to take greater risks as a result, in order to try to boost the share price. This may be against the wishes of shareholders and other stakeholders who may have a more risk-averse attitude.

The project appears to use new technology and ideas which, by their very nature, will be risky. There will therefore be uncertainty surrounding the income stream from the project – the extent of the risk should be assessed prior to progressing with the project. Are the current revenue and cost estimates realistic? What is the likelihood of competitors entering the market and the potential effects on revenue and market share? A full investigation, using such means as sensitivity analysis and duration, is required to answer such questions.

When assessing the extent of the value added by the project, it is important that risk is factored into the process. By doing so, directors will be in a better position (if necessary) to show stakeholders that they are not taking unacceptable risks in proceeding with the project. Other factors that must be investigated include the length of time it will take to get the product to market, any additional infrastructure required and potential expertise needed.

Key issue (2) – plant location

Positive factors

Mezza Co has identified an 'ideal' location for the plant, namely Maienar in Asia. This is due to Mezza already having a significant presence in Maienar and thus a well-developed infrastructure exists. There are also strong ties with senior government officials in this country and the government is keen to develop new industries. All of these factors are very positive for the potential development of the project. The ties to senior government officials are likely to be particularly useful when trying to deal with legal and administrative issues, thus reducing the time between development and production actually starting.

Other factors to consider

Despite the positive factors mentioned above, there are ethical and environmental issues to consider prior to making a final decision regarding plant location. The likely effect on the fishermen's livelihood could produce adverse publicity, as could potential damaging effects on the environment and wildlife. Environmental impact tends to generate considerable debate and Mezza will want to avoid any negative effects on its reputation (particularly as the project is supposed to be 'environmentally friendly').

The fact that Mezza has close ties with senior political figures and the government in general may create negative feeling if it is felt that Mezza could influence the government into making decisions that are not in the best interests of the locality and the country as a whole. This is a relationship that will have to be managed very carefully.

Risk mitigation

Given that Mezza has an excellent corporate image, it is unlikely that it will want to ignore the plight of the fishermen. It could try to work with the fishermen and involve them in the process, pointing out the benefits of the project to the environment as a whole (without ignoring the effects on their livelihood). It could offer the fishermen priority on new jobs that are created and emphasise the additional wealth that the project is likely to create.

Mezza could also consider alternative locations for the plant, although this is likely to be expensive, given the need for certain infrastructure already present in Maienar. Alternatively the company could try to find an alternative process for growing and harvesting the plant that would not have adverse effects on wildlife and fish stocks. Again, this is an expensive option and any such costs would have to be set against expected revenues to determine value added.

As mentioned, Mezza will have to manage its relationship with Maienar's government very carefully as it does not want to appear to be influencing government decisions. Mezza needs to make it very clear that it is following proper legal and administrative procedures – and is working with the government to protect and improve the country, rather than exploit it for its own gains.

Conclusion

It is important that Mezza considers all of the likely benefits and costs related to the project, not just to itself but also to the country and its inhabitants. While gaining prompt approval from the government will allow the project to proceed and become profitable more quickly, it is important that Mezza focuses on the effects of the project and alternative ways to proceed, in order to avoid an overall negative impact on its reputation.

(b) **Integrated reporting**

Integrated reporting looks at the ability of an organisation to create value and considers important relationships, both internally and externally. It involves considering the impact of the proposed project and six capitals as follows.

Financial

The integrated report should explain how commercialising the product should generate revenues over time, be an important element in diversification and make a significant contribution to the growth of Mezza. The report should also disclose the financial strategy implications if additional funding was required and what finance cost commitments Mezza will assume.

Manufactured

The report would identify the new facility as an important addition to Mezza's productive capacity. It would also show how the infrastructure that Mezza already has in Maienar will be used to assist in growing and processing the new plant.

Intellectual

The report should show how Mezza intends to protect the plant and hence its future income by some sort of protection, such as the patent. It should also highlight how development of the plant fulfils the aims of the subsidiary, to develop products that have beneficial impacts on other capitals.

Human

Mezza should show how the employment opportunities provided by the new facility link to how Mezza has been using local labour in Maienar. It should highlight the ways in which the new facility allows local labour to develop their skills. However, the report also needs to show whether Mezza is doing anything to help the fishermen deal with their loss of livelihood, since the adverse impact on the fishermen would appear to go against Mezza's strategy of supporting local farming communities.

Social and relationship

The development of the plant and the new facility should be reported in the context of Mezza's strategy of being a good corporate citizen in Maienar. It should explain how the new plant will assist economic development there and in turn how this will enhance the value derived to Mezza from operating in that country.

Natural

The report needs to set the adverse impact on the area and the fishing stock in the context of the longer-term environmental benefits that development of the plant brings. It also needs to show the commitments that Mezza is making to mitigate environmental damage.

2 Preparation question: Bournelorth

			Marks
(a)		Shareholder wealth maximisation and need for further investment	1–2
		Sell-off of IT services business	1–2
		Rights issue	2–3
		Debt finance	2–3
			Max 8
(b)	(i)	Risks associated with investment in development	Up to 4
		Controls over development	Up to 4
			Max 6
	(ii)	1 mark per point	3
(c)	(i)	Explanation that behavioural finance departs from rational decision-making	3
	(ii)	Impacts of behavioural factors on share price – up to 2 marks per well-explained point	Max 5
			25

(a) According to traditional finance theory, Bournelorth Co's directors will wish to strive for long-term shareholder wealth maximisation. The directors may not have been fully committed to long-term wealth maximisation, as they seemed to have focused on the development aspects which interested them most and left the original business mostly to others. However, now they are likely to come under pressure from the new external shareholders to maximise shareholder wealth and pay an acceptable level of dividend. To achieve this, it seems that Bournelorth Co will have to commit further large sums to investment in development of diagnostic applications (apps) in order to keep up with competitors.

Selling off the IT services business

At present the IT services business seems to be a reliable generator of significant profits. Selling it off would very likely produce a significant cash boost now, when needed. However, it would remove the safety net of reasonably certain income and mean that Bournelorth Co followed a much riskier business model. The IT services business also offers a possible gateway to reach customers who may be interested in the apps which Bournelorth Co develops.

Rights issue

If the executive directors wish to maintain their current percentage holdings, they would have to subscribe to 75% of the shares issued under the rights issue. Even though the shares would be issued at a discount, the directors might well not have the personal wealth available to subscribe fully. Previously they had to seek a listing to obtain enough funds for expansion, even though they were reluctant to bring in external investors, and this suggests their personal financial resources are limited.

However, the directors may need to take up the rights issue in order to ensure its success. If they do not, it may send out a message to external investors that the directors are unwilling to make a further commitment themselves because of the risks involved. There are also other factors which indicate that the rights issue may not be successful. The directors did not achieve the initial market price which they originally hoped for when Bournelorth Co was listed and shareholders may question the need for a rights issue soon after listing.

If the executive directors do not take up all of their rights, and the rights issue is still successful, this may have consequences for the operation of the business. The external shareholders would own a greater percentage of Bournelorth Co's equity share capital and may be in a position to reinforce the wishes of non-executive directors for improved governance and control systems and change of behaviour by the executive directors. Possibly they may also demand additional executive and non-executive directors, which would change the balance of power on the board.

The level of dividend demanded by shareholders may be less predictable than the interest on debt. One of the directors is also concerned whether the stock market is efficient or whether the share price may be subject to behavioural factors (discussed in (c) below).

Debt finance

Debt providers will demand Bournelorth Co commits to paying interest and ultimately repaying debt. This may worry the directors because of the significant uncertainties surrounding returns from new apps. Significant debt may have restrictive covenants built in, particularly if Bournelorth Co cannot provide much security. The directors may be faced with restrictions on dividends, for example, which may upset external shareholders.

Uncertainties surrounding funding may also influence directors' decisions. Loan finance may be difficult to obtain, but the amount and repayments would be fixed and could be budgeted, whereas the success of a rights issue is uncertain.

(b)   (i)   The main risks connected with development work are that time and resources are wasted on projects which do not generate sales or are not in line with corporate strategy. Directors may choose apps which interest them rather than apps which are best for the business. There is also the risk that projects do not deliver benefits, take too long or are too costly. Bournelorth Co's directors' heavy involvement in development activities may have made it easier to monitor them. However, the dangers with this are that the directors focus too much on their own individual projects, do not consider their projects objectively and do not step back to consider the overall picture.

        The board must decide on a clear strategy for investment in development and needs to approve major initiatives before they are undertaken. There must be proper planning and budgeting of all initiatives and a structured approach to development. The board must regularly review projects, comparing planned and actual expenditure and resource usage. The board must be prepared to halt projects which are unlikely to deliver benefits. One director should be given responsibility for monitoring overall development activity without being directly involved in any of the work. Post-completion reviews should be carried out when development projects have been completed.

   (ii)   Communication with shareholders and other important stakeholders, such as potential customers, may be problematic. Bournelorth Co faces the general corporate governance requirement of transparency and has to comply with the specific disclosure requirements of its local stock market.

        However, governance best practice also acknowledges that companies need to be allowed to preserve commercial confidentiality if appropriate, and clearly it will be relevant for Bournelorth Co. However, the less that it discloses, the less information finance providers will have on which to base their decisions.

        Another issue with disclosure is that product failures may be more visible now that Bournelorth Co has obtained a listing and may have to include a business review in its accounts.

(c)   (i)   Sewell defines behavioural finance as the influence of psychology on the behaviour of financial practitioners and the subsequent effect on markets. Behavioural finance suggests that individual decision-making is complex and will deviate from rational decision-making. Under rational decision-making, individual preferences will be clear and remain stable. Individuals will make choices with the aim of maximising utility, and adopt a rational approach for assessing outcomes.

Under behavioural finance, individuals may be more optimistic or conservative than appears to be warranted by rational analysis. They will try to simplify complex decisions and may make different decisions based on the same facts at different times.

(ii) Bournelorth Co's share price may be significantly influenced by the impact of behavioural factors, as it is a newly listed company operating in a sector where returns have traditionally been variable and unpredictable. The impact of behavioural factors may be complex, and they may exert both upward and downward pressures on Bournelorth Co's share price. Investors may, for example, compensate for not knowing much about Bournelorth Co by anchoring, which means using information which is irrelevant, but which they do have, to judge investment in Bournelorth Co.

The possibility of very high returns may add to the appeal of Bournelorth Co's shares. Some investors may want the opportunity of obtaining high returns even if it is not very likely that they will. The IT sector has also been subject to herd behaviour, notably in the dotcom boom. The herd effect is when a large number of investors have taken the same decision, for example to invest in a particular sector, and this influences others to conform and take the same decision.

However, even if Bournelorth Co produces high returns for some time, the fact that it is in a volatile sector may lead to investors selling shares before it appears to be warranted on the evidence, on the grounds that by the laws of chance Bournelorth Co will make a loss eventually (known as the gambler's fallacy).

Under behavioural finance, the possible volatility of Bournelorth Co's results may lead to downward pressure on its share price for various reasons. First some investors have regret aversion, a general bias against making a loss anyway. This, it is claimed, means that the level of returns on equity is rather higher than the returns on debt than is warranted by a rational view of the risk of equity.

Similarly under prospect theory, investors are more likely to choose a net outcome which consists entirely of small gains, rather than an identical net outcome which consists of a combination of larger gains and some losses. At present also, Bournelorth Co does not have much of a history of results for the market to analyse. Even when it has been listed for some time, however, another aspect of behavioural finance is investors placing excessive weight on the most recent results.

If the market reacts very well or badly to news about Bournelorth Co, the large rise or fall in the share price which results may also not be sustainable, but may revert back over time.

3 Cadnam

Marking scheme

			Marks
(a)	Interest	1	
	Tax	1	
	Investment in additional assets	2	
	Depreciation	$\underline{1}$	
		$\underline{5}$	
(b)	Calculations		
	Growth in PAT	1–2	
	Dividend payout ratios	1–2	
	Growth in dividends	1–2	
	Residual profit	1–2	
	Growth in share price	$\underline{1–2}$	
	Calculations		Max 6
	Discussion		
	Dividends	2–3	
	Gearing	2	
	Share price	$\underline{2}$	
			Max 12
(c)	Dividend policy statement	Up to 5	
	Directors' remuneration	Up to $\underline{5}$	
			Max 8
			$\underline{\underline{25}}$

(a)　**Dividend capacity**

	$m
Operating profit	2,678
Less: Interest (8% × $10,250m)	(820)
Less: Taxation (30% × ($2,678m – $820m))	(557)
Less: Investment in additional assets (25% × 0.03 × $2,678m/(1.03 × 0.02))	(975)
Forecast dividend capacity	326

(b)　**Growth in profit after tax**

	20X3	20X4	20X5	Geometric mean annual growth rate
	%	%	%	%
Cadnam	8.0	4.0	1.9	4.6
Holmsley	7.1	6.9	7.6	7.2

Geometric mean is the average compound growth over three years between 20X5 and 20X2 and is calculated as: [(value in 20X5 divided by 20X2 value) ^ (1/time period)] minus 1.

For example Cadnam = [(1,580 / 1,380) ^ (1/3)] - 1 = 0.046 or 4.6%

Dividend payout ratios (Profit after tax / dividends)

	20X2	20X3	20X4	20X5
	%	%	%	%
Cadnam	55.4	56.4	59.7	64.6
Holmsley	37.7	37.1	36.5	35.7

Growth in dividends

	20X3	20X4	20X5	Geometric mean annual growth rate
	%	%	%	%
Cadnam	9.8	10.1	10.3	10.1
Holmsley	5.4	5.3	5.3	5.3

Geometric mean is the average compound growth over three years between 20X5 and 20X2.

For example Cadnam = [(1,020/765)^(1/3)] - 1 = 0.101 or 10.1%

Residual profit (after tax-profit for the year – dividend – new investment)

	20X2	20X3	20X4	20X5
	$m	$m	$m	$m
Cadnam	333	338	41	(304)
Holmsley	330	375	419	486

Growth in share price

	20X3	20X4	20X5	Geometric mean annual growth rate
	%	%	%	%
Cadnam	9.6	4.9	2.5	5.6
Holmsley	3.8	6.1	6.8	5.6

Geometric mean is the average compound growth over three years between 20X5 and 20X2. For example Cadnam = [(5.75/4.88)^(1/3)] - 1 = 0.056 or 5.6%

Comments

Dividends

Both companies have shown fairly consistent increases over the last three years, with Cadnam Co's dividends increasing at around 10% each year, and Holmsley Co's dividends increasing at around 5% over the last three years. However, Holmsley Co's policy appears to be sustainable at present, whereas it is doubtful whether Cadnam Co's policy is sustainable.

Holmsley Co has managed to increase dividends, gradually also increasing investment in additional assets and residual profits, whilst at the same time having a decreasing dividend pay-out ratio.

In order to maintain its rate of dividend increase, however, Cadnam Co has had to pay out an increasing proportion of earnings each year. It seems that Cadnam Co may have sustained dividend increases up to 20X3 at the expense of additional investment, and is now having to increase additional investment significantly in order to make up for previous under-investment. In 20X5, Cadnam Co's residual profits became negative, and the dividend capacity calculation for 20X6 suggests that a much lower level of dividends would be appropriate.

Gearing

Holmsley Co's gearing appears to be stable at around the average for the industry, suggesting that perhaps it has found its optimum level. Up to 20X4, Cadnam Co could perhaps have been taking advantage of debt capacity to increase its debt towards this level. However, its gearing now appears to be on a rising trend of necessity increasing significantly in 20X5 to fund both additional investment and increasing dividends, despite the rise in its share price. Cadnam Co's gearing is predicted to increase further in 20X6, but how long this is sustainable is uncertain.

Share price

The average increase for both companies over the last four years has been the same. However, the percentage increases over the last two years for Holmsley Co has been higher than for Cadnam Co. This suggests that the market has placed more significance on the higher percentage growth in Holmsley Co's after-tax profits than in Cadnam Co's higher pertcentage growth in dividends, maybe seeing this as an indication that Holmsley Co's strategy has been more successful and is more likely in future to deliver higher share price growth.

(c) **Dividend policy**

One possible question is whether the statement in the annual report fairly reflects the likely future dividend policy of Cadnam Co. The report gives the impression that the current dividend policy will be sustained, whereas the figures suggest that this may not be the case. If the policy proves not to be sustainable, it would suggest a failure either of integrity (if the directors made a statement with a high risk that it would not be true) or due care (that they failed to take into account indicators which suggested their policy is not sustainable). The directors may be questioned by the auditors about whether this statement is true and fair.

There is also the question of balancing the interests of different stakeholders. To some degree, criticism of rises in dividend and director remuneration levels versus increases in employee salary levels could be said to be a matter of opinion.

However, the fact that there is a government enquiry into low pay in the sector suggests that pay levels are lower than society deems desirable. The force of the criticisms may be enhanced by the statements which Cadnam Co has made about developing an integrated reporting approach. Integrated reporting is not just about extra details in the annual report, but also reflects an underlying policy of carrying out business which includes responsiveness to the needs of different stakeholders.

The dividend capacity and gearing figures may also call into question whether Cadnam Co's board is taking excessive risks. Does paying out increasing dividends in future mean that the company is likely to have inadequate resources to sustain its business, and may be jeopardising the interests of lenders and employees as well as stakeholders? Certainly, there appear to be doubts about maintenance of future income levels with a number of contracts coming up for renewal and terms possibly being tightened by clients. Clients may be doubtful about renewing contracts if Cadnam Co's solvency appears doubtful.

Directors' remuneration

The directors' remuneration packages also raise concerns.

Comparison with Holmsley Co shows that salary, which is not dependent on performance, is a more significant element of the remuneration packages at Cadnam Co than Holmsley Co. Both companies have bonuses which depend to some degree on performance.

However, Cadnam Co's directors are also rewarded by loyalty bonuses, which again do not depend on performance but staying with the company. Holmsley Co has a share option scheme in place, which would seem to reward longer-term good performance, although it cannot be determined how significant a part of remuneration share options will be. Cadnam Co's remuneration scheme appears only to reward short-term profitability, possibly meaning that the directors may neglect the longer-term success and possibly even viability of the company.

4 Chawan

Workbook references. Chapter 2.

Top tips. This question required analysis of a company's past performance to help to decide whether or not to dispose of shares in the company. This is a tricky question to interpret; if rushed it can easily be misinterpreted as a valuations question (this was a common error in the exam). Once you have interpreted what is required this question is fairly straightforward in terms of the technical skills required.

Examining team's comments. Good answers for this part, which provided calculations in a tabular format and then discussed the results in a holistic manner, gained the majority of the marks. However, many responses tended to be unstructured, with few calculations to back up what was being said. Some responses also tended to be largely descriptive and piecemeal, where a ratio or trend was calculated and commented on, but the larger picture and discussion were missed. A surprising number of responses made errors in calculating the ratios and/or only gave ratios for one or two years. At this level, such an approach will not gain many marks. It is also difficult to discuss the key findings in any meaningful manner without examining a trend, but this cannot be done from examining one or two years' data.

Marking scheme

			Marks
(a)	Explanation of a dark pool network	3–4	
	Explanation of why Chawan Co may want to use one	1–2	
			Max 5
(b)	Profitability ratios	1–2	
	Investor ratios	3–4	
	Other ratios	1–2	
	Trends and other calculations	3–4	
			Max 10
	Note. Maximum 7 marks if only ratio calculations provided		
	Discussion of company performance over time	2–3	
	Discussion of company performance against competitors	2–3	
	Discussion of actual returns against expected returns	1–2	
	Discussion of need to maintain portfolio and alternative investments	1–2	
	Discussion of future trends and expectations	1–2	
	Discussion of takeover rumour and action as a result	1–2	
	Other relevant discussion/commentary	1–2	
			Max 10
			25

(a) A dark pool network allows shares to be traded anonymously, away from public scrutiny. No information on the trade order is revealed prior to it taking place. The price and size of the order are only revealed once the trade has taken place. Two main reasons are given for dark pool networks: first they prevent the risk of other traders moving the share price up or down; and second they often result in reduced costs because trades normally take place at the mid-price between the bid and offer; and because broker-dealers try to use their own private pools, thereby saving exchange fees.

Chawan Co's holding in Oden Co is 27 million shares out of a total of 600 million shares, or 4.5%. If Chawan Co sold such a large holding all at once, the price of Oden Co shares may fall temporarily and significantly, and Chawan Co may not receive the value based on the current price. By utilising a dark pool network, Chawan Co may be able to keep the price of the share largely intact, and possibly save transaction costs.

Although the criticism against dark pool systems is that they prevent market efficiency by not revealing bid-offer prices before the trade, proponents argue that in fact market efficiency is maintained because a large sale of shares will not move the price down artificially and temporarily.

(b) **Ratio calculations**

Focus on investor and profitability ratios

Oden Co	20X2	20X3	20X4	20X5
Operating profit/sales revenue		16.2%	15.2%	10.4%
Operating profit/capital employed		22.5%	20.4%	12.7%
Earnings per share		$0.27	$0.24	$0.12
Price to earnings ratio		9.3	10.0	18.3
Gearing ratio (debt/(debt + equity))		37.6%	36.9%	37.1%
Interest cover (operating profit/finance costs)		9.5	7.5	3.5
Dividend yield	7.1%	7.2%	8.3%	6.8%
Travel and leisure (T&L) sector				
Price to earnings ratio	11.9	12.2	13.0	13.8
Dividend yield	6.6%	6.6%	6.7%	6.4%

Other calculations

Oden Co sales revenue annual growth rate average between 20X3 and 20X5 =

$$\left(\frac{1,185}{1,342}\right)^{1/2} - 1 = -6.0\%$$

Between 20X4 and 20X5 = (1,185 − 1,335)/1,335 = −11.2%.

Oden Co average financing cost

20X3: 23/(365 + 88) = 5.1%
20X4: 27/(368 + 90) = 5.9%
20X5: 35/(360 + 98) = 7.6%

Share price changes	20X2–20X3	20X3–20X4	20X4–20X5
Oden Co	19.0%	−4.0%	−8.3%
T&L sector	15.8%	−2.3%	12.1%

Oden Co			
Return to shareholders (RTS)	20X3	20X4	20X5
Dividend yield	7.2%	8.3%	6.8%
Share price gain	19.0%	−4.0%	−8.3%
Total	26.2%	4.3%	−1.5%
Average: 9.7%			
Required return (based on capital asset pricing model (CAPM))	13.0%	13.6%	16.0%
Average: 14.2%			

T&L sector (RTS)	20X3	20X4	20X5
Dividend yield	6.6%	6.7%	6.4%
Share price gain	15.8%	−2.3%	12.1%
Total shareholder return	22.4%	4.4%	18.5%
Average: 15.1%			
Required return (based on CAPM)	12.4%	13.0%	13.6%
Average: 13.0%			

> **Tutorial Note**
>
> Dividend yield, when calculated as part of total shareholder return, is normally calculated as current dividend ÷ **closing** share price of the **previous** year. This is not the case in the calculations shown here because the closing share price is not given (the share price given is the average share price for the year) but a calculation based on the previous year share price would be acceptable in the exam.

Discussion

The following discussion compares the performance of Oden Co over time to the T&L sector and against expectations, in terms of it being a sound investment. It also considers the wider aspects which Chawan Co should take account of and the further information which the company should consider before coming to a final decision.

In terms of Oden Co's performance between 20X3 and 20X5, it is clear from the calculations above that the company is experiencing considerable financial difficulties. Profit margins have fallen and so has the earnings per share (EPS). While the amount of gearing appears fairly stable, the interest cover has deteriorated. The reason for this is that borrowing costs have increased from an average of 5.1% to an average of 7.6% over the three years. The share price has decreased over the three years as well and in the last year so has the dividend yield. This would indicate that the company is unable to maintain adequate returns for its investors (please also see below).

Although Oden Co has tried to maintain a dividend yield which is higher than the sector average, its price/earnings (P/E) ratio has been lower than the sector average between 20X3 and 20X4. It does increase significantly in 20X5, but this is because of the large fall in the EPS, rather than an increase in the share price. This could be an indication that there is less confidence in the future prospects of Oden Co, compared to the rest of the T&L sector. This is further corroborated by the higher dividend yield which may indicate that the company has fewer value-creating projects planned in the future. Finally, whereas the T&L sector's average share price seems to have recovered strongly in 20X5, following a small fall in 20X4, Oden Co's share price has not followed suit and the decline has gathered pace in 20X5. It would seem that Oden Co is a poor performer within its sector.

This view is further strengthened by comparing the actual returns to the required returns based on the capital asset pricing model (CAPM). Both the company and the T&L sector produced returns exceeding the required return in 20X3 and Oden Co experienced a similar decline to the sector in 20X4. However, in 20X5, the T&L sector appears to have recovered but Oden Co's performance has worsened. This has resulted in Oden Co's actual average returns being significantly below the required returns between 20X2 and 20X5.

Taking the above into account, the initial recommendation is for Chawan Co to dispose of its investment in Oden Co. However, there are three important caveats which should be considered before the final decision is made.

The first caveat is that Chawan Co should look at the balance of its portfolio of investments. A sale of $58 million worth of equity shares within a portfolio total of $360 million may cause the portfolio to become unbalanced and for unsystematic risk to be introduced into the portfolio. Presumably, the purpose of maintaining a balanced portfolio is to virtually eliminate unsystematic risk by ensuring that it is well diversified. Chawan Co may want to reinvest the proceeds from the sale of Oden Co (if it decides to proceed with the disposal) in other equity shares within the same sector to ensure that the portfolio remains balanced and diversified.

The second caveat is that Chawan Co may want to look into the rumours of a takeover bid of Oden Co and assess how realistic it is that this will happen. If there is a realistic chance that such a bid may happen soon, Chawan Co may want to hold onto its investment in Oden Co for the present time. This is because takeover bids are made at a premium and the return to Chawan Co may increase if Oden Co is sold during the takeover.

The third caveat is that Chawan Co may want to consider Oden Co's future prospects. The calculations above are based on past performance between 20X2 and 20X5 and indicate an increasingly poor performance. However, the economy is beginning to recover, albeit slowly and erratically. Chawan Co may want to consider how well placed Oden Co is to take advantage of the improving conditions compared to other companies in the same industrial sector.

If Chawan Co decides that none of the caveats materially affect Oden Co's poor performance and position, then it should dispose of its investment in Oden Co.

5 High K

> **Workbook references.** Analysis of financial strategy is covered in Chapter 2 of the Workbook.
>
> **Easy marks.** The ratio analysis required here should have been a source of easy marks.
>
> **Examining team's comments.** The performance of candidates who attempted this question was good. Sometimes candidates merely stated that a ratio/trend was increasing or decreasing, without attempting to address why this may be happening.

Marking scheme

		Marks
(a)	**Ratios**	
	Profitability	1–2
	Liquidity	1
	Solvency	1–2
	Investor	3–4
	Other ratios and trends	2–3
		Max 10
	Discussion	
	Profitability	2–3
	Liquidity	1–2
	Gearing	1–2
	Investor	2–3
	Stores and online sales	3–4
	Conclusion	1–2
		Max 11
(b)	1 mark per relevant point	Max 4
		<u>25</u>

(a)   Profitability

Revenues from the different types of store and online sales have all increased this year, despite a drop in store numbers. The increase in revenue this year may be largely due, however, to the government-induced pre-election boom in consumer expenditure, which appears unlikely to be sustained. Because the split of profits is not given, it is impossible to tell what has been the biggest contributor to increased profit. Profit as well as revenue details for different types of store would be helpful, also profit details for major product lines.

Improvements in return on capital employed derive from increases in profit margins and asset turnover.

The improvements in gross margins may be due to increased pressure being put on suppliers, in which case they may not be sustainable because of government pressure. The increased sales per store employee figures certainly reflects a fall in staff numbers, improving operating profit, although it could also be due to staff being better utilised or increased sales of higher value items in larger stores. If staff numbers continue to be cut, however, this could result in poorer service to customers, leading ultimately to decreased sales, so again it is questionable how much further High K Co can go.

The asset turnover shows an improvement which partly reflects the increase in sales. There have been only limited movements in the portfolio of the larger stores last year. The fall in non-current assets suggests an older, more depreciated, asset base. If there is no significant investment, this will mean a continued fall in capital employed and improved asset turnover. However, in order to maintain their appeal to customers, older stores will need to be refurbished and there is no information about refurbishment plans. Information about recent impairments in asset values would also be helpful, as these may indicate future trading problems and issues with realising values of assets sold.

Liquidity

The current ratio has improved, although the higher cash balances have been partly reflected by higher current liabilities. The increase in current liabilities may be due to a deliberate policy of taking more credit from suppliers, which the government may take measures to prevent. Being forced to pay suppliers sooner will reduce cash available for short-term opportunities.

Gearing

The gearing level in 20Y6 is below the 20Y4 level, but it would have fallen further had a fall in debt not been partly matched by a fall in High K Co's share price. It seems surprising that High K Co's debt levels fell during 20Y6 at a time of lower interest rates. Possibly lenders were (rightly) sceptical about whether the cut in central bank lending rate would be sustained and limited their fixed rate lending. Interest cover improved in 20Y6 and will improve further if High K Co makes use of revolving credit facilities. However, when High K Co's loans come up for renewal, terms available may not be as favourable as those High K Co has currently.

Investors

The increase in after-tax profits in 20Y5 and 20Y6 has not been matched by an increase in share price, which has continued to fall. The price/earnings ratio has been falling from an admittedly artificially high level, and the current level seems low despite earnings and dividends being higher. The stock market does not appear convinced by High K Co's current strategy. Return to shareholders in 20Y6 has continued to rise, but this has been caused by a significant % increase in dividend and hence increase in dividend yield. The continued fall in share price after the year end suggests that investors are sceptical about whether this increase can be maintained.

Revenue analysis

Town centre stores

High K Co has continued to close town centre stores, but closures have slowed recently and revenue increased in 20Y6. This suggests High K Co may have selected wisely in choosing which stores to keep open, although Dely Co believes there is no future for this type of store. Arguably though, town centre stores appeal to some customers who cannot easily get to out-of-town stores. Town centre stores may also be convenient collection points for customers using online click and collect facilities.

Convenience stores

High K Co has invested heavily in these since 20X3. The figures in 20Y4 suggest it may have over-extended itself or possibly suffered from competitive pressures and saturation of the market. The 20Y6 results show an improvement despite closures of what may have been the worst-performing stores. The figures suggest Dely Co's decision to close its convenience stores may be premature, possibly offering High K Co the opportunity to take over some of its outlets. Maintaining its convenience store presence would also seem to be in line with High K Co's commitment to be responsive to customer needs. Profitability figures would be particularly helpful here, to assess the impact of rental commitments under leases.

Out-of-town stores

Although the revenue per store for out-of-town stores has shown limited improvement in 20Y6, this is less than might have been expected. The recent consumer boom would have been expected to benefit the out-of-town stores particularly, because expenditure on the larger items which they sell is more likely to be discretionary expenditure by consumers which will vary with the business cycle. Where Dely Co sites its new out-of-town stores will also be a major issue for High K Co, as it may find some of its best-performing stores face more competition. High K Co again may need to consider significant refurbishment expenditure to improve the look of these stores and customer experience in them.

Online sales

Online sales have shown steady growth over the last few years, but it is difficult to say how impressive High K Co's performance is. Comparisons with competitors would be particularly important here, looking at how results have changed over the years compared with the level of investment made. It is also impossible to tell from the figures how much increases in online sales have been at the expense of store sales.

Conclusion

If High K Co's share price is to improve, investors need it to make some sort of definite decision about strategy the way its competitors have since its last year end. What the chief executive has been saying about flexibility and keeping a varied portfolio has not convinced investors. If High K Co is to maintain its competitive position, it may well have no choice but to make a significant further investment in online operations. Possibly as well it could review where its competitor is closing convenience stores, as it may be able to open, with limited investment, new stores in locations with potential.

However, it also must decide what to do about the large out-of-town stores, as their performance is already stagnating and they are about to face enhanced competition. High K Co will also need to determine its dividend policy, with maybe a level of dividend which is considered the minimum acceptable to shareholders allowed for in planning cash outflows.

Appendix

	20Y4	20Y5	20Y6
Profitability			
Gross profit %	4.33	5.07	6.19
Operating profit %	0.87	1.70	2.91
Asset turnover (sales revenue/(total assets – current liabilities))	2.36	2.42	2.53
Return on capital employed % (operating profit % × asset turnover)	2.05	4.11	7.36
Liquidity			
Current ratio	0.84	1.29	1.69
Solvency			
Gearing (non-current liabilities/non-current liabilities + share capital)			
(Market values of share capital) %	37.6	36.8	32.5
Interest cover	1.63	3.54	7.12
Investors			
Dividend cover	0.35	1.29	1.71
Price/earnings ratio	54.46	12.15	5.52

	20Y4	20Y5	20Y6
Return to shareholders			
Dividend yield %	5.30	6.36	10.60
Share price gain/(loss) %	(9.00)	(5.65)	(3.29)
Total	(3.70)	0.71	7.31
Revenue/store ($m)			
Town centre	31.91	33.05	33.93
Convenience	5.41	5.66	5.99
Out-of-town	46.45	46.16	46.46
Store revenue per store staff member ($'000)	247	258	272

Note. Credit will be given for alternative relevant calculations and discussion. Candidates are not expected to complete all of the calculations or evaluation above to obtain the available marks.

(b)   High K Co has not raised any equity finance over the last five years. Its falling share price means that a new share issue may not be successful. It may not only need debt finance to be renewed, but additional funding to be obtained.

High K Co intends to make more use of revolving credit facilities, which it need not draw on fully, rather than loans, which will mean that its finance costs are lower than on ordinary debt. However, these facilities are likely to be at floating rates, so if the government increases the central bank rate significantly, they could come at significant cost if High K Co decides to utilise them fully.

Finance costs on new debt, whatever form it takes, may therefore be significant and lower interest cover. High K Co may have to investigate selling some of the stores it owns either outright or on a sale or leaseback basis.

6 Tillinton

Workbook references. Analysis of financial strategy is covered in Chapter 2 of the Workbook.

Easy marks. The ratio analysis required here should have been a source of easy marks. Part (b) is also relatively straightforward in terms of applying knowledge of behavioural finance theory.

Examining team's comments. Every candidate should have aimed for the 10 marks available on the calculations as they are relatively easily earned. As only a mark is typically awarded for a ratio calculation, candidates who calculated well in excess of 10 ratios have done extra work without gaining more calculation marks. Equally, some answers produced only a few ratios or did not examine the full trend. Doing so, meant they obtained fewer marks than were available here. Some answers simply showed a percentage or figure without any workings at all. This meant that it is often difficult for markers to see how the ratio was arrived at. Therefore, own figure rule (OFR marks) cannot be awarded when the same mistake is applied to calculating another related ratio. It is also disappointing to see answers which used the wrong formulae to calculate basic ratios particularly, the return on capital employed, asset turnover, current ratio, gearing and price/earnings. Or mixed up dividend yield with payout ratio. These ratios and their interpretation are considered as assumed knowledge from the applied skills level.

Answers which interpreted and discussed the ratios calculated with reference to the question scenario and provided insight scored high marks. However, all too often, answers earned very few or no marks for the evaluation aspect as they merely described the increases and/or decreases in ratios and trends over the three-year period without further analysis.

In part (b) candidates were asked to discuss how behavioural factors may have affected the company's higher than expected share price. There were some excellent answers suggesting that these candidates may have read the AFM technical article published on this topic area.

Marks

(a) **Ratios**

Profitability	2–3
Liquidity	1
Solvency	1–2
Investor	3–4
Other ratios and trends	2–3
	Max 10

Discussion

Profitability	3–4
Liquidity	2–3
Solvency	2–3
Investor	2–3
Conclusion	2–3
	Max 10

(b) Up to 2 marks per relevant point   Max 5

25

(a) **Profitability**

Tillinton Co's chief executive is correct in saying that the absolute increase in revenue and gross profits on all products was greater in 20X3 than 20X2, but the % increase in revenue was smaller on all products, and the % increase in gross profit on toys was also lower. The % increase on the electronic toys shows the biggest fall, possibly indicating greater competition.

The improvements in operations mentioned by the chief executive seem to have maintained gross and operating profit margins and resulted in the absolute overall increases in gross and operating profits. However, this aspect of performance is almost all attributable to Tillinton Co's older products. The gross profit on electronic toys has hardly increased and the gross profit margin has fallen over the last two years. Although the margin remains higher than on the other products, even the 20X3 margin may not be sustainable. If competitors are starting to catch up with Tillinton Co, then the profit margin on the current range of electronic toys may continue to fall in future years, as prices fall to maintain market share.

Despite the emphasis on developing the products, the revenue generated by electronic toys is still below the revenue generated by non-electronic toys.

Asset turnover and return on capital employed have risen significantly over the last two years. However, part of the reason for the 20X3 increases was the significant increase in current liabilities. The further amount of investment which the chief executive appears to be contemplating suggests that asset turnover and return on capital employed may fall in future years, particularly if profit margins on electronic toys cannot be sustained.

Liquidity

The figures for other current assets seem to support the chief executive's contention that working capital is being managed better, as other current assets are falling as revenue and gross profits are rising.

However, the fall of the current ratio from 1.52 to 0.64 is significant, and the biggest reason for the fall in 20X3 was the large increase in current liabilities. Cash balances have remained at a low level, despite higher revenues and profit. Possibly there is now a bank overdraft, which could have contributed to the significant increase in finance costs between 20X2 and 20X3. It would seem that cash reserves have been exhausted by the combination of investment in non-current assets and the payments to finance providers (both interest and dividends), and Tillinton Co is more dependent on short-term liability

BPP
LEARNING
MEDIA

finance. Slowdown in any product area, particularly electronic toys, may result in significant liquidity problems.

Solvency

Gearing has fallen over the last two years, but this is due to share price increases which may not be sustainable. If book values rather than market values are used to calculate gearing, the fall in gearing is much smaller. More information is needed about an additional $30 million in long-term loans. Although costs on these may be higher than on its current loans, this would not account for all the increase in finance costs. As discussed above, Tillinton Co may be making use of overdraft finance. The fact that current liabilities have increased much more than non-current liabilities could be an indication that Tillinton Co is having problems raising all the longer term loan finance which it requires.

The figures suggest that Tillinton Co's board needs to review future financing carefully if the company wants to make further investment in electronic products. At some stage, the board will have to consider raising further finance, either through an issue of shares or through selling off parts of its operations.

Investor ratios

Both earnings and dividends per share have risen since 20X1, which could help explain the significant increase in share price. Dividend cover has remained around 2.0 despite an increase in earnings. Although dividends have increased, dividend yield has fallen since 20X1. The increase in total shareholder return is due solely to the increases in share price, which have also resulted in the price-earnings ratio increasing in 20X3. The current rate of share price increase does not appear to be warranted by the most recent results and may be partly due to generous dividend levels, which may not be sustainable if more cash is required for investment.

Conclusion

Despite the chief executive's optimistic message in the annual report, the benefits from the electronic toys development may be short-lived. There appears to be a mismatch between investment, dividend and financing policies. As discussed, margins on current products may fall further and there is no guarantee that margins on new electronic toys or other products will be higher if competition generally is increasing.

Further significant investment in electronic toys or other goods may be difficult to finance. Increased reliance on short-term finance is clearly not sustainable, but obtaining more debt may be problematic, particularly if gearing levels rise as share prices fall. Tillinton Co seems reluctant to take advantage of high share price levels to issue equity capital. This, plus the increase in dividends, may indicate Tillinton Co's board is unwilling to risk upsetting shareholders, despite the large increases in share price. The chief executive may be right in saying that funds may have to be obtained by selling off one of the other parts of the business, but revenue and profits from the older products may be more sustainable. An increased concentration on electronic products may be a high-risk strategy. Possibly, if investors become less positive towards the electronic goods sector, they may realise this, resulting in an increase in cost of capital and a fall in share price.

Note. Credit will be given for relevant, alternative approaches to the calculations and discussion.

Appendix

	20X1	20X2	20X3
Profitability			
% increase in revenue		18.1	17.0
Gross profit %	27.5	27.6	27.6
% increase in gross profit		18.4	17.1
Operating profit %	14.8	15.4	15.7
% increase in operating profit		22.9	19.0
Asset turnover (revenue/(total assets − current liabilities))	0.65	0.73	0.81
Return on capital employed %			
(operating profit % × asset turnover)	9.6	11.2	12.7

	20X1	20X2	20X3
Liquidity			
Current ratio	1.52	1.15	0.64
Solvency			
Gearing % (non-current liabilities/(non-current liabilities + market value of share capital))	29.4	25.8	22.0
Gearing % (non-current liabilities/(non-current liabilities + book value of share capital + reserves))	43.3	43.0	42.2
Interest cover	4.5	5.0	4.5
Investors			
Earnings per share ($)	0.15	0.19	0.21
Dividend per share ($)	0.075	0.09	0.105
Dividend cover	1.98	2.10	2.01
Market price per $0.50 share	2.76	3.49	4.44
Price/earnings ratio	18.4	18.4	21.1
Dividend yield % (dividend per share/share price)	2.72	2.58	2.36
Share price gain/(loss) %	10.40	26.45	27.22
Total shareholder return %	13.12	29.03	29.58
Types of product			
Electronic toys			
% increase in revenue		28.1	22.3
Gross profit %	40.2	35.1	29.0
% increase in gross profit		12.0	1.0
Other toys			
% increase in revenue		15.9	15.4
Gross profit %	23.8	25.1	26.0
% increase in gross profit		22.2	19.3
Clothing			
% increase in revenue		15.9	15.8
Gross profit %	25.1	26.0	27.7
% Increase in gross profit		20.1	23.5

Note. Credit will be given for alternative, relevant, calculations and discussion. Candidates will not be expected to complete all the calculations above to obtain 10 marks.

(b) Tillinton Co's shares may be overvalued because share prices generally are too high. The situation may be a stock market bubble. Share prices have been rising consistently recently and this could be encouraging investors to buy more shares, further increasing share prices.

The bubble could be more localised. Tillinton Co seems to be positioning itself as much in terms of producing technologically-advanced electronic products as manufacturing toys. The electronic goods sector may be more likely than other sectors to attract investors on the basis of future profit potential, with investors possibly following a herd instinct, investing because others have been investing in the expectation of future gains.

Possibly, investors are more persuaded by the chairman's confident language and future promises than they are by the concerns the figures suggest. They may also be paying excessive attention to the most recent set of results, rather than seeing them in the context of whether they can be sustained in the future.

If investors are attempting to make a valuation, they could prefer using a model which confirms what they believe the shares are worth (confirmation bias), rather than one which gives a more reliable indication of value. As discussed above, shareholders may be basing their estimates of value on the recent increases in dividend, even though it may be doubtful whether this is sustainable.

7 Limni Co

Marking scheme

			Marks
(a)	Evaluation of dividend policy	1–2	
	Evaluation of financing policy	3–4	
	Evaluation of risk management policy	1–2	
	Effect of dividends and share buybacks on the policies	2–3	
			Max 8
(b)	2 marks per evaluation of each of the three companies	6	
	Discussion of which company to invest in	2	
			8
(c)	Calculation of initial dividend capacity	3	
	Calculation of new repatriation amount	2	
	Comment	1–2	
			Max 6
(d)	1 mark per relevant point		Max 3
			25

(a) **Dividend policy**

Many high-growth companies, such as Limni Co, retain cash instead of paying dividends and use the cash to help fund the growth. Many such companies declare an intention not to pay dividends and as such the shareholders expect their wealth to increase through **capital gains** rather than dividend payments.

Financing

Capital structure theory suggests that to take advantage of the tax shield on interest payments, companies should have a capital structure which is a mixture of debt and equity. **Pecking order theory** suggests that companies typically use internally generated funds before seeking to raise external funds (initially debt, then equity). The two main factors in deterring companies from seeking external finance are **favouring one investor group at the expense of another** and the agency effect of providing additional information to the market.

Limni Co is following the pecking order theory to the extent that it is using internally generated funds first. However, it is then deviating from pecking order theory in looking to raise equity finance rather than debt even though it currently has insignificant levels of debt and is therefore not making full use of the tax shield. This may be explained by the fact that Limni Co operates in a **high-risk, rapidly changing industry**, where business risk is high. It may not want to take on **high levels of financial risk** by using significant levels of debt finance. Other issues such as potentially restrictive debt covenant may also be a factor in the financing decision.

Risk management

Managing the volatility of cash flows enables a company to plan its investment strategy more accurately. Limni Co needs to ensure that it will have **sufficient internally generated cash available when it is needed** for planned investments. More importantly, since Limni Co faces high levels of business risk, as discussed above, the company should look to manage the risks that are beyond the individual control of the company's managers.

Effect on policies by returning funds to shareholders

Returning funds to shareholders will affect each of these policies. The shareholder clientele could change, which may lead to share price fluctuations. However, since the change is being requested by shareholders, there is a good chance that this may not happen. The financing policy is likely to change since there will be less internally generated funds available, so Limni Co may consider taking on additional debt finance and therefore will have to look at the balance of business and financial risk. This could in turn change the risk management policy as interest rate risk will also have to be managed as well.

(b) **Theta**

Company Theta has a **fixed dividend payout ratio of 40%**. As a result the increase in dividends in recent years depends on the increase in profit after tax in these years rather than increasing at a steady rate, which is often preferred by shareholders. If profit after tax was to fall, Theta may reduce its dividend, which could send the wrong signals to shareholders and cause significant fluctuations in the share price. To avoid this, Theta may keep a stable dividend in years of reduced profits.

Omega

Company Omega has a policy of **increasing dividends at approximately 5% per year**, but earnings are only increasing at a rate of approximately 3% per year. This means the **dividend payout ratio is increasing**; it was 60% in 20X3 and is 65% in 20X7. Although this cannot continue in the long term, it suggests that there are less investment opportunities currently and Omega is reducing its retention ratio. This investment would be attractive to an investor looking for a high level of dividend income.

Kappa

Company Kappa has increased its payout ratio from 20% in 20X3 to 27% in 20X7. This is a fairly low payout ratio, but it is growing. **Earnings are growing rapidly** overall, but not at a constant annual rate (35% growth in 20X4, but only 3% in 20X5). Overall dividend growth is at a rate of 29% per year, and the annual dividend growth rate has been fairly constant. This policy seems consistent with a **growing company**, which is now **starting to pay more significant dividends** and return more funds to shareholders. This investment would be attractive to investors seeking a lower level of dividend income and higher levels of capital growth.

Due to uncertainty about whether Theta could decrease its future dividend payments, Limni Co is likely to prefer to invest in either Omega or Kappa. The choice between these two depends on whether Limni Co would **prefer higher dividends or higher capital growth**. Issues such as taxation position or length of time that the funds would be invested for may influence this choice too.

(c) **Current dividend capacity**

		$'000
Profit before tax	(23% × $600m)	138,000
Tax	(26% × $138m)	(35,880)
Profit after tax		102,120
Add back depreciation	(25% × 220m)	55,000
Less investment in assets		(67,000)
Overseas remittances		15,000
Additional tax	(6% × 15m)	(900)
Dividend capacity		104,220

Increase in dividend capacity = 104.22m × 0.1 = $10.422m

Gross up to allow for extra 6% tax = $10.422m/0.94 = $11,087,234

Percentage increase in remittances needed = (11,087,234/15,000,000) × 100% = 73.9%

Dividend repatriations would need to increase by approximately $11.1 million or 73.9% in order to increase dividend capacity by 10%. Limni Co needs to consider both whether this is **possible** for the subsidiaries and the **motivational and operational impact** of doing so on the subsidiaries.

(d) The main benefit of a share buyback scheme to a shareholder is that they can choose whether or not to sell their shares back to the company. This means they **can control the amount of cash they receive and in turn manage their own tax liability**. With dividend payments, especially with large special dividends, there may be a large tax liability as a result. Further benefits include the fact that, as share capital is reduced, the **earnings per share figure is likely to increase and share price may increase** too. Additionally share buybacks are often viewed positively by the markets and share price may increase.

8 Arthuro

Workbook references. Dividend capacity is covered in Chapter 1.

Top tips. The bulk of the marks relate to calculations in this question therefore it is important to show clear your workings. Add brief narrative where appropriate to explain your approach to the marker.

Easy marks. There are several easy marks to be gained in part (a) – for example, calculating operating profit, interest and tax. Part (b) is a straightforward discussion of benefits and problems.

Examining team's comments. In part (a) candidates were asked to calculate the dividend capacity of a company (based on free cash to equity method), and how much the subsidiary company would need to provide given an increase in the number of shares due to a rights issue. Only a minority of responses provided the correct answer for the initial dividend capacity. Common errors included not deducting interest before calculating the tax liability, errors in adding profit from sale of assets, cash received from sale of assets, investment in new assets and the remittances from the subsidiary company. Many responses were poorly presented and lacked evidence of a coherent approach. Because of this, very few candidates were able to calculate how much additional profits the subsidiary company would need to provide, in part (a)(ii).

In part (b), many candidates failed to recognise that companies face agency issues beyond just between shareholders and company's directors. Agency issues can also occur, for example, between debt holders and the company, or in this case, between the directorate of a subsidiary company and the directorate of the parent company.

Marking scheme

				Marks
(a)	(i)	Calculation of operating profit, interest and domestic tax	3	
		Depreciation	1	
		Profit on disposal of no-current assets and cash from disposal	2	
		Investment in new non-current assets	2	
		Investment in working capital	1	
		Calculation of dividend remittance from Bowerscots	1	
		Calculation of additional tax payable on Bowerscots profits	1	
				11
	(ii)	Dividend capacity required	1	
		Increase in dividend remittance	1	
		Revised dividend required (% or absolute amount)	1	
				3
(b)	(i)	Benefits of new policy	2–3	
		Problems of new policy	2–3	
				Max 5
	(ii)	Agency problems	3–4	
		Solutions to problems	3–4	
				Max 6
				25

(a) (i) Forecast dividend capacity is as follows:

	$'000
Operating profit (20% × 1.04 × $520m)	108,160
Less: Interest (8% × $135m)	(10,800)
	$'000
Less: Taxation (30% × ($108.16m – $10.8m))	(29,208)
Add: Depreciation	30,000
Less: Profit on disposal of NCA	(5,900)
Add: Cash received on disposal of NCA (W1)	16,300
Less: Investment in new NCA (W2)	(44,800)
Less: Investment in working capital (15% × 0.04 × $520m)	(3,120)
Add: Dividend remittance from Bowerscots Co (W3)	20,520
Less: Additional tax on Bowerscots Co's profits (10% × $45m)	(4,500)
Forecast dividend capacity	76,652

Workings

1 *Disposal of non-current assets*

	$'000
Profit on disposal	5,900
Cost	35,000
Less: Depreciation	(24,600)
Cash received on disposal	16,300

2   *Investment in non-current assets*

	$'000
Net book value at end of most recent year (start of 'normal' year)	110,000
Less: Depreciation in 'normal' year	(30,000)
Less: Net book value of assets disposed ($35m – $24.6m)	(10,400)
Net book value before investment in non-current assets	69,600
Required level of non-current assets ($110m × 1.04)	114,400
Investment in non-current assets	44,800

3   *Dividend remittance from Bowerscots*

	$'000
Profit before tax	45,000
Less: Tax at 20%	(9,000)
Profit after tax	36,000
Remitted to Arthuro Co (36,000 × 60% × 0.95)	20,520

(ii)   Dividend capacity required = (90 × 4/3)m × $0.74 = $88.8m

Increase in dividend remittances required = $88.8m – $76.652m = $12.148m

Total dividend remittance required = ($20.52m + $12.148m)/0.95 = $34.387m

Distribution % required = ($34.387m/$36m) × 100% = 95.5%

(b)   (i)   **Benefits of policy**

The change of policy appears to be viable. Arthuro Co would have had some slack if it had not undertaken the rights issue. The new policy takes up this slack and effectively tops up the amount required with an increase in dividends.

The new policy appears to ensure that Arthuro Co will have sufficient funds to pay the required level of dividends and fulfil its own investment requirements. It will mean that Bowerscots Co has less retained funds available for investment, but Arthuro Co's investment opportunities may be more profitable.

Problems with policy

Arthuro Co is now close to taking all of Bowerscots Co's post-tax earnings as dividends. Only a limited fall in Bowerscots Co's earnings would be needed for its dividends not to be enough to sustain Arthuro Co's dividend level. A fall could easily happen given the highly competitive environment in which Bowerscots Co operates. If Arthuro Co wanted to increase its dividends over time, it could not do so by receiving extra dividends from Bowerscots Co.

As mentioned, an increase in dividend will leave Bowerscots Co's management with less retained earnings to invest. The amount of investment they can undertake with the reduced funds available may be insufficient to sustain earnings levels and hence dividends for Arthuro Co.

The tax regime between the two countries means that the group will suffer more tax. The amount of additional tax payable by Arthuro Co on Bowerscots Co's profits will remain unchanged, but the increase in dividends will mean an increase in withholding tax, for which Arthuro Co will receive no credit. Given the lower tax rate in Owlia, for tax purposes higher retained earnings for Bowerscots Co would be preferable, possibly with funds loaned to Arthuro Co rather than paid as dividends.

(ii)   **Agency problems**

An agency situation arises between Arthuro Co's board (the principal) and Bowerscots Co's management (the agent). The proposals are likely to involve agency costs.

The policy limits the discretion of Bowerscots Co's management by restricting the amounts of retained funds available. However, this seems an inefficient way of exercising closer control, with agency costs including the increased liability for withholding tax. If Arthuro Co's board has concerns about Bowerscots Co's management, it would be better to make changes in the management team.

Even if Arthuro Co's board has confidence in Bowerscots Co's management team, it may nevertheless wish to oversee Bowerscots Co more closely, given the dependence of its dividend capacity on the amount received from the subsidiary. Again, increased supervision will involve increased agency costs in terms of time spent by Arthuro Co's management.

Bowerscots Co's management may feel that the new policy threatens their remuneration, as the limited funds available for investment will adversely affect the company's ability to maintain its profit levels. The managers may seek to join competitors, disrupting Bowerscots Co's management, jeopardising its ability to achieve its profit forecasts.

Resolving agency problems

Ways of motivating Bowerscots Co's management include making their remuneration less dependent on Bowerscots Co's results, for example, allowing them share options in Arthuro Co. If more of their remuneration depends on the group's results, Bowerscots Co's management may be happier with the suggested arrangement if they feel it will benefit the group. However, this motivational effect will be limited if Bowerscots Co's management feels that the group results are not influenced much by what they do.

Alternatively, a greater proportion of Bowerscots Co's management's remuneration could be by methods which are not dependent on its results, for example, increased salary or better benefits. However, by weakening the link between results and remuneration, it lessens their incentive to strive to produce the results needed to maintain the required level of dividend.

The decision-making on investments at group level may also have to change. Bowerscots Co will, under the new policy, have insufficient funds for major investments. Its management team should have the opportunity to make a case for retaining a greater percentage of funds, as they may have better investment opportunities than those available to the parent.

9 Lamri

Workbook references. Dividend capacity is covered in Chapter 1.

Top tips. The bulk of the marks relate to calculations in this question therefore it is important to show all your workings. However, there is a lot to do for 14 marks so try to identify shortcuts where you can – for example, the cash from domestic activities both prior to and subsequent to the implementation of the proposal is the same so there is no need to calculate this twice.

Don't be afraid to state what you might think is the obvious. There are marks available for identifying the irrelevance of adjusting for depreciation so make sure you mention your reasons for not including this calculation.

In part (b) it is important to recognise that the implementation of the proposal would result in a shortfall in dividend capacity (don't forget to uplift existing dividend by 8%). By recognising this issue, you can then make suggestions as to how the problem can be overcome.

Easy marks. There are several easy marks to be gained in part (a) – for example, calculating operating profit, interest and tax. Part (c) is a straightforward discussion of mechanisms to prevent transfer price manipulation.

Examining team's comments. This question required a logical and systematic approach as a lot was being asked (particularly in part (a)). Good attempts at part (a) achieved high marks but sometimes the answers were not appropriately structured which resulted in mixed-up answers. Few appropriate answers were received for part (b) and mostly reflected the disorganised approach to part (a).

Marks

(a)	Calculation of operating profit, interest and domestic tax	3
	Calculation of investments in working capital and non-current assets (including correct treatment of depreciation)	3
	Calculation of dividend remittance before new policy implementation	2
	Calculation of additional tax payable on Magnolia profits before new policy implementation	1
	Calculation of dividend remittance after new policy implementation	3
	Calculation of additional tax payable on Magnolia profits after new policy implementation	1
	Dividend capacity	1
		14
(b)	Concluding comments and explanation of reason	2
	Possible actions (1 mark per suggestion)	4
		6
(c)	1 mark per valid point	5
		25

(a) Dividend capacity

Prior to implementing TE's proposal

	$m
Operating profit (30% of $80m)	24.00
Less interest (8% of $35m)	(2.80)
Profit before tax	21.20
Less tax (28%)	(5.94)
Profit after tax	15.26
Less investment in working capital [15% of (20/120 × $80m)]	(2.00)
Less investment in non-current assets [25% of (20/120 × $80m)]	(3.33)
Less investment in new project	(4.50)
Cash flow from domestic activities	5.43
Overseas subsidiaries dividend remittances (W1)	3.16
Less tax paid on Magnolia's profits [(28 – 22)% of $5.40m]	(0.32)
Dividend capacity	8.27

Tutorial note

There is no need to add back depreciation to obtain cash flow as the investment that amounts to the total depreciation charged will cancel out this calculation. The effect is therefore neutral.

After implementing TE's proposal

	$m
Cash flows from domestic activities (see above)	5.43
Overseas subsidiaries dividend remittances (W2)	2.71
Additional tax on Magnolia's profits (6% of $3.12m)	(0.19)
Dividend capacity	7.95

Workings

1   *Overseas subsidiaries dividend remittances prior to TE's proposal*

	Magnolia	Strymon
	$m	$m
Sales revenue	15.00	5.70
Less variable costs	(2.40)	(3.60)
Less transferred costs	(5.70)	0
Less fixed costs	(1.50)	(2.10)
Operating profit	5.40	0
Less tax	(1.19)	0
Profit after tax	4.21	0
Remitted to Lamri	(3.16)	0
Retained in company	1.05	0

2   *Overseas subsidiaries dividend remittances after implementing TE's proposal*

	Magnolia	Strymon
	$m	$m
Sales revenue	15.00	7.98
Less variable costs	(2.40)	(3.60)
Less transferred costs	(7.98)	0
Less fixed costs	(1.50)	(2.10)
Operating profit	3.12	2.28
Less tax	(0.69)	(0.96)
Profit after tax	2.43	1.32
Remitted to Lamri	(1.82)	(0.89)
Withholding tax		(0.10)
Retained in company	0.61	0.33

(b) **Comments on impact of TE's proposal**

If the proposal is implemented, Lamri's dividend capacity will fall from $8.27 million to $7.95 million. Whilst the dividend capacity prior to implementation of the proposal exceeds the dividend to be paid ($7.5m × 1.08 = $8.1m), the proposal would lead to a shortfall in dividend capacity. The shortfall arises due to the high tax rate paid on Strymon's profits that Lamri cannot obtain credit for. Not only does Lamri lose the withholding tax on the remittances (10%), it is also paying an additional 14% in corporation tax (42% − 28%).

There are several ways in which the problem of this relatively small shortfall could be overcome. Lamri might consider reducing the growth rate of its dividends to a level that would be covered by the dividend capacity of $7.95 million. However, this might send adverse signals to the market given that a steady 8% growth has been maintained over the last few years.

Another alternative would be to borrow the shortfall. This may not be a popular option if Lamri wishes to avoid increasing its borrowings, particularly to fund dividend payments. Given that it would have to borrow to fund current shortfalls, there is a possibility that this problem would continue in the future, leading to even greater borrowings or the potential of having to reduce dividend growth.

Lamri might wish to consider postponing the project to a later date but the potential impact on company business would have to be evaluated. We are told in the scenario that a number of projects are in the pipeline for the future. Therefore postponing a current investment may not be feasible without impacting on future investments.

The final possibility would be to ask for a higher remittance from Strymon or Magnolia. The main problem with this would be the potential negative impact on morale of the subsidiaries' managers if they are required to pay over greater proportions of their profits (which may affect any profit-related benefits they may have).

BPP
LEARNING
MEDIA

(c) Transfer price manipulation is said to occur where Lamri uses transfer prices to avoid payment of taxes and tariffs, or other controls that the government of the host country has put in place.

The most common solution that tax authorities have adopted to reduce the probability of transfer price manipulation is to develop particular transfer pricing regulations as part of the corporate income tax code. These regulations are generally based on the concept of the arm's length standard, which states that all intra-firm activities of Lamri should be priced as if they took place between unrelated parties acting at arm's length in a competitive market.

The arm's length standard is defined as the prices which would have been agreed upon between unrelated parties engaged in the same or similar transactions under the same or similar conditions in the open market. In the absence of the existence of data to allow a reasonable estimate of the arm's length standard then the alternative methods used to establish the arm's length transfer price include:

(i) **Comparable uncontrolled price**

This method looks for a comparable product to the transaction in question being traded by Lamri in a comparable transaction with an unrelated party or the same or similar product being traded between two unrelated parties.

(ii) **Resale price method**

This method focuses on one side of the transaction, either the manufacturer or distributor, to estimate the transfer price using a functional approach.

(iii) **Cost plus method**

This method starts with the costs of production, measured using recognised accounting principles and then adds an appropriate mark-up over costs. The appropriate mark-up is estimated from those earned by similar manufacturers.

(iv) **Profit split method**

This method allocates the profit earned on a transaction between related parties.

10 Moonstar

> **Workbook references.** Securitisation is covered in Chapter 16, Islamic finance in Chapter 7, and interest rate swaps in Chapter 14.
>
> **Top tips.** It is important to review the articles on the ACCA website in the lead up to the exam; these often signal that a topic is likely to be tested. An article on securitisation appeared on the ACCA website shortly before this exam sitting.
>
> **Easy marks.** There are a few easy marks to be picked up in part (c) but only if you have a good working knowledge of this area.

Marking scheme

		Marks
(a)	Calculation of receivable	1
	Loan note amounts attributable to the A, B and C tranches	1
	Impact of swap	2
	Calculation of interest payable on interest for tranches A-, B- and C-rated tranches	3
	Estimation of return to subordinated certificates	1
	Comments and calculation relating to sensitivity	3
		11

(b) Benefits of securitisation   3–4
     Risks associated with securitisation   2–3
                                                                          Max 6

(c) (i)   Explanation/discussion of suitability of Sukuk finance   2–3
           Discussion of investors' views   1–2
                                                                          Max 4

     (ii) Explanation/discussion of suitability of Mudaraba contract   2–3
           Discussion of bank's views   1–2
                                                                          Max 4
                                                                            25

(a) An annual cash flow account compares the estimated cash flows receivable from the
     property against the liabilities within the securitisation process. The swap introduces
     leverage into the arrangement.

Cash flow receivable	$m	Cash flow payable	$m
$200m × 11%	22.00	A-rated loan notes	
Less service charge	(0.20)	Pay $108m (W1) × 11% (W2)	11.88
		B-rated loan notes	
		Pay $27m (W1) × 12%	3.24
		C-rated loan notes	
		Pay $27m (W1) × 13%	3.51
	21.80		18.63
		Balance to the subordinated certificates	3.17

Workings

1	Loan notes		$m
	A	$200m × 0.9 × 0.6	108
	B	$200m × 0.9 × 0.15	27
	C	$200m × 0.9 × 0.15	27

2	Swap	
	Pay fixed rate under swap	9.5%
	Pay floating rate	LIBOR + 1.5%
	Receive floating rate under swap	(LIBOR)
	Net payment	11%

The holders of the certificates are expected to receive $3.17 million on $18 million, giving
them a return of 17.6%. If the cash flows are 5% lower than the non-executive director has
predicted, annual revenue received will fall to $20.90 million, reducing the balance
available for the subordinated certificates to $2.07 million, giving a return of 11.5% on the
subordinated certificates, which is below the returns offered on the B- and C-rated loan
notes. The point at which the holders of the certificates will receive nothing and below
which the holders of the C-rated loan notes will not receive their full income will be an
annual income of $18.83 million (a return of 9.4%), which is 14.4% less than the income that
the non-executive director has forecast.

(b) **Benefits**

The finance costs of the securitisation may be lower than the finance costs of ordinary loan
capital. The cash flows from the commercial property development may be regarded as
lower risk than Moonstar Co's other revenue streams. This will impact upon the rates that
Moonstar Co is able to offer borrowers.

The securitisation matches the assets of the future cash flows to the liabilities to loan note
holders. The non-executive director is assuming a steady stream of lease income over the

next ten years, with the development probably being close to being fully occupied over that period.

The securitisation means that Moonstar Co is no longer concerned with the risk that the level of earnings from the properties will be insufficient to pay the finance costs. Risks have effectively been transferred to the loan note holders.

Risks

Not all of the tranches may appeal to investors. The risk-return relationship on the subordinated certificates does not look very appealing, with the return quite likely to be below what is received on the C-rated loan notes. Even the C-rated loan note holders may question the relationship between the risk and return if there is continued uncertainty in the property sector.

If Moonstar Co seeks funding from other sources for other developments, transferring out a lower risk income stream means that the residual risks associated with the rest of Moonstar Co's portfolio will be higher. This may affect the availability and terms of other borrowing.

It appears that the size of the securitisation should be large enough for the costs to be bearable. However, Moonstar Co may face unforeseen costs, possibly unexpected management or legal expenses.

(c)   (i)   Sukuk finance could be appropriate for the securitisation of the leasing portfolio. An asset-backed Sukuk would be the same kind of arrangement as the securitisation, where assets are transferred to a special purpose vehicle and the returns and repayments are directly financed by the income from the assets. The Sukuk holders would bear the risks and returns of the relationship.

         The other type of Sukuk would be more like a sale and leaseback of the development. Here the Sukuk holders would be guaranteed a rental, so it would seem less appropriate for Moonstar Co if there is significant uncertainty about the returns from the development.

         The main issue with the asset-backed Sukuk finance is whether it would be as appealing as certainly the A-tranche of the securitisation arrangement which the non-executive director has proposed. The safer income that the securitisation offers A-tranche investors may be more appealing to investors than a marginally better return from the Sukuk. There will also be costs involved in establishing and gaining approval for the Sukuk, although these costs may be less than for the securitisation arrangement described above.

   (ii)   A Mudaraba contract would involve the bank providing capital for Moonstar Co to invest in the development. Moonstar Co would manage the investment which the capital funded. Profits from the investment would be shared with the bank, but losses would be solely borne by the bank. A Mudaraba contract is essentially an equity partnership, so Moonstar Co might not face the threat to its credit rating which it would if it obtained ordinary loan finance for the development. A Mudaraba contract would also represent a diversification of sources of finance. It would not require the commitment to pay interest that loan finance would involve.

         Moonstar Co would maintain control over the running of the project. A Mudaraba contract would offer a method of obtaining equity funding without the dilution of control which an issue of shares to external shareholders would bring. This is likely to make it appealing to Moonstar Co's directors, given their desire to maintain a dominant influence over the business.

         The bank would be concerned about the uncertainties regarding the rental income from the development. Although the lack of involvement by the bank might appeal to Moonstar Co's directors, the bank might not find it so attractive. The bank might be concerned about information asymmetry – that Moonstar Co's management might be reluctant to supply the bank with the information it needs to judge how well its investment is performing.

11 Preparation question: Cathlynn

Workbook references. Chapter 4.

Top tips. If you can work your way through the formula and are able to use the normal distribution table, this question is actually not that bad. In (i), we need the standard deviation, so therefore we need to take the square root of the variance which we are given in the question. We have used interpolation to find the values in (ii).

(a) (i) Find (d_1) and (d_2).

Note. Standard deviation = square root of the variance so s = $\sqrt{0.12}$ = 0.346

$$d_1 = \frac{\ln(P_a / P_e) + (r + 0.5s^2)t}{s\sqrt{t}}$$

$$d_1 = \frac{\ln(3.5 / 3.3) + (0.08 + 0.5 \times 0.346^2)0.25}{0.346\sqrt{0.25}}$$

$$d_1 = \frac{0.059 + (0.14)0.25}{0.173}$$

$$d_1 = \frac{0.094}{0.173} = 0.54$$

$$d_2 = d_1 - s\sqrt{T}$$

$$d_2 = 0.54 - \left(\sqrt{0.12}\sqrt{0.25}\right)$$

$$= 0.54 - 0.17 = 0.37$$

(ii) Find N (d_1) and N (d_2) using normal distribution tables.

N (0.54) = 0.5 + 0.2054 = 0.7054

N (0.37) = 0.5 + 0.1443 = 0.6443

(iii) Using the Black-Scholes formula:

C_0 = (3.50 × 0.7054) − ((3.30e$^{-0.08 \times 0.25}$) × 0.6443)

= 2.47 − 2.08 = 0.39

(b) The main limitations of the Black-Scholes model are:

(i) The model is **only designed** for the valuation of **European call options**.

(ii) The basic model is based on the assumption that **shares pay no dividends**.

(iii) The model assumes that there will be **no transaction costs**.

(iv) The model assumes knowledge of the **risk-free rate of interest,** and also assumes the risk-free rate will be constant throughout the option's life.

(v) Likewise the model also assumes accurate knowledge of the **standard deviation of returns,** which is also assumed to be constant throughout the option's life.

12 Preparation question: Faoilean

Marking scheme

			Marks
(a)	Discussion of the idea of using options in making the project investment decision	7–8	
	Explanation of the assumptions	3–4	
			Max 11
(b)	Discussion of using options to value equity	4–5	
	Discussion of using options to assess default risk	2–3	
	Discussion of financial distress and time value of an option	2–3	
			Max 9
(c)	Explanation of why option values are determined by different risk factors	2–3	
	Explanation of what determines 'vega'	2–3	
			Max 5
			25

(a)   Conventional investment appraisal techniques such as net present value analysis often do not capture the full strategic benefits of a project in terms of either features of a project that allow risk to be managed or features that allow further follow-on gains to be made.

For example a situation may exist where a project is easy to abandon, or uses assets that are easy to switch to another use if the project fails. This **abandonment/redeployment option** adds value to a project because it limits the project's downside risk.

With this project Faoilean Co could negotiate a get-out clause which gives it the right to **sell the project back** to the government at a later date at a pre-agreed price. Alternatively, it could build facilities in such a way that it can **redeploy** them to other activities, or scale the production up or down more easily and at less cost. These options give the company the opportunity to step out of a project at a future date, if uncertainties today become negative outcomes in the future.

Another type of real option is the **option to delay**. A project can be structured to allow a company to react to improved information about the prospects of the project eg by staggering the capital expenditure over a period of time instead of investing in one block at the start of the project.

In the situation which Faoilean Co is considering, the initial **exploration rights** may give it the **option to delay** the decision of whether to undertake the **extraction** of oil and gas to a later date. In that time, using previous knowledge and experience, it can estimate the quantity of oil and gas which is present more accurately. It can also use its knowledge to assess the variability of the likely quantity. Faoilean Co may be able to negotiate a longer timescale with the government of Ireland for undertaking the initial exploration, before it needs to make a final decision on whether and how much to extract.

Finally, some projects may create an **option to expand into other areas** using the benefit of the experience gained during the project. For example, Faoilean Co can explore whether or not applying for the rights to undertake this exploration project could give it priority in terms of future projects, perhaps due to the new knowledge or technologies it builds during the current project. These opportunities would allow it to gain competitive advantage over rivals which, in turn, could provide it with greater opportunities in the future, but which are uncertain at present.

Faoilean Co can use the Black-Scholes option valuation formulae to assess the value of any real options associated with the project. This value can be added to the conventional net present value computation to give a more accurate assessment of the project's value.

The option price formula used with investment decisions is based on the BSOP model. The BSOP model makes a number of assumptions as follows:

(i)   The option is assumed to be exercised at a specific point in time (ie a European option); this may not be true in reality eg an option to redeploy may be exercised at any time.

(ii)   The BSOP model uses the risk-free rate of interest. It is assumed that this is known and remains constant, which may not be the case where the time it takes for the option to expire is long;

(iii)   The most significant drawback of the BSOP model is the **estimation of the standard deviation** of the price of the asset. The BSOP model assumes that volatility can be assessed and stays constant throughout the life of the project; again with long-term projects these assumptions may not be valid.

(iv)   The BSOP model assumes that the underlying asset can be traded freely. This is probably not accurate where the underlying asset is an investment project.

These assumptions mean that the value based around the BSOP model is indicative and not definitive.

Note. Credit will be given for alternative relevant comments.

(b)   The value of a firm can be thought of in these terms:

(i)   If the firm fails to generate enough value to repay its loans, then its value = 0; shareholders have the **option** to let the company die at this point.

(ii)   However, if the firm does generate enough value then the extra value belongs to the shareholders and in this case shareholders can pay off the debt (this is the **exercise price**) and continue in their **ownership** of the company.

Therefore, the BSOP model can be applied because shareholders have a **call option** on the business. The protection of limited liability creates the same effect as a call option because there is an upside if the firm is successful, but shareholders lose nothing other than their initial investment if it fails. So the value of a company can be calculated as the amount that you would pay as a **premium for this call option**.

If, at expiry of the debt, the value of the company is greater than the face value of debt, then the option is in-the-money, otherwise if the value of the firm is less than the face value of debt, then the option is out-of-the-money and equity is worthless.

Prior to expiry of the debt, the call option (value to holders of equity) will also have a time value attached to it.

The BSOP model can be used to assess the value of the option to the equity holders, the value of equity, which can consist of both time value and intrinsic value if the option is in-the-money, or just time value if the option is out-of-money.

Within the BSOP model, N(d1), the delta value, shows how the value of equity changes when the value of the company's assets changes. N(d2) depicts the probability that the call option will be in-the-money (ie have intrinsic value for the equity holders).

Debt can be regarded as the debt holders writing a put option on the company's assets, where the premium is the receipt of interest when it falls due and the capital redemption. If N(d2) depicts the probability that the call option is in-the-money, then 1 – N(d2) depicts the probability of default.

Therefore the BSOP model and options are useful in determining the value of equity and default risk.

Option pricing can be used to explain why companies facing severe financial distress can still have positive equity values. A company facing severe financial distress would presumably be one where the equity holders' call option is well out-of-money and therefore has no intrinsic value. However, as long as the debt on the option is not at expiry, then that call option will still have a time value attached to it. Therefore, the positive equity value reflects the time value of the option, even where the option is out-of-money, and this will diminish as the debt comes closer to expiry. The time value indicates that even though the option is currently out-of-money, there is a possibility that due to the volatility of asset values, by the time the debt reaches maturity, the company will no longer face financial distress and will be able to meet its debt obligations.

Note. Credit will be given for alternative relevant comments.

(c) According to the BSOP model, the value of an option is dependent on five variables: the value of the underlying asset, the exercise price, the risk-free rate of interest, the implied volatility of the underlying asset, and the time to expiry of the option. These five variables are input into the BSOP formula, in order to compute the value of a call or a put option. The different risk factors determine the impact on the option value of the changes in the five variables, and collectively these are known as the 'greeks'.

In the case of a call option the option will be more valuable if:

- The exercise price is lower; or

- The value of the underlying asset, the risk-free rate of interest, the volatility, or the time period is higher.

The 'vega' determines the sensitivity of an option's value to a change in the implied volatility of the underlying asset. Implied volatility is what the market is implying the volatility of the underlying asset will be in the future. The value of an option will rise as volatility increases because it will increase the potential extent to which an option may be in-the-money which will benefit the option holder – but if an option is out-of-the-money it will simply not be exercised and therefore if the extent to which an option is out-of-the-money rises then it has no impact on the option holder. Therefore as the 'vega' increases, so will the value of the option.

Note. Credit will be given for alternative relevant comments.

13 Fernhurst

> **Workbook references.** Investment appraisal methods are covered in Chapter 3.
>
> **Top tips.** In part (a) time management will be important, there are a lot of calculations to do (tax, inflation, working capital, duration) and it will be important to move on if a particular calculation is proving to be time consuming.
>
> **Easy marks.** Parts (b) and (c) are opportunities to score strongly. Part (b) asked for a calculation (and discussion) of the sensitivity of the project to a reduction in the selling price. Good exam technique could have been employed here to deal with the only area of complexity (the 15% chance of negative cash flows in Year 1) as a brief discussion point in your answer. Part (c) required a discussion of the meaning and significance of NPV and whether short-term measures were also important. This allowed candidates to identify the important of risk and uncertainty in investment appraisal.

Marking scheme

			Marks
(a)	Sales revenue	2	
	Variable costs	2	
	Fixed costs	1	
	Tax-allowable depreciation	2	
	Tax payable	1	
	Working capital	2	
	NPV of project	1	
	Comment on NPV	1	
	Duration calculation	2	
	Comment on duration	1	
			15
(b)	Reduction in selling price	3	
	Discussion	2–3	
		Max	5
(c)	Significance of net present value	1–2	
	Shareholders' attitude to the longer and shorter term	2–3	
	Time frame measures	1–2	
		Max	5
			25

(a)

	1 $'000	2 $'000	3 $'000	4 $'000
Sales revenue (W1)	13,250	16,695	22,789	23,928
Variable costs (W2)	(5,788)	(7,292)	(9,954)	(10,452)
Contribution	7,462	9,403	12,835	13,476
Marketing expenditure	(1,500)			
Fixed costs	(900)	(945)	(992)	(1,042)
Tax-allowable depreciation (W3)	(3,200)	(2,560)	(2,048)	(8,192)
Taxable profits/(losses)	1,862	5,898	9,795	4,242

BPP
LEARNING
MEDIA

	1 $'000	2 $'000	3 $'000	4 $'000
Taxation (25%)	(466)	(1,475)	(2,449)	(1,061)
Add back tax-allowable depreciation	3,200	2,560	2,048	8,192
Cash flows after tax	4,596	6,983	9,394	11,373
Initial investment				
Working capital	(41)	(53)	(56)	1,175
Cash flows	4,555	6,930	9,338	12,548
Discount factor	0.901	0.812	0.731	0.659
Present values	4,104	5,627	6,826	8,269
Present value	24,826			

Subtracting the cash outflows at time 0 ($16,000 for non-current assets and $1,025 for working capital) gives the project NPV:

$24,826 – $16,000 – $1,025 = **$7,801**

The net present value (NPV) is positive, which indicates the project should be undertaken.

Alternative approach using spreadsheet functionality:

Alternatively, the present value of the cash flows from time 1-4 can be calculated using the =NPV spreadsheet function. Either method is acceptable, but the spreadsheet function gives a slightly more precise answer and, with practice, should be quicker to use in the exam.

The spreadsheet extract shown in the following section shows the =NPV formula being applied using the cost of capital of 11%.

D16	▼	:	×	✓	f_x	=NPV(0.11,D15:G15)			
	A	B	C	D	E	F	G	H	I
15		Cash flows		4,555	6,930	9,338	12,548		
16		NPV		24,822					
17									
18									
19									

Note that the NPV function assumes that the first cash flow is in one year's time, so you then have to subtract the time 0 cash outflows as before to give the project NPV as:

$24,822 – $16,000 – $1,025 = **$7,797**

Workings

1   *Sales revenue*

Year		$'000
1	132,500 × 100	13,250
2	132,500 × 100 × 1.05 × 1.2	16,695
3	132,500 × 100 × 1.05² × 1.2 × 1.3	22,789
4	132,500 × 100 × 1.05³ × 1.2 × 1.3	23,928

2   *Variable costs*

Year		$'000
1	132,500 × 43.68	5,788
2	132,500 × 43.68 × 1.05 × 1.2	7,292
3	132,500 × 43.68 × 1.05² × 1.2 × 1.3	9,954
4	132,500 × 43.68 × 1.05³ × 1.2 × 1.3	10,452

3   *Tax-allowable depreciation*

Year		$'000
		16,000
1	Tax-allowable depreciation	(3,200)
		12,800
2	Tax-allowable depreciation	(2,560)
		10,240
3	Tax-allowable depreciation	(2,048)
		8,192
4	Balancing allowance	(8,192)
		0

Duration

Present value of inflows = NPV of project + outlay in Time 0 = 7,801 + 17,025 = **24,826**

Year	1	2	3	4
Present value (PV) $'000	4,104	5,627	6,826	8,269
PV × year	4,104	11,254	20,478	33,076

Duration = (4,104 + 11,254 + 20,478 + 33,076) / 24,286 = 2.78 years

The **project duration** is a measure of the **average time over which this project delivers its value,** ie it is the equivalent of a project that delivers 100% of its (present value) cash inflows in 2.78 years' time.

Alternative calculation:

Year	1	2	3	4
Present value (PV) $'000	4,104	5,627	6,826	8,269
Percentage of total PV	16.5%	22.7%	27.5%	33.3%

Duration = (1 × 0.165) + (2 × 0.227) + (3 × 0.275) + (4 × 0.333) = 2.78 years

(b)   **Reduction in selling price**

Discounted revenue cash flows = (13,250 × 0.75 × 0.901) + (16,695 × 0.75 × 0.812) + (22,789 × 0.75 × 0.731) + (23,928 × 0.75 × 0.659) = $43,441,000

Reduction in selling price = 7,801/43,441 = 18.0%

Fernhurst Co would appear to have some scope to reduce the price in order to guarantee the success of the product launch. It would be useful to know whether the finance director's views on the success of the product would change if the product was launched at a lower price. There may be scope to launch at a price which is more than 18.0% lower than the planned launch price, and increase the sales price subsequently by more than the rate of inflation if the launch is a success.

If the directors are unwilling to reduce the price, then their decision will depend on whether they are willing to consider other ways of mitigating a failed launch or take a chance that the product will make a loss and be abandoned. They will take into account both the probability (15%) of the loss and the magnitude (at least $1,000,000 but possibly higher).

Presumably the finance director's assessment of the probability of a loss is based more on doubts about the demand level rather than the level of costs, as costs should be controllable. Possibly Fernhurst Co's directors may consider a smaller-scale launch to test the market, but then Fernhurst Co would still be left with expensive facilities if the product were abandoned. The decision may therefore depend on what alternative uses could be made of the new facilities.

(c)   The non-executive director has highlighted the importance of long-term maximisation of shareholders' wealth. The NPV is the most important indicator of whether an investment is likely to do that. However, the assessment of investments using NPV has to be modified if the company is undertaking a number of different investments and capital is rationed. It is not necessarily the case that the investments with the highest NPV will be chosen, as account has to be taken of the amount of capital invested as well.

However, investors are not necessarily concerned solely with the long term. They are also concerned about short-term indicators, such as the annual dividend which the company can sustain. They may be concerned if the company's investment portfolio is weighted towards projects which will produce good long-term returns, but limited returns in the near future.

Risk will also influence shareholders' views. They may prefer investments where a higher proportion of returns are made in the shorter term, if they feel that longer-term returns are much more uncertain. The NPV calculation itself discounts longer-term cash flows more than shorter-term cash flows.

The payback method shows how long an investment will take to generate enough returns to pay back its investment. It favours investments which pay back quickly, although it fails to take into account longer-term cash flows after the payback period. Duration is a better measure of the distribution of cash flows, although it may be less easy for shareholders to understand.

14 Tisa Co

Workbook references. Investment appraisal is covered in Chapter 3.

Top tips. For part (a) you need to calculate the weighted average cost of capital (WACC). This can be done by estimating the project's asset beta, then using Tisa Co's capital structure to estimate the equity beta, then calculate the WACC.

Part (c)(i) requires an understanding of how to calculate VaR, but you could still get marks from the explanations of what the figures mean even if you have not calculated them correctly.

For part (b) do not neglect the requirement to explain the recommendation you have made.

Easy marks. Part (c)(ii) offers some straightforward discussion marks, some of which will be brought forward knowledge from FM.

Examining team's comments. In part (a) most candidates made a reasonably good attempt at determining the cost of capital, although few candidates were able to calculate the asset beta of other activities and therefore the component asset beta. A small number of candidates used an average of equity and debt weightings and, where this was done correctly, appropriate credit was given. Many responses did not give reasons for the approach taken and thereby did not achieve some relatively easy marks.

Few responses calculated the annual and five-year VaR figures in part (c), and very few provided explanations of the values obtained.

Marking scheme

		Marks	
(a)	Reasoning behind cost of capital calculation	2	
	Calculation of component asset beta	3	
	Calculation of component equity beta, and K_e and WACC	3	
			8
(b)	Calculation of IRR for Process Omega	3	
	Calculation of MIRR for Process Omega	1	
	Resolution and advice	4	
			8

(c) (i)   Annual and five-year VaR   2
           Explanation   2
                                                                      4
     (ii) 1 mark per relevant discussion point   Max   5
                                                                     25

(a) Use the information for Elfu Co to estimate the component project's asset beta. Then use Tisa Co's capital structure to estimate the project's equity beta and WACC. It is assumed that the beta of debt is zero.

Elfu Co MV_e = $1.20 × 400m shares = $480m

Elfu Co MV_d = $96 million

Elfu Co portfolio asset beta = 1.40 × $480m/($480m + $96m × (1 − 0.25)) = 1.217

Elfu Co asset beta of other activities = 1.25 × $360m/($360m + $76.8m × (1 − 0.25)) = 1.078

1.217 = component asset beta × 0.25 + 1.078 × 0.75

Component asset beta = (1.217 − (1.078 × 0.75))/0.25 = 1.634

Component equity beta based on Tisa Co capital structure

1.634 × [($18m + $3.6m × 0.75)/$18m] = 1.879

Using CAPM

K_e = 3.5% + 1.879 × 5.8% = 14.40%

WACC = (14.40% × $18m + 4.5% × $3.6m)/($18m + $3.6m) = 12.75%, say 13%

(b) **Process Omega**

Year	Cash flow $'000	Discount factor 13%	PV $'000	Discount factor 20%	PV $'000
0	(3,800)	1.000	(3,800)	1.000	(3,800)
1	1,220	0.885	1,080	0.833	1,016
2	1,153	0.783	903	0.694	800
3	1,386	0.693	960	0.578	801
4	3,829	0.613	2,347	0.482	1,846
			1,490		663

IRR is approximately 13% + (1,490/(1,490 − 663)) × (20% − 13%) = 25.6%

Tutorial note

You are unlikely to have used these exact discount rates, in which case you may reach a different conclusion in the discussion part of this question. As long as your conclusion is based on your calculations you will gain credit, whichever discount rates have been used.

Alternative approach using spreadsheet functionality:

Alternatively, the internal rate of return can be calculated using the =IRR spreadsheet function. Either method is acceptable, but the spreadsheet function gives a more precise answer and, with practice, should be quicker to use in the exam.

BPP
LEARNING
MEDIA

The spreadsheet extract shown in the following section shows the =IRR formula being applied:

D3		✕ ✓ f_x	=IRR(D2:H2)					
	A	B	C	D	E	F	G	H	I
1		**Time**		**0**	**1**	**2**	**3**	**4**	
2		Cash flows		- 3,800	1,220	1,153	1,386	3,829	
3		IRR		27.3%					

MIRR

$$MIRR = \left[\frac{PVr}{PVi}\right]^{1/n} \times (1+r_e) - 1$$

PVi = PV of investment phase = 3,800

PVr = PV of return phase   = 3,800 + NPV of 1,490 = 5,290

$$MIRR = \left[\frac{5,290}{3,800}\right]^{1/4} \times (1 + 0.13) - 1 = 0.227 \text{ or } \underline{\mathbf{22.7\%}}$$

Alternative approach using spreadsheet functionality:

Alternatively, the modified internal rate of return can be calculated using the =MIRR spreadsheet function. Either method is acceptable, but the spreadsheet function gives a slightly more precise answer and, with practice, should be quicker to use in the exam.

The spreadsheet extract shown in the following section shows the =MIRR formula being applied:

D3		✕ ✓ f_x	=MIRR(D2:H2,0.13,0.13)					
	A	B	C	D	E	F	G	H
1		**Time**		**0**	**1**	**2**	**3**	**4**
2		Cash flows		- 3,800	1,220	1,153	1,386	3,829
3		MIRR		22.8%					

Discussion

IRR assumes that positive cash flows are **reinvested and earn a return at the same rate as the project's IRR**. The MIRR assumes that positive cash flows are reinvested at the cost of capital. The assumption is more **reasonable** and the result produced is consistent with the net present value. Process Zeta should be adopted as a result, although the difference between the two projects is not significant.

(c)   (i)   A 99% confidence level requires the VaR to be within 2.33 standard deviations from the mean, based on a single tail measure.

Annual VaR = 2.33 × $800,000 = $1,864,000

Five-year VaR = $1,864,000 × $5^{0.5}$ = $4,168,031

This means that Elfu Co can be 99% confident that the cash flows will not fall by more than $1,864,000 in any one year or $4,168,031 in total over the five-year period. This means that it can be 99% sure that the returns will be at least ($2,200,000 – $1,864,000) = $336,000 each year. The company can also be 99% sure that the total five-year returns will be at least ($11,000,000 – $4,168,031) = $6,831,969 in total. There is only a 1% chance that the returns will be less than $336,000 each year or $6,831,969 in total.

(ii) Risk is most commonly dealt with by using **expected value** analysis, which involves assigning probabilities to all possible outcomes. The major drawback is that the assignment of probabilities is highly subjective. This method is also not suitable for a one-off project, as it may give an expected value that is not possible. It also does not indicate the maximum loss or the probability of making a loss, factors which will impact managers' decision making when they consider project risks.

Uncertainty can be dealt with using a variety of methods. One of these is **sensitivity analysis**. This involves altering the variables in the investment appraisal and seeing how this affects the outcome. The main drawbacks are that variables are looked at in isolation, but in reality they may be **interdependent** and that it does not assess the likelihood of the changes in the variables occurring.

Payback and **discounted payback** can be used to determine how long it will take to recover the initial cost of the investment. The major drawback is that any cash flows after payback has occurred are ignored.

15 Riviere

Workbook references. Project appraisal is covered in Chapter 3. Free trade areas are covered in Chapter 16.

Top tips. Make sure that you answer parts (a) and (c) in full – there are two aspects to both of these questions.

Easy marks. There are some easy marks to be gained in parts (a) and (c) for some straightforward discussion points; ensure where possible that these relate to the scenario.

Marking scheme

			Marks
(a)	Discussion of the EU as a free trade area	2–3	
	Discussion of the possible benefits to Riviere Co	2–3	Max 5
(b)	Calculation of IRR	2	
	Calculation of MIRR	2	
	Standard deviation calculations	1	
	Value at risk calculations	2	
	Discussion of merits of NPV and MIRR	2–3	
	Explanation of VaR	2–3	
	Recommendation	1–2	
			Max 13
(c)	Discussion of possible legal risks	3–4	
	Discussion of how to deal with these	3–4	
			Max 7
			25

(a) **A free trade area** like the EU aims to remove barriers to trade and allow **freedom of movement** of production resources such as capital and labour within the EU. The EU also has a **common legal structure** across all member countries and tries to **limit any discriminatory practice** against companies operating in these countries.

The EU also erects **common external trade barriers** to trade against countries which are not member states.

Riviere Co may benefit from operating within the EU in a number of ways.

It may be protected from non-EU competition because companies outside the EU may find it **difficult to enter the EU** markets due to barriers to trade.

A common legal structure should ensure that the standards of food quality and packaging apply equally across all the member countries. This will **reduce compliance costs** for Riviere, which may be an important issue for a small company with limited financial resources.

Having access to capital and labour within the EU may make it easier for the company to set up branches inside the EU, if it wants to. The company may also be able to access any grants which are available to companies based within the EU.

(b)   **Project Drugi internal rate of return (IRR)**

Net present value (NPV): €2,293,000 approximately using a cost of capital of 10%

Time	0	1	2	3	4	5
Cash flows (€'000)	(11,840)	1,230	1,680	4,350	10,240	2,200
Try 20%	1.0	0.833	0.694	0.579	0.482	0.402
Present value	(11,840)	1,025	1,166	2,519	4,936	884

NPV = €(1,310,000)

IRR = 10% + 2,293/(2,293 + 1,310) × 10% approximately = **16.4%**

Alternative approach using spreadsheet functionality:

Alternatively, the internal rate of return can be calculated using the =IRR spreadsheet function. Either method is acceptable, but the spreadsheet function gives a more precise answer and, with practice, should be quicker to use in the exam.

The spreadsheet extract shown in the following section shows the =IRR formula being applied:

C4	▼ ⋮	✕ ✓	fx	=IRR(C2:H2)				
	A	B	C	D	E	F	G	H
1		*Time*	*0*	*1*	*2*	*3*	*4*	*5*
2		Cash flows (€'000)	-11,840	1,230	1,680	4,350	10,240	2,200
3								
4		IRR	**15.9%**					
5								

Modified internal rate of return (MIRR)

Total present values (PVs) of inflows from Time 1 to 5 at 10% discount rate = outlay + NPV of project = €11,840,000 + €2,293,000 = €14,133,000

$$\text{MIRR (using formula provided)} = \left[\frac{PV_r}{PV_i}\right]^{1/n} \times (1+r_e)-1$$

$$\text{MIRR} = \left[\frac{14,133}{11,840}\right]^{1/5} \times (1+0.1)-1 = \underline{14\%}$$

Alternative approach using spreadsheet functionality:

Alternatively, the modified internal rate of return can be calculated using the =MIRR spreadsheet function. Either method is acceptable, but the spreadsheet function, with practice, should be quicker to use in the exam.

The spreadsheet extract shown in the following section shows the =MIRR formula being applied:

C4			:	×	✓	*fx*	=MIRR(C2:H2,0.1,0.1)		

	A	B	C	D	E	F	G	H
1		*Time*	0	1	2	3	4	5
2		Cash flows (€'000)	-11,840	1,230	1,680	4,350	10,240	2,200
3								
4		MIRR	**14.0%**					
5								
6								

Value at risk (VaR)

A 95% confidence level requires the annual present value VaR to be within approximately 1.645 standard deviations from the mean.

A 90% confidence level requires annual present value VaR to be within approximately 1.282 standard deviations from the mean.

Note. An approximation of standard deviations to two decimal places is acceptable.

95%, 5-year present value VaR = $400,000 × 1.645 × square root of 5 (since it is a 5-year project) = approx. **€1,471,000**

90%, 5-year present value VaR = $400,000 × 1.28 (approx.) × square root of 5 (since it is a 5-year project) = approx. **€1,145,000**

	Privi	Drugi
NPV (10%)	€2,054,000	€2,293,000
IRR	17.6%	16.4%
MIRR	13.4%	14.0%
VaR (over the project's life)		
95% confidence level	€1,103,500	€1,471,000
90% confidence level	€860,000	€1,145,000

The IRR for project Privi is higher. However, where projects are mutually exclusive, the **IRR can give an incorrect answer**. One reason for this is that the IRR assumes that returns are reinvested at the internal rate of return, whereas NPV and the MIRR assume that they are reinvested at the cost of capital (discount rate) which in this case is 10%. The cost of capital is a more realistic assumption as this is the minimum return required by investors in a company.

The NPV and the MIRR both indicate that project Drugi would create more value for Riviere Co.

Therefore, based purely on cash flows, **project Drugi should be accepted due to the higher NPV and MIRR, as they give the theoretically correct answer of the value created.**

The VaR provides an indication of the potential riskiness of a project. For example, if Riviere Co invests in project Drugi then it can be 95% confident that the PV will not fall by more than €1,471,000 over its life. Hence the project will still produce a positive NPV. However, there is a 5% chance that the loss could be greater than €1,471,000. With project Privi, the potential loss in value is smaller and therefore it is less risky.

When risk is also taken into account, the choice between the projects is not clear cut and depends on Riviere Co's attitude to risk and return. Project Drugi gives the higher potential NPV but is riskier, whereas project Privi is less risky but gives a smaller NPV. This is before taking into account additional uncertainties such as trading in an area in which Riviere Co is not familiar.

It is therefore recommended that Riviere Co should only proceed with project Drugi if it is willing to accept the higher risk and uncertainty.

BPP LEARNING MEDIA

(c) There are a number of possible **legal risks** which Riviere Co may face:

(i) The countries where the product is sold may have **different legal regulations** on food preparation, quality and packaging.

(ii) The legal regulations may be more lax in countries outside the EU but Riviere Co needs to be aware that **complying only with the minimum standards may impact its image negatively overall**, even if they are acceptable in the countries concerned.

(iii) There may be **trade barriers**, eg **import quotas** in the countries concerned which may make it difficult for Riviere Co to compete.

(iv) The legal system in some countries **may not recognise the trademarks** or production patents which the company holds on its packaging and production processes. This may enable competitors to copy the food and the packaging.

(v) Different countries may have different regulations regarding **product liability** from poorly prepared and/or stored food which cause harm to consumers.

Possible mitigation strategies:

(i) Riviere Co needs to undertake sufficient **research** into the countries' **current laws** and regulations to ensure that it complies with the standards required. It may even want to ensure that it exceeds the required standards to ensure that it maintains its reputation.

(ii) Riviere Co needs to ensure that it also keeps abreast of **potential changes** in the law. It may also want to ensure that it complies with best practice, even if it is not the law yet. Often current best practices become enshrined in future legislation.

(iii) Strict **contracts** need to be set up between Riviere Co and any agents it uses to transport and sell the food. These could be followed up by **regular checks** to ensure that the standards required are maintained.

Note. Credit will be given for alternative, relevant discussion for parts (a) and (c).

16 Arbore

Workbook references. Chapter 3 covers net present value and capital rationing.

Top tips. In part (a)(i) ensure you tackle both parts of the requirement. For part (ii) it is important to consider the factors which are different in a capital rationing scenario.

For part (d) ensure that you take the mark allocation for each sub-part into account when determining the length of your answer.

Easy marks. If you have studied multi-period capital rationing, full marks should be obtained on parts (b) and (c).

				Marks
(a)	(i)	Calculation of project PDur05 net present value	2	
		Calculation of percentage fall of selling price	3	
		Comment	1	
	(ii)	1 mark per relevant point		Max 5
(b)		Formulation of objective function	1	
		Formulation of constraints	2	
				3

			Marks
(c)	Category 1	1	
	Category 2	2	
	Category 3	<u>2</u>	
			5
(d)	(i) Explanation		2
	(ii) Explanation of the features of a CIMS	1–2	
	Benefits of maintaining a CIMS (1 mark per benefit)	<u>2–3</u>	
		Max	<u>4</u>
			<u>25</u>

(a) (i) **PDur05 NPV**

Annual sales revenue = $14 × 300,000 = $4.2m

Annual costs = $3.23 million

Annual cash flows = $0.97 million

This cash flow will be a 15-year annuity, starting from Year 4.

NPV = (2.5m) + (1.2m × 0.901) + (1.4m × 0.812) + (0.97m × 7.191 × 0.731)

= (2.5m) + (1.081m) + (1.137m) + 5.099m

= $0.381m

Sensitivity

To get an NPV of zero, the total present value (PV) of the project's annual cash flows needs to equal the sum of the PV of the investment amounts.

2.5m + 1.081m + 1.137m = $4.718m

This would mean annual cash flows would need to fall to:

4.718m/(7.191 × 0.731) = $0.897m

Sales revenue would need to fall to:

0.897m + 3.23m = $4.127m

Sales price would need to fall to:

4.127m/300,000 = $13.76

or a percentage decrease of:

(14 − 13.76)/14 × 100 = 1.7%

Conclusion

The NPV of the project is very sensitive to changes in the selling price of the product. Just a small decrease in the selling price could make the NPV zero or negative, meaning the project would not be worthwhile.

(ii) The **NPV method** gives an absolute figure which shows the increase in shareholders' funds as a result of the investment in a particular project. If capital is unlimited then this is the measure that should determine the projects to be invested in. If capital is limited then it is also necessary to consider the amount of limited capital required by the project.

Capital rationing decisions are often **more complicated** than identifying the ranking by NPV. Some of the complications of capital rationing problems are as follows:

(1) If capital is restricted in one period then it is highly likely to also be restricted in the next and **subsequent periods** as well. A multi-period model will therefore be required.

BPP LEARNING MEDIA

ANSWERS

(2) Projects are unlikely to possess the same characteristics. For example, some projects may contain real options with follow-on opportunities. Other projects may have greater **strategic significance**, which outweigh other financial considerations.

(3) Some projects may be **'one-off' opportunities** which can only be undertaken in a particular period. Other projects may be able to be delayed and then commence in the following period.

(b) A multi-period capital rationing model would use linear programming as follows:

Let: X1 = investment in project PDur01; X2 = investment in project PDur02; X3 = investment in project PDur03; X4 = investment in project PDur04; and X5 = investment in project PDur05

Then the objective is to maximise:

464X1 + 244X2 + 352X3 + 320X4 + 383X5

Given the following constraints:

Constraint Year 1: 4,000X1 + 800X2 + 3,200X3 + 3,900X4 + 2,500X5 ≤ 9,000

Constraint Year 2: 1,100X1 + 2,800X2 + 3,562X3 + 0X4 + 1,200X5 ≤ 6,000

Constraint Year 3: 2,400X1 + 3,200X2 + 0X3 + 200X4 + 1,400X5 ≤ 5,000

And where X1, X2, X3, X4, X5 ≥ 0

(c) **Category 1**

This figure is the maximum NPV that can be earned with the given constraints on capital expenditure. This is why this figure is less than the total NPV of all five of the projects.

Category 2

These are the proportions of each project that should be undertaken to achieve the maximum NPV given in Category 1. In this situation all of PDur05, 95.8% of PDur01, 73.2% of PDur03 and 40.7% of PDur02 should be undertaken. There should be no investment at all in project PDur04.

Category 3

These figures show the use of the constraints in each period and also any slack or investment funds unused in each period. As can be seen here, the constraints are fully utilised and there is no slack in any of the periods.

(d) (i) Generally speaking, a project with a positive NPV should be undertaken by a company and it **increases shareholder wealth** by generating returns in excess of the required rate. In this case, Arbore Co appears to be imposing **internal limits** on the amount of capital available for investment for each department. This may be due to budgetary limits on the amount the company wants to borrow. This is known as **soft capital rationing**.

(ii) A capital investment monitoring system (CIMS) is used to monitor the ongoing progress of a capital investment project once the decision to proceed has been taken. The CIMS will set a plan of how the project is to proceed and also a budget for the project. It will set project milestones and when they need to be achieved by. It will also consider the potential **external and internal risks** to the project. Contingency plans will be drawn up to deal with these identified risks if it is considered necessary. The CIMS will then ensure that the project progresses in line with the plan and the budget.

The benefits of a CIMS to Arbore include the fact that it attempts to ensure that the project **meets its budgeted revenue and expenditure**. It also helps to ensure that the project is completed on time and that the identified risk factors are still valid. Part of the role of the CIMS will be to identify a **critical path** of linked activities which will be vital to delivering the project on time. The participating departments should also take a **proactive** approach towards managing the risks of the project and may be able to reduce costs as a result. In addition, CIMS could be used as a means of communication between the project managers and the monitoring team.

Inspections are important...

① you'll get good feedback

② you can improve your skills for later

③ you can hear the honest opinions and point of views of different people

④ It will get you prepared for the future

⑤ you get can get a fun reward for doing it

...the Black-Scholes model are covered in Chapter 4.

...ng the values for the variables in the Black-Scholes
...roject (in this case the present value of its cash flows
...e 'exercise price'. Pe in this scenario is how much you will
...eting costs once the project actually starts (that is, the
...o delay is exercised).

...very easy to make a mistake in putting numbers into your
...r workings even if you don't get the correct answer.

...bles should be (eg Pa and Pe), make an assumption and
...correct. Remember to state your assumptions in your
...you are doing.

...are not difficult as you are already given the formulae
...some marks here. Part (c) is straightforward discussion if
...the Black-Scholes model.

...dents were able to determine the value of the option in
...entify the Pa and Pe values. In part (b) a significant
...discuss real options but merely talked about financial
...ne students did recognise that the value of the real option
...e.

	Marks	
...ng option to delay decision	2	
...ck-Scholes formula	1	
...oles formula	1	
...s formula	1	
	3	
	1	
	1	
...clusion	2	
		12
...oint		Max 7
...oint		Max 6
		25

(a) **Financial impact of option to delay**

First of all we calculate the present value (PV) of the project without the option to delay.

Year	0	1	2	3	4	5	6
	$m	$m	$m	$m	$m	$m	$m
Cash flows	(7.0)	(7.0)	(35.0)	25.0	18.0	10.0	5.0
Discount factor (11%)	1.000	0.901	0.812	0.731	0.659	0.593	0.535
DCF	(7.0)	(6.31)	(28.42)	18.28	11.86	5.93	2.68

NPV = $(2.98)m

Without the option to delay the project would be rejected.

Option to delay – use the Black-Scholes model to value this option

$c = P_aN(d_1) - P_eN(d_2)e^{-rt}$

Where $\quad d_1 = \dfrac{\ln\left(P_a / P_e\right) + (r + 0.5s^2)t}{s\sqrt{t}}$

$d_2 = d_1 - s\sqrt{t}$

P_a = current value of the project (that is the PV of its cash inflows)

      = $18.28m + $11.86m + $5.93m + $2.68m

      = $38.75m

P_e = 'exercise price' of the project (that is, the cost of production etc that can be delayed)

      = $35m

t = exercise date (that is, when the exercise price is paid) = 2 years

r = risk-free rate = 3.5%

s = standard deviation = 0.3

d_1 = [ln(38.75/35) + (0.035 + 0.5 × 0.3²) × 2]/[0.3 × $\sqrt{2}$] = 0.62

d_2 = 0.62 – (0.3 × $\sqrt{2}$) = 0.20

Using the normal distribution tables:

$N(d_1)$ = 0.5 + 0.2324 = 0.7324

$N(d_2)$ = 0.5 + 0.0793 = 0.5793

Value of option to delay = (38.75 × 0.7324) – (35 × 0.5793 × $e^{(-0.035 \times 2)}$) = $9.127m

Total value of project = $9.127m – $2.98m = $6.147m

The project would therefore be accepted with the option to delay included.

(b) **Implications of the results**

The option to delay the project gives management time to consider and monitor the potential investment before committing to its execution. This extra time will allow management to assess the popularity of similar launches and also to monitor competition. The success of the film will be heavily reliant on the marketing campaign launched by the film's promoters prior to its release – management will be able to monitor the extent of this campaign before committing to an expensive (and potentially unsuccessful) project.

However, the calculations of the value of the option to delay are subject to several limiting assumptions, primarily the volatility of the cash flows. The value of the option to delay ($9.127 million) is not an exact figure but rather an **indication** of how much management would value the opportunity to delay. The result shows that management should not dismiss the project immediately, despite the current negative NPV.

There may be other options embedded within the project. The technology used to develop the game may be used for other projects in the future (option to **redeploy**). Alternatively the project could lead to follow-on projects if the film is successful enough to generate sequels.

(c) The value of the option depends on the following variables.

(i) **The price of the security**

A decrease in the price of the security will mean that a call option becomes **less valuable**. Exercising the option will mean purchasing a security that has a lower value.

(ii) **The exercise price of the option**

A decrease in the exercise price will mean that a call option becomes **more valuable**; the profit that can be made from exercising the option will have increased.

(iii) **Risk-free rate of return**

A decrease in the risk-free rate will mean that a call option becomes **less valuable**. The purchase of an option rather than the underlying security will mean that the option holder has spare cash available which can be invested at the risk-free rate of return. A decrease in that rate will mean that it becomes less worthwhile to have spare cash available, and hence to have an option rather than having to buy the underlying security.

(iv) **Time to expiry of the option**

A decrease in the time of expiry will mean that a call option becomes **less valuable**, as the time premium element of the option price has been decreased.

(v) **Volatility of the security price**

A decrease in volatility will mean that a call option becomes **less valuable**. A decrease in volatility will decrease the chance that the security price will be above the exercise price when the option expires.

18 Marengo

Workbook references. Option pricing is covered in Chapter 4.

Top tips. There are several ways in which part (b) can be approached and the examining team stated that he would award marks for alternative relevant approaches. What is important is that you assess the advantages and disadvantages of each suggestion to provide a balanced discussion.

Easy marks. Part (a) offers some easy marks for calculating the delta of options and the number of options required.

Examining team's comments. Part (a) was either done well with candidates calculating the delta and then applying it correctly, or done poorly where candidates went on to calculate the value of a call and put option (which were not required). Very few candidates explained the numerical answer. Candidates need to be aware that some question parts may have more than a single requirement and all the requirements need to be addressed correctly in order to achieve full marks. Some reasonable points were made in part (b) but in many cases these lacked depth or substance.

		Marks
(a)	Identifying the need to calculate $N(d_1)$ for hedge ratio	2
	Calculation of d_1	2
	Calculation of $N(-d_1)$	2
	Calculation of number of put options required	1
		7
(b)	Discussing the theoretical argument for not hedging	3–4
	Discussing the limitations/risks/costs of selling the shares	3–4
	Discussing the risks/costs of using OTC options to hedge	2–3
	Discussing whether to hold shares at all	2–3
	Discussing the potential benefits of hedging and application to scenario	2–3
	Relevant concluding remarks	1–2
		Max $\frac{18}{25}$

(a) The number of put options to be purchased depends on the hedge ratio, which in turn is determined by the option's delta. We can estimate delta using $N(-d_1)$.

$$d_1 = \frac{\ln\left(P_a / P_e\right) + (r + 0.5s^2)t}{s\sqrt{t}}$$

d_1 = [ln(340/350) + (0.04 + 0.5 × 0.4²) × 2/12]/(0.4 × √(2/12))

d_1 = (−0.0290 + 0.02)/0.163

d_1 = −0.06

−d1 = 0.06

$N(-d1)$ = 0.5 + 0.0239 = 0.5239

Number of put options needed = 200,000 shares/(0.5239 × 1,000 shares) = 382 contracts

(b) **Possible reasons for the suggestions made by each of the three managers**

(i) *No hedging at all*

This argument is based on the theory that corporate risk should not be hedged. This theory states that, where a company holds a well-diversified portfolio and securities are priced correctly, unsystematic risk will be at least reduced to a minimal level or eliminated completely. There is, therefore, no apparent gain to shareholders of any further hedging or management of corporate risk (that is, unsystematic risk cannot be reduced further). Should hedging take place in a perfect market it is likely that shareholders will actually lose out, as the benefits derived from hedging will be outweighed by the costs of doing so.

In an imperfect market, however, shareholders are more likely to benefit from hedging. By reducing the volatility of the firm's earnings, cash flows are likely to increase, which will increase shareholders' wealth. Such a situation is likely to arise:

(1) If stable earnings increase the certainty of being able to pay for future investments which would encourage a more stable investment policy

(2) If tax rates are increasing

(3) If a high volatility of earnings could lead to financial distress for the company

None of the above reasons for hedging appears to exist for Marengo Co and the case for hedging seems to be weak. Marengo is a large company with numerous investments, therefore it is unlikely that reducing the volatility of one such investment will have a significant effect on its cash flows.

(ii) *Sell Arion Co's shares in order to eliminate risk of a fall in share price*

This is based on the assumption that Marengo will be protected from a fall in Arion's share price if it gets rid of the shares in Arion. However, there are a few issues with this proposal.

It is assumed that Marengo holds shares in Arion as an investment and generates a return greater than the risk-free rate. If Marengo sells these shares, an alternative investment offering similar returns should have to be found for the surplus funds, to prevent a reduction in Marengo's shareholder value. If such investments are not available, the shares should not be sold.

Another issue is the potential effect on Arion's share price if Marengo does 'dump' a large number of shares on the market. Managers have to ask whether they are likely to be able to sell such a large proportion of Arion's shares, although there is the chance that investors want to take the opportunity of purchasing shares at a lower price now, in the expectation that the price will increase again following the projected period of uncertainty.

(iii) *Hedge the investment using an appropriate derivative product*

If this proposal was undertaken, Marengo would be required to purchase 382 OTC put options from the bank (see calculations above). This could prove to be expensive, as Marengo will have to pay a premium on each option for the flexibility of having the right, but not the obligation, to exercise the options. Should the option not be exercised, Marengo will have suffered the cost of the premiums for no reason. However, if the options are exercised, Marengo will have protected itself against downside movements in the share price.

Hedging using options involves several risks. Delta is not stable, which means that the number of options that should have been taken out may change (thus Marengo may not be fully protected). Option values also change, the closer they come to the exercise date (measured by theta) and the underlying asset's volatility changes (measured by vega).

Despite the risks associated with derivative products, a stable hedging policy can be used to reduce agency conflicts between shareholders and managers. A single hedging transaction is unlikely to have much impact, but it is important to maintain a consistent approach to hedging against investment risks. This protects not only shareholders' wealth but also managers, who may not be as well diversified as the shareholders.

(iv)　*Do not hold any equity investments at all*

Edward may be correct that Marengo Co should not hold equity investments. This is not a core area of business for Marengo Co and it may be best not to focus on it and therefore sell all the shares. However, it is the job of the treasury department to manage excess funds and liquidity and it may be that the equity holdings deliver a valuable dividend stream which contributes to a healthy cash flow for the business. The treasury department will be able to show if their investment choices outperform the market return.

There is no easy way to justify or discourage hedging. Each case should be examined on its individual merits, but it is important for a company to have a risk management strategy on which such decisions can be based.

19 Furlion Co

Workbook references. The Black-Scholes model and its use in the valuation of real options are covered in Chapter 4, the World Bank is covered in Chapter 16 and rho is covered in Chapter 14.

Top tips. A number of articles on the Black-Scholes model were published on the ACCA website in the lead up to these exams, so make sure you are checking the ACCA website for recently published articles.

If you have studied – and are comfortable with – the valuation of real options using the Black-Scholes model, part (a) of this question should be relatively straightforward. The main issues you have to deal with are recognising that you are dealing with real options rather than traded options and appreciating that the option to delay is a call option.

Part (a) is a straightforward application of the Black-Scholes model. Make sure you make clear to the marker the value you are attaching to each of the components of the formulae being used. Remember to deal with the discussion areas of the question too – an easy thing to forget in the midst of large calculations!

Part (b), for five marks, required a discussion of the impact of changes in the interest rate on the value of a call option. The impact of changes in any of 'the greeks' is a commonly examined area.

Part (c) should be fairly brief. A couple of points about the role and limitations of the World Bank (and the International Development Association) are all that is needed.

Easy marks. Discussion of the limitations of Black-Scholes and other factors to be taken into account in part (a).

Marks

(a)   Current price variable (P_a) in BSOP formula   1
       Other variables in BSOP formula   1
       Calculation of d_1 and d_2 3
       Determination of $N(d_1)$ and $N(d_2)$ 2
       Value of the option to expand decision   1
       Revised value of projects and comments   Max   3
       Assumptions   Max   3
       Other factors   Max   3
                                                                                        Max   16

(b)   Explanation of rho   2
       Impact of interest rate movements   3
                                                                                               5

(c)   Role of World Bank   1
       Usefulness of World Bank as a source of finance   1–2
       Role of IDA   1
       Usefulness of IDA as a source of finance   1–2
                                                                                        Max   4
                                                                                               25

(a)   **Value of option to expand**

       Variables

       Volatility = 30%

       Current price (value of project including option exercise price) = $15m × 0.712 = $10.68m

       Exercise price (capital expenditure) = $15 million

       Exercise date = 3 years

       Risk-free rate = 4%

       d_1 = [ln(10.68/15) + (0.04 + 0.5 × 0.3²) × 3]/(0.3 × √3) = −0.1630

       d_2= −0.1630 − 0.3 × √3 = −0.6826

       $N(d_1)$ = 0.5 − 0.0636 = 0.4364 (using 0.16 for d_1)

       $N(d_2)$ = 0.5 − 0.2517 = 0.2483 (using 0.68 for d_2)

       Value of call option = P_a × $N(d_1)$ − P_e × $N(d_2)$ × e^{-rt}

       = (10.68 × 0.4364) − (15 × 0.2483 × $e^{-0.04 × 3}$)

       = 4.66 − 3.30

       = $1.36 million

       Overall value = $1.36m − $1.01m = $0.35m

       The investment has a positive net present value, so should be accepted on those grounds. Furlion Co should also consider the value of an abandonment option if results turn out to be worse than expected or a delay option if it wants to see how the reclamation programme is going to continue.

Assumptions made and other factors

Using real options for decision making has limitations. Real options are built around uncertainties surrounding future cash flows, but real option theory is only useful if management can respond effectively to these uncertainties as they evolve. The Black-Scholes model for valuing real options has a number of assumptions which may not be true in practice. It assumes that there is a market for the underlying asset and the volatility of returns on the underlying asset follows a normal distribution. The model also assumes perfect markets, a constant risk-free interest rate and constant volatility.

Furlion Co will also consider expectations about the future of the land reclamation programme. Has the programme been as quick and as effective as the Naswan government originally expected? Furlion Co will also want to consider how the programme will be affected by the amount of funding the government obtains and any conditions attached to that funding.

Furlion Co may also wish to consider whether its investment of this type will be looked on favourably by the Naswan government and whether tax or other concessions will be available. These may come with conditions, given the government's commitment to a sustainable economy, such as the way production facilities operate or the treatment of employees.

Given that this is a market which may expand in the future, Furlion Co should also consider the reaction of competitors. This may be a market where establishing a significant presence quickly may provide a significant barrier if competitors try to enter the market later.

As the investment is for the manufacture of specialist equipment, it is possible that there is insufficient skilled labour in the local labour pool in Naswa. As well as training local labour, supervision is likely to be required, at least initially, from staff based in other countries. This may involve cultural issues such as different working practices.

(b) The sensitivity of the valuation of options to interest rate changes can be measured by the option's rho. The option's rho is the amount of change in the option's value for a 1% change in the risk-free interest rate. The rho is positive for calls and so will be positive if the risk-free interest rate does increase.

However, interest rates tend to move quite slowly and the interest rate is often not a significant influence on the option's value, particularly for short-term options. However, many real options are longer term and will have higher rhos than short-term options. A change in interest rates will be more significant the longer the time until expiry of an option.

In addition, there are possible indirect economic effects of interest rate changes, such as on the return demanded by finance providers and hence on the cost of capital.

(c) The World Bank provides loans, often direct to governments, on a commercial basis, for capital projects. Loans are generally for a long-term period, which may suit the Naswan government. However, the terms of the loan may be onerous; not just the finance costs but the other conditions imposed on the scope of the projects.

Given the circumstances of the investment, Naswa may be able to obtain assistance from the International Development Association, which is part of the World Bank. This provides loans on more generous terms to the poorest countries. However, it is designed for countries with very high credit risk which would struggle to obtain funding by other means, and Naswa may not be eligible.

20 Toltuck

Marking scheme

		Marks	
(a)	Government yield curve	2	
	Toltuck Co spot-curve old and new	2	
	Bond valuation – old and new	3	
	Yield to maturity – old and new	3	
		—	10
(b)	Financial factors	4	
	Other factors	4	
	Limit marks for (b) to 3 marks in total if answer does not mention		
	Toltuck Co's position and performance	—	8
(c)	1–2 marks per impact discussed		Max 7
			25

(a) The government yield curve can be estimated from the data available:

Bond 1: $104 = $109/(1 + r_1)$

$r_1 = ($109/$104) - 1 = 4.81\%$

Bond 2: $102 = $7/1.0481 + $107/(1 + r_2)^2$

$r_2 = [107/(102 - 6.68)]^{1/2} - 1 = 5.95\%$

Bond 3: $98 = $6/1.0481 + $6/1.0595^2 + $106/(1 + r_3)^3$

$r_3 = [106/(98 - 5.72 - 5.35)]^{1/3} - 1 = 6.83\%$

Year	Govt yield curve %	Spread old rating %	Toltuck Co spot old rating %	Spread new rating %	Toltuck Co spot new rating %
1	4.81	0.18	4.99	0.54	5.35
2	5.95	0.31	6.26	0.69	6.64
3	6.83	0.45	7.28	0.86	7.69

Valuation of bond under old credit rating

Year	Payment $	Discount factor	Discounted cash flow $
1	8	1/1.0499	7.62
2	8	1/1.0626²	7.09
3	110	1/1.0728³	89.09
Bond valuation			103.80

Valuation of bond under new credit rating

Year	Payment $	Discount factor	Discounted cash flow $
1	8	1/1.0535	7.59
2	8	$1/1.0664^2$	7.03
3	110	$1/1.0769^3$	88.08
Bond valuation			102.70

Yield to maturity under old credit rating

Year	Payment $	Discount factor 8%	Discounted cash flow $	Discount factor 7%	Discounted cash flow $
0	(103.80)	1.000	(103.80)	1.000	(103.80)
1–3	8.00	2.577	20.62	2.624	20.99
3	102.00	0.794	80.99	0.816	83.23
			(2.19)		0.42

Using IRR approach, yield to maturity = 7 + ((0.42/(2.19 + 0.42)) × (8 − 7)) = 7.16%

Yield to maturity under new credit rating

Year	Payment $	Discount factor 8%	Discounted cash flow $	Discount factor 7%	Discounted cash flow $
0	(102.70)	1.000	(102.70)	1.000	(102.70)
1–3	8.00	2.577	20.62	2.624	20.99
3	102.00	0.794	80.99	0.816	83.23
			(1.09)		1.52

Using IRR approach, yield to maturity = 7 + ((1.52/(1.09 + 1.52)) × (8 − 7)) = 7.58%

Market value of $100 bond has fallen by $1.10 and the yield to maturity has risen by 0.42%.

(b) The credit agency will have taken the following criteria into consideration when assessing Toltuck C's credit rating:

Country

Toltuck Co's debt would not normally be rated higher than the credit ratings of its country of origin, Arumland. Therefore the credit rating of Arumland should normally be at least AA. The rating will also have depended on Toltuck Co's standing relative to other companies in Arumland. The credit agency may have reckoned that Toltuck Co's recent poor results have weakened its position.

Industry

The credit agency will have taken account of the impact of the recession on property construction companies generally in Arumland. Toltuck Co's position within the industry compared with competitors will also have been assessed. If similar recent developments by competitors have been more successful, this is likely to have had an adverse impact on Toltuck Co's rating.

Management

The credit agency will have made an overall assessment of management and succession planning at Toltuck Co. It will have looked at business and financing strategies and planning and controls. It will also have assessed how successful the management has been in terms of delivering financial results. The credit agency may have believed the poor returns on recent developments show shortcomings in management decision-making processes and it may have rated the current management team poorly.

Financial

The credit agency will have analysed financial results, using measures such as return on capital employed. The agency will also have assessed possible sources of future earnings growth. It may have been sceptical about prospects, certainly for the short term, given Toltuck Co's recent problems.

The credit agency will also have assessed the financial position of Toltuck Co, looking at its gearing and working capital management, and considering whether Toltuck Co has enough cash to finance its needs. The agency will also have looked at Toltuck Co's relationship with its bankers and its debt covenants, to assess how flexible its sources of finances are if it comes under stress. It may well have been worried about Toltuck Co's gearing being higher than the industry average and concerned about the high levels of cash it needs to finance operations. It will also have assessed returns on developments-in-progress compared with commitments to repay loans. Greater doubt about Toltuck Co's ability to meet its commitments is likely to have been a significant factor in the fall in its rating.

The agency will also have needed reassurance about the quality of the financial information it was using, so it will have looked at the audit report and accounting policies.

(c)   Toltuck Co may not have increased problems raising debt finance if debtholders do not react in the same way as the credit rating agency. They may attach different weightings to the criteria which they use. They may also come to different judgements about the quality of management and financial stability. Debtholders may believe that the recent problems Toltuck Co has had generating returns may be due more to external factors which its management could not have controlled.

However, it is probable that the fall in Toltuck Co's credit rating will result in it having more difficulty raising debt finance. Banks may be less willing to provide loans and investors less willing to subscribe for bonds. Even if debt finance is available, it may come with covenants restricting further debt or gearing levels. This will mean that if Toltuck Co requires substantial additional finance, it is more likely to have to make a rights issue or issue new equity on the stock market. Shareholders may be faced with the choice of subscribing large amounts for new capital or having their influence diluted. This may particularly worry the more cautious shareholders.

Even if Toltuck Co can obtain the debt it needs, the predicted increase in yield to maturity may be matched by debtholders demanding a higher coupon rate on debt. This will increase finance costs, and decrease profits and earnings per share, with a possible impact on share price. It will also mean that fewer funds are available for paying dividends. Toltuck Co has been faced with difficult decisions on balancing investment expenditure versus paying dividends and these difficulties may well increase.

Additional debt may have other restrictive covenants. They may restrict Toltuck Co's buying and selling of assets, or its investment strategy. Restrictions on Toltuck Co's decisions about the developments it undertakes may impact adversely on shareholder returns.

Loan finance or bonds will also come with repayment covenants. These may require Toltuck Co to build up a fund over time which will be enough to redeem the debt at the end of its life. Given uncertainties over cash flows, this commitment to retain cash may make it more difficult to undertake major developments or pay an acceptable level of dividend.

The fall in Toltuck Co's credit rating may result in its cost of equity rising as well as its cost of debt. In turn, Toltuck Co's weighted average cost of capital will rise. This will affect its investment choices and hence its ability to generate wealth for shareholders. It may result in Toltuck Co prioritising developments offering better short-term returns. This may suit the more cautious shareholders, but the current majority may worry that Toltuck Co will have to turn down opportunities which offer the possibility of high returns.

21 Coeden

Marking scheme

		Marks
(a)	*Prior to implementation of the proposal*	
	Cost of equity	1
	Cost of debt	1
	Market value of debt	2
	Market value of equity	3
	WACC	1
	After implementing the proposal	
	Coeden Co's current asset beta	1
	Asset beta of hotel services business only	2
	Equity beta of hotel services business only	2
	Cost of equity	1
	WACC	1
	Assumptions (1–2 marks per explained assumption)	2–3
	Discussion	2–3
		Max 20
(b)	Discussion (1–2 marks per point)	Max 5
		25

(a) **Before implementing proposal**

Cost of equity = 4% + (1.1 × 6%) = 10.6%

Cost of debt = 4% + 0.90 = 4.9%

Market value of debt (MV$_d$)

($5.20 × 1/1.049) + ($5.20 × 1/1.049^2) + ($105.20 × 1/1.049^3) = $100.82

Total value = $42m × 100.82/100 = $42,344,400

Market value of equity (MV$_e$)

As stated in the question the free cash flow to equity model provides a reasonable estimate of the market value of the company.

Assumption

The growth rate can be estimated using the rb model. It is assumed that the retained free cash flows to equity will be invested to generate a return at least equal to the shareholders' required rate of return.

r = 10.6% and b = 0.4

$g = rb = 10.6\% \times 0.4 = 4.24\%$

$MV_e = \dfrac{FCF \times g}{k_e - g} = 2.6m \times 1.0424/(0.106 - 0.0424) = \$42,614,000$ (rounded)

The proportion of MV_e to MV_d is close to 50:50, which will be used here to simplify the calculations.

$WACC = 10.6\% \times 0.5 + 4.9\% \times 0.5 \times 0.8 = 7.3\%$

After implementing the proposal

The estimate of the asset beta for Coeden Co is:

$\beta_a = 1.1 \times 0.5/(0.5 + 0.5 \times 0.8) = 0.61$

Asset beta for hotel services

It has been assumed that Coeden Co's asset beta is a weighted average of the average property company beta and the hotel services beta.

Therefore:

$0.61 = $ (Asset beta (hotel services) $\times 0.6) + (0.4 \times 0.4)$

$0.45 = $ Asset beta (hotel services) $\times 0.6$

Asset beta (hotel services) $= 0.75$

Equity beta for Coeden Co, hotel services only

MV_e is unchanged as stated in the question.

$MV_e = \$42,614,000$

$k_d = 4 + 0.6 = 4.6\%$

$MV_d = (\$5.20 \times 1/1.046) + (\$5.20 \times 1/1.046^2) + (\$105.20 \times 1/1.046^3) = \$101.65$

Total value $= \$12.6m \times 101.65/100 = \$12,808,000$ (rounded)

Equity beta calculation

$0.75 = \beta_e \times (42,614/(42,614 + 12,808 \times 0.8))$

$0.75 = \beta_e \times 0.806$

$\beta_e = 0.93$

Hotel services cost of equity and WACC

$k_e = 4\% + 0.93 \times 6\% = 9.6\%$

$WACC = 9.6\% \times (42,614/(42,614 + 12,808)) + 4.6\% \times 0.8 \times (12,808/(42,614 + 12,808)) = 8.2\%$

Comment

	Before proposal	After proposal
Cost of equity	10.6%	9.6%
WACC	7.3%	8.2%

The proposal will increase the asset beta of Coeden Co because the hotel services industry has a **higher business risk** than a business that also owns hotels. However, the equity beta and the cost of equity are both lower because of the **reduction in the level of debt**. This is because the reduction in debt means that the financial risk of Coeden Co is lower. However, the WACC increases because this lower debt level means there is less cheap debt in the financing mix. As a result the board of directors' assertion that the lower level of debt will reduce WACC is incorrect.

(b)   The assumption that the market value of equity will not change is unlikely to hold in reality. The change in the growth rate of free cash flows and sales revenue and the changes in the business and financial risks of the new business are all likely to have an effect.

In estimating the asset beta of Coeden Co for offering hotel services only there has been no consideration of the **change in business risk** as a result of renting rather than owning the hotels. A revised asset beta should be estimated to reflect the change in business risk.

The market value of equity has been used to estimate the post-implementation equity beta and cost of equity of the business. However, the market value of equity is dependent on the cost of equity, which is itself dependent on the equity beta. Therefore both the cost of equity and the market value of equity will **change** as a result of the implementation of this proposal.

22 Tippletine

Workbook references. Adjusted present value (APV) is covered in Chapter 6.

Top tips. For part (a)(i) you have to know which formula to use to calculate the ungeared cost of equity. It is the MM Proposition 2 formula which is given to you in the exam.

Easy marks. There are numerous easy marks to be picked up in part (a)(i) in the net present value calculations, although care will need to be taken over the timing of the tax cash flows because of the one year delay.

Examining team's comments. Part (a) required candidates to undertake an investment appraisal using the adjusted present value technique, where the loan that might be used to finance the investment had significant financing side effects. Most candidates scored reasonable marks on this part.

Part (b) required candidates to discuss an alternative form of loan finance (convertible loan notes) that could be used to fund the investment. This part was often omitted and generally was not well-answered when attempted, highlighting a number of weaknesses in student performance. There was a lack of knowledge with candidates failing to discuss important features of convertible loan finance, such as a company needing to have sufficient money to redeem the notes if necessary.

Candidates also failed to respond to the question verb 'discuss', which generally requires some coverage of both advantages and disadvantages. Few answers said anything about the advantages of the convertible loan notes. Many answers failed to examine the terms from the shareholders' viewpoint, as the question required.

Marking scheme

		Marks
(a)	Operating cash flow excluding marketing costs	1
	Tax allowable depreciation	1
	Taxation	2
	Working capital	2
	Discount factor	2
	Base case NPV	1
	Issue costs	1
	Tax shield on loan	2
	Subsidy	1
	Tax shield on subsidy	1
	Adjusted present value	1
	Comments and conclusion	2
		17
(b)	1–2 marks per point	Max 8
		25

BPP
LEARNING
MEDIA

BPP
LEARNING
MEDIA

Answers **145**

(a)

Year	0 $'000	1 $'000	2 $'000	3 $'000	4 $'000	5 $'000
Operating cash flow excluding marketing costs		2,000	14,500	15,225	15,834	
Marketing costs		(9,000)	(2,000)	(2,000)	(2,000)	
Cash flow before tax		(7,000)	12,500	13,225	13,834	
Taxation (W1)					(310)	(4,328)
Investment	(30,600)				13,500	
Working capital (W2)	(3,000)	(240)	(194)	(172)	3,606	
Cash flows	(33,600)	(7,240)	12,306	13,053	30,630	(4,328)
Discount factor 9% (W3)	1.000	0.917	0.842	0.772	0.708	0.650
Discounted cash flows	(33,600)	(6,639)	10,362	10,077	21,686	(2,813)
Base case NPV	(927)					

Alternative approach using spreadsheet functionality:

Alternatively, the present value of the cash flows from time 1 - 5 can be calculated using the =NPV spreadsheet function. Either method is acceptable, but the spreadsheet function gives a slightly more precise answer and, with practice, should be quicker to use in the exam.

The spreadsheet extract shown in the following section shows the =NPV formula being applied using the cost of capital of 9%.

C3	fx	=NPV(0.09,D2:H2)					
	A	B	C	D	E	F	G	H
1	**Time**		**0**	**1**	**2**	**3**	**4**	**5**
2		Cash flows		-7240	12306	13053	30630	-4328
3		Present value time 1-5	32,681					
4		less outlay at time 0	-33,600					
5		Base case NPV	- 919					
6								

Note that the NPV function assumes that the first cash flow is in one year's time, so you then have to subtract the time 0 cash outflows as before to give the project NPV.

Workings

1   Taxation

Year	TAD = Tax-allowable depreciation	Balance $'000
	Investment	30,600
1	TAD 25% reducing balance	(7,650)
		22,950
2	TAD 25% reducing balance	(5,738)
		17,212
3	TAD 25% reducing balance	(4,303)
		12,909
4	Balancing charge	591
		13,500

Year	1	2	3	4
	$'000	$'000	$'000	$'000
Cash flow before tax	(7,000)	12,500	13,225	13,834
Tax-allowable depreciation	(7,650)	(5,738)	(4,303)	591
Adjusted cash flow	(14,650)	6,762	8,922	14,425
Offset against previous losses		(14,650)	(7,888)	
Losses carried forward	(14,650)	(7,888)		
Taxable cash flow			1,034	14,425
Taxation at 30%			310	4,328
Year			4	5

2   Working capital

Year	1	2	3	4
	$'000	$'000	$'000	$'000
	3,000 × 0.08 = 240	(3,000 + 240) × 0.06 = 194	(3,000 + 240 + 194) × 0.05 = 172	3,000 + 240 + 194 + 172 = 3,606

3   Ungeared cost of equity

Humabuz Co

MV debt = $225m × 1.07 = $240.8m

MV equity = 125m × $3.20 = $400m

Ungeared cost of equity

$k_e = k^i_e + (1 - t)(k^i_e - k_d) V_d/V_e$

$10.5\% = k^i_e + (1 - 0.3)(k^i_e - 5.4\%)(240.8/400)$

$10.5\% + 2.28\% = 1.42 k^i_e$

$k^i_e = 9\%$

4   Issue costs

Debt: ($30,600,000/0.96) = $31,875,000

Debt issue costs: $31,875,000 × 0.04 = $1,275,000

5   Tax shield on loan

Use PV of an annuity (PVA) for years 2–5 at 5% (assume 5% is cost of debt).

Note. The risk-free rate of 2.5% could also be used for discounting.

Subsidised loan: $30,600,000 × (0.025 − 0.003) × 0.3 × (4.329 − 0.952) = $682,000

6   Subsidy

Benefit = $30,600,000 × (0.05 − 0.022) × 3.546 = $3,038,000

Tax relief lost = $30,600,000 × (0.05 − 0.022) × 0.3 × (4.329 − 0.952) = $868,000

7   Financing side effects

	$'000
Issue costs (W4)	(1,275)
Tax shield on loan (W5)	682
Subsidy benefit (W6)	3,038
Tax relief lost on subsidy benefit (W6)	(868)
Total benefit of financing side effects	1,577

Conclusion

If base case net present value is used, the project has a negative net present value of $927,000, and on that basis should be rejected. However, the financing side effects add $1,577,000 to the value of the project, giving a positive adjusted present value of $650,000. On that basis the project should be accepted. The revenues from the project appear to be uncertain and the realisable value at the end of the project may be optimistic. It would be useful to have an indication of the range of outcomes and an idea of the probability that the project will have a negative APV.

(b) **Advantages of convertible loan notes**

The investors may be happy that directors are demonstrating their commitment to the company by subscribing to convertible loan notes. The conversion rights mean that these directors will benefit if the share price increases, aligning their interests with shareholders.

The conversion terms also mean that the loan notes will not necessarily have to be repaid in a few years' time. This may be significant if Tippletine Co does not have the cash available for redemption then.

Drawbacks of convertible loan notes

The convertible loan notes would be treated as debt, increasing Tippletine Co's gearing, which may concern the other shareholders. The interest on the convertible loan notes will be payable before dividends and may leave less money for distribution to shareholders. Shareholders may doubt whether the higher interest burden on the convertible loan notes, compared with the subsidised loan, is compensated for by the lower costs of Tippletine Co not having to fulfil the government's requirements.

The other shareholders may be concerned by the interest rate on the convertible notes being Tippletine Co's normal cost of borrowing. The option to convert is an advantage for convertible loan note holders. They would often effectively pay for this option by receiving a lower rate of interest on the loan notes.

Shareholders would want to assess how likely conversion would be – that is, how likely it would be that the share price will rise above $2.75. The option to convert may also change the balance of shareholdings, giving the directors who held the notes a greater percentage of share capital and possibly more influence over Tippletine Co. The other shareholders may be unhappy with this.

The shareholders may also have reservations about the loan note holders having the option to redeem if Tippletine Co's share price is low. This reduces the risk of providing the finance from the loan note holders' viewpoint. However, if the share price is low, Tippletine Co's financial results and cash flows may be poor and it may struggle to redeem the loan notes. Shareholders may also be concerned that there is no cap the other way, allowing Tippletine Co to force conversion if the share price reaches a high enough level.

Note. Credit will be given for alternative relevant discussion.

23 Amberle

Marking scheme

		Marks
(a)	Working capital	2
	Discount rate	1
	Base case net present value	2
	Issue costs	1
	Tax shield benefit – subsidised loan	1
	Tax shield benefit – bank loan	4
	Subsidy benefit	1
	Adjusted present value	1
	Comments and conclusion	2
		15
(b)	Factors determining long-term finance policy	5–6
	Factors which cause policy to change	5–6
		Max 10
		Total 25

(a)

Year	0	1	2	3	4
	$m	$m	$m	$m	$m
Post-tax operating cash flows		28.50	36.70	44.40	50.90
Investment	(150.00)				
Realisable value					45.00
Working capital (W1)	(6.00)	(0.48)	(0.39)	(0.34)	7.21
Cash flows	(156.00)	28.02	36.31	44.06	103.11
Discount factor 12% (W2)	1.000	0.893	0.797	0.712	0.636
Present value	(156.00)	25.02	28.94	31.37	65.58
Base case net present value	(5.09)				

Base case net present value is approximately ($5.09 million) and on this basis, the investment should be rejected.

Alternative approach using spreadsheet functionality:

Alternatively, the present value of the cash flows from time 1–4 can be calculated using the =NPV spreadsheet function. Either method is acceptable, but the spreadsheet function gives a slightly more precise answer and, with practice, should be quicker to use in the exam.

The spreadsheet extract shown in the following section shows the =NPV formula being applied using the cost of capital of 12%.

C3	▼ : ✕ ✓ *fx*	=NPV(0.12,D2:G2)				
	A	B	C	D	E	F	G
1		Time	0	1	2	3	4
2		Cash flows	-156	28.02	36.31	44.06	103.11
3		Present value time 1-4	150.85				
4		less outlay at time 0	-156				
5		Base case net present value	-5.15				
6							

Note that the NPV function assumes that the first cash flow is in one year's time, so you then have to subtract the time 0 cash outflows as before to give the project NPV.

Workings

1   *Working capital*

Year	0 $m	1 $m	2 $m	3 $m	4 $m
Working capital		6.00	6.48	6.87	7.21
Required/(released)	6.00	0.48	0.39	0.34	(7.21)

2   *Discount rate*

Using asset beta

All-equity financed discount rate = 4% + (11% − 4%) 1.14 = 12%

3   *Issue costs*

$80m/0.97 = $82,474,227

Issue costs = 3% × $82,474,227 = $2,474,227

There will be no issue costs for the bank loan.

4   *Tax shield on subsidised loan*

Use PV of an annuity (PVA) years 1 to 4 at 8% (normal borrowing rate)

$80m × 0.031 × 30% × 3.312 = $2,464,128

Note to markers

Full credit should be given if tax shield is discounted at the government interest rate of 3.1% rather than the normal borrowing rate of 8%.

5   *Tax shield on bank loan*

Annual repayment = ($70m/PVA 8% Yr 1 – 4) = ($70m/3.312) = $21,135,266

Year	1 $'000	2 $'000	3 $'000	4 $'000
Opening balance	70,000	54,465	37,687	19,567
Interest at 8%	5,600	4,357	3,015	1,565
Repayment	(21,135)	(21,135)	(21,135)	(21,135)
Closing balance	54,465	37,687	19,567	(3)

Year	1 $'000	2 $'000	3 $'000	4 $'000
Interest cost	5,600	4,357	3,015	1,565
Tax relief at 30%	1,680	1,307	905	470
Discount factor 8%	0.926	0.857	0.794	0.735
Present value	1,556	1,120	719	345
Net present value	3,740			

6   *Subsidy benefit*

Benefit = $80m × (0.08 – 0.031) × 70% × 3.312 = $9,088,128

7   *Financing side effects*

	$'000
Issue costs (W3)	(2,474)
Tax shield on subsidised loan (W4)	2,464
Tax shield on bank loan (W5)	3,740
Subsidy benefit (W6)	9,088
Total benefit of financing side effects	12,818

Financing the project in this way would add around $12.82 million to the value of the project.

The adjusted present value of the project is around $7.73 million and so the project should be accepted. Sensitivity analysis should be undertaken on all the significant variables. Further analysis may be needed, particularly of the assumptions which lie behind the post-tax cash flows, such as sales and the tax rate. The realisable value of $45 million may be questionable. On the other hand, the time horizon of four years seems low and analysis should be done of potential cash flows beyond that time.

(b)   Amberle Co's board can use various principles to determine its long-term finance mix. The directors may aim to follow consistent long-term policies, or they may have preferences which change as circumstances change.

Long-term policy factors

At present Amberle Co is using a mix of finance, raising the question of whether the directors are aiming for an optimal level of gearing, or there is a level which they do not wish gearing to exceed. If the board wishes to maintain gearing at an optimal level, this is likely to be determined by a balance of risks and advantages. The main risks are not being able to maintain the required level of payment to finance providers, interest to debt providers or required level of dividend to shareholders. Advantages may include lower costs of debt, tax relief on finance costs as shown in the APV calculation or, on the other hand, not being legally required to pay dividends in a particular year.

Another issue is whether Amberle Co's board has preferences about what source of finance should be used and in what order. One example of this is following the pecking order of retained earnings, then debt, then equity. The board may prefer this pecking order on the grounds that avoiding a new equity issue means that the composition of shareholdings is unchanged, or because retained earnings and longer term debt are

BPP
LEARNING
MEDIA

judged low risk, or because the market will assume that an equity issue is being made because directors want to take advantage of Amberle Co's shares being over-priced. Other specific sources of finance may have benefits which attract the directors or drawbacks which deter them.

This investment highlights the aspect of whether the board prefers to match sources of finance with specific investments. Matching arguably gives greater flexibility and avoids committing Amberle Co to a long-term interest burden. However, to adopt this approach, the board will need assurance either that the investment will be able to meet finance costs and ultimately repayment burdens, or these can be met from surpluses from other operations.

Changing long-term financing policy

As well as deciding what financing mix or sources of finance they desire to use, the directors will also need to consider what factors would cause this decision to change.

A major change in the scope of the operations, with investment requirements being paramount, may cause a change in financing policy. Here the $150 million investment has been financed entirely by medium-term debt. Amberle Co may have chosen solely to use debt if it has made a recent equity issue and does not feel it can make another one so soon afterwards. In addition, if Amberle Co expands its manufacture of electric cars, it may decide to sell off its motorbike or cycles divisions if they are performing less well. If part of the business is sold, the sale proceeds could help finance new investment in the cars division.

The board may also be flexible at times and take advantage of whatever source of finance seems to be offering the best terms for Amberle Co. Here the board is taking advantage of loan finance being available at a low cost, thanks to the government loan scheme.

A change in the business or economic environment may also lead to the board rethinking how the company is financed. An economic recession, leading to falling share prices, may mean that the results of a share issue are uncertain. On the other hand, an increase in economic or business risk may mean that lenders are less likely to lend at acceptable rates or will impose greater restrictions. If the directors are risk-averse, they may not seek new finance during a recession but instead rely on retained earnings to finance any expansion.

24 Kerrin

Workbook references. Business valuations are covered in Chapters 8-10.

Top tips. Careful planning is required before starting your calculations. A sensible approach in part (b) (the main part of the question) is:

(1)   Identify the value of the acquired company (Danton) using the information on P/E ratios given and then increasing by 30% to reflect the return required.

(2)   Identify the post-acquisition value of the combined entity using the information on P/E ratios given.

(3)   Calculate the percentage of this that would be owned by the acquired company Danton, then the balance is the percentage owned by Kerrin.

(4)   Kerrin's 750 million shares = the percentage owned by Kerrin so the total number of shares can be estimated to determine the extra shares needed to be offered for Danton. This gives the terms of the share for share exchange.

The impact on shareholder wealth can be assessed by comparing the pre and post-acquisition values of each company.

There is quite a lot of thinking required here, but once a sensible approach is established the numbers are fairly straightforward.

Marking scheme

			Marks
(a)	Financial synergies	4–5	
	Overestimation of synergies	2–3	
	Proposed steps	1–2	
			Max 8
(b)	Kerrin PE ratio	2	
	Danton valuation	2	
	Post-acquisition valuation	3	
	Share-for-share offer terms	2	
	Advice	1	
	Impact on shareholder wealth	3	
		13	
(c)	Cash offer	2–3	
	Share-for-share offer	2–3	
			Max 4
			Total 25

Note. Credit will be given for alternative and valid comments.

(a) **Financial synergies**

Many acquisitions are justified on the basis that the combined organisation will be more profitable or grow at a faster rate than the companies operating independently. The expectation is that the acquisition will generate higher expected cash flows or a lower cost of capital, creating value for shareholders. The additional value created is known as synergy, the sources of which can be categorised into three types: revenue, cost and financial synergies.

Based on the scenario, there are a number of possible sources of financial synergy. As a private company, Danton Co is experiencing a funding constraint whereas Kerrin Co has significant cash reserves but limited growth opportunities. The combination of the two can create additional value since Danton Co may be able to utilise Kerrin Co's cash resources to fund its expansion in a way which would not have been possible otherwise, leading to an increase in the expected cash flows.

Assuming both companies' cash flows are less than perfectly correlated, those of the combined company will be less volatile than the individual companies operating independently. This reduction in volatility enables the combined company to borrow more and possibly cheaper financing than would otherwise have been possible. This increase in debt capacity, and therefore the present value of the tax shield, increases the value of the combined company in the form of a lower cost of capital.

BPP
LEARNING
MEDIA

Further benefits may arise if Kerrin Co is able to utilise Danton Co's unrelieved tax losses. Whilst Danton is no longer loss making and could offset these tax losses independently, the combined company may be able to obtain tax relief earlier, since the acquisition increases the availability of profits against which carried forward tax losses can be offset. The present value of the tax saved will therefore be greater in the combined company.

If both companies were publicly traded, there would be no benefit from diversification, since investors are capable of diversifying at a lower cost and with greater ease than the company. However, Danton Co is privately owned and the shareholders are therefore exposed to diversifiable unsystematic risk. Therefore the acquisition may lead to potential diversification and risk reduction benefits. The reduction in the cost of the capital increases the value of the combined company.

Overestimation of synergy value

There is evidence that bidding companies often overestimate the value of synergy arising from a potential acquisition with the result that companies pay too much for their target. When this happens, there is destruction in wealth for the bidding company's shareholders. There are a number of possible explanations for this problem.

First, merger and acquisition activity tends to be driven by the availability of cheap credit. At the peak of a wave of activity, there may be competition for targets, thereby increasing acquisition premiums.

Second, conflicts of interest may lead to a biased evaluation process. Deal advisers such as investment banks earn a large proportion of their fees from mergers and acquisitions. Their advice on whether an acquisition makes sense is potentially biased if they do not look after their clients' interests.

Third, management overconfidence may explain why this occurs. Acquiring companies may overestimate the acquisition synergy and/or underestimate the time it will take to deliver. Management may then be reluctant to admit mistakes when the facts change, even when there is still time to back out of a deal. Agency costs may also be a factor if managers are more interested in pursuing personal goals than maximising shareholder wealth.

Finally, there may be difficulties integrating the companies due to different work cultures and conflicts of interest.

Steps to address this problem

Kerrin Co's board needs to plan for synergy and take active steps to ensure that it is delivered. This responsibility needs to be allocated to someone who can ensure spare cash is utilised to invest in new growth opportunities, that tax losses are offset as efficiently as possible and that the combined company avails itself of cheaper financing. Companies which allocate this responsibility and monitor and review performance tend to be more successful in creating value. In order to avoid any bias, the deal advisers who stand to profit from an acquisition need to be separate from the evaluation process. Effective due diligence ensures the financial documents which form the basis of a valuation are scrutinised and inspected.

(b) 1 Identify the value of the acquired company (Danton):

Danton's P/E ratio:

Future maintainable earnings (FME) = ($381.9) × 0.8 = $305.5m

Kerrin Co number of shares = 375m/ $0.5 = 750m

Kerrin EPS = $305.5m / 750 = $0.4073

Price earnings (PE) ratio = $5.28/ 0.4073 = 12.96

Danton's estimated P/E ratio = 12.96 × 1.2 = 15.55

Danton Co future maintainable earnings:

= ($116.3m + $2.5m) × 0.8 = $95.0m

Danton's post-acquisition value:

Danton Co pre-acquisition PE valuation = 15.55 × $95m = $1,477.3m

Value increased by 30% post-acquisition = 1,477.3m × 1.3 = $1920.5m

2   Identify the post-acquisition value of the combined entity using the information on P/E ratios given.

Pre-tax value of synergies = $15.2m + $5.3m = $20.5m

Post-tax value of synergies = $20.5m × (1-0.2) = $16.4m

Combined Co future maintainable earnings = $305.5m (Kerrin) + $95m (Danton) + $16.4m (synergies) = $416.9m

Combined Co PE ratio 12.96 × 1.1 = 14.3

Combined Co post-merger valuation = 14.3 × $416.9m = $5,961.7m

3   Calculate the percentage of this that would be owned by the acquired company Danton, then the balance is the percentage owned by Kerrin.

The percentage of the post merger value that would be owned by Danton can be calculated as (1920.5/5961.7= 32.21%) and the balance (67.79%) is therefore the percentage owned by Kerrin.

4   Kerrin's 750 million shares = the percentage owned by Kerrin so the total number of shares can be estimated to determine the extra shares needed to be offered for Danton. This gives the terms of the share for share exchange.

Given that Kerrin has 750 million shares and that this is 67.79% of the total, then the total number of shares must be 750m/0.6779 = 1, 106.4m shares, so an extra 356.4 million shares need to be offered for Dantons 140 million shares (35m/$0.25 = 140m).

This gives the terms of the share for share exchange as approximately 2.55 Kerrin shares per Danton share (calculated as 356.4 / 140). Using an offer of 2.55 Kerrin shares means that Dantons' shareholders would own 2.55 × 140m = 357 million shares.

Impact on shareholder wealth

	Kerrin Co $m	Danton Co $m
Pre-acquisition valuation	3,960.0 (5.28 × 750m)	1,477.3
Cash offer		
Danton Co shareholders cash received:		
$13.10 × 140m shares		1,834.0
Kerrin Co post-acquisition equity valuation:		
$5,961.7m less acquisition cost of $1,834.0m	4,127.7	
Increase in shareholder wealth	4.2%	24.1%
Share-for-share offer		
Post-acquisition value		
Kerrin Co: (750/1,110) × $5,961.7	4,028.2	
Danton Co (357/1,110) × $5,961.7		1,917.4
Increase in shareholder wealth	1.7%	29.8%

The terms of the share-for-share offer meet the criteria specified by Danton Co's directors.

Note. Credit will be given for alternative valid approaches.

(c)   **Cash offer**

The main advantage of a cash offer is that it provides Danton Co's shareholders with a certain and immediate return. However, the premium is lower compared to the share-for-share offer and may be reduced even further if the realised gain gives rise to a tax liability. By indicating their preferred premium under both offers, it is possible the shareholders have priced in the risks associated with an uncertain share-for-share offer and on this basis may be indifferent between the two. The cash offer may give rise to agency issues since Danton Co's founders no longer have a stake in the business, even though Kerrin Co's board is keen to ensure the founders remain in position after the acquisition. The information provided is too limited to read too much into the intentions of the venture capitalist. However, typically a venture capitalist would be expected to exit within three to five years. In this case, they may prefer the certainty of the cash offer.

The cash offer transfers more of the added value to Kerrin Co without the need for dilution, which may appeal to the shareholders. As indicated in the question, Kerrin Co's existing reserves are sufficient to fund the cash offer, although this may constrain future dividends and/or investment decisions.

Share-for-share offer

Both sets of shareholders benefit from increased wealth as a result of the share offer, albeit only marginally so in the case of Kerrin Co's shareholders. Another drawback is that Kerrin Co's shareholders' percentages are also diluted under this method. However, a share-for-share offer would ensure that Danton Co's founders' interests are aligned with Kerrin Co's shareholders, reducing possible agency costs. It also provides Danton Co's shareholders with the right to participate in the future growth of the larger company, which the cash offer would prevent.

No basis has been provided for the synergistic benefits; the increase in shareholder wealth is so marginal even a minor deviation from the estimates could result in a reduction in shareholder wealth for the owners of Kerrin Co. On this basis, it is quite likely they will not approve a share-for-share offer without further negotiation around the acquisition premium.

Note. Credit will be given for alternative and valid comments.

25 Selorne

Workbook references. Acquisitions are covered in Chapters 8-10 of the Workbook.

Examining team's comments. In part (a)(i), common mistakes in the weaker attempts included getting the number of shares wrong for Selorne Co, mixing up free cash flow to equity with equity value and adding the two together, and miscalculating the additional value created.

Part (a)(ii) the majority of candidates answered this question part quite poorly probably because there were no standard valuation models to apply.

Part (b) candidates who described the various types of synergies available and how they could be achieved, received limited or no marks as they did not answer the question asked. Answers which scored high marks made good use of the scenario in the question and provided suggestions to explain why the synergy estimates might not be reliable.

In part (c), candidates received no marks when they compared the choice between a cash payment and a share-for-share exchange for the bid, as it is irrelevant to the question requirement. Secondly, it is disappointing to read in some answers which described that a rights issue would dilute the existing shareholders' control. Dilution of control would only happen if the said shareholders do not subscribe to their rights shares.

Marks

(a) (i) Valuation of Selorne Co — 1
Valuation of Chawon Co — 2
Valuation of Salorne Co's FCFE — 1
Valuation of combined company — 1
Additional value created — 1
6

(ii) Value per share combined company — 1
Value of Chawon's shareholding in combined company — 1
Share of gain created for Chawon — 1
Share of gain for Selorne's shareholders — 1
Comments — 2
6

(b) Up to 2 marks per relevant point discussed, discussion must relate
to Selorne to obtain 2 marks for a point
Reliability of estimates — 3–4
Problems with achieving synergies — 3–4
Max 7

Max 6

(c) Up to 2 marks per relevant factor discussed
25

(a) (i) Selorne Co current equity value = 50m shares × $6.50 = $325m

Chawon Co current equity value = $7m × 1.03/(0.15 − 0.03) = $60.1m

Selorne Co free cash flow to equity = $325m/8 = $40.6m

Combined company valuation = ($40.6m + $7m + $5m) × 8 = $420.8m

Additional value created = $420.8m − $325m − $60.1m = $35.7m

(ii) Chris Chawon will hold 2m × 5 = 10m shares in combined company

Value per share in combined company = $420.8m/(50m + 10m) = $7.01

Value of Chris Chawon's shareholding = 10m × $7.01 = $70.1m

Gain created for Chris Chawon = $70.1m − $60.1m = $10m

Gain created for Selorne Co shareholders = $35.7m − $10m = $25.7m

Chris Chawon will have a 16.7% (10m/(50m + 10m)) shareholding in the combined
company but 28.0% ($10m/$35.7m) of the gain on the combination will be
attributable to him. Shareholders who are doubtful about the merger may question
whether this is excessive, as possibly Chawon Co's desire to sell is being prompted
by the company struggling to remain solvent.

(b) **Reliability of synergy estimates**

The reliability of the estimates may vary depending on the synergies involved. The
synergies relating to size and services offered will depend on the ability to gain large
contracts and neither company has had recent success in doing this. However, the
contracts recently bid for by Chawon Co might have been won if the larger combined
company had bid. The synergies relating to operations and working practices may be
difficult to obtain if it is difficult to change the employment conditions of Selorne Co
drivers. Claims that improved driver utilisation may reduce spare capacity may be true, but
there is likely to be less spare capacity anyway if more contracts are won.

BPP
LEARNING
MEDIA

Other synergies may be easier to obtain. Duplication of premises in some locations should be eliminated easily, providing Chawon Co does not have onerous rental contracts and there is space on Selorne Co's sites. Combining central administrative functions should reduce some staffing costs, although these are likely to be smaller synergies than the potential operational synergies.

Problems with achieving synergies

A significant problem may be lack of unity at the top of the company. Selorne Co's directors are not all keen on the acquisition and this may spill over into being unable to agree on a clear post-acquisition plan. If lack of unity at board level becomes apparent to staff, it may be difficult to achieve unity at employee level.

Chris Chawon's role in the combined company may also make synergies difficult to achieve. He will have a significant shareholding and a place on the board, so it will be difficult for him not to be involved. Possibly he has the abilities and desire to achieve changes in operational practices which other board members lack. However, if Chris is given the leading role he requires, there may be a change in management style which may upset long-serving Selorne Co staff. Some may leave, jeopardising the continuity which seems to have been an important part of Selorne Co's success.

Another reason for possible problems with staff is the differing remuneration arrangements. Selorne Co's staff may have stayed with the company because both their job prospects and their remuneration have been safe. Attempts to change their employment conditions may lead to resistance and employee departures. Ex-Chawon Co employees who have been with the company for a while may expect salaries to be increased to be more in line with Selorne Co's employees, particularly if bonus arrangements become less generous.

The success of the acquisition may also depend on how well the staff of the two businesses integrate. Integration may be difficult to achieve. Many of Chawon Co's staff will not have the necessary licence to drive the Selorne Co lorries and may not wish to go through the process of obtaining this licence. Selorne Co drivers may be reluctant to drive the smaller vehicles. Staff sticking to what they have been used to driving is likely to prolong a 'them and us' culture.

(c) **Availability**

Although the finance director has identified possible sources of finance, there is no guarantee that they will necessarily be available. The success of a rights issue may well depend on the willingness and ability of the director-shareholders to subscribe. It may be difficult to find others willing to take up the directors' rights if they do not subscribe, as the directors' unwillingness may be seen as indicating a lack of confidence in the business. A rights issue may also take longer to arrange than other methods, which may be significant if Selorne Co needs the finance quickly to complete the acquisition.

Obtaining a bank loan or mezzanine finance may be difficult if Selorne Co takes on Chawon Co's debt and is viewed as too highly geared as a result. The success of a convertible debt issue may depend on the terms, also how possible subscribers view the future prospects of Selorne Co and the marketability of the shares.

Cost

Cost will be another significant factor. The cost of equity will normally be viewed as higher anyway than the cost of debt. Issue costs of equity are likely to be higher than those of debt. As Selorne Co's share price is stable, its current external shareholders appear content with the dividends paid, so there does not appear to be pressure to increase them. In any case, the board is not required to pay dividends every year.

Fixed interest cost on the bank loan may become a burden if interest rates fall, but the cost can be forecast with certainty. Because the mezzanine finance is unsecured, it is likely to have a higher interest cost than the bank loan. The rights of conversion to shares attaching to the convertible debt will mean a lower rate can be set for this, but the cost will depend on how appealing the possibility of conversion is. Again, the finance cost of debt will depend on the finance providers' attitude towards the increased debt burden resulting from the acquisition of Chawon Co.

Director preferences

The choice will also be determined by Selorne Co's board's attitude to gearing as well as how the possible finance providers view the company's gearing level. The board may feel that Selorne Co has reached, or exceeded, the gearing level which it would regard as desirable by taking on Chawon Co's debt. If this is the case, the board would have to use equity finance. The board may also be influenced by how gearing is likely to change over time. Over the next few years gearing may fall as Selorne Co makes profits and (hopefully) its share price increases. Chawon Co's debt may be repaid and not replaced. The convertible debt and mezzanine finance will also not be long-term sources of debt finance.

Control of Selorne Co

Selorne Co's board decision may also be determined by the implications of the different sources of finance for control of the company. The directors' control of the company will not be diminished if a rights issue is used and they take up their rights. An issue of shares arising from the convertible debt would change the balance of shareholdings, so the directors would have to decide how significant this would be. Mezzanine finance may also offer conversion rights, but possibly these could only be exercised if Selorne Co defaulted, which the board may view as unlikely.

Using a bank loan will have no impact on share capital, but the bank may impose restrictions which the directors are unwilling to bear, particularly if high gearing is an issue. These conditions could include restrictions on the sale of assets, limitations of dividends, or requiring accounting figures, for example, liquidity or solvency ratios, not to go beyond certain levels.

Mix of finance

Ultimately the board may also consider the possibility of a mix of finance. The offer could be backed by a core of equity finance from a rights issue, but if Selorne Co has to pay a higher price than expected, the difference could be made up by mezzanine finance.

Note. Credit will be given for alternative, relevant answers.

26 Chithurst

Workbook references. Valuing a firm using the dividend valuation model is covered in Chapter 8. Dividend policy is covered in Chapters 1 and 16.

Top tips. In part (a), the key is to spend time analysing the actual policies being followed, not in righting generalised answers on the relevance or irrelevance of dividend poliies in general. A similar question was set in June 2013.

Easy marks. Part (b), should have been easier because of the clear instructions as to the nature of the analysis that was required, however in the exam many students did not read the question properly and did not provide valuations based on two growth assumptions as specified by the question.

Marking scheme

			Marks
(a)	Benefits of dividend policy – 1–2 marks for each company	Max	5
	Drawbacks of dividend policy – 2–3 marks for each company	Max	7
	Calculations – Dividend payout ratios – 1 mark per company		3
	Other calculations		2
		Max	15
(b)	Comments on valuation of each company, max 4 marks per company		
	(max 5 marks for valuation calculation(s))	Max	10
			25

(a) **Dividend payout ratio**

	Chithurst Co %	Eartham Co %	Iping Co %
20X2	42.9	40.0	46.7
20X3	41.3	(150.0)	19.3
20X4	35.1	40.0	33.1
20X5	34.0	40.0	31.8

Residual profit (after-tax profit for the year – dividend – new investment)

	Chithurst Co $m	Eartham Co $m	Iping Co $m
20X2	26	27	3
20X3	18	(40)	7
20X4	38	24	4
20X5	43	43	6

Chithurst Co's policy

Benefits

Chithurst Co's policy provides shareholders with a stable, predictable income each year. As profits have grown consistently, dividend cover has increased, which suggests that, for now, dividend levels are sustainable. These are positive signals to the stock market.

Drawbacks

Chithurst Co's dividend policy is unpopular with some of its shareholders. They have indicated a preference for dividend levels to bear a greater relation to profit levels. Although they are still in a minority and cannot force the directors to pay more dividends, they are now possibly a significant minority. Ultimately, Chithurst Co's share price could fall significantly if enough shareholders sell their shares because they dislike the dividend policy.

The dividend policy may also have been established to meet the financial needs of the shareholders when Chithurst Co was unquoted. However, it is now difficult to see how it fits into Chithurst Co's overall financial strategy. The greater proportion of funds retained does not appear to be linked to the levels of investment Chithurst Co is undertaking. Chithurst Co's shareholders may be concerned that best use is not being made of the funds available. If there are profitable investments which Chithurst Co could be making but is not doing so, then Chithurst Co may find it more difficult in future to sustain the levels of profit growth. Alternatively, if profitable investments do not exist, some shareholders may prefer to have funds returned in the form of a special dividend or share repurchase.

Eartham Co

Benefits

For three out of four years, Eartham Co has been paying out dividends at a stable payout ratio. This may be attractive to some investors, who have expectations that the company's profits will keep increasing in the longer term and wish to share directly in increases in profitability.

The year when Eartham Co's dividend payout ratio differed from the others was 20X3, when Eartham Co made a loss. A dividend of $15 million was paid in 20X3, which may be a guaranteed minimum. This limits the downside risk of the dividend payout policy to shareholders, as they know they will receive this minimum amount in such a year.

Drawbacks

Although shareholders are guaranteed a minimum dividend each year, dividends have been variable. Eartham Co's shareholders may prefer dividends to increase at a steady rate which is sustainable over time, even if this rate is lower than the rate of increase in some years under the current policy.

If Eartham Co had another poor year of trading like 20X3, shareholders' expectations that they will be paid a minimum dividend may mean that cash has to be earmarked to pay the minimum dividend, rather than for other, maybe better, uses in the business.

Having a 'normal' dividend policy results in expectations about what the level of dividend will be. Over time Eartham Co's managers may be reluctant to change to a lower payout ratio because they fear that this will give shareholders an adverse signal. Even if its directors maintain a constant ratio normally, shareholders may question whether the proportion of funds being retained is appropriate or whether a higher proportion could be paid out as dividends.

Eartham Co appears to be linking investment and dividend policy by its normal policy of allocating a constant proportion of funds for dividends and therefore a constant proportion of funds to invest. However, the actual level of new investments does not seem to bear much relation to the proportion of funds put aside for investment. When deciding on investments, the directors would also take into account the need to take advantage of opportunities as they arise and the overall amount of surplus funds built up over the years, together with the other sources of external finance available.

Iping Co

Benefits

Iping Co seems to have adopted a residual dividend policy, which links investment and dividend decisions. The strategy appears to be to make investments if they offer sufficient return to increase long-term company value and only pay dividends if there are no more profitable investments. They are assuming that internal funds are cheaper than external funds, or maybe Iping Co cannot raise the funds required from external sources.

The policy is likely to appeal to shareholders who are more concerned with capital growth than short-term income.

Drawbacks

Dividend payments are totally unpredictable, as they depend on the investment choices. Shareholders cannot rely on having any dividend income in a particular year.

Many shareholders may be prepared to sacrifice dividends for a while in order for funds to be available for investment for growth. However, at some point they may consider that Iping Co is well established enough to be able to maintain a consistent dividend policy as well as invest sufficiently for future growth.

(b)   **Use of dividend valuation model**

Chithurst Co

Valuation = 33/0.11 = $300m

Chithurst Co's market capitalisation of $608 million is considerably in excess of the valuation suggested by the dividend valuation model. This may suggest that investors have some positive expectations about the company and the lower cost of equity compared with the other two companies suggests it is regarded as a more stable investment. Investors could also be valuing the company using earnings growth rather than dividend growth. However, the lower market capitalisation compared with the other two companies and the smaller increase in share price suggest that investors have higher expectations of long-term growth from Eartham Co and Iping Co.

Eartham Co

One-year growth rate = (48/44) − 1 = 9.1%

Valuation using one-year growth rate = 48 (1 + 0.091)/(0.14 − 0.091) = $1,068.7m

Three-year growth rate = $\sqrt[3]{(48/38)}$ − 1 = 8.1%

Valuation using three-year growth rate = 48 (1 + 0.081)/(0.14 − 0.081) = $879m

Eartham Co's market capitalisation is closer to the valuation suggested by the dividend growth model using the one-year growth rate between 20X4 and 20X5 rather than the three-year growth rate between 20X2 and 20X5. This, together with the recent increase in share price, suggests that Eartham Co's shareholders have an optimistic view of its ability to sustain the profit growth and hence the dividend growth of the last two years, although

BPP
LEARNING
MEDIA

its higher cost of equity than the other companies suggests that they are more wary about the risks of investing in Eartham Co. It indicates confidence in the directors' strategy, including the investments they have made.

Iping Co

One-year growth rate = (42/39) − 1 = 7.7%

Valuation using one-year growth rate = 42 (1 + 0.077)/(0.12 − 0.077) = $1,052.0m

Three-year growth rate = $\sqrt[3]{(42/35)}$ − 1 = 6.3%

Valuation using three-year growth rate = 42 (1 + 0.063)/(0.12 − 0.063) = $783.3m

The market capitalisation of Iping Co is higher than is suggested by the dividend valuation model, but the dividend valuation model may not provide a realistic valuation because dividends payable are dependent on investment opportunities.

The larger increase in share price compared with the other two companies suggests that Iping Co's investors expect its investments to produce high long-term returns and hence are presumably satisfied with its dividend policy.

27 Louieed

> **Workbook references.** Chapter 8 covers valuation of acquisitions, Chapter 9 covers strategic issues and, acquisitions, and Chapter 10 covers financing issues.
>
> **Top tips.** In part (a) ensure you use the clues in the scenario to discuss the pros and cons of the acquisition.
>
> Part (b) is only worth five marks, so it is important not to spend too much time here. The implied P/E ratio of the pure cash and pure paper offers is fairly straightforward.
>
> In part (c), for 14 marks, it is very important to answer the whole question. For example, answers that only answered the first aspect of the question (on finance required) would only have scored two marks.
>
> **Easy marks.** Candidates who focused on the simpler bids (pure cash and pure paper) would have been able to access most of the marks in parts (b) and (c).

Marking scheme

			Marks
(a)	Reasons for acquisition	3	
	Reasons against acquisition	3	
			6
(b)	Calculations: 1 mark for EPS, 1 mark each for P/E ratio for original offer, and for each of the three options for the proposed offer		5
(c)	Funding of bid: 1 mark for cash option, 1 mark for mixed option	2	
	Earnings per share: 1 mark for share-for-share option, 2 marks for cash option, 2 marks for mixed option	5	
	Gearing: 1 mark for each option	3	
	Comments	4–5	
			Max 14
			25

(a) **Advantages of the acquisition**

Louieed Co and Tidded Co appear to be a good strategic fit for a number of reasons. Louieed Co appears to have limited potential for further growth. Acquiring Tidded Co, a company with better recent growth, should hopefully give Louieed Co the impetus to grow more quickly.

Acquiring a company which has a specialism in the area of online testing will give Louieed Co capabilities quicker than developing this function in-house. If Louieed Co does not move quickly, it risks losing contracts to its competitors.

Acquiring Tidded Co will give Louieed Co access to the abilities of some of the directors who have led Tidded Co to becoming a successful company. They will provide continuity and hopefully will help integrate Tidded Co's operations successfully into Louieed Co. They may be able to lead the upgrading of Tidded Co's existing products or the development of new products which ensures that Louieed Co retains a competitive advantage.

It appears that Tidded Co's directors now want to either realise their investment or be part of a larger company, possibly because it will have more resources to back further product development. If Louieed Co does not pursue this opportunity, one of Louieed Co's competitors may purchase Tidded Co and acquire a competitive advantage itself.

There may also be other synergistic benefits, including savings in staff costs and other savings, when the two companies merge.

Disadvantages of the acquisition

It is not known what the costs of developing in-house capabilities will be. Although the process may be slower, the costs may be less and the process less disruptive to Louieed Co than suddenly adding on Tidded Co's operations.

It is not possible to tell which of Tidded Co's directors are primarily responsible for its success. Loss of the three directors may well represent a significant loss of its capability. This will be enhanced if the three directors join a competitor of Louieed Co or set up in competition themselves.

There is no guarantee that the directors who remain will fit into Louieed Co's culture. They are used to working in a less formal environment and may resent having Louieed Co's way of operating imposed upon them. This could result in departures after the acquisition, jeopardising the value which Tidded Co has brought.

Possibly Tidded Co's leadership in the online testing market may not last. If competitors do introduce major advances, this could mean that Tidded Co's current growth is not sustainable.

(b) **P/E ratio calculations**

Value of Louieed Co's share = $296m × 14/340m = $12.19

Value of Tidded Co share per original bid = $12.19 × (5/3) = $20.32

Tidded Co earnings per share = $128m/90 = $1.42

Tidded Co P/E ratio implied by original bid = $20.32/$1.42 = 14.3

Tidded Co P/E ratio implied by all Tidded Co's shareholders taking up the share offer = $12.19 × 2/$1.42 = 17.2

Tidded Co P/E ratio implied by mixed cash and share offer = ($22.75 × 0.4 + $12.19 × 2 × 0.6)/$1.42 = 16.7

Tidded Co P/E ratio implied by all Tidded Co's shareholders taking up the cash offer = $22.75/$1.42 = 16.0

(c)   **Funding of bid**

No extra finance will be required if all Tidded Co's shareholders take up the share offer.

All Tidded Co's shareholders take up cash offer

Cash required = 90m × $22.75 = $2,048m

Extra debt finance required = $2,048m – $220m – $64m = $1,764m

60% share-for-share offer, 40% cash offer

Cash required = 40% × 90m × $22.75 = $819m

Extra debt finance required = $819m – $220m – $64m = $535m

Impact of bid on earnings per share (EPS)

Louieed Co's EPS prior to acquisition = $296m/340 = $0.87

All Tidded Co's shareholders take up share offer

Number of shares after acquisition = 340m + (90m × 2) = 520m

EPS after acquisition = ($296m + $128m + $20m)/520m = $0.85

All Tidded Co's shareholders take up cash offer

Number of shares after acquisition = 340 million

EPS after acquisition = ($296m + $128m + $20m – $11.36m – $105.84m)/340m = $0.96

$105.84 million is the post-tax finance cost on the additional loan finding required of $1,764 million. Therefore $1,764m × 7.5% × 80% = $105.84m.

$11.36m is the post-tax opportunity cost of lost interest on the cash and cash equivalents surpluses of the two companies of $220m + $64m = $284m. Therefore $284m × 5% × 80% = $11.36m.

60% share-for-share offer, 40% cash offer

Number of shares after acquisition 340m + (90m × 2 × 0.6) = 448m

EPS after acquisition = ($296m + $128m + $20m – $11.36m – $32.1m)/448m = $0.89

$32.1 million is the post-tax finance cost on the additional loan funding required of $535 million. Therefore $535m × 7.5% × 80% = $32.1m.

Impact of bid on gearing (using market values)

Louieed Co's gearing (debt/(debt + equity)) prior to bid = 540/(540 + (340 × 12.19)) = 11.5%

All Tidded Co's shareholders take up share offer

Debt/(Debt + equity) after bid = (540 + 193)/(540 + 193 + (520 × $0.85 × 14)) = 10.6%

All Tidded Co's shareholders take up cash offer

Debt/(Debt + equity) after anticipated bid = (540 + 193 + 1,764)/(540 + 193 + 1,764 + (340 × $0.96 × 14)) = 35.3%

60% share-for-share offer, 40% cash offer

Debt/(Debt + equity) after bid = (540 + 193 + 535)/(540 + 193 + 535 + (448 × $0.89 × 14)) = 18.5%

Comments

The calculations suggest that if Tidded Co's shares are acquired on a share-for-share exchange on the terms required by its shareholders, Louieed Co's shareholders will suffer a fall in EPS attributable to them from $0.87 to $0.85. This is because Tidded Co is being bought on a higher P/E ratio than Louieed Co and the synergies arising from the acquisition are insufficient to compensate for this.

Use of loan finance to back a cash offer will attract tax relief on interest. The cost of debt will be lower than the cost of equity.

Issuing extra shares will lead to a dilution of the power of Louieed Co's existing shareholders. If all of Tidded Co's shareholders take up the share-for-share offer, they will hold around one-third of the shares of the combined company (180m/520m) and this may be unacceptable to Louieed Co's shareholders.

The benefits which Tidded Co's shareholders will gain will be fixed if they take up a cash offer and do not acquire shares in the combined company. If there are significant gains after the acquisition, these will mostly accrue to Louieed Co's existing shareholders if a significant proportion of Tidded Co's shareholders have taken a cash offer.

If the forecast for take-up of the offer is correct, even by combining the cash flows of the two companies, the new company will have insufficient funds to be able to pay all the shareholders who are expected to take up the cash offer. Further finance will be required.

The alternative to loan finance is financing the bid by issuing shares. Depending on the method used, this may also result in dilution of existing shareholders' ownership and also there is no guarantee that the issue will be successful.

There is also no guarantee that the forecast of 40% of the shareholders taking up the cash offer is correct. If all five of the major shareholders decide to realise their investment rather than just two, this will increase the cash required by $512 million (25% × $22.75 × 90m), for example.

Gearing will increase if loan finance is needed to finance the cash offer. If the mixed share and cash offer is taken up in the proportions stated, the gearing level of the combined company will increase from 11.5% to 18.5%. Current shareholders may not be particularly concerned about this. However, if all or most of the share capital is bought for cash, the gearing level of the combined company will be significantly greater, at a maximum of 35.3%, than Louieed Co's current gearing. This may be unacceptable to current shareholders and could mean an increase in the cost of equity, because of the increased risk, and also possibly an increase in the cost of debt, assuming in any case that debt finance at the maximum level required will be available. To guard against this risk, Louieed Co's board may want to limit the cash offer to a certain percentage of share value.

28 Makonis

> **Workbook references.** Acquisitions are covered in Chapters 8 and 10.
>
> **Top tips.** For part (a) make sure that you both state **and** discuss your assumptions; often candidates only stated their assumptions but did not discuss them.
>
> **Examining team's comments.** In part (a) common errors included not converting the asset beta into the equity beta; deducting tax from the free cash flows; growing cash flows from the wrong year; and not recognising that the debt value has to be deducted from the value of the company to find the value attributable to equity holders.
>
> Part (b) was not done well by many candidates. Few candidates could estimate the reduction in value to the equity holders of the acquiring company when the premium paid was increased. A sizeable number of candidates who chose this question left part (b) unanswered.
>
> Part (c) was answered reasonably well by many candidates but again weaker answers tended to state, rather than discuss, the possible financing methods. A number of candidates suggested using Islamic finance to finance the acquisition but, unless a specific asset or asset group can be identified to match with this form of finance, it is difficult to see how this can be an appropriate source of finance. The finance source(s) should be appropriate to what it is needed for. Therefore, again, contextualisation to the scenario is important.

BPP LEARNING MEDIA

		Marks
(a)	Market values of Makonis Co and Nuvola Co	1
	Combined company asset beta	1
	Combined company equity beta	1
	Combined company: cost of capital	1
	Combined company value: Years 1 to 4	3
	Combined company value: Years 5 to perpetuity	1
	Combined company value: value to equity holders and additional value	2
	Comment and discussion of assumptions	3–4
		Max 13
(b)	Impact on Makonis Co's equity holders if the premium paid to Nuvola Co's equity holders is 30%	2
	Impact on Makonis Co's equity holders if the premium paid to Nuvola Co's equity holders is 50%	2
	Impact	1
		5
(c)	Impact on the cash payable under each of 30% and 50% premiums	3
	Discussion of how Makonis Co would pay the high premium	4–5
		Max 7
		25

(a) **Combined company, cost of capital**

Asset beta

$(1.2 \times 480 + 0.9 \times 1{,}218)/(480 + 1{,}218) = 0.985$

Equity beta

$0.985 \times (60 + 40 \times 0.8)/60 = 1.51$

Cost of equity

$2\% + 1.51 \times 7\% = 12.57\%$

Cost of capital

$12.57\% \times 0.6 + 4.55\% \times 0.8 \times 0.4 = 9.00\%$

Combined company equity value

Year

	1 $m	2 $m	3 $m	4 $m
Free cash flows before synergy (growing at 5%)	226.80	238.14	250.05	262.55
Synergies	20.00	20.00	20.00	20.00
Free cash flows	246.80	258.14	270.05	282.55
PV of free cash flows at 9%	226.42	217.27	208.53	200.17

Note. The present value (PV) figures are slightly different if discount table factors are used, instead of formulae. Full credit will be given if discount tables are used to calculate PV figures.

Total PV of cash flows (Years 1 to 4) = $852.39 million

Total PV of cash flows (Years 5 to perpetuity) = 262.55 × 1.0225/(0.09 − 0.0225) × (1.09 to the power of − 4) = $2,817.51m

Total value to firm = $3,669.90m

Value attributable to equity holders = $3,669.90m × 0.6 = $2,201.94m

Additional value created from the combined company = $2,201.94m − ($1,218m + $480m) = $2,201.94m − $1,698.00m = $503.94m (or 29.7%)

Although the equity beta and therefore the risk of the combined company is more than Makonis Co on its own, probably due to Nuvola Co's higher business risk (reflected by the higher asset beta), overall the benefits from growth in excess of the risk-free rate and additional synergies have led to an increase in the value of the combined company of just under 30% when compared to the individual companies' values.

However, a number of assumptions have been made in obtaining the valuation, for example:

(i)   The assumption of growth of cash flows in perpetuity and whether this is realistic or not

(ii)   Whether the calculation of the combined company's asset beta when based on the weighted average of market values is based on good evidence or not

(iii)   It has been assumed that the figures such as growth rates, tax rates, free cash flows, risk-free rate of return and risk premium are accurate and do not change in the future

In all these circumstances, it may be appropriate to undertake sensitivity analysis to determine how changes in the variables would impact on the value of the combined company, and whether the large increase in value is justified.

(b)   If 30% premium is paid to Nuvola Co's equity holders, they will receive = 30% × $480m = $144m of the additional value created.

Makonis Co's equity holders will receive about $359.94 million or $1.71 per share of the additional value created, which is 29.5% of the current share price.

If 50% premium is paid to Nuvola Co's equity holders, they will receive = 50% × $480m = $240m of the additional value created.

Makonis Co's equity holders will receive about $263.94 million or $1.26 per share of the additional value created, which is 21.7% of the current share price.

Hence, Makonis Co's equity holders will receive almost 8% less return if a premium of 50% were paid.

(c)   One Makonis Co share for two Nuvola Co shares implies a premium of $0.50 ([$5.80 − $4.80]/2) per Nuvola Co share.

If a 30% premium is offered to Nuvola Co's equity holders, then they will expect $144 million premium or $0.72 per share, and therefore the cash paid will be $0.22 for each Nuvola Co share or $44 million in total.

If a 50% premium is offered to Nuvola Co's equity holders, then they will expect $240 million premium or $1.20 per share, and therefore the cash paid will be $0.70 per Nuvola Co share or $140 million in total.

The amount of cash required will increase substantially, by about $96 million, if Makonis Co agrees to the demands made by Nuvola Co's equity holders and pays the 50% premium. Makonis Co needs to determine how it is going to acquire the additional funds and the implications from this. For example, it could borrow the money required for the additional funds, but taking on more debt may affect the cost of capital and therefore the value of the company. It could raise the funds by issuing more equity shares, but this may not be viewed in a positive light by the current equity holders.

Makonis Co may decide to offer a higher proportion of its shares in the share-for-share exchange instead of paying cash for the additional premium. However, this will affect its equity holders and dilute their equity holding further. Even the current proposal to issue 100 million new shares will mean that Nuvola Co's equity holders will own just under one-third of the combined company and Makonis Co's shareholders would own just over two-thirds of the combined company.

Makonis Co should also consider what Nuvola Co's equity holders would prefer. They may prefer less cash and more equity due to their personal tax circumstances but, in most cases, cash is preferred by the target firm's equity holders.

BPP
LEARNING
MEDIA

29 Vogel

Marking scheme

			Marks
(a)	1–2 marks per point		Max 4
(b)	2–3 marks per point		Max 7
(c)	Cash gained from sales of Department C assets	1	
	Calculation of free cash flows for Ndege Co	2	
	Calculation of present values of Ndege Co cash flows and value	2	
	Vogel Co P/E ratios before and after acquisition	2	
	Tori Co P/E ratio and value	1	
	Value created from combining Department A with Vogel Co	1	
	Maximum premium payable	1	
	Approach taken	1–2	
	Assumptions made	2–3	
			Max 14
			25

(a) Vogel Co may have switched from a strategy of organic growth to one of growth by acquisition, if it was of the opinion that such a change would result in increasing the value for the shareholders.

Acquiring a company to gain access to new products, markets, technologies and expertise will almost certainly be quicker and may be less costly than developing these internally. Horizontal acquisitions may help Vogel Co eliminate key competitors and thereby reduce rivalry and possible overcapacity in its industry; they may also have enabled Vogel Co to take advantage of economies of scale and to compete against large rivals. Vertical acquisitions may help Vogel Co to secure the supply chain and maximise returns from its value chain.

Organic growth may take a long time, can be expensive and may result in little competitive advantage being established due to the time taken. Also organic growth, especially into a new area, would need managers to gain knowledge and expertise of an area or function, which they are not currently familiar with. Furthermore, in a saturated market, there may be little opportunity for organic growth.

Note. Credit will be given for alternative relevant comments.

(b)   Vogel Co can take the following actions to reduce the risk that the acquisition of Tori Co fails to increase shareholder value.

Since Vogel Co has a poor track record of adding value from its acquisitions it needs to review recent acquisitions to understand why they have not added value, ie it should do a post-audit of these acquisitions.

Vogel Co should also ensure that the valuation is based on reasonable input figures and that proper due diligence of the perceived benefits is undertaken prior to the offer being made. Often it is difficult to get an accurate picture of the target when looking at it from the outside. Vogel Co needs to ensure that it has sufficient data and information to enable a thorough and sufficient analysis to be undertaken.

The sources of synergy need to be properly assessed to ensure that they are achievable and to identify what actions Vogel Co needs to undertake to ensure their achievement. Targets should be set for all areas of synergy and responsibility for achieving these targets should be clearly allocated to members of Vogels' senior management team.

The board of directors of Vogel Co needs to ensure that there are good reasons to undertake the acquisition, and that the acquisition should result in an increase in value for the shareholders. The non-executive directors should play a crucial role in ensuring that acquisitions are made to enhance the value for the shareholders. Procedures need to be established to ensure that the acquisition is not overpaid. Vogel Co should determine the maximum premium it is willing to pay and not go beyond that figure. Research indicates that often too much is paid to acquire a company and the resultant synergy benefits are not sufficient to cover the premium paid. Often this is the result of the management of the acquiring company wanting to complete the deal at any cost, because not completing the deal may be perceived as damaging to both their own, and their company's, reputation. Vogel Co needs to ensure that it has proper procedures in place to integrate the staff and systems of the target company effectively, and also to recognise that such integration takes time. Vogel Co may decide instead to give the target company a large degree of autonomy and thus make integration less necessary; however, this may result in a reduction in synergy benefits.

Vogel Co should also have strategies in place to retain key staff in the companies that it is acquiring – these people need to be identified at an early stage and given assurances over their role and responsibilities post-acquisition. Vogel Co should also be mindful that its own and the acquired company's staff and management need to integrate and ensure a good working relationship between them.

Note. Credit will be given for alternative relevant comments.

(c)   **Approach taken**

The maximum premium payable is equal to the maximum additional benefit created from the acquisition of Tori Co, with no increase in value for the shareholders of Vogel Co. It should be noted that the shareholders of Vogel Co would probably not approve of the acquisition if they do not gain from it, but certainly they would not approve a bid in excess of this.

The additional benefit can be estimated as the sum of the cash gained (or lost) from selling the assets of Department C, spinning off Department B and integrating Department A, less the sum of the values of Vogel Co and Tori Co as separate companies.

Estimation of cash gained from selling the assets of Department C:

Non-current assets = (20% × $98.2m) = $19.64m

Current assets = (20% × $46.5m × 0.9) = $8.37m

Liabilities and closure costs = ($20.2 + $3m) = $23.2m

Total = $19.64m + $8.37m − $23.2m = **$4.81m**

BPP
LEARNING
MEDIA

Value created from spinning off Department B into Ndege Co

Free cash flow of Ndege Co	$m
Current share of PBDIT (0.4 × $37.4m)	14.96
Less PBIT attributable to Department C (10% × 14.96)	(1.50)
Less tax-allowable depreciation (0.4 × 98.2 × 0.10)	(3.93)
Profits before tax	9.53
Tax (20%)	(1.91)
Free cash flows	7.62

Value of Ndege Co =

Present value of $7.62 million free cash flow growing at 20% in the first year and discounted at 10%:

$7.62m × 1.2 × 0.909 = $8.31m

Add present value of cash flows from Year 2 onwards:

($9.14m × 1.052)/(0.1 − 0.052) × 0.909 = $182.11m

Less bond taken over by Ndege = $40 million

Value to shareholders of Ndege Co = 8.31 + 182.11 − 40 = $150.42m

Current values

Vogel Co's current value = $3 × 380m = $1,140m

Vogel Co, profit after tax = $158.2m × 0.8 = $126.56m

Vogel Co, P/E ratio before acquisition = $1,140.0m/$126.56m = 9.01 say 9

Vogel Co, P/E ratio after acquisition = 9 × 1.15 = 10.35

Tori Co, P/E ratio before acquisition = 9 × 1.25 = 11.25

Tori Co post-tax profit = $23m × 0.8 = $18.4m

Tori Co's current value = 11.25 × $18.4m = $207.0m

Value created from combined company

Post-acquisition 50% of Tori's earnings will remain after the disposal of Department C and the spin-off of Department B. So earnings will become:

$126.56m + (0.5 × $18.4m) + $7m synergy) = $142.76m

So the combined company should be worth the P/E of 10.35 × $142.76m = $1,477.57m.

Maximum premium =

	$m
Value of combined firm	1,477.57
Value of Ndege	150.42
Value for disposal of C	4.81
Less current value ($1,140m + $207.0m)	1,347.00
	285.80

Assumptions

Based on the calculations given above, it is estimated that the value created will be $285.80 million.

However, Vogel Co needs to assess whether the numbers it has used in the calculations and the assumptions it has made are reasonable. For example, Ndege Co's future cash flows seem to be growing without any additional investment in assets and Vogel Co needs to establish whether or not this is reasonable. It also needs to establish how the increase in its P/E ratio was determined after acquisition. Perhaps sensitivity analysis would be useful to show the impact on value changes, if these figures are changed. Given its poor record in generating value previously, Vogel Co needs to pay particular attention to these figures.

30 Newimber

Marking scheme

			Marks
(a)	Advantages of demerger	2–3	
	Disadvantages of demerger	2–3	
			Max 5
(b)	Market value of debt	2	
	Pre merger WACC	1	
	New equity beta and cost of equity of Newimber	1	
	New WACC Newimber	1	
	Pre-merger asset beta	1	
	Ponyins beta	1	
	Ponyins WACC	1	
	Discounted free cash flows Ponyins years 1 to 3	3	
	Discounted free cash flows Ponyins year 4 onwards	2	
	Discussion	2–3	
			Max 15
(c)	1-2 per relevant point		Max 5
			Total 25

(a) Advantages of demerger

If the managers of the sportswear division's belief that they can run the division better without the interventions of senior management at Newimber Co is well-founded, the business may be able to achieve operational efficiencies and increases in value.

The new company is not tied to the financial commitments associated with the formal clothing division in terms of finance cost and loan repayment. Its management will have the ability to determine the finance structure which best suits the new business.

Newimber Co's shareholders will continue to own both companies. If shareholders are concerned about the diversification of their portfolio, this will remain unchanged.

The demerger may allow Newimber Co's management team to focus on the formal clothing division. They should not need to spend time dealing with disagreements with the sportswear division's management team.

Disadvantages of demerger

There will be legal costs associated with the demerger, such as the cost of obtaining a listing for the new company arising out of the sportswear division. Also setting up the new company and establishing the new structure looks likely to take up significant management time. This may mean that neither company is focused on external opportunities and challenges for some time, maybe impacting results and competitive position.

Both the new companies may suffer adverse effects through being smaller entities. Economies of scale may be lost and the companies may find it less easy to raise new finance. Looking at the position across both companies in total, distributable profits may fall because of a rise of overheads, as each company will need its separate infrastructure and service departments.

The current arrangement may frustrate the management of the sportswear division, but the command structure is clear. Once the director-shareholders of Newimber Co merely become shareholders of the new company, they will not be able to intervene actively in its management and overrule its management team. Agency problems may arise if these shareholders have different attitudes to risk to Poynins Co's board or different views on the importance of short-term versus long-term objectives.

(b) **Current WACC Newimber Co**

k_e is 11.8% and k_d is 4.5%

Annuity factor 4.5% for 5 years $= 1 - (1 + 0.045)-5/0.045 = 4.390$

Loan value per $100 = ($5.90 × 4.390) + ($105.00 × 1.045–5) = $110.16 MVd = $110.16/100 × $200m = $220m

WACC = ((585 × 11.8%) + (220 × 4.5% × 0.72))/805 = 9.5%

New WACC Newimber Co

MVe is $351 million

$\beta_e = 1.21$ ((351 + (220 (1 – 0.28)/351) = 1.76 k_e = 3.4% + (1.76 × 6%) = 14.0%

WACC = ((351 × 14.0%) + (220 × 4.5% × 0.72))/571 = 9.9%, an increase of 0.4%

WACC Poynins Co

Current β_a of Newimber Co = 1.4(585/(585 + (220 (1 – 0.28)))) = 1.10

β Poynins Co = (1.10 – (0.6 × 1.21))/0.4 = 0.935

WACC Poynins Co = 3.4% + (0.935 × 6%) = 9.0% Free cash flows Poynins Co

Year	1 $m	2 $m	3 $m
Operating cash flows	45.0	54.0	62.1
Tax	(12.6)	(15.1)	(17.4)
Post-tax cash flows	32.4	38.9	44.7
Investment in assets	(20.0)	(22.0)	(22.0)
Free cash flows	12.4	16.9	22.7
Discount factor (9%)	0.917	0.842	0.772
Discounted cash flows	11.4	14.2	17.5

Discounted free cash flows Years 1 to 3 = $43.1 million

Discounted post-tax cash flows Year 4 onwards

= ($44.7m (1 + 0.02)/0.09 − 0.02) = $651.3m × 0.772 = $502.8m

Discounted investment in assets Year 4 onwards

= (25/0.09) = $277.8m × 0.772 = $214.5m

Poynins Co's valuation = $43.1m + $502.8m − $214.5m = $331.4m

> **Tutorial note**
>
> Alternatively the M&M formula for the cost of equity can be used to ungear and regear the cost of equity of Newimber.

Discussion

If the managers' estimates of the sportswear division's future free cash flows are realistic, then the valuation using free cash flows ($331.4m) exceeds the current valuation ($585m − $351m = $234m).

The valuation is dependent upon achieving ambitious growth targets in Years 1 to 3, particularly given the loss of economies of scale discussed above. The board and shareholders of Newimber Co would want details about the assumptions behind these figures, particularly as growth after that is only assumed to be 2%. The valuation is also dependent upon the investment figures being accurate, so directors and shareholders would again need more detail of these so that they can decide whether the extra investment is likely to generate the increased cash flows predicted.

They would also want to determine how the managers of the sportswear division plan to fund the investments, particularly if initial operating cash flows are not as high as expected.

The restructuring will lead to a marginal increase in the WACC of Newimber Co, as its financial risk increases with more gearing. The directors may be worried that Newimber Co's credit rating will fall.

(c) **Requirement for business review**

The directors of Poynins Co will have to fulfil the same statutory and listing requirements as Newimber Co currently fulfils. These are likely to include the requirements for a business review.

Investors are likely to be particularly interested in how future strategies for Poynins Co may differ from those which have been pursued recently. They are also likely to want to know about attitudes to risk management and risk management policies, as the new company appears to be likely to be more risk-seeking than the old division. They will also want to know about changes in finance policy, particularly if dividend policies are likely to differ.

Communication with stakeholders

Poynins Co's directors are likely to communicate with major shareholders on a regular basis; more than once a year. These will include the director-shareholders actively involved in Newimber Co and external investors. Poynins Co's directors will need to ensure that what they communicate keeps both sets of shareholders happy if the two groups have different priorities.

Poynins Co's directors will also have to be mindful of the need to communicate what their plans are to other important stakeholders. Employees and suppliers are particularly important here, as Poynins Co's board has plans for operational efficiencies. Employees may be interested in being informed about changes in working conditions. Attempts to impose tougher conditions on employees without communication or consultation may lead to employee departures or other disruptions. Suppliers will be interested in changes to payment arrangements. Suppliers may be concerned anyway about dealing with a new, smaller company, so may seek to impose shorter credit periods or lower credit limits if they do not have sufficient information.

BPP LEARNING MEDIA

Use of integrated reporting

In particular, Poynins Co's directors will have to consider if, and how, they use integrated reporting. They are not bound by the decision of Newimber Co's directors to prepare an integrated report. However, if they do not do so, it may suggest to investors and other stakeholders that the directors are not keen to disclose information about how the business is using its resources and maintaining relationships. This may affect their confidence in how the directors are running the company.

If the directors decide to prepare an integrated report for Poynins Co, readers of the accounts are likely to look for significant differences between this report and the integrated report of Newimber Co, and how the differences are justified. These may include differences in the approach to value creation, the outlook for the business and whether the information has been prepared and presented in different ways.

Note. Credit will be given for alternative, valid comments.

31 Flufftort

Workbook references. Financial reconstruction is covered in Chapter 14.

Easy marks. You should be able to pick up some relatively easy marks in part (b). This required an evaluation of the acceptability of the financing scheme to all parties. There were up to two marks per well-explained point. This should have picked up the breach of a loan covenant in part (a)(i) as well as issues relating to control and risk.

Examining team's comments. In part (a), it is worth reminding candidates that occasionally, as in this part of the question, there are marks available for relatively straightforward calculations without needing to apply complex techniques.

Marking scheme

				Marks
(a)	(i)	SOFP if shares purchased and cancelled		
		Cash and other assets	2	
		Equity	1	
		Liabilities	1	
				4
	(ii)	SOFP if full refinancing takes place		
		Cash and other assets	2	
		Equity	1	
		Liabilities	1	
				4
	(iii)	20X7 forecast	2	
		20X8 forecast	2	
				4
(b)		Up to 2 marks for each well-discussed point		Max 13
				25

(a) (i) **Statement of financial position (SOFP) if Gupte VC shares are purchased by Flufftort Co and cancelled**

	$m
Assets	
Non-current assets	69
Current assets excluding cash	18
Cash	–
Total assets	87
Equity and liabilities	
Share capital	40
Retained earnings	5
Total equity	45
Long-term liabilities	
Bank loan	30
Loan note	5
Total long-term liabilities	35
Current liabilities	7
Total liabilities	42
Total equity and liabilities	87

(ii) **SOFP if full refinancing takes place**

	$m
Assets	
Non-current assets	125
Current assets excluding cash	42
Cash (balancing figure)	5
Total assets	172
Equity and liabilities	
Share capital	90
Retained earnings	5
Total equity	95
Long-term liabilities	
Bank loan	65
Loan note	–
Total long-term liabilities	65
Current liabilities	12
Total liabilities	77
Total equity and liabilities	172

(iii) **Projected SOPL**

	20X7 $m	20X8 $m
Operating profit	20.0	25.0
Finance cost	(6.5)	(6.5)
Profit before tax	13.5	18.5
Taxation 20%	(2.7)	(3.7)
Profit after tax	10.8	14.8
Dividends	–	–
Retained earnings	10.8	14.8

(b) **Current situation**

Initial product developments have not generated the revenues required to sustain growth. The new Easicushion chair appears to offer Flufftort Co much better prospects of commercial success. At present, however, Flufftort Co does not have the resources to make the investment required.

Purchase of Gupte VC's shares

In the worst case scenario, Gupte VC will demand repayment of its investment in a year's time. The calculations in (a) show the financial position in a year's time, assuming that there is no net investment in non-current assets or working capital, the purchase of shares is financed solely out of cash reserves and the shares are cancelled. Repayment by this method would mean that the limits set out in the covenant would be breached (45/35 = 1.29) and the bank could demand immediate repayment of the loan.

The directors can avoid this by buying some of Gupte VC's shares themselves, but this represents money which is not being put into the business. In addition, the amount of shares which the directors would have to purchase would be greater if results, and therefore reserves, were worse than expected.

Financing the investment

The calculations in (a) show that the cash flows associated with the refinancing would be enough to finance the initial investment. The ratio of equity to non-current liabilities after the refinancing would be 1.46 (95/65), in line with the current limits in the bank's covenant. However, financing for the subsequent investment required would have to come from surplus cash flows.

Shareholdings

The disposition of shareholdings will change as follows:

	Current shareholdings		Shareholdings after refinancing	
	m	%	m	%
Directors	27.5	55.0	42.5	47.2
Other family members	12.5	25.0	12.5	13.9
Gupte VC	10.0	20.0	30.0	33.3
Loan note holder	–	–	5.0	5.6
	50.0	100.0	90.0	100.0

Gupte VC's percentage shareholding will rise from 20% to 33.3%, enough possibly to give it extra rights over the company. The directors' percentage shareholding will fall from 55% to 47.2%, which means that collectively they no longer have control of the company. The percentage of shares held by family members who are not directors falls from 25% to around 19.5%, taking into account the conversion of the loan note. This will mean, however, that the directors can still maintain control if they can obtain the support of some of the rest of the family.

Position of finance providers

The refinancing has been agreed by the chief executive and finance director. At present, it is not clear what the views of the other directors are, or whether the $15 million contributed by directors will be raised from them in proportion to their current shareholdings. Some of the directors may not be able to, or wish to, make a significant additional investment in the company. On the other hand, if they do not, their shareholdings, and perhaps their influence within the company, will diminish. This may be a greater concern than the board collectively losing control over the company, since it may be unlikely that the other shareholders will combine to outvote the board.

The other family shareholders have not been actively involved in Flufftort Co's management out of choice, so a reduction in their percentage shareholdings may not be an issue for them. They may have welcomed the recent dividend payment as generating a return on their investment. However, as they appear to have invested for the longer term, the new investment appears to offer much better prospects in the form of a capital gain on listing or buyout than an uncertain flow of dividends. The new investment appears only to have an upside for them in the sense that they are not being asked to contribute any extra funding towards it.

Rajiv Patel is unlikely to be happy with the proposed scheme. He is exchanging a guaranteed flow of income for an uncertain flow of future dividends sometime after 20X8. On the other hand, his investment may be jeopardised by the realisation of the worst case scenario, since his debt is subordinated to the bank's debt.

The most important issue from Gupte VC's viewpoint is whether the extra investment required is likely to yield a better outcome than return of its initial investment in a year's time. The plan that no dividends would be paid until after 20X8 is a disadvantage. On the other hand, the additional investment seems to offer the only prospect of realising a substantial gain by Flufftort Co being either listed or sold. The arrangement will mean that Gupte VC may be able to exercise greater influence over Flufftort Co, which may provide it with a greater sense of reassurance about how Flufftort Co is being run. The fact that Gupte VC has a director on Flufftort Co's board should also give it a clear idea of how successful the investment is likely to be.

The bank will be concerned about the possibility of Flufftort Co breaching the covenant limits and may be concerned whether Flufftort Co is ultimately able to repay the full amount without jeopardising its existence. The bank will be concerned if Flufftort Co tries to replace loan finance with overdraft finance. The refinancing provides reassurance to the bank about gearing levels and a higher rate of interest. The bank will also be pleased that the level of interest cover under the refinancing is higher and increasing (from 2.0 in 20X6 to 3.1 in 20X7 and 3.8 in 20X8). However, it will be concerned about how Flufftort Co finances the additional investment required if cash flows from the new investment are lower than expected. In those circumstances Flufftort Co may seek to draw on its overdraft facility.

Conclusion

The key players in the refinancing are Gupte VC, the bank and the directors other than the chief executive and the finance director. If they can be persuaded, then the scheme has a good chance of being successful. However, Rajiv Patel could well raise objections. He may be pacified if he retains the loan note. This would marginally breach the current covenant limit (90/70 = 1.29), although the bank may be willing to overlook the breach as it is forecast to be temporary. Alternatively, the refinancing would mean that Flufftort Co just had enough spare cash initially to redeem the loan note, although it would be more dependent on cash surpluses after the refinancing to fund the additional investment required.

32 Ennea

Workbook references. Chapter 1 for the role and responsibilities of management; Chapter 7 for sources of finance; Chapter 16 for securitisation.

Top tips. In part (a) it is important to include the discussion as well as the forecast statements of financial position and ratios. Don't state just what has happened, but also what this means for Ennea Co to get more marks.

Remember to relate the answer in part (b) to the scenario and the relatively small amount of finance makes a securitisation less likely to be appropriate.

Easy marks. There are some easy marks to be gained in part (a) in the forecasts under each of the three different proposals.

Examining team's comments. Part (a) revolved around the impact of changes in financing of a company and how the impact of changing financial structure affected the financial position, earnings per share and the gearing of the company.

The answers to this part tended to be varied. Candidates, who presented the changed financial position and calculated the changes in earnings for each proposal, which were then incorporated into the calculations of EPS and gearing, gained the majority of marks. However, overall this part of the question was not done well.

Many responses tended to discuss or try to explain the changes and therefore gained fewer marks. Many responses did not consider the impact on interest of increased or reduced debt financing, and therefore did not incorporate the impact into the profit after tax and the financial position. In a notable minority of responses, candidates did not calculate the earnings per share (EPS) and gearing correctly. Such responses gained few marks.

Part (b) tested what securitisation was and the key barriers to Ennea Co undertaking the process. This part was done poorly by most candidates. Few responses gave an adequate explanation of the securitisation process, often confusing it with what leasing was and/or assuming securitisation meant providing asset security or collateral for a loan. Very few responses considered the barriers to Ennea Co in any detail.

Marking scheme

		Marks	
(a)	Financial position calculations: proposal 1	3	
	Financial position calculations: proposal 2	2	
	Financial position calculations: proposal 3	3	
	Adjustments to forecast earnings		
	Interest payable on additional borrowing and higher coupon	2	
	Interest saved on lower borrowing and lower coupon	1	
	Return on additional investment	1	
	Return lost on less investment and profit on sale of non-current assets	1	
	Gearing and EPS calculations	2	
	Discussion of the results of the proposals	2–3	
	Discussion of the implications (eg risk, market reaction)	2–3	
			Max 20
(b)	Explanation of the process	2–3	
	Key barriers in undertaking the process	2–3	
			Max 5
			25

(a) Forecast financial position

	Current $'000	Proposal 1 $'000	Proposal 2 $'000	Proposal 3 $'000
Non-current assets	282,000	282,000	302,000	257,000
Current assets	66,000	64,720	67,720	63,682
Total assets	348,000	346,720	369,720	320,682
Current liabilities	37,000	37,000	37,000	37,000
Non-current liabilities	140,000	160,000	160,000	113,000
Total liabilities	177,000	197,000	197,000	150,000
Share capital (40c per share)	48,000	45,500	48,000	48,000
Retained earnings	123,000	104,220	124,720	122,682
Total equity	171,000	149,720	172,720	170,682
Total equity and capital	348,000	346,720	369,720	320,682

	Current $'000	Proposal 1 $'000	Proposal 2 $'000	Proposal 3 $'000
Initial profit after tax	26,000	26,000	26,000	26,000
Interest payable on additional borrowing ($20m × 6% × (1 – 0.2))		(960)	(960)	
Additional interest payable ($160m × 0.25% × (1 – 0.2))		(320)	(320)	
Interest saved on reduced borrowing ($27m × 6% × (1 – 0.2))				1,296
Interest saved on lower coupon ($113m × 0.15% × (1 – 0.2))				136
Return on additional investment ($20m × 15%)			3,000	
Return lost on reduced investment ($25m × 15%)				(3,750)
Profit on sale of non-current assets				2,000
Total assets	26,000	24,720	27,720	25,682
Gearing (non-current liabilities/ non-current liabilities + equity)	45.0%	51.7%	48.1%	39.8%
Number of shares ('000)	120,000 ($48m/$0.4 per share)	113,750 ($20m/$3.2 = 6.25m shares bought back)	120,000	120,000
Adjusted EPS	21.67c	21.73c	23.10c	21.40c

Note. Other calculations of gearing would be acceptable.

Tutorial note

These explanations are not required for the answer, but are presented here to aid understanding.

Explanations of figures above

Proposal 1

Non-current liabilities are increased by $20 million from the additional debt and capital is reduced by the same amount. Given that the share price is $3.20, the $20 million will buy back $20m/$3.20 = 6.25m shares. These shares have a nominal value of 6.25m × $0.4 = $2.5 million. The split between share capital and retained earnings will therefore be $2.5 million to share capital and the balance of $17.5 million to retained earnings (actually to the share premium account, but this is included in retained earnings for simplicity).

The additional interest payable of $1.28 million is taken off retained earnings due to the reduction in profit after tax and also deducted from cash as it is assumed to be paid in cash. It would be acceptable to include as a current liability if it was assumed to be unpaid.

Proposal 2

Non-current liabilities and non-current assets are increased by $20 million from the additional debt and purchase of assets. Additional interest is payable as for Proposal 1 and the new investment will generate an additional return of 15% which is $3 million in income. The net impact is income of $1.72 million, which is added to retained earnings and to current assets as it represents either cash or a receivable.

Proposal 3

Non-current assets are reduced by the net value at disposal ($25 million) and the proceeds of $27 million are used to reduce non-current liabilities. The profit of $2 million is added to retained earnings.

The reduction of investment in non-current assets means there will be a lower return on investment of 15% of the $25 million. However, interest will be saved on the non-current liabilities which will be paid off. The net impact is a loss of $2.318 million which is subtracted from retained earnings and deducted from current assets as a cash expense. Again it would be acceptable to include as a current liability if it was assumed to be unpaid.

Discussion

Proposal 1 would lead to a small increase in EPS, due to the reduction in the number of shares since earnings fall by about 5% because of the higher interest payments from the additional debt. However, gearing significantly increases by approximately 6%.

Under Proposal 3 EPS will fall, although total earnings will be higher than under Proposal 1. Total earnings fall because the interest saved and the profit on disposal are less than the loss of the return on the non-current asset investment. Gearing would also reduce significantly, by 5%.

Proposal 2 significantly increases EPS, which the other proposals do not. This is due to the return on the additional non-current asset investment. However, gearing will also increase by just over 3%, although this is less than under Proposal 1.

Proposal 1 is the least attractive. The choice between Proposals 2 and 3 will depend on whether the board of Ennea Co would prefer a higher EPS figure or a lower level of financial gearing. This may depend on industry averages for both of these figures, how the stock market would react to the proposals and the implications of the proposals on changes to the risk profile of the company and whether this would change the overall cost of capital. It should also be noted that the above forecasts and estimates and actual results may well differ from those stated.

(b)   Asset securitisation for Ennea Co would involve converting the future lease income, from the non-current asset leases, into assets and **selling these assets as bonds** now. The future income is then used to pay the coupons on the bonds. In effect Ennea Co forgoes the interest payments on the leases in favour of the bond sale proceeds.

The lease income would be aggregated and pooled and new bonds would be created based on these. The pooled assets are divided into **tranches** and the tranches are **credit rated**. The higher rated tranches would carry less risk and also have a lower return than tranches with a lower rating. If default occurs, the income of the lower tranches gets reduced first and any subsequent default is applied to the lowest tranche with any income left. This process means an asset with a low level of liquidity can be transformed into a security with high liquidity.

There are a number of barriers to undertaking a securitisation process. It is **very expensive** due to management costs, legal fees and ongoing administration and compliance costs. Ennea Co is looking at selling a relatively small amount of non-current assets and therefore the costs would be a significant proportion of the potential income. This high cost means that securitisation is **not feasible for a small asset pool**.

It is usual to not offer the full value of the asset in the form of securities, but to leave say 10% of the asset value as a buffer against default and converting the other 90% into securities. The method of credit enhancement would give the tranches a **higher credit rating** and therefore **improve their marketability**. However, if Ennea Co was to use this method it would not be able to take advantage of the full value of the assets.

33 Nubo

Marking scheme

		Marks
(a)	Sale of supermarkets division's assets	1
	Sale of supermarkets division as going concern	1
	Advice	2
	Extra cash after liabilities are paid	1
	Maximum debt which can be borrowed	1
	Additional funds available to Nubo Co	1
		7
(b)	1–2 marks per relevant point	Max 6
(c)	Discussion of why Ulap Bank might prefer a Musharaka contract	6–7
	Discussion of key concerns over the joint venture relationship	5–6
		Max 12
		25

(a)   Current and non-current liabilities = $387m + $95m = $482m

Sale of assets of supermarkets division

Proportion of assets to supermarkets division
Non-current assets = 70% × $550m = $385m; Current assets = 70% × $122m = $85.4m

Sale of assets = $385m × 1.15 + $85.4m × 0.80 = $511.07m

Sale of supermarkets division as a going concern

Profit after tax attributable to the supermarkets division: $166m/2 = $83m

Estimate of value of supermarkets division based on the P/E ratio of supermarket industry: $83 × 7 = $581m

Although both options generate sufficient funds to pay for the liabilities, the sale of the supermarkets division as a going concern would generate higher cash flows and the spare cash of $99m [$581m − $482m] can be used by Nubo Co for future investments.

BPP
LEARNING
MEDIA

This is based on the assumption that the value based on the industries' P/E ratios is accurate.

Proportion of assets remaining within Nubo Co

30% × ($550m + $122m) = $201.6m

Add extra cash generated from the sale of $99 million

Maximum debt capacity = $300.6 million

Total additional funds available to Nubo Co for new investments = $300.6m + $99m = $399.6m

(b)   A demerger would involve splitting Nubo Co into two separate companies which would then operate independently of each other. The equity holders in Nubo Co would continue to have an equity stake in both companies.

Normally demergers are undertaken to ensure that each company's equity values are fair. For example, the value of the aircraft parts production division based on the P/E ratio gives a value of $996m (12 × $83m) and the value of the supermarkets division as $581 million. If the current company's value is less than the combined values of $1,577 million, then a demerger may be beneficial. However, the management and shareholders of the new supermarkets company may not be keen to take over all the debt.

Nubo Co's equity holders may view the demerger more favourably than the sale of the supermarkets division. At present their equity investment is diversified between the aircraft parts production and supermarkets. If the supermarkets division is sold, then the level of their diversification may be affected. With the demerger, since the equity holders will retain an equity stake in both companies, the benefit of diversification is retained.

However, the extra $99 million cash generated from the sale will be lost in the case of a demerger. Furthermore, if the new aircraft parts production company can only borrow 100% of its asset value, then its borrowing capacity and additional funds available to it for new investments will be limited to $201.6 million instead of $399.6 million.

(c)   With a Mudaraba contract, the profits which Pilvi Co makes from the joint venture would be shared according to a pre-agreed arrangement when the contract is constructed between Pilvi Co and Ulap Bank. Losses, however, would be borne solely by Ulap Bank as the provider of the finance, although provisions can be made where losses can be written off against future profits. Ulap Bank would not be involved in the executive decision-making process. In effect, Ulap Bank's role in the relationship would be similar to an equity holder holding a small number of shares in a large organisation.

With a Musharaka contract, the profits which Pilvi Co makes from the joint venture would still be shared according to a pre-agreed arrangement similar to a Mudaraba contract, but losses would also be shared according to the capital or other assets and services contributed by both parties involved in the arrangement. Therefore a value could be put to the contribution-in-kind made by Pilvi Co and any losses would be shared by Ulap Bank and Pilvi Co accordingly. Within a Musharaka contract, Ulap Bank can also take the role of an active partner and participate in the executive decision-making process. In effect, the role adopted by Ulap Bank would be similar to that of a venture capitalist.

With the Mudaraba contract, Pilvi Co would essentially be an agent to Ulap Bank, and many of the agency issues facing corporations would apply to the arrangement, where Pilvi Co can maximise its own benefit at the expense of Ulap Bank. Pilvi Co may also have a propensity to undertake excessive risk because it is essentially holding a long call option with an unlimited upside and a limited downside.

Ulap Bank may prefer the Musharaka contract in this case, because it may be of the opinion that it needs to be involved with the project and monitor performance closely due to the inherent risk and uncertainty of the venture, and also to ensure that the revenues, expenditure and time schedules are maintained within initially agreed parameters. In this way, it may be able to monitor and control agency related issues more effectively and control Pilvi Co's risky actions and decisions. Being closely involved with the venture would change both Pilvi Co's and Ulap Bank's roles and make them more like stakeholders rather than principals and agents, with a more equitable distribution of power between the two parties.

Nubo Co's concerns would mainly revolve around whether it can work with Ulap Bank and the extra time and cost which would need to be incurred before the joint venture can start. If Pilvi Co had not approached Ulap Bank for funding, the relationship between Nubo Co and Pilvi Co would be less complex within the joint venture. Although difficulties may arise about percentage ownership and profit sharing, these may be resolved through negotiation and having tight specific contracts. The day to day running, management and decision-making process could be resolved through negotiation and consensus. Therefore having a third party involved in all aspects of the joint venture complicates matters.

Nubo Co may feel that it was not properly consulted about the arrangements between Pilvi Co and Ulap Bank, and Pilvi Co would need to discuss the involvement of Ulap Bank with Nubo Co and get its agreement prior to formalising any arrangements. This is to ensure a high level of trust continues to exist between the parties, otherwise the venture may fail.

Nubo Co may want clear agreements on ownership and profit-sharing. It would want to ensure that the contract clearly distinguishes it as not being part of the Musharaka arrangement which exists between Pilvi Co and Ulap Bank. Hence negotiation and construction of the contracts may need more time and may become more expensive.

Nubo Co may have felt that it could work with Pilvi Co on a day to day basis and could resolve tough decisions in a reasonable manner. It may not feel the same about Ulap Bank initially. Clear parameters would need to be set up on how executive decision making will be conducted by the three parties. Therefore, the integration process of bringing a third partner into the joint venture needs to be handled with care and may take time and cost more money. The above issues would indicate that the relationship between the three parties is closer to that of stakeholders, with different levels of power and influence, at different times, as opposed to a principal–agent relationship. This would create an environment which would need ongoing negotiation and a need for consensus, which may make the joint venture hard work. Additionally, it would possibly be more difficult and time consuming to accomplish the aims of the joint venture.

Note. Credit will be given for alternative relevant comments and suggestions for parts (b) and (c) of the question.

34 Bento

> **Workbook references.** MBOs are covered in Chapter 15.
>
> **Easy marks.** Part (a) offers easy marks if you address the question accurately.
>
> **Examining team's comments.** In part (b) few candidates could apply the annuity factor to calculate the annual amount payable. Instead they opted to do it on a straight-line basis but this ignored the time value of money. However, a good number of responses then structured the profit or loss statement appropriately to take account of interest, tax and dividends, to get to the retained earnings figures. Nonetheless, some responses did not do this and therefore kept the book value of equity unchanged, casting doubt about whether or not they understand the relationship between the profit or loss statement and the statement of financial position.
>
> In part (c), candidates were asked to assess whether or not the MBO was beneficial. Although not specified in the requirements, the appropriate way to assess benefit was to compare the value of the investment, the MBO in this case, with the cost of that investment, the price to be paid for the MBO. This part of the question was not done well.

Marks

(a)	Distinguish between an MBI and an MBO	2
	Discuss the relative benefits and drawbacks	4
		Max 5
(b)	Annual annuity on 8% bond	1
	Split between interest and capital repayment	2
	Operating profit for the first 4 years	1
	Finance costs	2
	Tax and dividend payable for the first 4 years (1 mark each)	2
	Book values of debt and equity in Years 1 to 4	2
	Gearing and concluding comment	2
		Max 12
(c)	Valuation methods (1 for net assets, 3 for dividend valuation)	4
	Discussion (1 to 2 marks per point)	4
		Max 8
		25

(a) An MBO involves the purchase of a business by the management team running that business. Hence, an MBO of Okazu Co would involve the takeover of that company from Bento Co by Okazu Co's current management team. However, an MBI involves purchasing a business by a management team brought in from outside the business.

The benefits of an MBO relative to an MBI to Okazu Co are that the existing management is likely to have detailed knowledge of the business and its operations. Therefore they will not need to learn about the business and its operations in a way which a new external management team may need to. It is also possible that an MBO will cause less disruption and resistance from the employees when compared to an MBI. If Bento Co wants to continue doing business with the new company after it has been disposed of, it may find it easier to work with the management team which it is more familiar with. The internal management team may be more focused and have better knowledge of where costs can be reduced and sales revenue increased, in order to increase the overall value of the company.

The drawbacks of an MBO relative to an MBI to Okazu Co may be that the existing management may lack new ideas to rejuvenate the business. A new management team, through their skills and experience acquired elsewhere, may bring fresh ideas into the business. It may be that the external management team already has the requisite level of finance in place to move quickly and more decisively, whereas the existing management team may not have the financial arrangements in place yet. It is also possible that the management of Bento Co and Okazu Co have had disagreements in the past and the two teams may not be able to work together in the future if they need to. It may be that an MBI is the only way forward for Okazu Co to succeed in the future.

(b) Annuity (8%, 4 years) = 3.312

Annuity payable per year on loan = $30,000,000/3.312 = $9,057,971

Interest payable on convertible loan, per year = $20,000,000 × 6% = $1,200,000

Annual interest on 8% bond

Year end	1	2	3	4
	$'000	$'000	$'000	$'000
Opening loan balance	30,000	23,342	16,151	8,385
Interest at 8%	2,400	1,867	1,292	671
Annuity	(9,058)	(9,058)	(9,058)	(9,058)
Closing loan balance	23,342	16,151	8,385	(2)*

v*The loan outstanding in Year 4 should be zero. The small negative figure is due to rounding.

Estimate of profit and retained earnings after MBO

Year end	1	2	3	4
	$'000	$'000	$'000	$'000
Operating profit	13,542	15,032	16,686	18,521
Finance costs	(3,600)	(3,067)	(2,492)	(1,871)
Profit before tax	9,942	11,965	14,194	16,650
Taxation	(1,988)	(2,393)	(2,839)	(3,330)
Profit for the year	7,954	9,572	11,355	13,320
Dividends	(1,989)	(2,393)	(2,839)	(3,330)
Retained earnings	5,965	7,179	8,516	9,990

Estimate of gearing

Year end	1	2	3	4
	$'000	$'000	$'000	$'000
Book value of equity	15,965 *	23,144	31,660	41,650
Book value of debt	43,342	36,151	28,385	20,000
Gearing	73%	61%	47%	32%
Covenant	75%	60%	50%	40%
Covenant breached?	No	Yes	No	No

* The book value of equity consists of the sum of the 5,000,000 equity shares which Dofu Co and Okazu Co's senior management will each invest in the new company (total 10,000,000), issued at their nominal value of $1 each, and the retained earnings from Year 1. In subsequent years the book value of equity is increased by the retained earnings from that year.

The gearing covenant is forecast to be breached in the second year only, and by a marginal amount. It is forecast to be met in all the other years. It is unlikely that Dofu Co will be too concerned about the covenant breach.

(c) **Net asset valuation**

Based on the net asset valuation method, the value of the new company to its investors (debt holders plus equity holders) is approximately:

$1.3 \times \$40,800,000$ (market value of non-current assets) + $12,300,000 (current assets) − $7,900,000 approx. (trade and other payables) = $57,440,000.

The new company will have $50 million of non-current liabilities so the value to equity investors will be $57,440,000 − $50,000,000 = $7,440,000.

Dividend valuation model

Year	Dividend	DF (12%)	PV
	$'000		$'000
1	1,989	0.893	1,776
2	2,393	0.797	1,907
3	2,839	0.712	2,021
4	3,330	0.636	2,118
Total			7,822

Annual dividend growth rate, Years 1 to 4 = $(3,330/1,989)1/3 - 1 = 18.7\%$

Annual dividend growth rate after Year 4 = 7.5% [40% × 18.7%]

Value of dividends after Year 4 = $(\$3,330,000 \times 1.075)/(0.12 - 0.075) \times 0.636 =$ $50,594,000 approximately

Based on the dividend valuation model, the value of the equity in the new company is approximately: $7,822,000 + $50,594,000 = $58,416,000

The $60 million asked for by Bento Co is payable as $50 million of debt finance and $10 million of equity; $10 million is higher than the current value of the new company's net assets ($7.44 million) but $10 million is considerably lower than the value of the company based on the present value of future dividends based on the dividend valuation model ($58.4 million).

BPP
LEARNING
MEDIA

It can be argued that the future growth potential of the company is better represented by the dividend valuation model, rather than the current value of the assets, so the price of $60 million does not seem excessive.

However, the dividend valuation model can produce a large variation in results if the model's variables are changed by even a small amount. Therefore, the basis for estimating the variables should be examined carefully to judge their reasonableness, and sensitivity analysis applied to the model to demonstrate the impact of the changes in the variables. The value of the future potential of the new company should also be estimated using alternative valuation methods including free cash flows and price/earnings methods.

It is therefore recommended that the MBO should be accepted.

Note. Credit will be given for alternative, relevant discussion for parts (a) and (c).

35 Eview Cinemas

Workbook references. Valuations are covered in Chapter 8, and reorganisations in Chapter 15.

Easy marks. Part (a) offers easy marks for determining the sales proceeds. In part (b) there were marks available that did not relate to the calculations in part (a) but instead were based on non-financial strategic factors relating to the scenario.

Examining team's comments. In part (a) the majority of candidates omitted to add back the interest saved from paying off the loan when calculating the adjusted earnings per share. A large number of candidates erroneously either included the loan already repaid or ignored the bank loans in determining the company's weighted average cost of capital. Quite a few candidates made a basic error in using market return instead of market premium when calculating a company's cost of equity.

Part (b) required an evaluation of the decision to sell off the unbundled part of the company. Most discussions were too narrowly focused on the results from the calculations produced in part (a).

Marking scheme

		Marks	
(a)	PV of free cash flows Years 1–4	1	
	PV of free cash flows Years 5 onwards	2	
	Desired sales proceeds	1	
	Impact on statement of financial position	4	
	Impact on eps	5	
	Impact on WACC		
	Equity beta – cinemas	2	
	Revised cost of equity – cinemas	1	
	Revised WACC	1	
			17
(b)	Arguments against sale	4–5	
	Arguments for sale	4–5	
		Max	8
			25

(a) **Proceeds from sales of EV clubs**

Year (all figures $m)	1	2	3	4
Free cash flows	390	419	455	490
Discount factor 12%	0.893	0.797	0.712	0.636
Present value	348	334	324	312
Present value	1,318			

Present value in Year 5 onwards = $490m × 1.052/(0.12 − 0.052) × 0.636 = $4,821m
Total present value = $1,318m + $4,821m = $6,139m

Desired sales proceeds (25% premium) = $6,139m × 1.25 = $7,674m

Impact on statement of financial position ($m)

Profit on sale = $7,674m − $3,790m = $3,884m

Current assets increase = current liabilities $2,166m × current ratio of 1.5 = $3,249m = increase of $902m compared to current level of $2,347m

Increase in non-current assets = increase in non-current assets = proceeds from sale of $7,674m less $902m increase in working capital, less $3,200m loan note repayment = $3,572m increase. This is then reduced by the sale of EV clubs with non-current asset value given as $3,790m. So the net change is a fall of $3,790m − $3,572m = $218m.

	Original $m	Adjustments $m	Final $m
Assets			
Non-current assets	15,621	(218)	15,403
Current assets	2,347	902	3,249
Total assets	17,968		18,652
Equity and liabilities			
Called-up share capital	1,000		1,000
Retained earnings	7,917	3,884	11,801
Total equity	8,917		12,801
Non-current liabilities			
10% loan notes	3,200	(3,200)	–
Other loan notes	2,700		2,700
Bank loans	985		985
Total non-current liabilities	6,885		3,685
Current liabilities	2,166		2,166
Total equity and liabilities	17,968		18,652

Impact on eps ($m)

	Current forecast	Revised forecast
Predicted post tax profits	1,135	1,135
($454m × 10/4)		
Less: profits from EV clubs		(454)
Add: interest saved, net of tax		256
($3,200m × 10% × (1 − 0.2))		
Add: return on additional non-current assets		343
($3,572m × 12% × (1 − 0.2))		
Add: return on additional current assets		51
($902m × 7% × (1 − 0.2))		
Adjusted profits	1,135	1,331
Number of shares	1,000m	1,000m
Adjusted eps	$1.135	$1.331

Impact on WACC

Equity beta

V_e = $15,750m × 1.1 = $17,325m

V_d = ($2,700 × 0.93) + $985m = $3,496m

βe = 0.952 ((17,325 + 3,496 (1 − 0.2))/17,325 = 1.106

Revised cost of equity

$k_e = 4 + (10 - 4)1.106 = 10.64\%$

Revised WACC

$WACC = 10.64 (17,325/(17,325 + 3,496)) + 8 (1 - 0.2) (3,496/(17,325 + 3,496)) = 9.93\%$

(b) Shareholders would appear to have grounds for questioning the sale of the EV clubs. It would mean that Eview Cinemas Co was no longer diversified into two sectors. Although shareholders can achieve diversification themselves in theory, in practice transaction costs and other issues may mean they do not want to adjust their portfolio.

The increase in gym membership brought about by the forthcoming sports festival could justify the predicted increases in free cash flows made in the forecasts. Although increased earnings per share are forecast once the EV clubs are sold, these are dependent on Eview Cinemas Co achieving the sales price which it desires for the EV clubs and the predicted returns being achieved on the remaining assets.

The proposed expansion of multiscreen cinemas may be a worthwhile opportunity, but the level of demand for big cinema complexes may be doubtful and there may also be practical problems like negotiating change of use. In Year 1 the EV clubs would be forecast to make a post-tax return on assets of $(454/3,790) = 12.0\%$ compared with 9.6% ($12\% \times 0.8$) on the additional investment in the cinemas.

Investors may also wonder about the motives of Eview Cinemas Co's board. Selling the EV clubs offers the board a convenient way of resolving the conflict with the management team of the EV clubs and investors may feel that the board is trying to take an easy path by focusing on what they are comfortable with managing.

There may be arguments in favour of the sale, however. The lower WACC will be brought about by a fall in the cost of equity as well as the fall in the cost of debt. A reduction in the complexity of the business may result in a reduction in central management costs.

Eview Cinemas Co may also be selling at a time when the EV clubs chain is at its most attractive as a business, in the period before the sports festival. The premium directors are hoping to obtain (on top of a valuation based on free cash flow figures which may be optimistic) suggest that they may be trying to realise maximum value while they can.

36 Kenduri

Workbook references. Hedging foreign currency transactions is covered in Chapter 12. Gamma is covered in Chapter 11.

Top tips. In part (b) make sure you don't confuse payments and receipts in your matrix. Also it was important to read the scenario carefully to see that the spot mid-rate should be used, rather than any other rate.

For part (c) don't waste time if you don't know what a gamma value is.

Easy marks. There are some easy marks to be gained in part (a) for money market hedging and forward market calculations as these should be brought forward knowledge from FM.

Examining team's comments. For part (a), in many cases the advice was limited to a recommendation but without proper justification, and therefore few marks were gained.

Answers to part (c) were poor and few candidates were aware of what gamma is and what a high gamma meant in relation to a long call option. There also appeared to be some confusion about what a long call meant. A long call is buying the right to buy an underlying asset at a predetermined price, whereas a short call is selling the right to buy an underlying asset at a predetermined price (and similarly for put options).

Marks

(a) Calculation of net US$ amount — 1
Calculation of forward market US$ amount — 1
Calculation of US$ money market amount — 2
Calculation of one put option amount (1.60 or 1.62) — 3
Calculation of the second put option amount or if the preferred
  exercise price is explained — 2
Advice and recommendation — 3–4

Max 12

(b) Construction of the transactions matrix — 1
Calculation of the £ equivalent amounts of US$, CAD and JPY — 4
Calculation of the net receipt/payment — 2
Explanation of government reaction to hedging — 3

10

(c) 1 mark per valid point — Max 3

25

(a) Only transactions between Kenduri Co and Lakama Co are relevant, which are:

Payment of $4.5 million

Receipt of $2.1 million

Net payment = $2.4 million

The hedging options are: using the forward market, money market hedging and currency options.

Forward market

As selling £ for $, receive at lower rate.

2,400,000/1.5996 = £1,500,375

Money market hedge

Invest US$ now: 2,400,000/(1 + 0.031/4) = $2,381,543

Converted at spot: 2,381,543/1.5938 = £1,494,255

Borrow in £ now: 1,494,255 × (1 + 0.04/4) = £1,509,198

The forward market is cheaper and therefore is preferred.

Options

Kenduri would buy sterling put options to protect against a depreciating £.

Exercise price $1.60/£1

£ payment = 2,400,000/1.6 = £1,500,000

1,500,000/62,500 = 24 contracts

24 3-month put options purchased

Premium = 24 × 0.0208 × 62,500 = $31,200

Premium in £ = 31,200/1.5938 = £19,576

Total payments = 1,500,000 + 19,576 = £1,519,576

BPP LEARNING MEDIA

Exercise price $1.62/£1

£ payment = 2,400,000/1.62 = £1,481,481

1,481,481/62,500 = 23.7 contracts

23 3-month put options purchased

£ payment = 23 × 62,500 = £1,437,500

Premium = 23 × 0.0342 × 62,500 = $49,163

Premium in £ = 49,163/1.5938 = £30,846

Unhedged amount = 2,400,000 − (1,437,500 × 1.62) = $71,250

Hedging using forward market = 71,250/1.5996 = £44,542

Total payments = 1,437,500 + 30,846 + 44,542 = £1,512,888

Both options hedges are worse than using the forward or money markets as a result of the premiums payable for the options. However, options have an advantage over forwards and money markets because the prices are not fixed and the buyer can let the option lapse if exchange rates move favourably. Therefore the options have a limited downside, but an unlimited upside. Only with options can Kenduri Co take advantage of the $ weakening against the £.

Conclusion

The forward market is preferred to the money market hedge. The choice between options and forwards will depend on whether management wants to risk the higher cost for the potential upside if exchange rates move in Kenduri Co's favour.

(b)   Spot mid-rates are as follows:

US$1.5950/£1

CAD 1.5700/£1

JPY 132.75/£1

Paying subsidiary

Receiving subsidiary	UK £'000	US £'000	Canada £'000	Japan £'000	Total receipts (add across) £'000	Total payments (add down) £'000	Net receipt / (payment) £'000
UK	–	1,316.6	2,165.6	–	3,482.2	3,521.9	(39.7)
US	2,821.3	–	940.4	877.7	4,639.4	3,727.1	912.3
Canada	700.6	–	–	2,038.2	2,738.8	3,106.0	(367.2)
Japan	–	2,410.5	–	–	2,410.5	2,915.9	(505.4)

Kenduri Co will make a payment of £39,700 to Lakama Co.

Jaia Co will make a payment of £367,200 to Lakama Co.

Gochiso Co will make a payment of £505,400 to Lakama Co.

Multilateral netting will minimise the number of transactions taking place through the banks of each country. This limits the amount paid in fees to these banks. Governments which do not allow multilateral netting are therefore looking to **maximise the transactions and fees** that the local banks will receive. Other countries may choose to allow multilateral netting in the belief that this makes them more attractive to multinational companies and the lost banking fees are **more than compensated for** by the extra business brought to the country.

(c)   Gamma measures the **rate of change of the delta** of an option. Deltas can be near zero for a long call option which is deep out-of-the-money, where the price of the option will be insensitive to changes in the price of the underlying asset. Deltas can also be near 1 for a long call option which is deep in-the-money, where the price of the option and the value of the underlying asset move mostly in line with each other. When a long call option is at-the-money, the delta is 0.5 but also changes rapidly. Therefore, the **highest gamma values are when a call option is at-the-money**. Gamma values are also higher when the option is closer to expiry. In this case, it appears that the option is trading near at-the-money and that it has a relatively short period before expiry.

37 Massie

Workbook references. Chapters 11 and 12.

Top tips. Don't rush into hedging questions without reading the scenario carefully. A number of candidates assumed that because Europe was mentioned, the netting would be in euros which was not in fact the case.

Examining team's comments. Very few candidates demonstrated the knowledge to calculate the effective cost of the collar hedge.

Marking scheme

				Marks
(a)	(i)	Dollar amounts owed and owing	2	
		Totals owed and owing	3	
		Net amounts owed	1	
		Payments and receipts	$\underline{2}$	
			8	
	(ii)	1–2 marks per problem discussed		Max 3
(b)		Recommendation to purchase calls		1
		Number and month of contracts		1
		Calculation of basis		1
		Options contracts calculations		
		(only one option contract needs to be used, with a justification		
		for choosing this exercise price, lose 1 mark if no justification)	4	
		Collars approach and calculations	5	
		Comments and conclusion	$\underline{2\text{–}3}$	
				Max 14
				$\underline{\underline{25}}$

(a) (i)

Owed by	Owed to	Local currency (m)	$m
Armstrong (US)	Horan (South Africa)	US$12.17	12.17
Horan (South Africa)	Massie (Europe)	SA R42.65	3.97
Giffen (Denmark)	Armstrong (US)	D Kr21.29	3.88
Massie (Europe)	Armstrong (US)	US$19.78	19.78
Armstrong (US)	Massie (Europe)	€1.57	2.13
Horan (South Africa)	Giffen (Denmark)	D Kr16.35	2.98
Giffen (Denmark)	Massie (Europe)	€1.55	2.11

Owed to	Giffen (De) $m	Armtg (US) $m	Owed by Horan (SA) $m	Massie (Eu) $m	Total $m
Giffen (De)			2.98		2.98
Armtg (US)	3.88			19.78	23.66
Horan (SA)		12.17			12.17
Massie (Eu)	2.11	2.13	3.97	_____	8.21
Owed by	(5.99)	14.30	(6.95)	(19.78)	
Owed to	2.98	23.66	12.17	8.21	
Net	(3.01)	9.36	5.22	(11.57)	

Under the terms of the arrangement, Massie, as the company with the largest debt, will pay Horan $5.22 million, as the company with the smallest amount owed. Then Massie will pay Armstrong $6.35 million and Giffen will pay Armstrong $3.01 million.

(ii)   The Armstrong Group may have problems if any of the governments of the countries where the subsidiaries are located object to multilateral netting. However, this may be unlikely here.

The new system may not be popular with the management of the subsidiaries because of the length of time before settlement (up to six months). Not only might this cause cash flow issues for the subsidiaries, but also the length of time may mean that some of the subsidiaries face significant foreign exchange risks. The system may possibly have to allow for immediate settlement in certain circumstances, for example, if transactions are above a certain size or if a subsidiary will have significant cash problems if amounts are not settled immediately.

(b)   Need to hedge against a fall in interest rate, therefore buy call options. Require 50 contracts (25,000,000/1,000,000) × 6/3.

As Massie is looking to invest on 30 November, December contracts are needed.

Basis

Futures price – current price (1 September) = basis

95.76 – (100 – 3.6) = –0.64

Unexpired basis = ¼ × 0.64 = –0.16

Option

Amount received will be (LIBOR – 0.4%) × 25,000,000 × 6/12

If interest rates increase by 0.5% to 4.1%

Expected futures price = (100 – 4.1) – 0.16 = 95.74

Exercise price	97.00	96.50
Futures price	95.74	95.74
Exercise option?	No	No
Gain in basis points	–	–

	€	€
Interest received (€25m × 6/12 × (4.1 – 0.4)%)	462,500	462,500
Gain on options	–	–
Premium		
(3.2 × €25 × 50)	(4,000)	
(18.2 × €25 × 50)		(22,750)
Net receipt	458,500	439,750
Effective interest rates	3.67%	3.52%

Alternative solution:

Exercise rate (100 – price)	3%	3.5%
Futures rate (100 – price)	4.26%	4.26%
Exercise option?	No	No
Gain in %	–	–

	%	%
Interest received (4.1 – 0.4)%	3.7	3.70
Gain on options	–	–
Premium		
	(0.032)	(0.182)
Effective interest rates	3.668%	3.518%
Net receipt (€25m × effective interest rate × 6/12)	458,500	439,750

If interest rates fall by 0.5% to 3.1%

Expected futures price = (100 – 3.1) – 0.16 = 96.74

Exercise price	97.00	96.50
Futures price	96.74	96.74
Exercise option?	No	Yes
Gain in basis points	–	24
	€	€
Interest received		
(€25m × 6/12 × (3.1 – 0.4)%)	337,500	337,500
Gain on options		
(0 and 24 × €25 × 50)	–	30,000
Premium		
(3.2 × €25 × 50)	(4,000)	
(18.2 × €25 × 50)		(22,750)
Net receipt	333,500	344,750
Effective interest rates	2.67%	2.76%

Alternative solution:

Exercise rate (100 – price)	3%	3.5%
Futures rate (100 – price)	3.26%	3.26%
Exercise option?	No	Yes
Gain in %	–	0.24%
	%	%
Interest received		
(3.1 – 0.4)%	2.7	2.70
Gain on options	–	0.24
Premium		
	(0.032)	(0.182)
Effective interest rates	2.668%	2.758%
Net receipt (€25m × effective interest rate × 6/12)	333,500	344,750

Using a collar

Buy December call at 97.00 for 0.032 and sell December put at 96.50 for 0.123. Net premium received = 0.091.

If interest rates increase to 4.1%

	Buy call	Sell put
Exercise price	97.00	96.50
Futures price	95.74	95.74
Exercise option?	No	Yes
Gain in basis points	–	
	€	
Interest received	462,500	
Loss on exercise		
(76 × €25 × 50)	(95,000)	
Premium		
(9.1 × €25 × 50)	11,375	
Net receipt	378,875	
Effective interest rates	3.03%	

Alternative solution:

Futures rate	4.26%
Exercise call option at 3%?	No
Exercise put option at 3.5%?	Yes
Loss on option (futures rate 4.26 – 3.5% put rate)	(0.76)%

	%
Interest received (4.1 – 0.4)%	3.7
Loss on options	(0.76)
Premium (cost of call – revenue from put)	0.091
Effective interest rates	3.031%
Net receipt (€25m × effective interest rate × 6/12)	378,875

If interest rates fall to 3.1%

	Buy call	Sell put
Exercise price	97.00	96.50
Futures price	96.74	96.74
Exercise option?	No	No
Gain in basis points	–	

	€
Interest received	337,500
Loss on exercise	–
Premium (9.1 × €25 × 50)	11,375
Net receipt	348,875
Effective interest rates	2.79%

Alternative solution:

Futures price	3.26%
Exercise call option at 3%?	No
Exercise put option at 3.5%?	No

	%
Interest received (3.1 – 0.4)%	2.7
Premium (cost of call – revenue from put)	0.091
Effective interest rates	2.791%
Net receipt (€25m × effective interest rate × 6/12)	348,875

Summary

	97.00	96.50	Collar
Interest rates rise to 4.1%	3.67%	3.52%	3.03%
Interest rates fall to 3.1%	2.67%	2.76%	2.79%

The collar gives a significantly worse result than either of the options if interest rates rise, because Massie cannot take full advantage of the increase. It is marginally the better choice if interest rates fall.

The recommendation would be to choose the option with the 97.00 exercise price, which has a cheaper premium, unless interest rates are virtually certain to fall.

38 Adverane

Marks

(a)	Calculation of net US$ receipt	1	
	Money market hedge	2	
	Futures		
	Buy futures	1	
	Predicted futures rate based on basis reduction	2	
	Expected receipt	1	
	Number of contracts	1	
	Conclusion	1–2	
			Max 9
(b)	(i) CHF amounts owed and owing	2	
	Totals owed and owing	2	
	Net amounts owed	1	
	Payments and receipts	2	
		7	
	(ii) Advantages – 1 mark each		Max 3
(c)	Performance assessment	2–3	
	Work of central treasury	2–3	
	Buying internally	2–3	
			Max 6
			25

(a)   Net receipt = $10,150,000 – $3,700,000 = $6,450,000

Adverane Co will have a net dollar receipt in four months' time and needs to hedge against the Swiss Franc strengthening.

Money market

Borrow US$: US$6,450,000/(1 + [0.037/3]) = US$6,371,419

Convert into CHF at spot rate: US$6,371,419/1.1222 = CHF5,677,615

Invest in CHF: CHF5,677,615 × (1 + [0.027/3]) = CHF5,728,714

Futures

Buy Swiss Franc futures and use six-month futures contracts.

Basis

Assume that basis reduces to zero at contract maturity in a linear fashion.

Opening basis with six months to expiry of future = future – spot = 1.1204 – 1.1222 = -0.0018

In four months' time, there are two months until the expiry of the future, so the closing basis is estimated as -0.0018 × 2/6 = -0.0006.

The effective futures rate is therefore opening future – closing basis = 1.1204 – –0.0006 = 1.1210.

Expected receipt = $6,450,000/1.1210 = CHF5,753,791

Number of contracts = CHF5,753,791/125,000 = 46.03 contracts, approximately 46 contracts

On the basis that futures give the higher expected receipt, they should be chosen, but Adverane Co should assess whether basis risk is likely to be significant. Adverane Co should also consider, as regards money market hedging, that CHF receipts could be used to pay off any existing CHF loans or for other investment purposes, in which case the benefit to Adverane Co could be greater than hedging using futures.

(b) (i) Use mid-spot rates to translate amounts.

Owed by	Owed to	Local currency m	CHF m
Adverane (Switzerland)	Bosha (Eurozone)	CHF15.90	15.90
Adverane (Switzerland)	Diling (Brazil)	CHF4.46	4.46
Bosha (Eurozone)	Cogate (USA)	€24.89	26.60
Bosha (Eurozone)	Diling (Brazil)	€18.57	19.84
Cogate (USA)	Adverane (Switzerland)	US$27.08	24.16
Cogate (USA)	Diling (Brazil)	US$5.68	5.07
Diling (Brazil)	Adverane (Switzerland)	BRL38.80	12.29
Diling (Brazil)	Bosha (Eurozone)	BRL51.20	16.22

Owed to	Owed by				
	Adverane (Switzerland) CHFm	Bosha (Eurozone) CHFm	Cogate (USA) CHFm	Diling (Brazil) CHFm	Total CHFm
Adverane (Switzerland)			24.16	12.29	36.45
Bosha (Eurozone)	15.90			16.22	32.12
Cogate (USA)		26.60			26.60
Diling (Brazil)	4.46	19.84	5.07		29.37
Owed by	(20.36)	(46.44)	(29.23)	(28.51)	
Owed	36.45	32.12	26.60	29.37	
Net	16.09	(14.32)	(2.63)	0.86	

Under the terms of the arrangement, Bosha, the company with the largest debt, will pay Diling, the company with the smallest amount owed to it, CHF0.86 million. Bosha will pay Adverane CHF13.46 million and Cogate will pay Adverane CHF2.63 million.

(ii) The advantage of using a central treasury for multilateral netting is that the central treasury can coordinate the information about inter-group balances. There will be a smaller number of foreign exchange transactions, which will mean lower commission and transmission costs. There will be less loss of interest through money being in transit. The foreign exchange rates available may be more advantageous as a result of large transaction sizes resulting from consolidation. The netting arrangements should make cash flow forecasting easier in the group.

(c) Setting the transfer price at market price should enable a fair assessment of the performance of both the buying and selling divisions. Both internal and external sales will be accounted for at the same price. However, this may distort performance in that the costs of internal sales may be lower than external sales. For example, administration costs should be lower and there should be no costs of bad debts. These cost savings should be shared between the two divisions to give a fair picture. If the selling division has spare capacity, selling at incremental cost rather than market price may provide greater certainty that the buying division will use the selling division.

In theory, using market price should mean that the central treasury function has to intervene less. Simple market price provides an objective measure over which the divisions should agree. However, in reality, there may be complications that require central intervention. The market price may be difficult to determine or may fluctuate wildly, and central treasury may have to decide which price to use. If it is decided that an allowance should be made for costs of internal transfer being lower, central treasury may have to determine what this should be as it may vary significantly between products and divisions.

BPP
LEARNING
MEDIA

Specifying the transaction takes place at market price is designed to ensure that the buying division buys from the selling division, rather than an external supplier if the buying and selling division have failed to agree a price. The implicit assumption is that the buying division will use the selling division because of better service from, and greater dependability of, dealing within the group. This may not necessarily be the case. If the buying division previously purchased internally as a result of a low transfer price, forcing it to pay market price may mean it chooses an external supplier for non-price reasons.

39 Nutourne

Workbook references. Currency hedging is covered in Chapter 12.

Top tips. As ever, do not get obsessed with the parts of the question that seem (on first reading) especially difficult, eg how to demonstrate the outcome if the option is not exercised in part (a) and the numerical part of part (c). In AFM a solid answer to the majority of the question will secure a pass mark even if you do not manage to deal with the more complicated issues. Take care with the key issues in the question without worrying about getting everything right.

Easy marks. In part (b) and the first part of part (c), the discussion points should be easy as long as you do not make your points too briefly.

ACCA examining team's comments. Common errors included errors in calculating remaining basis, dividing by the exchange rates instead of multiplying and calculating the income received using forwards when the question scenario did not require this.

Marking scheme

			Marks
(a)	**Futures**		
	Sell futures now	1	
	Number of contracts	1	
	Forward hedge	1	
	Predicted futures rate using basis	1	
	Overall expected receipt	1	
	Options		
	Purchase June put	1	
	Premium	1	
	Overall expected receipt	1	
	Calculation of when option is a better choice	2	
	Comments	2	
		12	
(b)	Advantages of forward contract	2–3	
	Disadvantages of forward contract	2–3	
	Reasons for using exchange-traded derivatives	1–2	
			Max 7
(c)	Significance of initial and maintenance margins	2	
	Mark-to-market explanation	1	
	Numerical illustration using Nutourne Co's figures	3	
		6	
			25

(a) Nutourne Co will have a Swiss Franc receipt in six months' time and needs to hedge against the dollar strengthening.

Futures

Sell Swiss futures and use June futures contracts.

No. of contracts = CHF12,300,000/125,000 = 98.4, say 98, hedging CHF12,250,000

Remainder to be hedged on the forward market is CHF12,300,000 – CHF12,250,000 = CHF 50,000

Receipt = CHF50,000 × 1.0358 = $51,790

Calculation of futures price

Assume that basis reduces to zero at contract maturity in a linear fashion.

Estimate from opening June futures rate of 1.0369, with seven months to expiry; this means that opening basis is 0.0077 (since the future is above the current spot of 1.0292 by this amount). At the end of May, with only one month until expiry this basis should fall to 1/7 × 0.0077 = 0.0011.

Predicted futures rate at the end of May = 1.0369 – 0.0011 = 1.0358

Expected receipt = CHF12,250,000 × 1.0358 = $12,688,550

Outcome

	$
Futures	12,688,550
Remainder on forward market	51,790
	12,740,340

Or

Calculation of futures price

Alternatively, use spot rate = 1.0292

Predicted futures rate at the end of May = 1.0292 + (6/7 × (1.0369 – 1.0292)) = 1.0358 (when the June futures contract is closed out in May).

Expected receipt = CHF12,250,000 × 1.0358 = $12,688,550

Outcome

	$
Futures	12,688,550
Remainder on forward market	51,790
	12,740,340

Options contract

Nutourne Co would purchase CHF June put options.

Number of contracts 98, as before.

Amount not hedged, hedged by forward contract CHF translated as $51,790 as before.

Assuming the options are exercised:

	$
Receipt (W1)	12,709,375
Premium (W2)	(105,350)
Forward contract	51,790
	12,655,815

Workings

1   *Receipt*

CHF125,000 × 98 × 1.0375 = $12,709,375

2   *Premium*

1.0375 options = 98 × 125,000 × 0.0086 = $105,350

The options would give the higher receipt if they were not exercised and the spot rate moved sufficiently in Nutourne Co's favour. If Nutourne Co allowed the option to lapse, it would obtain the same receipt as under the futures if the US$/CHF spot rate was x, such that:

12,692,225 = 12,250,000x − 105,350

12,250,000x = 12,692,225 + 105,350

so that x is US$1.0447 = CHF1.

Or

12,688,550 = 12,250,000x − 105,350

12,250,000x = 12,688,550 + 105,350

so that x is US$1.0444 = CHF1.

Comments

If the options are exercised, the futures would give the higher receipt. The options give a lower receipt because of the premium which Nutourne Co has to pay. The futures will be subject to the risk that basis (the difference between the futures price and the spot price) may not decrease linearly as the futures approach maturity, as assumed in the above calculations. This will mean that the hedge of the CHF 12,250,000 is imperfect, and the receipt may be unpredictable despite a futures hedge being taken out.

The options can also be allowed to lapse if for some reason the contract is not completed. If this happens, Nutourne Co will only have to settle the forward contract.

(b)   ### Benefits of a forward contract

A forward contract would not involve payment of a large premium upfront to the counterparty.

A forward contract is a simple arrangement to understand, whereas the basis of calculation of the premium for an over☺the☺counter (OTC) option may be unclear.

A forward contract gives a certain receipt for the purposes of budgeting.

Drawbacks of a forward contract

A forward contract has to be fulfilled, even if the transaction which led to the forward contract being purchased is cancelled. Exchange rate movements may mean that the contract has to be fulfilled at an unfavourable rate. An OTC option can be allowed to lapse if it is not needed.

A forward contract does not allow the holder to take advantage of favourable exchange rate movements. An OTC option need not be exercised if the exchange rate moves in the holder's favour.

A forward contract may only be available for a short time period, depending on what currencies are involved. An OTC option may be purchased for a longer time period, over a year.

The rate offered on a forward contract will be determined by a prediction based on expected interest rates. The rate offered on an OTC option may be more flexible. This may suit a holder who is prepared to tolerate the risk of some loss in order to have the opportunity to take advantage of favourable exchange rate movements, but who wishes to use the option to set a limit to possible losses.

Reasons why exchange-traded derivatives are used

One of the main reasons why the treasury function uses exchange-traded derivatives is that the contracts can be bought and sold as required. Also, because the markets are regulated by an exchange, counterparty risk (the risk of the other party to the transaction defaulting) should be minimised.

(c) The mark-to-market process begins with Nutourne Co having to deposit an amount (the initial margin) in a margin account with the futures exchange when it takes out the futures. The margin account will remain open as long as the futures are open. The profit or loss on the futures is calculated daily and the margin account is adjusted for the profit or loss.

The maintenance margin is the minimum balance which has to be maintained on the margin account.

If the losses on the futures are so large that the balance on the margin account is less than the maintenance margin, then the futures exchange will make a demand (a margin call) for an extra payment (the variation margin) to increase the balance on the account back to the maintenance margin.

In the example, initial margin = $1,450 \times 98 = $142,100

Maintenance margin = $1,360 \times 98 = $133,280

Loss in ticks = 0.0011/0.0001 = 11

Total loss = 11 ticks $\times$ $12.50 $\times$ 98 = $13,475

Balance on margin account = $142,100 – $13,475 = $128,625

This is less than the maintenance margin, so Nutourne Co would have to deposit an extra ($133,280 – $128,625) = $4,655 (the variation margin) to bring the balance on the margin account up to the maintenance margin.

Alternative solution

In some exchanges, a variation margin may be required to increase the balance on the account back to its initial margin level. Therefore, in this case, the variation margin amount would be $13,475 (ie $142,100 – $128,625).

40 Buryecs

Workbook references. Foreign currency hedging is covered in Chapter 12.

Top tips. Part (a), 6 marks, this asked for an analysis of the pros and cons of currency swaps. There was clearly the opportunity for some 'text-book' points to be made here but the marking guide caps the marks at 3 if no reference is made to the scenario (eg the swap did not cover the full amount of the currency inflows).

Part (b)(i), 4 marks, this required a brief analysis of the benefits from the swap and explanation of how it would work. There was quite a lot of work to do here for 4 marks, but no issues that have not been seen before in similar interest rate swap questions.

Part (b)(ii), 8 marks, this required an NPV analysis of the project. This required a careful projection of future exchange rates using PPP theory and recognising that exchange rates were being quoted to 1 unit of the foreign currency.

Part (c), 7 marks, this was an assessment of the outcome of using two OTC option contracts. It would have been sensible to assess these against the swap but 5 of the marks were available for simple showing the outcome of the option contracts. Care had to be take here to understand the currency the option contracts were in and whether calls or puts were needed.

A similar question was set in June 2011.

Examining team comments. In part (c) a large number of candidates showed a lack of understanding when they chose call instead of put options. Many attempted to treat the currency options as if they were exchange traded when they were not. Finally, few candidates discussed whether the currency option is a preferred hedging method to a currency swap, hence many missed out on the marks allocated to this part of the question.

Marks

(a) Advantages 2–3
     Disadvantages 3–4
     Limit marks for (a) to 3 marks in total if answer does not mention Max 6
     Buryecs Co's situation

(b) (i) Recognition that swap gives advantage 1
          Swap mechanism 2
          Net benefit after bank charges 1
                                                                    4

     (ii) Exchange rates 2
          Correct translation of amounts swapped 1
          Correct translation of other amounts 1
          Net present value 1
          Gain in € from the swap of the initial fee amount 1
          Comments 2–3
                                                                    8

(c) Put option 1
     $7.25 option calculations 2
     $7.75 option calculations 2
     Comments 2–3
                                                                    7
                                                                   25

(a) The currency swap will involve Buryecs Co taking out a loan in € and making an arrangement with a counterparty in Wirtonia, which takes out a loan in $. Buryecs Co will pay the interest on the counterparty's loan and vice versa.

Advantages

Payment of interest in $ can be used to match the income Buryecs Co will receive from the rail franchise, reducing foreign exchange risk.

Buryecs Co will be able to obtain the swap for the amount it requires and may be able to reverse the swap by exchanging with the other counterparty. Other methods of hedging risk may be less certain. The cost of a swap may also be cheaper than other methods of hedging, such as options.

The swap can be used to change Buryecs Co's debt profile if it is weighted towards fixed-rate debt and its directors want a greater proportion of floating rate debt, to diversify risk and take advantage of probable lower future interest rates.

Drawbacks

The counterparty may default. This would leave Buryecs Co liable to pay interest on the loan in its currency. The risk of default can be reduced by obtaining a bank guarantee for the counterparty.

The swap may not be a worthwhile means of hedging currency risk if the exchange rate is unpredictable. If it is assumed that exchange rates are largely determined by inflation rates, the predicted inflation rate in Wirtonia is not stable, making it more difficult to predict future exchange rates confidently. If the movement in the exchange rate is not as expected, it may turn out to have been better for Buryecs Co not to have hedged.

Buryecs Co is swapping a fixed rate commitment in the Eurozone for a floating rate in Wirtonia. Inflation is increasing in Wirtonia and there is a risk that interest rates will increase as a result, increasing Buryecs Co's finance costs.

The swap does not hedge the whole amount of the receipt in Year 3. Another method will have to be used to hedge the additional receipt from the government in Year 3 and the receipts in the intervening years.

If the government decides to impose exchange controls in Wirtonia, Buryecs Co may not be able to realise the receipt at the end of Year 3, but will still have to fulfil the swap contract.

(b) (i)

	Buryecs Co	Counterparty	Interest rate benefit
Eurozone	4.0%	5.8%	1.8%
Wirtonia	Bank rate + 0.6%	Bank rate + 0.4%	0.2%
Gain on swap (60:40)	1.2%	0.8%	2.0%
Bank fee (60:40)	(0.3%)	(0.2%)	(0.5%)
Gain on swap after bank fee	0.9%	0.6%	1.5%

The swap arrangement will work as follows:

	Buryecs Co	Counterparty
Buryecs Co borrows at	4.0%	
Counterparty borrows at		Bank rate + 0.4%
Swap		
Counterparty receives		(Bank rate)
Buryecs Co pays	Bank rate	
Counterparty pays		4.6%
Buryecs Co receives	(4.6%)	
Advantage	120 basis points	80 basis points
Net result	Bank rate – 0.6%	5.0%

After paying the 30 point basis fee, Buryecs Co will effectively pay interest at the bank rate – 0.3% and benefit by 90 basis points or 0.9%. The counterparty will effectively pay interest at 5.2% and benefit by 60 basis points or 0.6%.

(ii) Using the purchasing power parity formula to calculate exchange rates:

$$S_1 = S_0 \times (1 + h_c)/(1 + h_b)$$

Year	1	2	3
	$0.1430 \times 1.06/1.03 =$	$0.1472 \times 1.04/1.08 =$	$0.1417 \times 1.03/1.11 =$
	0.1472	0.1417	0.1315

At Year 3, $5,000 million will be exchanged at the original spot rate as per the agreement and the remaining inflows will be exchanged at the Year 3 rate.

Year	0	1	2	3
	$m	$m	$m	$m
Initial fee	(5,000)			
Payment at end of franchise				7,500
Annual income		600	600	600
Year 0 Exchange rate	0.1430			
Years 1–3 Exchange rates		0.1472	0.1417	0.1315
	€m	€m	€m	€m
Swap translated at 0.1430	(715)			715
Amount not covered by swap (7,500 – 5,000) translated at 0.1315				329
Annual income		88	85	79
Cash flows in home country	(715)	88	85	1,123
Discount factor 14%	1.000	0.877	0.769	0.675
Present value	(715)	77	65	758

The net present value of the project is €185 million, indicating that it should go ahead. However, the value is dependent on the exchange rate, which is worsening for the foreign income. If there are also uncertainties about the variability of returns during the three years, the directors may consider the project to be in excess of their risk appetite and decline the opportunity.

As a result of the exchange rates on the initial fee being fixed at the year 0 spot rate, Buryecs Co has gained $5,000m × (0.1430 − 0.1315) × 0.675 = €39m.

(c) Receipt using swap arrangement = €715m + €329m = €1,044m

Receipt if transaction unhedged = $7,500m × 0.1315 = €986m

Predicted exchange rate at Year 3 is €0.1315 = $1 or $7.6046 = €1

Options

Buy $ put options as receiving $.

$7.75 exercise price

Do not exercise

Net receipt = €986m − (1.6% × $7,500m × 0.1430) = €969m

$7.25 exercise price

Exercise

Receipt from government = $7,500m/7.25 = €1,034m

Net receipt = €1,034m − (2.7% × $7,500m × 0.1430) = €1,005m

The $7.25 option gives a better result than not hedging, given the current expectations of the exchange rate. However, it gives a worse result than the swap even before the premium is deducted, because of the exchange rate being fixed on the swap back of the original amount paid. These calculations do not take into account possible variability of the finance costs associated with the swap, caused by swapping into floating rate borrowing.

41 Lurgshall

Workbook references. Interest rate hedging is covered in Chapter 13.

Top tips. Make sure in interest rate option questions that you carefully and clearly specify the type of option needed, the number of contracts, the basis remaining and the decision over whether or not to exercise.

Examining team's comments. In part (a) a significant minority of candidates also spent time calculating the impact of the futures and FRA, even though these were given. This resulted in poor time management and was due to not reading the question properly. Most candidates made relevant comments, but quite often these were brief and did not gain full marks.

Swaps

Comparative advantage and recognition of benefit	2
Initial decision to borrow floating by Lurgshall & fixed by counterparty	1
Swap impact	2
Net benefit after charges	1
Comments	3–4
	Max 15

(b) Advantages of swaps   2–3

     Disadvantages of swaps   2–3

                                Max 5

(c) 1-2 marks per relevant point   5

                                     25

(a) **Options**

Buy put options as need to hedge against a rise in interest rates.

Number of contracts required: $84,000,000/$2,000,000 × 6/3 = 84

Total basis = futures price 4.95% − 4.50% current rate (1 May) = 0.45%

Unexpired basis on 1 September = 0.45 × 1/5 = 0.09

Expected futures rate if rates rise by 0.6% = 4.5% + 0.6% + 0.09% = 5.19%

Exercise %	4.75%
Futures %	5.19%
Exercise?	Yes
Gain in %	0.44%
	%
Interest paid (4.5% + 0.6% + 0.5%)	5.6
Gain from options	(0.44)
Premium	0.411
Net payment	5.571%

Effective in $ annual interest rate

$84m × 0.05571 × 6/12   = $2,339,820

Alternative options calculations

Buy put options as need to hedge against a rise in interest rates.

Number of contracts required: $84,000,000/$2,000,000 × 6/3 = 84

Total basis = current price (1 May) − futures price = (100 − 4.50) − 95.05 = 0·45

Unexpired basis on 1 September = 0.45 × 1/5 = 0.09

Expected futures price = 100 − 5.1 − 0.09 = 94.81

Exercise price	95.25
Futures price as above	94.81
Exercise?	Yes
Gain in basis points	44

	$
Interest paid ($84,000,000 × 5.6% × 6/12)	2,352,000
Gain from options	
0.0044 × $2,000,000 × 3/12 × 84	(184,800)
Premium	
0.00411 × $2,000,000 × 3/12 × 84	172,620
Net payment	2,339,820
Effective annual interest rate	
2,339,820/84,000,000 × 12/6	= 5.57%

Swaps

	Lurgshall Co	Counterparty	Interest rate differential
Fixed rate	5.60%	6.10%	0.50%
Floating rate	LIBOR + 0.50%	LIBOR + 1.50%	1.00%

Lurgshall Co has an advantage in borrowing at both fixed and floating rates, but the floating rate advantage is larger. Gain % for Lurgshall Co = 50% (1 − 0.5 − 0.2) = 0.15

	Lurgshall Co	Counterparty
Rate without swap	(5.60%)	(LIBOR + 1.50%)
Benefit	0.15%	0.15
Net result	(5.45%)	(LIBOR + 1.35%)
Swap Borrows at	(LIBOR + 0.50%)	(6.10)
Lurgshall Co pays	(4.85%)	4.85%
Counterparty pays	LIBOR	(LIBOR)
Bank fee	(0.10%)	(0.10%)
Net result	(5.45%)	(LIBOR + 1.35%)

Comments

The swap gives a result which is marginally worse than the forward rate agreement and the futures. The options give a worse result than the other choices.

Risks which might be considered include counterparty risk for the forward rate agreement and swap. Using Birdam Bank should mean that this risk is low for forward rate agreements, and also for swaps, assuming that the bank bears the risk of the counterparty defaulting.

Basis risk should be considered for the traded futures. Here, because the differences between the instruments are small, a failure to estimate basis accurately may mean that futures are chosen when they do not offer the lowest borrowing cost. For the swaps, if Lurgshall Co swaps into fixed rate debt, it faces the market risk of an unexpected fall in interest rates.

Other factors to consider include the possibility that rates will increase rather less than forecast, meaning that the option would not be exercised and at some point would be the lowest cost choice. The length of time of the swap also needs to be considered. Although it commits Lurgshall Co to the fixed rate, if the borrowing turns out to be longer than the six months, the swap may provide a better time match than the other hedging opportunities.

(b) **Advantages of swaps**

Transaction costs are generally relatively low. If Lurgshall Co arranged the swap itself, the costs would be limited to legal fees. The transaction costs may also be lower than the costs of terminating one loan and arranging another.

Lurgshall Co can, as here, swap a commitment to pay a variable rate of interest which is uncertain with a guaranteed fixed rate of interest. This allows Lurgshall Co to forecast finance costs on the loan with certainty.

Swaps are over-the-counter arrangements. They can be arranged in any size and for whatever time period is required, unlike traded derivatives. The period available for the swap may be longer than is offered for other interest rate derivatives.

Swaps make use of the principle of comparative advantage. Lurgshall Co can borrow in the market where the best deal is available to it, and then use the swap to access the loan finance it actually wants at an overall cheaper cost.

Disadvantages of swaps

Swaps are subject to counterparty risk, ie the risk that the other party to the arrangement may default on the arrangement. This would apply in particular if Lurgshall Co arranged the swap itself. If it is arranged through a bank, the bank can provide a guarantee that the swap will be honoured.

If Lurgshall Co swaps into a fixed rate commitment, it cannot then change that commitment. This means it cannot take advantage of favourable interest rate changes as it could if it used options. This may be a particular problem if the swap period is more than a few months and interest rates are expected to be volatile.

As swaps are over-the-counter instruments, they cannot be easily traded or allowed to lapse if they are not needed or become no longer advantageous. It is possible that a bank may allow a reswapping arrangement to reverse a swap that is not required, but this will incur further costs.

(c) The chief executive appears to underestimate the degree of knowledge required for day-to-day work. Less experienced staff may be able to arrange borrowing if the lender has already been chosen or, for example, arrange forward rate agreements to be used if they are prescribed.

However, if judgement is required as to, for example, which lender or hedging instrument to use, using less experienced staff may mean that a sub-optimal decision is taken. Poor decisions may result in opportunity costs, for example, not using the lender who gives the best deal or being committed to a fixed forward rate agreement when an option would have allowed the business to take advantage of favourable rate movements. These opportunity costs may not be as clear as the salary costs of experienced staff.

As the business operates internationally, the treasury department will need to monitor financial market conditions and exchange rates, and other issues which may be significant such as political developments. Because of their previous experiences, longer-serving staff are more likely to appreciate the implications of developments and whether treasury policies and decisions need to change in response to changes in risk. Senior staff are also needed to manage the work of less experienced staff to prevent or mitigate the effect of mistakes which may be costly.

Experienced staff are also needed to establish overall guidelines and policies for treasury activities. Their judgement will be required to establish principles which will mean that actions taken by staff are in line with the risk appetite of the business and are sufficiently prudent from the viewpoint of risk management. Experienced staff will also have greater knowledge of law, accounting standards and tax regulations, which can help the business avoid penalties and perhaps structure its dealings so that it can, for example, minimise the level of tax paid.

The chief executive has plans for a major expansion of the business, involving significant investment and financing decisions. Advice from experienced treasury staff will be invaluable in supporting the decisions required. If Lurgshall Co is planning a major acquisition, the treasury function can provide advice on the structure of consideration and financing implications. If, as here, a major investment is being contemplated, experienced staff can advise on translating views on risk into a relevant cost of capital, which will help ensure that the financial appraisal of the investment is realistic.

42 Awan

Marking scheme

		Marks	
(a)	Calculation of impact of FRA for interest rate increase and decrease	4	
	Decision to go long on futures	1	
	Selection of March futures and options	1	
	Unexpired basis calculation	1	
	Impact of interest rates increase/decrease with futures	4	
	Decision to buy call options	1	
	Impact of interest rates increase/decrease with options	5	
	Discussion	2–3	
			Max 19
(b)	1–2 marks per well-explained point		Max 6
			25

(a) **Using FRAs**

FRA rate 4.82% (3–7), since the investment will take place in three months' time for a period of 4 months.

If interest rates increase by 0.9% to 4.99%

Investment return = 4.79% × 4/12 × $48,000,000 =	$766,400
Payment to Voblaka Bank = (4.99% − 4.82%) × $48,000,000 × 4/12 =	$(27,200)
Net receipt =	$739,200
Effective annual interest rate = 739,200/48,000,000 × 12/4 =	4.62%

If interest rates decrease by 0.9% to 3.19%

Investment return = 2.99% × 4/12 × $48,000,000 =	$478,400
Receipt from Voblaka Bank = (4.82% − 3.19%) × $48,000,000 × 4/12 =	$260,800
Net receipt =	$739,200
Effective annual interest rate (as above)	4.62%

Using futures

Need to hedge against a fall in interest rates, therefore go long in the futures market. Awan Co needs March contracts as the investment will be made on 1 February.

No. of contracts needed = $48,000,000/$2,000,000 × 4 months/3 months = 32 contracts.

Basis
Current price (on 1/11) – futures price = total basis
(100 – 4.09) – 94.76 = 1.15
Unexpired basis = 2/5 × 1.15 = 0.46

If interest rates increase by 0.9% to 4.99%

Investment return (from above) =	$766,400
Expected futures price = 100 – 4.99 – 0.46 =	94.55
Loss on the futures market = (0.9455 – 0.9476) × $2,000,000 × 3/12 × 32 =	$(33,600)
Net return =	$732,800
Effective annual interest rate = $732,800/$48,000,000 × 12/4 =	4.58%

If interest rates decrease by 0.9% to 3.19%

Investment return (from above) =	$478,400
Expected futures price = 100 – 3.19 – 0.46 = 96.35	
Gain on the futures market = (0.9635 – 0.9476) × $2,000,000 × 3/12 × 32 =	$254,400
Net return =	$732,800
Effective annual interest rate (as above) =	4.58%

Using options on futures

Need to hedge against a fall in interest rates, therefore buy call options. As before, Awan Co needs 32 March call option contracts ($48,000,000/$2,000,000 × 4 months/3 months).

If interest rates increase by 0.9% to 4.99%

Exercise price	94.50	95.00
Futures price	94.55	94.55
Exercise?	Yes	No
Gain in basis points	5	0
Underlying investment return (from above)	$766,400	$766,400
Gain on options (0.0005 × 2,000,000 × 3/12 × 32)	$8,000	$0
Premium		
0.00432 × $2,000,000 × 3/12 × 32	$(69,120)	
0.00121 × $2,000,000 × 3/12 × 32		$(19,360)
Net return	$705,280	$747,040
Effective interest rate	4.41%	4.67%

If interest rates decrease by 0.9% to 3.19%

Exercise price	94.50	95.00
Futures price	96.35	96.35
Exercise?	Yes	Yes
Gain in basis points	185	135
Underlying investment return (from above)	$478,400	$478,400
Gain on options		
(0.0185 × 2,000,000 × 3/12 × 32)	$296,000	
(0.0135 × 2,000,000 × 3/12 × 32)		$216,000
Premium		
As above	$(69,120)	
As above		$(19,360)
Net return	$705,280	$675,040
Effective interest rate	4.41%	4.22%

Discussion

The FRA offer from Voblaka Bank gives a slightly higher return compared to the futures market; however, Awan Co faces a credit risk with over-the-counter products like the FRA, where Voblaka Bank may default on any money owing to Awan Co if interest rates should fall. The March call option at the exercise price of 94.50 seems to fix the rate of return at 4.41%, which is lower than the return on the futures market and should therefore be rejected. The March call option at the exercise price of 95.00 gives a higher return compared to the FRA and the futures if interest rates increase, but does not perform as well if the interest rates fall. If Awan Co takes the view that it is more important to be protected against a likely fall in interest rates, then that option should also be rejected. The choice between the FRA and the futures depends on Awan Co's attitude to risk and return; the FRA gives a small, higher return, but carries a credit risk. If the view is that the credit risk is small and it is unlikely that Voblaka Bank will default on its obligation, then the FRA should be chosen as the hedge instrument.

(b) The delta value measures the extent to which the value of a derivative instrument, such as an option, changes as the value of its underlying asset changes. For example, a delta of 0.8 would mean that a company would need to purchase 1.25 option contracts (1/0.8) to hedge against a rise in price of an underlying asset of that contract size, known as the hedge ratio. This is because the delta indicates that when the underlying asset increases in value by $1, the value of the equivalent option contract will increase by only $0.80.

The option delta is equal to $N(d_1)$ from the Black-Scholes option pricing formula. This means that the delta is constantly changing when the volatility or time to expiry change. Therefore even when the delta and hedge ratio are used to determine the number of option contracts needed, this number needs to be updated periodically to reflect the new delta.

43 Wardegul

Workbook references. Interest rate risk and hedging are covered in Chapter 13.

Top tips. If you are familiar with interest rate hedging using derivatives, this should be a relatively straightforward question. Use the BPP proforma for setting up futures and options to ensure you do not forget any of the steps.

In part (b) read the question and its requirements carefully; in this question, many candidates misread the question and answered it in terms of national or global functions, some without even mentioning regional functions, which was asked for in the question. These answers indicated the question had not been properly understood, and candidates mistakenly reproduced their textbook knowledge of centralised (global) versus decentralised (country) treasury functions instead of applying their knowledge to the question asked.

Easy marks. Part (a) is a commonly examined area, offering an opportunity to show your knowledge of this area.

Examining team's comments. Part (a) Some candidates omitted to identify which hedging instruments they had chosen for example, a buy vs sell futures or a put vs call options, making it difficult for markers to award marks. A number of candidates omitted to discuss their results and/or make a recommendation meaning that they could not be awarded these marks.

Marks

(a) Impact of FRA for rate increase and decrease — 2
Go long on futures — 1
Selection of March futures and options — 1
Number of contracts — 1
Basis calculation — 1
Impact of interest rate increase/decrease with futures — 3
Buy call options — 1
Premium calculations — 1
Exercise options? — 1
Impact of interest rate increase/decrease with options — 3
Discussion — 3–4

Max 18

(b) Regional functions compared with national functions — 4–5
Regional functions compared with global function — 3–4

Max 7

25

(a) **Forward rate agreement**

FRA 5.02% (4–9) since the investment will take place in four months' time for a period of five months.

If interest rates increase by 1.1% to 5.3%

	D
Investment return 5.0% × 5/12 × D27,000,000	562,500
Payment to bank (5.3% – 5.02%) × 5/12 × D27,000,000	(31,500)
Net receipt	531,000
Effective annual interest rate 531,000/27,000,000 × 12/5	4.72%

If interest rates fall by 0.6% to 3.6%

	D
Investment return 3.3% × 5/12 × D27,000,000	371,250
Receipt from bank (5.02% – 3.6%) × 5/12 × D27,000,000	159,750
Net receipt	531,000
Effective annual interest rate as above	4.72%

Futures

Go long in the futures market, as the hedge is against a fall in interest rates. Use March contracts, as investment will be made on 31 January.

Number of contracts = D27,000,000/D500,000 × 5 months/3 months = 90 contracts

Basis

Current price (1 October) – futures price = basis

(100 – 4.20) – 94.78 = 1.02

Unexpired basis on 31 January = 2/6 × 1.02 = 0.34

If interest rates increase by 1.1% to 5.3%

	D
Investment return as above	562,500
Expected futures price: 100 − 5.3 − 0.34 = 94.36	
Loss on the futures market: (0.9436 − 0.9478) × D500,000 × 3/12 × 90	(47,250)
Net return	515,250
Effective annual interest rate 515,250/27,000,000 × 12/5	4.58%

If interest rates fall by 0.6% to 3.6%

	D
Investment return as above	371,250
Expected futures price: 100 − 3.6 − 0.34 = 96.06	
Profit on the futures market: (0.9606 − 0.9478) × D500,000 × 3/12 × 90	144,000
Net receipt	515,250
Effective annual interest rate as above	4.58%

Options on futures

Buy call options as need to hedge against a fall in interest rates. As above, 90 contracts required.

If interest rates increase by 1.1% to 5.3%

Exercise price	94.25	95.25
Futures price as above	94.36	94.36
Exercise?	Yes	No
Gain in basis points	11	0
	D	D
Investment return (as above)	562,500	562,500
Gain from options (0.0011 × 500,000 × 3/12 × 90)	12,375	0
Premium		
0.00545 × D500,000 × 3/12 × 90	(61,313)	
0.00098 × D500,000 × 3/12 × 90		(11,025)
Net return	513,562	551,475
Effective interest rate		
513,562/27,000,000 × 12/5	4.56%	
551,475/27,000,000 × 12/5		4.90%

If interest rates fall by 0.6% to 3.6%

Exercise price	94.25	95.25
Futures price as above	96.06	96.06
Exercise?	Yes	Yes
Gain in basis points	181	81
Investment return (as above)	371,250	371,250
Gain from options		
Gain from options: 0.0181 × D500,000 × 3/12 × 90	203,625	
Gain from options: 0.0081 × D500,000 × 3/12 × 90		91,125
Premium as above	(61,313)	(11,025)
Net return	513,562	451,350

Effective interest rate		
513,562/27,000,000 × 12/5	4.56%	
451,350/27,000,000 × 12/5		4.01%

Alternative presentation of calculations:

Forward rate agreement:

FRA 5.02% (4–9) since the investment will take place in four months' time and last for five months.

Possible scenarios:	Rates rise by 1.1%	Rates fall by 0.6%
Base rate (now = 4.2%)	5.3%	3.6%
Return on investment (Base – 0.3%)	5.0%	3.3%
Impact of FRA (5.02% vs Base)	(0.28%)	1.42%
Net outcome as %	4.72%	4.72%
In Ds (% × D27,000,000 × 5/12)	531,000	531,000

Futures agreement:

March contracts to buy at 94.78 or 5.22% (100 – 94.78) are need to cover to the start of the investment (31 January). The number of contracts required will be D27m/D0.5m contract size × 5 months (investment term) divided by 3 months (contract term) = 90.

Opening basis on 1 Oct: future – base = 5.22% – 4.20% = 1.02% with six months to expiry of March future.

Estimated closing basis on 31 January = 1.02% × 2/6 = 0.34% with two months to expiry of March future.

So if rates rise to a base rate of 5.3% the estimated futures price is 5.3% + 0.34% = 5.64%.

If rates fall to a base rate of 3.6% the estimated futures price is 3.6% + 0.34% = 3.94%.

Possible scenarios:	Rates rise by 1.1%	Rates fall by 0.6%
Base rate (now = 4.2%)	5.3%	3.6%
Return on investment (Base – 0.3%)	5.0%	3.3%
Impact of Future:		
Opening rate 1 Oct (to receive)	5.22%	5.22%
Closing rate 31 January (to pay)	5.64%	3.94%
Net outcome on future	(0.42%)	1.28%
Overall net outcome (actual + future)	4.58%	4.58%
In Ds (% × D27,000,000 × 5/12)	515,250	515,250

Options agreement:

March call options at 5.75% (94.25) or 4.75% (95.25) can be chosen. There is an argument for either, this solution illustrates the outcome if 4.75% is chosen, which is the rate closest to the current base rate and provides compensation if interest rates fall at a lower premium compared to the 5.75% rate. Again 90 contracts will be needed, and contracts are closed out against the futures price on 31 January.

Possible scenarios:	Rates rise by 1.1%	Rates fall by 0.6%
Base rate (now = 4.2%)	5.3%	3.6%
Return on investment (Base – 0.3%)	5.0%	3.3%

Impact of Future:

	Rates rise by 1.1%	Rates fall by 0.6%
Call option rate 1 Oct	4.75%	4.75%
Closing rate 31 January (to pay)	5.64%	3.94%
Net outcome on future	Do not exercise	0.81%
Premium	(0.098)%	(0.098)%
Outcome (actual + option– premium)	4.902%	4.012%
In Ds (% × D27,000,000 × 5/12)	551,475	451,350

Discussion

The forward rate agreement gives the highest guaranteed return. If Wardegul Co wishes to have a certain cash flow and is primarily concerned with protecting itself against a fall in interest rates, it will most likely choose the forward rate agreement. The 95.25 option gives a better rate if interest rates rise, but a significantly lower rate if interest rates fall, so if Wardegul Co is at all risk averse, it will choose the forward rate agreement.

This assumes that the bank which Wardegul Co deals with is reliable and there is no risk of default. If Wardegul Co believes that the current economic uncertainty may result in a risk that the bank will default, the choice will be between the futures and the options, as these are guaranteed by the exchange. Again the 95.25 option may be ruled out because it gives a much worse result if interest rates fall to 3.6%. The futures give a marginally better result than the 94.25 option in both scenarios but the difference is small. If Wardegul Co feels there is a possibility that interest rates will be higher than 5.41%, the point at which the 94.25 option would not be exercised, it may choose this option rather than the future.

(b) **Regional functions compared with national functions**

Organising treasury activities on a regional basis would be consistent with what is happening in the group overall. Other functions will be organised regionally. A regional treasury function may be able to achieve synergies with them and also benefit from information flows being organised based on the regional structure.

If, as part of a reorganisation, some treasury activities were to be devolved outside to a bank or other third party, it would be simpler to arrange for a single provider on a regional basis than arrange for separate providers in each country.

A regional function will avoid duplication of responsibilities over all the countries within a region. A regional function will have more work to do, with maybe a greater range of activities, whereas staff based nationally may be more likely to be under-employed. There may be enough complex work on a regional basis to justify employing specialists in particular treasury areas which will enhance the performance of the function. It may be easier to recruit these specialists if recruitment is done regionally rather than in each country.

Regional centres can carry out some activities on a regional basis which will simplify how funds are managed and mean less cost than managing funds on a national basis. These include pooling cash, borrowing and investing in bulk, and netting of foreign currency income and expenditure.

Regional centres could in theory be located anywhere in the region, rather than having one treasury function based in each country. This means that they could be located in the most important financial centres in each region or in countries which offered significant tax advantages.

From the point of view of Wardegul Co's directors and senior managers, it will be easier to enforce common standards and risk management policies on a few regional functions than on many national functions with differing cultures in individual countries.

Regional functions compared with global function

Wardegul Co is being reorganised on a regional basis because of the demands of its global expansion. As discussed above, reorganising treasury functions regionally will be consistent with the way other functions are organised. Reorganising the treasury function regionally will be one way of dealing with the problem of having a single, overstretched, global function.

A regional function could employ experts with knowledge of the regulations, practices and culture of the major countries within the region. It may be more difficult for a global function to recruit staff with local expertise.

There may be practical issues why individual countries prefer to deal with regional functions rather than a global function, for example, a regional function will be based in the same, or similar, time zone as the countries in its region.

A regional function may have better ideas of local finance and investment opportunities. There may, for example, be better alternatives for investment of the surplus funds than the centralised function has been able to identify.

44 Keshi

Marking scheme

		Marks	
(a)	Buy put options and number of contracts	1	
	Future prices if interest rates rise or fall	1	
	Option contract calculations for any exercise price	3	
	Second set of option calculations if provided	1	
	Swap and resulting advantage	2	
	Swap impact	2	
	Effective borrowing rate	2	
	Discussion and recommendation	3–4	
			Max 15
(b)	Discussion of merits of centralising	3–4	
	Discussion of merits of decentralising	2–3	Max 6
(c)	1–2 marks per well-explained point		Max 4
			25

(a) **Options**

Keshi needs to hedge against a rise in interest rates, therefore it needs to buy **put options**.

Keshi Co needs 42 March put option contracts ($18,000,000/$1,000,000 × 7 months/3 months).

Basis

Current March futures price – spot price = total basis = 44 basis points as at 1 December

Unexpired basis as at 1 February = 22 **or 0.22% (given in the question)**

If 95.50 options (ie 4.5%) are used:

	Rates fall − 0.5%	Rates rise + 0.5%
	%	%
LIBOR rate (currently 3.8%)	3.3	4.3
Borrowing rate for Keshi	3.7	4.7
Closing future LIBOR + basis of 0.22%	3.52	4.52
Exercise option at 4.5%?	No	Yes
	Rates fall − 0.5%	Rates rise + 0.5%
Premium	(0.662)	(0.662)
Option gain/(loss)		0.02
Net effective annual interest rate	**4.362%**	**5.342**
	(3.7 + 0.662)	(4.7 + 0.662 − 0.02)

Alternative solution:

Expected futures price on 1 February if interest rates increase by 0.5% =

100 − (3.8 + 0.5) − 0.22 = 95.48

Expected futures price on 1 February if interest rates decrease by 0.5% =

100 − (3.8 − 0.5) − 0.22 = 96.48

If interest rates increase by 0.5% to 4.3%

Exercise price 95.50

Futures price 95.48

Exercise?   Yes

Gain in basis points 2

Underlying cost of borrowing

4.7% × 7/12 × $18,000,000 = $493,500

Gain on options

0.0002 × $1,000,000 × 3/12 × 42 = $2,100

Premium

0.00662 × $1,000,000 × 3/12 × 42 = $69,510

Net cost $560,910

Effective interest rate **5.342%** (560,910 / 18,000,000 × 12/7)

If interest rates decrease by 0.5% to 3.3%

Exercise price 95.50

Futures price 96.48

Exercise?   No

Underlying cost of borrowing

3.7% × 7/12 × $18,000,000 = $388,500

Premium $69,510

Net cost $458,010

Effective interest rate **4.362%** (458,010 / 18,000,000 × 12/7)

Using swaps

Keshi will want to swap into fixed rate finance in order to hedge the risk of interest rates rising.

With this type of swap the outcome will be as follows:

		Keshi Co
No swap:		(5.5%)
Swap:		
Loan		(LIBOR + 0.4%)
Fixed rate paid		(4.6%)
Floating rate received	LIBOR + 0.3%	
Net cost pre-fee		(4.7%)
Total gain (5.5 vs 4.7)		0.8%
Gain to Keshi (70% of 0.8)		0.56%
Outcome pre-fees (5.5 − 0.56)		4.94%
Outcome post-fees (4.94 + 0.1)		**5.04%**

Discussion and recommendation

Under each choice the interest rate cost to Keshi Co will be as follows:

	Doing nothing	95.50 option	Swap
If rates increase by 0.5%	4.7% floating; 5.5% fixed	5.342%	5.04%
If rates decrease by 0.5%	3.7% floating; 5.5% fixed	4.362%	5.04%

Borrowing at the floating rate and undertaking a **swap** effectively fixes the rate of interest at 5.04% for the loan, which is **significantly lower than the market fixed rate of 5.5%**.

On the other hand, **doing nothing** and borrowing at the floating rate minimises the interest rate at 4.7%, against the next best choice which is the swap at 5.04% if interest rates increase by 0.5%. And, should interest rates decrease by 0.5%, then doing nothing and borrowing at a floating rate of 3.7% minimises cost, compared to the next best choice which is the 95.50 option.

On the face of it, **doing nothing and borrowing at a floating rate seems to be the better choice** if interest rates increase or decrease by a small amount, but if interest rates increase substantially then this choice will no longer result in the lowest cost.

The swap minimises the variability of the borrowing rates, while doing nothing and borrowing at a floating rate maximises the variability. If Keshi Co wants to eliminate the risk of interest rate fluctuations completely, then it should borrow at the floating rate and swap it into a fixed rate.

(b) A **centralised** treasury department should be able to evaluate the financing requirements of Keshi Co's group as a whole and it may be able to **negotiate better rates when borrowing in bulk**. The department could operate as an internal bank and undertake **matching** of funds. Therefore it could transfer funds from subsidiaries which have spare cash resources to ones which need them, and thus **avoid going into the costly external market to raise funds**.

The department may be able to undertake **multilateral internal netting** and thereby reduce costs related to hedging activity. **Experts** and resources within one location could **reduce duplication costs**.

The concentration of experts and resources within one central department may result in a **more effective decision-making** environment and higher quality risk monitoring and control. Further, having access to the Keshi Co group's entire cash funds may give the company access to larger and more diverse investment markets.

Decentralising Keshi Co's treasury function to its subsidiary companies may be beneficial in several ways. Each subsidiary company may be better placed to take **local regulations and customs** into consideration. An example is the case of Suisen Co's need to use Salam contracts instead of conventional derivative products which the centralised treasury department may use as a matter of course.

Giving subsidiary companies more **autonomy** over how they undertake their own fund management may result in increased **motivation** and effort from the subsidiary's senior management and thereby increase future income. Subsidiary companies which have access to their own funds may be able to respond to opportunities **quicker** and establish competitive advantage more effectively.

(c) Islamic principles stipulate the need to avoid uncertainty and speculation. In the case of Salam contracts, payment for the commodity is made at the start of the contract. The buyer and seller of the commodity know the price, the quality and the quantity of the commodity and the date of future delivery with certainty. Therefore, **uncertainty and speculation** are avoided.

On the other hand, futures contracts are marked to market daily and this could lead to uncertainty in the amounts received and paid every day. Furthermore, **standardised futures contracts have fixed expiry dates and predetermined contract sizes**.

This may mean that the underlying position is not hedged or covered completely, leading to limited speculative positions even where the futures contracts are used entirely for hedging purposes.

Finally, only a few commodity futures contracts are offered to cover a range of different quality grades for a commodity, and therefore price movement of the futures market may not be completely in line with the price movement in the underlying asset.

Note. Credit will be given for alternative, relevant discussion for parts (b) and (c).

45 Daikon

Workbook references. Interest rate hedging is covered in Chapter 13.

Easy marks. You should be able to pick up some relatively straightforward marks in part (a) for the option calculations. Ensure your recommendation is based on your calculations.

Examining team's comments. Part (b) was done unsatisfactorily by most candidates. Very few candidates got the calculations of the marked to market correct. What was required was to identify the change in ticks or basis points and multiply the three numbers together.

(a)   Borrowing period is 6 months (11 months – 5 months).

Current borrowing cost = $34,000,000 × 6 months/12 months × 4.3% = $731,000

Borrowing cost if interest rates increase by 80 basis points (0.8%) = $34,000,000 × 6/12 × 5.1% = $867,000

Additional cost = $136,000 [$34,000,000 × 6/12 × 0.8%]

Using futures to hedge

Need to hedge against a rise in interest rates, therefore go short (contracts to sell) in the futures market.

Borrowing period is 6 months

No. of contracts needed = $34,000,000/$1,000,000 × 6 months/3 months = 68 contracts.

Basis

Current price (on 1 June 20X5) – futures price = total basis

(100 – 3.6) – 95.84 = 0.56

Unexpired basis (at beginning of November) = 2/7 × 0.56 = 0.16

Assume that interest rates increase by 0.8% (80 basis points) to 4.4%

Expected futures price = 100 – 4.4 – 0.16 = 95.44 (or 100 – 95.44 = 4.56%)

Gain on the futures market = (95.84 – 95.44) × $25 × 68 = $68,000 (or 4.56% closing future – 4.16% opening future = 0.4%)

Net additional cost = ($136,000 – $68,000) $68,000 (or 0.8% – 0.4% gain on future = 0.4%)

Using options on futures to hedge

Need to hedge against a rise in interest rates, therefore buy put options. As before, 68 put option contracts are needed ($34,000,000/$1,000,000 × 6 months/3 months).

Assume that interest rates increase by 0.8% (80 basis points) to 4.4%

Exercise price	95.50	96.00
Futures price	95.44	95.44
Exercise?	Yes	Yes
Gain in basis points	6	56
Gain on options		
6 × $25 × 68	$10,200	
56 × $25 × 68		$95,200
Premium		
30.4 × $25 × 68	$51,680	
50.8 × $25 × 68		$86,360
Option benefit/(cost)	$(41,480)	$8,840
Net additional cost		
($136,000 + $41,480)	$177,480	
($136,000 – $8,840)		$127,160

Alternative solution (shown in %)

	%		%
Borrow	–5.1		–5.1
Opening	4.5		4.0
Closing	4.56		4.56
	0.06		0.56
Premium	–0.304		–0.508
NET	–5.344		–5.048
Extra vs 4.3%	–1.044		–0.748
	(0.01044 × $34m × 6/12)		(0.00748 × $34m × 6/12)
In $s	**–177,480**		**–127,160**

Using a collar on options to hedge

Buy put options at 95.50 for 0.304 and sell call at 96.00 for 0.223

Net premium payable = 0.081

Assume that interest rates increase by 0.8% (80 basis points) to 4.4%

	Buy put	Sell call
Exercise price	95.50	96.00
Futures price	95.44	95.44
Exercise?*	Yes	No

(*The put option is exercised since, by exercising the option, the option holder has the right to sell the instrument at 95.50 instead of the market price of 95.44 and gain 6 basis points per contract. The call option is not exercised since, by not exercising the option, the option holder can buy the instrument at a lower market price of 95.44 instead of the higher option exercise price of 96.00.)

Gain on options
6 × $25 × 68	$10,200
Premium payable	
8.1 × $25 × 68	$13,770
Net cost of the collar	$3,570
Net additional cost	
($136,000 + $3,570)	$139,570

Alternative solution for collar (in %)

	%	
Borrow	−5.1	
Put	0.06	gain (as before)
Call not exercised		
Premium	−0.081	(0.304% − 0.223%)
	−5.121	
	−0.821%	extra vs 4.3%

in $s this is a cost of −$139,570

(0.00821 × $34m × 6/12)

Based on the assumption that interest rates increase by 80 basis points in the next five months, the futures hedge would lower the additional cost by the greatest amount and is significantly better than either the options hedge or the collar hedge. In addition to this, futures fix the amount which Daikon Co is likely to pay, assuming that there is no basis risk. The benefits accruing from the options are lower, with the 95.50 option and the collar option actually increasing the overall cost. In each case, this is due to the high premium costs. However, if interest rates do not increase and actually reduce, then the options (and to some extent the collar) provide more flexibility because they do not have to be exercised when interest rates move in the company's favour. But the movement will need to be significant before the cost of the premium is covered.

On that basis, on balance, it is recommended that hedging using futures is the best choice as they will probably provide the most benefit to Daikon Co.

However, it is recommended that the points made in part (b) are also considered before a final conclusion is made.

(b)   **Mark to market: Daily settlements**

2 June: 8 basis points (95.76 − 95.84) × $25 × 50 contracts = $10,000 loss

3 June: 10 basis points (95.66 − 95.76) × $25 × 50 contracts + 5 basis points (95.61 − 95.66) × $25 × 30 contracts = $16,250 loss

[Alternatively: 15 basis points (95.61 − 95.76) × $25 × 30 contracts + 10 basis points (95.66 − 95.76) × $25 × 20 contracts = $16,250 loss]

4 June: 8 basis points (95.74 − 95.66) × $25 × 20 contracts = $4,000 profit

Both mark to market and margins are used by markets to reduce (eliminate) the risk of non-payment by purchasers of the derivative products if prices move against them.

Mark to market closes all the open deals at the end of each day at that day's settlement price, and opens them again at the start of the following day. The notional profit or loss on the deals is then calculated and the margin account is adjusted accordingly on a daily basis. The impact on Daikon Co is that if losses are made, then the company may have to deposit extra funds with its broker if the margin account falls below the maintenance margin level. This may affect the company's ability to plan adequately and ensure it has enough funds for other activities. On the other hand, extra cash accruing from the notional profits can be withdrawn from the broker account if needed.

Each time a market-traded derivative product is opened, the purchaser needs to deposit a margin (initial margin) with the broker, which consists of funds to be kept with the broker while the position is open. As stated above, this amount may change daily and would affect Daikon Co's ability to plan for its cash requirements, but also open positions require that funds are tied up to support these positions and cannot be used for other purposes by the company.

The value of an option prior to expiry consists of time value, and may also consist of intrinsic value if the option is in-the-money. If an option is exercised prior to expiry, Daikon Co will only receive the intrinsic value attached to the option but not the time value. If the option is sold instead, whether it is in-the-money or out-of-the-money, Daikon Co will receive a higher value for it due to the time value. Unless options have other features, like dividends, attached to them, which are not reflected in the option value, they would not normally be exercised prior to expiry.

46 Sembilan

Workbook references. Chapter 13 for interest rate hedging, Chapter 14 for debt-equity swaps.

Top tips. For part (a) you need to use the forward rates rather than the current yield curve rates for Years 2 to 4. Don't forget the second part of the requirement!

For part (b)(ii) it is important to note that the bank has guaranteed the swap.

Part (c) requires you to think about the implications of raising equity to pay off debt, including the willingness of the shareholders to participate.

Easy marks. Part (b)(i) is fairly straightforward, it just requires you to choose a higher and lower rate to use for the illustration.

Examining team's comments. Part (a) required the candidates to calculate the variable amounts received and the fixed amounts paid by Sembilan Co to Ratus Bank based on forward rates. A number of candidates incorrectly included the 60 basis points, which is part of the original loan contract but would not be part of the swap; and some answers used the spot rates instead of the forward rates. It is surprising that the responses contained basic errors when there was a recent article in the Student Accountant on how a swap contract can be valued based on forward rates and a fixed rate. Few candidates could explain why the fixed rate was lower than the four-year spot rate.

In part (b) many responses gave explanations, rather than a demonstration, that the payment liability did not change. Many of the explanations lacked adequate detail. The requirement 'Demonstrate' means that the candidates should show, by examples or otherwise, that the payment does not change whether interest rates increase or decrease. Few managed to do this with any clarity.

Marking scheme

				Marks
(a)		Gross amount receivable by Sembilan Co	1	
		Gross amounts payable by Sembilan Co	1	
		Net amounts receivable or payable every year	2	
		Explanation of why fixed rate is less than the four-year yield curve rate	2	
				6
(b)	(i)	Demonstration of impact of interest rate changes	4	
		Explanation and conclusion	1	
				5
	(ii)	1 mark per relevant discussion point		Max 5
(c)		1–2 marks per relevant discussion point		Max 9
				25

BPP
LEARNING
MEDIA

(a) Gross amounts of interest receivable from Ratus Bank based on Year 1 spot rate and Years 2–4 forward rates.

Year 1 = 0.025 × $320m = $8m

Year 2 = 0.037 × $320m = $11.84m

Year 3 = 0.043 × $320m = $13.76m

Year 4 = 0.047 × $320m = $15.04m

Fixed gross amount of interest payable to Ratus Bank in each of the Years 1–4

3.7625% × $320m = $12.04m

Therefore the expected receipts/(payments) are:

Year 1 = $8.00m – $12.04m = ($4.04m)

Year 2 = $11.84m – $12.04m = ($0.20m)

Year 3 = $13.76m – $12.04m = $1.72m

Year 4 = $15.04m – $12.04m = $3.00m

The equivalent fixed rate of 3.7625% is less than the 3.8% four-year yield curve rate because the 3.8% represents a zero-coupon bond with one payment in the fourth year. The relevant bond here pays coupons at different time periods when the yield curve rates are lower, hence the fixed rate is lower.

(b) (i)

	% impact %	Yield interest 3% $m	Yield interest 5% $m
Borrow at yield + 60 basis points	(Yield + 0.6)	(11.52)	(17.92)
Receive yield	Yield	9.60	16.00
Pay fixed	(3.7625)	(12.04)	(12.04)
Fee 20 basis points	(0.2)	(0.64)	(0.64)
	4.5625	(14.60)	(14.60)

The receipt and payment based on the yield curve remove the fluctuating element, leaving the 60 basis points borrowing charge, the 20 basis points fee and the fixed payment rate: 0.6% + 3.7625% + 0.2% = 4.5625%.

(ii) Sembilan Co is using the swap to manage its **interest rate risk** and is protecting against a rise in interest rates. This has been done without changing the initial debt of $320 million, which is already in issue.

The interest rate payments are fixed, which means that it is much easier for Sembilan Co to **forecast its future cash flows** and also helps to budget accurately.

The cost to Sembilan Co is relatively small, especially when compared to **potential losses** if interest rates are to rise. Other derivatives, such as options, are typically more expensive.

The swap will be relatively **straightforward**, with the bank undertaking all the relevant administration and organisation. Other derivatives would be more time consuming to arrange.

The main disadvantage is that Sembilan Co will be unable to take advantage of a **favourable movement** in interest rates.

There is no **counterparty risk** involved as the bank is guaranteeing the swap and will make good any default.

(c)   Issuing equity and using the proceeds to reduce the amount of debt will **change the capital structure** of Sembilan Co and there are a number of implications of this which need to be considered.

As the proportion of debt compared to equity increases, **financial distress also increases** and associated costs along with it. Companies with high levels of financial distress may find that suppliers demand more onerous credit terms, and that they may have to give longer credit terms to attract customers and pay higher wages to attract employees. Also providers of equity may **demand a higher level of return** because financial risk has increased. In addition, there may be restrictive covenants that make it more difficult to raise funds (either debt or equity). On the other hand, there will be greater levels of tax relief from the higher interest payments. However, this is only available while the company is making taxable profits or **tax exhaustion** will set in. Sembilan Co is assumed to have judged the relative benefits of high and low levels of financial gearing in making its original decision on debt and equity levels.

The proposed equity issue will change the existing balance and therefore the value of Sembilan Co may not be maximised. However, a **lower debt level** would result in a **higher credit rating** for the company as well as reduce the scale of restrictive covenants. Increasing the level of equity would also increase the debt capacity of the company, which would help to raise finance for future projects more easily. Reduced financial distress may make it easier to deal with stakeholders such as suppliers and customers.

Changing the financial structure of a company can be expensive. There are likely to be costs for the early redemption of debt which can be found in the contractual clauses of the debt to be repaid. **A new issue of equity may also be expensive**, especially if shares are offered to new shareholders as there will be marketing costs and underwriting costs as well. Although a rights issue may be less expensive, the costs may still be significant.

If a rights issue is undertaken, Sembilan Co will need to decide on whether the current shareholders will be able to take up the rights and the level of discount to the current market price that should be offered to ensure a full take-up of rights. The impact of the rights issue on the current price should be considered as well. Studies have shown that **typically markets view rights issues positively** and the share price does not reduce to the theoretical ex-rights price. However, this is because the funds are usually spent on profitable projects and the reaction may not be so positive if the funds are to be used to repay debt.

The move will need to be justified to the market and so Sembilan Co will need to provide information to existing and any new shareholders which shows that one group will not be favoured at the expense of another. Sufficient information is required to **prevent issues with information asymmetry**, but if too much information is produced it may reduce the competitive position of Sembilan Co.

47 Pault

Workbook references. Chapter 13 for interest rate hedging, Chapter 14 for debt-equity swaps.

Top tips. It is important to read articles produced by the examining team, this question was covered by an article that was published in the lead up to the September exam. It is important not to panic with this type of question, for example part (a)(ii) required the evaluation of a swap after 1 year; this did not require anything from (a)(i) and should have been accessible even to candidates that had struggled with (a)(i).

Easy marks. Part (b), 4 marks – required advice on the factors influencing the value of a swap. Part (c), 9 marks – required a discussion of the advantages and disadvantages of simply continuing with floating rate finance compared to using a swap. This was well answered and was the easiest, and most important part of the question.

Marks

(a) (i) Gross amount payable by Pault Co — 1
Calculation of forward rates — 3
Basis point reduction — 1
Net amounts receivable or payable each year — $\underline{1}$
$\underline{6}$

(ii) Yield interest calculations — 5
Comment on interest payment liability — $\underline{1}$
$\underline{6}$

(b) Up to 2 marks per point — Max 4

(c) Advantages (up to 2 marks per relevant point) — Max 5
Disadvantages (up to 2 marks per relevant point) — Max 5
9
$\underline{\underline{25}}$

(a) (i) Gross amount of annual interest paid by Pault Co to Millbridge Bank = 4.847% × $400m = $19.39m.

Gross amounts of annual interest receivable by Pault Co from Millbridge Bank, based on Year 1 spot rates and Years 2–4 forward rates:

Year

1    $0.0350 \times \$400m = \$14m$

2    $0.0460 \times \$400m = \$18.4m$

3    $0.0541 \times \$400m = \$21.64m$

4    $0.0611 \times \$400m = \$24.44m$

Workings

Year 2 forward rate: $(1.0425^2/1.037) - 1 = 4.80\%$

Year 3 forward rate: $(1.0470^3/1.0425^2) - 1 = 5.61\%$

Year 4 forward rate: $(1.0510^4/1.0470^3) - 1 = 6.31\%$

Rates are reduced by 20 basis points in calculation.

At the start of the swap, Pault will expect to pay or receive the following net amounts at each of the next four years:

Year

1    $14m – $19.39m = $(5.39m) payment
2    $18.4m – $19.39m = $(0.99m) payment
3    $21.64m – $19.39m = $2.25m receipt
4    $24.44m – $19.39m = $5.05m receipt

(ii) **Interest payment liability**

	Impact %	Yield interest 2.9% $m	Yield interest 4.5% $m
Borrow at yield interest + 50 bp	(Yield + 0.5)	(13.60)	(20.00)
Receive yield – 20 bp	Yield – 0.2	10.80	17.20
Pay fixed 4.847%	(4.847)	(19.39)	(19.39)
Bank fee – 25 bp	(0.25)	(1.00)	(1.00)
	(5.797)	(23.19)	(23.19)

The interest payment liability will be $23.19 million, whatever the yield interest, as the receipt and payment are based on the yield curve net of interest rate fluctuations.

(b) At the start of the contract, the value of the swap will be zero. The terms offered by Millbridge Bank equate the discounted value of the fixed rate payments by Pault Co with the variable rate payments by Millbridge Bank.

However, the value of the swap will not remain at zero. If interest rates increase more than expected, Pault Co will benefit from having to pay a fixed rate and the value of the swap will increase. The value of the swap will also change as the swap approaches maturity, with fewer receipts and payments left.

(c) **Disadvantages of swap arrangement**

The swap represents a long-term commitment at a time when interest rates appear uncertain. It may be that interest rate rises are lower than expected. In this case, Pault Co will be committed to a higher interest rate and its finance costs may be higher than if it had not taken out the finance arrangements. Pault Co may not be able to take action to relieve this commitment if it becomes clear that the swap was unnecessary.

On the basis of the expected forward rates, Pault Co will not start benefiting from the swap until Year 3. Particularly during Year 1, the extra commitment to interest payments may be an important burden at a time when Pault Co will have significant development and launch costs.

Pault Co will be liable for an arrangement fee. However, other methods of hedging which could be used will have a cost built into them as well.

Advantages of swap arrangement

The swap means that the annual interest payment liability will be fixed at $23.19 million over the next four years. This is a certain figure which can be used in budgeting. Having a fixed figure may help planning, particularly as a number of other costs associated with the investment are uncertain.

The directors will be concerned not just about the probability that floating rates will result in a higher commitment than under the swap, but also about how high this commitment could be. The directors may feel that rates may possibly rise to a level which would give Pault Co problems in meeting its commitments and regard that as unacceptable.

Any criticism after the end of the loan period will be based on hindsight. What appeared to be the cheapest choice at that stage may not have been what appeared most likely to be the cheapest choice when the loan was taken out. In addition, criticism of the directors for not choosing the cheapest option fails to consider risk. The cheapest option may be the most risky. The directors may reasonably take the view that the saving in cost is not worth the risks incurred.

The swap is for a shorter period than the loan and thus allows Pault Co to reconsider the position in four years' time. It may choose to take out another swap then on different terms, or let the arrangement lapse and pay floating rate interest on the loan, depending on the expectations at that time of future interest rates.

48 Conejo

Marking scheme

				Marks
(a)	Being able to bear higher levels of financial risk		Up to 3	
	Better protection from predatory takeover bids		Up to 3	
	Taxation benefit of higher levels of debt finance		Up to 2	
				Max 7
(b)	(i)	Appendix 1		
		Conejo Co's yield curve based on BBB rating	1	
		Bond value based on BBB rating and spot yieald rates	1	
		Comment on reason for virtually no change in value	1	
		Calculation of the coupon rate of the new bond	2	
		Comment on coupon rate	1	
			6	
	(ii)	Appendix 2		
		Duration based on annual coupon and balloon payment of $100 in Year 5	2	
		Amount of fixed annual repayments of capital and interest	2	
		Duration based on annual equivalent payments	2	
			6	
	(iii)	Appendix 3		
		Financial position, Proposal 1	3	
		Financial position, Proposal 2	3	
		Interest payable on additional new debt finance	1	
		Interest payable on higher coupon for current debt finance	1	
		Return on additional investment	1	
		Gearing calculations	1	
		Earnings per share calculations	1	
			11	
	(iv)	Discussion in report		
		Impact on Conejo Co	Up to 6	
		Credit migration, credit rating agencies and CEO's opinion	Up to 6	
		Impact on Conejo Co's equity holders	Up to 4	
		Impact on Conejo Co's debt holders: current and new	Up to 3	
				Max 16
		Professional marks for part (b)		
		Report format	1	
		Structure and presentation of the report	3	
			4	
				50

(a) Increasing the debt finance of a company relative to equity finance increases its financial risk, and therefore the company will need to be able to bear the consequences of this increased risk. However, companies face both financial risk, which increases as the debt levels in the capital structure increase, and business risk, which is present in a company due to the nature of its business.

In the case of Conejo Co, it could be argued that as its profits and cash flows have stabilised, the company's business risk has reduced, in contrast to early in its life, when its business risk would have been much higher due to unstable profits and cash flows. Therefore, whereas previously Conejo Co was not able to bear high levels of financial risk, it is able to do so now without having a detrimental impact on the overall risk profile of the company. It could therefore change its capital structure and have higher levels of debt finance relative to equity finance.

The predatory acquisition of one company by another could be undertaken for a number of reasons. One possible reason may be to gain access to cash resources, where a company which needs cash resources may want to take over another company which has significant cash resources or cash generative capability. Another reason may be to increase the debt capacity of the acquirer by using the assets of the target company. Where the relative level of debt finance is increased in the capital structure of a company through a financial reconstruction, like in the case of Conejo Co, these reasons for acquiring a company may be diminished. This is because the increased levels of debt would probably be secured against the assets of the company and therefore the acquirer cannot use them to raise additional debt finance, and cash resources would be needed to fund the higher interest payments.

Many tax jurisdictions worldwide allow debt interest to be deducted from profits before the amount of tax payable is calculated on the profits. Increasing the amount of debt finance will increase the amount of interest paid, reducing the taxable profits and therefore the tax paid. Modigliani and Miller referred to this as the benefit of the tax shield in their research into capital structure, where their amended capital proposition demonstrated the reduction in the cost of capital and increase in the value of the firm, as the proportion of debt in the capital structure increases.

(b) **Report to the board of directors (BoD), Conejo Co**

Introduction

This report discusses whether the proposed financial reconstruction scheme which increases the amount of debt finance in Conejo Co would be beneficial or not to the company and the main parties affected by the change in the funding, namely the equity holders, the debt holders and the credit rating companies. Financial estimates provided in the appendices are used to support the discussion.

Impact on Conejo Co

Benefits to Conejo Co include the areas discussed in part (a) above and as suggested by the CFO. The estimate in Appendix 3 assumes that the interest payable on the new bonds and the extra interest payable on the existing bonds are net of the 15% tax. Therefore, the tax shield reduces the extra amount of interest paid. Further, it is likely that because of the large amount of debt finance which will be raised, the company's assets would have been used as collateral. This will help protect the company against hostile takeover bids. Additionally, Proposal 2 (Appendix 3) appears to be better than proposal 1, with a lower gearing figure and a higher earnings per share figure. However, this is dependent on the extra investment being able to generate an after-tax return of 12% immediately. The feasibility of this should be assessed further.

Conejo Co may also feel that this is the right time to raise debt finance as interest rates are lower and therefore it does not have to offer large coupons, compared to previous years. Appendix 1 estimates that the new bond will need to offer a coupon of 3.57%, whereas the existing bond is paying a coupon of 5.57%.

The benefits above need to be compared with potential negative aspects of raising such a substantial amount of debt finance. Conejo Co needs to ensure that it will be able to finance the interest payable on the bonds and it should ensure it is able to repay the capital amount borrowed (or be able to re-finance the loan) in the future. The extra interest payable (Appendix 3) will probably not pose a significant issue given that the profit after tax is substantially more than the interest payment. However, the repayment of the capital amount will need careful thought because it is significant.

The substantial increase in gearing, especially with respect to Proposal 1 (Appendix 3), may worry some stakeholders because of the extra financial risk. However, based on market values, the level of gearing may not appear so high. The expected credit migration from A to BBB seems to indicate some increase in risk, but it is probably not substantial.

The BoD should also be aware of, and take account of, the fact that going to the capital markets to raise finance will require Conejo Co to disclose information, which may be considered strategically important and could impact negatively on areas where Conejo Co has a competitive advantage.

Reaction of credit rating companies

Credit ratings assigned to companies and to borrowings made by companies by credit rating companies depend on the probability of default and recovery rate. A credit migration from A to BBB means that Conejo Co has become riskier in that it is more likely to default and bondholders will find it more difficult to recover their entire loan if default does happen. Nevertheless, the relatively lower increase in yield spreads from A to BBB, compared to BBB to BB, indicates that BBB can still be considered a relatively safe investment.

Duration indicates the time it takes to recover half the repayments of interest and capital of a bond, in present value terms. Duration measures the sensitivity of bond prices to changes in interest rates. A bond with a higher duration would see a greater fluctuation in its value when interest rates change, compared to a bond with a lower duration. Appendix 2 shows that a bond which pays interest (coupon) and capital in equal annual instalments will have a lower duration. This is because a greater proportion of income is received earlier and income due to be received earlier is less risky. Therefore, when interest rates change, this bond's value will change by less than the bond with the higher duration. The CEO is correct that the bond with equal annual payments of interest and capital is less sensitive to interest rate changes, but it is not likely that this will be a significant factor for a credit rating company when assigning a credit rating.

A credit rating company will consider a number of criteria when assigning a credit rating, as these would give a more appropriate assessment of the probability of default and the recovery rate. These criteria include, for example, the industry within which the company operates, the company's position within that industry, the company's ability to generate profits in proportion to the capital invested, the amount of gearing, the quality of management and the amount of financial flexibility the company possesses. A credit rating company will be much less concerned about the manner in which a bond's value fluctuates when interest rates change.

Impact on equity holders

The purpose of the financial reconstruction would be of interest to the equity holders. If, for example, Conejo Co selects Proposal 1 (Appendix 3), it may give equity holders an opportunity to liquidate some of their invested capital. At present, the original members of the company hold 40% of the equity capital and Proposal 1 provides them with the opportunity to realise a substantial capital without unnecessary fluctuations in the share price. Selling large quantities of equity shares in the stock exchange may move the price of the shares down and cause unnecessary fluctuations in the share price.

If, on the other hand, Proposal 2 (Appendix 3) is selected, any additional profits after the payment of interest will benefit the equity holders directly. In effect, debt capital is being used for the benefit of the equity holders.

It may be true that equity holders may be concerned about the increased risk which higher gearing will bring, and because of this, they may need higher returns to compensate for the higher risk. However, in terms of market values, the increased gearing may be of less concern to equity holders. Conejo Co should consider the capital structure of its competitors to assess what should be an appropriate level of gearing.

Equity holders will probably be more concerned about the additional restrictive covenants which will result from the extra debt finance, and the extent to which these covenants will restrict the financial flexibility of Conejo Co when undertaking future business opportunities.

Equity holders may also be concerned that because Conejo Co has to pay extra interest to debt holders, its ability to pay increasing amounts of dividends in the future could be affected. However, Appendix 3 shows that the proportion of interest relative to after-tax profits is not too high and any concern from the equity holders is probably unfounded.

Impact on debt holders

Although the current debt holders may be concerned about the extra gearing which the new bonds would introduce to Conejo Co, Appendix 1 shows that the higher coupon payments which the current debt holders will receive would negate any fall in the value of their bonds due to the credit migration to BBB rating from an A rating. Given that currently Conejo Co is subject to low financial risk, and probably lower business risk, it is unlikely that the current and new debt holders would be overly concerned about the extra gearing. The earnings figures in Appendix 3 also show that the after-tax profit figures provide a substantial interest cover and therefore additional annual interest payment should not cause the debt holders undue concern either.

The current and new debt holders would be more concerned about Conejo Co's ability to pay back the large capital sum in five years' time. However, a convincing explanation of how this can be achieved or a plan to roll over the debt should allay these concerns.

The current and new debt holders may be concerned that Conejo Co is not tempted to take unnecessary risks with the additional investment finance, but sensible use of restrictive covenants and the requirement to make extra disclosures to the markets when raising the debt finance should help mitigate these concerns.

Conclusion

Overall, it seems that the proposed financial reconstruction will be beneficial, as it will provide opportunities for Conejo Co to make additional investments and/or an opportunity to reduce equity capital, and thereby increasing the earnings per share. The increased gearing may not look large when considered in terms of market values. It may also be advantageous to undertake the reconstruction scheme in a period when interest rates are low and the credit migration is not disadvantageous. However, Conejo Co needs to be mindful of how it intends to repay the capital amount in five years' time, the information it will disclose to the capital markets and the impact of any negative restrictive covenants.

Report compiled by:

Date

Appendices:

Appendix 1: Change in the value of the current bond from credit migration and coupon rate required from the new bond (Question (b)(i))

Spot yield rates (yield curve) based on BBB rating

1 year	2.20%
2 year	2.51%
3 year	2.84%
4 year	3.25%
5 year	3.62%

Bond value based on BBB rating

$5.57 \times 1.0220^{-1} + \$5.57 \times 1.0251^{-2} + \$105.57 \times 1.0284^{-3} = \$107.81$

Current bond value = $107.80

Although the credit rating of Conejo Co declines from A to BBB, resulting in higher spot yield rates, the value of the bond does not change very much at all. This is because the increase in the coupons and the resultant increase in value almost exactly matches the fall in value from the higher spot yield rates.

Coupon rate required from the new bond

Take R as the coupon rate, such that:

$(\$R \times 1.0220^{-1}) + (\$R \times 1.0251^{-2}) + (\$R \times 1.0284^{-3}) + (\$R \times 1.0325^{-4}) + (\$R \times 1.0362^{-5}) + (\$100 \times 1.0362^{-5}) = \$100$

$4.5665R + 83.71 = 100$

$R = \$3.57$

Coupon rate for the new bond is 3.57%.

If the coupon payments on the bond are at a rate of 3.57% on the face value, it ensures that the present values of the coupons and the redemption of the bond at face value exactly equals the bond's current face value, based on Conejo Co's yield curve.

Appendix 2: Macaulay durations (Question (b)(ii))

Macaulay duration based on annual coupon of $3.57 and redemption value of $100 in Year 5:

$[(\$3.57 \times 1.0220^{-1} \times 1 \text{ year}) + (\$3.57 \times 1.0251^{-2} \times 2 \text{ years}) + (\$3.57 \times 1.0284^{-3} \times 3 \text{ years}) + (\$3.57 \times 1.0325^{-4} \times 4 \text{ years}) + (\$103.57 \times 1.0362^{-5} \times 5 \text{ years})]/\$100$

$= [3.49 + 6.79 + 9.85 + 12.57 + 433.50]/100 = 4.7 \text{ years}$

Macaulay duration based on fixed annual repayments of interest and capital:

Annuity factor: (3.57%, 5 years) = $(1 - 1.0357^{-5})/0.0357 = 4.51$ approximately

Annual payments of capital and interest required to pay back new bond issue = $100/4.51 = $22.17 per $100 bond approximately

$[(\$22.17 \times 1.0220^{-1} \times 1 \text{ year}) + (\$22.17 \times 1.0251^{-2} \times 2 \text{ years}) + (\$22.17 \times 1.0284^{-3} \times 3 \text{ years}) + (\$22.17 \times 1.0325 - 4 \times 4 \text{ years}) + (\$22.17 \times 1.0362^{-5} \times 5 \text{ years})]/\$100$

$= [21.69 + 42.20 + 61.15 + 78.03 + 92.79]/100 = 3.0 \text{ years}$

Alternative presentation of duration calculations:

(Discount factors are based on the interest rates shown in previous presentation)

Based on annual rate of 3.57% and redemption in Year 5:

Time	1	2	3	4	5	Total
$	3.57	3.57	3.57	3.57	103.57	
df	0.978	0.952	0.919	0.880	0.837	
PV	3.5	3.4	3.3	3.1	86.7	100.0
% PV	0.04	0.03	0.03	0.03	0.87	1.0
% × year	0.04	0.06	0.09	0.12	4.35	**4.7**

Based on fixed annual repayments of interest and capital:

$	22.17	22.17	22.17	22.17	22.17	Total
df	0.978	0.952	0.919	0.880	0.837	
PV	21.7	21.1	20.4	19.5	18.6	101.3
% PV	0.22	0.21	0.20	0.20	0.19	1.0
% × year	0.22	0.42	0.60	0.80	0.95	**3.0**

Appendix 3: Forecast earnings, financial position, earnings per share and gearing (Question (b)(iii)) Adjustments to forecast earnings

Amounts in $m	Current	Proposal 1	Proposal 2
Forecast after-tax profit	350.00	350.00	350.00
Interest payable on additional borrowing (based on a coupon rate of 3.57%)			
3.57% × $1,320m × (1 – 0.15)		(40.06)	(40.06)
Additional interest payable due to higher coupon			
0.37% × $120m × (1 – 0.15)		(0.38)	(0.38)
Return on additional investment (after tax)			
12% × $1,320m			158.40
Adjusted profit after tax	350.00	309.56	467.96

Forecast financial position

Amounts in $m	Current	Proposal 1	Proposal 2
Non-current assets	1,735.00	1,735.00	3,055.00
Current assets	530.00	489.56	647.96
Total assets	2,265.00	2,224.56	3,702.96
Equity and liabilities			
Share capital ($1 per share par value)	400.00	280.00	400.00
Reserves	1,700.00	459.56	1,817.96
Total equity	2,100.00	739.56	2,217.96
Non-current liabilities	120.00	1,440.00	1,440.00
Current liabilities	45.00	45.00	45.00
Total liabilities	165.00	1,485.00	1,485.00
Total liabilities and capital	2,265.00	2,224.56	3,702.96
Gearing % (non-current liabilities/equity)	5.7%	194.7%	64.9%
Earnings per share (in cents)			
(Adjusted profit after tax/no. of shares)	87.5c	110.6c	117.0c

Note. If gearing is calculated based on non-current liabilities/(non-current liabilities + equity) and/or using market value of equity, instead of as above, then this is acceptable as well.

Proposal 1

Additional interest payable is deducted from current assets, assuming it is paid in cash and this is part of current assets. Reserves are also reduced by this amount. (Other assumptions are possible.)

Shares repurchased as follows: $1 × 120m shares deducted from share capital and $10 × 120m shares deducted from reserves. $1,320 million, consisting of $11 × 120m shares, added to non-current liabilities.

Proposal 2

Treatment of additional interest payable is as per Proposal 1.

Additional debt finance raised, $1,320 million, is added to non-current liabilities and to non-current assets, assuming that all this amount is invested in non-current assets to generate extra income.

It is assumed that this additional investment generates returns at 12%, which is added to current assets and to profits (and therefore to reserves).

(Explanations given in notes are not required for full marks, but are included to explain how the figures given in Appendix 3 are derived.)

Note. Credit will be given for alternative relevant presentation of financial positions and discussion.

49 Chrysos

Workbook references. Reverse takeovers are covered in Chapter 9; business reorganisations are covered in Chapter 15.

Top tips. This question required careful reading because it was complicated to understand what was going on and, as you would expect, some of the numerical parts to the question were challenging. It is important to target the easier areas and not to worry about getting every aspect of the calculations correct (this is unlikely to be achievable under exam conditions). Part (b)(i), for 18 marks, was the hardest part of question 1. It was important here to keep your nerve and to score the easier marks; these were available for evaluating whether to sell or unbundle a division (6 marks), calculating the cost of capital for the remaining business (2 marks) and using it to

attempt a cash flow valuation (5 marks). It was important not to panic, and to adopt a logical approach, for example:

- First decide whether the company sells a division to a supplier or to an MBO team.

- Next estimate the revised SOFP using a balancing figure for reserves to all it to balance, don't worry too much if it doesn't because this does not affect your ability to value the company.

- Now re-gear the given cost of equity to reflect company's given gearing.

- Now attempt a cash flow valuation and if your cash flow valuation is before interest return to the previous step and calculate a WACC using the given cost of debt.

Easy marks. It is important to target the easier discussion areas and not to worry about getting every aspect of the calculations correct (this is unlikely to be achievable under exam conditions). The discussion parts of this question – parts (a), (b)(iii) and (c) were worth about half of the marks and therefore need (almost) as much effort as the numerical areas.

Marking scheme

				Marks
(a)		Explanation of what a reverse takeover involves	2	
		Advantages (up to 2 marks per well explained advantage)		Max 4
		Disadvantages (up to 2 marks per well explained disadvantage)		Max 4
				Max 9
(b)	(i)	Extract of financial position after restructuring programme **Appendix 1**		
		Manufacturing business unit unbundled through an MBO		
		Estimate of cash flows	3	
		Estimate of amount payable to ChrysosCo	2	
		Selection of higher value unbundling option	1	
		Appendix 2		
		Chrysos Co, cost of equity	1	
		Chrysos Co, cost of capital	1	
		Appendix 3		
		Estimate of cash flows	3	
		Estimate of equity value	2	
				18
	(ii)	Explanation of approach taken	1–2	
		Explanation of assumptions made (up to 2 marks per assumption)	3–4	
				Max 5
	(iii)	**Appendix 4**		
		Value from increased ownership	1	
		Additional value	1	
		Discussion of restructuring programme on the VCOs	3–4	
		Discussion of restructuring programme on Chrysos Co	4–5	
				Max 10
		Professional marks for part (b)		
		Report format	1	
		Structure and presentation of the report	3	
				4
(c)		1–2 marks per relevant point		Max 4
				50

(a) A reverse takeover enables a private, unlisted company, like Chrysos Co, to gain a listing on the stock exchange without needing to go through the process of an initial public offering (IPO). The private company merges with a listed 'shell' company. The private company initially purchases equity shares in the listed company and takes control of its board of directors. The listed company then issues new equity shares and these are exchanged for equity shares in the unlisted company, thereby the original private company's equity shares gain a listing on the stock exchange. Often the name of the listed company is also changed to that of the original unlisted company.

Advantages relative to an IPO

(1)   An IPO can take a long time, typically between one and two years, because it involves preparing a prospectus and creating an interest among potential investors. The equity shares need to be valued and the issue process needs to be administered. Since with the reverse takeover shares in the private company are exchanged for shares in the listed company and no new capital is being raised, the process can be completed much quicker.

(2)   An IPO is an expensive process and can cost between 3% and 5% of the capital being raised due to involvement of various parties, such as investment banks, law firms, etc, and the need to make the IPO attractive through issuing a prospectus and marketing the issue. A reverse takeover does not require such costs to be incurred and therefore is considerably cheaper.

(3)   In periods of economic downturn, recessions and periods of uncertainty, an IPO may not be successful. A lot of senior managerial time and effort will be spent, as well as expenditure, with nothing to show for it. On the other hand, a reverse takeover would not face this problem as it does not need external investors and it is not raising external finance, but is being used to gain from the potential benefits of going public by getting a listing.

Disadvantages relative to an IPO

(1)   The 'shell' listed company being used in the reverse takeover may have hidden liabilities and may be facing potential litigation, which may not be obvious at the outset. Proper and full due diligence is necessary before the process is started. A company undertaking an IPO would not face such difficulties.

(2)   The original shareholders of the listed company may want to sell their shares immediately after the reverse takeover process has taken place and this may affect the share price negatively. A lock-up period during which shares cannot be sold may be necessary to prevent this. Note. An IPO may need a lock-up period as well, but this is not usually the case.

(3)   The senior management of an unlisted company may not have the expertise and/or understanding of the rules and regulations which a listed company needs to comply with. The IPO process normally takes longer and is more involved, when compared to a reverse takeover. It also involves a greater involvement from external experts. These factors will provide the senior management involved in an IPO, with opportunities to develop the necessary expertise and knowledge of listing rules and regulations, which the reverse takeover process may not provide.

(4)   One of the main reasons for gaining a listing is to gain access to new investor capital. However, a smaller, private company which has become public through a reverse takeover may not obtain a sufficient analyst coverage and investor following, and it may have difficulty in raising new finance in future. A well-advertised IPO will probably not face these issues and find raising new funding to be easier.

(b)   **Report to the board of directors (BoD), Chrysos Co**

This report provides extracts from the financial position and an estimate of the value of Chrysos Co after it has undertaken a restructuring programme. It also contains an explanation of the process used in estimating the value and of the assumptions made. Finally, the report discusses the impact of the restructuring programme on the company and on venture capital organisations.

It is recommended that the manufacturing business unit is unbundled through a management buy-out, rather than the assets being sold separately, and it is estimated that Chrysos Co will receive $3,289 million from the unbundling of the manufacturing business unit (Appendix 1). This amount is recorded as a cash receipt in the extract of the financial position given below.

Extract of Chrysos Co's financial position following the restructuring programme

	$m
Non-current assets	
Land and buildings (80% × $7,500m)	6,000
Equipment ((80% × $5,400m) + $1,200m)	5,520
Current assets	
Inventory (80% × $1,800m)	1,440
Receivables (80% × $900m)	720
Cash ($3,289m + $400m − $1,200m − $1,050m)	1,439
Total assets	15,119
Equity	
Share capital ($1,800 + $600m)	2,400
Reserves **	10,319
Non-current liabilities	
Bank loan	1,800
Current liabilities	
Payables (80% × $750m)	600
Total equity and liabilities	15,119

** Balancing figure

Estimate of Chrysos Co's equity value following the restructuring programme

It is estimated that Chrysos Co's equity value after the restructuring programme has taken place will be just over $46 billion (Appendix 3).

Process undertaken in determining Chrysos Co's equity value

The corporate value is based on a growth rate of 4% on cash flows in perpetuity, which are discounted at Chrysos Co's cost of capital (Appendix 2). The cash flows are estimated by calculating the profit before depreciation and tax of the unbundled firm consisting of just the mining and shipping business unit and then deducting the depreciation and taxation amounts from this.

The bank loan debt is then deducted from the corporate value to estimate the value of the firm which is attributable to the equity holders (Appendix 3).

Assumptions made in determining Chrysos Co's equity value

It is assumed that Sidero Co's ungeared cost of equity is equivalent to Chrysos Co's ungeared cost of equity, given that they are both in the same industry and therefore face the same business risk. Modigliani and Miller's Proposition 2 is used to estimate Chrysos Cos's restructured cost of equity and cost of capital.

It is assumed that deducting depreciation and tax from the profit before depreciation, interest and tax provides a reasonably accurate estimate of the free cash flows (Appendix 3). Other adjustments such as changes in working capital are reckoned to be immaterial and therefore not considered. Depreciation is not added back because it is assumed to be the same as the capital needed for reinvestment purposes.

It is assumed that the cash flows will grow in perpetuity. The assumption of growth in perpetuity may be over-optimistic and may give a higher than accurate estimate of Chrysos Co's equity value.

Note. Credit will be given for alternative and relevant assumptions.

Impact of the restructuring programme on Chrysos Co and on the venture capital organisations (VCOs)

By acquiring an extra 600 million equity shares, the proportion of the VCOs' equity share capital will increase to 40% ((600m + 20% × 1,800)/(1,800 + 600)) from 20%. Therefore, the share of the equity value the VCOs will hold in Chrysos Co will increase by $9,229 million, which is 77.5% more than the total of the value of bonds cancelled and extra payment made (Appendix 4). As long as the VCOs are satisfied that the equity value of Chrysos Co after the restructuring programme has been undertaken is accurate, the value of their investment has increased substantially. The VCOs may want undertake a feasibility study on the annual growth rate in cash flows of 4% and the assumption of growth in perpetuity. However, the extent of additional value created seems to indicate that the impact for the VCOs is positive.

By cancelling the VCOs' unsecured bonds and repaying the other debt in non-current liabilities, an opportunity has been created for Chrysos Co to raise extra debt finance for future projects. Based on a long-term capital structure ratio of 80% equity and 20% debt, and a corporate value of $47,944 million (Appendix 3), this equates to just under $9,600 million of possible debt finance which could be accessed. Since the bank loan has a current value of $1,800 million, Chrysos Co could raise just under an extra $7,800 million debt funding and it would also have $1,439 million in net cash available from the sale of the machinery parts manufacturing business unit.

Chrysos Co's current value has not been given and therefore it is not possible to determine the financial impact of the equity value after the restructuring has taken place on the company as a whole. Nevertheless, given that the company has access to an extra $7,800 million debt funding to expand its investment into new value-creating projects, it is likely that the restructuring programme will be beneficial. However, it is recommended that the company tries to determine its current equity value and compares this with the proposed new value. A concern may be that both the five senior equity holders' group and the 30 other equity holders group's proportion of equity shares will reduce to 30% from 40% each, as a result of the VCOs acquiring an additional 600 million shares. Both these shareholder groups need to be satisfied about the potential negative impact of these situations against the potential additional benefits accruing from the restructuring programme, before the company proceeds with the programme.

Conclusion

The restructuring programme creates an opportunity for Chrysos Co to have access to extra funding and additional cash for investment in projects in the future. The VCOs are likely to benefit financially from the restructuring programme as long as they are satisfied about the assumptions made when assessing the value created. However, Chrysos Co will need to ensure that all equity holder groups are satisfied with the change in their respective equity holdings.

Report compiled by:

Date:

Note. Credit will be given for alternative and relevant points.

Appendices

Appendix 1: Unbundling the manufacturing business unit

Option 1: Sale of assets

Net proceeds to Chrysos Co from net sale of assets of the manufacturing business unit are $3,102 million.

Option 2: Management buy-out

	$m
Sales revenue (20% × $16,800m)	3,360
Operating costs (25% × 10,080m)	(2,520)
Profit before depreciation, interest and tax	840
Depreciation (12% × 20% × ($7,500m + $5,400m))	(310)
	530
Tax (18% × $530m)	(95)
Cash flows	435

Estimated value = ($435m × 1.08)/0.10 = $4,698m

Amount payable to Chrysos Co = 70% × $4,698m = $3,289m

The option to unbundle through a management buy-out (option 2) is marginally better for Chrysos Co and it will opt for this.

Appendix 2: Calculation of cost of equity and cost of capital

Chrysos Co, estimate of cost of equity (Ke) and cost of capital (CoC)

$$Ke = 12.46\% + [0.82 \times (12.46\% - 4.5\%) \times (0.2/0.8)]$$

$$Ke = 14.09\%$$

$$CoC = 0.8 \times 14.09\% + 0.2 \times 4.5\% \times 0.82 = 12.01, \text{ say } 12\%$$

Appendix 3: Estimate of value

	$m
Sales revenue (80% × $16,800m)	13,440
Costs prior to depreciation, interest and tax (75% × 10,080m)	(7,560)
Profit before depreciation and tax	5,880
Depreciation (12% × ($6,000m + $5,520m))	(1,382)
	4,498
Tax (18% × $4,498m)	(810)
Cash flows	3,688

Cost of capital to be used in estimating Chrysos Co's value is 12% (Appendix 2)
Estimated corporate value = ($3,688m × 1.04)/(0.12 − 0.04) = $47,944m
Estimated equity value = $47,944m − $1,800m = $46,144m

Note. It is also acceptable to calculate cash flows after interest payment and use the cost of equity to estimate the equity value based on cash flows to equity instead of cash flows to firm.

Appendix 4: Value created for VCOs

Value attributable to the VCOs = 40% × $46,144m = $18,458m
Value from increased equity ownership (this has doubled from 20% to 40%)

50% × $18,458m = $9,229m

Value of unsecured bonds foregone by the VCOs = $4,800m
Additional capital invested by the VCOs = $400m
Total of additional capital invested and value of bonds forgone = $5,200m
Additional value = ($9,229m − $5,200m)/$5,200m = 77.5% (or $4,029m)

(c) As a private company, Chrysos Co is able to ensure that the needs of its primary stakeholder groups –finance providers, managers and employees – are taken into account through the supervisory board. The supervisory board has representatives from each of these groups and each group member has a voice on the board. Each stakeholder group should be able to present its position to the board through its representatives, and decisions will be made after agreement from all group representatives. In this way, no single stakeholder group holds primacy over any other group.

Once Chrysos Co is listed and raises new capital, it is likely that it will have a large and diverse range of equity shareholders, who will likely be holding equity shares in many other companies. Therefore there is likely to be pressure on Chrysos Co to engage in value creating activity aimed at keeping its share price buoyant and thereby satisfying the equity shareholders. It is, therefore, likely that the equity shareholders' needs will hold primacy over the other stakeholder groups and quite possibly the power of the supervisory board will diminish as a result of this.

50 Yilandwe

Examining team's comments. Many candidates found the calculations required in this question difficult and appeared to spend a significant amount of time on them. This created pressure on them to complete the rest of the requirements of the question in less time and also the structure of the report was often unsatisfactory. This meant that candidates failed to gain many of the easier marks available for discussing the assumptions and the majority of the professional marks. Many candidates' scripts which had marks of between 40% and 49% could have passed if these marks had been gained.

In part (a), generally this part of the question was done well with many candidates getting between three and five marks out of five. Where marks were lower, the candidates did not compare between the two options but merely talked about the benefits and drawbacks of setting up a plant in another country. Sometimes candidates made too many points on this part and spent too long on it. Good time management within questions, as well as between questions, is essential.

In part (b), unsatisfactory answers tried to convert all cash flows into dollars from the outset, instead of keeping them in Yilandwe currency. This was not a good approach, as it made the subsequent inflationary impact very difficult to calculate and often the answers were incorrect. Therefore, such answers received few marks.

Easy marks. There are numerous easy marks to be picked up in part (a) and (b)(ii) of this question.

Marking scheme

				Marks
(a)	Benefits		2–3	
	Drawbacks		2–3	
				Max 5
(b)	(i)	Sales revenue	3	
		Parts costs	3	
		Variable costs	2	
		Fixed costs	1	
		Royalty fee	1	
		Tax payable in Yilandwe	3	
		Working capital	2	
		Remittable cash flows ($)	1	
		Contribution from parts ($)	2	
		Tax on parts' contribution and royalty	1	
		Impact of lost contribution and redundancy	1	
		NPV of project	1	
				21
	(ii)	Up to 2 marks per assumption discussed	Up to 9	
		2–3 marks per issue/risk discussed	Up to 11	
				Max 17
	(iii)	Reasoned recommendation		3
		Professional marks		
		Report format	1	
		Layout, presentation and structure	3	
				4
				50

(a)   **Benefits of own investment as opposed to licensing**

Imoni Co may be able to benefit from setting up its own plant as opposed to licensing in a number of ways.

First, Yilandwe wants to attract foreign investment and is willing to offer a number of financial concessions to foreign investors which may not be available to local companies.

The company may also be able to control the quality of the components more easily, and offer better and targeted training facilities, if it has direct control of the labour resources.

The company may also be able to maintain the confidentiality of its products, whereas assigning the assembly rights to another company may allow that company to imitate the products more easily.

Investing internationally may provide opportunities for risk diversification, especially if Imoni Co's shareholders are not well diversified internationally themselves.

Finally, direct investment may provide Imoni Co with new opportunities in the future, such as follow-on options.

Drawbacks of own investment as opposed to licensing

Direct investment in a new plant will probably require higher, upfront costs from Imoni Co compared to licensing the assembly rights to a local manufacturer. It may be able to utilise these saved costs on other projects.

Imoni Co will most likely be exposed to higher risks involved with international investment, such as political risks, cultural risks and legal risks. With licensing these risks may be reduced somewhat.

The licensee, because it would be a local company, may understand the operational systems of doing business in Yilandwe better. It will therefore be able to get off the ground quicker. Imoni Co, on the other hand, will need to become familiar with the local systems and culture, which may take time and make it less efficient initially.

Similarly, investing directly in Yilandwe may mean that it costs Imoni Co more to train the staff and possibly require a steeper learning curve from them. However, the scenario does say that the country has a motivated and well-educated labour force and this may mitigate this issue somewhat.

Note. Credit will be given for alternative, relevant suggestions.

(b)   **Report on the proposed assembly plant in Yilandwe**

This report considers whether or not it would be beneficial for Imoni Co to set up a parts assembly plant in Yilandwe. It takes account of the financial projections, presented in detail in Appendices 1 and 2, discusses the assumptions made in arriving at the projections and discusses other non-financial issues which should be considered. The report concludes by giving a reasoned recommendation on the acceptability of the project.

Assumptions made in producing the financial projections

It is assumed that all the estimates such as sales revenue, costs, royalties, initial investment costs, working capital, and costs of capital and inflation figures are accurate. There is considerable uncertainty surrounding the accuracy of these and a small change in them could change the forecasts of the project quite considerably. A number of projections using sensitivity and scenario analysis may aid in the decision-making process.

It is assumed that no additional tax is payable in the US for the profits made during the first two years of the project's life when the company will not pay tax in Yilandwe either. This is especially relevant to Year 2 of the project.

No details are provided on whether or not the project ends after four years. This is an assumption which is made, but the project may last beyond four years and therefore may yield a positive net present value. Additionally, even if the project ceases after four years, no details are given about the sale of the land, buildings and machinery. The residual value of these non-current assets could have a considerable bearing on the outcome of the project. It is assumed that the increase in the transfer price of the parts sent from the US directly increases the contribution which Imoni Co earns from the transfer. This is probably not an unreasonable assumption. However, it is also assumed that the negotiations with Yilandwe's government will be successful with respect to increasing the transfer price and the royalty fee. Imoni Co needs to assess whether or not this assumption is realistic.

The basis for using a cost of capital of 12% is not clear and an explanation is not provided about whether or not this is an accurate or reasonable figure. The underpinning basis for how it is determined may need further investigation.

Although the scenario states that the project can start almost immediately, in reality this may not be possible and Imoni Co may need to factor in possible delays.

It is assumed that future exchange rates will reflect the differential in inflation rates between the respective countries. However, it is unlikely that the exchange rates will move fully in line with the inflation rate differentials.

Other risks and issues

Investing in Yilandwe may result in significant political risks. The scenario states that the current political party is not very popular in rural areas and that the population remains generally poor. Imoni Co needs to assess how likely it is that the government may change during the time it is operating in Yilandwe and the impact of the change. For example, a new government may renege on the current government's offers and/or bring in new restrictions. Imoni Co will need to decide what to do if this happens.

Imoni Co needs to assess the likelihood that it will be allowed to increase the transfer price of the parts and the royalty fee. Whilst it may be of the opinion that currently Yilandwe may be open to such suggestions, this may depend on the interest the government may get from other companies to invest in Yilandwe. It may consider that agreeing to such demands from Imoni Co may make it obligated to other companies as well.

The financial projections are prepared on the basis that positive cash flows from Yilandwe can be remitted back to the US. Imoni Co needs to establish that this is indeed the case and that it is likely to continue in the future.

Imoni Co needs to be careful about its ethical stance and its values, and the impact on its reputation, given that a school is being closed in order to provide it with the production facilities needed. Whilst the government is funding some of the transport costs for the children, the disruption this will cause to the children and the fact that after six months the transport costs become the parents' responsibility may have a large, negative impact on the company's image and may be contrary to the ethical values which the company holds. The possibility of alternative venues should be explored.

Imoni Co needs to take account of cultural risks associated with setting up a business in Yilandwe. The way of doing business in Yilandwe may be very different and the employees may need substantial training to adapt to Imoni Co's way of doing business. On the other hand, the fact that the population is well educated, motivated and keen may make this process easier to achieve.

Imoni Co also needs to consider fiscal and regulatory risks. The company will need to assess the likelihood of changes in tax rates, laws and regulations, and set up strategies to mitigate eventualities which can be predicted. In addition to these, Imoni Co should consider and mitigate, as far as possible, operational risks such as the quality of the components and maintenance of transport links.

Imoni Co should assess and value alternative real options which it may have. For example, it could consider whether licensing the production of the components to a local company may be more financially viable; it could consider alternative countries to Yilandwe, which may offer more benefits; it could consider whether the project can be abandoned if circumstances change against the company; and entry into Yilandwe may provide Imoni Co with other business opportunities.

Recommendation

The result from the financial projections is that the project should be accepted because it results in a positive net present value. It is recommended that the financial projections should be considered in conjunction with the assumptions, the issues and risks, and the implications of these, before a final decision is made.

There is considerable scope for further investigation and analysis. It is recommended that sensitivity and scenario analysis be undertaken to take into consideration continuing the project beyond four years and so on. The value of any alternative real options should also be considered and incorporated into the decision.

Consideration must also be given to the issues, risks and factors beyond financial considerations, such as the impact on the ethical stance of the company and the impact on its image, if the school affected is closed to accommodate it.

Report compiled by:

Date:

Appendices

Appendix 1

Year	0	1	2	3	4
	YRm	YRm	YRm	YRm	YRm
Sales revenue (W2)		18,191	66,775	111,493	60,360
Parts costs (W2)		(5,188)	(19,060)	(31,832)	(17,225)
Variable costs (W2)		(2,921)	(10,720)	(17,901)	(9,693)
Fixed costs		(5,612)	(6,437)	(7,068)	(7,760)
Royalty fee (W3)		(4,324)	(4,813)	(5,130)	(5,468)
Tax-allowable depreciation		(4,500)	(4,500)	(4,500)	(4,500)
Taxable profits/(loss)		(4,354)	21,245	45,062	15,714
Tax loss carried forward				(4,354)	
				40,708	
Taxation (40%)		0	0	(16,283)	(6,286)
Add back loss carried fwd				4,354	
Add back depreciation		4,500	4,500	4,500	4,500
Cash flows after tax		146	25,745	33,279	13,928
Working capital	(9,600)	(2,112)	(1,722)	(1,316)	14,750
Land, buildings and machinery	(39,000)				
Cash flows (YRm)	(48,600)	(1,966)	24,023	31,963	28,678

Year	0	1	2	3	4
	YRm	YRm	YRm	YRm	YRm
Exchange rate	101.4	120.1	133.7	142.5	151.9
Remittable flows	(479,290)	(16,370)	179,678	224,302	188,795
Contribution (parts sales) ($120 + inflation per unit, W4)		18,540	61,108	95,723	48,622
Royalty (W3)		36,000	36,000	36,000	36,000
Tax on contribution and royalty (20%)		(10,908)	(19,422)	(26,345)	(16,924)
Cash flows	(479,290)	27,262	257,364	329,680	256,493
Discount factors (12%)	1	0.893	0.797	0.712	0.636
Present values	(479,290)	24,345	205,119	234,732	163,130

Net present value of the project before considering the impact of the lost contribution and redundancy is approximately $148.0 million.

Alternative approach using spreadsheet functionality:

Alternatively, the present value of the cash flows from time 1–4 can be calculated using the =NPV spreadsheet function. Either method is acceptable, but the spreadsheet function gives a slightly more precise answer and, with practice, should be quicker to use in the exam.

The spreadsheet extract shown in the following section shows the =NPV formula being applied using the cost of capital of 12%.

	A	B	C	D	E	F	G
C3			fx =NPV(0.12,D2:G2)				
1		**Time**	**0**	**1**	**2**	**3**	**4**
2		Cash flows		27,262	257,364	329,680	256,493
3		Present value	627,176				
4		less outlay at time 0	- 479,290				
5		Net present value	147,886				

Note that the NPV function assumes that the first cash flow is in one year's time, so you then have to subtract the time 0 cash outflows to obtain the project's NPV.

Lost contribution and redundancy cost

The lost contribution and redundancy costs are small compared to the net present value and would therefore have a minimal impact of reducing the net present value by $0.1 million approximately.

Note. Full credit will be given if the assumption is made that the amounts are in $'000 instead of $.

Appendix 2

Workings

1 *Unit prices and costs including inflation*

Year	1	2	3	4
Selling price (€)	735	772	803	835
Parts ($)	288	297	306	315
Variable costs (YR)	19,471	22,333	24,522	26,925

2 *Sales revenue and costs*

Year	1 YRm	2 YRm	3 YRm	4 YRm
Sales revenue	150 × 735 × 165 = 18,191	480 × 772 × 180.2 = 66,775	730 × 803 × 190.2 = 111,493	360 × 835 × 200.8 = 60,360
Parts costs	150 × 288 × 120.1 = 5,188	480 × 297 × 133.7 = 19,060	730 × 306 × 142.5 = 31,832	360 × 315 × 151.9 = 17,225
Variable costs	150 × 19,471 = 2,921	480 × 22,333 = 10,720	730 × 24,522 = 17,901	360 × 26,925 = 9,693

3 *Royalty fee*

$20m × 1.8 = $36m

This is then converted into YR at the YR/$ rate for each year: 120.1, 133.7, 142.5 and 151.9 for Years 1 to 4 respectively.

4 *Contribution from parts*

Year	1	2	3	4
Revenue per unit in $	280 × 1.03 = $288.4	288.4 × 1.03 = $297.052	297.052 × 1.03 = $305.964	305.964 × 1.03 = $315.143
Parts costs	200 (current price) – 40 (contribution at current price) = $160 So $160 × 1.03 = $164.8	$164.8 × 1.03 = $169.744	169.744 × 1.03 = $174.836	174.836 × 1.03 = $180.081

Year	1	2	3	4
Contribution per unit	288.4 – 164.8 = $123.6	297.052 – 169.744 = $127.308	305.964 – 174.836 = $131.128	315.143 – 180.081 = $135.062
Contribution in $m	123.6 × 150m (volume) = $18,540m	127.308 × 480m = $61,108m	131.128 × 730m = $95,723m	135.062 × 360m = $48,622m

Note. Credit will be given for alternative, relevant approaches to the calculations, and to the discussion of the assumptions, risks and issues.

51 Avem

Workbook references. Acquisition strategies and valuation issues are covered in Chapters 9 and 10 of the Workbook.

Top tips. For part (a) make sure that you answer **both** aspects to the question (risk diversification **and** identifying undervalued companies).

For part (b) you can score some easy marks by referring to general concerns of competition authorities.

To tackle part (c)(i) you need to realise that what is required is an assessment of the value of the combined entity compared to the value of the two companies as independent entities. If you are working on these lines then you are likely to score a pass mark even if your answer is not perfect.

Part (c)(ii) requires an attempt to assess the present value of the project and also whether to accept an offer at the end of Year 1 to abandon the project. There are many possible approaches here, but the ingredients to success are to have a reasonable attempt at a project-specific cost of capital and to use expected values in a sensible way.

Part (c)(iii) should be attempted even if the numerical analysis in (c)(i) and (c)(ii) has not been completed and gives an opportunity to score some easy marks.

Easy marks. There are numerous easy marks to be picked up in part (a), (b) and (c)(iii) of this question.

Marking scheme

				Marks
(a)		Risk diversification	2–3	
		Purchasing undervalued companies	4–5	
				Max 7
(b)		1–2 marks per point	1	Max 4
(c)	(i)	Avem current value	1	
		Avem free cash flow to equity	1	
		Fugae estimated growth rate	2	
		Fugae estimate of current value	2	
		Combined company – value created	2	
		Gain to Nahara	1	
		Gain to Avem	1	
				10

		Marks
(ii)	Reka asset beta	2	
	Project asset beta	1	
	Fugae market value of debt	2	
	Project equity beta and cost of equity	2	
	Project risk-adjusted cost of capital	1	
	Annual PVs of project	1	
	PVs of different outcomes	2	
	Expected NPV before Limni offer	3	
	PV of Limni offer	1	
	Expected NPV of project with Limni offer	3	
			18

(iii)	Benefits with and without the project	2–3	
	Assumptions	3–4	
	Conclusion	1–2	
			Max 7

Professional marks

Report format	1	
Layout, presentation and structure	3	
		4
		50

(a)   Like individuals holding well-diversified portfolios, a company could reduce its exposure to unsystematic risk by creating a number of subsidiaries in **different sectors**.

This may lead to a **reduction in the volatility of cash flows**, which may lead to a better credit rating and a **lower cost of capital**.

The argument against this states that since **individual shareholders can do this themselves both quickly and cheaply**, there is little reason for companies to do this. Indeed, research suggests that markets do not reward this risk diversification because diversified portfolios are **often managed inefficiently** because head office struggles to cope with the different issues facing each subsidiary. As a result decision making may be **ineffective and slow**.

For Nahara Co, undertaking mergers and acquisitions (M&As) may have beneficial outcomes **if the sovereign fund has its entire investment in the holding company and is not well-diversified itself**. In such a situation unsystematic risk reduction can be beneficial. The case study does not state whether or not this is the case and therefore a definitive conclusion cannot be reached.

If Nahara Co is able to identify undervalued companies and after purchasing the company can increase the value for the holding company overall, by increasing the value of the undervalued companies, then such activity would benefit their shareholders. However, for this strategy to work, Nahara Co must:

(1)   Possess a superior capability or knowledge in identifying bargain buys ahead of its competitor companies. To achieve this, it must have access to better information, which it can tap into quicker and/or have superior analytical tools. This implies that the stock market is **less than semi-strong form efficient**; if the stock market is accurately valuing companies using all available public information then share prices are unlikely to be undervalued.

(2)   Ensure that it has quick access to the necessary funds to pursue an undervalued acquisition. Even if Nahara Co possesses superior knowledge, it is unlikely that this will last for a long time before its competitors find out; therefore it needs to have the funds ready, **to move quickly**. Given that it has access to sovereign funds from a wealthy source, access to funds is probably not a problem.

(3)   Ensure it has competences in turning around underperforming companies – this will require a measure of understanding of the sector that the acquired company is operating in. It is likely that Nahara can develop expertise in a wide range of sectors, but not in all sectors. So there will be **limits to the validity of a diversification strategy**.

(b)   In a similar manner to the Competition and Markets Authority in the UK, the EU will assess significant M&A impact in terms of whether they will lead to **a substantial lessening** of competition within a country's market.

It will, for example, use tests such as worldwide revenue and European revenue of the group after the M&A.

It may **block the M&A** if it feels that the M&A will give the company monopolistic powers or enable it to carve out a dominant position in the market so as to negatively affect consumer choice and prices.

Sometimes the EU may ask for the company to **sell some of its assets** to reduce its dominant position rather than not allow an M&A to proceed. It would appear that this may be the case behind the EU's concern and the reason for its suggested action.

(c)   **Report**

To: Board of Directors, Avem Co
From: AN Consultant
Subject: Proposed acquisition of Fugae Co
Date: XX/XX/XX

Introduction

This report considers whether Avem Co should acquire Fugae Co. In order to assess the additional value created from bringing the two companies together the value of the two companies is determined separately and then as a combined entity. The report concludes by considering whether or not the acquisition will be beneficial to Avem Co and to Nahara Co.

(i)   **Additional value created for Avem without considering the luxury transport project**

Appendix 1 shows that the additional value created from combining the two companies is approximately $451.5 million. $276.8 million of this will go to Nahara Co, which represents a premium of about 30% which is the minimum acceptable to Nahara Co. The balance of the additional value will go to Avem Co which is about $174.7 million. This represents an increase in value of 1.46% [$174.7 million /$12,000 million].

(ii)   **Additional value created for Avem including the luxury transport project**

Appendix 2 shows that accepting **the project would increase Fugae Co's value** as the expected net present value is positive.

After taking into account Lumi Co's offer, the expected net present value is higher. Therefore, it would be **beneficial for Fugae Co to take on the project and accept Lumi Co's offer, if the tourism industry does not grow as expected**, as this will increase Fugae Co's value.

(iii) **Assumptions**

It is assumed that all the figures relating to synergy benefits, betas, growth rates, multipliers, risk-adjusted cost of capital and the probabilities are accurate. There is considerable **uncertainty** surrounding the accuracy of these. A **sensitivity analysis** is probably needed to assess the impact of these uncertainties.

It is assumed that the br model provides a reasonably good estimate of the growth rate, and that perpetuity is not an unreasonable assumption when assessing the value of Fugae Co.

It is assumed that the **capital structure would not change substantially when the new project is taken on**. Since the project is significantly smaller than the value of Fugae Co itself, this is not an unreasonable assumption.

There may be more outcomes in practice than the ones given and financial impact of the outcomes may not be known with such certainty. The **Black-Scholes option pricing model** may provide an alternative and more accurate way of assessing the value of the project.

It is assumed that Fugae Co can rely on Lumi Co paying the $50 million at the beginning of Year 2 with certainty. Fugae Co may want to assess the reliability of Lumi Co's offer and whether formal contracts should be drawn up between the two companies.

Concluding comments

Although Nahara Co would gain more than Avem Co from the acquisition both in percentage terms and in monetary terms, **both companies benefit from the acquisition**. As long as all the parties are satisfied that the value is reasonable despite the assumptions highlighted above, it would appear that the acquisition should proceed.

Appendices

Appendix 1: Additional value created from combining Avem Co and Fugae Co

Avem Co, current value = $7.5/share × 1,600m shares = $12,000m

To estimate Fugae's current value we need to estimate the growth rate. This is calculated on the basis of the bre model.

b = 1 − 0.773 = 0.267

re = 0.11

Fugae Co, estimate of growth rate = 0.227 × 0.11 = 0.025 = 2.5%

Fugae Co, current value estimate = $76.5m × 1.025/(0.11 − 0.025) = $922.5m

So the value of the two companies before the combination is approximately $12,000m + $922.5m = $12,922.5m.

The **combined company** is expected to have a value that is 7.5 times its free cash flow. Avem Co's free cash flow to equity = $12,000m/7.2 = $1,666.7m

Fugae's free cash flow is $76.5 million and is expected to increase by the expected synergy of $40 million.

So we can estimate the additional value created by the combined company as:

Value as a combined company − value of Avem and Fugae as independent companies

([$1,666.7m + $76.5m + $40m] × 7.5) − ($12,922.5m) = **$451.5m**

Nahara will expect a 30% return so the gain to Nahara for selling Fugae Co, 30% × $922.5m = **$276.8m**

Therefore Avem Co will gain $174.7m of the additional value created, $451.5m − $276.8m = **$174.7m**

Appendix 2: Value of project to Fugae Co

Appendix 2.1 Project cost of capital

Estimate of risk-adjusted cost of capital to be used to discount the project's cash flows

The project value is calculated based on its cash flows which are discounted at the project's risk-adjusted cost of capital, to reflect the business risk of the project.

BPP
LEARNING
MEDIA

To determine the beta of the project we first need to calculate Reka Co's asset beta

Reka Co equity value = $4.50 × 80m shares = $360m

Reka Co debt value = 1.05 × $340m = $357m

Asset beta = 1.6 × $360m/($360m + $357m × 0.8) = 0.89

Now we can calculate the project's asset beta

0.89 = project's asset beta × 0.15 + 0.80 × 0.85

Project's asset beta = 1.4

Before we can calculate the cost of equity for this project we will need to adjust it for Fugae Co's debt levels.

Fugae has $380 million of debt in terms of its book value. To calculate the market value of this debt we need to take into account the return required by debt holders. This can be estimated as

Cost of debt = Risk-free rate of return plus the credit spread

= 4% + 0.80% = 4.80%

So the current market value of a $100 bond =

$5.4 × 1.048^{-1} + $5.4 × 1.048^{-2} + $5.4 × 1.048^{-3} + $105.4 × 1.048^{-4} =

$102.14 per $100 book value

So the total market value of debt = 1.0214 × $380m = $388.1m

The market value of Fugae's equity has been previously estimated as $922.5 million

So now we can take the asset beta of 1.4 and estimate the project's risk-adjusted equity beta using

$$\beta a = \left(\frac{Ve}{(Ve + Vd(1-t))} \right) \beta e + \left(\frac{Vd(1-t)}{(Ve + Vd(1-t))} \right) \beta d$$

so

1.4 = ($922.5m/($922.5m + $388.1m × 0.8) βe

1.4 × ($922.5m + $388.1m × 0.8)/$922.5m = βe = 1.87

So the project's risk-adjusted cost of equity is:

(ri) = R_f + β (E(R_m − R_f))

4% + 1.87 × 6% = **15.2%**

And finally the project's risk-adjusted cost of capital

$$WACC = \left(\frac{V_e}{(V_e + V_d)} \right) K_e + \left(\frac{V_d}{(V_e + V_d)} \right) K_d (1 - t)$$

(922.5/(922.5 + 388.1)) 15.2% + (388.1m/($922.5m + 388.1m)) 4.8% × 0.8

= 11.84%, say 12%

Appendix 2.2 Estimate of expected value of the project without the offer from Lumi Co

If the first year is as expected

($'000)

Year	1	2	3	4
Cash flows	3,277.6	16,134.3	36,504.7	35,683.6
Discount factor 12%	0.893	0.797	0.712	0.636
Present values	2,926.9	12,859.0	25,991.3	22,694.8
Probabilities	1.0	0.8	0.8	0.8
Expected value	**2,926.9**	**10,287.8**	**20,793.0**	**18,155.8**
Present values (40% Time 2 – 4)		12,859.0 × 0.4 = 5,143.6	25,991.3 × 0.4 = 10,396.5	22,694.8 × 0.4 = 9.077.9
Probabilities		0.2	0.2	0.2
Expected value		**1,029.3**	**2,079.3**	**1,815.6**
Total expected value	**2,926.9**	**11,317.1**	**22,872.3**	**19,971.4**

Total expected value from time 1–4 if the first year is as expected is therefore 2,926.9 + 11,317.1 + 22,872.3 + 19,971.4 = $57,087.7 (000).

There is a 75% chance of this occurrence.

If the first year is NOT as expected

($'000)

Year	1	2	3	4
Present values (50% fall from original projections)	2,926.9 × 0.5 = 1,463.5	12,859.0 × 0.5 = 6,429.5	25,991.3 × 0.5 = 12,995.7	22,694.8 × 0.5 = 11,347.4

Total expected value from time 1–4 if the first year is **not** as expected is therefore 1,463.5 + 6,429.5 + 12,995.7 + 11,347.4 = $32,236.1 (000).

There is a 25% chance of this occurrence.

The **overall present value (PV) of the project inflows** is (75%×57,087.7) + (25% × 32,236.1) = $50,874.8 (000).

So the **project net present value (NPV)** is 50,874.8 – 42,000 = **$8,874.8 (000)**.

Estimate of expected value of the project with the offer from Lumi Co

PV of $50m = $50,000,000 × 0.893 = $44,650,000

If the tourism industry does not grow as expected in the first year, then it is more beneficial for Fugae Co to exercise the offer made by Lumi Co, given that Lumi Co's offer of $44.65 million (PV of $50 million) is greater than the PV of the Years 2 to 4 cash flows for that outcome. This figure is then incorporated into the expected NPV calculations.

So, if the first year is **not** as expected the PV of the inflows becomes 1,463.5 + 44,650 = $46,113.5 (000).

There is a 25% chance of this occurrence.

The **overall PV of the project inflows** now becomes (75% × 57,087.7) + (25% × 46,113.5) = $54,344.2 (000).

So the **project NPV** is 54,344.2 – 42,000 = **$12,344.2 (000)**.

Note. Credit will be given for alternative, relevant approaches to the calculations, comments and suggestions/recommendations.

52 Talam

> **Workbook references.** Advanced investment appraisal and real options are covered in Chapters 2 and 4 respectively. Sustainability and ethical issues are covered in Chapter 1.
>
> **Top tips.** It is important to take time to get to grips with what is being required with this question, and it is vital to allocate time to planning to make sure that the requirements are fully understood before you start writing. This is especially important with this question.
>
> **Easy marks.** There are numerous easy marks to be picked up in the discussion parts (a) and (c) of this question. However, you will need to apply your knowledge to the scenario to score well and not simply repeat technical knowledge (see Examining Team comments below). Also, the first part of the calculations was a standard NPV and should have been, and was, handled well.
>
> **Examining team's comments.** Surprisingly, part (a) was not done very well. Only a minority of candidates considered the full range of discursive points. Many answers simply stated the different kinds of real options, such as the option to expand, delay a decision or discontinue, and then went on to mention that real options were helpful in situations where there was flexibility in making the decisions. Very few responses then progressed to discuss how this could be incorporated into investment decisions, and whether or not real options were helpful.
>
> In part (b)(ii) some candidates tried to calculate the N(d1) and N(d2), although these were provided.
>
> In part (b)(iii) some candidates did little in the way of an assessment and/or just listed the assumptions but did not discuss them.
>
> In part (c) few responses considered the full range of strategic commercial interests which a company would consider.

Marking scheme

				Marks
(a)		1–2 marks per well-explained comment		5
(b)	(i)	(Appendix 1)		
		Sales revenue		2
		Variable costs		2
		Fixed costs		1
		Training costs		2
		Tax		2
		Working capital		2
		Uwa project NPV		1
				12
	(ii)	(Appendix 2)		
		Jigu project underlying asset value		2
		Honua Co Offer: exercise price		1
		Honua Co Offer: underlying asset value		2
		Honua Co Offer: other variables used in option calculation		1
		Honua Co Offer: call value		1
		Honua Co Offer: put value		2
				9

		Marks
(iii)	Initial assessment of value of the Uwa project	2
	Up to 2 marks per well discussed assumption (max 4 marks if assumptions relating to real options are not discussed)	8
		10
	Professional marks for part (b)	
	Report format	1
	Structure and presentation of the report	3
		4
(c)	Discussion of the issues	4–5
	Discussion of how the issues may be addressed	5–6
		Max 10
		50

(a) When making decisions following investment appraisals of projects, net present value assumes that a decision must be made immediately or not at all, and once made, it cannot be changed. Real options, on the other hand, recognise that many investment appraisal decisions have some flexibility.

For example, decisions may not have to be made immediately and can be delayed to assess the impact of any uncertainties or risks attached to the projects. Alternatively, once a decision on a project has been made, to change it, if circumstances surrounding the project change. Finally, to recognise the potential future opportunities, if the initial project is undertaken, like the Jigu Project.

Real options give managers choices when making decisions about whether or not to undertake projects, by estimating the value of this flexibility or choice. Real options take into account the time available before a decision on a project has to be made, as well as taking into account the risks and uncertainties attached to the project. It uses these factors to estimate an additional value which can be attributable to the project. Real options view risks and uncertainties as opportunities, where upside outcomes can be exploited, and a company has the option to disregard any downside impact.

By incorporating the value of any real options available into an investment appraisal decision, Talam Co will be able to assess the full value of a project.

(b) **Report to Talam Co Board**

Introduction

This report assesses whether or not the Uwa Project should be undertaken based on its value from an initial net present value (NPV) calculation, and then taking into account the options provided by the offer from Honua Co and the Jigu Project. As part of the assessment, a discussion of the assumptions and their impact on the assessment is provided.

Assessment

The value of the Uwa Project based on just the initial NPV is a small negative amount of $(6,000) approximately (Appendix 1). This would indicate that the project is not worth pursuing, although the result is very marginal. The offer from Honua Co, and the Jigu Project, using the real options method, gives an estimated value of $17,668,000 (Appendix 2), which is positive and substantial. This indicates that the Uwa Project should be undertaken.

Assumptions

The following assumptions have been made when calculating the values in Appendices 1 and 2.

(1)   Since the Uwa Project is in a different industry to Talam Co's current activities, the project-specific, risk-adjusted cost of capital of 11% based on Honua Co's asset beta is used. It is assumed that Honua Co's asset beta would provide a good approximation of the business risk inherent in drone production.

(2)   It is assumed that all the variables used to calculate the values of the projects in Appendices 1 and 2 are correct and accurate. Furthermore, it is assumed all the variables such as inflation rates, tax rates, interest rates and volatility figures remain as forecast through the period of each project. It is also assumed that the time periods related to the projects and the offer from Honua is accurate and/or reasonable.

(3)   The Black-Scholes option pricing (BSOP) model is used to estimate the real option values of the Jigu Project and the Honua Co offer. The BSOP model was developed for financial products and not for physical products, on which real options are applied. The BSOP model assumes that a market exists to trade the underlying project or asset without restrictions, within frictionless financial and product markets.

(4)   The BSOP model assumes that the volatility or risk of the underlying asset can be determined accurately and readily.

   Whereas for traded financial assets this would most probably be reasonable, as there is likely to be sufficient historical data available to assess the underlying asset's volatility, this is probably not going to be the case for real options. For large, one-off projects, there would be little or no historical data available. Volatility in such situations would need to be estimated using simulation models, such as the Monte-Carlo simulation, with the need to ensure that the model is developed accurately and the data input used to generate outcomes reasonably reflects what is likely to happen in practice.

(5)   The BSOP model assumes that the real option is a European-style option which can only be exercised on the date when the option expires. In some cases, it may make more strategic sense to exercise an option earlier. The real option is more representative of an American-style option which can be exercised before expiry. Therefore, the BSOP model may underestimate the true value of an option.

(6)   Real options models assume that any contractual obligations involving future commitments made between parties will be binding and will be fulfilled. For example, it is assumed that Honua Co will fulfil its commitment to purchase the project from Talam Co at the start of the third year for $30 million and there is therefore no risk of non-fulfilment of that commitment.

(7)   The BSOP model does not take account of behavioural anomalies which may be displayed by managers when making decisions.

Conclusion

The initial recommendation is that the Uwa Project should be undertaken when the offer from Honua Co and going ahead with the Jigu Project are included. Taken together, these result in a significant positive NPV. However, one or more of the above assumptions may not apply and therefore NPV value is not a 'correct' value. Instead, the appendices provide indicative value, which can be attached to the flexibility of a choice of possible future actions that are embedded with the Uwa Project and indicate that it should be undertaken.

Report compiled by:

Date

Note. Credit will be given for alternative valid discussion comments.

APPENDICES:

Appendix 1

(Part (b)(i)):

Net present value computation of the Uwa Project before incorporating the offer from Honua Co and the financial impact of the Jigu Project. All figures are in $000s.

Year	0	1	2	3	4
Sales revenue (W1)		5,160	24,883	49,840	38,405
Less:					
Variable costs (W2)		2,064	9,581	18,476	13,716
Fixed costs		2,700	2,970	3,267	3,594
Tax allowable depreciation (TAD) (W3)		5,250	5,250	5,250	12,250
Training costs		4,128	5,749	1,848	1,372
Cash flows before tax		(8,982)	1,333	20,999	7,473
Tax (W3)		1,796	(267)	(4,200)	(1,495)
Add back TAD (W3)		5,250	5,250	5,250	12,250
Working capital	(1,032)	(1,972)	(2,496)	1,144	4,356
Machinery purchase and sale	(35,000)				7,000
Net cash flows	(36,032)	(3,908)	3,820	23,193	29,584
Present value of cash flows (discounted at 11%)					
	(36,032)	(3,521)	3,100	16,959	19,488

Approximate NPV = $(6,000)

Tutorial note

The present value of the cash flows from time 1–4 can be calculated using the =NPV spreadsheet function. This is shown in the following spreadsheet extract:

C3		▼ :	× ✓	fx	=NPV(0.11,D2:G2)			
	A	B	C	D	E	F	G	
1			Time	1	2	3	4	
2				-3908	3820	23193	29584	
3		Present value time 1-4 cash flows	36,026					
4		Less outlay	- 36,032					
5								
6		NPV	- 6					
7								

Note that the NPV function assumes that the first cash flow is in one year's time, so you then have to subtract the time 0 cash outflows to obtain the project's NPV.

BPP
LEARNING
MEDIA

Workings:

1   *Sales revenue*

Year	1	2	3	4
Units produced and sold	4,300	19,200	35,600	25,400
Selling price ($) (inflated at 8%)	1,200	1,296	1,400	1,512
Sales revenue ($000s)	5,160	24,883	49,840	38,405

2   *Variable costs*

Year	1	2	3	4
Units produced and sold	4,300	19,200	35,600	25,400
Variable costs per unit ($) (inflated at 4%)	480	499	519	540
Total variable costs ($000s)	2,064	9,581	18,476	13,716

3   *Tax*

Year	1	2	3	4
Straight-line $35,000 \times 0.15 = \$5,250$				
Written down value (WDV) start year	35,000	29,750	24,500	19,250
WDV end year (written down to scrap value)	29,750	24,500	19,250	(7,000)
Balancing allowance				12,250

Appendix 2

(Part (b)(ii):

Jigu Project:

Asset value

Asset value of Jigu Project of $46,100,000 is estimated as present value of future cash flows related to the project:

$\$70,000,000 \times 1.11^{-4}$, where $\$70,000,000 = \$60,000,000 + \$10,000,000$.

Honua Co offer, initial variables used to calculate the d_1, d_2, $N(d_1)$ and $N(d_2)$ figures: Asset value (P_a) = $16,959,000 + $19,488,000 = $36,447,000 (cash flows foregone) Exercise price (P_e) = $30,000,000

Exercise date (t) = 2 years Risk-free rate (r) = 2.30% Volatility (s) = 30%

Value of Honua Co's offer

Call value: $\$36,447,000 \times 0.7821 - \$30,000,000 \times 0.6387 \times e^{(-0.023 \times 2)} = \$10,205,640$

Honua Co's offer is equivalent to a put option.

Put value: $\$10,205,640 - \$36,447,000 + \$30,000,000 \times e^{(-0.023 \times 2)} = \$2,409,899$

Estimated total value arising from the two real options

Value of Jigu Project: $15,258,399

Value of Honua Co's offer: $2,409,899

Estimated total value from the two real options: $2,409,899 + $15,258,399 = $17,668,298

(c)   The overarching issue is that of conflict between the need to satisfy shareholders and the financial markets, and Talam Co's stated aims of bringing affordable environmentally friendly products to market and maintaining high ethical standards. This overarching issue can be broken down into smaller related issues.

Producing profitable products will presumably result in positive NPV projects, thus ensuring a continued strong share price performance. This should satisfy the markets and shareholders. However, if the products cannot be sold at a reasonable selling price because some farmers are not able to afford the higher prices, then this may compromise Talam Co's aim of bringing environmentally friendly products to market and making them affordable.

A possible solution is to lower production costs by shifting manufacturing to locations where such costs are lower. Talam Co's BoD thus considered the move to Dunia to lower production costs. This presumably would allow Talam Co to reduce prices and make the drones more affordable, but at the same time ensure that the projects result in positive NPVs. However, the issue here is that supplier companies in Dunia, whom Talam Co trades with, use young teenage children as part of their workforce. This may impact negatively on Talam Co's stated aim of maintaining high ethical standards. In fact, Talam Co may need to rethink its links with companies it trades with in Dunia entirely. Otherwise there is a real risk that Talam Co could suffer from long-term loss of reputation, and this may cause substantial and sustained financial damage to the company.

Talam Co may decide that maintaining its share price and its reputation should take the highest priority and therefore it may reach a decision that the best way to address the issue(s) is to not try to reduce costs, and to withdraw from Dunia completely But this would prevent many agriculturalists from taking advantage of the biodegradable drones. Therefore, Talam Co may want to explore alternative ways to meet all the aims.

Talam Co could consider moving to another location, if this was feasible. It is not known from the narrative whether or not viable alternatives are available, but Talam Co would need to ensure that possible alternative locations would have the infrastructure to produce the components at the same or lower costs. Talam Co may also want to consider the softer issues; for example, it will want a good working relationship and network in the new locations, which it has with the companies in Dunia. These may need to be developed and would take time, and probably incur additional costs.

For these reasons, Talam Co may decide to explore the existing production facilities in Dunia further. It is possible that the supplier companies are not exploiting the young teenage children but are supporting their education and their families in a positive way. Stopping the relationship may jeopardise this support. Talam Co would need to investigate the working conditions of the children and the manner in which they are rewarded and supported. It may want to consult the guardians of the young teenage children and see if there are other feasible solutions. For example, could the guardians be employed instead of the young teenage children or are they already engaged in alternative employment?

After all factors are considered, Talam Co may conclude that the best way to achieve all its aims is to continue in Dunia and also have the production of drone components located there. If this is the case and young teenage children continue to be employed there, then Talam Co would need a sustained public relations campaign to defend its position and demonstrate how it ensures that the teenage children have not been exploited, but are gainfully employed and receiving a good education to help them progress in life.

Note. Credit will be given for alternative valid discussion comments.

53 Washi

> **Workbook references.** International investment appraisal is covered in Chapter 5, and currency hedging is covered in Chapter 13.
>
> **Examining team's comments.** Part (b) required a discussion of the comparative advantages and disadvantages between exchange traded and over-the-counter option (OTC) contracts. While some candidates did well for this part, others received no marks when they mixed up exchange traded with over-the-counter options or compared options with futures/forwards. A number of candidates made the same point for example, tailor-made hedge for OTC options as an advantage, and not tailor-made hedge for exchange traded options as a disadvantage, therefore not gaining any extra marks for double the effort.
>
> Part (c) On futures hedging, many candidates omitted to identify whether futures contracts were to be sold or bought at the start of the hedge. Quite a few candidates incorrectly hedged using call options instead of put options. A large majority of candidates made no attempt to calculate the proceeds from the six-month investment of the JPY receivable which would reduce the additional debt finance needed, thus receiving no marks for this part. The main difficulty that many candidates encountered was calculating the ARD/JPY spot cross rates from the given JPY/EUR and ARD/EUR spot exchange rates and then forecasting ARD/JPY exchange rates using purchasing power parity. These spot cross rates and forecast exchange rates are then used to convert the initial investment amount in ARD currency to JPY currency to determine the debt finance required as well as for the investment appraisal in part (c)(ii).
>
> Common mistakes in the answers include not showing workings for the exchange rates produced, therefore no 'own figure rule' (OFR) marks could be awarded if the exchange rates were wrong; not labelling the currencies making it difficult for markers to identify the exchange rate referred to in the calculation; cross rates incorrectly calculated and purchasing power parity wrongly applied in forecasting the ARD/JPY exchange rates.
>
> Part (d) required candidates to discuss the validity of decentralising the one treasury department for the whole group into individual treasury departments for the major subsidiary companies. Most candidates demonstrated a good understanding in contrasting the benefits of both centralised and individual treasury departments and scored high marks. Answers which focussed only on the benefits of decentralisation or centralisation of the treasury function scored limited marks.

Marking scheme

			Marks
(a)	1–2 marks per valid point		Max 5
(b)	Advantages	2–3	
	Disadvantages	2–3	
			Max 5
(c)	(i) **(Appendix 1)**		
	Amount to be received based on forward rate	1	
	Decision to go short on futures	1	
	Estimate of futures rate in six months based on basis	1	
	Amount to be received based on futures market	1	
	Decision to purchase put options	1	
	Premium payable	1	
	Amount to be received based on options market	1	
	Decision: select appropriate hedge instrument	1	

	JPY receivable following further six months of investment	1
	Estimate of current cross rate(s)	1
	Estimate of ARD/JPY rate in one year's time	1
	Debt borrowing required	1
		12

(ii) **(Appendix 2)**

Estimate of future ARD/JPY rates	1
Lost contribution	1
Tax saving on lost contribution	1
Contribution from sales of components	2
Tax on contribution from components sales	1
Additional tax payable in Japan	2
Present values and net present value	1
	9

(iii) **(Report on project and funding evaluation)**

Evaluation of hedge choice and debt finance required	3–4
Evaluation of Airone project	3–4
Conclusion	1–2
	Max 8

Professional marks for part (c)

Report format	1
Structure and presentation of the report	3
	4

(d)

Benefits of a centralised treasury department	3–4
Benefits of decentralised treasury departments	2–3
Over-arching commentary	1
Note. Max 6 marks if no over-arching commentary.	—
	Max 7
	50

(a) Washi Co may want to invest in overseas projects for a number of reasons which result in competitive advantage for it, for example:

Investing overseas may give Washi Co access to new markets and/or enable it to develop a market for its products in locations where none existed before. Being involved in marketing and selling products in overseas markets may also help it gain an understanding of the needs of customers, which it may not have had if it merely exported its products.

Investing overseas may give Washi Co easier and cheaper access to raw materials it needs. It would therefore make good strategic sense for it to undertake the overseas investment.

Investing in projects internationally may give Washi Co access to cheaper labour resources and/or access to expertise which may not be readily available in Japan. This could therefore lead to reduction in costs and give Washi Co an edge against its competitors.

Closer proximity to markets, raw materials and labour resources may enable Washi Co to reduce its costs. For example, transportation and other costs related to logistics may be reduced if products are manufactured close to the markets where they are sold.

Risk, such as economic risk resulting from long-term currency fluctuations, may be reduced where costs and revenues are matched and therefore naturally hedged.

Washi Co may increase its reputation because it is based in the country within which it trades leading to a competitive edge against its rivals.

International investments might reduce both the unsystematic and systematic risks for Washi Co if its shareholders only hold well diversified portfolios in domestic markets, but not internationally.

Note. Credit will be given for alternative valid areas of discussion.

(b) **Advantages**

Exchange traded options are readily available on the financial markets, their price and contract details are transparent, and there is no need to negotiate these. Greater transparency and tight regulations can make exchange traded options less risky. For these reasons, exchange traded options' transaction costs can be lower.

The option buyer can sell (close) the options before expiry. American style options can be exercised any time before expiry and most traded options are American style options, whereas over-the-counter options tend to be European style options.

Disadvantages

The maturity date and contract sizes for exchange traded options are fixed, whereas over-the-counter options can be tailored to the needs of parties buying and selling the options.

Exchange traded options tend to be of shorter terms, so if longer term options are needed, then they would probably need to be over-the-counter.

A wider range of products (for example, a greater choice of currencies) is normally available in over-the-counter options markets.

(c) **Report to the board of directors (BoD), Washi Co**

Introduction

This report evaluates whether or not Washi Co should invest in the Airone project and the amount of debt finance required of JPY 3,408.6 million (Appendix 1) to fund the project. The evaluation considers both the financial and the non-financial factors.

Evaluation of the preferred hedge choice and debt finance required

The income from the sale of the European subsidiary is maximised when futures contracts are used. Therefore, these are chosen as Washi Co will borrow the least amount of debt finance as a result. However, compared to the forward contract, futures are marked-to-market daily and require a margin to be placed with the broker. This could affect Washi Co's liquidity position. The assumption has been made that basis reduces proportionally as the futures contracts approach expiry, but there is no guarantee that this will be the case. Therefore, basis risk still exists with futures contracts. Although forward contracts give a smaller return, there is no basis risk and margin requirements. However, they do contain a higher risk of default as they are not market traded. Options give the lowest return but would give Washi Co the flexibility of not exercising the option should the Euro strengthen against the Yen.

Although the EUR 80 million receipt from the sale of the subsidiary has been agreed, there may be a risk that the sale may fall through and/or the funds or some proportion of the funds are not received. Washi Co may need to assess and factor in this risk, however small it may be.

The amount of interest on deposit is based on the current short-dated Japanese treasury bills and the estimate of the borrowing requirement is computed from the predicted exchange rate between ARD and JPY in a year's time, based on the purchasing power parity. Both these estimates could be inaccurate if changes occur over the coming months. Although insufficient information is provided for a financial assessment, Washi Co should explore the possibility of converting the EUR into ARD immediately on receipt and keeping it in an ARD bank account until needed, instead of first converting EUR into JPY and then into ARD.

Using debt finance to make up any shortfall in the funding requirement may be appropriate for Washi Co given that it is an unlisted company and therefore access to other sources of funding may be limited. Nevertheless, Washi Co should assess how the extra borrowing would affect any restrictive covenants placed on it and the impact on its cost of capital. Since the amount seems to be small in the context of the project as a whole, this may not be a major problem.

Washi Co should also explore whether or not investing in the Airone project restricts its ability to fund other projects or affects its ability to continue normal business activity, especially if Washi Co is facing the possibility of hard capital rationing.

Evaluation of the Airone project

The net present value of the Airone project is estimated to be JPY (457) million (Appendix 2). Given the negative net present value, the initial recommendation would be to reject the project. However, given that the result is marginal, Washi Co should consider the following factors before rejecting the project.

At present, Washi Co does not have a significant presence in the part of the world where Airone is located. Taking on the project may make good strategic sense and provide a platform for Washi Co to establish its presence in that part of the world.

Furthermore, once Washi Co has established itself in Airone, it may be able to develop further opportunities and new projects. The value of these follow-on options has not been incorporated into the financial assessment. Washi Co should explore the possibility of such opportunities and their possible value.

The financial assessment ends abruptly at the end of the four years. No indication is given on what would happen to the project thereafter. It may be sold as a going concern or, if closed, its land and assets may be sold. The cash flows from these possible courses of action need to be incorporated into the assessment, and these could make the project worthwhile.

A number of assumptions and estimates would have been made in the financial assessment. For example, the rate of inflation used for future figures is the current rate and the tax rate used is the current rate, these may well change in the coming years. Therefore, it is best to undertake sensitivity analysis and produce a number of financial assessments before making any firm commitment to proceed with the project or deciding to reject it.

Conclusion and recommendation

The income from the sale of the European subsidiary is maximised when futures contracts are used, but Washi Co should weigh this against the benefits and drawbacks of all hedging instruments before making a final decision.

Although the project is currently giving a negative net present value, rejecting it at the outset is premature. A number of factors, discussed above, need to be considered and assessed before a final decision is made. Sensitivity analysis would be very helpful in this respect.

Finally, Washi Co should consider alternative uses for the funding which will be dedicated to the project. These alternative uses for the finance need to be considered before any decision is made, especially if Washi Co is facing the possibility of hard capital rationing.

Report compiled by:

Date

APPENDICES:

Appendix 1 (Part (c)(i)): Japanese Yen receivable from sale of European subsidiary under each hedging choice and the additional debt finance needed to fund the Airone project

Forward rate

Since it is a EUR receipt, the lock-in rate of JPY125.3 per EUR will be used.

Expected receipt from sale: EUR 80m × 125.3 = JPY 10,024m

Futures contracts

The futures contracts need to show a gain when the Euro depreciates against the Yen, therefore a short position is needed, using the seven-month contracts. It is assumed that basis will depreciate proportionally to the time expired.

Predicted futures rate

$125.2 + 1/3 \times (126.9 - 125.2) = 125.8$

Or: $125.2 + 1/7 \times (129.2 - 125.2) = 125.8$

Number of contacts sold = EUR 80,000,000/EUR 125,000 = 640 contracts

Expected receipt from sale: EUR 125,000 × 640 × 125.8 = JPY 10,064m

Options contracts

640 seven-month put options contracts will be purchased to protect against a depreciation of Euro.

If options are exercised:

EUR 125,000 × 640 × 126 = JPY 10,080m

Premium payable = JPY 3.8 × 125,000 × 640 = JPY 304m

Net income = JPY 10,080m – JPY 304m = JPY 9,776m

Conclusion

Futures contracts give the highest receipt and will, therefore, be used to hedge the expected Euro receipt.

Receipt invested

Invested for further six months till needed for the Airone project.

JPY 10,064m × (1 + (0.012/2)) = JPY 10,124.4m

Spot cross rates: 0.70 – 0.74 ARD per JPY 1

[92.7/132.4 = 0.70 and 95.6/129.2 = 0.74]

Expected ARD/JPY conversion spot rate in 12 months = 0.70 × 1.09/1.015 = 0.75

Additional debt finance needed to fund Airone project

Investment amount required = ARD 10,150m/0.75 = JPY 13,533m

Debt finance required = JPY 13,533m – JPY 10,124.4m = JPY 3,408.6m

Appendix 2 (Part (c)(ii): Airone project net present value

Project year	0	1	2	3	4
Cash flows in ARD (millions)	(10,150)	2,530	5,760	6,780	1,655
Future exchange rate ARD/JPY (W1)	0.75	0.81	0.87	0.93	1.00
In JPY million					
Project year	0	1	2	3	4
Cash flows	(13,533)	3,123	6,621	7,290	1,655
Lost contribution		(110)	(112)	(113)	(115)
Tax saving on lost contribution (30%)		33	34	34	35
Contribution: components (W2)		300	609	644	79
Tax on components cont. (30%)		(90)	(183)	(193)	(24)
Additional tax payable (15%) (W3)		(333)	(966)	(1,097)	(45)
Net cash flows	(13,533)	2,923	6,003	6,565	1,585
Present value (discounted at 12%)	(13,533)	2,610	4,784	4,674	1,008

Expected net present value is JPY (457)m

Workings

1   *Predicted future exchange rate (ARD/JPY)*

Project year	0	1	2	3	4
	0.70 × 1.09/1.015	0.75 × 1.09/1.015	0.81 × 1.09/1.015	0.87 × 1.09/1.015	0.93 × 1.09/1.015
Exchange rate ARD/JPY	0.75	0.81	0.87	0.93	1.00

2   *Components contribution*

Project year	1	2	3	4
In JPY millions				
Components revenue (post inflation)	1,200	2,436	2,576	314
Contribution (25%)	300	609	644	79

3   *Additional tax payable*

Project year	1	2	3	4
Pre-tax profits (ARD m)	1,800	5,600	6,800	300
Additional tax payable at 15% (JPY m)	1,800/0.81 × 0.15 = 333	5,600/0.87 × 0.15 = 966	6,800/0.93 × 0.15 = 1,097	300/1.0 × 0.15 = 45

(d)   It is difficult to conclude definitively whether a centralised treasury department is beneficial or not in all circumstances and for all companies. It depends on each company itself and the circumstances it faces. Washi Co should take this into account before making a final decision.

Benefits of a centralised treasury department

Having a centralised treasury management function avoids the need to have many bank accounts and may therefore reduce transactions costs and high bank charges.

Large cash deposits may give Washi Co access to a larger, diverse range of investment opportunities and it may be able to earn interest on a short-term basis, to which smaller cash deposits do not have access. On the other hand, if bulk borrowings are required, it may be possible for Washi Co to negotiate lower interest rates, which it would not be able to do on smaller borrowings.

A centralised treasury function can offer the opportunity for Washi Co to match income and expenditure and reduce the need for excessive risk management, and thereby reduce costs related to this.

A centralised treasury management department could hire experts, which smaller, diverse treasury management departments may not have access to.

A centralised treasury function may be better able to access what is beneficial for Washi Co as a whole, whereas local treasury functions may lead to dysfunctional behaviour.

Benefits of separate (decentralised) treasury departments

It could be argued that decentralised treasury departments are better able to match and judge the funding required with the need for asset purchases for investment purposes on a local level. Therefore, they may be able to respond quicker when opportunities arise and so could be more effective and efficient.

Individual departments within a subsidiary may have better relationships with the treasury departments of that subsidiary and are therefore able to present their case without lengthy bureaucratic delays.

Ultimately, the benefits may be implicit rather than explicit. Having decentralised treasury departments may make the subsidiary companies' senior management and directors more empowered and have greater autonomy. This in turn may increase their levels of motivation, as they are more in control of their own future, resulting in better decisions being made.

54 Chikepe

Marking scheme

			Marks
(a)	Compare and contrast the two directors' opinions	4–5	
	Discussion of types of synergy benefits	4–5	
			Max 9
(b)	1–2 marks per point		Max 5
(c)	(i) (Appendix 1)		
	Estimate of future growth rate	1	
	Exclude interest from free cash flows	1	
	Estimate of free cash flows	2	
	Estimate of Foshoro Co's value	1	
	Estimate of equity value of Foshoro Co	1	
		6	

		Marks
(ii)	(Appendix 2)	
	Combined company asset beta	1
	Combined company equity beta	1
	Combined company cost of equity	1
	Combined company cost of capital	1
	Combined company sales revenue (or operating profits) (Years 1 to 4)	1
	Combined company taxation amounts (Years 1 to 4)	1
	Combined company additional asset investment (Years 1 to 4)	1
	Combined company total value (Years 1 to 4)	1
	Combined company value after first four years	1
	Combined company total market value	1
	Combined company market value of equity	1
		11

(iii)	(Discussion in report and Appendix 3)	
	Evaluation of benefit to Chikepe Co shareholders	3–4
	Discussion of the limitations of the valuation method used	4
		Max 7

Professional marks for part (c)	
Report format	1
Structure and presentation of the report	3
	4

(d)	Discussion of mandatory-bid rule and principle of equal treatment	3–4
	Discussion of effectiveness of poison pills and disposal of crown jewels	4–5
		Max 8
		50

(a) Director A's focus is on reducing the risk in the business through diversification and thereby increasing its value. A strategy of risk diversification resulting in greater value can work in situations where the equity holders are exposed to both unsystematic and systematic risks, for example, when their investment is concentrated in one company. In such situations, the shareholders would be subject to unsystematic risk and diversification would reduce this risk.

In the case of Chikepe Co, this is unlikely to be the case, as a large proportion of shares are owned by institutional shareholders, and it is likely that their investment portfolios are already well-diversified and therefore they are not exposed to unsystematic risk. Further diversification will be of no value to them. In fact, it may be construed that managers are only taking this action for their own benefit, as they may be closely tied to the company and therefore be exposed to total risk (both unsystematic and systematic risks). This may then become a source of agency-related conflict between the management and the shareholders.

However, diversification overseas into markets which have some barriers to entry might reduce both systematic and unsystematic risks as well.

Director B, on the other hand, seems to be suggesting that Chikepe Co should focus on its core business and increase value through identifying areas of synergy benefits. It may be the case that Chikepe Co's management and directors are well placed to identify areas where the company can gain value by acquiring companies with potential synergy benefits.

BPP
LEARNING
MEDIA

The types of synergy benefits, which may arise in established pharmaceutical companies, can include:

(1) Identifying undervalued companies, where the management is not effective in unlocking the true value of company. By replacing the existing management, Chikepe Co may be able to unlock the value of the company.

(2) Acquiring companies which have strategic assets or product pipelines. Chikepe Co may be well-placed to identify companies which have a number of product pipelines, which those companies are not exploiting fully. By acquiring such companies, Chikepe Co may be able to exploit the product pipelines.

(3) Through acquisitions, Chikepe Co may be able to exploit economies of scope by eliminating process duplication, or economies of scale where its size may enable it to negotiate favourable terms.

(4) Foshoro Co may benefit if Chikepe Co acquires it because it is struggling to raise funding for its innovative products. Chikepe Co is an established company but has few new product innovations coming in the future. Therefore, it may have spare cash resources which Foshoro Co may be able to utilise.

Note. Credit will be given for alternative valid discussion.

(b) Traditional investment appraisal methods such as net present value assume that an investment needs to be taken on a now or never basis, and once undertaken, it cannot be reversed. Real options take into account the fact that in reality, most investments have within them certain amounts of flexibility, such as whether or not to undertake the investment immediately or to delay the decision; to pursue follow-on opportunities; and to cancel an investment opportunity after it has been undertaken. Where there is increasing uncertainty and risk, and where a decision can be changed or delayed, this flexibility has value, known as the time value of an option.

Net present value captures just the intrinsic value of an investment opportunity, whereas real options capture both the intrinsic value and the time value, to give an overall value for an opportunity. When a company still has time available to it before a decision needs to be made, it may have opportunities to increase the intrinsic value of the investment through the strategic decisions it makes.

Investing in new companies with numerous potential innovative product pipelines may provide opportunities for flexibility where decisions can be delayed and the intrinsic value can be increased through strategic decisions and actions taken by the company. Real options try to capture the value of this flexibility within companies with innovative product pipelines, whereas net present value does not.

(c) **Report to the board of directors (BoD), Chikepe Co**

Introduction

This report evaluates whether the acquisition of Foshoro Co would be beneficial to Chikepe Co's shareholders by estimating the additional equity value created from the synergies resulting when the two companies are combined. The market values of equity of the two companies as separate entities are considered initially and then compared with the equity value of the two companies together. The free cash flow to firm valuation method is used to estimate the values of the companies and the limitations of this method are discussed.

The market value of equity of Chikepe Co is given as $12,600 million.

Based on the free cash flow to firm valuation method:

- The current market value of equity of Foshoro Co is estimated at $986 million (Appendix 1); and

- The market value of equity of the combined company is estimated at $14,993 million (Appendix 2).

Therefore, the additional market value of equity arising from synergy benefits when the two companies are combined is estimated at $1,407 million (Appendix 3), which is then split between Foshoro Co's shareholders receiving $296 million (a 30% premium) and

Chikepe Co's shareholders receiving the balance of $1,111 million, which is approximately 8.8% excess over the original equity value (Appendix 3).

However, the valuation method used has a number of limitations, as follows:

(i) The values of both Foshoro Co and the combined company are based on estimations and assumptions, for example:

    (1) Foshoro Co's future growth rate of free cash flows is based on past growth rates and it is assumed that this will not change in the future.

    (2) It is not explained how Foshoro Co's cost of capital is estimated/calculated. Such an estimate may be more difficult to make for private companies.

    (3) The assumption of perpetuity is made when estimating the values of Foshoro Co and the combined company, and this may not be valid.

(ii) The basis for the synergy benefits, such as higher growth rates of sales revenue and profit margins, needs to be explained and justified. It is not clear how these estimates have been made.

(iii) Whereas it may be possible to estimate the asset beta of a listed company such as Chikepe Co, it may be more difficult to provide a reasonable estimate for the asset beta of Foshoro Co. Therefore, the estimate of the cost of capital of the combined company may not be accurate.

(iv) The costs related to the acquisition process would need to be factored in.

Therefore, whereas the free cash flow method of estimating corporate values is theoretically sound, using it in practice to estimate values is open to errors and judgements.

Conclusion

The valuations indicate that Chikepe Co's shareholders would benefit from the acquisition of Foshoro Co and the value of their shares should increase by 8.8%. However, the method used to estimate the value created makes a number of estimates and assumptions. It is therefore recommended that a range of valuations is made under different assumptions and estimates, through a process of sensitivity analysis, before a final decision is made. As well as this, the limitations of the valuation method used should be well understood and taken into account.

Report compiled by:

Date

APPENDICES:

Appendix 1 (Part (c)(i)): Foshoro Co, estimate of current value

Cost of capital = 10%

Growth rate of profits and free cash flows = $(\$91.0m/\$83.3m)1/3 - 1 = 0.03 = 3\%$

Free cash flow to firm (FCFF) = PBIT + non-cash expenses − additional cash investment − tax

FCFF = $192.3m + $112.0m − $98.2m − (20% × $192.3m) = $167.6m

Foshoro Co, estimated value = ($167.6m × 1.03)/(0.10 − 0.03) = $2,466.1m

Current estimated market value of equity of Foshoro Co = $2,466.1m × 40% = $986.4m, say $986m approximately.

Appendix 2 (Part (c)(ii)): Estimate of value created from combining Chikepe Co and Foshoro Co

Asset beta of combined company = (0.800 × $12,600m + 0.950 × $986.4m)/($12,600m + $986.4m) = 0.811

Equity beta of combined company = 0.811 × (0.70 + 0.30 × 0.80)/0.70 = 1.089

Cost of equity, combined company = 2% + 1.089 × 7% = 9.6% approx.

Cost of capital, combined company = 9.6% × 0.7 + 5.3% × 0.3 × 0.8 = 8% approx.

Combined company, free cash flows and value computation ($ millions)

Sales growth rate, Years 2 to 4 = 7% per year; operating profit margin = 20%

Year	1	2	3	4
Sales revenue	4,200	4,494	4,809	5,146
Operating profit	840	899	962	1,029
Less tax (20%)	(168)	(180)	(192)	(206)
Less additional investment in assets	(200)	(188)	(202)	(216)
Free cash flows	472	531	568	607
PV of free cash flows (8%)	437	455	451	446

	$m
Present value (first four years)	1,789
Present value (after four years)	
$607 \times 1.056/(0.08 - 0.056) \times 0.735$	19,630
Estimated market value of the combined company	21,419

Market value of equity of the combined company = 70% × $21,419m = $14,993m

Appendix 3: Synergy benefits and their distribution

Additional market equity value created by combining the two companies

$14,993m – ($12,600m + $986m) = $1,407m

Therefore, synergy benefits resulting from combining the two companies: $1,407 million

Premium payable to Foshoro Co shareholders: 30% × $986m = $296m

Balance of synergy benefits going to Chikepe Co's shareholders: $1,111 million

As a percentage of current value: $1,111m/$12,600m × 100% = 8.8%

(d) Both the mandatory bid rule and the principle of equal treatment are designed to protect minority shareholders, where an acquirer has obtained a controlling interest of the target company. The mandatory bid rule provides minority shareholders with the opportunity to sell their shares and exit the target company at a specified fair share price. This price should not be lower than the highest price paid for shares, which have already been acquired within a specified period. The principle of equal treatment requires the acquiring company to offer the same terms to minority shareholders as were offered to the earlier shareholders from whom the controlling interest was acquired. Both these regulatory devices are designed to ensure that the minority shareholders are protected financially and are not exploited by the acquirer.

The purpose of both poison pills and disposal of crown jewels is to make the target company unattractive to the acquirer. Poison pills give existing shareholders in the target company the right to buy additional shares in their company at a discount once the acquiring company has bought a certain number of shares in the target company. The aim is to make the target company more expensive to purchase, as the acquirer needs to buy more shares. Disposal of crown jewels involves selling the target company's most valuable assets, and therefore making the target company less attractive to the acquirer. The effectiveness of either defence tactic can be limited, as the company's management would need its shareholders to authorise such moves (although there are ways in which poison pills can be incorporated without gaining prior authorisation from shareholders). Shareholders may not be willing to do this as they normally get premiums on their shares during takeover battles. Additionally, disposing of key strategic assets could substantially weaken a company's competitive advantage and therefore its future potential. Such action may be detrimental to the company and therefore shareholders would probably not approve that course of action.

55 Cigno

Marks

(a) Up to 2 marks for distinguishing the two forms of unbundling | 4

(b) (i) Appendix 1

Anatra Co, manufacturing business, P/E ratio	1
Estimate of the value created from sell-off	3
Appendix 2	
Cigno Co asset beta	1
Combined company asset beta	1
Combined company equity beta	1
Combined company cost of capital	1
Appendix 3	
Sales revenue, Years 1 to 4	1
Operating profit, Years 1 to 4	1
Taxation, Years 1 to 4	1
Capital investment, Years 1 to 4	1
Value from Years 1 to 4	1
Value from Year 5 onwards	1
Value for Cigno Co shareholders before impact of savings from tax and employee cost reduction	2
Appendix 4	
Value created from tax and employee cost savings	1
Value for Cigno Co shareholders after impact of savings from tax and employee cost reduction	1
	18

(ii) Discussion of values for the equity holders, additional costs/benefits not given | 3–4

Methods used and assumptions made | 4–5

Max 8

(iii) Reputation factors | 1–2

Ethical factors | 1–2

Comment on value | 1–2

Max 4

Professional marks for part (b)

Report format | 1

Structure and presentation of the report | 3

4

(c) 1 to 2 marks per point | Max 6

(d) Up to 2 marks for explaining the purpose of each condition | 6

50

(a) Both forms of unbundling involve disposing of the non-core parts of the company.

The divestment through a sell-off normally involves selling part of a company as an entity or as separate assets to a third party for an agreed amount of funds or value. This value may comprise of cash and non cash based assets. The company can then utilise the funds gained in alternative, value-enhancing activities.

The MBI is a particular type of sell-off which involves selling a division or part of a company to an external management team, who will take up the running of the new business and have an equity stake in the business. An MBI is normally undertaken when it is thought that the division or part of the company can probably be run better by a different management team compared to the current one.

(b)   **Report to the BoD, Cigno Co**

This report assesses the potential value of acquiring Anatra Co for the equity holders of Cigno Co, both with and without considering the benefits of the reduction in taxation and in employee costs. The possible issues raised by reduction in taxation and in employee costs are discussed in more detail below. The assessment also discusses the estimates made and the methods used.

Assessment of value created

Cigno Co estimates that the premium payable to acquire Anatra Co largely accounts for the benefits created from the acquisition and the divestment, before considering the benefits from the tax and employee costs saving. As a result, before these savings are considered, the estimated benefit to Cigno Co's shareholders of $128 million (see Appendix 3) is marginal. Given that there are numerous estimations made and the methods used make various assumptions, as discussed below, this benefit could be smaller or larger. It would appear that without considering the additional benefits of cost and tax reductions, the acquisition is probably too risky and would probably be of limited value to Cigno Co's shareholders.

If the benefits of the taxation and employee costs saved are taken into account, the value created for the shareholders is $5,609 million (see Appendix 4), and therefore significant. This would make the acquisition much more financially beneficial. It should be noted that no details are provided on the additional pre-acquisition and post-acquisition costs or on any synergy benefits that Cigno Co may derive in addition to the cost savings discussed. These should be determined and incorporated into the calculations.

Basing corporate value on the P/E method for the sell-off, and on the free cash flow valuation method for the absorbed business, is theoretically sound. The P/E method estimates the value of the company based on its earnings and on competitor performance. With the free cash flow method, the cost of capital takes account of the risk the investors want to be compensated for and the non-committed cash flows are the funds which the business can afford to return to the investors, as long as they are estimated accurately.

However, in practice, the input factors used to calculate the organisation's value may not be accurate or it may be difficult to assess their accuracy. For example, for the free cash flow method, it is assumed that the sales growth rate, operating profit margin, the taxation rate and incremental capital investment can be determined accurately and remain constant. It is assumed that the cost of capital will remain unchanged and it is assumed that the asset beta, the cost of equity and cost of debt can be determined accurately. It is also assumed that the length of the period of growth is accurate and that the company operates in perpetuity thereafter. With the P/E model, the basis for using the average competitor figures needs to be assessed; for example, have outliers been ignored; and the basis for the company's higher P/E ratio needs to be justified as well. The uncertainties surrounding these estimates would suggest that the value is indicative, rather than definitive, and it would be more prudent to undertake sensitivity analysis and obtain a range of values.

Key factors to consider in relation to the redundancies and potential tax savings

It is suggested that the BoD should consider the impact of the cost savings from redundancies and from the tax payable in relation to corporate reputation and ethical considerations.

At present, Cigno Co enjoys a good reputation and it is suggested that this may be because it has managed to avoid large-scale redundancies. This reputation may now be under threat and its loss could affect Cigno Co negatively in terms of long-term loss in revenues, profits and value; and it may be difficult to measure the impact of this loss accurately.

Whilst minimising tax may be financially prudent, it may not be considered fair. For example, currently there is ongoing discussion and debate from a number of governments and other interested parties that companies should pay tax in the countries they operate and derive their profits, rather than where they are based. Whilst global political consensus in this area seems some way off, it is likely that the debate in this area will increase in the future. Companies that are seen to be operating unethically with regard to this may damage their reputation and therefore their profits and value.

BPP LEARNING MEDIA

Nonetheless, given that Cigno Co is likely to derive substantial value from the acquisition, because of these savings, it should not merely disregard the potential savings. Instead it should consider public relations exercises it could undertake to minimise the loss of reputation, and perhaps meet with the government to discuss ways forward in terms of tax payments.

Conclusion

The potential value gained from acquiring and unbundling Anatra Co can be substantial if the potential cost savings are taken into account. However, given the assumptions that are made in computing the value, it is recommended that sensitivity analysis is undertaken and a range of values obtained. It is also recommended that Cigno Co should undertake public relations exercises to minimise the loss of reputation, but it should probably proceed with the acquisition, and undertake the cost saving exercise because it is likely that this will result in substantial additional value.

Report compiled by:

Date:

Appendix 1: Estimate of value created from the sell-off of the equipment manufacturing business

Average industry P/E ratio = $2.40/$0.30 = 8

Anatra Co's equipment manufacturing business P/E ratio = 8 × 1.2 = 9.6

Value from sell-off of equipment manufacturing business

Share of pre-tax profit = 30% × $2,490m = $747m

After-tax profit = $747m × (1 − 0.22) = $582.7m

Value from sell-off = $582.7m × 9.6 = $5,594m (approximately)

Appendix 2: Estimate of the combined company cost of capital

Anatra Co, asset beta = 0.68

Cigno Co, asset beta:

Equity beta = 1.10

Proportion of market value of debt = 40%; Proportion of market value of equity = 60%

Asset beta = 1.10 × 0.60/(0.60 + 0.40 × 0.78) = 0.72

Combined company, asset beta

Market value of equity, Anatra Co = $3 × 7,000m shares = $21,000m

Market value of equity, Cigno Co = 60% × $60,000m = $36,000m

Asset beta = (0.68 × 21,000 + 0.72 × 36,000)/(21,000 + 36,000) = 0.71 (approximately)

Combined company equity beta = 0.71 × (0.6 + 0.4 × 0.78)/0.6 = 1.08

Combined company, cost of equity = 4.3% + 1.08 × 7% = 11.86%

Combined company, cost of capital = 11.86% × 0.6 + 6.00% × 0.78 × 0.4 = 8.99, say 9%

Appendix 3: Estimate of the value created for Cigno Co's equity holders from the acquisition

Anatra Co, medical R&D value estimate:

Sales revenue growth rate = 5%

Operating profit margin = 17.25%

Tax rate = 22%

Additional capital investment = 40% of the change in sales revenue

Cost of capital = 9% (Appendix 2)

Free cash flow growth rate after 4 years = 3%

Current sales revenue = 70% × $21,400m = $14,980m

Cash flows, Years 1 to 4

Year	1	2	3	4
	$m	$m	$m	$m
Sales revenue	15,729	16,515	17,341	18,208
Profit before interest and tax	2,713	2,849	2,991	3,141
Tax	597	627	658	691
Additional capital investment	300	314	330	347
Free cash flows	1,816	1,908	2,003	2,103
Present value of cash flows (9% discount)	1,666	1,606	1,547	1,490

Value, Years 1 to 4: $6,309m

Value, Year 5 onwards: $[\$2,103 \times 1.03/(0.09 - 0.03)] \times 1.09^{-4} = \$25,575m$

Total value of Anatra Co's medical R&D business area = $31,884 million

Total value of Anatra Co following unbundling of equipment manufacturing business and absorbing medical R&D business:

$5,594m (Appendix 1) + $31,884m = $37,478m (approximately)

Anatra Co, current market value of equity = $21,000 million

Anatra Co, current market value of debt = $9,000 million

Premium payable = $21,000m × 35% = $7,350m

Total value attributable to Anatra Co's investors = $37,350 million

Value attributable to Cigno Co's shareholders from the acquisition of Anatra Co before taking into account the cash benefits of potential tax savings and redundancies = Value following unbundling ($37,478m) – Anatra's debt ($9,000m) – price paid for Anatra ($21,000m + $7,350m) = $128m

Appendix 4: Estimate of the value created from savings in tax and employment costs following possible redundancies

Cash flows, Years 1 to 4

Year	1	2	3	4
	$m	$m	$m	$m
Cash flows (4% increase p.a.)	1,600	1,664	1,731	1,800
Present value of cash flows (9%)	1,468	1,401	1,337	1,275

Total value = $5,481 million

Value attributable to Cigno Co's shareholders from the acquisition of Anatra Co after taking into account the cash benefits of potential tax savings and redundancies = $5,609 million

(c)   The feasibility of disposing of assets as a defence tool against a possible acquisition depends upon the type of assets sold and how the funds generated from the sale are utilised.

If the type of assets are fundamental to the continuing business then this may be viewed as disposing of the corporation's 'crown jewels'. Such action may be construed as being against protecting the rights of shareholders (similar to the conditions discussed in part (d) below). In order for key assets to be disposed of, the takeover regulatory framework may insist on the corporation obtaining permission from the shareholders first before carrying it out.

On the other hand, the assets may be viewed as not being fundamental to the core business and may be disposed of to generate extra funds through a sell-off (see part (a) above). This may make sense if the corporation is undertaking a programme of restructuring and reorganisation.

In addition to this, the company needs to consider what it intends to do with the funds raised from the sale of assets. If the funds are used to grow the core business and therefore enhancing value, then the shareholders would see this positively and the value of the corporation will probably increase. Alternatively, if there are no profitable alternatives, the funds could be returned to the shareholders through special dividends or share buybacks. In these circumstances, disposing of assets may be a feasible defence tactic.

However, if the funds are retained but not put to value-enhancing use or returned to shareholders, then the share price may continue to be depressed. And the corporation may still be an attractive takeover target for corporations which are in need of liquid funds. In these circumstances, disposing of assets would not be a feasible defence tactic.

(d)   Each of the three conditions aims to ensure that shareholders are treated fairly and equitably.

The mandatory-bid condition through sell out rights allows remaining shareholders to exit the company at a fair price once the bidder has accumulated a certain number of shares. The amount of shares accumulated before the rule applies varies between countries. The bidder must offer the shares at the highest share price, as a minimum, which had been paid by the bidder previously. The main purpose for this condition is to ensure that the acquirer does not exploit their position of power at the expense of minority shareholders.

The principle of equal treatment condition stipulates that all shareholder groups must be offered the same terms, and that no shareholder group's terms are more or less favourable than another group's terms. The main purpose of this condition is to ensure that minority shareholders are offered the same level of benefits as the previous shareholders from whom the controlling stake in the target company was obtained.

The squeeze-out rights condition allows the bidder to force minority shareholders to sell their stake, at a fair price, once the bidder has acquired a specific percentage of the target company's equity. The percentage varies between countries but typically ranges between 80% and 95%. The main purpose of this condition is to enable the acquirer to gain a 100% stake of the target company and prevent problems arising from minority shareholders at a later date.

Note. Credit will be given for alternative, relevant approaches to the calculations, comments and suggestions/recommendations.

56 Lirio

Workbook references. Purchasing power parity theory is covered in chapter 5. Dividend capacity is covered in Chapter 16. Currency hedging is covered in Chapter 12.

Top tips. Where a 50-mark question covers a wide range of syllabus areas, as here, you need to focus on maximising your marks in the areas that you can do and not get too distracted by the areas that you find more difficult.

Part (a) – as is often the case, the 50-mark question starts with a basic area, here requiring an explanation of purchasing power parity theory.

Part (b)(i) required an assessment of the dividend capacity of the company. This is a topic that has been examined before.

Part (b)(ii) asked for assessment of the outcome of a currency hedge using either forwards, futures or options. This required a careful analysis of the appropriate part of the 'spread' to use and recognition that the $ was the contract currency for the futures and options contracts. Apart from this, the calculations here have been tested many times in previous exam sittings.

In part (b)(iii) the question gave information about the impact of the project on the pattern of future dividends. This suggested the use of the dividend valuation model (DVM) to establish the value of the company before and after the project to see if the project would 'add value'. Those candidates who realised that the DVM was needed scored well here. However, in general this part of the question was poorly done because candidates were not able to see the need for DVM.

Part (b)(iv) asked for a discussion of the proposed methods of financing the project.

This could have been satisfactorily answered by using the details provided in the scenario.

The implication of the changing patterns of dividend (given in the question) resulting from the project is that a cut in the dividend was being considered to finance the project. However, many candidates missed this and therefore failed to discuss the potential impact of the project on dividend policy. This was the key issue in this part of the question.

Easy marks. There were easier marks in many elements of this compulsory question (part (a), some of (b)(i), (b)(ii), some of (b)(iv) and the presentation marks in part (b)). Targeting these easier marks is an essential element in exam technique for AFM.

Marking scheme

				Marks
(a)		Up to 2 marks per well-explained point		Max 6
(b)	(i)	Appendices 1 and 1.1		
		Operating profit	1	
		Interest paid	1	
		Tax paid for normal activities	1	
		Investment in working capital	1	
		Investment in additional non-current assets	1	
		Correct treatment of depreciation	1	
		Cash flows remitted from Pontac Co	2	
		Additional tax payable	1	
			9	
	(ii)	Appendix 2		
		Amount received based on forward contracts	1	
		Correctly identifying long contracts and purchasing call options	1	
		Expected futures price based on linear narrowing of basis	1	
		Amount received based on futures contracts	1	
		Recognition of small over-hedge when using futures contracts	1	
		Option contracts or futures contracts purchased	1	
		Premium paid in dollars	1	
		Amount received based on options contracts	2	
		1–2 marks for each well-discussed point	4	
		Reasonable recommendation	1	
			14	
	(iii)	Appendix 3 and project assessment		
		Estimate of dividend growth rate (prior to project undertaken)	2	
		Estimate of corporate value (prior to project undertaken)	1	
		Annual dividend per share after transfer of funds to project	2	
		Estimate of value after project is undertaken	2	
		Concluding comments on project assessment	1	
			8	
	(iv)	Discussion of issues		
		Limitations of method used	1–2	
		Signalling impact of change in dividend policy	1–2	
		Clientele impact of change in dividend policy	2–3	
		Rationale for not considering debt or equity	3–4	
		Other relevant discussion points	2–3	
			9	

Professional marks for part (b)
Structure and presentation of the discussion paper   3
Clearly highlighting/emphasising areas for further discussion/detailed summary   1
             4

50

(a)   Purchasing power parity (PPP) predicts that the exchange rates between two currencies depend on the relative differences in the rates of inflation in each country. Therefore, if one country has a higher rate of inflation compared to another, then its currency is expected to depreciate over time. However, according to PPP the 'law of one price' holds because any weakness in one currency will be compensated by the rate of inflation in the currency's country (or group of countries, in the case of the euro).

Economic exposure refers to the degree by which a company's cash flows are affected by fluctuations in exchange rates. It may also affect companies which are not exposed to foreign exchange transactions, due to actions by international competitors.

If PPP holds, then companies may not be affected by exchange rate fluctuations, as lower currency value can be compensated by the ability to raise prices due to higher inflation levels. This depends on markets being efficient.

However, a permanent shift in exchange rates may occur, not because of relative inflation rate differentials, but because a country (or group of countries) lose their competitive positions. In this case the 'law of one price' will not hold, and prices readjust to a new and long-term or even permanent rate. For example, the UK £ to US$ rate declined in the 20th century, as the US grew stronger economically and the UK grew weaker. The rate almost reached parity in 1985 before recovering. Since the financial crisis in 2009, it has fluctuated between roughly $1.5 to £1 and $1.7 to £1.

In such cases, where a company receives substantial amounts of revenue from companies based in countries with relatively weak economies, it may find that it is facing economic exposure and its cash flows decline over a long period of time.

(b)   **Discussion paper to the BoD, Lirio Co**

Discussion paper compiled by:

Date:

Purpose of the discussion paper

The purpose of this discussion paper is:

(i)   To consider the implications of the BoD's proposal to use funds from the sale of its equity investment in the European company and from its cash flows generated from normal business activity over the next two years to finance a large project, instead of raising funds through equity and/or debt

(ii)   To assess whether or not the project adds value for Lirio Co or not

Background information

The funds needed for the project are estimated at $40,000,000 at the start of the project. $23,118,000 of this amount is estimated to be received from the sale of the equity investment (Appendices 2 and 3). This leaves a balance of $16,882,000 (Appendix 3), which will be obtained from the free cash flows to equity (the dividend capacity) of $21,642,000 (Appendix 1) expected to be generated in the first year. However, this would leave only $4,760,000 available for dividend payments in the first year, meaning a cut in expected dividends from $0.27/share to $0.0595/share (Appendix 3). The same level of dividends will be paid in the second year as well.

Project assessment

Based on the dividend valuation model, Lirio Co's market capitalisation, and therefore its value, is expected to increase from approximately $360 million to approximately

$403 million, or by just under 12% (Appendix 3). This would suggest that it would be beneficial for the project to be undertaken.

Possible issues

(1) The dividend valuation model is based on a number of factors such as: an accurate estimation of the dividend growth rate, a non-changing cost of equity and a predictable future dividend stream growing in perpetuity. In addition to this, it is expected that the sale of the investment will yield €20,000,000 but this amount could increase or reduce in the next three months. The dividend valuation model assumes that dividends and their growth rate are the sole drivers of corporate value, which is probably not accurate.

(2) Although the dividend irrelevancy theory proposed by Modigliani and Miller suggests that corporate value should not be affected by a corporation's dividend policy, in practice changes in dividends do matter for two main reasons. First, dividends are used as a signalling device to the markets and unexpected changes in dividends paid and/or dividend growth rates are not generally viewed positively by them. Changes in dividends may signal that the company is not doing well and this may affect the share price negatively.

(3) Second, corporate dividend policy attracts certain groups of shareholders or clientele. In the main this is due to personal tax reasons. For example, higher rate taxpayers may prefer low dividend payouts and lower rate taxpayers may prefer higher dividend payouts. A change in dividends may result in the clientele changing and this changeover may result in excessive and possibly negative share price volatility.

(4) It is not clear why the BoD would rather not raise the required finance through equity and/or debt. The BoD may have considered increasing debt to be risky. However, given that the current level of debt is $70 million compared to an estimated market capitalisation of $360 million (Appendix 3), raising another $40 million through debt finance will probably not result in a significantly higher level of financial risk. The BoD may have been concerned that going into the markets to raise extra finance may result in negative agency type issues, such as having to make proprietary information public, being forced to give extra value to new equity owners, or sending out negative signals to the markets.

Areas for further discussion by the BoD

Each of these issues should be considered and discussed further by the BoD. With reference to point (i), the BoD needs to discuss whether the estimates and the model used are reasonable in estimating corporate value or market capitalisation. With reference to points (ii) and (iii), the BoD needs to discuss the implications of such a significant change in the dividend policy and how to communicate Lirio Co's intention to the market so that any negative reaction is minimised. With reference to point (iv), the BoD should discuss the reasons for any reluctance to raise finance through the markets and whether any negative impact of this is perhaps less than the negative impact of points (ii) and (iii).

Appendix 1: Expected dividend capacity prior to large project investment

	$'000
Operating profit (15% × (1.08 × $300m))	48,600
Less interest (5% of $70m)	(3,500)
Less taxation (25% × ($48.6m – 3.5m))	(11,275)
Less investment in working capital ($0.10 × (0.08 × $300m))	(2,400)
Less investment in additional non-current assets ($0.20 × (0.08 × $300m))	(4,800)
Less investment in projects	(8,000)
Cash flows from domestic operations	18,625
Cash flows from Pontac Co's dividend remittances (see Appendix 1.1)	3,297
Additional tax payable on Pontac Co's profits (5% × $5.6m)	(280)
Dividend capacity	21,642

Appendix 1.1: Dividend remittances expected from Pontac Co

	$'000
Total contribution $24 × 400,000 units	9,600
Less fixed costs	(4,000)
Less taxation (20% × $5.6m)	(1,120)
Profit after tax	4,480
Remitted to Lirio Co (80% × $4.48m × 92%)	3,297

Appendix 2: Euro (€) investment sale receipt hedge

Lirio Co can use one of forward contracts, futures contracts or option contracts to hedge the € receipt.

Forward contract

Since it is a € receipt, the 1.1559 rate will be used.

€20,000,000 × 1.1559 = $23,118,000

Futures contracts

Go long to protect against a weakening € and use the June contracts to hedge as the receipt is expected at the end of May 20X6 or beginning of June 20X6 (in three months' time).

Opening basis = futures rate − spot rate

Here the June futures rate (per $) is 0.8656 and the March spot rate (per $) = 1 / 1.1585 = 0.8632.

So opening basis is 0.8656 − 0.8632 = 0.0024

There are four months to the expiry of the June futures contract so we can assume that when the futures contracts are closed out, one month before expiry, then ¼ of this basis will remain. So closing basis is estimated as 0.0024 × ¼ = 0.0006.

The effective futures rate can be estimated as opening futures rate − closing basis

Tutorial note. Other methods are possible.

Here this gives 0.8656 − 0.0006 = 0.8650.

Expected receipt = €20,000,000/0.8650 = $23,121,387

Number of contracts bought = $23,121,387/$125,000 = approximately 185 contracts (resulting in a very small over-hedge and therefore not material)

(Full credit will be given where the calculations are used to show the correction of the over-hedge using forwards.)

Option contracts

Purchase the June call option to protect against a weakening € and because receipt is expected at the end of May 20X6 or beginning of June 20X6.

Exercise price is 0.86, therefore expected receipt is €20,000,000/0.8600 = $23,255,814

Contracts purchased = $23,255,814/$125,000 = 186.05, say 186
Amount hedged = $125,000 × 186 = $23,250,000
Premium payable = 186 × 125,000 × 0.0290 = €674,250
Premium in $ = €674,250 × 1.1618 = $783,344
Amount not hedged = €20,000,000 − (186 × 125,000 × 0.8600) = €5,000
Use forward contracts to hedge €5,000 not hedged. €5,000 × 1.1559 = $5,780

(Full credit will be given if a comment on the under-hedge being immaterial and therefore not hedged is made, instead of calculating the correction of the under-hedge.)

Total receipts = $23,250,000 + $5,780 − $783,344 = $22,472,436

Advice and recommendation

Hedging using options will give the lowest receipt at $22,472,436 from the sale of the investment, while hedging using futures will give the highest receipt at $23,127,387, with the forward contracts giving a receipt of $23,118,000.

The lower receipt from the option contracts is due to the premium payable, which allows the option buyer to let the option lapse should the € strengthen. In this case, the option would be allowed to lapse and Lirio Co would convert the € into $ at the prevailing spot rate in three months' time. However, the € would need to strengthen significantly before the cost of the option is covered. Given market expectation of the weakness in the € continuing, this is not likely to be the case.

Although futures and forward contracts are legally binding and do not have the flexibility of option contracts, they both give higher receipts. Hedging using futures gives the higher receipt, but futures require margin payments to be made upfront and contracts are marked to market daily. In addition to this, the basis may not narrow in a linear fashion and therefore the amount received is not guaranteed. All these factors create uncertainty in terms of the exact amounts of receipts and payments resulting on a daily basis and the final receipt.

On the other hand, when using forward contracts to hedge the receipt exposure, Lirio Co knows the exact amount it will receive. It is therefore recommended that Lirio Co use the forward markets to hedge the expected receipt.

Note. It could be argued that in spite of the issues when hedging with futures, the higher receipt obtained from using futures markets to hedge means that they should be used. This is acceptable as well.

Appendix 3: Estimate of Lirio Co's value based on the dividend valuation model

If the large project is not undertaken and dividend growth rate is maintained at the historic level

Dividend history

Year to end of February	20X3	20X4	20X5	20X6
Number of $1 equity shares in issue ('000)	60,000	60,000	80,000	80,000
Total dividends paid ($'000)	12,832	13,602	19,224	20,377
Dividend per share	$0.214	$0.227	$0.240	$0.255

Average dividend growth rate = $(0.255/0.214)^{1/3} - 1 = 1.0602$ (or say 6%)

Expected dividend in February 20X7 = $0.255 × 1.06 = $0.270

Lirio Co, estimate of value if large project is not undertaken =

$0.270/(0.12 − 0.06) = $4.50 per share or $360 million market capitalisation

If the large project is undertaken

Funds required for project	$40,000,000
Funds from sale of investment (Appendix 2)	$23,118,000
Funds required from dividend capacity cash flows	$16,882,000
Dividend capacity funds before transfer to project (Appendix 1)	$21,642,000
Dividend capacity funds left after transfer	$4,760,000
Annual dividend per share after transfer	$0.0595
Annual dividend paid (end of February 20X7 and February 20X8)	$0.0595
Dividend paid (end of February 20X9)	$0.3100
New growth rate	7%

Lirio Co, estimate of value if large project is undertaken =

$0.0595 × 1.12^{-1} + $0.0595 × 1.12^{-2} + $0.3100 × 1.12^{-3} + [$0.3100 × 1.07/(0.12 − 0.07)] × 1.12^{-3}
= $5.04 per share or $403 million market capitalisation

Note. A discussion paper can take many formats. The answer provides one possible format. Credit will be given for alternative and sensible formats; and for relevant approaches to the calculations and commentary.

57 Morada

> **Workbook references.** Risk management is covered in Chapter 2; cost of capital in Chapter 7.
>
> **Top tips.** Part (b)(i) 17 marks – this was the hardest part of this question. It was important here to keep your nerve and to score the easier marks; these were available for calculating the current cost of equity and cost of capital (6 marks were available for this).
>
> The key points in calculating the revised cost of capital were:
>
> - Remembering that the market value of debt is needed for a WACC calculation and that this is not the same as the book value of debt. To work out the market value you need to calculate the present value of the future cash flows and discount at the company's pre-tax cost of debt.
>
> - Read the question carefully, this told you to assume that the value of equity is unchanged under any proposal.
>
> - Being aware that the information provided on movements in assets and liabilities was mainly relevant to part (bii).
>
> **Easy marks.** Parts of this question are extremely challenging but it is important to target the easier areas and not to worry about getting every aspect of the calculations correct (this is unlikely to be achievable under exam conditions).
>
> The discussion parts of this question – parts (a), (b)(iii) and (c) were worth about half of the marks (including the professional marks in part (b) and therefore need (almost) as much effort as the numerical areas.
>
> In part (b)(iii) the easiest marks are for stating your assumptions – this was requested in the question and was worth up to 3 marks. Key assumptions include the assumption that the value of equity is unaffected by each proposal (which seems highly unlikely) and that the weightings used to calculate the asset beta in proposal 2 are accurate, and that any increase in earnings affects retained profits.

Marking scheme

				Marks
(a)		Relationship between business and financial risk		3
		Risk mitigation and risk diversification as part of a company's risk management strategy		$\underline{3}$
				$\underline{6}$
(b)	(i)	Appendix 1		
		Prior to implementation of any proposal		
		Cost of equity		1
		Cost of debt		1
		Market value of equity		1
		Market value of debt		2
		Cost of capital		1
		After implementing the first director's proposal		
		Market value of debt		2
		Morada Co, asset beta		1
		Asset beta of travel services only		1
		Equity beta of travel services only		1
		Cost of equity		1
		Cost of capital		1
		After implementing the second director's proposal		
		Market value of debt		2
		Cost of equity		1
		Cost of capital		$\underline{1}$
				$\underline{17}$

(ii) Appendix 2

Adjusted earnings, first director's proposal	2	
Financial position, first director's proposal	2	
Adjusted earnings, second director's proposal	2	
Financial position, second director's proposal	$\frac{1}{7}$	

(iii)

Discussion	5–6	
Assumptions	2–3	
Reasoned recommendation	$\underline{1–2}$	
Note. Maximum 8 marks if no recommendation given.		Max 9

Professional marks for part (b)

Report format	1	
Structure and presentation of the report	$\frac{3}{4}$	

(c) 1 to 2 marks per point

Max $\underline{\quad 7}$

$\underline{\underline{50}}$

(a) The owners or shareholders of a business will accept that it needs to engage in some risky activities in order to generate returns in excess of the risk-free rate of return. A business will be exposed to differing amounts of business and financial risk depending on the decisions it makes. Business risk depends on the decisions a business makes with respect to the services and products it offers and consists of the variability in its profits. For example, it could be related to the demand for its products, the rate of innovation, actions of competitors, etc. Financial risk relates to the volatility of earnings due to the financial structure of the business and could be related to its gearing, the exchange rate risk it is exposed to, its credit risk, its liquidity risk, etc. A business exposed to high levels of business risk may not be able to take excessive financial risk, and vice versa, as the shareholders or owners may not want to bear risk beyond an acceptable level.

Risk management involves the process of risk identification, of assessing and measuring the risk through the process of predicting, analysing and quantifying it, and then making decisions on which risks to assume, which to avoid, which to retain and which to transfer. As stated above, a business will not aim to avoid all risks, as it will want to generate excess returns. Dependent on factors such as controllability, frequency and severity of the risk, it may decide to eliminate or reduce some risks from the business through risk transfer. Risk mitigation is the process of transferring risks out of a business through, for example, hedging or insurance, or avoiding certain risks altogether. Risk diversification is a process of risk reduction through spreading business activity into different products and services, different geographical areas and/or different industries to minimise being excessively exposed by focusing exclusively on one product/service.

(b) **Report to the BoD, Morada Co**

This report provides a discussion on the estimates of the cost of equity and the cost of capital and the impact on the financial position and the earnings after tax, as a result of the proposals put forward by the first director and the second director. The main assumptions made in drawing up the estimates will also be explained. The report concludes by recommending which of the two directors' proposals, if any, should be adopted.

Discussion

The table below shows the revised figures of the cost of equity and the cost of capital (Appendix 1), and the forecast earnings after tax for the coming year (Appendix 2), following each proposal from the first and second directors. For comparison purposes, figures before any changes are given as well.

	Cost of equity Appendix 1	Cost of capital Appendix 1	Earnings after tax Appendix 2
Current position	12.2%	10.0%	$28.0m
Following first director's proposal	11.6%	11.1%	$37.8m
Following second director's proposal	12.3%	9.8%	$30.8m

Under the first director's proposal, although the cost of equity falls due to the lower financial risk in Morada Co because of less debt, the cost of capital actually increases. This is because, even though the cost of debt has decreased, the benefit of the tax shield is reduced significantly due to the lower amount of debt borrowing. Added to this is the higher business risk, reflected by the asset beta, of Morada Co just operating in the travel services sector. This higher business risk and reduced tax shield more than override the lower cost of debt resulting in a higher cost of capital.

Under the second director's proposal, the cost of equity is almost unchanged. There has been a significant increase in the cost of debt from 4.7% to 6.2%. However, the cost of capital has not reduced significantly because the benefit of the tax shield is also almost eroded by the increase in the cost of debt.

If no changes are made, then the forecast earnings after tax as a percentage of non-current assets is 10% ($28m/$280m). Under the first director's proposal, this figure almost doubles to 19.3% ($37.8m/$196m) and, even if the one-off profit from the sale of non-current assets is excluded, this figure is still higher at 12.9% ($25.2m/$196m). Under the second director's proposal, this figure falls to 8.8% ($30.8m/$350m).

Assumptions

(1) It is assumed that the asset beta of Morada Co is a weighted average of the asset betas of the travel services and the maintenance services business units, using non-current assets invested in each business unit as a fair representation of the size of each business unit and therefore the proportion of the business risk which that business unit represents within the company.

(2) The assumption of the share price not changing after either proposal is not reasonable. It is likely that due to changes in the business and financial risk from implementing either proposal, the risk profile of the company will change. The changes in the risk profile will influence the cost of equity, which in turn will influence the share price.

(3) In determining the financial position of Morada Co, it is assumed that the current assets will change due to changes in the profit after tax figure; therefore this is used as the balancing figure for each proposal.

Recommendation

It is recommended that neither the first director's proposal nor the second director's proposal should be adopted. The second director's proposal results in a lower return on investment and a virtually unchanged cost of capital. So there will not be a meaningful benefit for Morada Co. The first director's proposal does increase the return on investment but results in a higher cost of capital. If the reason for adopting either proposal is to reduce risk, then this is not achieved. The main caveat here is that where the assumptions made in the calculations are not reasonable, they will reduce the usefulness of the analysis.

Report compiled by:

Date:

Note. Credit will be given for alternative and relevant points.

Appendix 1: Estimates of cost of equity and cost of capital

Before either proposal is implemented

Cost of equity (Ke) = 3.8% + 1.2 × 7% = 12.2%
Cost of debt (Kd) = 3.8% + 0.9% = 4.7%

Market value of equity (MVe) = $2.88 × 125m shares = $360m

Market value of debt (MVd)

Per \$100 $\$6.20 \times 1.047^{-1} + \$6.20 \times 1.047^{-2} + \$6.20 \times 1.047^{-3} + \$106.20 \times 1.047^{-4} = \$105.36$

Total MVd = \$105.36/\$100 × \$120m = \$126.4m

Cost of capital = (12.2% × \$360m + 4.7% × 0.8 × \$126.4m)/\$486.4m = 10.0%

If the first director's proposal is implemented

MV_e = \$360m
BV_d = \$120m × 0.2 = \$24m
Kd = 4.4%

MV_d per \$100 $\$6.20 \times 1.044^{-1} + \$6.20 \times 1.044^{-2} + \$6.20 \times 1.044^{-3} + \$106.20 \times 1.044^{-4} = \$106.47$

Total MV_d = 106.47/\$100 × \$24 = \$25.6m

Morada Co, asset beta

1.2 × \$360m/(\$360m + \$126.4m × 0.8) = 0.94

To calculate the asset beta of travel services it will be assumed that it represents 70% of the value of the company (the question says that the % of the total book value of non-current assets can be used to represent the total size of each division, and says that 30% of the non-current assets belong to the repairs and maintenance division).

This means that the asset beta of travel × 0.7 + asset beta of the repairs and maintenance division × 0.3 = 0.94.

We are told that the asset beta of the repairs and maintenance division is 0.65 so:

Beta of travel × 0.7 + 0.65 × 0.3 = 0.94

So beta of travel × 0.7 = 0.94 − 0.195

So asset beta of travel = 0.745 / 0.7 = 1.06

This is now re-geared to calculate the equity beta of travel services.

Equity beta of travel services = 1.06 × (\$360m + \$25.6m × 0.8)/\$360m = 1.12

K_e = 3.8% + 1.12 × 7% = 11.6%

Cost of capital = (11.6% × \$360m + 4.4% × 0.8 × \$25.6m)/\$385.6 = 11.1%

If the second director's proposal is implemented

MV_e = \$360 million

The basis points for the Ca3 rated bond is 240 basis points higher than the risk-free rate of interest, giving a cost of debt of 6.2%, therefore:

MV_d = BV_d = \$190m

Equity beta of the new, larger company = 1.21

Ke = 3.8% + 1.21 × 7% = 12.3%

Cost of capital = (12.3% × \$360m + 6.2% × 0.8 × \$190m)/\$550m = 9.8%

Appendix 2: Estimates of forecast after-tax earnings and forecast financial position

MORADA CO EXTRACTS FROM THE FORECAST AFTER-TAX EARNINGS
FOR THE COMING YEAR

	Current forecast \$'000	Forecast: first director proposal \$'000	Forecast: second director proposal \$'000
Current forecast after-tax earnings	28,000	28,000	28,000
Interest saved due to lower borrowing (\$96m × 6.2% × 0.8)		4,762	
Interest payable on additional borrowing (\$70m × 6.2% × 0.8)			(3,472)

	Current forecast $'000	Forecast: first director proposal $'000	Forecast: second director proposal $'000
Reduction in earnings due to lower investment (9% × $84m)		(7,560)	
Additional earnings due to higher investment (9% × $70m)			6,300
Profit on sale of non-current assets (15% × $84m)		12,600	
Revised forecast after-tax earnings	28,000	37,802	30,828
Increase in after-tax earnings		9,802	2,828

MORADA CO EXTRACTS FROM THE FORECAST FINANCIAL POSITION FOR THE COMING YEAR

	Current forecast $'000	Forecast: first director proposal $'000	Forecast: second director proposal $'000
Non-current assets	280,000	196,000	350,000
Current assets (balancing figure)	48,000	43,702	57,828
Total assets	328,000	239,702	407,828
Equity and liabilities			
Share capital (40c/share)	50,000	50,000	50,000
Retained earnings**	137,000	146,802	139,828
Total equity	187,000	196,802	189,828
Non-current liabilities (6.2% redeemable bonds)	120,000	24,000	190,000
Current liabilities	21,000	18,900	28,000
Total liabilities	141,000	42,900	218,000
Total liabilities and capital	328,000	239,702	407,828

** Note. With the two directors' proposals, the retained earnings amount is adjusted to reflect the revised forecast after-tax earnings.

(c)   Note. This is an open-ended question and a variety of relevant answers can be given by candidates depending on how the question requirement is interpreted. The following answer is just one possible approach which could be taken. Credit will be given for alternative, but valid, interpretations and answers therein.

According to the third director, risk management involves more than just risk mitigation or risk diversification as proposed by the first and second directors. The proposals suggested by the first and the second directors are likely to change the makeup of the company, and cause uncertainty amongst the company's owners or clientele. This in turn may cause unnecessary fluctuations in the share price. She suggests that these changes are fundamental and more than just risk management tools.

Instead, it seems that she is suggesting that Morada Co should follow the risk management process suggested in part (a) above, where risks should be identified, assessed and then mitigated according to the company's risk appetite.

The risk management process should be undertaken with a view to increasing shareholder wealth, and therefore the company should consider what drives this value and what are the risks associated with these drivers of value. Morada Co may assess that some of these risks are controllable and some not controllable. It may assess that some are severe and others less so, and it may assess that some are likely to occur more frequently than others.

Morada Co may take the view that the non-controllable, severe and/or frequent risks should be eliminated (or not accepted). On the other hand, where Morada Co is of the opinion that it has a comparative advantage or superior knowledge of risks, and therefore is better able to manage them, it may come to the conclusion that it should accept these. For example, it may take the view that it is able to manage events such as flight delays or hotel standards, but would hedge against currency fluctuations and insure against natural disasters due to their severity or non-controllability.

Theory suggests that undertaking risk management may increase the value of a company if the benefits accruing from the risk management activity are more than the costs involved in managing the risks. For example, smoothing the volatility of profits may make it easier for Morada Co to plan and match long-term funding with future projects or to take advantage of market imperfections by reducing the amount of taxation payable, or it may reduce the costs involved with incidences of financial distress. In each case, though, the benefits accrued should be assessed against the costs involved.

Therefore, a risk management process is more than just mitigating risk through reducing financial risk as the first director is suggesting or risk diversification as the second director is suggesting. Instead it is a process of risk analysis and then about judgement of which risks to hedge or mitigate, and finally, which risk reduction mechanisms to employ, depending on the type of risk, the cost of the risk analysis and mitigation, and the benefits accruing from the mitigation.

58 Opao

> **Workbook references.** Business re-organisation is covered in Chapter 15, reverse takeovers in Chapter 9 and valuation techniques in Chapter 10. Financing a takeover is covered in Chapter 11.
>
> **Top tips.** Don't panic - this question is not as bad as it looks on first read through (they rarely are). Use your first read through to actively plan parts (a) and (b) to help manage stress and to ensure that your first read through actually achieves something.
>
> **Easy marks.** Over 60% of the marks (including professional marks) from parts (a), (b), (c)(i) and (d) are relatively manageable. **Don't rush** these sections in order to concentrate on the harder areas; it is important to maximise you marks in areas that you are strong in.
>
> **ACCA examining team's comments.** In terms of professional marks, some candidates did not provide a reasonable structure in their answer, nor put the answer to part (c) in a report format. These marks are relatively easy to obtain, and a well-structured response would provide candidates with a useful framework within which to provide a response. Such an approach will result in a much higher chance of success in the examination. Nevertheless, many candidates' answers were good, and they earned the majority of the professional marks.

Marking scheme

			Marks	
(a)		Distinguishing between MBO and MBI	1–2	
		Discussion of choice of MBI	2–3	
				Max 4
(b)		Explanation of portfolio restructuring and organisational restructuring	2	
		Discussion of reason(s) for change in business focus	3	
			5	
(c)	(i)	**(Appendix 1)**		
		Equity value of Opao Co	1	
		Tai Co, free cash flow to firm	2	
		Estimate of value of Tai Co	1	
		Estimate of equity value of Tai Co	1	
		Combined company, free cash flows	2	
		Value of combined company, Years 1 to 4	1	
		Value of combined company, after Year 4	1	
		Equity value of combined company	1	
			10	

(ii)   **(Appendix 2)**

Cash offer, percentage gain, Tai Co	1
Cash offer, percentage gain, Opao Co	2
Share-for-share offer, share of additional value	1
Share-for-share offer, Opao Co share value	1
Share-for-share offer, total shares allocated to Tai Co	1
Share-for-share offer, 2 Opao Co shares for 1 Tai Co share	1
Share-for-share offer, percentage gain, Tai Co	1
Share-for-share offer, percentage gain, Opao Co	1
Mixed offer, percentage gain, Tai Co	1
Mixed offer, percentage gain, Opao Co	2
	12

(iii) **(Report on proposed acquisition)**

Evaluation: Opao Co	3–4
Evaluation: Tai Co	3–4
	Max 7

Professional marks for part (c)

Report format	1
Structure and presentation of the report	3
	4

(d)

Explanation of difference between an IPO and reverse takeover	3
Discussion of using an IPO or reverse takeover to obtain a listing	5
	8
	50

(a)   A management buy-out (MBO) involves the purchase of a company by the management running that company. Hence, Burgut Co's current management team would be buying Burgut Co from Opao Co. A management buy-in (MBI) involves selling Burgut Co to a management team brought in from outside the company.

Opao Co may have sold Burgut Co through a MBI for the following reasons. Opao Co's BoD may have felt that Burgut Co's current management team lacked fresh ideas and strategies which could have driven Burgut Co forward successfully. Instead, it may have felt that a fresh team, with skills and expertise gained externally, would have had the required innovative ideas and skills. It may be that the external team of managers may have had the finance available to move quickly, whereas the internal team of managers may not have had the finance in place to purchase Burgut Co at that time. It is also possible that the management teams within Burgut Co and Opao Co had disagreements in the past, and Opao Co's BoD may have believed the two management teams would not be able to work together in the future, if needed. Thus, the BoD may have felt that a fresh management team was the better option going forwards.

(b)   Portfolio restructuring involves the acquisition of companies, or disposals of assets, business units and/or subsidiary companies through divestments, demergers, spin-offs, MBOs and MBIs. Organisational restructuring involves changing the way a company is organised. This may involve changing the structure of divisions in a business, business processes and other changes such as corporate governance.

The aim of either type of restructuring is to increase the performance and value of the business.

Opao Co, in going from a conglomerate business to one focusing on just two business areas, can be seen as restructuring its portfolio, as businesses and assets that are not part of financial services and food manufacturing are disposed of, and businesses focusing on these areas are acquired. Financial markets may take the view that focusing on food manufacturing and financial services has enabled Opao Co's senior management to concentrate on areas in which they have expertise. Whereas other businesses in which the senior management are not experts are disposed of. This activity leads to the maximisation of business value.

Shareholders are interested in maximising returns from their investments, which companies achieve through maximizing business value, whilst minimising the risks inherent in their investment activity. Shareholders who are closely linked to a particular business do not hold diversified investment portfolios, and therefore benefit from diversification of risk undertaken by a company, investing in many different areas. On the other hand, institutional shareholders and other shareholders, who hold diversified portfolios, would not benefit from a company undertaking risk management through diversification by becoming a conglomerate. Instead, such companies would increase value by focusing on areas in which they have relative expertise, as Opao Co seems to do. So Opao Co's changing owner clientele has forced it to change its overall strategy. This strategy change was implemented through portfolio restructuring.

(c) **Report to the board of directors (BoD), Opao Co**

Introduction

This report provides an estimate of the additional value created if Opao Co were to acquire Tai Co, and the gain for each company's shareholders based on a cash offer, a share-for-share offer and a mixed offer. It evaluates the likely reaction of the two companies' shareholders to each payment method.

Summary of the estimates from the appendices

From Appendix 1

Opao Co equity value pre-acquisition: $5,000 million

Tai Co equity value pre-acquisition: $1,000 million

Combined company equity value post-acquisition: $6,720 million

From Appendix 2

Therefore, additional value based on synergy benefits is $720m or 12% ($720m/$6,000m)

Estimated percentage gain in value

	Opao Co	Tai Co
Cash offer	11.2%	15.8%
Share-for-share offer	6.4%	40.0%
Mixed offer	9.7%	23.4%

Likely reactions

Tai Co's shareholders are likely to consider all the offers made, because they all fall within the range of premiums paid in previous acquisitions of 15% to 40%. The cash offer is at the lower end of the range, the share-for-share offer at the top end of the range and the mixed offer in between. It is likely that Tai Co's shareholders will be more attracted to the share-for-share offer as it maximises their return. However, this offer is reliant on the fact that the expected synergy benefits will be realised and Tai Co will probably need to analyse the likelihood of this. Cash payment, although much lower, gives a certainty of return. The mixed offer provides some of the certainty of a cash payment, but also offers a higher return compared to the cash offer. This return is roughly in the middle of the premium range. It may therefore prove to be the better option for Tai Co's shareholders.

Opao Co's shareholders benefit less from the acquisition compared to Tai Co's shareholders. In each case, they get less than the additional value created of 12%, with the cash payment offering the highest return of 11.2%, which is just below the 12% overall return. The share-for-share offer gives the least return at just over half (6.4%) of the overall return of 12%. Nevertheless, with this option, cash is retained within Opao Co and can be used for other value creating projects. Opao Co's shareholders may also prefer the mixed offer, because the return they are expecting to receive is between the cash and share-for-share offers. Also, less cash resources are used compared to the cash offer, and they still benefit from a significant proportion of the additional value created.

BPP
LEARNING
MEDIA

Conclusion

Based on the benefits accruing to both sets of shareholders, it is not possible to conclusively say that one method of acquisition payment would be acceptable to both sets of shareholders. However, both sets of shareholders may be persuaded that the mixed offer provides a reasonable compromise between the wholly cash and the wholly share-for-share prices. Given that synergy benefits are shared (even if not equally), both companies' share prices should increase if the acquisition proceeds, as long as the estimates when estimating the valuations are reasonably accurate.

Report compiled by:

Date

APPENDICES:

Appendix 1 (Part (c)(i)):

Equity value of Opao Co prior to acquisition

$2.50/share × 2,000m shares = $5,000m

Equity value of Tai Co prior to acquisition

Free cash flows to firm = $132.0m + $27.4m − $24.3m − ($132.0m × 0.2) = $108.7m

Company value = $108.7m × 1.03/(0.11 − 0.03) = $1,399.5m, say $1,400m

Equity value = $1,400m − $400m = $1,000m

Equity value of combined company post acquisition

All amounts in $ millions

Year	1	2	3	4
Sales revenue (5.02% growth, yrs 2 to 4)	7,351	7,720	8,108	8,515
Pre-tax profit (15.4% of sales revenue)	1,132	1,189	1,249	1,311
Less: Tax (20%)	(226)	(238)	(250)	(262)
Less: Additional investment ($0.31 per $1, yrs 2 to 4)	(109)	(114)	(120)	(126)
Free cash flows	797	837	879	923
Present value of free cash flows (10%)	724	691	660	630

Combined company value: years 1 to 4 = $2,705 million

Combined company value: after year 4 = 923 × 1.024/(0.1 − 0.024) × 1.1^{-4} = $8,494m

Total combined company value = $11,199 million

Equity value (60% × $11,199m) = $6,719.4m, say $6,720 million

Appendix 2 (Part (c)(ii): Percentage gains for Tai Co and Opao Co shareholders under each payment method

Estimate of additional value created from acquisition due to synergy benefits

$6,720m − ($5,000m + $1,000m) = $720m

Tai Co, value per share = $1,000m/263m shares = $3.80/share approx.

Cash offer

Tai Co shareholders, percentage gain

($4.40 − $3.80)/$3.80 = $0.60/$3.80 = 15.8%

Opao Co shareholders, percentage gain

Amount of additional value created going to Tai Co shareholders = $0.60 × 263m shares = $157.8m

Amount of additional value created going to Opao Co shareholders = $720m − $157.8m = $562.2m

As a percentage = ($562.2m/2,000m shares)/$2.50 = 11.2%

Share-for-share offer

Share of additional value to Tai Co shareholders = $720m × 0.555 = $399.6m

Share of additional value to Opao Co shareholders = $720m × 0.445 = $320.4m

Opao Co equity value after acquisition = $5,320.4 million

Opao Co, estimated share price after acquisition = $5,320.4m/2,000m shares = $2.66/share

Opao Co shares to be allocated to Tai Co shareholders = ($1,000m + $399.6m)/$2.66 = 526m shares approximately

Therefore, share-for-share offer will be 2 Opao Co shares for 1 Tai Co share (526/263 = 20)

Tai Co shareholders, percentage gain

($2.66 × 2 shares − $3.80 × 1 share)/($3.80 × 1 share) = 40%

Opao Co shareholders, percentage gain

($2.66 − $2.50)/$2.50 = 6.4%

Mixed offer

Tai Co shareholders, percentage gain

(($2.60 + $2.09) − $3.80)/$3.80 = $0.89/$3.80 = 23.4%

Opao Co shareholders, percentage gain

Amount of additional value going to Tai Co shareholders = $0.89 × 263m = $234.1m

Amount of additional value created going to Opao Co shareholders = $720m − $234.1m = $485.9m

As a percentage = ($485.9m/2,000m shares)/$2.50 = 9.7%

Tutorial note

Credit would also be given for using the post-acquisition price provided in the question to analyse the impact on Opao Co's shareholders with the mixed offer.

(d)   The initial public offering (IPO) is the conventional way to obtain a listing where a company issues and offers shares to the public. When doing this, the company will follow the normal procedures and processes required by the stock exchange regarding a new issue of shares and will comply with the regulatory requirements.

Undertaking a reverse takeover enables a company to obtain a listing without going through the IPO process. The BoD of Burgut Co would initially take control of a 'shell' listed company by buying some shares in that company and taking over as its BoD. The 'shell' listed company was probably a normal listed company previously, but is no longer trading. New equity shares in the listed company would then be exchanged for Burgut Co's shares, with the external appearance that the listed company has taken over Burgut Co. But in reality Burgut Co has now effectively got a listing, having taken control of the listed company previously. Normally, the name of the original listed company would then be changed to Burgut Co.

Compared with an IPO, the main benefits of undertaking a reverse takeover are that it is cheaper, takes less time and ensures that Burgut Co will obtain a listing on a stock exchange. An IPO can cost between 3% and 5% of the capital being raised because it involves investment banks, lawyers, and other experts. A marketing campaign and issuing a prospectus are also needed to make the offering attractive and ensure shares to the public do get sold. A reverse takeover does not need any of these and therefore avoids the related costs. The IPO process can typically take one or two years to complete due to hiring the experts, the marketing process and the need to obtain a value for the shares. Additionally, the regulatory process and procedures of the stock exchange need to be complied with. With a reverse takeover, none of these are required and therefore the process is quicker. Finally, there is no guarantee that an IPO will be successful. In times of

BPP
LEARNING
MEDIA

uncertainty, economic downturn or recession, it may not attract the attention of investors and a listing may not be obtained. With reverse takeover, because the transaction is an internal one, between two parties, it will happen and Burgut Co will be listed.

However, obtaining a listing through a reverse takeover can have issues attached to it. The listed 'shell' company may have potential liabilities which are not transparent at the outset, such as potential litigation action. A full due diligence of the listed company should be conducted before the reverse takeover process is started. The IPO process is probably better at helping provide the senior management of Burgut Co with knowledge of the stock exchange and its regulatory environment. The involvement of experts and the time senior management need to devote to the listing process will help in this regard. Due to the marketing effort involved with an IPO launch, it will probably have an investor following, which a reverse takeover would not. Therefore, a company which has gone through an IPO would probably find it easier to raise extra funds, whilst a company which has gone through a reverse takeover may find it more difficult to raise new funding.

Overall, neither option of obtaining a listing has a clear advantage over the other. The choice of listing method depends on the company undertaking the listing and the purpose for which it is doing so.

Note. Credit will be given for alternative valid areas of discussion.

59 Okan

> **Workbook references.** Ethics is covered in Chapter 1 and risk in Chapter 2. Adjusted present value is covered in Chapter 6. Currency risk is covered in Chapter 13.
>
> **Top tips.** You will need to be very strict on your time management with this question – it is easy to overrun especially if you are attempting to produce a 100% perfect answer to part (b)(ii).
>
> **Easy marks.** Over 60% of the marks are available for discussion but ensure your points are addressed to the scenario to maximise marks.
>
> **ACCA examining team's comments.** Professional marks in part (b) were awarded for the format, structure and presentation of the report. While many candidates presented their answers in a report format as required, thereby gaining the majority or all the professional marks, a significant minority of candidates did not address this requirement fully, or not at all. These relatively easy marks to obtain could make the difference between a pass or a fail for some candidates.

Marking scheme

			Marks
(a)	1–2 marks per well-discussed comment		Max 4
(b)	(i)	**(Appendix 1)**	
		Forward market hedge	1
		Money markets hedge	2
		Minimum borrowing required	1
			4
	(ii)	**(Appendix 2a)**	
		Sales revenue	2
		Production costs	1
		Component costs	3
		Tax	2
		Working capital	2
		Project Alpha base case NPV	1
		Project Beta base case NPV	1
			12

(Appendix 2b)

Issue costs	1
Annual tax shield	1
Annual subsidy	1
Present value of tax shield and subsidy	1
Project Alpha adjusted present value	1
Project Beta adjusted present value	1
	6

(Appendix 2c)

	Project Alpha duration	2
(iii)	Discussion of the assumptions made	4–5
	Evaluation and justification	3–4
	(Maximum 7 marks if no considered justification given)	Max 8

Professional marks for part (b)

Report format	1
Structure and presentation of the report	3
	4

(c)	Explanation of economic risk faced by Okan Co	2–3
	Discussion of management of economic risk	1–2
		Max 4

(d) Discussion of management of each of the four risk categories (Maximum 2 marks per risk category discussed. Maximum of 5 marks if not all categories discussed)	Max 6
	50

ANSWERS

(a) Adjusted present values (APVs) separate out a project's cash flows and allocate a specific discount rate to each type of cash flow, dependent on the risk attributable to that particular type of cash flow. Net present value (NPV) discounts all cash flows by the average discount rate attributable to the average risk of a project.

One reason why APV may be preferable to NPV is because by separating out different types of cash flows, the company's managers will be able to see which part of the project generates what proportion of the project's value. Furthermore, allocating a specific discount rate to a cash flow part helps determine the value added or destroyed. In this example, Okan Co is able to determine how much value is being created by the investment and how much by the debt financing. For complex projects, investment related cash flows could be further distinguished by their constituent risk factors, where applicable.

(b) **Report to the board of directors (BoD), Okan Co**

Introduction

This report evaluates, and provides a justification and decision on, whether Okan Co should pursue Project Alpha or Project Beta, based on the important factors identified by the company, namely the returns generated by the projects, the projects' risks and non-financial aspects.

Evaluation

Financing

Using forward markets to hedge the expected receipt in six months' time results in the higher receipt equalling Y$25,462,000 approximately. If the money markets hedge is used the receipt is Y$25,234,936 (Appendix 1).

Using forward markets to hedge the expected receipt would therefore minimise the amount of debt borrowing. However, the amount receivable from the money markets hedge is based on the annual bank investment rate available to Okan Co of 2.4%.

Okan Co may be able to use the funds borrowed to generate a higher return than the bank investment, and therefore using money markets to undertake the hedge may be financially advisable. Okan Co should investigate any opportunities for higher income but based on the current results, the forward market hedge is recommended to minimise the amount of debt finance needed.

Minimum amount of debt borrowing required is Y$24,538,000 approximately.

Project returns and risk

	Project Alpha	*Project Beta*
Base case net present value (NPV) (in six months' time)	Y$5,272,000 (Appendix 2a)	Y$5,100,000 (Appendix 2a)
Adjusted present value (APV)	Y$6,897,218 (Appendix 2b)	Y$6,725,218 (Appendix 2b)
Project duration	3.04 years (Appendix 2c)	2.43 years (given)

Project Alpha's and Project Beta's base case NPVs and APVs are similar to each other, with Project Alpha expected to yield a small amount in excess to the yield expected from Project Beta. However, Project Beta's project duration is significantly lower.

This is because a higher proportion of Project Beta's cash flows come earlier in the project's life, compared to Project Alpha.

There is more certainty to earlier cash flows and this is reflected in the lower duration for Project Beta. Project Beta's risk is lower than Project Alpha.

In estimating the base case NPV and APV for Project Alpha, it is assumed that the cash flows are known with reasonable certainty and the inflation rates will not change during the life of the project. It is also assumed that the future exchange rate between the Y$ and the £ will change in accordance with the purchasing power parity differential. Furthermore, it is assumed that the prices and costs related to Project Alpha will increase in line with inflation during the six months before the project starts. For Project Alpha, it is assumed that the initial working capital requirement is funded by the company and not from the funds raised from the subsidised loan, similar to the assumption made for Project Beta. However, for both projects, Okan Co needs to consider, and take account of, the opportunity costs related to this.

In terms of the Project Alpha's discount rate, it is assumed that the given discount rate accurately reflects the business risk of the project.

Whilst this level of detail is not provided for Project Beta, it is assumed that similar assumptions will have been made for Project Beta as well. In the case of both projects, Okan Co should assess the accuracy or reasonableness of the assumptions, and if necessary, conduct sensitivity analysis to observe how much the projects' values change if input variables are altered.

Notwithstanding the assumptions and caveats made above, it would appear that Project Beta would be preferable to Project Alpha, given that it has a similar APV but a significantly lower risk.

Nevertheless, there may be good strategic reasons why Okan Co may select Project Alpha over Project Beta. For example, these reasons may include providing access to new markets, enabling Okan Co to erect barriers to entry against competitors or looking at follow-on opportunities as possible real options.

Justification

Due to the substantially lower risk (as measured by the project duration) and similar APV, it is recommended that Project Beta be selected by Okan Co. It is also recommended that forward markets are used to hedge the income expected in six months' time to part fund the project. This would minimise the debt borrowing needed.

However, this decision is predicated on the fact that the implications of the assumptions and the wider strategic reasons discussed above have been carefully considered by Okan Co.

Report compiled by:

Date

Note. Credit will be given for alternative and valid evaluative comments.

Appendices:

Appendix 1 (Part (b)(i)):

Expected receipt in six months' time, using forward markets:

€10,000,000 × 2.5462 = Y$25,462,000

Expected receipt in six months' time, using money markets:

€10,000,000/(1 + 0.022/2) = €9,891,197
€9,891,197 × 2.5210 = Y$24,935,708

Y$24,935,708 × (1 + 0.024/2) = Y$25,234,936

Minimum amount of debt borrowing Okan Co would require:

Y$50,000,000 − Y$25,462,000 = Y$24,538,000

Appendix 2a (Part (b)(ii)): Projects Alpha and Beta, base case net present value, in six months' time

Base case net present value before considering financing side effects. All figures are in Y$000s.

Year	0	1	2	3	4
Sales revenue (W1)		17,325	34,304	62,890	33,821
Less:					
Production costs (W2)		(6,365)	(11,584)	(24,095)	(9,546)
Component costs (W3)		(3,708)	(5,670)	(11,877)	(4,578)
Cash flows before tax		7,252	17,050	26,918	19,697
Tax (W4)		1,050	(1,535)	(3,977)	(1,721)
Working capital	(1,733)	(2,547)	(4,288)	4,360	4,208
Plant purchase and sale	(50,000)				10,000
Net cash flows	(51,733)	5,755	11,227	27,301	32,184
Base case present value of cash flows (discounted at 10%)	(51,733)	5,232	9,279	20,512	21,982

Approximate, base case net present value (NPV) of Project Alpha = Y$5,272,000.

Base case net present value (NPV) of Project Beta = Y$(8,450,000 + 19,360,000 + 22,340,000 + 4,950,000) − Y$50,000,000 = Y$ 5,100,000

Workings:

1   *Sales revenue*

Year	1	2	3	4
Pre-inflated revenues (Y$ 000s)	15,750	28,350	47,250	23,100
Inflation	× 1.1^1	× 1.1^2	× 1.1^3	× 1.1^4
Post-inflated revenues (Y$ 000s)	17,325	34,304	62,890	33,821

2 Production costs

Year	1	2	3	4
Pre-inflated production costs (Y$ 000s)	6,120	10,710	21,420	8,160
Inflation	$\times 1.04^1$	$\times 1.04^2$	$\times 1.04^3$	$\times 1.04^4$
Post-inflated production costs (Y$ 000s)	6,365	11,584	24,095	9,546

Component costs are not inflated, but future exchange rates are based on purchasing power parity (PPP).

3 Component cost

Year	1	2	3	4
PPP multiplier	3.03 × 1.04/1.02	3.09 × 1.04/1.02	3.15 × 1.04/1.02	3.21 × 1.04/1.02
Forecast Y$ per £1	3.09	3.15	3.21	3.27
Component cost (£)	1,200	1,800	3,700	1,400
Component cost (Y$)	3,708	5,670	11,877	4,578

4 Tax

Year	1	2	3	4
Cash flows before tax	7,252	17,050	26,918	19,697
Tax allowable depreciation	(12,500)	(9,375)	(7,031)	(11,094)
Taxable cash flows	(5,248)	7,675	19,887	8,603
Tax payable (20%)	(1,050)	1,535	3,977	1,721

Appendix 2b (Part (b)(ii)): Projects Alpha and Beta, adjusted present value (APV), in six months' time

Issue costs = 3/97 × Y$24,538,000 = Y$758,907
Annual tax shield = 2.1% × Y$24,538,000 × 20% = Y$103,060
Annual interest saved on subsidised loan = 2.9% × Y$24,538,000 × 80% = Y$569,282
Annuity factor, Years 1 to 4 at 5% interest = 3.546

Present value of the tax shield and loan subsidy benefit = (Y$103,060 + Y$569,282) × 3.546
= Y$2,384,125

Project Alpha APV	Y$
Base case NPV of Project Alpha (appendix 2a)	5,272,000
Issue costs	(758,907)
Present value of the tax shield and loan subsidy benefit	2,384,125
APV	6,897,218

Project Beta APV	Y$
Base case NPV of Project Beta (appendix 2a)	5,100,000
Issue costs	(758,907)
Present value of the tax shield and loan subsidy benefit	2,384,125
APV	6,725,218

Appendix 2c (Part (b)(ii)): Project Alpha's duration based on its base case present values of cash flows Project Alpha

Year	1	2	3	4
PVs × years	5,232,000 × 1 = 5,232,000	9,279,000 × 2 = 18,558,000	20,512,000 × 3 = 61,536,000	21,982,000 × 4 = 87,928,000

Total PVs × time = 173,254,000 approximately
Total PVs = 57,005,000 approximately
Project Alpha duration = 173,254,000/57,005,000 = 3.04 years

(c) **Explanation of why the subsidiary company may be exposed to economic risk and how it may be managed**

Companies face economic exposure when their competitive position is affected due to macroeconomic factors such as changes in currency rates, political stability, or changes in the regulatory environment. Long-term economic exposure or economic shocks can cause a permanent shift in the purchasing power and other parity conditions. Normally, companies face economic exposure when they trade internationally. However, even companies which do not trade internationally nor rely on inputs sourced internationally may still face economic exposure.

In the case of Okan Co's subsidiary company, economic risk may have occurred because interest rates have been kept at a high level, causing the original parity conditions to break down. High interest rates will be attractive to international investors, as they can get higher returns and higher rates may lead to the Y$ becoming stronger relative to other currencies. This in turn would allow international competitors to produce goods more cheaply than the subsidiary company and thereby enhance their competitive position relative to the subsidiary company.

Managing economic exposure is difficult due to its long-lasting nature and because it can be difficult to identify. Financial instruments, such as derivatives, and money markets cannot normally be used to manage such risks. Okan Co's subsidiary company can try tactics such as borrowing in international or eurocurrency markets, sourcing input products from overseas suppliers and ultimately shifting production facilities overseas. None of these are easy or cheap and can expose the company to new types of risks. Okan Co would also need to assess that any action it takes to manage economic risk fits into its overall risk management strategy.

(d) **How each category or risk may be managed**

Risks which fall into the severe and frequent category need immediate attention, as they could threaten the company's survival or derail its long-term strategy. The aim here would be to reduce the severity of the risks and the frequency with which they occur quickly. It may mean avoiding certain actions or abandoning certain projects, even if they could be profitable in the long term. Where a company has a real option and does not need to take action which will result in high frequency and high severity of risk, it may prefer to wait and see what happens.

Where the frequency of risks occurring is high but their impact is not severe, action needs to be taken so that such risks do not become severe in the future. For example, the company could put systems into place to detect these risks early and plans to deal with them if they do occur. Where the same kind of risks occur often, the company may decide to have set processes for dealing with them. For example, where there is a loss of relatively unskilled staff, the company may decide to replace staff quickly with casual workers, but also have appropriate training facilities in place.

If there are risks which are severe but only happen occasionally or infrequently, the company should try to insure against these. Contingency plans could also be put into place to mitigate the severity. For example, if the consequences of IT failure are high when a business decides to move to a new system, it could put appropriate contingencies into place. These may include secondary backup IT systems or initially trialling the new system on a few business units before undertaking a complete role out.

Risks which are neither severe, nor frequent, should be monitored and kept under review, but no significant action should be taken. It is possible that any significant action would incur costs which would likely be higher than the benefits derived from eliminating such risks. Monitoring such risks will ensure that should they move out of this category into the more severe/frequent categories, the company can start to take appropriate action.

Note. Credit will be given for alternative and valid explanatory and discussion comments.

BPP
LEARNING
MEDIA

Mock exams

ACCA

Advanced Financial Management

Mock Examination 1

Sample questions

Questions
Time allowed 3 hours and 15 minutes
Section A   THIS question is compulsory and MUST be attempted Section B   BOTH questions to be attempted

DO NOT OPEN THIS EXAM UNTIL YOU ARE READY TO START UNDER EXAMINATION CONDITIONS

SECTION A: THIS QUESTION is compulsory and MUST be attempted

Question 1

Mlima Co is a private company involved in aluminium mining. About eight years ago, the company was bought out by its management and employees through a leveraged buyout (LBO). Due to high metal prices worldwide, the company has been growing successfully since the LBO. However, because the company has significant debt borrowings with strict restrictive covenants and high interest levels, it has had to reject a number of profitable projects. The company has currently two bonds in issue, as follows:

- A 16% secured bond with a nominal value of $80 million, which is redeemable at par in five years. An early redemption option is available on this bond, giving Mlima Co the option to redeem the bond at par immediately if it wants to.

- A 13% unsecured bond with a nominal value of $40 million, which is redeemable at par in 10 years.

Mlima Co's board of directors (BoD) has been exploring the idea of redeeming both bonds to provide it with more flexibility when making future investment decisions. To do so, the BoD has decided to consider a public listing of the company on a major stock exchange. It is intended that a total of 100 million shares will be issued in the newly listed company. From the total shares, 20% will be sold to the public, 10% will be offered to the holders of the unsecured bond in exchange for redeeming the bond through an equity-for-debt swap, and the remaining 70% of the equity will remain in the hands of the current owners. The secured bond would be paid out of the funds raised from the listing.

The details of the possible listing and the distribution of equity were published in national newspapers recently. As a result, potential investors suggested that, due to the small proportion of shares offered to the public and for other reasons, the shares should be offered at a substantial discount of as much as 20% below the expected share price on the day of the listing.

Mlima Co, financial information

It is expected that after the listing, deployment of new strategies and greater financial flexibility will boost Mlima Co's future sales revenue and, for the next four years, the annual growth rate will be 120% of the previous two years' average growth rate. After the four years, the annual growth rate of the free cash flows to the company will be 3.5%, for the foreseeable future. Operating profit margins are expected to be maintained in the future. Although it can be assumed that the current tax-allowable depreciation is equivalent to the amount of investment needed to maintain the current level of operations, the company will require an additional investment in assets of 30c per $1 increase in sales revenue for the next four years.

EXTRACTS FROM MLIMA CO'S PAST THREE YEARS' STATEMENT OF PROFIT OR LOSS

Year ended	31 May 20X3	31 May 20X2	31 May 20X1
	$m	$m	$m
Sales revenue	389.1	366.3	344.7
Operating profit	58.4	54.9	51.7
Net interest costs	17.5	17.7	18.0
Profit before tax	40.9	37.2	33.7
Taxation	10.2	9.3	8.4
Profit after tax	30.7	27.9	25.3

Once listed, Mlima Co will be able to borrow future debt at an interest rate of 7%, which is only 3% higher than the risk-free rate of return. It has no plans to raise any new debt after listing, but any future debt will carry considerably fewer restrictive covenants. However, these plans do not take into consideration the Bahari project (see below).

Bahari project

Bahari is a small country with agriculture as its main economic activity. A recent geological survey concluded that there may be a rich deposit of copper available to be mined in the north-east of the country. This area is currently occupied by subsistence farmers, who would have to be relocated to other parts of the country. When the results of the survey were announced, some farmers protested that the proposed new farmland they would be moved to was less fertile and that their communities were being broken up. However, the protesters were intimidated and violently put down by the government, and the state-controlled media stopped reporting about them. Soon afterwards, their protests were ignored and forgotten.

In a meeting between the Bahari government and Mlima Co's BoD, the Bahari government offered Mlima Co exclusive rights to mine the copper. It is expected that there are enough deposits to last at least 15 years. Initial estimates suggest that the project will generate free cash flows of $4 million in the first year, rising by 100% per year in each of the next two years, and then by 15% in each of the two years after that. The free cash flows are then expected to stabilise at the Year 5 level for the remaining ten years.

The cost of the project, payable at the start, is expected to be $150 million, comprising machinery, working capital and the mining rights fee payable to the Bahari government. None of these costs is expected to be recoverable at the end of the project's 15-year life.

The Bahari government has offered Mlima Co a subsidised loan over 15 years for the full $150 million at an interest rate of 3% instead of Mlima Co's normal borrowing rate of 7%. The interest payable is allowable for taxation purposes. It can be assumed that Mlima Co's business risk is not expected to change as a result of undertaking the Bahari project.

At the conclusion of the meeting between the Bahari government and Mlima Co's BoD, the president of Bahari commented that working together would be like old times when he and Mlima Co's chief executive officer (CEO) used to run a business together.

Other information

Mlima Co's closest competitor is Ziwa Co, a listed company which mines metals worldwide. Mlima Co's directors are of the opinion that after listing Mlima Co's cost of capital should be based on Ziwa Co's ungeared cost of equity. Ziwa Co's cost of capital is estimated at 9.4%, its geared cost of equity is estimated at 16.83% and its pre-tax cost of debt is estimated at 4.76%. These costs are based on a capital structure comprising of 200 million shares, trading at $7 each, and $1,700 million 5% irredeemable bonds, trading at $105 per $100. Both Ziwa Co and Mlima Co pay tax at an annual rate of 25% on their taxable profits.

It can be assumed that all cash flows will be in $ instead of the Bahari currency and therefore Mlima Co does not have to take account of any foreign exchange exposure from this venture.

Required

(a)   Prepare a report for the BoD of Mlima Co that:

   (i)   Explains why Mlima Co's directors are of the opinion that Mlima Co's cost of capital should be based on Ziwa Co's ungeared cost of equity and, showing relevant calculations, estimate an appropriate cost of capital for Mlima Co.   **(7 marks)**

   (ii)   Estimates Mlima Co's value without undertaking the Bahari project and then with the Bahari project. The valuations should use the free cash flow methodology and the cost of capital calculated in part (i). Include relevant calculations.   **(14 marks)**

   (iii)   Advises the BoD whether or not the unsecured bond holders are likely to accept the equity-for-debt swap offer. Include relevant calculations.   **(5 marks)**

(iv) Advises the BoD on the listing and the possible share price range, if a total of 100 million shares are issued. The advice should also include:

    (1) A discussion of the assumptions made in estimating the share price range

    (2) In addition to the reasons mentioned in the scenario above, a brief explanation of other possible reasons for changing its status from a private company to a listed one

    (3) An assessment of the possible reasons for issuing the share price at a discount for the initial listing   **(12 marks)**

Professional marks will be awarded in part (a) for the format, structure and presentation of the report.   **(4 marks)**

(b) Discuss the possible impact on, and response of, Mlima Co to the following ethical issues, with respect to the Bahari project:

(i) The relocation of the farmers

(ii) The relationship between the Bahari president and Mlima Co's CEO

Note. The total marks will be split equally between each part.   **(8 marks)**

(Total = 50 marks)

SECTION B: BOTH QUESTIONS to be attempted

Question 2

Casasophia Co, based in a European country that uses the euro (€), constructs and maintains advanced energy efficient commercial properties around the world. It has just completed a major project in the US and is due to receive the final payment of US$20 million in four months.

Casasophia Co is planning to commence a major construction and maintenance project in Mazabia, a small African country, in six months' time. This government-owned project is expected to last for three years during which time Casasophia Co will complete the construction of state-of-the-art energy efficient properties and provide training to a local Mazabian company in maintaining the properties. The carbon-neutral status of the building project has attracted some grant funding from the European Union, and these funds will be provided to the Mazabian government in Mazabian Shillings (MShs).

Casasophia Co intends to finance the project using the US$20 million it is due to receive and borrow the rest through a € loan. It is intended that the US$ receipts will be converted into € and invested in short-dated treasury bills until they are required. These funds, plus the loan, will be converted into MShs on the date required, at the spot rate at that time.

Mazabia's government requires Casasophia Co to deposit the MShs2.64 billion it needs for the project, with Mazabia's central bank, at the commencement of the project. In return, Casasophia Co will receive a fixed sum of MShs1.5 billion after tax, at the end of each year for a period of three years. Neither of these amounts is subject to inflationary increases. The relevant risk-adjusted discount rate for the project is assumed to be 12%.

Financial information

Exchange rates available to Casasophia

	Per €1	Per €1
Spot	US$1.3585–US$1.3618	MShs116–MShs128
4-month forward	US$1.3588–US$1.3623	Not available

Currency futures (Contract size €125,000, Quotation: US$ per €1)

2-month expiry	1.3633
5-month expiry	1.3698

Currency options (Contract size €125,000, Exercise price quotation: US$ per €1, cents per euro)

	Calls		Puts	
Exercise price	2-month expiry	5-month expiry	2-month expiry	5-month expiry
1.36	2.35	2.80	2.47	2.98
1.38	1.88	2.23	4.23	4.64

Casasophia Co local government base rate	2.20%
Mazabia government base rate	10.80%
Yield on short-dated euro treasury bills	1.80%

(assume 360-day year)

Mazabia's current annual inflation rate is 9.7% and is expected to remain at this level for the next six months. However, after that, there is considerable uncertainty about the future and the annual level of inflation could be anywhere between 5% and 15% for the next few years. The country where Casasophia Co is based is expected to have a stable level of inflation at 1.2% per year for the foreseeable future. A local bank in Mazabia has offered Casasophia Co the opportunity to swap the annual income of MShs1.5 billion receivable in each of the next three years for euros, at the estimated annual MShs/€ forward rates based on the current government base rates.

Required

(a) Advise Casasophia Co on, and recommend, an appropriate hedging strategy for the US$ income it is due to receive in four months. Include all relevant calculations. **(15 marks)**

(b) Given that Casasophia Co agrees to the local bank's offer of the swap, calculate the net present value of the project in six months' time, in €. Discuss whether the swap would be beneficial to Casasophia Co. **(10 marks)**

(Total = 25 marks)

Question 3

Staple Group is one of Barland's biggest media groups. It consists of four divisions, organised as follows:

- **Staple National** – the national newspaper, the *Daily Staple*. This division's revenues and operating profits have decreased for the last two years.

- **Staple Local** – a portfolio of 18 local and regional newspapers. This division's operating profits have fallen for the last five years and operating profits and cash flows are forecast to be negative in the next financial year. Other newspaper groups with local titles have also reported significant falls in profitability recently.

- **Staple View** – a package of digital channels showing sporting events and programmes for a family audience. Staple Group's board has been pleased with this division's recent performance, but it believes that the division will only be able to sustain a growth rate of 4% in operating profits and cash flows unless it can buy the rights to show more major sporting events. Over the last year, Staple View's biggest competitor in this sector has acquired two smaller digital broadcasters.

- **Staple Investor** – established from a business which was acquired three years ago, this division offers services for investors including research, publications, training events and conferences. The division gained a number of new clients over the last year and has thus shown good growth in revenues and operating profits.

Some of Staple Group's institutional investors have expressed concern about the fall in profitability of the two newspaper divisions.

The following summarised data relates to the group's last accounting year. The percentage changes in pre-tax profits and revenues are changes in the most recent figures compared with the previous year.

	Total	National	Local	View	Investor
			Division		
Revenues ($m)	1,371.7	602.4	151.7	496.5	121.1
Increase/(decrease) in revenues (%)		(5.1)	(14.7)	8.2	16.5
Pre-tax profits ($m)	177.3	75.6	4.5	73.3	23.9
Increase/(decrease) in pre-tax profits (%)		(4.1)	(12.6)	7.4	19.1
Post-tax cash flows ($m)	120.2	50.7	0.3	53.5	15.7
Share of group net assets ($m)	635.8	267.0	66.6	251.2	51.0
Share of group long-term liabilities ($m)	230.9	104.4	23.1	93.4	10.0

Staple Group's board regards the *Daily Staple* as a central element of the group's future. The directors are currently considering a number of investment plans, including the development of digital platforms for the *Daily Staple*. The finance director has costed the investment programme at $150 million. The board would prefer to fund the investment programme by disposing of parts or all of one of the other divisions. The following information is available to help assess the value of each division:

1   One of Staple Group's competitors, Postway Co, has contacted Staple Group's directors asking if they would be interested in selling 15 of the local and regional newspapers for $60 million. Staple Group's finance director believes this offer is low and wishes to use the net assets valuation method to evaluate a minimum price for the Staple Local division.

2   Staple Group's finance director believes that a valuation using free cash flows would provide a fair estimate of the value of the Staple View division. Over the last year, investment in additional non-current assets for the Staple View division has been $12.5 million and the incremental working capital investment has been $6.2 million. These investment levels will have to increase at 4% annually in order to support the expected sustainable increases in operating profit and cash flow.

3   Staple Group's finance director believes that the valuation of the Staple Investor division needs to reflect the potential it derives from the expertise and experience of its staff. The finance director has calculated a value of $118.5 million for this division, based on the earnings made last year but also allowing for the additional earnings which he believes that the expert staff in the division will be able to generate in future years.

Assume a risk-adjusted, all-equity financed, cost of capital of 12% and a tax rate of 30%. Goodwill should be ignored in any calculations.

Staple Group's finance and human resources directors are looking at the staffing of the two newspaper divisions. The finance director proposes dismissing most staff who have worked for the group for less than two years, two years' employment being when staff would be entitled to enhanced statutory employment protection. The finance director also proposes a redundancy programme for longer-serving staff, selecting for redundancy employees who have complained particularly strongly about recent changes in working conditions. There is a commitment in Staple Group's annual report to treat employees fairly, communicate with them regularly and enhance employees' performance by structured development.

Required

(a)   Evaluate the options for disposing of parts of Staple Group, using the financial information to assess possible disposal prices. The evaluation should include a discussion of the benefits and drawbacks to Staple Group from disposing of parts of Staple Group.

(19 marks)

(b)   Discuss the significance of the finance director's proposals for reduction in staff costs for Staple Group's relationships with its shareholders and employees and discuss the ethical implications of the proposals.

(6 marks)

(Total = 25 marks)

Answers

DO NOT TURN THIS PAGE UNTIL YOU HAVE
COMPLETED THE MOCK EXAM

Exam success skills

In any AFM exam it will be important to apply good general exam technique by using the six exam success skills identified at the start of the Revision Kit, in the section covering 'essential skills.' These skills are: 1. Case scenario: Managing information; 2. Correct interpretation of requirements; 3. Answer planning: Priorities, structure and logic; 4. Efficient numerical analysis; 5. Effective writing and presentation; and 6. Good time management.

Skill	Examples
Managing information	It is crucially important to assimilate the information in the question scenario.
	In longer questions, such as the 50 mark question, it is difficult to assimilate information by simply starting at the beginning and read to the end because there is so much information to take in.
	Instead it is sensible to take an **active approach** to reading each question. Read enough of the question to get an idea of the basic scenario and then read the initial requirements so that you understand the first things that you are expected to do with this information.
	For example, in Question 1 the lengthy scenario makes a lot more sense if, before reading all of it, you are aware that the first requirements require a free cash flow valuation using an ungeared cost of equity based on another company in the same industry.
Correct Interpretation of requirements	Be careful to interpret the verbs used in the question requirements carefully.
	For example, in Q3a the verb 'evaluate' clearly implies that calculations are expected.
	Also be careful to identify where a question requirement contains more than one instruction.
	For example, in Q1b where discussion of the impact on AND response of various stakeholders is requested, and in Q3b where there are two areas that need to be discussed.
Answer planning	This is always important in AFM questions.
	For example, in risk management questions (such as Q2), it is especially important that your plan correctly identifies (i) the risk being faced and (ii) the relevant timings. If you get these wrong, then there will be a cap on the number of marks that you can score (however accurate your answers are).
Efficient numerical analysis	It is essential that the marker can follow your workings and your logic.
	It is also important that you accept that under exam conditions you will not get <u>all</u> the calculations correct, and that this is not necessary in order to score a strong pass mark.
	If you make a mistake early in your calculations that affects your later calculations then the marker will only penalise the error you have made, and not its follow-on impact on other calculations. This means that it is not normally a good use of your time to correct such errors during the exam.
	For example, in Question 2 it is important that your calculations of the futures hedge clearly shows the type of futures contract and the number of contracts, but the exact accuracy (eg whether or not to use a forward contract to hedge any over or under hedge arising from the future) is not crucial.

ANSWERS

Skill	Examples
Effective writing and presentation	In Q1 there are four marks available for professional structure (eg use of sub-headings, appendices etc). Many of the techniques used here are good practice in all questions throughout the exam.
	It is also very important to relate your points to the scenario and to the requirement wherever possible. This does not mean simply repeating the details from the question but using this information to help to explain the point you are making.
	For example, in Q3(b) there is a commitment in the annual report to treat employees fairly, but why is this relevant in a discussion of ethics?
Good Time Management	The exam is 3 hours 15 minutes long, which translates to 1.95 minutes per mark.
	If you build in an allowance of 20% of your time for assimilating the scenario and planning, this falls to 1.56 minutes per mark (1.95 × 0.8).
	It is essential that you do not allow yourself to become bogged down in the harder numerical areas of the exam.
	For example, it is especially easy to get bogged down in Q1(a) (ii) in this exam.
	At the beginning of a question, work out the amount of time you should be spending on
	(a) Planning:
	(i) for a 25 mark question this will be about 1.95 × 25 marks × 20% = 10 minutes
	(ii) for a 50 mark question this should be about 20 mins.
	(b) Writing your answer to each requirement:
	(iii) Take the mark allocation and multiply by 1.56 minutes per mark.

Diagnostic

Did you apply these skills when reading, planning, and writing up your answer? Identify the exam success skills where you think you need to improve and capture your thoughts here of what you want to achieve when attempting questions in future.

Question 1

Marking scheme

			Marks	
(a)	(i)	Explanation of Mlima Co's cost of capital based on Ziwa Co's ungeared cost of equity	3	
		Ziwa Co, cost of ungeared equity	4	
				7
	(ii)	Sales revenue growth rates	1	
		Operating profit rate	1	
		Estimate of free cash flows and PV of free cash flows for Years 1 to 4	4	
		PV of free cash flows after Year 4	2	
		Base case Bahari project value	2	
		Annual tax shield benefit	1	
		Annual subsidy benefits	1	
		PV of tax shield and subsidy benefits	1	
		Value of the Bahari project	1	
				14
	(iii)	Calculation of unsecured bond value	2	
		Comment	2	
		Limitation	1	
				5

	Marks
(iv) Comments on the range of values	3–4
Discussion of assumptions	3–4
Explanation for additional reasons for listing	2–3
Assessment of reasons for discounted share price	2–3
Conclusion	1–2
	Max 12

Professional marks

Report format	1
Layout, presentation and structure	3
	4

(b) Discussion of relocation of farmers	4–5
Discussion of relationship between Bahari president and Mlima Co CEO	4–5
	Max 8
	50

(a) **Report**

To: Board of directors, Mlima Co
From: AN Consultant
Subject: Initial public listing: price range and implications
Date: XX/XX/XX

This report considers a range of values for Mlima Co to consider in preparation for the proposed public listing. These values are based on 100 million shares being issued. The assumptions made in determining these values are discussed and the likelihood of the equity-for-debt swap being successful is also considered. Finally the report will evaluate other reasons for listing and also why the shares should be issued at a discount.

Mlima Co cost of capital

Ziwa Co's ungeared cost of equity represents the return Ziwa Co's shareholders would require if Ziwa Co was financed entirely by equity. This return would compensate the shareholders for the business risk of Ziwa Co's operations.

Since Mlima Co is in the same industry, and therefore faces the **same business risk**, this required rate of return should also compensate Mlima Co's shareholders. This rate would be used as Mlima Co's cost of capital as it is expecting to have no debt and therefore this rate **does not need adjusting for financial risk**. Therefore the cost of equity is also the cost of capital. This cost of capital is calculated in Appendix 1 as 11%.

Mlima Co estimated value

Using the cost of capital of 11%, the value of Mlima Co is calculated as $564.9 million (see Appendix 2 for full calculation), before considering the proposed Bahari project. The value of the Bahari investment, without considering the tax shield and subsidy benefits from the subsidised government loan, does not exceed the initial investment. When the tax and subsidy benefits are considered, the present value of the Bahari project is $21.5 million (see Appendix 3 for full calculation). This gives a total value for Mlima Co of just over $586 million. This gives the **following potential share prices**, based on 100 million shares, including the effect of the suggested 20% share price discount.

Potential share price	Excluding Bahari project	Including Bahari project
Full value	$5.65 per share	$5.86 per share
20% discount	$4.52 per share	$4.69 per share

Equity-for-debt swap

The unsecured bond is currently estimated to be worth $56.8 million (see Appendix 4 for full calculation). It is proposed that the existing bond holders will be offered a 10% stake in Mlima Co post-listing, which means that **only the value at $5.86 per share would leave the bond holders better off**, and therefore would be the only acceptable price. If the lowest price of $4.52 per share is used, then the equity stake would need to be around 12.6% for the bond holders to accept the offer (56.8m/4.52 = 12.566).

The bond value is based on a yield to maturity of 7%, because Mlima Co can borrow at 7%, so this is therefore its current yield. The yield could be **more accurately estimated** if it was based on future risk-free rates and the credit spreads for the company.

Assumptions

The main assumptions are over the **accuracy of the estimates** used in producing the valuation. The value of Mlima Co is based on estimated future growth rates, profit margins, tax rates and capital investment. The future growth rates and margins are based on **past data, which may not be a reliable indicator of future prospects**. The Bahari project includes estimated cash flows for 15 years and the reasonableness of these estimates needs to be considered to see if they are realistic.

The cost of capital used for Mlima Co is based on Ziwa Co's ungeared cost of equity, on the basis that the business risk is the same for both companies as they operate in the same industry. However, it is possible that the **business risks are different**, for example due to geographical locations, and therefore the cost of capital is not appropriate for Mlima Co. Accepting the Bahari project could also affect the business risk of Mlima Co.

The value of the Bahari project is based on the Bahari government providing the promised subsidised loan. Mlima Co needs to consider whether the full subsidy will definitely be provided for the full 15 years and whether a change of government may change the position. There may also be other **political risks** which need to be assessed fully.

Transaction costs for the listing have been ignored as they are assumed to be insignificant. It should be confirmed that this is the case before making a final decision.

Reasons for a public listing

The main reason behind this public listing is to remove the debt from the company. Other reasons for pursuing a public listing include: a **gain in prestige** for the company by listing on a recognised stock exchange, having **greater access to sources of finance** and being able to raise funds more quickly as a result, providing shareholders with a value for their equity stake and enabling them to **realise their investment** if they wish to do so.

Issuing shares at a discount

Since the public will only be issued 20% of the share capital from the initial listing, they will be **minority shareholders** and have a limited ability to influence the decision making of Mlima Co. Even if they voted as a bloc, they would not be able to overturn the decision on their own. The discounted share price, would therefore compensate the shareholders for the **additional risk** of being minority shareholders. The position of the unsecured bond holders should also be considered. On the assumption that they hold 12.6% of the equity (as discussed earlier) they could form a bloc with the new shareholders of 32.6%, which would be **enough to influence company decisions**. Whether they would form a bloc with new shareholders or are more closely aligned with the interests of the current owners is something that should be looked into.

Shares are often issued at a discount to ensure that they all get sold. This is even more common for a new listing and the price of the shares does usually rise immediately after the listing.

Conclusion

A price range for the listing of between $4.52 and $5.86 per share has been calculated, depending on whether the Bahari project is undertaken and whether the shares are offered at a discount of 20%. It is recommended that Mlima Co consults the underwriters for the share issue, to carry out book-building to assess the price that potential investors are willing to pay.

If 20% of the shares (20 million shares) are sold to the public at $4.52 per share, the listing will raise just over $90 million. $80 million would then be spent redeeming the secured bond, leaving just in excess of $10 million of funds remaining. Mlima Co needs to consider whether these funds will be **sufficient to carry on its operations**. The Bahari investment may result in a change to the desired capital structure of the company, which may also have an impact on the cost of capital.

Becoming a listed company will also result in listing costs and **additional annual costs** to meet compliance and reporting requirements. These factors will need to be balanced against the benefits of listing before making a decision whether or not to proceed.

Appendices

Appendix 1: Mlima cost of capital

Ziwa Co market value of debt = 105/100 × 1,700m = $1,785m

Ziwa Co market value of equity = 200m × $7 = $1,400m

Ziwa Co ungeared cost of equity using $k_{eg} = k_{eu} + (1 - t)(k_{eu} - k_d)$ D/E

$16.83\% = k_{eu} + 0.75(k_{eu} - 4.76\%) \times 1,785/1,400$

$16.83\% + 4.55\% = 1.9563 k_{eu}$

$k_{eu} = 10.93\%$ (say 11%)

Appendix 2: Value of Mlima Co prior to Bahari project

Past 2 years' sales growth = $\sqrt{\dfrac{389.1}{344.7}} - 1 = 0.0625$ or 6.25%

Expected growth for 4 years = 1.2 × 6.25% = 7.5%

Operating profit margin (historic)

20X3 58.4/389.1 = 0.150

20X2 54.9/366.3 = 0.150

20X1 51.7/344.7 = 0.150

Operating profit margin is expected to be 15%.

Year	1 $m	2 $m	3 $m	4 $m	4+ $m
Sales revenue (increasing at 7.5%)	418.3	449.7	483.4	519.7	
Operating profit (15%)	62.7	67.5	72.5	78.0	
Tax at 25%	(15.7)	(16.9)	(18.1)	(19.5)	
Additional capital investment (W1)	(8.8)	(9.4)	(10.1)	(10.9)	
Free cash flows	38.2	41.2	44.3	47.6	49.3*
Discount factor (11%)	0.901	0.812	0.731	0.659	8.787**
PV of free cash flows	34.4	33.5	32.4	31.4	433.2

Value of company = $564.9 million

* 47.6 × 1.035 = 49.3

** 1/(0.11 − 0.035) × 0.659 = 8.787

Working

Year	1 $m	2 $m	3 $m	4 $m
Sales revenue	418.3	449.7	483.4	519.7
Increase in revenue	29.2	31.4	33.7	36.3
30% of increase	8.8	9.4	10.1	10.9

Appendix 3: Value of Bahari project

Base case

Year	Free cash flow	Discount factor 11%	PV
	$m		$m
0	(150)	1.000	(150.0)
1	4	0.901	3.6
2	8	0.812	6.5
3	16	0.731	11.7
4	18.4	0.659	12.1
5	21.2	0.593	12.6
6–15	21.2	3.492	74.0
			(29.5)

10-year annuity discounted for 5 years = 5.889 × 0.593

Annual tax shield benefit = 3% × 150m × 25% = $1.1m

Subsidy benefit = 4% × 150m × 0.75 = $4.5m

Total annual benefit = $5.6 million

Annuity factor (7%, 15 years) = 9.108

PV of tax shield and subsidy benefit = 5.6m × 9.108 = $51.0m

APV = ($29.5m) + $51.0m = $21.5m

Appendix 4: Value of unsecured bond

Annual interest = 13% × 40m = $5.2m

Assume a yield to maturity of 7%. A 10-year annuity factor at 7% is 7.024

Discount factor for redemption of bond (7%, 10 years) is 0.508

Bond value = 5.2m × 7.024 + 40m × 0.508 = $56.8m

(b) The activities of Mlima Co are likely to be of greater interest and be **scrutinised more closely** once it is listed. The company needs to consider the ethical implications of both situations and whether Mlima Co is complying with its own ethical code (if it has one). Regarding the relocation of the farmers, Mlima Co needs to judge where its responsibility lies. It may decide that this is a **matter between the farmers and the government**, and that Mlima Co is not responsible (either directly or indirectly) for the current situation. If Mlima Co does not agree to the offer, it seems likely that the **mining rights would be given to another company** and so the farmers' situation would not improve by Mlima Co walking away from the deal. Mlima may be better off by influencing the government over this issue by asking it to keep the farmers together and to offer them more fertile land. In addition, Mlima Co could offer jobs and training to any farmers who choose to remain where they are.

In the case of the Bahari president and Mlima Co's CEO, Mlima Co must ensure that any negotiation was transparent and there was **no bribery or other illegal practice involved**. If the company and the government can show that decisions have been made in the **best interests** of the country and Mlima Co, and no individuals benefited from the decision, then it should not be seen negatively. Indeed, it is good for business to have strong relationships and this can create a **competitive advantage**.

Mlima should consider how it would respond to public scrutiny of these issues, possibly even pre-empting issues by releasing press statements to explain positions.

Question 2

Marking scheme

			Marks
(a)	Forward contract calculation	1	
	Forward contract comment	1	
	Futures contracts calculations	3	
	Futures contracts comments	2	
	Option contracts calculations	4	
	Option contracts comments	2–3	
	Conclusion	1	
			Max 15
(b)	Estimates of forward rates	3	
	Estimates of present values and net present value in euros	3	
	Discussion	4–5	
			Max 10
			25

(a) **Hedging strategy**

Forward contract

The company will be receiving US$ therefore we use US$1.3623 as the rate.

Receipt in € = US$20m/1.3623 = €14,681,054

The hedge fixes the rate at €1 = US$1.3623. This rate is legally binding.

Futures contract

A two-month contract is too short for the required hedge period therefore we must use a five-month contract. The contract will be closed out in four months' time.

Number of contracts = €14,624,159/€125,000 = 117 contracts

You can estimate the futures rate using the five-month price, the spot rate and the four-month forward rate:

We could estimate the number of contracts needed as:

$'000	€'000	Contract size		No contracts
20,000	1.3698	14,601	125	117

Outcome

The outcome will depend on the spot and future prices. The futures price can be estimated as follows:

	Now	4 months
5-month future	1.3698	1.3714 balance
Spot rate	1.3618	1.3698 assumed
Basis	0.0080 × 1/5 =	0.0016
	5 months	1 month remaining

Assuming that the spot rate in four months is the same as the futures rate, the outcome will be:

	$'000	€'000
Actual	$20,000	
Assumed spot in 4 months		1.3698 (alternative assumptions are possible)
In euros ('000)		€14,601

Future

Opening	1.3698	to buy
Closing	1.3714	to sell
Ticks	(0.0016)	

Profit ('000) €17
(117 × 125,000 × 0.0016/spot 1.3698)

		€14,618
Effective rate	(20,000/14,618)	1.3682

Alternative shortcut approach

Opening future rate – closing basis = 1.3698 – 0.0016 = effective rate 1.3682

Comments

The futures rate is worse than the forward rate. Futures contracts are marked to market on a daily basis and require margin payments as a result. As with forward contracts, futures contracts fix the rates and are legally binding.

Options

With options the holder has the right but not the obligation to exercise the option (that is, the option will be exercised if it is beneficial to the holder). However, there is a premium to be paid for this flexibility, making options more expensive than futures and forward contracts.

To protect itself against a weakening US$, Casasophia will purchase euro call options.

Exercise price = $1.36

Receipts = $20m/1.36 = €14,705,882

Number of contracts = €14,705,882/€125,000 = 117.6 contracts (117 contracts)

With 117 contracts, receipts = €125,000 × 117 = €14,625,000

Premium payable = $0.0280 × 117 × 125,000 = $409,500 (or $409,500/1.3585 = €301,435)

Amount not hedged = US$20m – (117 × €125,000 × 1.36) = US$110,000

This amount can be hedged using a 4-month forward contract as follows:

US$110,000/1.3623 = €80,746

Total receipts = €14,625,000 – €301,435 + €80,746 = **€14,404,311**

Exercise price = $1.38

Receipts = $20m/1.38 = €14,492,754

Number of contracts = €14,492,754/€125,000 = 115.9 contracts (purchase 115 contracts)

With 115 contracts, receipts = €125,000 × 115 = €14,375,000

Premium payable = $0.0223 × 115 × 125,000 = US$320,563 (or $320,563/1.3585 = €235,968)

Amount not hedged = US$20m – (115 × €125,000 × 1.38) = US$162,500

This amount can be hedged using a 4-month forward contract as follows:

US$162,500/1.3623 = €119,284

Total receipts = €14,375,000 – €235,968 + €119,284 = **€14,258,316**

The receipts from either of the options are considerably lower than those from either the futures contract or the forward contract. This is primarily due to the premiums payable to secure the flexibility that options offer. The US$ would have to move significantly against the € to allow Casasophia to cover the cost of the premiums.

Conclusion

Based on the calculations above, it is recommended that Casasophia uses forward contracts to hedge against the US$ depreciating against the € in order to maximise receipts. The company should be aware that once the contract is agreed, the price is fixed and is legally binding. In addition, there is no formal exchange for forward contracts, thus giving rise to default risk.

(b) **Project NPV**

Expected forward rates (using interest rate parity)

$$F_0 = S_0 \times \frac{\left(1 + i_c\right)}{\left(1 + i_b\right)}$$

Year	Forward rate (€1 = MShs)
Half year	128 × (1.108/1.022) = 138.77
	128 + [(138.77 – 128)/2] = 133.38
1.5 years	133.38 × (1.108/1.022) = 144.60
2.5 years	144.60 × (1.108/1.022) = 156.77
3.5 years	156.77 × (1.108/1.022) = 169.96

NPV calculation (note that Year 1 actually means 1.5 years from now as project starts in six months' time)

Year	1	2	3
Income (MShs, million)	1,500	1,500	1,500
Forward rate	144.60	156.77	169.96
Income (€m)	10.37	9.57	8.82
Discount factor (12%)	0.893	0.797	0.712
DCF	9.26	7.63	6.28

Total present value = €23.17 million

Expected spot rate (MShs) in 12 months' time (using purchasing power parity):

$$S_1 = S_0 \times \frac{\left(1+h_c\right)}{\left(1+h_b\right)}$$

$S_1 = 116 \times (1 + 0.097)/(1 + 0.012) = 125.74$

In six months' time expected spot rate = $116 + (125.74 - 116)/2 = 120.9$

Total investment required in € = MShs2.64b/120.9 = €21.84m

NPV = €1.33m

Will the swap be beneficial for Casasophia?

Forward rates based on interest rate parity show that MShs is depreciating against the € as interest rates are much higher in Mazabia (10.8%) than in the European country (2.2%). However, even with a depreciating MShs the project is still worthwhile (positive NPV).

When forward rates are estimated using purchasing power parity, it is assumed that forward rates will change according to differences between the two countries' inflation rates. If Mazabia's inflation rate is greater than the European country's rate, the MShs will depreciate against the €.

We are told that Mazabia's inflation rate could vary between 5% and 15% over the next few years, therefore a swap would appear to be advantageous (as it would fix the future exchange rates). Without the swap there will be uncertainty over the NPV of the project.

Default risk should also be taken into consideration and Casasophia may ask the government of Mazabia to act as a guarantor in order to reduce the risk.

The grant funding will be provided directly to the Mazabian government in MShs. It may be worthwhile for Casasophia to explore the possibility of receiving the grant directly in € as this would reduce currency exposure.

Question 3

Workbook references. Valuations are covered in Chapter 8, and reorganisations in Chapter 15.

Easy marks. Part (b) offers easy marks if you address both parts of the question.

Examining team's comments. A sizeable number of candidates attempted to value the whole of the company instead of parts of the company.

Marking scheme

		Marks	
(a)	Sale of Staple Local		
	Calculations/comments on figures	2	
	Discussion of benefits/drawbacks	3–4	
	Sale of Staple View		
	Calculations/comments on figures	3	
	Discussion of benefits/drawbacks	3–4	
	Sale of Staple Investor		
	Comments on figures	2	
	Discussion of benefits/drawbacks	3–4	
	Other points/conclusion	2–3	
			Max 19
(b)	Discussion of importance of different stakeholders and possible conflicts	3–4	
	Discussion of other ethical issues	2–3	
			Max 6
			25

(a) **Staple Local**

Net assets valuation = 15/18 × $66.6m = $55.5m.

It is assumed that the titles in this division are equal in size.

The division's pre-tax profits are $4.5 million and post-tax cash flows are $0.3 million, with losses forecast for the next year. Therefore any valuation based on current or future expected earnings is likely to be lower than the net assets valuation.

Benefits of selling Staple Local

The local newspapers seem to have the poorest prospects of any part of the group. Further investment may not make a big difference, if the market for local newspapers is in long-term decline.

The offer from Postway Co gives Staple Group the chance to gain cash immediately and to dispose of the papers. The alternative of selling the titles off piecemeal is an uncertain strategy, both in terms of the timescale required and the amounts which can be realised for individual titles. It is very likely that the titles with the best prospects would be sold first, leaving Staple Group with a remaining portfolio which is of very little value.

Drawbacks of selling Staple Local

The offer is not much more than a net asset valuation of the titles. The amount of cash from the sale to Postway Co will be insufficient for the level of investment required in the *Daily Staple*.

The digital platforms which will be developed for the *Daily Staple* could also be used to boost the local papers. Staff on the local titles could have an important role to play in providing content for the platforms.

Loss of the local titles may mean loss of economies of size. In particular, printing arrangements may be more economic if both national and local titles are printed at the same locations.

Staple View

Free cash flows to equity = $53.5m − $12.5m − $6.2m = $34.8m

Free cash flow valuation to equity = $34.8m (1.04)/(0.12 − 0.04) = $452.4m

The assumption of constant growth is most important in this valuation. It is possibly fairly conservative but, just as faster growth could be achieved by gaining the rights to broadcast more sporting events, results may be threatened if Staple View loses any of the rights which it currently has.

Benefits of selling Staple View

Present circumstances may be favourable for selling the television channels, given their current profitability. Staple Group may be able to obtain a better offer from a competitor than in the future, given recent acquisition activity in this sector.

Selling Staple View will certainly generate more cash than selling either of the smaller divisions. This will allow investment not only in the *Daily Staple*, but also in the other divisions, and possibly targeted strategic acquisitions.

Drawbacks of selling Staple View

The television channels have become a very important part of Staple Group. Investors may believe that the group should be focusing on further investment in this division rather than investing in the *Daily Staple*, which may be in decline.

Selling the television channels removes an important opportunity for cross-selling. Newspaper coverage can be used to publicise important programmes on the television channels and the television channels can be used for advertising the newspaper.

Staple View is a bigger part of the group than the other two divisions and therefore selling it is likely to mean a bigger reduction in the group's borrowing capacity.

Staple Investor

The valuation made by the finance director is questionable as it is based on one year's profits, which may not be sustainable. There is no information about how the additional earnings have been calculated whether the finance director has used a widely accepted method of valuation or just a best estimate. If a premium for additional earnings is justified, there is also no information about whether the benefit from staff's expertise and experience is assumed to be perpetual or just to last for a certain number of years.

Benefits of selling Staple Investor

This division appears to have great potential. Staple Group will be able to sell this division from a position of strength, rather than it being seen as a forced sale like selling the Staple Local division might be.

The division is in a specialist sector which is separate from the other areas in which Staple Group operates. It is not an integral part of the group in terms of the directors' current core strategy.

Drawbacks of selling Staple Investor

The division currently has the highest profit margin at 19.7% compared with Staple National (12.5%), Staple Local (3.0%) and Staple View (14.8%). It seems likely to continue to deliver good results over the next few years. Investors may feel that it is the part of the group which offers the safest prospect of satisfactory returns.

Investors may be happy with the structure of the group as it is, as it offers them some diversification. Selling the Staple Investor division and focusing more on the newspaper parts of the group may result in investors seeking diversification by selling some of the shareholding in Staple Group and investing elsewhere.

Although Staple Group's management may believe that the valuation gives a good indication of the division's true value, they may not be able to sell the division for this amount now. If the division remains within the group, they may achieve a higher price in a few years' time. Even if Staple Investor could be sold for the $118.5 million valuation, this is less than the $150 million required for the planned investment.

Conclusion

Selling the Staple View division offers the directors the best chance to obtain the funds they require for their preferred strategy of investment in the *Daily Staple*. However, the directors are not considering the possibility of selling the *Daily Staple*, perhaps in conjunction with selling the local newspapers as well. Although this could be seen as selling off the part of the group which has previously been essential to its success, it would allow Staple Group to raise the funds for further investment in the television channels and the Staple Investor division. It could allow the directors to focus on the parts of the group which have been the most successful recently and offer the best prospects for future success.

(b) **Stakeholder conflicts**

If Staple Group takes a simple view of the role of stakeholders, it will prioritise the interest of shareholders over other stakeholders, particularly employees here, and take whatever actions are required to maximise profitability. However, in Staple Group's position, there may be a complication because of the differing requirements of shareholders. Some may want high short-term profits and dividends, which may imply significant cost cutting in underperforming divisions. Other shareholders may wish to see profits maximised over the long term and may worry that short-term cost cutting may result in a reduction of investment and adversely affect staff performance at an important time.

Transformational change of the newspaper business is likely to require the co-operation of at least some current employees. Inevitably redundancy will create uncertainty and perhaps prompt some staff to leave voluntarily. Staple Group's management may want to identify some key current employees who can lead the change and try to retain them.

Also the policy of making employees who have not been with the group very long redundant is likely to make it difficult to recruit good new employees. The group will probably create new roles as a result of its digital investment, but people may be unwilling to join the group if it has a reputation for bad faith and not fulfilling promises to develop its staff.

Ethical issues

The significance of what the firm's annual report says about its treatment of employees may depend on how specific it is. A promise to treat employees fairly is rather vague and may not carry much weight, although it broadly commits the firm to the ethical principle of objectivity. If, however, the policy makes more specific statements about engaging with employees and goes further in the statement beyond what is required by law, then Staple Group is arguably showing a lack of honesty if it does not fulfil the commitments it has made.

The suggestion that managers should ensure that employees who are perceived to be 'troublemakers' should be the first to be chosen for redundancy is dubious ethically. If managers do this, then they may be breaking the law, and would certainly be acting with a lack of honesty and transparency.

ACCA

Advanced Financial Management

Mock Examination 2
Specimen exam

Questions	
Time allowed 3 hours and 15 minutes	
Section A	THIS question is compulsory and MUST be attempted
Section B	BOTH questions to be attempted

DO NOT OPEN THIS EXAM UNTIL YOU ARE READY TO START
UNDER EXAMINATION CONDITIONS

SECTION A: THIS QUESTION is compulsory and MUST be attempted

Question 1

Cocoa-Mocha-Chai (CMC) Co is a large, listed company based in Switzerland and uses Swiss Francs as its currency. It imports tea, coffee and cocoa from countries around the world, and sells its blended products to supermarkets and large retailers worldwide. The company has production facilities located in two European ports where raw materials are brought for processing, and from where finished products are shipped out. All raw material purchases are paid for in US dollars (US$), while all sales are invoiced in Swiss francs (CHF).

Until recently CMC Co had no intention of hedging its foreign currency exposures, interest rate exposures or commodity price fluctuations, and stated this intent in its annual report. However, after consultations with senior and middle managers, the company's new board of directors (BoD) has been reviewing its risk management and operations strategies.

You are a financial consultant hired by CMC to work on the following two proposals which have been put forward by the BoD for further consideration:

Proposal one

Setting up a treasury function to manage the foreign currency and interest rate exposures (but not commodity price fluctuations) using derivative products. The treasury function would be headed by the finance director. The purchasing director, who initiated the idea of having a treasury function, was of the opinion that this would enable her management team to make better decisions. The finance director also supported the idea as he felt this would increase his influence on the BoD and strengthen his case for an increase in his remuneration.

In order to assist in the further consideration of this proposal, the BoD wants you to use the following upcoming foreign currency and interest rate exposures to demonstrate how they would be managed by the treasury function:

(i)   A payment of US$5,060,000 which is due in four months' time; and

(ii)   A four-year CHF60,000,000 loan taken out to part-fund the setting up of four branches (see proposal two below). Interest will be payable on the loan at a fixed annual rate of 2.2% or a floating annual rate based on the yield curve rate plus 0.40%. The loan's principal amount will be repayable in full at the end of the fourth year.

Additional information relating to proposal one

The current spot rate is US$1.0635 per CHF1. The current annual inflation rate in the US is three times higher than Switzerland.

The following derivative products are available to CMC Co to manage the exposures of the US$ payment and the interest on the loan:

Exchange-traded currency futures

Contract size CHF125,000 price quotation: US$ per CHF1

3-month expiry 1.0647

6-month expiry 1.0659

Exchange-traded currency options

Contract size CHF125,000, exercise price quotation: US$ per CHF1, premium: cents per CHF1

	Call options		Put options	
Exercise price	3-month expiry	6-month expiry	3-month expiry	6-month expiry
1.06	1.87	2.75	1.41	2.16
1.07	1.34	2.22	1.88	2.63

It can be assumed that futures and option contracts expire at the end of the month and transaction costs related to these can be ignored.

 BPP LEARNING MEDIA

Over-the-counter products

In addition to the exchange-traded products, Pecunia Bank is willing to offer the following over-the-counter derivative products to CMC Co:

(i)   A forward rate between the US$ and the CHF of US$1.0677 per CHF1.

(ii)   An interest rate swap contract with a counterparty, where the counterparty can borrow at an annual floating rate based on the yield curve rate plus 0.8% or an annual fixed rate of 3.8%. Pecunia Bank would charge a fee of 20 basis points each to act as the intermediary of the swap. Both parties will benefit equally from the swap contract.

Alternative loan repayment proposal

As an alternative to paying the principal on the loan as one lump sum at the end of the fourth year, CMC Co could pay off the loan in equal annual amounts over the four years similar to an annuity. In this case, an annual interest rate of 2% would be payable, which is the same as the loan's gross redemption yield (yield to maturity).

Proposal two

This proposal suggested setting up four new branches in four different countries. Each branch would have its own production facilities and sales teams. As a consequence of this, one of the two European-based production facilities will be closed. Initial cost-benefit analysis indicated that this would reduce costs related to production, distribution and logistics, as these branches would be closer to the sources of raw materials and also to the customers. The operations and sales directors supported the proposal as, in addition to the above, this would enable sales and marketing teams in the branches to respond to any changes in nearby markets more quickly. The branches would be controlled and staffed by the local population in those countries. However, some members of the BoD expressed concern that such a move would create agency issues between CMC Co's central management and the management controlling the branches. They suggested mitigation strategies would need to be established to minimise these issues.

Response from the non-executive directors

When the proposals were put to the non-executive directors, they indicated that they were broadly supportive of the second proposal if the financial benefits outweigh the costs of setting up and running the four branches. However, they felt that they could not support the first proposal, as this would reduce shareholder value because the costs related to undertaking the proposal are likely to outweigh the benefits.

Required

(a)   Advise CMC Co on an appropriate hedging strategy to manage the foreign exchange exposure of the US$ payment in four months' time. Show all relevant calculations, including the number of contracts bought or sold in the exchange-traded derivative markets.

(15 marks)

(b)   Demonstrate how CMC Co could benefit from the swap offered by Pecunia Bank.

(6 marks)

(c)   Calculate the modified duration of the loan if it is repaid in equal amounts and explain how duration can be used to measure the sensitivity of the loan to changes in interest rates

(7 marks)

(d)   Prepare a memorandum for the board of directors (BoD) of CMC Co which:

(i)   Discusses proposal one in light of the concerns raised by the non-executive directors; and

(9 marks)

(ii)   Discusses the agency issues related to proposal two and how these can be mitigated.

(9 marks)

Professional marks will be awarded in part (d) for the presentation, structure, logical flow and clarity of the memorandum.

(4 marks)

(Total = 50 marks)

SECTION B: BOTH QUESTIONS to be attempted

Question 2

You have recently commenced working for Burung Co and are reviewing a four-year project which the company is considering for investment. The project is in a business activity which is very different from Burung Co's current line of business.

The following net present value estimate has been made for the project:

All figures are in $ million

Year	0	1	2	3	4
Sales revenue		23.03	36.60	49.07	27.14
Direct project costs		(13.82)	(21.96)	(29.44)	(16.28)
Interest		(1.20)	(1.20)	(1.20)	(1.20)
Profit		8.01	13.44	18.43	9.66
Tax (20%)		(1.60)	(2.69)	(3.69)	(1.93)
Investment/sale	(38.00)				4.00
Cash flows	(38.00)	6.41	10.75	14.74	11.73
Discount factors (7%)	1	0.935	0.873	0.816	0.763
Present values	(38.00)	5.99	9.38	12.03	8.95

Net present value is negative $1.65 million, and therefore the recommendation is that the project should not be accepted.

Notes to NPV proposal

In calculating the net present value of the project, the following notes were made:

1   Since the real cost of capital is used to discount cash flows, neither the sales revenue nor the direct project costs have been inflated. It is estimated that the inflation rate applicable to sales revenue is 8% per year and to the direct project costs is 4% per year.

2   The project will require an initial investment of $38 million. Of this, $16 million relates to plant and machinery, which is expected to be sold for $4 million when the project ceases, after taking any taxation and inflation impact into account.

3   Tax-allowable depreciation is available on the plant and machinery at 50% in the first year, followed by 25% per year thereafter on a reducing balance basis. A balancing adjustment is available in the year the plant and machinery is sold. Burung Co pays 20% tax on its annual taxable profits. No tax-allowable depreciation is available on the remaining investment assets and they will have a nil value at the end of the project.

4   Burung Co uses either a nominal cost of capital of 11% or a real cost of capital of 7% to discount all projects, given that the rate of inflation has been stable at 4% for a number of years.

5   Interest is based on Burung Co's normal borrowing rate of 150 basis points over the ten-year government yield rate.

6   At the beginning of each year, Burung Co will need to provide working capital of 20% of the anticipated sales revenue for the year. Any remaining working capital will be released at the end of the project.

7   Working capital and depreciation have not been taken into account in the net present value calculation above, since depreciation is not a cash flow and all the working capital is returned at the end of the project.

Further financial information

It is anticipated that the project will be financed entirely by debt, 60% of which will be obtained from a subsidised loan scheme run by the government, which lends money at a rate of 100 basis points below the 10-year government debt yield rate of 2.5%. Issue costs related to raising the finance are 2% of the gross finance required. The remaining 40% will be funded from Burung Co's

BPP
LEARNING
MEDIA

normal borrowing sources. It can be assumed that the debt capacity available to Burung Co is equal to the actual amount of debt finance raised for the project.

Burung Co has identified a company, Lintu Co, which operates in the same line of business as that of the project it is considering. Lintu Co is financed by 40 million shares trading at $3.20 each and $34 million debt trading at $94 per $100. Lintu Co's equity beta is estimated at 1.5. The current yield on government treasury bills is 2% and it is estimated that the market risk premium is 8%. Lintu Co pays tax at an annual rate of 20%.

Both Burung Co and Lintu Co pay tax in the same year as when profits are earned.

Required

(a)   Calculate the adjusted present value (APV) for the project, correcting any errors made in the net present value estimate above, and conclude whether the project should be accepted or not. Show all relevant calculations.   **(15 marks)**

(b)   Comment on the corrections made to the original net present value estimate and explain the APV approach taken in part (a), including any assumptions made.   **(10 marks)**

(Total = 25 marks)

Question 3

Hav Co is a publicly listed company involved in the production of highly technical and sophisticated electronic components for complex machinery. It has a number of diverse and popular products, an active research and development department, significant cash reserves and a highly talented management who are very good in getting products to market quickly.

A new industry that Hav Co is looking to venture into is biotechnology, which has been expanding rapidly, and there are strong indications that this recent growth is set to continue. However, Hav Co has limited experience in this industry. Therefore, it believes that the best and quickest way to expand would be through acquiring a company already operating in this industry sector.

Strand Co

Strand Co is a private company operating in the biotechnology industry and is owned by a consortium of business angels and company managers. The owner-managers are highly skilled scientists who have developed a number of technically complex products, but have found it difficult to commercialise them. They have also been increasingly constrained by the lack of funds to develop their innovative products further.

Discussions have taken place about the possibility of Strand Co being acquired by Hav Co. Strand Co's managers have indicated that the consortium of owners is happy for the negotiations to proceed. If Strand Co is acquired, it is expected that its managers would continue to run the Strand Co part of the larger combined company.

Strand Co is of the opinion that most of its value is in its intangible assets, comprising intellectual capital. Therefore, the premium payable on acquisition should be based on the present value to infinity of the after-tax excess earnings the company has generated in the past three years, over the average return on capital employed of the biotechnological industry. However, Hav Co is of the opinion that the premium should be assessed on synergy benefits created by the acquisition and the changes in value, due to the changes in the price/earnings (P/E) ratio before and after the acquisition.

Financial Information

Given below are extracts of financial information for Hav Co for 20X3 and Strand Co for 20X1, 20X2 and 20X3:

Year ended 30 April	Hav Co 20X3	Strand Co 20X3	Strand Co 20X2	Strand Co 20X1
	$m	$m	$m	$m
Earnings before tax	1,980	397	370	352
Non-current assets	3,965	882	838	801
Current assets	968	210	208	198

Year ended 30 April	Hav Co 20X3	Strand Co 20X3	20X2	20X1
	$m	$m	$m	$m
Share capital (25c/share)	600	300	300	300
Reserves	2,479	183	166	159
Non-current liabilities	1,500	400	400	400
Current liabilities	354	209	180	140

The current average P/E ratio of the biotechnology industry is 16.4 times and it has been estimated that Strand Co's P/E ratio is 10% higher than this. However, it is thought that the P/E ratio of the combined company would fall to 14.5 times after the acquisition. The annual after-tax earnings will increase by $140 million due to synergy benefits resulting from combining the two companies.

Both companies pay tax at 20% per year and Strand Co's annual cost of capital is estimated at 7%. Hav Co's current share price is $9.24 per share. The biotechnology industry's pre-tax return on capital employed is currently estimated to be 20% per year.

Acquisition proposals

Hav Co has proposed to pay for the acquisition using one of the following three methods:

1   A cash offer of $5.72 for each Strand Co share;

2   A cash offer of $1.33 for each Strand Co share plus 1 Hav Co share for every two Strand Co shares; or

3   A cash offer of $1.25 for each Strand Co share plus one $100 3% convertible bond for every $5 nominal value of Strand Co shares. In 6 years, the bond can be converted into 12 Hav Co shares or redeemed at par.

Required

(a)   Distinguish between the different types of synergy and discuss possible sources of synergy based on the above scenario.   **(9 marks)**

(b)   Based on the two different opinions expressed by Hav Co and Strand Co, calculate the maximum acquisition premium payable in each case.   **(6 marks)**

(c)   Calculate the percentage premium per share that Strand Co's shareholders will receive under each acquisition payment method and justify, with explanations, which payment method would be most acceptable to them.   **(10 marks)**

(Total = 25 marks)

Answers

DO NOT TURN THIS PAGE UNTIL YOU HAVE
COMPLETED THE MOCK EXAM

Exam success skills

In any AFM exam it will be important to apply good general exam technique by using the six exam success skills identified at the start of the Revision Kit, in the section covering 'essential skills'. These skills are: 1. Case scenario: Managing information; 2. Correct interpretation of requirements; 3. Answer planning: Priorities, structure and logic; 4. Efficient numerical analysis; 5. Effective writing and presentation; and 6. Good time management.

Some examples of how to apply these skills in this exam are provided in the table below.

Skill	Examples
Managing information	It is crucially important to assimilate the information in the question scenario.
	In longer questions, such as the 50 mark question, it is difficult to assimilate information by simply starting at the beginning and reading to the end because there is so much information to take in.
	Instead, it is sensible to take an **active approach** to reading each question. Read enough of the question to get an idea of the basic scenario and then read the initial requirements so that you understand the first things that you are expected to do with this information.
	For example, in Question 1 the lengthy scenario makes a lot more sense if, before reading all of it, you are aware that the first requirements relate to currency hedging and to an interest rate swap.
Correct Interpretation of requirements	Be careful to interpret the verbs used in the question requirements carefully. For example, in Q1(d), the verb 'discuss' implies that an element of critical analysis (discussing from different viewpoints) is appropriate. Also be careful to identify where a question requirement contains more than one instruction. For example, in Q1© where calculation AND explanation is asked for, and again in Q3(c).
Answer planning	This is always important in AFM questions.
	For example, in risk management questions such as Q1(a), it is especially important that your plan correctly identifies (i) the risk being faced (ii) the relevant timings. If you get these wrong, then there will be a cap on the number of marks that you can score (however accurate your answers are).
Efficient numerical analysis	It is essential that the marker can follow your workings and your logic.
	It is also important that you accept that under exam conditions you will not get <u>all</u> the calculations correct, and that this is not necessary in order to score a strong pass mark.
	If you make a mistake early in your calculations that affects your later calculations, then the marker will only penalise the error you have made, and not its follow-on impact on other calculations. This means that it is not normally a good use of your time to correct such errors during the exam.
	For example, in Question 2(a) an error early on in your calculations would only attract a small penalty despite its impact on the final APV.

Skill	Examples
Effective writing and presentation	In Q1 there are four marks available for professional structure (eg use of sub-headings, appendices etc). Many of the techniques used here are good practice in all questions throughout the exam.
	It is also very important to relate your points to the scenario and to the requirement wherever possible. This does not mean simply repeating the details from the question but using this information to help to explain the point you are making.
	For example, in 2(b) it is not enough to state the assumptions, you need to explain their relevance.
Good Time Management	The exam is 3 hours 15 minutes long, which translates to 1.95 minutes per mark.
	If you build in an allowance of 20% of your time for assimilating the scenario and planning, this falls to 1.56 minutes per mark (1.95 × 0.8).
	It is essential that you do not allow yourself to become bogged down in the harder numerical areas of the exam.
	For example, in Q1 it is vital to leave enough time to answer the discursive parts, especially part (d).
	(a) At the beginning of a question, work out the amount of time you should be spending on:Planning:
	(i) for a 25 mark question this will be about 1.95 × 25 marks × 20% = 10 minutes
	(ii) for a 50 mark question this should be about 20 mins.
	(b) Writing your answer to each requirement:
	(iii) Take the mark allocation and multiply by 1.56 minutes per mark.

Diagnostic

Did you apply these skills when reading, planning, and writing up your answer? Identify the exam success skills where you think you need to improve and capture your thoughts here of what you want to achieve when attempting questions in future.

Question 1

Marking scheme

		Marks	
(a)	Calculation of payment using the forward rate	1	
	Going short on futures and purchasing put options	2	
	Predicted futures rate based on basis reduction	1	
	Futures: Expected payment and number of contracts	2	
	Options calculation using either 1.06 or 1.07 rate	3	
	Options calculation using the second rate (or explanation)	2	
	Advice (1 to 2 marks per point)	4–5	
			Max 15
(b)	Comparative advantage and recognition of benefit as a result	2	
	Initial decision to borrow fixed by CMC Co and floating by counterparty	1	
	Swap impact	2	
	Net benefit after bank charges	1	
		6	

			Marks
(c)	Calculation of annual annuity amount		1
	Calculation of Macaulay duration		2
	Calculation of modified duration		1
	Explanation		$\frac{3}{7}$
(d)	(i) 2–3 marks per point		Max 9
	(ii) Discussion of the agency issues	3–4	
	Discussion of mitigation strategies and policies	$\frac{4-6}{}$	
			Max 9

Professional marks

Memorandum format	1
Structure and presentation of the memorandum	$\frac{3}{4}$
	$\underline{\underline{50}}$

(a) The US$ payment of 5.06 million due in four months' time exposes CMC to the risk of a devaluation in the CHF over this period.

This risk can be managed in a number of ways.

(i) **Forward contracts**

The forward rate being offered of US$1.0677 per CHF would mean that the cost of this payment would be fixed at:

$5.06m/1.0677 = 4,739,159 CHF

This would completely remove the possibility of negative (or positive) exchange rate movements impacting on the cost of this payment in CHF.

Forward contracts are a simple way of starting to hedge risk and carry no transaction costs, although they do carry default risk.

(ii) **Futures**

CMC would need to enter into contracts to sell CHF on the futures exchange. Six-month contracts would be needed.

The effective exchange rate on the futures market can be estimated as follows:

	Now	In 4 months
6-month future	1.0659	
Spot	1.0635	
Basis	0.0024	0.0008
	6 months remaining	2 months remaining
		$(0.0024 \times 2/6)$

The closing future price is estimated at spot in six months (assume this is 1.0659) + 0.0008 = 1.0667.

The futures contracts would be set up as follows:

Number of contracts to sell ($5.06m/1.0659/125,000) = 38

In reality a margin payment would be needed to cover potential losses on these contracts.

Assuming that the closing spot = 1.0659 then the situation would be:

Actual transaction = a payment of $5.06m/1.0659 = 4,747,162 CHF

Contract to sell at opening future 1.0659

Contract to buy at closing future rate 1.0667

Loss on future = 0.0008

Total losses = 0.0008 × 38 contracts × 125,000 = $3,800 converted into CHF at closing spot = 3,800/1.0659 = 3,565 CHF

Final outcome = actual + future = 4,747,162 + 3,565 = 4,750,727 CHF

This is an effective rate of $5,060,000/4,750,727 = 1.0651

This can also be estimated as the opening futures price – closing basis = 1.0659 – 0.0008 = 1.0651

The treasury department would have to ensure that the future was closed out on the same date as the actual transaction.

There may be variation margin payments during the next four months if potential losses on these contracts exceed the initial margin.

This is less attractive than the forward contract.

(iii) **Currency options**

Because the contracts are in CHF, the contracts required will be to sell CHF ie put options. Six-month contracts will be needed.

As with futures, 38 contracts will be needed.

There is a choice of 2 options, 1.06 and 1.07 $ to the CHF. The 1.07 is the better rate and therefore is more expensive.

The potential outcome of using both is set out below.

	1.06	1.07
Cost of setting up 38 put options (in $)	102,600	124,925
	(2.16 premium)	(2.63 premium)
Cost in CHF at today's spot rate of 1.0635	96,474	117,466

Assuming that the option is exercised

	Use option			Use option	
	$5,035,000	$		$5,082,500	$
Cost in CHF	−4,750,000			−4,750,000	
		shortage in $ ($5.06m − $5.035m)			surplus in $ ($5.06m − $5.0825m)
	−25,000		22,500		in CHF at 1.0677
		CHF at 1.0677			fwd rate
	−23,415	(fwd rate)	21,073		
Premium in CHF	−96,474		−117,466		
Net in CHF	−4,869,889		−4,846,393		

This is an uncertain outcome, and may be better if the CHF gets stronger over the next four months (because then the option would not need to be exercised).

Summary	CHF
Forward	4,739,159
Future	4,750,728
Option at 1.06	4,869,889
Option at 1.07	4,846,393

Based on this analysis I recommend using forwards which in any case are a simple and low cost way of beginning to hedge currency risk.

(b)

	CMC Co	Counterparty	Interest rate differential
Fixed rate	2.2%	3.8%	1.6%
Floating rate	Yield rate + 0.4%	Yield rate + 0.8%	0.4%

CMC Co has a comparative advantage in borrowing at the fixed rate and the counterparty has a comparative advantage in borrowing at the floating rate. Total possible benefit before Pecunia Bank's fee is 1.2% (1.6 −0.4), which if shared equally results in a benefit of 0.6% each, for both CMC Co and the counterparty.

	CMC Co	Counterparty
CMC Co borrows at	2.2%	
Counterparty borrows at		Yield rate + 0.8%
Advantage	60 basis points	60 basis points
Net result	Yield rate − 0.2%	3.2%
SWAP		
Counterparty receives		Yield rate
CMC Co pays	Yield rate	
Counterparty pays		2.4%
CMC Co receives	2.4%	

After paying the 20 basis point fee, CMC Co will effectively pay interest at the yield curve rate and benefit by 40 basis points or 0.4%, and the counterparty will pay interest at 3.4% and benefit by 40 basis points or 0.4% as well.

Note. Full marks will be given where the question is answered by estimating the arbitrage gain of 1.2% and deducting the fees of 0.4%, without constructing the above table.

(c) Annuity factor, 4 years, 2% = 3.808

Equal annual amounts repayable per year = CHF60,000,000/3.808 = CHF15,756,303

Time	1	2	3	4	Total
Repayments (CHF'000)	15,756.3	15,756.3	15,756.3	15,756.3	
Df 2%	0.980	0.961	0.942	0.924	
PV ('000)	15,441.2	15,141.8	14,842.4	14,558.8	59,984.2
% of present value	15,441.2 ÷ 59,984.2 = 0.26	15,141.8 ÷ 59,984.2 = 0.25	14,842.4 ÷ 59,984.2 = 0.25	14,558.8 ÷ 59,984.2 = 0.24	

Macaulay duration

(0.26 × 1 year +
0.25 × 2 years +
0.25 × 3 years +
0.24 × 4 years)
= 2.47 years

Modified duration = 2.47/1.02 = 2.42 years

The size of the modified duration will determine how much the value of a bond or loan will change when there is a change in interest rates. A higher modified duration means that the fluctuations in the value of a bond or loan will be greater, hence the value of 2.42 means that the value of the loan or bond will change by 2.42 times the change in interest rates multiplied by the original value of the bond or loan.

The relationship is only an approximation because duration assumes that the relationship between the change in interest rates and the corresponding change in the value of the bond or loan is linear. In fact, the relationship between interest rates and bond price is in the form of a curve which is convex to the origin (ie non-linear). Therefore duration can only provide a reasonable estimation of the change in the value of a bond or loan due to changes in interest rates, when those interest rate changes are small.

(d) **MEMORANDUM**

From:

To: The board of directors, CMC Co

Date: XX/XX/XXXX

Subject: Discussion of the proposal to manage foreign exchange and interest rate exposures, and the proposal to move operations to four branches and consequential agency issues

This memo discusses the proposal of whether or not CMC Co should undertake the management of foreign exchange and interest rate exposure, and the agency issues resulting from the proposal to locate branches internationally.

(i)   **Proposal One: Management of foreign exchange and interest rate exposure**

The non-executive directors are correct if CMC Co is in a situation where markets are perfect and efficient, where information is freely available and where securities are priced correctly. In this circumstance, risk management or hedging would not add value and, if shareholders hold well-diversified portfolios, unsystematic risk will be largely eliminated.

The position against hedging states that in such cases companies would not increase shareholder value by hedging or eliminating risk because there will be no further reduction in unsystematic risk. Furthermore, the cost of reducing any systematic risk will equal or be greater than the benefit derived from such risk reduction. Shareholders would not gain from risk management or hedging; in fact, if the costs exceed the benefits, then hedging may result in a reduction in shareholder value.

There are two main situations where reduction in volatility or risk may increase cash flows – where a firm could face significant financial distress costs due to high volatility in earnings; and where stable earnings increase certainty and the ability to plan for the future, thus resulting in stable investment policies by the firm.

Active hedging may also reduce agency costs. For example, unlike shareholders, managers and employees of the company may not hold diversified portfolios. Hedging allows the risks faced by managers and employees to be reduced. Additionally, hedging may allow managers to be less concerned about market movements which are not within their control and instead allow them to focus on business issues over which they can exercise control. This seems to be what the purchasing director is contending. On the other hand, the finance director seems to be more interested in increasing his personal benefits and not necessarily in increasing the value of CMC Co.

A consistent hedging strategy or policy may be used as a signalling tool to reduce the conflict of interest between bond holders and shareholders, and thus reduce restrictive covenants.

It is also suggested that until recently CMC Co had no intention of hedging and communicated this in its annual report. It is likely that shareholders will therefore have created their own risk management policies. A strategic change in the policy may have a negative impact on the shareholders and the clientele impact of this will need to be taken into account.

The case of whether to hedge or not is not clear cut and CMC Co should consider all the above factors and be clear about why it is intending to change its strategy before coming to a conclusion. Any intended change in policy should be communicated to the shareholders. Shareholders can also benefit from risk management because the risk profile of the company may change, resulting in a reduced cost of capital.

(ii)   **Proposal Two: International branches, agency issues and their mitigation**

Principal–agent relationships can be observed within an organisation between different stakeholder groups. With the proposed branches located in different

BPP
LEARNING
MEDIA

countries, the principal–agent relationship will be between the directors and senior management at CMC Co in Switzerland, and the managers of the individual branches. Agency issues can arise where the motivations of the branch managers, who are interested in the performance of their individual branches, diverge from the management at CMC Co headquarters, who are interested in the performance of the whole organisation.

These issues may arise because branch managers are not aware of, or appreciate the importance of, the key factors at corporate level. They may also arise because of differences in cultures and divergent backgrounds.

Mitigation mechanisms could involve:

- Monitoring policies

- Compensation policies

- Communication policies

Monitoring policies: These would involve ensuring that key aims and strategies are agreed between all parties before implementation, and results monitored to ensure adherence with the original agreements. Where there are differences, for example due to external factors, new targets need to be agreed. Where deviations are noticed, these should be communicated quickly.

Compensation packages: These should ensure that reward is based on achievement of organisational value and therefore there is every incentive for the branch managers to act in the best interests of the corporation as a whole.

Communication: Branch managers should be made fully aware of the organisational objectives, and any changes to these, and how the branch contributes to these, in order to ensure their acceptance of the objectives. The management at CMC Co headquarters should be fully aware of cultural and educational differences in the countries where the branches are to be set up and fully plan for how organisational objectives may nevertheless be achieved within these differences.

Note. Credit will be given for alternative, relevant approaches to the calculations, comments and suggestions/recommendations.

Question 2

Workbook references. APV technique is covered in Chapter 6.

Top tips. Make sure that you underline the key requirement words to identify all the aspects of a question. For example in part (b) there are three aspects to the question that will all score marks; these are regarding the corrections made (1), the approach taken (2) and the limitations of the method (3).

Easy marks. The comments in part (b) are an easy source of marks.

Examining team's comments. It was pleasing that candidates approached this question in a structured and systematic manner, and the majority of the responses achieved a pass mark.

Part (a) focused on the calculation of the APV with candidates being given the opportunity to make corrections to the original NPV calculations. This part was done well in most cases and the flexibility in marking allowed credit to be awarded for the follow-on approach even if errors were made earlier. Although many candidates knew the approach for the APV, some of the financing side-effect calculations were also not done correctly.

Part (b) focused on the comment on the corrections and explanation of the approach taken and assumptions made. This part was generally done well, although some answers did not make a sufficient number of good points to warrant a good pass being awarded. Many answers tended to repeat the points in slightly different ways and therefore got no additional marks.

		Marks
(a)	Inflated incremental profit	2
	Taxation	2
	Working capital	2
	Estimate of discount rate	2
	Net present value	1
	Issue costs	1
	Tax shield benefit	2
	Subsidy benefit	1
	Adjusted present value and conclusion	2
		15
(b)	Corrections made	4–5
	Approach taken	2–3
	Assumptions made	3–4
		Max 10
		25

ANSWERS

(a) **All figures are in $ million – corrections are numbered**

Year	0	1	2	3	4
(error 1) Sales revenue (inflated, 8% p.a.)		24.87	42.69	61.81	36.92
(error 1) Costs (inflated, 4% p.a.)		(14.37)	(23.75)	(33.12)	(19.05)
Incremental profit		10.50	18.94	28.69	17.87
(error 2) Interest (not relevant)		n/a	n/a	n/a	n/a
(error 3) Tax (W1)		(0.50)	(3.39)	(5.44)	(3.47)
(error 4) Working capital (W2)	(4.97)	(3.57)	(3.82)	4.98	7.38
Investment/sale of machinery	(38.00)				4.00
Cash flows	(42.97)	6.43	11.73	28.23	25.78
(error 5) Discount factors (12%, W3)	1	0.893	0.797	0.712	0.636
Present values	(42.97)	5.74	9.35	20.10	16.40

Base case net present value is approximately $8.62 million.

Workings

1   *All figures are in $ million*

Year	0	1	2	3	4
Incremental profit		10.50	18.94	28.69	17.87
Capital allowances		8.00	2.00	1.50	0.50
Taxable profit		2.50	16.94	27.19	17.37
Tax (20%)		0.50	3.39	5.44	3.47

2   *All figures are in $ million*

Year	0	1	2	3	4
Working capital (20% of sales revenue)		4.97	8.54	12.36	7.38
Working capital required/(released)	4.97	3.57	3.82	(4.98)	(7.38)

3 $$\beta a = \left(\frac{V_e}{(V_e + V_d(1-t))} \right) \beta_e + \left(\frac{V_d(1-t)}{(V_e + V_d(1-t))} \right) \beta_d$$

Assuming the beta of debt = 0, Lintu Co's asset beta =

[$128m/($128m + $31.96m × 0.8] × 1.5 approx. = 1.25

Using the CAPM $E(ri) = R_f + \beta(E(R_m - R_f))$

So the all-equity financed discount rate = 2% + 1.25 × 8% = 12%

(error 6) Financing side effects

	$'000
Issue costs 2/98 × $42.97m	(876.94)
Tax shield	
Annual tax relief =	
On the subsidised loan = $42.97m × 60% × 0.015 × 20% = $77,346	
On the rest of the loan = $42.97m × 40% × 0.04 × 20% = $137,504	
Total = 77,346 + 137,504 = $214,850m p.a. for 4 years	
This is discounted at the normal cost of debt which is 1.5% above the risk-free rate of 2.5% ie = 4%.	
The present value of the tax relief annuity = 214.85 × 3.63	779.91
Annual subsidy benefit	
$42.97m × 60% × 0.025 × 80% = 515.64 ('000)	
The present value of the subsidy benefit annuity = 515.64 × 3.63	1,871.77
Total benefit of financing side effects	1,774.74

Financing the project entirely by debt would add just under $1.78 million to the value of the project, or approximately an additional 20% to the all-equity financed project.

The APV of the project is just under $10.4 million and therefore it should be accepted.

Note. In calculating the present values of the tax shield and subsidy benefits, instead of the discount factor being based on the normal borrowing/default risk of the company, alternatively, 2% or 2.5% could be used depending on the assumptions made. Credit will be given where these are used to estimate the annuity factor, where the assumption is explained.

(b) **Corrections made to the original net present value (numbers are referenced in the above calculations)**

(i) Cash flows are inflated and the nominal rate based on Lintu Co's all-equity financed rate is used (see below). Where different cash flows are subject to different rates of inflation, applying a real rate to non-inflated amounts would not give an accurate answer because the effect of inflation on profit margins is being ignored.

(ii) Interest is not normally included in the net present value calculations. Instead, it is normally imputed within the cost of capital or discount rate. In this case, it is included in the financing side effects.

(iii) The approach taken to exclude depreciation from the net present value computation is correct, but capital allowances need to be taken away from profit estimates before tax is calculated, reducing the profits on which tax is payable.

(iv) The impact of the working capital requirement is included in the estimate as, although all the working capital is recovered at the end of the project, the flows of working capital are subject to different discount rates when their present values are calculated.

Approach taken (relates to errors 5 and 6)

The value of the project is initially assessed considering only the business risk involved in undertaking the project. The discount rate used is based on Lintu Co's asset beta which measures only the business risk of that company. Since Lintu Co is in the same line of business as the project, it is deemed appropriate to use its discount rate, instead of 11% that Burung Co uses normally.

The impact of debt financing and the subsidy benefit are then considered. In this way, Burung Co can assess the value created from its investment activity and then the additional value created from the manner in which the project is financed.

Assumptions made

It is assumed that all figures used are accurate and any estimates made are reasonable. Burung Co may want to consider undertaking a sensitivity analysis to assess this.

It is assumed that the initial working capital required will form part of the funds borrowed but that the subsequent working capital requirements will be available from the funds generated by the project. The validity of this assumption needs to be assessed since the working capital requirements at the start of Years 2 and 3 are substantial.

It is assumed that Lintu Co's asset beta and all-equity financed discount rate represent the business risk of the project. The validity of this assumption also needs to be assessed. For example, Lintu Co's entire business may not be similar to the project, and it may undertake other lines of business. In this case, the asset beta would need to be adjusted so that just the project's business risk is considered.

It is also assumed that there are no adverse side effects of taking on the extra debt eg a worsening credit rating which could impact Burung's trading position.

Note. Credit will be given for alternative, relevant explanations.

Question 3

Workbook references. Acquisitions are covered in Chapters 8 and 9.

Top tips. For part (a) make sure any synergies suggested are consistent with the given scenario, rather than a generic list. For example, research and development (R&D) synergies are more applicable in this scenario than in a general acquisition question.
For part (b) you may have slightly different numbers depending on roundings. Do not worry about this as full marks will still be given where roundings are sensible.

For part (c) you need to use the maximum premiums calculated in part (b). Ensure that you use whatever numbers you have calculated in order to gain any follow through marks. Also for part (c) ensure that you justify the recommendation you have made and that it is supported by the calculations.

Easy marks. You should be able to pick up some relatively straightforward marks in part (a) for distinguishing the different types of synergies as well as suggesting potential synergies in this scenario.

Examining team's comments. Part (b) was not done well on the whole. Few candidates knew how to approach answering this question and most tried to use the figures given in innovative but incorrect ways to get to an answer.

For part (c) some reasonable answers were provided for the cash only and the cash and shares methods of payment. The bond payment method was done less well and few answers justified the payment method that Strand Co's shareholders (the target company's shareholders) would prefer.

		Marks
(a)	Distinguish between different synergies	1–2
	Evaluating possible financial synergies	2–3
	Evaluating possible cost synergies	1–2
	Evaluating possible revenue synergies	3–4
	Concluding comments	1–2
		Max 9
(b)	Average earnings and capital employed	1
	After-tax premium	1
	PV of premium (excess earnings)	1
	Hav Co and Strand Co values	1
	Combined company value	1
	Value created/premium (P/E method)	1
		6
(c)	Strand Co, value per share	1
	Cash offer premium (%)	1
	Cash and share offer premium (%)	2
	Cash and bond offer premium (%)	2
	Explanation and justification	4–5
		Max 10
		25

(a) Synergies arise from an acquisition when the value of the new, combined entity is greater than the sum of the two individual values before the acquisition. There are three types of synergies: revenue, cost and financial.

Revenue synergies create higher revenues for the combined entity, also creating a higher return on equity and an extended period of competitive advantage.

Cost synergies arise from eliminating duplication of functions and also from economies of scale due to the size of the new entity.

Financial synergies may result from the ability to increase debt capacity or from transferring group funds to companies where they can be best utilised.

In this scenario, there may be financial synergies available as Hav Co has significant cash reserves, but Strand Co is constrained by a lack of funds. This means that the new entity may have the funds to **undertake projects** that would have been rejected by Strand Co due to a lack of funds. The larger company may also have an increased debt capacity and therefore additional access to finance. It is also possible that the new entity will have a lower cost of capital as a result of the acquisition.

Cost synergies may be available, through the removal of duplication in areas such as head office functions, but also in R&D. These synergies are likely to be more short term. Other cost synergies may arise from a **stronger negotiating position** with suppliers due to the size of the new entity, meaning better credit terms and also lower costs.

Revenue synergies have the potential to be the biggest synergies from this acquisition, although they are likely to be the hardest to achieve, and also to sustain. Hav Co can help Strand Co with the marketing of its products, which should result in **higher revenues** and a longer period of **competitive advantage**. Combining the R&D activity and the technologies of both companies may mean products can be brought to market faster too. To achieve these synergies it is important to retain the services of the scientist managers of Strand Co. They have been used to complete autonomy as the managers of Strand Co, so this relationship should be managed carefully.

A major challenge in an effective acquisition is to **integrate processes and systems** between the two companies efficiently and effectively in order to gain the full potential benefits. Often, this is done poorly and can mean that the acquisition is ultimately seen as a failure. Hav Co needs to plan for this before proceeding with the acquisition.

(b) **Maximum premium based on excess earnings**
Average pre-tax earnings of Strand Co = (397 + 370 + 352)/3 = $373m
Average capital employed = [(882 + 210 − 209) + (838 + 208 − 180) + (801 + 198 − 140)]/3 = $869.3m
Excess annual premium (pre-tax) = 373 − (869.3 × 0.2) = $199.1m
Post-tax annual premium = $199.1 × 0.8 = $159.3m
PV of annual premium in perpetuity = 159.3/0.07 = $2,275.7m

The maximum premium payable is $2,275.7m.

Maximum premium based on P/E ratio

Strand Co's estimated P/E ratio = 16.4 × 1.10 = 18.04
Strand Co's post-tax profit (most recent) = 397m × 0.8 = $317.6m
Hav Co's post-tax profit = 1,980 × 0.8 = $1,584m

Hav Co current value = $9.24 × 2,400m shares = $22,176m

Strand Co current value = 18.04 × $317.6 = $5,729.5m

Value of combined company = (1,584 + 317.6 + 140) × 14.5 = $29,603.2m

Maximum premium = 29,603.2 − (22,176 + 5,729.5) = $1,697.7m

(c) Current value of a Strand Co share = $5,729.5m/1,200m shares = $4.77 per share
Maximum premium % based on excess earnings = 2,275.7/5,729.5 × 100 = 39.7%
Maximum premium % based on P/E ratio = 1,697.7/5,729.5 × 100 = 29.6%

Cash offer: premium % to Strand Co shareholder

(5.72 − 4.77)/4.77 × 100 = 19.9%

Cash and share offer: premium % to Strand Co shareholder

1 Hav Co share for 2 Strand Co shares

Hav Co share price = $9.24

Price per Strand Co share = 9.24/2 = $4.62

Cash payment per Strand Co share = $1.33

Total return = 4.62 + 1.33 = $5.95

Premium = (5.95 − 4.77)/4.77 × 100 = 24.7%

Cash and bond offer: premium % to Strand Co shareholder

Each share has nominal value of $0.25 so $5 is 20 shares

Bond value $100/20 shares = $5 per share

Cash payment per Strand Co share = $1.25

Total return = 5 + 1.25 = $6.25

Premium = (6.25 − 4.77)/4.77 × 100 = 31.0%

Tutorial note. Although these evaluations have been carried out using the current share price given in the question, an equally valid approach would have been to have used a post-acquisition share price based on earlier calculations (although this would take longer and is less advisable given that it is likely that about half of the marks are available for the numerical element of this question).

Based on the calculations above, the cash plus bond offer will give the highest return to Strand Co shareholders. In addition, the **bond can be converted** to 12 Hav Co shares, giving a value per share of $8.33($100/12), which is below the current share price and so already **in-the-money**. If the share price increases over the 6-year period, then the value of the bond should also increase. The bond will also earn interest of 3% per year for the holder.

The 31% return is the closest to the maximum premium based on excess earnings and higher than the maximum premium based on P/E ratios. Thus this method appears to **transfer more of the value** to the owners of Strand Co.

However, this payment method gives the **lowest initial cash payment** of the three methods being considered. This may make it seem more attractive to the Hav Co shareholders as well, although they stand to have their shareholding diluted most by this method, but not until six years have passed.

The cash and share offer gives a return in between the other options. Although the return is lower than the cash and bond offer, Strand Co's shareholders could **sell the Hav Co shares immediately** if they wish to. However, if the share price of Hav Co falls between now and the acquisition, the return to Strand Co shareholders will be lower.

The cash only offer gives an immediate return to Strand Co shareholders, but it is the **lowest return** and may also place a **strain on the cash flow** of Hav Co, which may need to increase borrowings as a result.

It seems most likely that Strand Co's shareholder/managers, who will continue to work in the new entity, will accept the mixed cash and bond offer. This maximises their current return and also gives them the chance to gain in the future when converting the bond. The choice of payment method could be influenced by the impact on personal taxation situations, though.

ACCA

Advanced Financial Management

Mock Examination 3

March 2020 exam

Questions
Time allowed 3 hours and 15 minutes
Section A THIS question is compulsory and MUST be attempted Section B BOTH questions to be attempted

DO NOT OPEN THIS EXAM UNTIL YOU ARE READY TO START
UNDER EXAMINATION CONDITIONS

SECTION A: This question is compulsory and MUST be attempted

Question 1

Exhibit 1: Introduction

Westparley Co is a listed retailer, mainly selling food and small household goods. It has outperformed its competitors over the last few years as a result of providing high quality products at reasonable prices, and also having a stronger presence online. It has kept a control on costs, partly by avoiding operating large stores on expensive city centre sites. Instead, it has had smaller stores on the edge of cities and towns, and a limited number of larger stores on convenient out-of-town sites, aiming at customers who want their journeys to shops to be quick. One of its advertising slogans has been: 'We are where you want us to be.'

Westparley Co's share price has recently performed better than most companies in the retail sector generally. Share prices in the retail sector have been relatively low as a result of poor results due to high competition, large fixed cost base and high interest rates. The exception has been shares in retailers specialising in computer and high-technology goods. These shares appear to have benefited from a boom generally in share prices of high-technology companies. Some analysts believe share prices of many companies in the high-technology sector are significantly higher than a rational analysis of their future prospects would indicate.

Exhibit 2: Matravers Co

Westparley Co has identified the listed retailer Matravers Co as an acquisition target, because it believes that Matravers Co's shares are currently undervalued and part of Matravers Co's operations would be a good strategic fit for Westparley Co.

Matravers Co operates two types of store:

Matravers Home mainly sells larger household items and home furnishings. These types of retailer have performed particularly badly recently and one major competitor of Matravers Home has just gone out of business. Matravers Home operates a number of city centre sites but has a much higher proportion of out-of-town sites than its competitors.

Matravers Tech sells computers and mobile phones in much smaller outlets than those of Matravers Home.

Extracts from Matravers Co's latest annual report are given below:

	$m
Pre-tax profit	1,950
Long-term loan	6,500
Share capital ($1 shares)	5,000

The share of pre-tax profit between Matravers Home and Matravers Tech was 80:20.

The current market value of Matravers Co's shares is $12,500m and its debt is currently trading at its book value. Westparley Co believes that it will have to pay a premium of 15% to Matravers Co's shareholders to buy the company.

Westparley Co intends to take advantage of the current values attributed to businesses such as Matravers Tech by selling this part of Matravers Co at the relevant sector price earnings ratio of 18, rather than a forecast estimate of Matravers Tech's present value of future free cash flows of $4,500m.

The company tax rate for both companies is 28% per year.

Exhibit 3: Post-acquisition cost of capital

The post-acquisition cost of capital of the combined company will be based on its cost of equity and cost of debt. The asset beta post-acquisition can be assumed to be both companies' asset betas weighted in proportion to their current market value of equity.

Westparley Co has 4,000 million $1 shares in issue, currently trading at $8.50. It has $26,000m debt in issue, currently trading at $105 per $100 nominal value. Its equity beta is 1.02.

Matravers Co's asset beta is 0.75. The current market value of Matravers Co's shares is $12,500m and its long-term loan is currently trading at its book value of $6,500m.

The risk-free rate of return is estimated to be 3.5% and the market risk premium is estimated to be 8%.

The pre-tax cost of debt of the combined company is expected to be 9·8%. It can be assumed that the debt:equity ratio of the combined company will be the same as Westparley Co's current debt:equity ratio in market values.

The company tax rate for both companies is 28% per year.

Exhibit 4: Plans for Matravers Co

The offer for Matravers Co will be a cash offer. Any funding required for this offer will be a mixture of debt and equity. Although for the purposes of the calculation it has been assumed that the overall mix of debt and equity will remain the same, the directors are considering various plans for funding the purchase which could result in a change in Westparley Co's gearing.

As soon as it acquires all of Matravers Co's share capital, Westparley Co would sell Matravers Tech as it does not fit in with Westparley Co's strategic plans and Westparley Co wishes to take advantage of the large values currently attributed to high-technology businesses. Westparley Co would then close Matravers Home's worst-performing city centre stores. It anticipates the loss of returns from these stores would be partly compensated by higher online sales by Matravers Co, generated by increased investment in its online operations. The remaining city centre stores and all out-of-town stores would start selling the food and household items currently sold in Westparley Co's stores, and Westparley Co believes that this would increase profits from those stores.

Westparley Co also feels that reorganising Matravers Co's administrative functions and using increased power as a larger retailer can lead to synergies after the acquisition.

Exhibit 5: Post-acquisition details

Once Matravers Tech has been sold, Westparley Co estimates that sales revenue from the Matravers Home stores which remain open, together with the online sales from its home business, will be $43,260m in the first year post-acquisition, and this figure is expected to grow by 3% per year in years 2 to 4.

The profit margin before interest and tax is expected to be 6% of sales revenue in years 1 to 4.

Tax allowable depreciation is assumed to be equivalent to the amount of investment needed to maintain existing operations. However, an investment in assets (including working capital) will be required of $630m in year 1. In years 2 to 4, investment in assets each year will be $0.50 of every $1 increase in sales revenue.

After four years, the annual growth rate of free cash flows is expected to be 2% for the foreseeable future.

As well as the free cash flows from Matravers Co, Westparley Co expects that post-tax synergies will arise from its planned reorganisation of Matravers Co as follows in the next three years:

Year	1	2	3
	$m	$m	$m
Free cash flows	700	750	780

The current market value of Matravers Co's shares is $12,500m and its debt is currently trading at its book value of $6,500m.

Required

(a) Discuss the behavioural factors which may have led to businesses such as Matravers Tech being valued highly. **(6 marks)**

(b) Prepare a report for the board of directors of Westparley Co which:

    (i) Compares the additional value which Westparley Co believes can be generated from the sale of Matravers Tech based on the P/E ratio, with that of the projected present value of its future free cash flows; **(4 marks)**

(ii)   Calculates the weighted average cost of capital for the combined company;

(6 marks)

(iii)   Estimates the total value which Westparley Co's shareholders will gain from the acquisition of Matravers Co; and

(10 marks)

(iv)   Assesses the strategic and financial value to Westparley Co of the acquisition, including a discussion of the estimations and assumptions made.

(12 marks)

Professional marks will be awarded in part (b) for the format, structure and presentation of the report.

(4 marks)

(c)   Discuss the factors which may determine how the offer for Matravers Co will be financed and hence the level of gearing which Westparley Co will have.

(4 marks)

(Total = 50 marks)

SECTION B: BOTH questions to be attempted

Question 2

Exhibit 1: Boullain Co

Boullain Co is based in the Eurozone and manufactures components for agricultural machinery. The company is financed by a combination of debt and equity, having obtained a listing five years ago. In addition to the founder's equity stake, the shareholders consist of pension funds and other institutional investors. Until recently, sales have been generated exclusively within the Eurozone area but the directors are keen to expand and have identified North America as a key export market. The company recently completed its first sale to a customer based in the United States, although payment will not be received for another six months.

Exhibit 2: Hedging policy and key stakeholders

At a recent board meeting, Boullain Co's finance director argued that the expansion into foreign markets creates the need for a formal hedging policy and that shareholder value would be enhanced if this policy was communicated to the company's other stakeholders. However, Boullain Co's chief executive officer disagreed with the finance director on the following grounds. First, existing shareholders are already well diversified and would therefore not benefit from additional risk reduction hedging strategies. Second, there is no obvious benefit to shareholder value by communicating the hedging policy to other stakeholders such as debt providers, employees, customers and suppliers. You have been asked to provide a rationale for the finance director's comments in advance of the next board meeting.

Exhibit 3: Hedging products

Assume today's date is 1 March 20X0. Boullain Co is due to receive $18,600,000 from the American customer on 31 August 20X0. The finance director is keen to minimise the company's exposure to foreign exchange risk and has identified forward contracts, exchange traded futures and options as a way of achieving this objective.

The following quotations have been obtained.

Exchange rates (quoted as €/US$1)

Spot	0.8707–0.8711
Six months forward	0.8729–0.8744

Currency futures (contract size €200,000; exercise price quoted as US$ per €1)

	Exercise price
March	1.1476
June	1.1449
September	1.1422

Currency options (contract size €200,000; exercise price quoted as US$ per €1, premium: US cents per €1)

	Calls			Puts		
Exercise price	March	June	September	March	June	September
1.1420	0.43	0.59	0.77	0.62	0.78	0.89

Assume futures and options contracts mature at the month end and that there is no basis risk. The number of contracts to be used should be rounded down to the nearest whole number in calculations. If the full amount cannot be hedged using an exact number of futures or options contracts, the balance is hedged using the forward market.

Exhibit 4: Margin information

Once the position is open, the euro futures contract outlined above will be marked-to-market on a daily basis. The terms of the contract require Boullain Co to deposit an initial margin of $3,500 per contract with the clearing house. Assume the maintenance margin is equivalent to the initial margin. The tick size on the contract is $0.0001.

Your manager is concerned about the impact of an open futures position on Boullain Co's cash flow and has asked you to calculate and explain the impact of the following hypothetical changes in the closing settlement price in the first three days of the contract.

Closing settlement prices (US$ per €1)

Date	Settlement price
1 March	1.1410
2 March	1.1418
3 March	1.1433

Required

(a) Explain the rationale for the policy of hedging Boullain Co's foreign exchange risk and the potential benefits to shareholder value if that policy is effectively communicated to the company's key stakeholders. **(7 marks)**

(b) Recommend a hedging strategy for Boullain Co's foreign currency receipt in six months' time based on the hedging choices the finance director is considering. Support your recommendation with appropriate discussion and relevant calculations. **(11 marks)**

(c) Calculate and explain the impact of the open futures position on Boullain Co's US$ cash flow, based on the settlement prices provided. **(7 marks)**

(Total = 25 marks)

Question 3

Exhibit 1: Hathaway Co

Hathaway Co operates in the aviation industry, manufacturing safety equipment for commercial aircraft. The company has a policy of carefully appraising new investment opportunities, including the detailed analysis of all cost and revenue assumptions prior to their approval.

Exhibit 2: Project chi

Hathaway Co's board is reviewing a potential investment, project chi. The company's engineers have developed a new technology which can detect the potential for mechanical failure with a greater degree of accuracy than has previously been the case. Early test results have been extremely encouraging.

If the board accepts the engineers' proposal, Hathaway Co would need to submit an application to the relevant regulatory authority. It is expected regulatory approval would be granted in one year's time. Manufacturing and sales would commence immediately after being granted regulatory approval. Hathaway Co's chief engineer presented an investment case for project chi to the board, including a summary of the following cost and revenue forecasts and assumptions.

Hathaway Co is expected to sell 3,000 units in the first year of production with demand increasing by 5% in each subsequent year of its four-year life. These sales forecasts are based on a contribution of $5,000 per unit in the first year of production and increasing at 2% per year in subsequent years. Annual fixed costs of $8.7m are expected in the first year of production, increasing at 3% per year throughout the life of the project.

An investment in plant and machinery of $12m will be required as soon as regulatory approval has been granted. Tax allowable depreciation is available on the plant and machinery at an annual rate of 20% on a straight-line basis. A balancing adjustment is expected at the end of the project when the plant and machinery will be scrapped.

Tax is payable at 20% in the year in which profits are made. The relevant cost of capital to be used in the appraisal is 12%.

Exhibit 3: Project chi extra information

The finance director, however, raised the following objections and consequences to the chief engineer's presentation.

The chief engineer's cost and revenue assumptions ignore the possibility of a recession, which has a 20% probability of occurring. In a recession, the total present values for the four years of production are likely to be 40% lower. The finance director also believes there is an alternative, mutually exclusive, development opportunity based on the new technology although this would still depend on it being granted regulatory approval. This alternative option would incur an identical investment cost of $12m but generate annual, inflation adjusted, post-tax cash flows of $3.43m over its seven-year life from year two onwards.

The investment case assumes regulatory approval is certain whereas historically only 70% of Hathaway Co's applications have been approved. In one year's time, if the regulatory application is not approved, it is assumed that the concept can be sold to Gepe Co for $1.0m at that time. If the board rejects the proposal now, assume the concept can be sold for $4.3m immediately.

Exhibit 4: Projects lambda and kappa

A recent board meeting discussed two recent investments, projects lambda and kappa, both involving the construction of new manufacturing plants for safety equipment. Both projects are now operational although project lambda experienced significant time delays and cost overruns while project kappa was under budget and within schedule.

On closer examination, the directors noticed that project lambda's revenue far exceeded initial expectations, whereas project kappa's revenue was much less than originally expected. On balance, Hathaway Co's chief executive officer suggested that each project's successes compensated for their respective failings and that this was to be expected when making predictions about the future in an investment plan. However, one of the directors suggested the company could benefit from the introduction of a capital investment monitoring system and post-completion audit. The directors agreed to discuss this in greater depth at the next board meeting.

Required

(a)   (i)   Evaluate the financial acceptability of the project chi investment proposal based on the chief engineer's forecasts, assuming regulatory approval is granted in one year's time.   **(6 marks)**

       (ii)   Calculate the expected net present value of the proposal based on the finance director's assumptions about the likelihood of a recession and the potential impact on project chi's cash flows.   **(2 marks)**

       (iii)   Calculate the net present value of the finance director's alternative option for the technology and advise the board whether this is worth pursuing.   **(3 marks)**

       (iv)   Recommend whether the board should proceed with the application for regulatory approval after taking into consideration Hathaway Co's 70% approval rate with its regulatory applications or to sell the concept now to Gepe Co. Include in your analysis any comments on your findings.   **(6 marks)**

(b)   Explain the rationale for implementing capital investment monitoring systems and post-completion audits. Suggest ways in which Hathaway Co may have benefited if these procedures had been applied to projects lambda and kappa.   **(8 marks)**

(Total = 25 marks)

Answers

DO NOT TURN THIS PAGE UNTIL YOU HAVE
COMPLETED THE MOCK EXAM

Exam success skills

In any AFM exam it will be important to apply good general exam technique by using the six exam success skills identified at the start of the Revision Kit, in the section covering 'essential skills'. These skills are: 1. Case scenario: Managing information; 2. Correct interpretation of requirements; 3. Answer planning: Priorities, structure and logic; 4. Efficient numerical analysis; 5. Effective writing and presentation; and 6. Good time management.

Some examples of how to apply these skills in this exam are provided in the table below.

Skill	Examples
Managing information	It is crucially important to assimilate the information in the question scenario.
	In longer questions, such as the 50 mark question, it is difficult to assimilate information by simply starting at the beginning and reading to the end because there is so much information to take in.
	Instead it is sensible to take an active approach to reading each question. Read enough of the question to get an idea of the basic scenario and then read the initial requirements so that you understand the first things that you are expected to do with this information.
Correct Interpretation of requirements	Be careful to interpret the verbs used in the question requirements carefully.
	Also be careful to identify where a question requirement contains more than one instruction.
	For example, in Q1(biv) the question requires an assessment of strategic AND financial issues.
Answer planning	This is always important in AFM questions.
	For example, in risk management questions such as Q2(b), it is especially important that your plan correctly identifies the risk being faced; the relevant timings; and basis. If you get these wrong, then there will be a cap on the number of marks that you can score (however accurate your answers are).
Efficient numerical analysis	It is essential that the marker can follow your workings and your logic.
	It is also important that you accept that under exam conditions you will not get all the calculations correct, and that this is not necessary in order to score a strong pass mark.
	If you make a mistake early in your calculations that affects your later calculations then the marker will only penalise the error you have made, and not its follow-on impact on other calculations. This means that it is not normally a good use of your time to correct such errors during the exam.
	For example, in Question 2(b) an error in the number of contracts (rounding up instead of down as instructed in the question) would only attract a small penalty despite its impact on the final numbers.
Effective writing and presentation	In Q1 there are four marks available for professional structure (eg use of sub-headings, appendices etc). Many of the techniques used here are good practice in all questions throughout the exam.
	It is also very important to relate your points to the scenario and to the requirement wherever possible. This does not mean simply repeating the details from the question but using this information to help to explain the point you are making.
	For example, in 1(b)(iv) it is not enough to state the assumptions, you need to discuss their relevance.

Skill	Examples
Good Time Management	The exam is 3 hours 15 minutes long, which translates to 1.95 minutes per mark.
	If you build in an allowance of 20% of your time for assimilating the scenario and planning, this falls to 1.56 minutes per mark (1.95 × 0.8).
	It is essential that you do not allow yourself to become bogged down in the harder numerical areas of the exam
	For example, in Q(1) it is vital to leave enough time to answer the discursive parts, especially part (c).
	At the beginning of a question, work out the amount of time you should be spending on:
	(a) Planning:
	(i) for a 25 mark question this will be about 1.95 × 25 marks × 20% = 10 minutes
	(ii) for a 50 mark question this should be about 20 mins.
	(b) Writing your answer to each requirement:
	(i) Take the mark allocation and multiply by 1.56 minutes per mark.

Diagnostic

Did you apply these skills when reading, planning, and writing up your answer? Identify the exam success skills where you think you need to improve and capture your thoughts here of what you want to achieve when attempting questions in future.

BPP LEARNING MEDIA

Question 1

Marking scheme

				Marks
(a)		1–2 marks per relevant point (examples may include asking price, opportunity to purchase and information available is positive, herd instinct, following fashion and confirmation bias)		Max 6
(b)	(i)	Share of pre-tax profit	1	
		After-tax profit	1	
		Proceeds from sell-off	1	
		Comparison with free cash flow valuation	$\underline{1}$	
			$\underline{4}$	
	(ii)	Westparley Co MV debt and equity	1	
		Westparley Co asset beta	1	
		Combined company asset beta	1	
		Combined company equity beta	1	
		Combined company cost of equity	1	
		Combined company cost of capital	$\underline{1}$	
			$\underline{6}$	
	(iii)	Sales revenue		
		Profit before interest and tax	1	
		Tax	1	
		Additional capital investment	1	
		PV of free cash flows years 1–4	1	
		PV of free cash flows year 5 onwards	1	
		Present value of synergies	2	
		Premium payable	1	
		Value attributable to Westparley Co's shareholders	1	
			$\underline{1}$	
			$\underline{10}$	

(iv)	Strategic value	
	Financial value	3–4
	Estimations made	2–3
	Assumptions made	3–4
		3–4
		Max 12

Professional marks for part (b)

Report format	1
Structure and presentation of the report	3
	4

(c) 1–2 marks per relevant point
(examples may include available security, available tax relief,
shareholder attitude to debt, industry norms)   Max 8

50

(a) Individual business

A number of behavioural factors, to do with the individual company as well as the sector as a whole, may lead to Matravers Tech being valued higher than appears to be warranted by rational analysis of its future prospects. One possible factor is the asking price, even if it is not a fair one, may provide a reference point which significantly influences the purchaser's valuation of the business.

The fact that Matravers Tech is available for purchase may help raise its price. Purchasers may see this as a rare opportunity to buy an attractive business in this retail sector. This will be made more likely if investors have loss aversion bias, a desire to buy Matravers Tech now because otherwise the opportunity will be lost.

Matravers Tech being offered for sale will mean that information about the company, showing it in a positive light, will be available for purchasers. This could result in availability bias, investors taking particular note of this information because they can readily obtain it, rather than other information which may be more difficult or costly to find.

Sector

There are a number of possible behavioural reasons why share prices in this sector appear generally higher than rational analysis indicates. One is the herd instinct, investing in the sector because other investors have also been buying shares, not wishing to make judgements independently of other investors.

The herd instinct may be generated by previous share price movements. Investors may believe once prices start rising in the sector, they will continue to do so indefinitely.

Following fashion may also be a factor. Fund managers who wish to give the impression that they are actively managing their portfolio by making regular changes to it, may have a preference for companies which appear up-to-date and are currently popular. This may be linked to an expectation that sales of technologically-advanced goods are likely to generate high returns.

There is also confirmation bias, the idea that investors will pay attention to evidence which confirms their views that the sector is a good one in which to invest, and ignore evidence which contradicts their beliefs. In the past, technology companies have been valued using methods which support the beliefs of investors that they are of high value, rather than traditional methods, such as cash flow analysis, which suggest a lower business value is more realistic.

(b) (iv) Report to the board of directors, Westparley Co

This report evaluates whether the acquisition of Matravers Co would be beneficial to Westparley Co's shareholders by estimating the future value generated by Matravers Co (i.e. Matravers Home currently), the proceeds from selling Matravers Tech and the additional value created from synergies immediately after the companies are combined.

Strategic fit

The strategic case for taking over the business appears to be strongest for the out-of-town stores and the online business. The acquisition would provide an additional out-of-town presence for Westparley Co. Better usage in the out-of-town stores could generate higher returns. Having the food and home businesses on the same site could generate some cross-sales between the two. Possibly combining the two companies' online presence and investing further could mean Matravers Home benefiting from the factors which have driven strong performance by Westparley Co.

Taking over the city centre stores, even the successful ones, seems to have less strategic logic, however. Westparley Co would be taking on a high cost burden. The success of the food business in city centres is doubtful, as food shops sited there will be less convenient for customers who do not live in the city centres, and Westparley Co has marketed itself as being easily accessible for customers. There is, perhaps, wider incompatibility between the two businesses. The food business is characterised by quick shopping for often a limited number of items, whereas purchases in the home business, particularly of larger items, are likely to take longer and site convenience be less of an issue.

Financial aspects

Based on the predictions for future cash flows and required premiums from Matravers Co's shareholders, the acquisition would add value to Westparley Co's shareholders, if, and only if, the excess value on selling Matravers Tech and the synergies are both largely achieved. Together they add up to $2,400m ($558m + $1,842m) compared with total added value of $1,897m. There are questions about the estimates for these figures and also the estimates for the future free cash flows of the current Matravers Home business.

Synergies

Most of the additional value is due to synergies and it is difficult to see how the synergies are calculated. There is likely to be scope for some administrative savings. However, operational cost synergies appear less obvious as the two companies are operating in different retail sectors. Any synergy figures will also have to take account of costs in achieving synergies, such as store closure costs, and also commitments such as leases which may be a burden for some time. Synergies may also not be achieved because of lack of co-operation by staff or problems integrating the two businesses.

Current Matravers Home business

The suggested increase in cash flows appears doubtful for a number of reasons. If stores being closed are making positive cash flow contributions, these will have to be replaced. Whether they can be is doubtful given the problems in this part of the retail sector. It may be a more profitable use of store space to have an area for food sales, but the food sales generated in Matravers Co's shops may take business from Westparley Co's existing shops. Similarly, increased online sales may be at the expense of sales in stores.

Sale of Matravers Tech

There is no indication of how interested buyers will be in the business. The industry price-earnings (P/E) ratio used may be an average which does not reflect Matravers Tech's circumstances. It would be better to find a P/E ratio for a proxy company with similar financial and business risk. As Matravers Tech would not be listed, this would suggest a discount to the P/E ratio should be applied. Since also Westparley Co has an estimate of future free cash flow, potential buyers may be able to come up with their own estimates and base the price they are prepared to pay on their estimates.

Other assumptions

One important assumption is the 15% premium expected to be required by Matravers Co's shareholders. Other assumptions made in the calculations include operating profit margin and tax rates remaining constant and cash flows being assumed to increase to perpetuity. Incremental capital investment is assumed to be accurate. It is assumed that the cost of debt will remain unchanged and that the asset beta, cost of equity and cost of debt can be determined accurately. Given all the assumptions, Westparley Co should carry out sensitivity analysis using different assumptions and obtaining a range of values.

Conclusion

On the assumptions made, the acquisition appears to add financial value for the shareholders of Westparley Co. However, the figures are subject to a significant number of uncertainties and the strategic logic for buying the whole Matravers business appears unclear. On balance, Westparley Co may want to consider a more limited acquisition of just the out-of-town stores if these are available, as their acquisition appears to make better strategic sense.

Report compiled by:

Date

Appendix 1 Estimate of additional value created from sell-off of Matravers Tech (b)(i)

Share of pre-tax profit = 20% × $1,950m = $390m

After-tax profit = $390m × (1 − 0.28) = $281m

Proceeds from sell-off based on P/E ratio = $281m × 18 = $5,058m

Excess value from sell-off = $5,058m − $4,500m = $558m

Appendix 2 Estimate of combined company cost of capital (b)(ii)

Matravers Co asset beta = 0.75

Westparley Co asset beta

Market value of debt = 1.05 × $26,000m = $27,300m

Market value of equity = 4,000 million × $8.50 = $34,000m

Asset beta = 1.02 × (34,000)/(34,000 + (27,300 × 0.72)) = 0·65

Combined company, asset beta

Market value of Matravers Co equity = $12,500m

Asset beta = ((0.75 × 12,500) + (0.65 × 34,000))/(12,500 + 34,000) = 0.68

Equity beta = 0.68 ((34,000 + (27,300 × 0.72))/34,000) = 1.07

Combined company cost of equity = 3.5% + (1.07 x 8%) = 12.1%

Combined company cost of capital = ((34,000 × 12.1%) + (27,300 × 9.8% × 0.72))/ (34,000 + 27,300) = 9.9%, say 10%

Appendix 3 Estimate of the value created for Westparley Co's shareholders (b)(iii)

Cash flows, years 1 to 4

Year	1	2	3	4
	$m	$m	$m	$m
Sales revenue	43,260	44,558	45,895	47,272
Profit before interest and tax	2,596	2,673	2,754	2,836
Tax	(727)	(748)	(771)	(794)
Additional capital investment	(630)	(649)	(669)	(689)
Free cash flows	1,239	1,276	1,314	1,353
Discount factor	0.909	0.826	0.751	0.683
Present value of free cash flows	1,126	1,054	987	924

Present value years 1 to 4 = $4,091m

Present value year 5 onwards (($1,353m × 1.02)/(0.1 − 0.02)) × 1.10^{-4} = $11,781m

Total present value = $4,091m + $11,781m = $15,872m

Synergies

Year	1	2	3
	$m	$m	$m
Free cash flows	700	750	780
Discount factor	0.909	0.826	0.751
Present value of cash flows	636	620	586

Present value of synergies = $1,842m

Amount payable for Matravers Co's shares = $12,500m × 1.15 = $14,375m

Value attributable to Matravers Co's investors = $14,375m + $6,500m = $20,875m

Value attributable to Westparley Co shareholders = present value of cash flows + proceeds from sell-off + value of synergies − value to Matravers Co's investors

= $15,872m + $5,058m + $1,842m − $20,875m = $1,897m

(c) **Calculation of gearing**

If gearing is calculated on the basis of market values, a fall in the share price will result in the level of gearing rising. Westparley Co's board may be worried about a fall in the share price given the problems affecting many companies' share prices in the retail sector and the possibility that the stock market may react adversely to the acquisition.

Directors' preferences

Directors may have their own preferences about financing. They may be able to choose a mix of sources and a level of gearing which reflects these preferences. Directors may be concerned about too high a burden of payment to finance providers, in terms of cost or ultimately repayment of debt. They may not wish to commit the company to conditions imposed by finance providers. By contrast, they may be concerned about how a change in the shareholder base as a result of a share issue may impact upon their own position. Directors may also be concerned about the impression given by their choice of finance. Pecking order theory states that equity issue is seen as the last resort for financing, so if the purchase is financed by an equity issue, it may be seen as a sign of a lack of confidence by directors that Westparley Co can sustain its current share price.

Costs and cash flows

Gearing decisions may not just be determined by their own preferences but by external conditions or constraints. Choosing more debt could lower the overall cost of capital, due to lower cost and tax relief, making investments such as Matravers Co appear more profitable. Higher levels of debt may result in the cost of equity rising, reducing the overall impact on the cost of capital. Against that, higher levels of debt mean increased finance cost commitments, even though Westparley Co may need further cash for investment in stores. This may be an important concern if interest rates are high. By contrast, dividends to shareholders do not have to be paid when returns are low or money is required for investment, although failure to meet dividend expectations may result in the board being pressurised by shareholders.

Availability

The availability of finance may also be a significant issue, particularly if an acquisition has to be completed quickly. An equity issue may take time to arrange and require shareholder approval. Sufficient debt finance may be difficult to obtain if lenders feel that Westparley Co already has significant commitments to debt finance providers. The timescale over which finance is available may be significant. Westparley Co may seek longer-term finance if existing debt finance is due to be repaid soon or if significant cash

 BPP LEARNING MEDIA

ANSWERS

is needed for short-term investment, not just in Matravers Co's stores, but also in Westparley Co's existing stores.

Mix

Other external factors may influence the mix of finance chosen. Westparley Co's directors may be concerned about keeping the level of gearing at or below the industry average, because of finance providers becoming worried if gearing exceeds industry levels. Keeping debt as a significant element in overall finance may act as a deterrent to acquirers becoming interested in making a bid for Westparley Co. Directors may also not have a target figure in mind but be content if gearing is within a range of values.

Question 2

> **Workbook references.** The rationale for risk management is covered in Chapters 2 and 11, and foreign currency hedging is covered in Chapter 12.
>
> **Top tips.** It is important to answer all parts of a requirement. For example, there are two aspects to parts (a) and part (c) but many candidates ignored one of these two aspects and therefore limited the number of marks that they could score to half the marks available for that requirement.
>
> **Easy marks.** One twist in this question is that the question specifically says that "If the full amount cannot be hedged using an exact number of futures or options contracts, the balance is hedged using the forward market". This complicates the calculations but if this aspect to the calculations had been ignored then it was still possible to score 10 of the 11 marks, so ignoring this complication would have been understandable / sensible under exam conditions.
>
> **Examining team's comments.** The examining team made the point that answers need to make clear which currency is being used to avoid basic errors such as adding together amounts that are in different currencies.

Marking scheme

			Marks
(a)	Rationale for hedging policy		
	Communication of policy with stakeholders	3–4	
		3–4	
(b)	Forward		Max 7
	Buy September futures	1	
	Number of futures contracts	1	
	Predicted futures rate	1	
	Underhedge futures	1	
	Buy September calls	1	
	Option premium	1	
	Futures outcome	1	
	Outcome	1	
	Discussion and recommendation	2–3	
			Max 11
(c)	Initial and/or maintenance margins	1	
	Daily profit or loss calculations	3	
	Explanation	3	
		7	
			25

(a) **Rationale for hedging policy**

Within the framework of Modigliani and Miller, Boullain Co's CEO is correct in stating that a company's hedging policy is irrelevant. In a world without transaction or agency costs, and where markets are efficient and information symmetrical, hedging creates no value if shareholders are well diversified. Shareholder value may even be destroyed if the costs associated with hedging exceed the benefits.

However, in the real world where market imperfections exist, including the transaction costs of bankruptcy and other types of financial distress, hedging protects shareholder value by avoiding the distress costs associated with potentially devastating foreign exchange fluctuations.

Active hedging may also benefit debt-holders by reducing the agency costs of debt. A clearly defined hedging policy acts as a signalling tool between shareholders and debt-holders. In this sense, hedging allows for higher leverage and a lower cost of debt and reduces the need for restrictive covenants.

Communication of policy with stakeholders

Even when foreign exchange risks are hedged, the funding of variation margin payments on exchange traded futures can create financial distress. A well communicated hedging strategy allows debt providers to make informed decisions about Boullain Co's ability to service its debt.

Agency costs and the risk of financial distress also impact the expected wealth of employees who, unlike shareholders, may not enjoy the risk reduction benefits of a diversified portfolio. A consistent hedging policy reduces the risks faced by employees which may serve to benefit Boullain Co in the form of motivational and productivity improvements.

Customers and suppliers have claims on a company which create shareholder value but are conditional upon Boullain Co's survival. Suppliers may invest in production systems which create value in the form of lower costs. For customers, these claims reflect promises of quality and after-sales service levels which enable Boullain Co to charge higher prices. In both cases, shareholder value is created as long as the customers and suppliers believe these claims will be honoured. One way of achieving this is by implementing a hedging strategy and communicating it to stakeholders.

In conclusion, management should attempt to communicate the principles underlying its hedging strategy and the benefits to shareholder value in the form of reduced agency and distress costs. In this way, stakeholders can make informed decisions about the potential risks and impact on their expected wealth.

(b) **Forward contract**

$18,600,000 × 0.8729 = €16,235,940

Futures

Buy September € futures

Calculation of futures price

Spot rate (US$/€1) = 1/0.8707 = 1.1485

Predicted futures using spot rate = 1.1422 + ((1.1485 − 1.1422) × 1/7) = 1.1431

Or using futures: 1.1422 + ((1.1449 − 1.1422) × 1/3)) = 1.1431

Number of contracts

Expected receipt = $18,600,000/1.1431 = €16,271,542

Number of contracts = €16,271,542/€200,000 = 81.4, say 81 contracts

Amount underhedged = $18,600,000 − (81 × €200,000 × 1.1431$/€) = $81,780

(Note that this is a minor area worth 1 mark; credit will be given for recognising the underhedged amount, whatever exchange rate is applied to it.)

Receipt at forward rate = $81,780 × 0.8729€/$ = €71,386

Outcome

	€
Futures (81 × 200,000)	16,200,000
Forward market	71,386
	16,271,386

Options

September € call options

Number of contracts

Payment = $18,600,000/1.1420$/€ = €16,287,215

Number of contracts = €16,287,215/€200,000 = 81.4, say 81 contracts

Premium

Premium = 81 × €200,000 × 0.0077$/€ = $124,740

Translate at spot = $124,740 × 0.8711€/$ = €108,661

Amount underhedged = $18,600,000 − (81 × €200,000 × 1.1420$/€) = $99,600

Receipt at forward rate = $99,600 × 0.8729€/$ = €86,941

Outcome

	€
Options (81 × €200,000)	16,200,000
Premium	(108,661)
Forward market	86,941
	16,178,280

Recommendation

The forward and futures contracts fix the exchange rate with the futures contract generating a slightly higher euro receipt compared to the forward. However, the futures contract is exposed to basis risk and is marked-to-market daily. The initial margin and variation margins need to be funded and would impact cash flow in the short term.

The option outcome of €16,178,280 provides a worst-case scenario based on the option being exercised. The option premium is expensive which results in a lower receipt if the option is exercised. Unlike the forward and futures contracts, however, the option allows Boullain Co to retain the upside whilst also protecting against the downside risk. Based on the forward and futures markets, the dollar is expected to strengthen and it is therefore unlikely the option would be exercised.

The final hedging choice depends on the board's attitude to risk. However, assuming there is no default risk associated with the forward contract, this may be the best choice under the circumstances. The board may also wish to consider the possibility of not hedging since the dollar is expected to strengthen.

(c) **Marking-to-market**

Initial margin = maintenance margin = $3,500 × 81 = $283,500

1 March:

((1.1410 − 1.1422)/0.0001) × $20 × 81 = $19,440 loss

Maintenance margin is 100% of initial margin:

Therefore variation margin = $19,440

2 March:

((1.1418 − 1.1410)/0.0001) × $20 × 81 = $12,960 profit

3 March:

((1.1433 − 1.1418)/0.0001) × $20 × 81 = $24,300 profit

In order to reduce counter-party risk, Boullain Co deposits the initial margin of $283,500 with the clearing house when the futures position is opened. The notional profit or loss at each day's closing settlement price is added to or subtracted from the margin account balance. If the margin account balance falls below the level of the maintenance margin, Boullain Co is required to deposit additional funds to top up the margin account.

Boullain Co makes a notional loss at the end of the first day and would therefore pay a variation margin to return the margin account to the level of the specified maintenance margin. Since Boullain Co makes a notional profit on the subsequent two days, the amount in the margin account will be greater than the specified maintenance margin and no variation margin is required. The profit on each of those days may be withdrawn in cash.

Question 3

Workbook references. Project appraisal is mainly covered in Chapter 3.

Easy marks. There are easy numerical marks in part (a) if you read the question carefully and produce the required analysis.

Examining team's comments. A significant number of candidates lost a mark in part (a)(iv) by omitting a justification for their recommendation on whether to accept or reject the project. A significant number of candidates made unsatisfactory attempts at part (b), mistaking capital investment monitoring to mean assessing whether a potential investment project should be accepted or not.

Marking scheme

			Marks
(a)	(i)	Contribution	2
		Fixed costs	1
		Tax (including tax allowable)	2
		NPV	1
			6
	(ii)	Expected NPV	2
	(iii)	Alternative option NPV	2
		Decision outcome	1
			3
	(iv)	Decision	2
		Comments	4
			6
(b)	Capital investment monitoring:		
	Rationale		2
	Benefits		2–3
	Post-completion audit:		
	Rationale		2–3
	Benefits		8
			Max 8
			25

(a) (i) **Net present value (NPV):** All figures are in $ms unless otherwise indicated

Year	1	2	3	4	5
Contribution (w1)		15.00	16.07	17.21	18.43
Fixed costs		(8.70)	(8.96)	(9.23)	(9.51)
Tax allowable depreciation		(2.40)	(2.40)	(2.40)	(2.40)
Balancing adjustment					(2.40)
Taxable profits		3.90	4.71	5.58	4.12
Taxation (20%)		(0.78)	(0.94)	(1.12)	(0.82)
Add back depreciation		2.40	2.40	2.40	4.80
Investment cost	(12.00)				
Cash flows	(12.00)	5.52	6.17	6.86	8.1
Discount factors (12%)	0.893	0.797	0.712	0.636	0.567
NPV	(10.72)	4.40	4.39	4.36	4.59
	7.02				

(Alternatively this can be calculated using the =NPV function to work out the value of the cash flows from time 1-5)

Workings

1   *Working 1 (W1): Contribution*

Year	2	3	4	5
Volume (000s)	3.00	3.15	3.31	3.47
Contribution per unit ($000s)	5.00	5.10	5.20	5.31
Contribution ($m)	15.00	16.07	17.21	18.43

(ii) **Incorporating finance director's objections**

Expected NPV of chief engineer's proposal:

PV of years 2–5 = $17.74m

60% PV of years 2–5 = $10.64m

Expected PV of years 2–5 = (0.8 × $17.74m + 0.2 × $10.64m) = $16.32m

Expected NPV = $16.32m – $10.72m = $5.6m

(iii) **Alternative option NPV**

Annuity factor (12%, t2 – t8) = 4.968 – 0.893 = 4.075

PV of years 2–8 = 4.075 × $3.43m = $13.98m

NPV = $13.98m – $10.72m = $3.26m

Therefore, it is more beneficial to follow the chief engineer's proposal.

(iv) **Apply for regulatory approval or sell**

Next, consider decision to sell to Gepe Co now or continue with application for regulatory approval.

NPV of sale to Gepe Co now = $4.3m

Expected NPV = 0.7 × $5.6m + 0.3 × (0.893 × $1.0m) = $4.19m

Therefore, more beneficial to sell immediately to Gepe Co.

Recommendation:

Immediate sale to Gepe Co for $4.3 million.

Comments

Based on the chief engineer's assumptions, the project generates a positive NPV of $7.02 million and should therefore be accepted in preference to the option to sell the concept for $4.3 million. On the other hand, when the finance director's objections are incorporated into the appraisal, the expected NPV is only $4.19 million and should therefore be rejected in favour of the option to sell.

It should be noted that the expected NPV of $4.19 million is an average. In other words, it is the average NPV if the project is carried out repeatedly which may not be useful in the case of a one-off development opportunity. Based on the calculations above, there is a 30% chance that the NPV will be only $893,000, which may pose a risk the directors are not prepared to take. The directors' attitude to risk will be an important factor in the final decision.

Furthermore, the analysis largely depends upon the values of the probabilities prescribed, the range of possible outcomes and the accuracy of the revenue and cost assumptions. Sensitivity analysis may be useful in testing the impact of variations in each of these variables on the final outcome.

(b)   Whilst Hathaway Co's investment plans are based on a detailed analysis of all cost and revenue assumptions, projects lambda and kappa highlight failings in the appraisal and implementation phases.

Capital investment monitoring

Capital investment monitoring involves reviewing the implementation of an investment project to ensure it progresses according to the original investment plan, timescale and budget. This involves assessing the risks associated with the implementation phase and identifying deviations from the investment plan so that remedial action can be taken where necessary. Controls should be established to ensure effective delivery of the project.

Effective investment monitoring may have avoided the cost overruns and time delays experienced by Hathaway Co's project lambda. The appointment of a project manager would have ensured ownership of the project and provided accountability for time delays and cost increases. The original investment plan, including cost estimates, provides a benchmark against which actual performance can be assessed. An effective monitoring system would ensure that any changes to the cost estimates would be justified and authorised. Where significant deviations are encountered, it may be necessary to terminate the project. A project steering committee would ensure greater scrutiny and accountability and oversee the implementation phase.

Post-completion audit

A post-completion audit is an objective, after the fact, appraisal of all phases of the capital investment process regarding a specific project. Each project is examined from conception until as much as a few years after it has become operational. It examines the rationale behind the initial investment decision, including the strategic fit, and the efficiency and effectiveness of the outcome. The key objective is to improve the appraisal and implementation of future capital investment projects by learning from past mistakes and successes.

An effective post-completion audit may have identified the reasons behind the failure of Hathaway Co's project kappa to achieve its forecast revenues. By comparing the actual project outcome with the original projections, an audit will examine whether the benefits claimed prior to approval ever materialise. The audit is not an academic exercise; an effective audit would identify failings and help Hathaway Co learn from past mistakes as well replicate its successes. Project kappa's principal failing seems to be the inaccuracy of the revenue assumptions. An audit would establish the reasons behind that failing and identify ways in which this can be addressed. For example, it is possible the initial assumptions failed to predict future competitor actions or the full range of potential economic scenarios. In this way, Hathaway Co's managers benefit by learning how to appraise investment proposals more accurately and implement them more efficiently than before.

(**Note.** *Credit will be given for alternative and valid discursive comments*)

ACCA
Advanced Financial Management
Mock Examination 4
Sep/Dec 2020
Sample questions

Questions	
Time allowed 3 hours and 15 minutes	
Section A	THIS question is compulsory and MUST be attempted
Section B	BOTH questions to be attempted

DO NOT OPEN THIS EXAM UNTIL YOU ARE READY TO START
UNDER EXAMINATION CONDITIONS

SECTION A: THIS QUESTION is compulsory and MUST be attempted

Question 1

Exhibit 1: Kingtim Co

Kingtim Co is a nationwide chain of garden centres, selling products such as plants, fertilisers, tools and garden furniture. It was established 20 years ago by the current team of executive directors and achieved a listing on its local stock market four years ago. Since listing, the company has made consistent profits and has been able to increase its dividends each year. The executive directors collectively own between them 25% of issued share capital. The remaining shares are held by a number of investors, with none of them owning more than 10% of issued share capital.

Two of Kingtim Co's major competitors have been taken over in the last two years. Media coverage suggests that further takeovers are possible. Potential acquirers include other chains of garden centres, property developers and supermarket chains looking to diversify their business into the profitable garden centre sector. As yet, no potential acquirer has approached Kingtim Co to buy the whole chain, although Kingtim Co has had enquiries from other businesses wanting to purchase individual garden centres. Kingtim Co can sell a number of individual garden centres without threatening its continued existence.

Exhibit 2: Takeover defences

Kingtim Co's executive directors remain committed to the business. They are fearful of a takeover, believing that the new owners will want some, or all of them, to leave the company. They have therefore been considering possible defences against a takeover bid. Kingtim Co's chief executive has received two proposals from directors:

(1)   Sell individual garden centres which would be particularly attractive to purchasers. Disposal of these centres would make Kingtim Co, overall, a less attractive purchase.

(2)   Pay the executive directors higher remuneration and change their contracts so that they would receive much higher compensation for loss of office if their contracts were terminated early.

Kingtim Co's chief executive believes, however, that any defence Kingtim Co adopts should also strengthen the company's future. They are therefore proposing to expand the company's current limited sales of camping products in its garden centres by establishing a chain of Kingtim outdoor shops, selling camping, walking and other outdoor equipment. The outdoor retail sector is competitive, but the chief executive believes that Kingtim Co will be successful. The establishment of the chain of outdoor shops would be funded solely by debt, the idea being that changing Kingtim Co's finance structure by having significantly more debt would make it less attractive to acquirers.

Exhibit 3: Financial details

Kingtim Co currently has 25 million $1 shares in issue, with a current share price of $5.56 per share. It also has 0.45 million 6.5% bonds in issue. Each 6.5% bond has a nominal value of $100 and is currently trading at $104 per $100. The premium on redemption of the bonds in three years' time is 2%. Based on a yield to maturity approach, the after-tax cost of the bonds is 4.1%.

Kingtim Co's quoted equity beta for its existing garden centre business is 0.9.

Kingtim Co plans to issue 0.6 million, 7.5%, new bonds, each with a nominal value of $100. These bonds will be redeemable in four years' time at a premium of 8%. The coupon on these bonds will be payable on an annual basis. These bonds are anticipated to have a credit rating of BBB–. The issue of the new 7.5% bonds will not affect the market value of Kingtim Co's shares or the existing 6.5% bonds.

The market value of the new bonds will be determined by using information relating to Kingtim Co's credit rating and the four bonds which the government has issued to estimate Kingtim Co's yield curve. All the bonds are of the same risk class. Details of the bonds are as follows:

Bond	Annual yield (based on spot rate)	Redeemable in
Ga	4%	1 year
Th	4.3%	2 years
De	4.7%	3 years
Ro	5.2%	4 years

Credit spreads, shown in basis points, are as follows:

Rating	1 year	2 years	3 years	4 years
BBB–	56	78	106	135

Kingtim Co plans to invest $60m in non-current assets for the outdoor shops (working capital requirements can be ignored). Currently, Kingtim Co's non-current assets have a net book value of $150m. It is assumed that the proportion of the book value of non-current assets which will be invested in the outdoor shops and the garden centres will give a fair representation of the size of each business within Kingtim Co. The asset beta of similar companies in the outdoor retail sector is assumed to be 0.88.

Before taking into consideration the impact of this new investment, Kingtim Co's forecast pre-tax earnings for the coming year is $24m. It is estimated that the new investment will make a 10% pre-tax return.

The corporation tax rate applicable to all companies is 25% per year. The current risk-free rate of return is estimated to be 4% and the market risk premium is estimated to be 9%.

Exhibit 4: Employee remuneration

Kingtim Co's annual report contains a general commitment to act with social responsibility, in line with society's expectations. It also commits to paying its staff fairly in accordance with their responsibilities and states that its staff are vital to its success.

To try to improve the situation of low-paid employees, the government has recommended a basic hourly wage as the minimum level employees should be paid, although this minimum is not legally enforceable. A newspaper investigation has revealed that some staff in Kingtim Co's garden centres in the northern region of the country are paid up to 15% less per hour than the recommended minimum wage. Most of these staff are part-time staff, working limited hours each week.

The manager of Kingtim Co's northern region centres, when asked to comment, stated that Kingtim Co had obligations to its shareholders to control staff costs. Lower pay levels were necessary to differentiate between staff, ensuring that managers and staff with experience and expertise were appropriately rewarded. The manager commented that pay levels also reflected the lower commitment to Kingtim Co which part-time staff made compared with full-time staff.

Required

(a) Discuss the feasibility and effectiveness of the defence strategies of selling off individual garden centres and enhancing directors' remuneration. **(7 marks)**

(b) Prepare a report for the board of directors of Kingtim Co which:

(i) Estimates the company's cost of capital before the new bonds are issued;

(4 marks)

(ii) Estimates the market value and yield to maturity of the new bonds; **(7 marks)**

(iii) Estimates the revised cost of equity and revised cost of capital if the new bonds are issued; **(7 marks)**

(iv)   Estimates the impact of the chief executive's proposal on forecast after-tax earnings for the coming year; and   **(3 marks)**

(v)   Discusses the impact on Kingtim Co's cost of capital and the reaction of equity and bond holders to the chief executive's proposal. The discussion should include an explanation of any assumptions made in the estimates in (b) (i) – (iv) above.

                                                                                                         (10 marks)

Professional marks will be awarded in part (b) for the format, structure and presentation of the report.   **(4 marks)**

(c)   Discuss the approach taken to employee remuneration by Kingtim Co's Northern region and the issues associated with it.   **(8 marks)**

                                                                                                         (50 marks)

SECTION B: BOTH questions to be attempted

Question 2

Exhibit 1: Colvin Co

Colvin Co is based in the eurozone region and was established ten years ago to manufacture competition standard bicycles for professional road racers. When the company obtained a listing five years ago, the founder retained a small minority shareholding. The remaining shares are held by a number of institutional investors.

The board recently decided to expand the range of models and to look for new growth opportunities abroad. Whilst manufacturing is currently restricted to the eurozone, the board of directors has identified Canvia as a key growth market and is considering a potential investment project to manufacture and sell a new model there. This would involve establishing a subsidiary in Canvia.

Exhibit 2: Project information

The currency in Canvia is the Canvian lira (CL) and the current exchange rate is CL9.91 per euro (€). The annual rate of inflation in Canvia is expected to remain at 10% throughout the four-year duration of the project.

The finance director estimates the project's sales volumes, inflation-adjusted, pre-tax contribution and fixed costs as follows:

Year	1	2	3	4
Sales volume (units)	109,725	121,795	148,590	197,624
Pre-tax contribution (CLm)	419.4	500.2	671.3	961.2
Fixed costs (CLm)	270.0	291.6	314.9	340.1

The project will require an immediate investment of CL75m in land and buildings and CL700m in plant and machinery. Tax allowable depreciation is available on plant and machinery on a straight-line basis at an annual rate of 25% on cost. Colvin Co's finance director believes the plant and machinery will have a zero residual value at the end of the four years. The land and buildings will be disposed of at the end of the project and their tax-exempt value is expected to increase at an annual rate of 30% throughout the four-year life of the investment.

The project will also require an immediate investment in working capital of CL25m. The annual working capital requirement is expected to increase in line with inflation in Canvia and will be released back in full at the end of the project. Colvin Co has a policy of extracting remittable cash flows as dividends at the earliest possible opportunity.

All components for the new bicycle will be produced or purchased in Canvia except for a gearing system component which will be manufactured by Colvin Co in the eurozone. The cost of acquiring this component from the eurozone is already included in the pre-tax contribution estimates, based on a transfer price of €10 per component. The finance director estimates a manufacturing cost of €2 per component. Both the transfer price and manufacturing cost are expected to increase in line with eurozone annual inflation of 4% in the first two years of the project and 2% in years three and four.

Corporation tax in Canvia is payable annually at 25% and companies are allowed to carry losses forward to be offset against future trading profits. Colvin Co pays corporation tax in its home country at an annual rate of 20%. Taxes are payable in both countries in the year the liability is incurred. A bi-lateral tax treaty exists between the two countries, which permits the offset of overseas tax against any domestic tax liability incurred on overseas earnings.

Exhibit 3: Discount rate

The board proposes financing the project with a mix of equity and debt in such a way that the existing capital structure remains unchanged. For the purposes of this project, the chief executive believes Colvin Co's weighted average cost of capital of 13% should be adjusted to include a country risk premium on the basis that Canvia is a developing economy and appears to be economically less stable than the eurozone countries. She made this decision after consulting a country risk index, which compares the standard deviation of market returns in various countries.

Additional factors taken into consideration include foreign exchange risk, the fact that there have been frequent changes of government in Canvia and the main opposition party has threatened to reintroduce controls on dividend remittances if elected. You have therefore been asked to use a discount rate of 16% to appraise this investment project.

Required

(a) Evaluate the suitability of the investment proposal in Canvia, including the impact of the country risk premium on the net present value of the project. **(15 marks)**

(b) Explain possible strategies Colvin Co could adopt to avoid a block on dividend remittances if Canvia's opposition party was to win the election. **(4 marks)**

(c) Discuss the validity of the chief executive's reasons for adjusting the discount rate used in appraising the project in Canvia. **(6 marks)**

(25 marks)

Question 3

Exhibit 1: Fitzharris Co

Fitzharris Co is a large construction company. Its treasury department uses a variety of derivatives regularly to manage interest rate and commodity price risk.

Fitzharris Co's chief executive has recently been reviewing how the treasury department uses derivatives, in particular options, to hedge risk. She has raised queries about aspects of option pricing which she does not understand. In particular, she wants to know the impact upon option price of the time until expiry of the option and the interest rate.

Exhibit 2: Transaction to be hedged

Today's date is 1 August. Fitzharris Co plans to borrow an amount of $48m on 1 December, to finance a major construction project, for a period of up to three years. Its treasury department has decided to hedge the risk associated with this borrowing, as there is some uncertainty about how interest rates will move over the rest of this year. The current central bank base rate is 3.7%, but predictions in the media suggest that it could rise or fall by 0.4% by 1 December. Fitzharris Co can currently borrow funds at a floating rate of central bank base rate plus 50 basis points.

Fitzharris Co's treasury department is considering hedging the interest rate risk by using:

(1) An interest rate swap arranged through Fitzharris Co's bank

(2) A collar on options on interest rate futures

Swap

Fitzharris Co's bank has found a possible counterparty for a swap with Fitzharris Co. The counterparty can borrow at an annual floating rate of base rate plus 130 basis points, or a fixed rate of 4.8%. Fitzharris Co's bank has quoted it a nominal fixed rate of 4.6% for it to borrow. The bank would charge a fee of five basis points to each party individually to act as the intermediary of the swap. Both parties would share equally the potential gains from the swap.

Collar

Options on three-month December $ futures, $1,000,000 contract size, option premiums are in annual %

Strike price	Calls	Puts
96.25	0.198	
95.75		0.211

The current three-month $ futures price for December futures is 95.85.

Futures and options contracts are assumed to be settled at the end of each month. Basis is assumed to diminish to zero at contract maturity at a constant rate, based on monthly time intervals. It is also assumed that there is no basis risk and there are no margin requirements.

Required

(a)   Calculate, in percentage terms, the results of the hedging strategies that are being considered for the $48m loan, if the central bank base rate increases to 4.1% or falls to 3.3%. Your calculations should demonstrate the rates at which payments between counterparties should be made.
                                                                                        (13 marks)

(b)   Comment on the results of your calculations in (a) and discuss the advantages and drawbacks for Fitzharris Co of interest rate swaps compared with traded collars. **(8 marks)**

(c)   Explain the significance of the time until expiry and the interest rate in the context of option valuation.
                                                                                        (4 marks)

                                                                                        (25 marks)

Answers

DO NOT TURN THIS PAGE UNTIL YOU HAVE
COMPLETED THE MOCK EXAM

Exam success skills

In any AFM exam it will be important to apply good general exam technique by using the six exam success skills identified at the start of the Revision Kit, in the section covering 'essential skills'. These skills are: 1. Case scenario: Managing information; 2. Correct interpretation of requirements; 3. Answer planning: Priorities, structure and logic; 4. Efficient numerical analysis; 5. Effective writing and presentation; and 6. Good time management.

Some examples of how to apply these skills in this exam are provided in the table below.

Skill	Examples
Managing information	It is crucially important to assimilate the information in the question scenario.
	In longer questions, such as the 50 mark question, it is difficult to assimilate information by simply starting at the beginning and reading to the end because there is so much information to take in.
	Instead, it is sensible to take an **active approach** to reading each question. Read enough of the question to get an idea of the basic scenario and then read the initial requirements so that you understand the first things that you are expected to do with this information.
	For example, in Question 1 the lengthy scenario makes a lot more sense if, before reading all of it, you are aware of the theme of the report in part (b).
Correct Interpretation of requirements	Be careful to interpret the verbs used in the question requirements carefully. For example, in Q1(a), the verb 'discuss' implies that an element of critical analysis (discussing from different viewpoints) is appropriate. Also be careful to identify where a question requirement contains more than one instruction. For example, in Q1(b)(ii) and (iii).
Answer planning	This is always important in AFM questions.
	For example, in risk management questions such as Q1(a), it is especially important that your plan correctly identifies (i) the risk being faced (ii) the relevant timings. If you get these wrong, then there will be a cap on the number of marks that you can score (however accurate your answers are).
Efficient numerical analysis	It is essential that the marker can follow your workings and your logic.
	It is also important that you accept that under exam conditions you will not get <u>all</u> the calculations correct, and that this is not necessary in order to score a strong pass mark.
	If you make a mistake early in your calculations that affects your later calculations, then the marker will only penalise the error you have made, and not its follow-on impact on other calculations. This means that it is not normally a good use of your time to correct such errors during the exam.
	For example, in Question 2(a) an error early on in your calculations would only attract a small penalty despite its impact on the final NPV.

Skill	Examples
Effective writing and presentation	In Q1 there are four marks available for professional structure (eg use of sub-headings, appendices etc). Many of the techniques used here are good practice in all questions throughout the exam.
	It is also very important to relate your points to the scenario and to the requirement wherever possible. This does not mean simply repeating the details from the question but using this information to help to explain the point you are making.
	For example, in Q1(b)(v) it is not enough to state the assumptions, you need to explain their relevance.
Good Time Management	The exam is 3 hours 15 minutes long, which translates to 1.95 minutes per mark.
	If you build in an allowance of 20% of your time for assimilating the scenario and planning, this falls to 1.56 minutes per mark (1.95 × 0.8).
	It is essential that you do not allow yourself to become bogged down in the harder numerical areas of the exam.
	For example, in Q1 it is vital to leave enough time to answer the discursive parts, especially part (d).
	(a) At the beginning of a question, work out the amount of time you should be spending on:Planning:
	(i) for a 25 mark question this will be about 1.95 × 25 marks × 20% = 10 minutes
	(ii) for a 50 mark question this should be about 20 mins.
	(b) Writing your answer to each requirement:
	(iii) Take the mark allocation and multiply by 1.56 minutes per mark.

Diagnostic

Did you apply these skills when reading, planning, and writing up your answer? Identify the exam success skills where you think you need to improve and capture your thoughts here of what you want to achieve when attempting questions in future.

Question 1

> **Workbook references.** Ethics is covered in Chapter 1 and cost of capital Chapters 2 and 7. Defence strategies are covered in Chapter 9.
>
> **Top tips.** You will need to be very strict on your time management with this question - it is easy to overrun especially if you are attempting to produce a 100% perfect answer to part (b)(ii).
>
> **Easy marks.** About 60% of the marks are available for discussion but ensure your points are addressed to the scenario to maximise marks remember the professional marks can be obtained by:
>
> 1.   Providing a suitable, simple, heading to the answer (eg a simple report format)
> 2.   Providing a short introduction paragraph outlining the structure of the report
> 3.   Providing a clear answer (e.g. referencing spreadsheet calculations where appropriate).
> 4.   Providing a conclusion to complete the report.

Marking scheme

Marks

(a)		Sell-off assets	3–4
		(examples of points could include company less appealing, use of proceeds from sell-off, how Kingtim Co will be	
		Onerous contracts	
		(examples of points could include cost burden, acquirer may be prepared to bear it, corporate governance	3–4
			Max 7
(b)	(i)	Cost of equity	1
		Value of equity	1
		Value of existing bonds	1
		WACC	1
			4
	(ii)	Annual spot yield curve	1
		Value of new bonds	3
		Market value of new bonds	1
		Yield to maturity of proposed bonds	2
			7
	(iii)	Asset beta garden centre business	1
		Weighted asset beta	2
		Revised equity beta	1
		Revised cost of equity	1
		Revised WACC	2
			7
	(iv)	Revised P/L	3
			3
	(v)	Cost of capital	1–2
		Assumptions	3–4
		Equity holders	3–4
		(examples of points could include inadequate returns, higher business and financial risks, threat to earnings/dividend/ share price, covenant/repayment commitments, forecast extra earnings insufficient, sale of shares/changes in shareholder base)	
		Bond holders	2–3
			Max 10

Professional marks for part (b)

Report format $\underline{}$ 1

Structure and presentation of the report $\dfrac{3}{4}$

(c) Up to 2 marks for each well-explained issue
(issues could include rewarding expertise/seniority fairly,
balancing shareholder and employee interests, unfair to
question staff's commitment, society's expectations/law,
expectations raised by Kingtim Co's statements,
employee/customer reaction to poor practices) $\underline{8}$

Max 8

$\underline{50}$

(a) **Sell-off of garden centres**

Selling some of the most desirable garden centres, known as selling the crown jewels, may deter some acquirers looking to buy the whole chain if Kingtim Co sells the assets they most desire. Kingtim Co could take this option if it is able to sell off individual centres without jeopardising its overall existence.

However if no particular use is made of the cash raised from the sales, Kingtim Co would still remain a tempting takeover target due to its cash surpluses. Returning the surplus cash to shareholders in the form of a one-off dividend might be popular with shareholders, but equally they might be concerned about their future returns given the sale of assets generating significant income. Shareholders and others interested in Kingtim Co might also question what future strategies the board had in mind if it did not use these cash surpluses for investment.

Also, if the money was distributed to shareholders, Kingtim Co would become a smaller company and perhaps more affordable to some potential acquirers.

Enhanced directors' remuneration and contracts

The enhanced commitments to the directors would represent an increased burden for acquirers, either the costs of honouring them, or the cost and the time involved in terminating the directors' employment and compensating them. This burden may deter acquirers, particularly if the decision to acquire is marginal.

However, enhancing the commitments to the directors could be ineffective. The acquirer could decide to keep the directors on and pay the increased remuneration. Alternatively, the acquirer may feel that buying out the directors' contracts and compensating them is a necessary cost that it is prepared to bear.

Corporate governance aspects are also important. As a listed company, Kingtim Co should have a remuneration committee made up of non-executive directors, who should be reviewing the executive directors' remuneration packages. Kingtim Co may have to publish a remuneration report to explain the rationale for directors' remuneration, and to allow shareholders to discuss and perhaps vote on the report.

Shareholders may believe that the directors are being given a better compensation package without having earned it, and for no other reason than to try to protect their own positions. They may doubt whether directors are acting in the best interests of the company and its shareholders.

(b) (v) **Report to board of directors, Kingtim Co**

Introduction

This report indicates the impact of the proposed investment in outdoor shops and the consequent increase in debt finance. It also discusses the possible reactions of equity and bond holders to the proposals. Financial estimates provided in the appendices are used to support the discussion and assumptions underlying the estimates are set out below.

Cost of capital

There are two impacts, in opposite directions, on the weighted average cost of capital.

Kingtim Co's cost of equity has risen significantly. This is due to increased business risk, resulting from the investment in the outdoor shops and increased financial risk from the additional debt. The increase in the cost of equity has pushed the weighted average cost of capital upwards.

However, the higher proportion of debt in the company's finance structure, with debt having a lower cost than equity and also being tax-deductible, has pushed the weighted average cost of capital downwards.

Overall, however, the weighted average cost of capital has risen, meaning the increase in the cost of equity has had the greater impact.

Assumptions

The assumptions about the returns from the new investment may depend on how much Kingtim Co can attract customers away from competitors rather than finding a new market niche itself. Competitor reaction may also impact upon returns.

The CAPM model used is assumed to be a good predictor of equity returns, although some published evidence suggests that it may not be.

The asset beta used for the outdoor shops is a representative beta for similar companies and may not be accurate for Kingtim Co. The asset beta used to calculate the revised cost of equity is a weighted average of the asset betas of the two businesses. The weighting used is the non-current assets in each business, which is assumed to approximate to the size of each business. This assumes that non-current assets currently held are valued fairly, and that their valuation represents their income-generating potential and the proportion of business risk that each business represents.

The share price and price of the existing bonds are assumed to remain unchanged when the new investment is made. As discussed below, there is a strong possibility of changes in the shareholder base leading to changes in the share price and hence in the cost of capital.

Equity holders

Equity holders may consider the returns from the new investment to be insufficient. The pre- tax return of 10% is lower than the 16% pre-tax return on the existing garden centres, and is not much above the 7.5% pre-tax finance cost of the bonds used to finance the investment.

Equity holders are likely to be concerned about the increases in both business and financial risks. The increase in business risk is due to the higher business risk for the outdoor shops, due to the competition in that sector. Equity holders will be concerned about the possible variability of returns and also of dividends, as the company is committed to an increased operating cost burden in terms of extra premises and increased finance costs. Variability of returns may also result in the share price becoming more volatile.

Other aspects concerning equity holders might be any restrictive covenants attached to the new bonds that affect payment of dividends and also the planned repayment of the bonds.

Kingtim Co already has a significant commitment to repay the $45m bonds in three years' time. The new bonds would mean an additional commitment to repay $60m just a year later. The alternative is refinancing, but the terms that would be available are currently unknown,

These risks may mean that equity holders reconsider their investment in Kingtim Co, if they are risk-averse and do not feel that the additional returns compensate for the risk. They will take into account that the return on investment in the new business is lower than the current return on investment in the garden centres, although they are

BPP
LEARNING
MEDIA

not required to make any additional investment themselves for the return on the outdoor shops. The share price will fall if a significant number of shareholders decide to sell their shares, although Kingtim Co may attract a new clientele of shareholders who are more risk-seeking.

Bond holders

Bond holders are likely to be most concerned about Kingtim Co's ability to meet its interest and repayment commitments. Holders of the new bonds are particularly likely to be concerned about the ability to repay their capital, given the commitment to repay existing bond holders. Bond holders may also be concerned about whether the financing of the investment allows Kingtim Co to take undue risks. They may wonder about the motivation for undertaking the new investment using debt finance, particularly if they are not convinced about its business case.

Conclusion

Assuming a strong business case can be made for the investment and the estimates are robust, Kingtim Co may be able to justify financing it solely by debt and claim that the increase in financial risk is within acceptable levels. However, before committing to further debt, Kingtim Co must provide a clear plan for repayment of both the current and new bonds, or offer sufficient assurance that it will be able to refinance its debt when it is due for repayment.

Appendix 1 Estimate of existing cost of capital (b)(i)

Cost of equity

$k_e = 4.0\% + (0.9 \times 9.0\%) = 12.1\%$

Value of equity (V_e) = $5.56 × 25 million shares = $139m

Value of existing bonds

$V_d = \$104 \times 0.45$ million = $46.8m

Current WACC

WACC = ((12.1% × 139) + (4.1% × 46.8))/(139 + 46.8) = 10.1%

Appendix 2 Estimate of cost of new bonds (b)(ii)

Annual yield curve

Bond	Government annual yield curve	Credit spread	Kingtim Co annual yield curve
Ga	4%	56	4.56%
Th	4.3%	78	5.08%
De	4.7%	106	5.76%
Ro	5.2%	135	6.55%

Value of new bonds based on annual yield curve

$\$7.50 \times 1.0456^{-1} + \$7.50 \times 1.0508^{-2} + \$7.50 \times 1.0576^{-3} + \$115.50 \times 1.0655^{-4} = \$109.92$

Market value of new bonds

$109.92 × 0.6m = $65.952m

Yield to maturity of new bonds

Year		$	5%	$	3%	$
0	Market value	(109.92)	1.000	(109.92)	1.000	(109.92)
1 – 4	Interest (post-tax)	5.63	3.546	19.96	3.717	20.93
4	Redemption	108.00	0.823	88.88	0.888	95.90
				(1.08)		6.91

YTM (k_d) = 3% + ((6.91/(6.91 + 1.08)) × (5% – 3%)) = 4.7%

(Alternatively this can be worked out using the =IRR spreadsheet function, although the numbers will have to be laid out separately for each year for this to work.)

Appendix 3 Revised cost of equity and WACC (b)(iii)

β_a garden centre business = $0.9 \times (139/(139 + (46.8 \times 0.75))) = 0.72$

Weighted average $\beta_a = (0.72 \times (150/(150 + 60))) + (0.88 \times (60/(150 + 60))) = 0.77$

$\beta_e = 0.77 \times ((139 + ((46.8 + 65.952) \times 0.75))/139) = 1.24$

$k_e = 4.0\% + (1.24 \times 9.0\%) = 15.2\%$

WACC = $((15.2\% \times 139) + (4.1\% \times 46.8) + (4.7\% \times 65.952))/(139 + 46.8 + 65.952) = 10.4\%$

Appendix 4 Revised earnings forecast (b) (iv)

Forecast statement of profit or loss for the coming year

	$000
Forecast after-tax earnings ($24m × 0.75)	18,000
Additional finance cost ($60m × 7.5% × 0.75)	(3,375)
Additional after-tax earnings due to new investment ($60m × 10% × 0.75)	4,500
Revised forecast after-tax earnings	19,215
Increase in after-tax earnings	1,125

(c) **Approach taken**

The stated approach to employee remuneration has some business logic. Expertise, experience, seniority and commitment are all attributes that staff have that could be reflected in extra rewards for them, not only out of fairness to the staff but also because of their value to the business. If staff with these attributes believe they are not being rewarded fairly, they may leave and perhaps join a competitor.

Kingtim Co also has a duty to enhance the wealth of its shareholders and has raised expectations by recently increasing dividends. There is a stakeholder conflict, as increasing the wages of many employees would lead to lower profits and less money available for distribution to shareholders.

Issues with approach

The statement about part-time staff not having the same level of commitment may well be unjust, as they may be as committed as full-time staff during the hours they work.

The current approach raises a number of ethical issues, which may also harm Kingtim Co's reputation. It has made commitments to act in accordance with society's expectations and to treat its staff fairly. Although the basic wage is not legally enforceable, it does represent society's expectations about what employees should be paid. Limiting rewards to staff who may only be able to work part-time because of other commitments could also be something that society judges to be discriminatory and may be against the law.

In addition, if Kingtim Co's directors are given more lucrative contracts as a takeover defence mechanism, this undermines the argument for limiting staff costs in order to maintain shareholder returns.

The consequences of these threats to reputation might again be that lower-paid staff eventually decide to leave. A high staff turnover will mean few staff develop experience and expertise over time, which may impact on customer quality. Kingtim Co may also have problems recruiting staff for its new outdoor business. Customers may also stop shopping at Kingtim Co in protest at the poor treatment of staff.

BPP
LEARNING
MEDIA

Question 2

Marking scheme

		Marks
(a)	Exchange rates	2
	Tax	2
	Working capital	2
	Land and buildings residual value	1
	Remittable cash flows in euros	1
	Contribution from component	2
	Tax on contribution	1
	Net present values	2
	Comment	2–3
		Max 15
(b)	Up to 2 marks per point (eg transfer price, royalty)	Max 4
(c)	Up to 2 marks per point (eg argument for WACC, total risk vs market risk, correlation across countries)	Max 6
		25

(a) **Project cash flows:** All figures are in CL millions

Year	0	1	2	3	4
Contribution		419.4	500.2	671.3	961.2
Fixed costs		(270.0)	(291.6)	(314.9)	(340.1)
Tax allowable depreciation		(175.0)	(175.0)	(175.0)	(175.0)
Taxable profit / (loss)		(25.6)	33.6	181.4	446.1
Tax loss carried forward		25.6	(25.6)		
Adjusted taxable profit		0.0	8.0	181.4	446.1
Taxation (25%)			(2.0)	(45.4)	(111.5)
Add loss carried forward		(25.6)	25.6		
Add depreciation		175.0	175.0	175.0	175.0
Cash flows after tax		149.4	206.6	311.0	509.6
Working capital (W2)	(25.0)	(2.5)	(2.8)	(3.0)	33.3
Investment cost	(775.0)				214.2
Cash flows	(800.0)	146.9	203.8	308.0	757.1

Cash flows: All figures are in € millions

Year	0	1	2	3	4
Exchange rate (W1)	9.91	10.48	11.09	11.96	12.89
Total investment cost	(80.7)				
Remittable cash flows		14.0	18.4	25.8	58.7
Component contribution (W3)		0.9	1.1	1.3	1.8
Tax on net contribution (20%)	___	(0.2)	(0.2)	(0.3)	(0.4)
Cash flows	(80.7)	14.7	19.3	26.8	60.1

Net present value using 16% discount rate: All figures are in € millions

Year	0	1	2	3	4
Cash flows	(80.7)	14.7	19.3	26.8	60.1
Discount rate (16%)	1.000	0.862	0.743	0.641	0.552
Present values	(80.7)	12.7	14.3	17.2	33.2

Net present value (€3.3m)

Net present value using 13% discount rate: All figures are in € millions

Year	0	1	2	3	4
Cash flows	(80.7)	14.7	19.3	26.8	60.1
Discount rate (13%)	1.000	0.885	0.783	0.693	0.613
Present values	(80.7)	13.0	15.1	18.6	36.8

Net present value €2.8m

[It is quicker to use the spreadsheet function =NPV to calculate the two NPVs, although remember that this calculates the present value from time 1 onwards so you need to subtract the time cash outflow after doing this.]

Workings

Working 1 (W1): Exchange rates

Year	1	2	3	4
CL/€	9.91 × 1.10/1.04 = 10.48	10.48 × 1.10/1.04 = 11.09	11.09 × 1.10/1.02 = 11.96	11.96 × 1.10/1.02 = 12.89

Working 2 (W2): Working capital (CLm)

Year	0	1	2	3	4
Inflation		10%	10%	10%	10%
Increase with inflation	(25.0)	(27.5)	(30.3)	(33.3)	
Incremental working capital	(25.0)	(2.5)	(2.8)	(3.0)	33.3

Working 3 (W3): Component contribution (€)

Year	1	2	3	4
Contribution /€	109,725 × 8 × 1.04 = 0.9m	121,795 × 8 × 1.04² = 1.1m	148,590 × 8 × 1.04² × 1.02 = 1.3m	197,624 × 8 × 1.04² × 1.02² = 1.8m

Comment

The decision whether to accept or reject the project critically depends on the discount rate, switching from a negative net present value of €3.3m when the discount rate includes a country risk premium to a positive net present value of €2.8m when there is no premium. This adjustment to the weighted average cost of capital requires further investigation because it is possible Colvin Co could reject projects that increase shareholder wealth.

The outcome assumes the contribution and other cash flows are reliably estimated. Other critical inputs include the assumption that land and buildings will increase in value at an annual rate of 30% and that any disposal is tax exempt.

(b) There are a number of possible strategies to avoid exchange controls on remittances. Colvin Co could increase the transfer price paid by the Canvian subsidiary for the gearing system component. This would increase Colvin Co's profit to the detriment of the subsidiary's profit. Alternatively, Colvin Co doesn't curretly levy a management charge or royalty but if these were introduced it would transfer profit from the subsidiary without the need for a dividend.

These methods assume the exchange controls imposed in Canvia are not applied to repatriations in general. An alternative would be for Colvin Co's subsidiary tò make a loan to the Canvian subsidiary of another Eurozone based parent company which, in return, would lend an equivalent amount in Euros to Colvin Co. The same objective could be achieved with a currency swap although counterparty risk would be a factor in both cases.

(c) Colvin Co's investment in Canvia does not involve a change in business risk or capital structure. The company's weighted average cost of capital would normally be expected to provide a reasonable measure of risk for the new project. The chief executive's justification for a risk premium is based on the increased risk the company is exposed to in Canvia, a developing economy, compared to the company's existing business in the Eurozone. This perception of increased risk is based on a country risk index, which compares the standard deviation of market indices around the world. The chief executive has incorporated other factors, such as political risk and foreign exchange risk in determining this premium.

However, standard deviation is not the appropriate measure of risk for Colvin Co's investment since any portion of total risk that is uncorrelated across different markets can be diversified away at no cost to investors. For example, adverse political events in Canvia may be partially offset by more favourable events in other parts of the world. No rational investor would pay a premium for risk that can be avoided. In this sense, although Colvin Co's investment in Canvia is exposed to foreign exchange risk, this too can be mitigated by an appropriate hedging policy.

Furthermore, Colvin Co's institutional shareholders are likely to be well diversified across global markets and asset classes. The potential for further risk reduction by Colvin Co from diversifying operations globally is therefore limited when the shareholders can achieve this more efficiently on their own.

The only component of total risk that could justify a premium to Colvin Co's cost of capital is market risk or undiversifiable risk. This assumes returns across countries are significantly positively correlated. For example, there is a strong possibility that a recession in the Eurozone may lead to a downturn in Canvia too rather than offset it, transmitted through trade links and closer integration between markets. This tendency for markets across the world to move together means reduced risk reduction benefits from diversification, hence a higher cost of capital. The key issue therefore is whether the risk of the new investment is diversifiable or not. If returns across markets are significantly positively correlated and the risk undiversifiable, the new project in Canvia may therefore command a risk premium although no justification is provided for the chief executive's premium of 3% which would require further investigation and analysis.

Question 3

Workbook references. Interest rate hedging is covered in Chapter 13 and option valuation is covered in Chapters 4 and 11..

Top tips.

Part (a). A complication here is that a swap would cover the whole period of the loan whilst a collar would only cover a short initial period unless it was rolled forward. Under exam conditions it is best to ignore this and prepare some standard % calculations, this issue can then be raised in the discussion part of this question.

Part (b). A comment should be brief – here it was only worth 1 mark. The discussion should compare the two forms of hedging and not just list all of the general pros and cons of collars and swaps. The key point is that these instruments have to be compared to each other.

Part (c). There were up to 3 marks for both concepts, to an overall maximum of 4 marks for this part of the question. This required two short paragraphs, one explaining how time value affects the value of call and put options (time value increases the value of both call and put options), the other explaining how interest rates affects the value of call and put options (higher rates increase the value of call options but decreases the value of put options).

Marking scheme

		Marks
(a)	**Swaps**	
	Comparative advantage of 0.6%	1
	Initial decision to borrow floating by Fitzharris Co and fixed by counterparty	1
	Advantage of 0.25% per party after the bank fee	1
	Suitable swap rates	1
	Final rate to be paid by Fitzharris Co	1
	Collars	1
	Number of contracts	1
	Basis calculation	1
	Buy put and sell call options	1
	Premium calculation	1
	Exercise options?	2
	Impact of interest rate increase/decrease with collars	$\underline{2}$
		$\underline{13}$
(b)	Comment on calculations	1
	Advantages of swaps compared with collars	3–4
	(advantages could include flexibility, longer time period, certainty of finance costs, comparative advantage)	
	Disadvantages of swaps compared with collars	
	(disadvantages could include counterparty risk, inability take advantage of favourable rate movements, swaps cannot be traded)	$\underline{3–4}$
		Max 8
(c)	Time (Theta)	2–3
	Interest rate (Rho)	$\underline{2–3}$
		Max 4
		$\underline{\underline{25}}$

(a) **Swap**

	Fitzharris Co	Counterparty	Interest rate differential
Fixed rate	4.60%	4.80%	0.20%
Floating rate	Base rate + 0.50%	Base rate + 1.30%	0.80%

Fitzharris Co has an advantage in borrowing at both fixed and floating rates, but the floating rate advantage is larger.

Gain % for Fitzharris Co = 50% (0.8 – 0.2 – 0.1) = 0.25

	Fitzharris Co	Counterparty
Rate without swap	(4.60%)	(Base rate + 1.30%)
Benefit	0.25%	0.25%
Net result	(4.35%)	(Base rate + 1.05%)
Swap		
Borrows at	(Base rate + 0.50%)	(4.80%)
Fitzharris Co pays	(3.80%)	3.80%
Counterparty pays	Base rate	(Base rate)
Bank fee	(0.05%)	(0.05%)
Net result	(4.35%)	(Base rate + 1.05%)

Collar

Buy December put options at 95.75 for 0.211 and sell December call options at 96.25 for 0.198

Number of contracts = ($48,000,000/$1,000,000) × (36 months/3 months) = 576**

Basis = Current price (1 August) – futures price

(100 – 3.70) – 95.85 = 0.45

Unexpired basis on 1 December = 1/5 × 0.45 = 0.09

Premium = (0.00211 – 0.00198) = 0.013%

If base rate rises by 0.4% to 4.1%

Futures price = 100 – 4.1 – 0.09 = 95.81

	Buy put	Sell call
Exercise price	95.75	96.25
Futures price	95.81	95.81
Exercise?*	No	No
Loss in basis points	–	–

*The put option is not exercised, because Fitzharris Co can sell the futures at the futures market price of 95.81 rather than the option exercise price of 95.75. The call option is not exercised, as the option holder can buy the futures at the lower futures market price of 95.81 rather than the exercise price of 96.25.

	%
Borrowing cost (4.1% + 0.5%)	4.600
Premium	0.013
Total payment	4.613

If base rate falls by 0.4% to 3.3%

Futures price = 100 – 3.3 – 0.09 = 96.61

	Buy put	Sell call
Exercise price	95.75	96.25
Futures price	96.61	96.61
Exercise?*	No	Yes
Loss in basis points	–	36

* The put option is not exercised, as by not exercising the option Fitzharris Co can sell the futures at the higher futures market price of 96.61 rather than the lower exercise price of 95.75. The call option is exercised, because the option holder can buy the futures at the option exercise price of 96.25 rather than the futures market price of 96.61.

	%
Borrowing cost (4.1% + 0.5%)	3.800
Loss on options (0.0036 × 100)	0.360
Premium	0.013
Effective annual interest rate	4.173

> **Tutorial note**
>
> It is possible to justify a range of different hedging periods for this situation. Any justified hedging period from the four-month period of uncertainty, outlined in the question, up to 36 months was awarded credit. It was recognised that in reality a collar for 36 months would not happen and instead there would be a rolling series of hedges.
>
> Answers which calculated costs in dollar amounts based on their number of contracts and then calculated an effective annual rate, were also eligible for full credit.

(b) **Comment**

The calculations do not give a clear indication of which strategy should be chosen. The swap gives a better result if base rate rises by 0.4%, the options if base rate falls by 0.4%. The decision may be determined by whether the company views a rise or fall in interest rates as being more likely, or how it views the advantages and disadvantages of the strategies.

Advantages of swaps

As swaps are over-the counter arrangements, they can be arranged in any size. The amount covered by collars based on traded options is determined by the size of the option contract. There may be over and under hedging.

The traded options available may last for a short period, perhaps up to two years, less maybe than the period of the loan. Swaps can be arranged for a much longer period.

Fitzharris Co is swapping here a commitment to pay a variable rate of interest that is uncertain with a guaranteed fixed rate of interest. This allows Fitzharris Co to forecast finance costs on the loan with certainty. The net payments on the collar will depend on how interest rates move.

Unlike collars, swaps make use of the principle of comparative advantage. Fitzharris Co can borrow in the market where the best deal is available to it.

Disadvantages of swaps

Swaps are subject to counterparty risk, the risk that the other party may default on the arrangement. This should not generally be a problem if Fitzharris Co arranges the swap through the bank. It may, however, be a problem if it arranges the swap itself. As the options that the collar is based on are traded on the derivatives markets, this should guarantee there will be no counterparty risk.

As Fitzharris Co is swapping into a fixed rate commitment, it cannot take advantage of favourable interest rate changes as it could, to some extent, if it used collars. Here the swap results in a lower cost than the collar if interest rates rise, but the collar is better if interest rates fall.

As swaps are over-the-counter instruments, they cannot be traded or allowed to lapse if they are not needed. The options can be traded on a derivative market.

(c) **Time**

An option's price consists of two elements, its intrinsic value and its time premium. The time premium diminishes over time to zero at the point that the option expires. Theta measures how much time value is lost over time. It is generally expressed as an amount lost per day. Theta reduces the value of both put and call options for holders.

BPP
LEARNING
MEDIA

The change in theta for in the money and out of the money options is broadly linear. At the money options have the greatest time premium and greatest theta. Theta for at the money options does not change in a linear fashion, but changes more rapidly as the expiry date approaches.

Interest rate

Rho measures how the option price varies with changes in interest rates. An option's rho is the amount of change in value for a 1% change in the option's risk free interest rate. The rho is positive for call options if the risk-free interest rate increases and negative for put options.

Compared with other factors affecting option price, the interest rate is not a significant influence, as interest rates often move slowly. A change in interest rates will be more significant the longer the time until expiry of an option.

Mathematical tables and formulae

Formulae

Modigliani and Miller Proposition 2 (with tax)

$$k_e = k_e^i + (1-T)(k_e^i - k_d)\frac{V_d}{V_e}$$

The Capital Asset Pricing Model

$$E(r_i) = R_f + \beta_i \ (E(r_m) - R_f)$$

The asset beta formula

$$\beta_a = \left[\frac{V_e}{(V_e + V_d(1-T))}\beta_e\right] + \left[\frac{V_d(1-T)}{(V_e + V_d(1-T))}\beta_d\right]$$

The Growth Model

$$P_o = \frac{D_o(1+g)}{(r_e - g)}$$

Gordon's growth approximation

$$g = br_e$$

The weighted average cost of capital

$$WACC = \left[\frac{V_e}{V_e + V_d}\right]k_e + \left[\frac{V_d}{V_e + V_d}\right]k_d(1-T)$$

The Fisher formula

$$(1+i) = (1+r)(1+h)$$

Purchasing power parity and interest rate parity

$$S_1 = S_0 \times \frac{(1+h_c)}{(1+h_b)} \qquad F_0 = S_0 \times \frac{(1+i_c)}{(1+i_b)}$$

Modified Internal Rate of Return

$$MIRR = \left[\frac{PV_R}{PV_I}\right]^{\frac{1}{n}}(1+r_e) - 1$$

The Black-Scholes option pricing model

$$c = P_a N(d_1) - P_e N(d_2)e^{-rt}$$

Where:

$$d_1 = \frac{\ln(P_a / P_e) + (r + 0.5s^2)t}{s\sqrt{t}}$$

$$d_2 = d_1 - s\sqrt{t}$$

The Put Call Parity relationship

$$p = c - P_a + P_e e^{-rt}$$

Present value table

Present value of 1 ie $(1 + r)^{-n}$

Where   r = discount rate

        n = number of periods until payment

Discount rate (r)

Periods (n)	1%	2%	3%	4%	5%	6%	7%	8%	9%	10%	
1	0.990	0.980	0.971	0.962	0.952	0.943	0.935	0.926	0.917	0.909	1
2	0.980	0.961	0.943	0.925	0.907	0.890	0.873	0.857	0.842	0.826	2
3	0.971	0.942	0.915	0.889	0.864	0.840	0.816	0.794	0.772	0.751	3
4	0.961	0.924	0.888	0.855	0.823	0.792	0.763	0.735	0.708	0.683	4
5	0.951	0.906	0.863	0.822	0.784	0.747	0.713	0.681	0.650	0.621	5
6	0.942	0.888	0.837	0.790	0.746	0.705	0.666	0.630	0.596	0.564	6
7	0.933	0.871	0.813	0.760	0.711	0.665	0.623	0.583	0.547	0.513	7
8	0.923	0.853	0.789	0.731	0.677	0.627	0.582	0.540	0.502	0.467	8
9	0.914	0.837	0.766	0.703	0.645	0.592	0.544	0.500	0.460	0.424	9
10	0.905	0.820	0.744	0.676	0.614	0.558	0.508	0.463	0.422	0.386	10
11	0.896	0.804	0.722	0.650	0.585	0.527	0.475	0.429	0.388	0.350	11
12	0.887	0.788	0.701	0.625	0.557	0.497	0.444	0.397	0.356	0.319	12
13	0.879	0.773	0.681	0.601	0.530	0.469	0.415	0.368	0.326	0.290	13
14	0.870	0.758	0.661	0.577	0.505	0.442	0.388	0.340	0.299	0.263	14
15	0.861	0.743	0.642	0.555	0.481	0.417	0.362	0.315	0.275	0.239	15

(n)	11%	12%	13%	14%	15%	16%	17%	18%	19%	20%	
1	0.901	0.893	0.885	0.877	0.870	0.862	0.855	0.847	0.840	0.833	1
2	0.812	0.797	0.783	0.769	0.756	0.743	0.731	0.718	0.706	0.694	2
3	0.731	0.712	0.693	0.675	0.658	0.641	0.624	0.609	0.593	0.579	3
4	0.659	0.636	0.613	0.592	0.572	0.552	0.534	0.516	0.499	0.482	4
5	0.593	0.567	0.543	0.519	0.497	0.476	0.456	0.437	0.419	0.402	5
6	0.535	0.507	0.480	0.456	0.432	0.410	0.390	0.370	0.352	0.335	6
7	0.482	0.452	0.425	0.400	0.376	0.354	0.333	0.314	0.296	0.279	7
8	0.434	0.404	0.376	0.351	0.327	0.305	0.285	0.266	0.249	0.233	8
9	0.391	0.361	0.333	0.308	0.284	0.263	0.243	0.225	0.209	0.194	9
10	0.352	0.322	0.295	0.270	0.247	0.227	0.208	0.191	0.176	0.162	10
11	0.317	0.287	0.261	0.237	0.215	0.195	0.178	0.162	0.148	0.135	11
12	0.286	0.257	0.231	0.208	0.187	0.168	0.152	0.137	0.124	0.112	12
13	0.258	0.229	0.204	0.182	0.163	0.145	0.130	0.116	0.104	0.093	13
14	0.232	0.205	0.181	0.160	0.141	0.125	0.111	0.099	0.088	0.078	14
15	0.209	0.183	0.160	0.140	0.123	0.108	0.095	0.084	0.074	0.065	15

Annuity table

Present value of an annuity of 1 ie $\dfrac{1-(1+r)^{-n}}{r}$

Where   r = discount rate

          n = number of periods

Discount rate (r)

Periods (n)	1%	2%	3%	4%	5%	6%	7%	8%	9%	10%	
1	0.990	0.980	0.971	0.962	0.952	0.943	0.935	0.926	0.917	0.909	1
2	1.970	1.942	1.913	1.886	1.859	1.833	1.808	1.783	1.759	1.736	2
3	2.941	2.884	2.829	2.775	2.723	2.673	2.624	2.577	2.531	2.487	3
4	3.902	3.808	3.717	3.630	3.546	3.465	3.387	3.312	3.240	3.170	4
5	4.853	4.713	4.580	4.452	4.329	4.212	4.100	3.993	3.890	3.791	5
6	5.795	5.601	5.417	5.242	5.076	4.917	4.767	4.623	4.486	4.355	6
7	6.728	6.472	6.230	6.002	5.786	5.582	5.389	5.206	5.033	4.868	7
8	7.652	7.325	7.020	6.733	6.463	6.210	5.971	5.747	5.535	5.335	8
9	8.566	8.162	7.786	7.435	7.108	6.802	6.515	6.247	5.995	5.759	9
10	9.471	8.983	8.530	8.111	7.722	7.360	7.024	6.710	6.418	6.145	10
11	10.368	9.787	9.253	8.760	8.306	7.887	7.499	7.139	6.805	6.495	11
12	11.255	10.575	9.954	9.385	8.863	8.384	7.943	7.536	7.161	6.814	12
13	12.134	11.348	10.635	9.986	9.394	8.853	8.358	7.904	7.487	7.103	13
14	13.004	12.106	11.296	10.563	9.899	9.295	8.745	8.244	7.786	7.367	14
15	13.865	12.849	11.938	11.118	10.380	9.712	9.108	8.559	8.061	7.606	15

(n)	11%	12%	13%	14%	15%	16%	17%	18%	19%	20%	
1	0.901	0.893	0.885	0.877	0.870	0.862	0.855	0.847	0.840	0.833	1
2	1.713	1.690	1.668	1.647	1.626	1.605	1.585	1.566	1.547	1.528	2
3	2.444	2.402	2.361	2.322	2.283	2.246	2.210	2.174	2.140	2.106	3
4	3.102	3.037	2.974	2.914	2.855	2.798	2.743	2.690	2.639	2.589	4
5	3.696	3.605	3.517	3.433	3.352	3.274	3.199	3.127	3.058	2.991	5
6	4.231	4.111	3.998	3.889	3.784	3.685	3.589	3.498	3.410	3.326	6
7	4.712	4.564	4.423	4.288	4.160	4.039	3.922	3.812	3.706	3.605	7
8	5.146	4.968	4.799	4.639	4.487	4.344	4.207	4.078	3.954	3.837	8
9	5.537	5.328	5.132	4.946	4.772	4.607	4.451	4.303	4.163	4.031	9
10	5.889	5.650	5.426	5.216	5.019	4.833	4.659	4.494	4.339	4.192	10
11	6.207	5.938	5.687	5.453	5.234	5.029	4.836	4.656	4.486	4.327	11
12	6.492	6.194	5.918	5.660	5.421	5.197	4.988	4.793	4.611	4.439	12
13	6.750	6.424	6.122	5.842	5.583	5.342	5.118	4.910	4.715	4.533	13
14	6.982	6.628	6.302	6.002	5.724	5.468	5.229	5.008	4.802	4.611	14
15	7.191	6.811	6.462	6.142	5.847	5.575	5.324	5.092	4.876	4.675	15

Standard normal distribution table

	0.00	0.01	0.02	0.03	0.04	0.05	0.06	0.07	0.08	0.09
0.0	0.0000	0.0040	0.0080	0.0120	0.0160	0.0199	0.0239	0.0279	0.0319	0.0359
0.1	0.0398	0.0438	0.0478	0.0517	0.0557	0.0596	0.0636	0.0675	0.0714	0.0753
0.2	0.0793	0.0832	0.0871	0.0910	0.0948	0.0987	0.1026	0.1064	0.1103	0.1141
0.3	0.1179	0.1217	0.1255	0.1293	0.1331	0.1368	0.1406	0.1443	0.1480	0.1517
0.4	0.1554	0.1591	0.1628	0.1664	0.1700	0.1736	0.1772	0.1808	0.1844	0.1879
0.5	0.1915	0.1950	0.1985	0.2019	0.2054	0.2088	0.2123	0.2157	0.2190	0.2224
0.6	0.2257	0.2291	0.2324	0.2357	0.2389	0.2422	0.2454	0.2486	0.2517	0.2549
0.7	0.2580	0.2611	0.2642	0.2673	0.2704	0.2734	0.2764	0.2794	0.2823	0.2852
0.8	0.2881	0.2910	0.2939	0.2967	0.2995	0.3023	0.3051	0.3078	0.3106	0.3133
0.9	0.3159	0.3186	0.3212	0.3238	0.3264	0.3289	0.3315	0.3340	0.3365	0.3389
1.0	0.3413	0.3438	0.3461	0.3485	0.3508	0.3531	0.3554	0.3577	0.3599	0.3621
1.1	0.3643	0.3665	0.3686	0.3708	0.3729	0.3749	0.3770	0.3790	0.3810	0.3830
1.2	0.3849	0.3869	0.3888	0.3907	0.3925	0.3944	0.3962	0.3980	0.3997	0.4015
1.3	0.4032	0.4049	0.4066	0.4082	0.4099	0.4115	0.4131	0.4147	0.4162	0.4177
1.4	0.4192	0.4207	0.4222	0.4236	0.4251	0.4265	0.4279	0.4292	0.4306	0.4319
1.5	0.4332	0.4345	0.4357	0.4370	0.4382	0.4394	0.4406	0.4418	0.4429	0.4441
1.6	0.4452	0.4463	0.4474	0.4484	0.4495	0.4505	0.4515	0.4525	0.4535	0.4545
1.7	0.4554	0.4564	0.4573	0.4582	0.4591	0.4599	0.4608	0.4616	0.4625	0.4633
1.8	0.4641	0.4649	0.4656	0.4664	0.4671	0.4678	0.4686	0.4693	0.4699	0.4706
1.9	0.4713	0.4719	0.4726	0.4732	0.4738	0.4744	0.4750	0.4756	0.4761	0.4767
2.0	0.4772	0.4778	0.4783	0.4788	0.4793	0.4798	0.4803	0.4808	0.4812	0.4817
2.1	0.4821	0.4826	0.4830	0.4834	0.4838	0.4842	0.4846	0.4850	0.4854	0.4857
2.2	0.4861	0.4864	0.4868	0.4871	0.4875	0.4878	0.4881	0.4884	0.4887	0.4890
2.3	0.4893	0.4896	0.4898	0.4901	0.4904	0.4906	0.4909	0.4911	0.4913	0.4916
2.4	0.4918	0.4920	0.4922	0.4925	0.4927	0.4929	0.4931	0.4932	0.4934	0.4936
2.5	0.4938	0.4940	0.4941	0.4943	0.4945	0.4946	0.4948	0.4949	0.4951	0.4952
2.6	0.4953	0.4955	0.4956	0.4957	0.4959	0.4960	0.4961	0.4962	0.4963	0.4964
2.7	0.4965	0.4966	0.4967	0.4968	0.4969	0.4970	0.4971	0.4972	0.4973	0.4974
2.8	0.4974	0.4975	0.4976	0.4977	0.4977	0.4978	0.4979	0.4979	0.4980	0.4981
2.9	0.4981	0.4982	0.4982	0.4983	0.4984	0.4984	0.4985	0.4985	0.4986	0.4986
3.0	0.4987	0.4987	0.4987	0.4988	0.4988	0.4989	0.4989	0.4989	0.4990	0.4990

This table can be used to calculate $N(d)$, the cumulative normal distribution functions needed for the Black-Scholes model of option pricing. If $d_i > 0$, add 0.5 to the relevant number above. If $d_i < 0$, subtract the relevant number above from 0.5.

Review Form – Advanced Financial Management (AFM) (02/21)

Name: _____   Address: _____

_____

_____

How have you used this Kit?
(Tick one box only)

☐ On its own (book only)

☐ On a course: college _____

☐ With 'correspondence' package

☐ Other _____

Why did you decide to purchase this Kit?
(Tick one box only)

☐ Have used the Workbook

☐ Have used other BPP products in the past

☐ Recommendation by friend/colleague

☐ Recommendation by a lecturer at college

☐ Saw advertising

☐ Other _____

During the past six months do you recall seeing/receiving any of the following?
(Tick as many boxes as are relevant)

☐ Our advertisement in *Student Accountant*

☐ Our advertisement in *Pass*

☐ Our advertisement in *PQ*

☐ Our brochure with a letter through the post

☐ Our website www.bpp.com

Which (if any) aspects of our advertising do you find useful?
(Tick as many boxes as are relevant)

☐ Prices and publication dates of new editions

☐ Information on product content

☐ Facility to order books off-the-page

☐ None of the above

Which BPP products have you used?

Workbook	☐	Other	☐
Kit	☑		

Your ratings, comments and suggestions would be appreciated on the following areas.

	Very useful	Useful	Not useful
Passing AFM	☐	☐	☐
Questions	☐	☐	☐
Top Tips etc in answers	☐	☐	☐
Content and structure of answers	☐	☐	☐
Mock exam answers	☐	☐	☐

Overall opinion of this Kit   Excellent ☐   Good ☐   Adequate ☐   Poor ☐

Do you intend to continue using BPP products?
Yes ☐   No ☐

Please visit https://www.bpp.com/request-support to provide your feedback for this material.

Review Form (continued)

TELL US WHAT YOU THINK

Please note any further comments and suggestions/errors below.